James
COOK

James
COOK

The Story Behind the Man who Mapped the World

PETER
FITZSIMONS

CONSTABLE

CONSTABLE

First published in Australia and New Zealand in 2019 by Hachette Australia
First published in Great Britain in 2020 by Constable

10 9 8 7 6 5 4 3 2

ISBN: 978-1-4721-3140-9

Cover design by Luke Causby/Blue Cork

Cover images: Captain James Cook by William Hodges, courtesy of National Maritime
Museum, Greenwich, London; world map by John Tallis, 1851; sextant and compass
images courtesy of iStock and Adobe Stock

Author photo courtesy of Peter Morris/Sydney Heads
Maps by Jane Macaulay

Typeset in 11.1/14.1 pt Sabon LT Pro by Bookhouse, Sydney
Printed and bound in Great Britain by Clays Ltd, Elcograf S.p.A.

Papers used by Constable are from well-managed forests
and other responsible sources.

MIX
Paper from
responsible sources
FSC® C104740

Constable
An imprint of
Little, Brown Book Group
Carmelite House
50 Victoria Embankment
London EC4Y 0DZ

An Hachette UK Company
www.hachette.co.uk

www.littlebrown.co.uk

To the late John Cawte Beaglehole OM CMG of
New Zealand, the historian to whom all who attempt
to tell the story of James Cook will be most indebted.

And to my late friend, Professor John Molony of
Australia who, not long before he died at the age of 91,
encouraged me down the path of writing this book,
and gave me wise counsel as to how to do it.

CONTENTS

LIST OF MAPS

ACKNOWLEDGEMENTS AND NOTES

So many thank you's, so little time . . .

As mentioned in my dedication, it was Professor John Molony who gave me the most cogent advice on how to do this book, and I will always treasure the memory of his learning, kindness and sagacity.

To lay the groundwork I did much the same as I did with my book *Mutiny on the Bounty* – with the assistance of one of my researchers, my cousin Angus FitzSimons, I began by going after Captain Cook – the person *behind* the legend – to dig as deeply as possible into the primary documents to pursue the man and peruse his key relationships, influences and influencers. I needed to work out just how much of his life and times could be effectively reconstituted so I could in turn build a portrait of his life that would allow the reader to, ideally, be *in* it, not just reading about it. The answer was, it would be bloody difficult, but it could be done!

Another researcher, Barb Kelly, was equally assiduous in trying to fill gaps, trawling every obscure document she could get her digital hands on to bring precious and often previously unrevealed detail to the account, and was wonderful for the energy and care she put into the whole thing – like all of us becoming ever more impassioned with the story as we went along. In the areas where this book breaks new ground in terms of documenting the life on board the *Endeavour*, the rivalries, feuds and friendships, etc., it was more often than not Barb who found the relevant account that enabled me to bring it to life, and I warmly thank her. As with my most recent book *The Catalpa Rescue*, it was great that both her son Lachlan and my son Jake were able to lend valuable assistance.

Dr Libby Effeney has worked with me for the better part of the last decade and is without peer. Her work on this, going into what we call the FD, Fine Detail, was stronger than ever, and her ability to cross-reference different sources giving differing accounts – and work out which one was on the money – was as outstanding as ever. Her input was wonderful across the board but, again, if this book breaks new ground on Cook's life before setting foot on the *Endeavour*, Libby is the one to whom I owe the greatest debt. And she worked *hard*!

She is living in Mexico, so it meant that just as I was flagging near midnight, she took the watch and kept on sailing through the night, always getting me back on course when I strayed from the historical record. It was a privilege to be able to harness her massive intellect in the service of finding Cook, and I will long treasure her final note to me on this – 'I think we found the Cap'n.' I think we did, too!

My warm thanks also to Dr Peter Williams, the Canberra military historian who first started working with me on my book about Gallipoli, and has stayed with me thereafter. He joined this project late in the piece, but proved to know more about maritime history and lore than all of the rest of us put together.

For the last decade I have worked like this, with a great team of researchers contributing across the board, and so intense was this particular exercise – with so much material to work through, looking for pearls – that this book owes them an even greater debt than usual. I thank them all profusely, though whatever mistakes you might find are mine alone!

I also relied on the help of many experts in specific fields. I offer my thanks once again to Colonel Renfrey Pearson for finding rare documents in archives in the United Kingdom, and Gregory Blake for his expert advice on all things to do with the weapons of the time, particularly the muskets and cannon. Jonathan Nally, the expert on all things astronomical, provided valuable input on everything to do with the Transit of Venus and the instruments they used to record it. The New Zealand chapters were vetted by Owen Hughes, with input from Ngāpuhi man Julian Wilcox, who I have previously worked with on Māori Television. For the Australian chapter on Botany Bay, I relied on Gweagal man Dr Shayne Williams, and Ray Ingrey, the Chairman of the Gujaga Foundation. Professor John Maynard, the Director of the Purai Global Indigenous and Diaspora Research Studies Centre, was also extremely helpful in vetting those sections concerning the Gadigal and Wangal peoples. For the North Queensland chapters, my old friend from my Burke and Wills book, Dave Phoenix, was extremely helpful, and I was very grateful for vetting and input from Guugu Yimithirr man Harold Ludwick. Throughout the whole book, my dear friend Sally Aitken, the series producer and director of the documentary series *The Pacific, In the Wake of Captain Cook with Sam Neill*, was a great and generous adviser to me, as she had already sailed these waters.

There were a few complications in telling a story from so long ago in modern English. To begin with, in Cook's time the idea that we should all spell words the same way – that there was a correct and incorrect way at all – had not quite taken *holed . . . hol'd . . .* hold. With a few exceptions to give it historical flavour I have taken the liberty of using modern spelling to give the story clarity, and for the same reason have sometimes used modern language, such as changing 'darts' and 'lances' to 'spears'. The same applies to 'Native' names, with even a Cook contemporary, Johann Forster, complaining, 'Some of the names [of the Natives] were strangely spelt, as there never were two persons, in the last and former voyages, who spelt the same name in the same manner.'*

As to dates and times, there was another complication in that, although he was many years at sea, Joseph Banks always recorded his journal using civilian time, whereas Captain Cook nautically marked each midday as the start of a new day. (This was emblematic in so many ways of the story itself: that you have these two extraordinary men, not on the same page or the same date, even when they experience the same thing at the same time.) Just to add to that complication, when staying on shore for a while, such as in Tahiti, Cook would use civilian time, then when back at sea he'd change it to nautical time: 'I shall, during our stay at this island . . . no longer reckon the day according to the civil account.'†

It took some work, but all the dates are now sorted . . . !

As ever, and as I always recount concerning my historical writing, I have tried to bring the *story* part of this hi*story* alive, by putting it in the present tense, and constructing it in the manner of a novel, albeit with 1200 footnotes, give or take, as the pinpoint pillars on which the story rests. For the sake of the storytelling, I have occasionally created a direct quote from reported speech in a journal, diary or letter, and changed pronouns and tenses to put that reported speech in the present tense. When the story required generic dialogue – such as in the things

---

* Johann Reinhold Forster, *Observations Made During a Voyage Round the World, on Physical Geography, Natural History, and Ethic Philosophy*, G. Robinson, London, 1778, p. 512.
† Cook, Log, 13 June 1769.

a Captain of that time would say to his Master when bringing the *Endeavour* into port – I have taken the liberty of using that dialogue to help to bring the story to life.

Always, my goal has been to determine what were the words used, based on the primary documentary evidence presented, and what the feel of the situation was. For the same reason of remaining faithful to the language of the day, I have stayed with the imperial system of measurement.

All books used are listed in the Bibliography, but here I cite most particularly the works of J.C. Beaglehole, as well as the work of Cook's two earliest biographers, Andrew Kippis and Walter Besant; Richard Hough's work on Cook; Patrick O'Brian's and John Gascoigne's biography of Banks; and also Anne Salmond's masterwork, *The Trial of the Cannibal Dog*.

Once the broad manuscript was finished, my long-time editor and friend from the *Sydney Morning Herald*, Harriet Veitch, took the fine-tooth comb to the whole thing, untangling hopelessly twisted sentences, eliminating many grammatical errors and giving my work a sheen that does not properly belong to it. She has strengthened my stuff for three decades now, and I warmly thank her. In all my books, I give a draft of the near finished product to my eldest brother David, who has the best red pen in the business. When his interest flags, it is a fair bet so too will that of the reader, and I generally slash what doesn't grab him, so long as it is not key to the story. In this case I am not my brother's keeper, I rather follow his direction to throw things out. In this book, he was as astute as ever, and I record my gratitude.

My thanks also, as ever, to my highly skilled editor Deonie Fiford, who has honoured my request that she preserve most of the sometimes odd way I write, while only occasionally insisting that something come out because it just doesn't work.

I am also grateful to my friend and publisher, Matthew Kelly of Hachette, with whom I have worked many times over the last three decades, and who was enthusiastic and supportive throughout, always giving great guidance – apart from getting on my tits in the last few days or so.

I have loved doing this book, and hope you enjoy it.

Peter FitzSimons
Neutral Bay, Sydney
10 August 2019

James Cook is a hard as well as an easy man to talk about, and character studies have an evil propensity to degenerate into hypothesis. Everybody knows Cook's name; yet, I have always felt, extraordinarily little is known about him. He is an exceptionally difficult man to get inside. Certainly he was a great man . . . The more I dig . . . the more I am convinced of the stature of his genius.[1]

James Cook's defining biographer, J.C. Beaglehole, 1956

He was, to begin with, over six feet high, thin and spare; his head was small; his forehead was broad; his hair was of a dark brown; rolled back and tied behind in the fashion of the time; his nose was long and straight; his nostrils clear and finely cut; his cheekbones were high – a feature which illustrated his Scotch descent; his eyes were brown and small, but well set, quick, and piercing; his eyebrows were large and bushy; his chin was round and full; his mouth firmly set; his face long. It is an austere face, but striking. One thinks, perhaps wrongly, that without having been told whose face this is, in the portrait, we might know it is the face of a man remarkable for patience, resolution, perseverance, and indomitable courage. The portraits of naval worthies are sometimes disappointing . . . That of James Cook satisfies. It is a face worthy of the navigator. Such was the appearance of the man: tall, thin, grave . . .[2]

A description of James Cook by his second biographer, Sir Walter Besant, 1890

INTRODUCTION

In its first conception, the plan for this book was relatively simple and it came from my wife, Lisa Wilkinson.

'Captain Cook,' she noted to me in mid-2017, 'is the most mythological figure in Australian history, the one most constantly raised through the ages, and yet none of us really have a feel for the man himself. Who was he? What was he like? You should do a book and try to find out.'

Yes, dear.

But I really took her point, particularly with the focus on Cook growing as the 250th anniversary of his landing at Botany Bay approaches. He really is the most iconic figure in these parts since, well, since his arrival – with perhaps only Ned Kelly to argue the toss – and I had previously noted the ubiquity of Captain Cook in my own first studies of Australian history while at Peats Ridge Public School in the latter part of the 1960s. That man was everywhere, in every account from the so-called 'beginning' of Australian history.

(I know, but we'll get to that.)

I wrote in my childhood memoirs, A Simpler Time: 'In fact, in all of the history lessons, I don't recall anyone else at all, bar the good Cap'n, being present in the saga. It was almost as if after sailing the Endeavour across the Seven Seas, one morning Captain Cook in the crow's nest shouted "Land Ho!" to Captain Cook on the bridge, who had in turn shouted to a dozen Captain Cooks on the deck to heave-ho, me hearties, haul on the ropes, trim the main-sails, and Nor' by Nor'west let's bring her round into Botany Bay, singing too-ra-li-oo-ra-li-atterly, singing too-ra-li-oo-ra-li-ay. Or something like that.'

Or something like that, indeed.

But who was he? What formed him, ignited his passion, what made him laugh, cry, sing? Who was the *man* behind the monument? Of course he was all the rage when Imperialism and Colonialism were regarded as a very good thing, only for his popularity to plummet when the Empire struck back and Cook came to be regarded as one of the prime instruments of imperial invasion. But who really was the actual *person* behind the misunderstood, misremembered and mythologised man so many have come to know, love and, in recent times . . . sniff unpleasantly at?

One way or another, though, I wanted to get to the bottom of how the humble James Cook – who must have come from somewhere, I guess – became the iconic 'Captain Cook' I'd heard so much about; how that first remarkable voyage encompassing Tahiti, New Zealand and Australia transformed him from a man into a legend, and to see if I could breathe life into that man again in these pages.

Clearly, it was not going to be easy to find the man himself. Nearing the end of his life, the master writer and historian John Cawte Beaglehole OM CMG confessed to the difficulty of getting to the core of this blurry legend.

'Searching around, as I do, for the man,' he noted with an air of resignation in 1969, 'some leading characteristic, some not very secret spring, I light on . . . stubbornness.'[1]

I concur! It just wasn't stubbornness of the expressive variety. My reckoning is that, even as a child, if James Cook had badly stubbed his toe he would have been unlikely to cry out. And even as a sea-captain, and then legendary English figure, so buttoned-down was his nature that precious few utterances of any real interest made it into the diaries and letters of his contemporaries – at least not from the first of his three major voyages, which is the one that interested me.

Even James Boswell, the great British diarist and chronicler of his times, a dragnet for people and quotes of interest in the latter part of the 1700s, noted that he simply found Cook, 'a plain, sensible man with an uncommon attention to veracity . . . I talked a great deal with him today as he was very obliging and communicative. He seemed to have no desire to make people stare, and being a man of good steady moral principles as I thought, did not try to make theories out of what he had seen to confound virtue and vice.'[2]

Cook not only understated things, he barely stated anything at all. The world would prove to be his oyster, but he left behind barely any quotable pearls of wisdom.

The brilliant writer Fanny Burney also met Cook, and was equally underwhelmed at his conversation, albeit with a rider. Here she is at a dinner party with Cook after the return of the *Endeavour* from Southern climes: 'This truly great man appeared to be full of sense and thought; well-mannered, and perfectly unpretending; but studiously wrapped up in his own purposes and pursuits; and apparently under a pressure of mental fatigue when called upon to speak, or stimulated to deliberate, on any other.'[3]

And yet when Burney is confronted by his stilted ineptitude after she asks James Cook to compare his journey with others he has embarked upon, the not so ancient Mariner suddenly comes good, by nimbly showing her in a fashion that thrills: 'Captain Cook instantly took a pencil from his pocket-book, and said he would trace the route; which he did in so clear and scientific a manner, that I would not take fifty pounds for the book. The pencil marks having been fixed by skin milk, will always be visible.'[4]

That is Cook – a man of few words and many extraordinary actions.

Joseph Banks, by contrast, burst from every page he wrote, every diary entry written by his contemporaries, everything he *did*. In my book *Mutiny on the Bounty*, which briefly covered the *Endeavour* voyage insofar as it concerned their arrival at Tahiti, I had already been stunned by Joseph Banks' sexual proclivities when he had first visited that fair island – from a man who used to be on our $5 note, dammit! – and now here he was again, cutting a swathe through the whole Cook story on their First Voyage to the Pacific.

It became ever more clear that Captain Cook and Mr Banks were a peculiar pair, a daring duo, totally different in background, temperament, personality and character – and yet they formed a brilliant if uneasy partnership that achieved extraordinary things. Their relationship, in particular, came to fascinate me in the course of researching this book, and I hope what follows will bring out much of its particularities.

In terms of that research, my starting point – like every Cook biographer – was the life's work of the aforementioned great historian J.C. Beaglehole, a man so serious about getting to the heart of his subject that he was not content merely to read the published account of Cook's journals. Oh no, as he later recounted, to get to the bottom of James Cook one could not be content, 'merely to read between the printed lines, but [must] go to the originals and study the deletions and alterations, the drafts and the second thoughts, the doubts and surmises as well as the decisions, the blots as well as the fair copies'.[5]

This bloke was as thorough as any writer who ever lived, and I must make clear I am not so presumptuous as to claim to have found an answer that differs from Beaglehole's. (Though I certainly differ from him in emphasis, and never more than in the scene of Cook's landing at Botany Bay.) He is the master, and everyone who follows Beaglehole into the realms of Captain Cook must . . . do precisely that. But what I at least hope I have added to the plethora of works on Cook is an attempt, if not to get inside his head, at least to get as far as possible inside his life and times that, as much as possible, the reader can be *in* the moment, not merely observing it from afar. And given that every oft-told story will be told differently according to the age in which it is told, as we see things through the lens of our own times, I record the three angles of Captain Cook that interest me most: Cook's time in Australia and New Zealand, his role in asserting British sovereignty over lands with peoples that had been there for thousands of years – in Australia's case, 65,000 years – and his interaction with the Indigenous peoples of those lands.

In Australia, late in this second decade of the new millennium, the issues of sovereignty and British dealings with the First Peoples are particularly important as we try to come to terms with our history, and turn the page to a new and more equitable chapter. Where does Captain Cook fit into all that?

Exactly.

'Not long ago, the Australian government dismissed the latest attempt by Indigenous Australians to present their own vision for the future, in the Uluru Statement from the Heart,' Professor Bruce Buchan of Griffith University recently wrote. 'Cook is not the appropriate avatar of Empire to embody this continued denial, but his persistent enrolment as national icon ensures that his legacy will continue to shadow the nation's future. Would it be too much to ask that, instead of avatar or icon, hero or villain, we begin to see Captain Cook with fresh eyes? We might then begin to see beyond him, beyond the reflection of our wished-for selves, and begin to perceive new possibilities.'[6]

Ahem. Give me some room, please, Professor. I'm going to give it a shot . . .

PROLOGUE

'I want to go to sea, sir.'[1]

James Cook to his master at age 17

At the entrance of a little nameless river, scarce indeed worth a name, stands Whitby, which, however, is an excellent harbour, and where they build very good ships for the coal trade, and many of them, too, which makes the town rich.[2]

Daniel Defoe, 1724, on the port which launched the maritime career of James Cook

1746, Staithes, England, from threads to ropes

James Cook is a scurrilous thief.

Can it be? The worst kind of abomination. A lad whose honest, hard-working and easy-going appearance is nothing but a façade for evil skullduggery which has seen him take advantage of those who trust him most.

And yes, it pains Mr William Sanderson – the gentle shopkeeper in the village of Staithes, clinging precariously to the shore of the North Sea, at the base of the highest cliffs in England – to come to such a conclusion, but there is no way around either his conviction or his extreme disappointment. Why, he couldn't have been more kind to this farming lad, who he had treated as if his own son! Yes, he had taken young Cook into his drapery-cum-grocery store 18 months ago at the age of 16, fed him well and paid him a basic wage to sweep out and prepare the shop each morning and attend to customers during the day. In the evenings, after the day's trade is done, the till is tallied with no dilly-dally and the last of the items on the countertops are safely sealed and stored, the floor is swept and the door locked, Mr Sanderson climbs the stairs to his family dwelling above the shop leaving James to take his supper alone at the counter. Young James pauses only to glory in that deliciously tangy waft that rises off the fried fish before he wolfs it down, followed by a rough knob of bread and the whole lot washed down by a small mug of ale, a frothy brown warm brew with a woody flavour that is like mother's milk to a baby.

After supper, the lad often roams the shoreline, breathing deep on the intoxicating sea air, gazing at the bobbing vessels and visiting the taverns – the Shoulder of Mutton, the Black Lion and, most particularly, the place just a few doors down the cobbled street from Mr Sanderson's shop, the Cod and Lobster. It is in this smoky tavern, one of a row of ramshackle establishments lining the seashore while the craggy cliffs of Yorkshire crowd in from behind, that young James can talk long and late to the heavily weathered fishermen – known as 'coblemen', after their flat-bottomed boats called 'cobles' – who are downing their ales and puffing on their pipes even as they tell tales of whales, of larks with sharks and fierce North Sea[3] gales which generate waves so big they were higher than the sails, I tell you, young James.

The stories they tell of travelling the world! The lure of the sea! The sense of being afloat on infinity ... with the possibility of going anywhere!

Yes, and as they talk of distant ports, of New York, New France, the Cape of Good Hope, Batavia, and the mysterious South Seas – that largely unknown watery expanse ruled jealously if not quite zealously by the Spaniards since the days of Balboa – young James soaks it up like a sponge, remembering details, conjuring distant worlds with all that he can muster of what, in another more expressive lad, might pass for delight. It is the same when some of the men talk of their adventures serving in His Majesty's Navy – close cannon battles with French ships with masts falling, men dying and His Majesty's Jack still flying, narrow escapes from the mighty Spanish fleet, the horrors of salt pork rations for weeks on end and – *wait, while I remove my shirt!* – see here, young James, the gnarled scars that tell of the time I was flogged before the mast for speaking back to the Captain. I never did that again, I can tell you.

James Cook is not put off. He wants to experience such things himself, all bar the brutal flogging. The stories are a siren song with every telling, the call ever stronger, shaping his dreams and guiding his days to the point that he positively needs to leave this lubber's life on land and sail off into a perpetually bobbing and oft dangerous world.

If you learn enough, you can tame it, master it, survive – just as these men have survived, to tell their tales.

James Cook sits enthralled, night after night, hungry for more, and is often still there at midnight, at which point the men must leave to take their boats out fishing and he must plod back to the store.

And the fishermen like the lad so well in turn – noting his 'affability of conversation'[4] and his eagerness to learn everything he could about their lives at sea – that they encourage him, occasionally letting him come along on their cobles, venturing a little way out to sea in the inky night.

Yes, perhaps Sanderson has given James Cook too much rope. The earnest if slightly dreamy lad has practically been one of the family – albeit one who returns each night to sleep on a straw mattress under the shop counter, where there are 'fewer cockchafers, beetles and earwigs'[5] than in the rest of the shop. But so industrious had the gangly young Cook seemed, so good-natured, so attentive in his work – weighing herbs and flour with precision, measuring lengths of cloth and ribbon, then measuring them again before cutting them straight as an arrow with an unwavering hand, counting out buttons one by one – that Mr Sanderson could already see the day when the young fellow might become a partner in the business and allow his master and mentor to live an easier life, filled with more prayer and rest.

But now, suddenly, such hopes are shattered.

For, just today young James has *stolen* from him, robbed the cash box of a shilling.

That James Cook is a scurrilous thief.

Again and again, his brow furrowed, his heart breaking, Mr Sanderson goes over the events which prove it. In the morning a well-heeled lady had come in to purchase her groceries and paid with a shiny shilling, the lustre of which had nearly matched her own. Mr Sanderson had put it in the cash box and now that trade is done and he is toting up the day's takings it is . . . gone. Of course it has to be young James, as he is the only other person with access to the cash box. How disappointed the Lord of the Manor of Acton in Yorkshire, Thomas Skottowe, will be to hear the news. For it had been M'Lud himself who had noted the promise and nimble mind of this young fellow – the son of one of his labourers – and after paying for his schooling had arranged for his apprenticeship with Mr Sanderson.

And now, all of that is destroyed over a stolen shilling.

Mr Sanderson, taking his cane in hand – he uses it as infrequently as he does reluctantly, but this would appear to be such an occasion – walks into the drapery looking for the lad, only to find him missing.

And so Sanderson, by now an angry squall with darkened brow, ready to boom thunder and crack lightning, sticks his head out into the street, a waft of sea air filling his nose.

'*Men*,' he calls to a couple of fishermen leaning against a post across the street. '*Have yer seen James Cook? He's run away and robbed me of a shilling.*'

But the fishermen won't have it. They're fond of this broth of a boy and will never believe for a moment that he is capable of such a thing.

'*Robbed you? Tha' robbed it thissen last night to pay t'reckonin'. Are tha' too drunk yet to mind gooing out for t'money?*'[6]

It is, frankly, a fair point – if not the drinking part, at least the sheer unlikeliness that young James had robbed him. Shaking his head, Sanderson walks back to the box to check once again. Surely, it must be there. Alas, alas, still no shiny shilling.

Ah, but in fact James hasn't run away at all, for here he is now, returning from an errand, for all the world as if he has done nothing at all!

James, come in here please?

The old man looks the young fellow up and down and asks the question he must: Did you steal the shilling?

The answer from the shaken lad – for you *must* believe me, Mr Sanderson, as my whole future life depends on it – is yes and . . . no.

The thing is, Mr Sanderson, I *did* take the shiny shilling, but I replaced it with *another* shilling.

What?

And *why?*

Outside, the horses clip-clop by on the cobble-stones, pulling wagons filled with herring, cod and other fish freshly hauled off the water-worn fishing boats drawn up at the harbour's edge. Underneath their fishy cargo are carefully secreted duty-free bottles of wine, brandy and perfumes, smuggled in by the fishermen to satisfy the locals' growing appetite for such luxuries at a price they can afford. But on this day the shopkeeper has ears only for young James as, in his strong Yorkshire accent – a curious combination of the labourer's argot he had grown up with, all sharp vowels and dropped consonants, their words cut short and strung together wherever possible, and the more sophisticated words he has picked up from his ceaseless reading after hours – the lad makes his case . . .

Whilst I took yon shillin', I nae took it for all. I am nowt thief. It were replaced, straight, wit' mine own shillin', sir.

For you see, sir, while I did take the shiny shilling, I instantly replaced it with one of my own. I am *not* a thief.

But why, James? Why replace one shilling with another?

James Cook takes the shiny shilling from his pocket, enjoying its lustre, its delicious weight, and shows one side of it to Mr Sanderson. For as you can see, sir, the remarkable thing about this shilling is not just its shine, it is where it comes from. While on the obverse there is the standard depiction of His Majesty King George I, and the reverse has the unremarkable British arms in four crowned shields, please look *there*, Mr Sanderson, look closely and you will see the letters: SSC. This, sir, is a South Sea Shilling, minted from silver found in the East Indies by the South Sea Company back in the 1720s . . . and *that* is why I took it.

Clip-clop . . . clip-clop . . . clip-clop.

A pungent fishy cloud hovers in the wagon's wake and drifts through the open front door of Mr Sanderson's shop.

Still Mr Sanderson is none the wiser.

So what if it is from the South Seas? What is that to you, young James?

'I want to go to sea, sir,'[7] James says simply. For a year and a half, he has been a dutiful apprentice shopkeeper and done his best. He's halfway done. For many a lad, whose father is a mere day-labourer turned farm bailiff on a farm outside the coastal industrial town of Whitby – nearly as poor as the dirt he tills – just the idea that he will likely run a store of his own would be enough of a step up in life. But one cannot spend hours, days, weeks, months and now *years* in a dull store by the seaside watching ships come and go and not wonder about where they have come from, where they are going to, and not hunger to experience some of that himself.

He wants to go to sea, sir.

Infinitely relieved at least that the fine young man really *is* a fine young man after all and has not let him down terribly, Mr Sanderson goes from disappointment to deliverance. He loosens his grip on his cane, and on the spot, he grants James a release from his indenture. Over the coming days, the kindly shopkeeper even uses his good offices to secure young James an apprenticeship with his friend John Walker, a local ship-owner and fellow Quaker, who, in partnership with his brother Henry, runs colliers out of Whitby, ferrying coal from Newcastle just to the North down the East coast of England and up the Thames to feed the rapidly multiplying factories of a booming industrial London, which burns over a million tons a year.

For young Cook, taking 10 such round-trips a year down the coast and back is a perfect opportunity to 'learn the ropes'.

Yes, it means that the 18 months of hard work as a shop apprentice are effectively thrown away, but as it happens his time in Staithes had been extremely valuable in any case. The colourful, rough breed of men who are the local fishermen had taught the young fellow to dream. It had all become so intoxicating that, even back in the shop lately, on the busiest of days, he could think of little else. Well, now it is time to try to turn his dreams into reality.

And so, one day in late autumn when the leaves are just starting to fall and there is the beginning of a bite in the air, it happens. The scraggly long-limbed James Cook – newly turned 18 years old – puts all of his worldly belongings into one sack, throws it over his shoulder and sets off.

On the cliff tops above Staithes, he takes one last look behind to the tiny town far below and, buttoning his coat against the now strong wind, begins walking Southward a dozen miles cross-country over the moors – not for nothing does a local saying have it that 'the only road to Whitby is the sea'[8] – until he reaches the Western cliff above the destination of his dreams.

And there it is!

Just below is the bustling medieval port town of Whitby, a vista of tightly packed red-tiled roofs cluttered together on steep slopes.

Young Cook skips down the rough-hewn stone steps that wind between the houses, all the way to the port proper built around the River Esk, which flows into the North Sea at this point.

Around the narrow river mouth – a veritable harbour when the tide is high, and a shallow inlet laced with intertidal mud flats when it's low – bustling shipyards jostle against each other for position along the river's silty banks, astir with maritime industry. Ship skeletons sit half-built on dry docks, sooty smoke billows from fires at the rope-works.

Taking it all in, glorying in being a part of this busy seaside port, limber young James now wanders along the cobbled paths to the port proper – through the mass of captains, sailors, workers and street urchins – and begins to make inquiries.

Hello, my name is James Cook, and I am looking for the house of John Walker, if you could help me?

Yes, as a matter of fact they can. Captain Walker is well known in this tight-knit community and young James is soon making his way to the house, delighting in all the booming industry going on around him, the smell of fish, tar, hemp and freshly sawn timber all mingling in the smoky air. He has arrived!

Captain Walker's three-storey higgledy-piggledy house is just 20 feet from the water's edge, at the end of Grape Lane – formerly Grope Lane and before that Gropecunt Lane, when it was infamous for prostitution – a thoroughfare so narrow that one of the many drunk men lying across it over the centuries could have his boots touching one side of it, and his hands the other.

Just as many a life has suddenly and radically altered course on the flip of a coin, so too has young James gone from one life to another in a very short time, all because his own shiny shilling has come up with neither heads nor tails, but sails – the call of the South Seas.

•

Like all the ship-owners of this port, John Walker and his brother Henry – who prove to be friendly men, at least so far as oft cantankerous ship-owners go – run small colliers of the type known as 'Whitby cats', a lightly rigged vessel of around 105 feet in length with a remarkably shallow draught. They are 'round in the bow, broad and square in the stern; her lines are laid for room rather than speed; her length is about three times her breadth'.[9] With a crew of just a dozen or less, a Whitby cat (the 'cat' part is thought to have come from the Norwegian 'kati', meaning ship) can carry 30 keels of coal in its hold – some 600 tons – and, most importantly, do so with remarkable safety as its shallow draught and wide waist allow it to ride out nearly any storm and sail with impunity over all bar the most shallow of shoals – those trouble-some sandbanks often found just below the water's surface. The key is to 'touch and go', touch so lightly in shallow waters that you can still keep going, effectively nudging your way forward.

Not for the cat any ornamental figure on the prow, though, for it is built for work not beauty.

Like a short fat lad with a snub nose and feet set wide apart, the Whitby cat cannot move particularly fast, but it can carry a very heavy load and be exceedingly difficult to knock over. If it were of equine nature it would be all pit-pony and no show-pony, with the heart of a thoroughbred.

Of course the great day soon arrives when young James sets foot on the deck of a Whitby cat for the first time, and it is like a lad from a thatched cottage – rather like that of his parents' – first setting foot in a cathedral, gazing at the towering masts high above, the shimmering furled sails like the wings of a giant bird.

James Cook, who is also put together with no frills and an enormous capacity for work, is soon springing up into a very tall and striking lad indeed – over six feet tall with a strong nose and earnest gaze – and, to the delight of Mr Walker, he proves extraordinarily adept at grasping even complex concepts. At the local school for apprentices, over his first wintry Whitby months, he plunges confidently straight into learning the basic principles of 'navigation, the meaning of latitude and longitude, how to read a chart and much more'.[10]

Whitby's apprentice schools are nothing like the grammar schools or public schools of larger towns across Great Britain. You don't need Greek, Latin or literature to run a ship, so why learn it? In these parts they teach practical skills for budding 'jack tars', sailors, to give them the tools to turn themselves into fine seamen.

For his part, the practical James could not be happier. As a child he had benefited from the kindly attentions of his wealthy master's kindly wife, Mrs Skottowe, who had recognised his sharpness and taken time to teach him 'his letters'[11] – giving him a key which he had delighted thereafter in turning in every lock he could find. Yes, though a mere labourer's child in the tiny village of Marton, what had set him apart had been his thirst for knowledge, and immediately thereafter the four happy years spent at the village school in Great Ayton, surrounded by other children, improving his reading, learning how to write and 'the first rules of arithmetic'[12] had been a pleasure. And he now realises how much he had missed those days of learning while in the shop with Mr Sanderson. Now, back at it, in a classroom among many other lads just like himself – there are no fewer than 1256 apprentices listed in Whitby this year – and learning all about subjects that will directly help him to live his sea-going dream, young James Cook learns as never before, growing intellectually with every week that passes, to the delight of his teachers.

So too is his 'home life' happy, as he is truly welcomed into Mr Walker's household, where, at the insistence of dear Mrs Walker, he eats with the family and, at the meal's conclusion, is not obliged to retreat to sleep under a shop counter, but may retire gracefully to the perfectly comfortable attic in their 'plain Quaker-like house'.[13]

The Walkers' house, like the Walkers themselves, exudes a solid old-world integrity, built from hard work, for stability and with no façade whatsoever. Their home is a fitting sanctuary in which a young man like James Cook might learn the value of patience and humility. Sharing these lodgings are other apprentices, their bunks closely grouped just like the hammocks on a real ship.

But here, he does not sleep. No, he has retired to do more study, for the Walkers' housekeeper, Mary Prowd, his 'trusty old nurse'[14] who has taken such a shine to the lad she calls him 'Honey James',[15] always ensures that his chair is in position before a table bearing many freshly sharpened pencils on the right-hand side, illuminated by many candle ends for him to burn so that he can pore over his books and tables into the night, usually making endless calculations designed to hone his capacity for working out where in the world – literally – he might be.

It's all a luxury he's never known before – with time to devote himself exclusively to learning, with a base that fully facilitates the same. Not only does James feel at home, he *is* at home, with his buttoned-down personality fitting in well with the Quaker values of modesty, hard work, diligence and a markedly gentle way of dealing with the world.

In fact, the entire port of Whitby, with a strong Quaker community forming the backbone of its 5000 residents, is an equally fertile environment for a young man like him who is eager to work hard, improve himself and gain a maritime education above all other things. For Whitby judges a man on devotion to those values far more than the mere class concerns that prevail in much of the rest of England. And just as a Quaker cares not for class and is not intimidated by aristocracy, nor does he drink too much, nor does he visit brothels or engage in brawling. He is moderate in all things, bar hard work.

Still, as John Walker knows only too well – as he has been disappointed by bright sparks before – excelling at book learning is one thing. Prospering at sea is another thing entirely.

Ah, but young James Cook proves adept at that, too, for from the moment he plants his feet on the deck of his first vessel, the *Freelove*, in February 1747, it is as though the rocking of his cradle must have been the precursor to the rocking of this ship – for it is like he was born to go to sea.

Young Cook is, in a word, indefatigable. Mr Walker, like so many people after him, finds young James a fellow of surprising and extraordinary gifts, capable of relentless focus over long periods and a singular capacity to get the job done, come what may; a fellow of action who is hungry to learn 'practical seamanship . . . all the parts of a ship and her rigging; the sails, the running and the standing gear, and how to use them'.[16]

These are the foundations to turn a lad from land-lubber to sailor.

Now, see here. This here raised deck just behind the mainmast is the quarter-deck and this is where the Captain commands the vessel from, as it allows full vision of all the ship's workings without turning your head. Just behind him is the tiny poop deck, which can also be used for observation, but is essentially the roof of the Captain's cabin – the most comfortable spot on the ship. In terms of sleeping quarters, you can judge your importance by how close to that cabin you are, 'aft the mast', with all the officers' quarters high and towards the stern of the ship, away from the part that must bash through the waves. The common seamen however are 'before the mast'. The further forward and lower down you are, the lower you are in the hierarchy.

And while here at sea, we don't talk about miles. We talk of 'furlongs' and 'leagues', with nearly eight furlongs to a mile and 28 furlongs to a league – so a league is a wee bit under three-and-a-half miles, do you see? And a cable is some 185 yards. As to 25 *miles* in total of rope you see that makes up the spiderweb of lines and rigging about all the masts, that will take a little more explaining . . .

While at sea Cook watches the old salts working in the rigging, he memorises the coastline between Whitby and London and he learns to navigate around the treacherous shoals and hidden rocks of England's East coast and the notorious Thames Estuary. By the time he instinctively thinks in terms of 'larboard' and 'starboard', instead of 'left' and 'right', he is granted his dearest wish of all and sent to more distant and dangerous horizons, on voyages even beyond the North Sea coal trade. He even gets an exhilarating taste of the oft treacherous Baltic Sea when he takes coal to the Low Countries and returns with timber, pitch, hemp and iron to supply Whitby's ship-building industry. He even joins voyages in the government's service, ferrying 'foreign mercenaries and their horses from Middleburg in Flanders to Dublin and Liverpool',[17] allowing him to sail the Channel and the Irish Sea, to weather storms with towering waves, find his sea-legs and grow in confidence with every passing day.

Most impressively, once on shore, the lad shows no interest in downing copious amounts of liquor at the taverns and no interest in whorehouses, unlike so many of the other young sailors. Instead, with Walker's strong encouragement, he concentrates on his studies.

As the Walker brothers beam just to see the lad blossoming in this fashion, young James evolves into a young man who is never idle, but always at work on something, just like his masters. Occasionally he can make it back home to his own family at Great Ayton, where, as the second of eight children, he is greeted as the conquering hero – with his beloved mother, Grace, always preparing a special meal for the occasion. But even while he is with them the truth is he is always hungering to get back to Whitby and get to sea.

Certainly, it takes three years of seafaring for James Cook to finish his apprenticeship and be promoted from 'Boy' to 'Able Seaman' in the Merchant Navy, but by the time he gets there in 1750, he is a highly qualified Able Seaman. For he is not only capable of rigging, operating and maintaining the sails, scrubbing the decks, caulking leaky seams in the wooden hull by using a mallet and caulking iron to force the sticky black pitch into the gaps just so, but he can also speak fluent sailor – *'Abaft the beam!'* *'Catch a turn there!'* *'Paul there, my hearty'* *'Predy the main deck'* *'Ready with the lead!'*[18] – and also has the hang of accurate depth sounding, not to mention knowing how to read the barometer to predict the weather.

Depth sounding, at least, or 'swinging the lead' as it is more commonly known, is fairly easy – in fact one of the easiest jobs on the ship as you stand on the special platform built outside the hull, by the bows of the ship, and swing a long thin piece of rope, on which is attached a heavy piece of lead, into the water. The rope has regularly spaced pieces of material wrapped around it – made of leather, calico, serge and different pieces of rope – and by seeing how many knots, one fathom (6 feet) per knot, disappear beneath the waves before you hit the bottom, you can easily determine the depth of water you are in – and, most crucially, whether the ship is in danger by being in water that is too shallow.

Reading the barometer, too, is fairly straightforward.

Oh, say it one more time, James: *When the glass falls low; Prepare for a blow; When it rises high; Let your kites fly*[19] . . .

Again and again:

Winds at night are always bright; but winds in the morning, sailors take warning.[20]

Bit by bit, the young fellow builds up a deep well of experience by being in a difficult sea off a windswept coast of uncertain contours. Week after week, month after month, Cook is in the prow of the bow as the Whitby cat nudges through the storm-ravaged North and Baltic seas, regularly darting in to shore to load and unload coal, through thick mists and waters littered with shifting sands, dangerous shoals and tidal estuaries.

In fact, James Cook is such a promising prospect that in December 1752, at the age of 24, he sits and passes the formal exams to be a Mate – one of the Captain's officers – and in 1755, when 'young James' is now an imposing 26-year-old man of no little accomplishment after completing 16 voyages without blemish, John Walker even offers to make him Captain of the Whitby cat *Friendship*, on which he is currently serving.

But again Cook surprises . . .

For as global tension between the imperial giants Britain and France rises over trade, territory and established colonies, it becomes obvious that armed confrontation beckons, not merely a fight between countries but an actual world war. And one cold morning in the late spring of 1755, just as the *Friendship* sails up the Thames, the attention of the young Mariner is drawn to a bustle of men on the wharf at Wapping. *What is going on?* There appears to be a group of armed, uniformed men from the Royal Navy escorting a gaggle of dishevelled and clearly unhappy merchant sailors along the wharf to a waiting carriage.

Oh. It is a press gang, a forced rounding up of young merchant sailors to man Royal Navy ships as Great Britain prepares to force the issue with France over their North American colonies. Britain is moving from a peace footing to a war footing. Perhaps it is only a matter of time before *all* merchantmen will be so compelled?

Why wait?

Watching as the sailors are bustled along the wharf, Cook comes to a key decision. He will decline Mr Walker's offer of Captaincy, and volunteer in the Royal Navy. Despite the fact he is now on the edge of everything he has been working for and more – becoming the Captain of a ship – Cook has looked at the life of such Captains, endlessly trawling familiar waters with dull coal, and has decided he can do *much* better. For James Cook is quietly developing another key attribute – *ambition*, a stirring in his soul that he can do something not done before, achieve things undreamt of by anyone, let alone one of low birth. But he will need to take real risks to achieve this ambition.

He will need, once more, to throw away certainty for the lure of adventure, the hope of glory. Somehow this man of such humble beginnings, James Cook, has decided that even something so vaulted as being the Captain of a ship in the Merchant Navy is not enough for him. He can do better still. For he wants to be an officer in *His Majesty's Royal Navy*. Of course it is highly unlikely that he could ever make Captain – for such an exalted post is simply never reached by the lower orders – but simply to be an officer of the quarter-deck would be an extraordinary achievement. Beyond that, he wants adventure – there is no doubt that war is looming – and so he promptly resigns.

Three days later the muster roll of one of His Majesty's fleet of the Royal Navy, HMS *Eagle*, records the arrival of a 26-year-old sailor more unremarkable than a stray dog: '161. From London Rendezvous, James Cook, rating, AB [able seaman] date of entry June 17th, 1755.'[21]

James Cook doesn't mind the Able Seaman's dismal wage of £1/4s a month, or the demotion from his rank of Mate in the Merchant fleet, as it is a sacrifice he's willing to make, content to begin again and trust that he will rise on merit. After all, while advancement in the British Army frequently turns on your class, your familial and classmate connections – the latter all the more powerful depending on what school or university you graduated from – the Royal Navy is much more open. So esoteric are many of the skills required, so dependent on hours spent at sea actually sailing a ship, that tried and true sailors of sufficiently sound character are likely to rise to the position of Master's Mate, or even Master, even if, like Cook, they come from origins as humble as a garden potato.

CHAPTER ONE

THE ROYAL NAVY

The Royal Navy of England hath ever been its greatest defence and ornament; it is its ancient and natural strength, the floating bulwark of our island.

William Blackstone, Justice of Court of the King's Bench, 1765

Mr Cook frequently expressed to me the obligation he was under to Capt. Simcoe, and on my meeting him in London . . . he confessed most candidly that the several improvements and instructions he had received on board the Pembroke *had been the sole foundation of the services he had been enabled to perform.*[1]

Samuel Holland on Cook's time under Captain Simcoe

So, on the scene of our scrutiny, into this busy age, steps the figure of Joseph Banks, the gifted, the fortunate youth: enthusiastic, curious, the voyager, the disciple of Linnaeus, the botanist and zoologist, the devotee of savages; not yet, as one examines his early career, a Public Figure, but certainly a Gentleman, certainly a figure typical of his age; and certainly as much as anyone, and more than most, the Gentleman Amateur of Science.

J.C. Beaglehole, *The Endeavour Journal of Joseph Banks 1768–1771*

July 1755, HMS *Eagle*, The Channel, a tall ship and a star to steer her by

The tall and imposing figure standing at the prow of HMS *Eagle* – one of His Majesty's ships, a 1222-ton ship of the line, carrying 58 guns – radiates pride and ability.

James Cook has taken to life in the Royal Navy with great gusto, enormous diligence and even greater delight . . . and has already hugely impressed his commander, Captain Joseph Hamar. For while it is one thing for Hamar to have a skeleton crew substantially filled by those who have been press-ganged, it is quite another to have a more than

1

competent young man who wants to be there, and really knows what he is doing.

For the real problem the good Cap'n has been experiencing is that most of those press-ganged are land-lubbers not seamen; and are consequently both distressed to be on board and uninterested in learning any sea skills. Captain Hamar has already written his concerns to the Admiralty – the London land office of the Lords of the Sea, those who not only rule the waves, but also the lives of every British sailor from cabin boy to Admiral – 'I do not believe there is a worse man'd ship in the Navy.'[2]

It means that James Cook is precious indeed, and from the first day had stood out to the Captain as a real sailor, a brilliant diamond in the land-lubber roughs, even a shiny shilling among dull pennies. It is not just that he knows what to do, it is that he even has a way with the men, an understanding of the common man – for he clearly is one himself – which allows him to coax out of them work that even the Captain struggles to extract. And so, just one month and seven days after signing on to the Royal Navy, Able Seaman James Cook has been made Master's Mate James Cook, if you please, and carefully records that fact in his understated way, in his first journal of record:

> Log Book on Board his Maj[s] Ship Eagle, Kept by Jam[s] Cook Masters Mate Commencing the 27th June 1755 . . .[3]

It is a key breakthrough, clearly a sign that the Captain considers Cook to be warrant officer material, perhaps one day a Master himself, as Master's Mate is a key lower rung on that ladder for competent seamen who are not gentlemen; whereas if you are high-born and went to the right school, you are liable to be made, even with no seamanship, one of the 'Midshipmen' – so called because these junior commissioned officers berth amidships – based on your pedigree.

So be it.

It is not in Cook's nature to bridle against the unfairness of the class system. He just wants to work, understand more and get better at what he does. On this day he turns from the prancing white horses of the frothy waves that lie ahead on the Channel and looks back at the receding vision of Portsmouth. It is wonderful to be at sea, on such an exciting mission, his first venture into a war arena, as they must patrol between Southern Ireland and the Scilly Islands with orders to intercept and capture any French ships of war that they encounter. The bonus for Cook is the actual bounty he will collect as his share of the spoils, should they capture any French vessels. It's a potential fortune, which encourages every Captain to engage.

As it turns out, the misadventure of a broken mast during a bad storm means this first mission is all too brief, and just four weeks later the Admiralty replaces Captain Hamar with a man of considerably more firepower: 32-year-old Captain Hugh Palliser, the son of an Army Captain and – herewith, his instant rapport with Cook – a Yorkshireman.

They both know what it is to be branded with the first sound out of your mouth as 'Yorkshireman', and they are proud of that brand. Stubborn, industrious, and proud of their humility, as only a Yorkshireman can be.

Other sailors might look blankly at Captain Palliser when he says, '*Put wood in 'ole!*' but Cook grew up in a house where his father said that all the time, and knows to *shut the door*.

He is more than happy to have Captain Palliser as his '*gaffer*', boss, and works each day and into the evening hours until he is completely '*jiggered*', exhausted.

Their bond is as instant as it is deep, and, while on their first voyage – this time patrolling the Western approaches to the Channel – Palliser makes time to instruct the eager young fellow on the practical aspects of navigation, the many things that Cook has not been able to pick up from his book studies. Before long, he is methodically recording observations so that he can begin drawing charts that show an accurate outline of the coast.

And now, James takes this sextant, and 'shoots the sun', measuring the angle of the sun above the horizon at a specific time to calculate our latitude.

Night after night, after mess, when the ship is secure under watch, Captain Palliser sits up late with this enthusiastic student of the sea, talking all matters maritime, including how science is closing in on achieving the Holy Grail of navigation: longitude – how far they are to the East or West of the meridian line passing through Greenwich outside London, which is far more difficult to assess than the latitude.

And of course Captain Palliser is also an able tutor in such grand traditions of the Royal Navy as always passing the port to the left, and *sliding* it along the table, so that not a drop is spilled even in heavy seas – and, in fact, even when you are on land. In similar spirit, while the first toast of the night will always be 'God Save the King', it was after King Charles II himself was returning to England on the *Royal Charles* and hit his head on the low ceiling of the Captain's cabin when replying to a toast that he personally established the tradition for Officers of the Royal Navy to remain seated for the toast. Superstitions? There are many, but always remember: 'Stop a glass ringing and save a man's life', the idea being that if a glass is bumped and starts to ring, you must immediately put your finger on it to stop it, as somewhere in the world a sailor's life is threatened. Yes, perhaps a silly superstition, but do it anyway.

So much to learn!

In November 1755, the bond between Captain Palliser and Master's Mate Cook is deepened further when the Cap'n rides shotgun with young Cook through his first naval battle, though it is less a real battle than giving a good pounding to a storm-ravaged French warship they find in the Bay of Biscay. The French surrender but their ship is not worth saving so the British set her afire. The worthy and always humane Captain Palliser – a Captain's Captain that a young naval man can always get his bearings for life from – has his crew take the *Eagle*'s small boats to pick up 26 of the some 200 surviving Frenchmen.

James Cook records the day in his log with typically even temperament: 'Received on board from the *Esperance* 26 prisoners at 4 o'clock. *Esperance* on fire and there being no possibility of keeping her above water.'[4]

As she sinks beneath the waves, so too does any chance of a bounty, but as Great Britain and France declare war six months later – they'd effectively been at war for 18 months but until then neither had bothered with a formal declaration – there will be more opportunities to come. Indeed, the following year James Cook and his good Cap'n have the *Eagle* swoop, all guns blazing, on a 50-gun French ship, *Duc d'Aquitaine*, just two days out of Plymouth, which they capture after a 45-minute clash.

Who can take the French ship back to port?

Why that would be, of course, Master's Mate James Cook, and he arrives a wealthier man than he's ever been, courtesy of his share of the bounty – in his case £15, more than half of his annual pay of £28-14s-0d.

So it goes for the remarkable James Cook. By October 1757, just before his 29th birthday, he receives his first warrant, making him no less than Master James Cook of HMS *Pembroke*. In just a decade, labourer's son James Cook has gone from a boy whose maritime experience was no more than the wetness behind his ears, as he set foot on a merchant Whitby cat for the first time, to Master in the Royal Navy, generally regarded as the highest naval office that a non-gentleman might aspire to. The Master is usually the one in control of a ship's navigation, setting the best course, keeping the logbook, inspecting all stores and provisions, observing coasts, shoals and rocks. In other words he is 'the chief executive officer on board',[5] often getting paid more than the Lieutenants and Surgeons, while the gentleman Captain merely oversees the whole operation.

The *Pembroke*'s commander is Captain John Simcoe, a Royal Navy man who – as well as being an experienced naval commander with a reputation as a 'fighting Captain'[6] – is a devoted man of science, well versed in the art of navigation and forever reading the latest advances in the area. Like Palliser, Simcoe is ahead of the Admiralty on this and has realised sooner than my Lords that proficiency in navigation is the key to unlocking the world, and it can only come through dedicated training by experts. What is more, Captain Simcoe is by nature both ambitious and accomplished – having received his Lieutenant's commission at the ripe age of 28 – and seeing the same ambition in his new Master, takes him under his wing and resolves to teach his willing pupil all that he can.

Another bonus for Cook in being Master of a newly built 60-gun ship of 1222 tons is the long voyage it promises – the direct fulfilment of his earliest dreams back in Staithes. Soon he will be setting out on a long voyage across a vast ocean, on this occasion no less than the mighty Atlantic. He could be slicing sides of bacon or measuring lengths of tartan for an old Yorkshire biddy, perhaps still sleeping under a dark counter ... but here he is master of his fate and Captain of his soul for some time already, but now, now, he is also Master of HMS *Pembroke*!

The sea has been good to him.

•

There can be few things more impressive than a gathering of His Majesty's grand ships of the line sailing off to serve Britain, and this morning, 22 February 1758, is a case in point, as no fewer than 15 of them leave Plymouth bound for North America and an upcoming battle with the French and their Native allies. William Pitt, Great Britain's Secretary of State, has ordered the combined British naval and land forces to wrest control of the major fort at Louisburg on Île Royale before sailing up the St Lawrence River to capture Quebec. Thus shall Britain put a definitive end to the interests of the haughty and strutting French in North America.

Louisburg is a fortress town established for purely military purposes and sits menacingly at the mouth of the St Lawrence River, the critical artery that delivers the lifeblood to the French colony's beating heart – Quebec, the capital of New France. It is garrisoned by about '3000 regulars, 1000 armed inhabitants and a band of Indians'.[7] Up on the walls are mounted 219 cannon and 17 mortars, while below in the harbour five ships of the line and seven frigates manned by 3000 men, bristle with a total of 546 guns. If the English can take Louisburg and so prevent supply to the heavily garrisoned Quebec, then it can only be a matter of time before they can sail the fleet up the St Lawrence and take Quebec, too.

The grand armada looks majestic as the ships make their way through the Channel and onwards to the Atlantic.

And down there, sailing among them, is HMS *Pembroke*.

Look closely, on the quarter-deck. You see that austere yet elegant-looking man standing by Captain John Simcoe, over six feet and well built, looking ship-shape in his pristine warrant officer's uniform? He's too busy with his duties to be on the prow for this magnificent moment, but it's him all right, the humble Yorkshireman, Master James Cook. And oh how his eyes glitter, just to look at the mighty warships flanking his own. His first long voyage. Across the Atlantic to the New World!

And yet, such is the nature of long voyages at sea: the shine turns to rust with time. The wind in the sails of the fresh seafarer blows out. After six weeks of battering headway against oncoming waves and gales, of eating stale food and drinking oft slimy water, many of those aboard this armada are beginning to suffer the scourge of scurvy, a foe far more devastating and persistent than the French. Aboard the *Pembroke*, dozens of sailors with swollen gums and aching joints are incapable of rising from their berths. Within days, one afflicted sailor dies in his hammock, toothless and bloated. Many more follow.

Most frustrating for Cook, a problem-solver and man of action who has never seen so many healthy men struck down so quickly, is that the disease has no seeming cause, no rhyme in time or reason from season. It hits day and night, as shipmate after shipmate starts to feel the dreaded stiffness in his joints and the swelling of his gums, which always mark the onset of the oft fatal illness. Soon, splotchy blotches of purple start to appear on thighs and legs and often turn into suppurating, stinking sores – that make even friends turn away in horror, and fear. Teeth fall out and the skin takes on a lifeless pallor even as nostrils, lips and anus suffer from prolonged bleeding. Shocking cases of diarrhoea – never welcome at the best of times but a disaster in the confined spaces of a ship, with men sleeping on hammocks – run through the ship's company on the lower decks. But there is nothing Master Cook and his fellow officers can do to stop it. A devastating 26 men out of their crew of 324 succumb to the infamous sailors' disease, to be buried at sea in ceremonies where all are clearly wondering *Who will be next?*

Almost as if he is the chosen one, however, as if the gods have chosen to smile upon him, none of the horror touches James Cook. His robust constitution holds as strong as ever and his capacity to bear hardship shines for all to see, even as his seafaring skills continue to leap forward with remarkable alacrity, powered by his acute intellect and his drive to improve himself.

What doesn't leap forward is the *Pembroke*, as it must proceed Westwards into the teeth of contrary winds, and it is not until the second week of May 1758 – 11 weeks after departure, on a journey that was meant to take just three weeks – that Captain John Simcoe finally orders the anchor to be dropped in the deep harbour at Halifax, Nova Scotia. Dozens of the crew are immediately rushed to the naval hospital, and half a dozen of those who remain that evening steal the *Pembroke*'s yawl and desert. It leaves the ship so unalterably undermanned that at the end of the month it cannot sail out of Halifax with the rest of the 157 vessels of the British fleet bound for the battle at Louisburg.

It is no less than a month before the *Pembroke* can muster the manpower through local press-ganging to get going again, and when they drop anchor at Gabarus Bay, a few miles West of Louisburg, they drop into that grinding, still state of conflict known as a siege. The French are content to wait, however, knowing that the rocky spine of the coast will serve as insurance against any incursion from the *Pembroke* and its ilk. And what have they to worry about? The *Pembroke* settles solemnly into place with a fleet of 30 ships of the line, flanked by frigates, sloops and fire ships, vessel upon vessel. The 12,600 troops land to prosecute the siege, while on the ships – bobbing, waiting, enduring the endless boredom that sieges provide in abundance – are 8000 sailors. The French have noted that despite this, yes, some English may have already landed South of Louisburg with heavy artillery. But it is no matter, their arrival will amount to a pinprick, not a punch. There is precious little chance that the French walls shall be breached by foot, and no chance by sail or oar. What the French do not know is that their citadel is already under siege, not by men . . . but by maps.

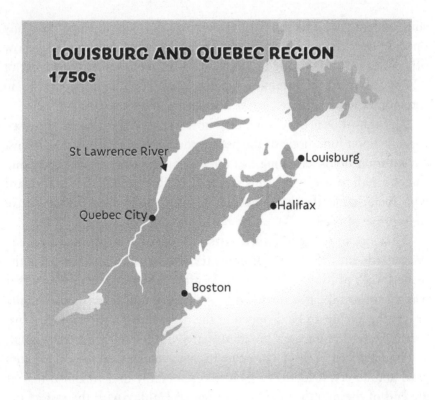

It is 3 o'clock in the morning, on 25 July 1758. Securely hidden under a comforting blanket of fog and darkness, some 50 boats filled with 600 British sailors from the *Pembroke* and other ships, make their way into the bay at Louisburg. The men on the oars row as silently as possible, each oar slipping beneath the surface and pulled with a muffled grunt. They come up alongside the two French warships charged with guarding Louisburg. In the dark, British sailors shinny up ropes to the deck above.

In his log, James Cook reports the night's events: '50 boats manned and armed rowed into the harbour ... in order to cut away the Men of War and tow them into the NE Harbour, on which they did Viz the [*Bienfaisant*] of 64 guns, the [*Prudent*] being aground she was set on fire, at which the firing ceased on both sides.'[8]

The next day, 26 July 1758, the French Governor of Île Royale hauls up the white flag above Louisburg's stone fortress and the British now have control over both the gulf and the river mouth, with one significant problem to overcome before they can reach their goal of capturing

Quebec, further upriver. That is, they have nothing beyond a single rudimentary chart of the St Lawrence River – done by an Englishman, its title, *Exact Chart of the River St Lawrence*, is patently absurd – and they know nothing of its shoals, tides and outcrops, and nor do they have any idea of the lie of the land surrounding the New French capital.

The most urgent task now for General James Wolfe of the Army and Admiral Saunders of the Navy is to find the safest route for the fleet to move upriver, as well as the best cove to secure so they can land their infantry and artillery *en masse*. (And although the French have direction buoys littered along the river to guide their own boats, they will surely remove them with the threat of the British lion at their doorstep.)

Wolfe has just the man for the job, and calls up his brilliant engineer and master military surveyor, Lieutenant Samuel Holland, to begin charting the area around the Gulf of St Lawrence and the river, and moving up as far as he dare, as close to Quebec as possible, so they can form a plan based on solid information. Snapping off a salute, Lieutenant Holland is quickly on his way to collect his instruments from his quarters.

27 July 1758, Kennington Cove, the master pieces it together

For now, at least, this fleet of the Royal Navy is able to drop anchor in the harbour that lies below Louisburg, and disgorge its sailors and soldiers into the fort, as well as the town itself.

Master James Cook, with some unexpected time on his hands, goes on land to look around Kennington Cove just South of Louisburg, where the British troops and artillery were first landed back in June. Now, usually when he had any spare time he would retire to a quiet spot to delve deeply into the intricacies of highly complicated mathematics and the endless wonders of astronomy, both key to honing his navigational skills. But on this day, he is going for a walk along the recently conquered shore, which is littered with the debris of tens of British boats smashed up by the heavy surf during the landings, when he stops . . . and stares.

Pray tell, what is that?

And who is that?

What is that figure in yonder dunes doing?

It proves to be a Lieutenant from His Majesty's Army with some sort of contraption in front of him . . . it looks like a tripod, atop which is a metallic square, like the top of a table, supporting a triangular instrument, which the man keeps adjusting, before scribbling something upon the table-like surface – whereupon he fidgets with the instrument atop the square once more then scribbles again. And again and again!

Cook stands quietly, staring, until the inevitable . . .

. . .

. . .

Presently, the other officer becomes aware of a tall figure hovering close.

Yes . . . ?

It is a Master James Cook of HMS Pembroke, *sir, and he is eager to know what is going on, for it is all Double-Dutch to him.*

Captain Lieutenant Samuel Holland grins to hear it. Holland is a Dutchman, an accomplished surveyor and military engineer so highly regarded he has become General Wolfe's engineer of choice for all thorny problems, despite being foreign-born. It's just James Cook's luck to not only come across him at this time, but that Holland is of a friendly disposition, surprised at the interest shown by this naval officer of about his age, but happy to answer questions. After all, most of Holland's own contemporaries have turned their backs on his complex obsession as a military surveyor, whatever that is – the mathematics of it all tends to send their minds reeling into confusion – so, yes, he is happy to talk to Master Cook and explain his occupation.

Now look. What I have here is a 'plane table'. With this device, backed by deep concentration, the patience of Job and a knowledge of mathematics, an extraordinary thing can be accomplished – you can develop a precise map, which will allow you to formulate an equally precise plan of attack, do you see?

Cook's eyes narrow, his thick brows furrowing. No words are needed, Holland knows the question behind that face.

How, sir?

Holland beams to have found such a willing pupil. He gestures to the setup in front of him, and begins to explain.

Well, the method is called 'triangulation', and it relies on the plane table – this flat square here on top of the tripod – being absolutely horizontal, which you can ensure by virtue of this spirit level. With a sheet of paper secured to the top of the plane table, we next use this alidade – like a telescope and a ruler in one – to record the angle from our current position to particular features, like yonder headlands, river entrance and beaches. And now, here is the thing. By now moving the plane table a known precise distance, as if along the base of a very long triangle and taking different angles to the same features, and marking the points those lines intersect, we can work out their precise distances from each other, and our plane table! An accurate map starts to form up beneath your very fingers! If you do this while on a ship, taking constant angles and measurements you can map an entire coastline with superb accuracy. You've surely learnt that as a Master in the Navy?

James Cook shakes his head regretfully. No, he has not. He has heard of the concept, from Captain Palliser mostly, but as far as he knows His Majesty's Royal Navy has no interest and an equal number of instruments.[9]

As to surveying features of the land, it is not even discussed in naval circles – and yet, to his credit, James Cook immediately recognises how learning Holland's sophisticated land surveying techniques could revolutionise the work of the Royal Navy. He has chanced upon the man to know in the world of land surveying. A lantern has been illuminated above his head, and he suddenly understands the significance of Holland's work.

To this point, most charts that he has both seen, and roughly sketched under Captain Palliser's instruction, have been just that – *rough* – no more than an indication of the contours of a coastline as seen by the naked eye and scrawled by an untrained hand. A hit-and-miss affair whereby if you trusted the map of a shoreline, let's say, you were just as likely to hit a cruel reef as to miss a dangerous shoal – and to finish on a fatal shore. To this point, working in the coal trade and Navy alike, a premium is always placed on the old salts – those sailors who personally know each nook and cranny of the coastline, who know where the dangers lie in the harbour entrance at low tide. They've seen friends lost on those reefs, and will never forget the agony of hitting them.

But if a map could be precise, a thing to be trusted rather than warily consulted, if they could achieve that for nautical charts, why such a thing could transform the world of the sailor, and perhaps even open up the unknown world to one willing to embrace this new way. Cook is just such a man and begs Holland to give him more in-depth instruction.

Please, do go on, Lieutenant Holland.

The Dutchman does and is thrilled as Cook questions him closely, noting the Englishman's keen intelligence, hunger to learn, and quick grasp of the essentials. In fact, Cook is so keen that Holland instantly makes him an offer.

As I am currently tasked with surveying and charting not just the town of Louisburg, but the whole of St Lawrence Bay and its shoreline, including as much of the river as possible, in preparation for the British land and naval attack on Quebec City . . . would you like to be one of my assistants and learn on the job? We have one imprecise English chart, and some French charts newly seized from Louisburg, but at first glance they look hopelessly inaccurate and we can certainly not trust the lives of our men and fate of our ships to their accuracy. We need to move fast and form accurate new charts. Will you help?

Well, Cook would love to, and on the spot Holland organises a meeting with Cook for the 'the next day in order to make him acquainted with the whole process'.[10]

The next day, bright and early, Cook returns to shore with the permission of Captain Simcoe, along with an invitation from the same for Holland to come this evening to dine on the *Pembroke* with the Captain and Master Cook, not forgetting, 'to bring the plane table pieces along'.[11] (Despite his own vast experience, even Captain Simcoe has never come across or even heard of this plane table that has his brilliant Master in such a stir, and is eager to see it.)

Lieutenant Holland and Master Cook spend an interesting and satisfying day surveying the shoreline of Gabarus Bay, where some of the fleet is still at anchor. Holland delights in teaching his willing pupil, whom he will ever after regard as one of the sharpest minds with whom he has dealt.

That evening, Holland is further impressed when, after accepting Captain Simcoe's invitation to dine, he notes that the *Pembroke*'s Great Cabin is nothing less than an incubator for science and learning.

These particular English officers are a rare breed: devoted to improving their knowledge and determined to gather books, charts, instruments and, yes, people.

The Dutchman further delights to find in Captain Simcoe another keen intellect, as well as a man of great wisdom and experience.

For his part, Simcoe is impressed by Holland, and entirely agrees with young Cook. This is a man from whom his Master can learn an enormous amount, but his significance goes well beyond that. The art he is teaching has the potential to change marine navigation deeply.

From this day forth, Cook is consumed with the business of surveying and making charts, and, after fulfilling his official duties every day, fills every hour he can with both refining his craft and executing it in the service of Great Britain – the charts they are making will be key to the capture of Quebec – and the service of science, mathematics, navigation and draughtsmanship.

Summer 1758, Revesby Abbey, to the manor born

> *For you can't but be sensible that there is a great inattention in him, and an immoderate love of play . . . which we must endeavour to get the better of in some degree, or it will be a constant obstacle to his improvement. This sometimes occasions quarrels between us; tho' in other respects we agree extremely well together; as I really think him a very good-tempered and well-disposed boy.*[12]
>
> Assistant Master at Eton, Edward Young, in a letter to William Banks, the father of Joseph Banks, in February 1757

On this beautiful day, as a jaunty, tireless 15-year-old lad, lithe of limb and fresh of face, with the constitution of an ox, Joseph Banks is intent on enjoying his holidays from Eton out in the sunshine and fresh air, without a care in the world. As a matter of fact, as the scion of a family as long established in these parts as it is wealthy – with a whole *string* of estates – there are few things that concern Joseph in the first place. Everything is taken care of for him. And on this day he is strolling along a quaint country lane near his family's large and stately home, Revesby Abbey, 'a rather heavy, graceless mass'[13] of a manor set on a vast 340-acre estate in Lincolnshire with 'vast woods behind, vast fens in front',[14] surrounds that offer unlimited opportunity for fishing, one of young Joe's favourite hobbies.

After spending a wonderful afternoon bathing in the river with his friends, Joseph finds the light of the setting sun strikes perfectly on the wildflowers lining his path – pansies, violets, mignonette, hollyhocks, marigold, lavender and monk's hood – no less than the path of his future.

For now, in a moment he will remember ever afterwards, he stops and stares at the sheer wondrous beauty of the flowers and foliage that flank his steps. The *colour* of these blossoms! The *variety*! The *patterns* in all their splendour!

Yes, he has walked these green lanes all his life, but never has he seen revealed what he sees now, this impossibly glorious array of colours arranged in mysterious order.

'How beautiful!' he says to himself. 'Would it not be far more reasonable to make me learn the nature of these plants than the Greek and Latin I am confined to?'[15]

Right here and now, he resolves to become a student of the natural world, his mind blossoming at the very idea of blossoms.

Starting . . . now.

Skipping on, just a little further down the lane he comes across – *hulloa!* – an old woman collecting wild herbs and flowers, known locally as 'culling simples', to be sold to the local apothecaries.

'What is the name of that flower?'[16] he asks her, only to see her wrinkles of wisdom rising in surprise at the vision of a young *gentleman* of just 15 years taking an interest in her humble labours. All these years, and here again is something new she has never experienced before.

She tells this young gentleman with the flowing auburn hair that goes all the way to his shoulders the name of the flower and then stoops back down to work. But the boy stays hovering over her.

'What is that one?' he persists, pointing at the plant she is pulling out from the earth, its dirt-covered roots hanging limp like the hair of a vagabond.

The old woman, knowing the boy comes from the old abbey estate just up the way, is shrewd.

For the princely sum of sixpence I will teach you all I know of these 'wildflowers, their seasons, and where they can be collected'.[17]

The lad nods enthusiastically and hurries home to tell his bemused parents, William and Sarah Banks.

Their lad is interested in . . . what?

Plants? Herbs? Wildflowers?

It's all a bit . . . *common?*

Besides which, in his whole life young Joseph has only ever shown interest in 'games and sports' like fishing and cricket on the village green . . . until this? It is all very odd. Still, they agree to indulge this strange new passion, so long as he promises to not drop behind in his lessons.

Done. And it is not a passing fancy.

The next morning the sun creeping over their sprawling Lincoln estate finds Joseph crawling, gathering wildflowers . . . and soon enough, insects, butterflies, beetles, and whatever other wonders of nature he can find.

After several weeks, Joseph's stern father thinks this natural history fad of his son's has all gone too far and insists the lad spend more time reading his Greek and Latin at his desk than meandering outdoors.

Joseph's mother, Sarah, however, decides to actively encourage his strange pursuit. Certainly they are gentry, but they are landed gentry, which means the lad has grown up fairly earthy to begin with, surrounded by animals, and not afraid to get his hands dirty.

And after all, she may well have been responsible for his lack of fear of even the ugliest side of nature in the first place. As a wee one he would take toads into his hands and bring them right into contact with his nose and face, with her complete blessing as she had always insisted that, 'the toad is actually a harmless animal; and to whose manner of life man is certainly under some obligation as its food is chiefly those insects which devour his crops and annoy him in various ways'.[18]

It is just the way his beloved mother is, and before long she gives him a copy of the iconic *Gerard's Herball – or Generall Historie Of Plants* to consult, which he does every day thereafter, taking it back to Eton, where its pages are soon ripped, ear-marked and smudged with both soil and the sweat from his dripping brow from an afternoon's exertion.

Back in the boarding house at Eton, few friends understand this latest obsession of 'Joe' Banks, but they too watch his love of natural history – the study of animal, vegetable and mineral – grow with bemusement rather than disdain. A charismatic and popular lad among his peers, Joe is even able to convince that fine fellow Henry Brougham to come out botanising with him. Decades later, Brougham would fondly reminisce to his son about those lazy, hazy afternoons collecting flowers, leaves and whole plants with Joe.

'He was a remarkably fine-looking, strong and active boy, whom no fatigue could subdue, and no peril daunt. His whole time out of school was given up to hunting after plants and insects, making a *hortus siccus* of the one, and forming a cabinet of the other. As often as Banks could induce me to quit my tasks in reading or in verse-making, he would take me on his long rambles.'[19] It's no wonder Brougham kept 'so many butterflies, beetles, and other insects, as well as a cabinet of shells and fossils'[20] in his home for the rest of his days.

As to young Joseph at the time, however, his whole attitude to his formal studies has changed.

He used to feel a bit bad about his lack of ardour for his Classical studies, as though he was letting his teachers and parents down. But what does he care now? He has all of natural history to study; a discipline of practical import, now opening up like a gorgeous rose in early spring. Something he can read about *and DO! Outdoors!* And though he is learning rapidly on a scale never before reached in his life – understanding the basic foundation stones on which the study of nature is based – it just doesn't feel like study used to. This is not a chore; it is a positive joy!

And yes, his teacher and his father become ever more frustrated at his waning reports – especially as they know what potential he has, as one so obviously highly intelligent – but their disappointment does not even make a scratch on the surface of his deep satisfaction. He is learning so much, of so many wondrous things.

His teachers continue to argue, but Joseph cares not. From now he will do only the bare minimum of what is required in his formal lessons – while reserving his passion for his natural history studies (indulging a little more in his particular passion for the botanical world, more than the animal and mineral).

And yes, perhaps it does come at a certain cost, in that the more time he spends botanising, the less time he has to learn the social mores for a man of his position, for it will later be noted of him by the leading salon sophisticate of the latter part of 18th century London, Fanny Burney, that 'if instead of going round the world he had only fallen from the moon, he could not appear less versed in the usual modes of a tea-drinking party',[21] while another contemporary would observe, 'his manners are rather coarse and heavy'.[22]

But he simply doesn't care, don't you see?

He wants to botanise, and that is *that is that!*

Winter 1758–59, Halifax, Nova Scotia, chartered account

It is so cold even the ice is shivering.

For sailors, the cold creeps from the depths, stalks the ship, engulfs it, and in the silent watch of the night finally works its way into not just the marrow of their bones, but into their very souls.

Shaking, shuddering, they emerge on deck in the morning to brave constant freezing storms and squalls that howl down upon them, leaving snow on even the low peaks. All around them the arctic currents and subzero temperatures are forming sea ice that infests the shallow waters close to land and threatens to block the British fleet's entry to the Gulf of St Lawrence. And yet it is not merely the gelid gloom which persuades the British Admirals and Generals of the wisdom in waiting until the following summer before launching their planned attack on Quebec. For they have captured Louisburg too late in the season; the St Lawrence River will soon be frozen over until spring comes to thaw it the next year.

The only useful thing that can be done meantime is to prepare charts of the route up the river, at least as far up as the wall of ice.

With frozen eyes, thus, the British brass look to the likes of Lieutenant Holland and the inexhaustible Master, James Cook, to do what needs to be done, to begin surveying the whole area and keep doing so through what looks likely to be the coldest North American winter on record. Though he is desperately cold, James Cook does not particularly care. As one who cut his maritime teeth in the North and Baltic Seas in even more challenging conditions – with waves as tall as pine trees thundering down upon you for days on end – the current conditions are luxurious. Yes, of course it's cold, but when you are bobbing at anchor in a safe and well-supplied harbour, it is nothing to complain about. And in any case, the task at hand is not only one he was born to, but, as he prefers constant industry to idleness of any sort, his spirits lift even further.

Given there are so few other official duties to engage him over this terrible winter, and the *Pembroke* is at anchor in a safe harbour, the ever kind Captain John Simcoe – himself taken a little ill with the bitter cold – allows James Cook to dedicate his every waking hour, and even a few hours that ordinarily would have been devoted to sleeping, to surveying.

Hence the dim figure you can see right there, every morning at the barest glimmer of first light, being rowed away from the *Pembroke* in a long-boat all the way to Gaspe Bay at the Southern head of the entrance to the St Lawrence River.

Landing on this rocky shore, he carefully sets up the plane table and sighting rule he has borrowed from Lieutenant Holland and, all day long right until just before sunset, works away on his chart – the first full survey he has attempted alone. He wants it to be *perfect*. As he grows more confident, Cook even adds some techniques of his own, eschewing Lieutenant Holland's exclusively land-based trigonometric surveying to take the boat out and survey different features from the sea itself. At other times he has his crew carry large and colourful flags to various points, so he can measure different angles to distinct points, rather than amorphous masses. He also keeps the crew busy by taking soundings at various points, so he can include this data too, in a comprehensive land–sea survey. It is slow, painstaking work but, bit by bit, the chart forms up beneath his ever more skilled hands, recording every peak, every bluff, every promontory or point of interest. The plane tabling and the soundings 'correct and elaborate on the existing charts, taking precise soundings and "sailing directions"'.[23]

When, by late November, the cold becomes so severe that it actually threatens to freeze the British fleet in at the Gulf of St Lawrence, most of the ships are ordered by the Admiralty to return to Halifax until spring.

(At least it also guarantees that no French ships will be able to get through the sea ice that guards the newly captured Louisburg. Winter brings peace for both sides – and time to prepare for the battles to come.)

In Halifax, Holland and Cook use the *Pembroke*'s Great Cabin – a room with so many books they practically counted as cargo – for their masterwork, the complete chart of the mouth of the St Lawrence River, and the safest way for the fleet to get there. Day after day, and into the night, the three men – for Captain Simcoe, though ailing with pneumonia, joins them – work on their chart, as they consult all of their notes and previous measurements and bring them to bear on this one master copy. It is a room unlike any other on a Royal Navy ship, just as these are unlikely officers of the Royal Navy. As Holland himself will later recall of Simcoe's Great Cabin aboard the *Pembroke*, 'dedicated to scientific purposes and mostly taken up with a drawing table, [it] furnished no room for idlers'.[24]

His bushy eyebrows practically throwing wispy shadows, Captain Simcoe is like the wise old man of the three. No, he is not versed in the latest techniques, but he does have decades of experience in drawing charts to bring to the plane table, and is able to make great contributions to the emerging chart. For his part, Holland brings his own sharp mind, commitment to precision and vast practical experience of land surveying and chart making, enlightening his new friends about the latest innovations.

Under the tutelage of Captain Simcoe and Holland, James Cook remains the eager pupil, reserved but relentless, but both of his teachers recognise not just his talent, but what is likely his genius, as the chart takes shape. What soon becomes obvious is that the chart they have been using really is, as Holland expresses it, 'so erroneously heretofore laid down'[25] that Captain Simcoe sends a missive to the Admiralty insisting that all of Newfoundland, and indeed the whole North-east coastline, needs a fresh survey.

'I have mentioned to several of my friends in power,' he tells Master Cook one day in the Great Cabin, 'the necessity of having surveys of these parts and astronomical observations made as soon as peace is restored.'[26]

With which, looking earnestly at his Master through his rheumy eyes, he says, 'I recommend you make yourself competent to the business by

learning spherical trigonometry and the practical part of astronomy,'
and hands him a book, Leadbetter's *A Compleat System of Astronomy*,
published in 1728.

James Cook runs his palm across the leather cover, still listening to
his Captain, then opens to the front contents page:

Containing
The Description and use of the laws of spherical geometry; the
projection of the sphere orthographically and stereographic-
ally upon the planes of the meridian, ecliptic and horizon; the
doctrine of the sphere; and the eclipses of the sun and moon for
thirty-seven years . . .[27]

When Captain Simcoe takes his leave – gone to rest again as his health is
only getting worse – James Cook sits down and begins to read Leadbetter's
book (the first of many readings).

The author begins:

> There have been great contentions among the learned of different
> nations about the origin of this study, every one claiming an interest
> in it; as the Babylonians, Egyptians, Grecians, Scythians, &c. But
> be that as it will, we now enjoy it in a very clear light, to the
> immortal honour of those two great geometricians, the late Sir Isaac
> Newton and Dr Edmund Halley, our present Astronomer-Royal.
>
> Upon this science depend navigation, geography and dialing;
> without which 'tis impossible they should be maintained. For,
> first, the Mariner cannot conduct a ship thro' the unbeaten
> paths of the ocean with the help of it; but being well skilled in
> astronomy, he may, by the knowledge of eclipses, the immersions
> and emersions of Jupiter's satellites, and the times and transits
> of the moon by the fixed stars and planets, determine . . . the
> true longitude found at sea. And for this reason I would advise
> every man who has the care of a ship, or of a school, that he
> both well inform himself, and also those under his instructions,
> of the following work.[28]

James Cook is immediately engrossed, just as he is soon also absorbed
by studying another of Captain Simcoe's recommendations – the work
of Euclid, the Father of Geometry. While all of his maritime comrades
complain bitterly about the winter of early 1759, as it immobilises them
and keeps them on shore, Cook is in his hay, refining his art.

'During that hard winter,' he will later recall, 'I first read Euclid and applied myself to the study of mathematics and astronomy, without any other assistance than what a few books and my own industry afforded me.'[29]

•

And yet, even as Cook's mind continues to open to the possibilities of the Earth and its position in the universe *vis-a-vis* the sun and the other planets, so too does the Earth continue to orbit that sun in such a manner that, by early May 1759, the weather has so warmed that Admiral Charles Saunders gives the orders to his British fleet: 'Sail for St Lawrence.'

Within a month an intimidating 35 ships of the line, flanked by numerous smaller men-o'-war and transports – a grand armada of 200 ships – sail out of the safe port of Halifax to begin the journey to Quebec.

For his part, James Cook is filled with pride and wonder to see among this grand fleet of His Majesty's Royal Navy no fewer than 50 capacious, steady and sturdy, humble and hard-working Whitby cats being used as troop transports.

Cook is as dour as a day in deep December, because, even while thrilled to be paving the way for this grand armada aboard the *Pembroke*, he is aware that the man to whom he owes so much, Captain Simcoe, is so gravely ill that he is confined to his cabin.

By his bedside not long afterwards, the ship's Surgeon is so sure of what will happen soon that he asks the beloved commander if he wishes his body preserved for a burial ashore?

Simcoe looks his doctor right in the eyes and, with feeble breath, rasps a reply that will be long celebrated: 'Apply your pitch to its proper purpose; keep your lead to mend the shot holes, and commit me to the deep.'[30]

A truly worthy officer of His Majesty's Royal Navy right to the bitter end, the 49-year-old Captain John Simcoe finally breathes his rasping last on 16 May 1759.

Typically of Master James Cook – though gripped by deep emotion, aware of what he has lost, the debt he owes to a fine man now gone – his words as expressed in his journal are muted: 'At 6 buried the corpse of Captain John Simcoe and fired 20 guns, half a minute between each gun.'[31]

Whatever Cook feels, it is simply not in his nature to give expression to it.

In Quebec the Marquis de Montcalm, the commander of French forces in North America, receives a report from his scouts to the East, along the banks of the St Lawrence. They have heard the rolling boom of the guns piercing the night, saluting Captain Simcoe, and they understand everything only too well.

Winter is over. The British have arrived.

Merde.

•

In June of 1759, the fleet is 300 miles up the St Lawrence, the worst of the waters behind them. There remains a single river obstacle, perhaps the greatest they will face, La Traverse. It is a trouble they must take arms against, however, for there is no alternative route. It is imperative that the British soldiers be brought as close to the city of Quebec as possible if they want to take it. Their advance will be far from a solitary affair, backed by the great black guns slumbering aboard the ships. It is simply their only chance, the only avenue of victory against the entrenched French under the Marquis de Montcalm.

Admiral Saunders is quick to order the best four Masters from his fleet, James Cook there among them, to sound along the narrows of La Traverse to find a way through.

Captain Gordon has already been ordered to take command of six ships – which includes the *Pembroke*, boasting one James Cook – and go ahead of the fleet, marking the way. As the French have sensibly removed all their own direction buoys – floating empty barrels, tethered by cables on the river bed – they must start from scratch.

The next day, 8 June, finds Cook back in one of the *Pembroke*'s boats, standing in the bow with his lead line, as six terrified sailors follow his order to row him back and forth as he sounds the treacherous Traverse. The cliffs tower over them on both sides, jagged rocks threaten them from below, all while, from the heights, the French cannon rain shot down upon them, with many near-misses regularly splashing them. With just one direct hit, they will be killed. But Cook barely blinks and, with a gaze every bit as steady as his hands, continues to mark down his measurements over the next few days as they return again and again to move back and forth through the Traverse. After he has worked out a rough path through the rocks and shoals they follow it again, testing its suitability. Nothing is left to chance, apart from being killed by a cannonball.

No matter, by 10 June, he is confident that he has accomplished his task, including having gained familiarity with the Traverse's big tidal swings and shallow sandbanks, which really do make it similar to the Thames Estuary, and is finally able to record in his log: 'Retired satisfied with being acquainted with the channel.'[32]

His charts are compared with the work of his colleagues, copied, and the resultant charts distributed to the entire fleet. Now, aided by several French pilots who know the Traverse waters, who have been captured and must now navigate for their lives to be spared, the British ships slowly move up the river, and through the Traverse, aided immeasurably by their small boats who position themselves right by the most difficult spots, to help guide them through. James Cook is, of course, among them and is proud to help the *Pembroke* make it through, just as all the other ships are able to get through to the other side.

By 27 June 100 warships of the Royal Navy are through to the other side, with not a single one lost – a triumph of navigation, due in no small part to the genius and courage of one Master James Cook. The achievement is deeply appreciated not just by the Navy brass, but also by the Army's soldiers, too, as they are now able to safely disembark on to land, Île d'Orleans, a large island that lies five miles downriver from Quebec.

With the ships in place, and the troops safely encamped for the moment, all that remains is to find the right landing place as close to Quebec as possible, to launch the assault on the city. As leaders of the grandest Royal Navy/Army landing operation in British history, Admiral Saunders and General Wolfe are insistent that nothing be left to chance. And so the Masters of the fleet's ships – Cook among them – are ordered to their boats the next day, this time to observe and chart the waters and shoreline upriver from the Traverse, which is all new to them.

The French, meanwhile, have a plan of their own . . .

CHAPTER TWO

A BATTLE ROYAL

I beg leave to inform their Lordships, that from my Experience of Mr Cook's Genius and Capacity, I think him well qualified for the Work he has performed, and for greater Undertakings of the same kind.[1]

Admiral Colville, Commodore and Commander in Chief of His Majesty's Ships and Vessels in North America, in a letter to the Secretary of the Admiralty, December 1762

Every blockhead does that; my Grand Tour shall be one round the whole globe.[2]

Joseph Banks at the age of 21, after being advised by a friend to take the traditional 'Grand Tour' of Europe

Midnight, 27 June 1759, Bason de Quebec, floating fire ahoy!
It is the silent watch of the night, with the only noise being the gentle lapping of the waves against the hulls of the British ships, the murmurs of the men on watch and . . .

And suddenly a cry of alarm rings out, carrying far across the water and arousing the attention of all the watches.

And another! And another!

Within moments, there is uproar as fearful screams carry across the dark waters.

'Fire ships!'

Among those soon rushing up on deck across all the ships is James Cook, who pushes his way to the *Pembroke*'s upper deck to join a jostling group of sailors crowding the gunwale.

Fire ships!

Coming at them on the current from upriver are several roaring balls of flame – a tactic perfected by Sir Francis Drake against the Spanish Armada at the Battle of Gravelines in 1588 – small unmanned ships filled with raging combustibles to cause chaos among an anchored enemy fleet.

By the hurried count of Master Cook there are seven big fire ships and three smaller fire rafts. It is going to take quick action to avoid catastrophe and the Master is the man for the job.

Lower the boats! Sailors, man the boats! Take grappling irons! NOW! *Move! Row!* The men are unsure what the Master has in mind but trust his judgement and spring into action. For his part, Cook looks across the inky expanse. Silhouetted against the glow from the approaching fires are dozens of British sailors bustling around the upper decks of the two ships closest to the approaching fire ships.

The crew scramble to find anything with a sharp edge – a cutlass, a saw, a knife, even a piece of broken bottle – and start cutting, chopping and hacking at the snaking hemp fibres that bind their ships to the anchors in the deep. Hemp makes way for sharpened steel with each blow, the top of the cables fall limply to water below and, just before the fire ships – now roaring infernos – drift onto them, the British ships are hauled away by their own sailors pulling them to safety in their own small boats.

In the meantime James Cook has now descended into the *Pembroke*'s yawl and taken command of the plan to get the fire ships under control. With nerves of iron, Cook has the yawl brought as close as they dare to one of the fire ships, just as several other boats from the fleet go after the others, and together, they manage to throw their grappling hooks upon this floating menace, and together, they successfully tow all of the fire ships and flaming rafts well clear of the British armada.

It is the first of many ruses that the desperate French will try over the next weeks as the two great powers engage in this arm wrestle for the ages for the city of Quebec.

Late one afternoon, James Cook is once more out in the yawl, this time reconnoitring a prospective landing place, when, alerted by the sound of splashing, Cook and his men look up to see dozens of canoes filled with North American Indians and French soldiers – the two have formed a curious alliance – furiously paddling towards them.

'ROW!' Cook orders, with uncharacteristic sharpness.

Like mad things, his men do exactly that and, though it is a close-run thing, they are, *in extremis*, able to make it to Île d'Orleans, and the fortified British camp.

Quickly, men, on to shore!

So closely do the Abenaki Indians follow, that while the British sailors are jumping with Cook from the bow of the yawl, the Natives are boarding her at the stern – and Cook and his men are only saved by several armed British soldiers who have been attracted by the commotion and charge into the fray.

Among other things, his survival means that James Cook can continue his survey work with Lieutenant Holland, charting the area upriver from La Traverse, and by the middle of August the latter is ready to hand over to General Wolfe, 'A Plan of the River St. Lawrence, from the Falls of Montmorenci to Sillery'.[3]

Wolfe is so impressed that Holland is immediately promoted to the rank of Captain.

Indeed, Holland's chart is the key that may unlock the door to Quebec, and to the war. Militarily, the value of having accurate maps is about to be tested. The French have no doubt where the British will land – the obvious spot, the notably accessible beach at Beauport, just a few miles North of Quebec, where they send their troops accordingly. The heavy French presence notwithstanding, General Wolfe insists the attack go ahead right there and, betraying his lack of knowledge when it comes to landings, has them attack at low tide – meaning the boats cannot get closer than 200 yards to the beach. The equipment-laden soldiers must struggle through shallows and mud, making them sitting ducks for the French to hunt from the shore – only a little less mobile. The landing fails with the tragic loss of 450 men. Quebec will have to be captured some other way, but where, and how?

12 September 1759, Quebec, a fight for the fate of empire

Is this the breakthrough they have been looking for? On a reconnaissance expedition a short way upriver just a mile or two South-west of Quebec, General Wolfe spots what he has been looking for – a possible weakness in the French defences. It is a small cove on the West side, which appears to have only a skeleton crew of soldiers manning its posts as the French prefer to concentrate their troops to the North of the city at Beauport. Even better, as he gazes intently through his telescope, it seems that there is a defined path with a gentle slope to get up the cliffs to the 'Plains of Abraham', above.

The key will be to launch an attack there, while convincing the French that the British truly intend to attack again at Beauport – with much of the latter responsibility falling to perhaps the most reliable officer Wolfe has, James Cook.

And so it is, on the night of 12 September, the dark figure at the bow of the *Pembroke*'s boat being gently stroked forward is none other than

Cook, as his men lay out buoys in a line to the Beauport shore. Behind him, many other ships' boats are also in line. Cook returns, mission accomplished, to record in his log:

> Moderate and cloudy weather at 6 p.m. Unmoored and hoved in to half a cable on the best bower anchor. At midnight all the rowboats in the fleet made a feint to land at Beauport in order to draw the enemy's attention that way to favour the landing of the troops above the town . . .[4]

Speaking of which, at exactly the same time, General Wolfe himself leads an imposing 4400 of his troops to the reconnoitred shore and, after a minimal struggle against what little French resistance there is, has them climbing to the Plains of Abraham in the darkness and in position by sunrise.

Of course, it does not take the French long to realise they have been duped, and by mid-morning no fewer than 4000 gaily uniformed French troops – their felt tricorn hats trimmed with gold lace and trailing a white ribbon cockade that wafts around their blue waistcoats – are marching from the walled city in glorious formation, towards the invaders. The two sides quickly get to grips, hand-to-hand, sword-to-sword, and even General-to-General as both Wolfe and Montcalm are in the thick of it throughout. Alas, though Wolfe's troops gradually get on top, the British General himself takes a mortal blow. The officer closest to him is none other than Captain Samuel Holland, who stoops down to talk to his commander as a soldier near Wolfe shouts, 'They run, see how they run.'[5] Wolfe opens his eyes and asks who is running. Assured that it is the French, he just manages to get out his last words, 'Now, God be praised, I will die in peace.'[6]

Five days later, in the absence of General Montcalm, who has also been killed, France surrenders Quebec to the British. This feat of arms – which has fundamentally decided that North America will be British, not French – becomes a textbook example of how His Majesty's Navy and Army can work together in perfect harmony. And it's all because they were informed by precise charts of both land and sea put together by Captain Holland, who was assisted by an unknown Navy Master . . . who was it again? . . . *This* fellow, James Cook.

His efforts have not gone unnoticed, and a fortnight later this rising star of the Royal Navy receives word that he has been promoted to be Master of the squadron's flagship, *Northumberland,* under command of

Captain Lord Colville. A further success comes in November when James Cook's very own 'Gaspe bay and harbor' is published by the Admiralty among Holland's charts of the area. And there underneath is his name: 'James Cook Master of his Majesty's Ship the *Pembroke*'.[7] (It appears that, in a final act of goodwill, mentoring and promoting the virtues of his charge before his death, Captain Simcoe had sent Cook's Master's chart to the Admiralty.) Its obvious value to the Admiralty and Great Britain makes Cook even more determined to develop his draughting and navigational skills. He now wants nothing less than to be able to ply his map-making craft in every part of the globe in which he finds himself, and to place those maps at the service of the Admiralty.

Nor are the commercial implications being ignored by the British. Maps like the ones Cook draws – precise and with particular attention to shoals, reefs, rivers, headlands, harbours and bays, drawn from the perspective of one to whom such things are crucial – are important to every merchant Mariner in the world, as they will help prevent precious cargo ships from running aground. In fact, so new is the art, that the copyright for each map is held by the map-maker, meaning a pretty penny can be guaranteed to the man who makes maps that can be relied upon. James Cook is determined that he will be such a man. (No matter that he has made the maps while serving in the Royal Navy – the copyright remains his.) So lucrative are his royalties that he could possibly earn a greater annual income simply by providing definitive maps than an Admiral would get in salary.

Yes, he is so good, and so rare in the ranks, that his services are placed at a very high premium.

•

Another long cold winter in Halifax to endure, and things follow the familiar pattern. Most of the *Northumberland*'s sailors busy themselves drinking and wenching, interspersed with a little wenching and drinking . . . all while 'Honey James' Cook throws himself into his studies. Again he buries himself in the work of Euclid – the Father of Geometry – and also delves ever deeper into the science of astronomy and how it can be applied to navigation.

In London, meanwhile, the chart of the Gulf of St Lawrence that he has worked on is being reproduced by the Admiralty, and though Cook's name is absent, what counts is that it is known in Navy circles that he had a large part in it. It means that, upon their return to Halifax, he and Captain Holland are put to work charting further up the St Lawrence River, towards Quebec city, and the results are so impressive that Captain Lord Colville gives an order for his Master James Cook to be paid a bonus of £50, 'in consideration of his indefatigable industry in making himself master of the Pilotage of the River Saint Lawrence'.[8]

All of which is good news for Master Cook. The bad news is that the men he commands are suffering ever more from ill-health – mostly the ailments that come with the cold, together with malnourishment from living on Navy rations – and are becoming ever more ill-disciplined, engaging in swearing, rudeness and laxness when on duty.

Master Cook tries to tackle both and, when it comes to scurvy, starts to form the idea that it comes from lack of sufficient fresh food. Obviously there is something that the men usually eat on land that they are not eating at sea – it is just that no-one can work out what it is. Groping for an answer, Cook insists his men eat whatever fresh food they can get their hands on – a bit of a problem when the Halifax winter sets in, but Cook's zeal is enough to defeat and eat the coldest quarry and find any greenery buried beneath the snowy scenery.

As for the ill-discipline, the traditional method of dealing with that in the Royal Navy is to hand out extra lashings of the lash, soaked in saltwater, and turn the backs of recalcitrant men into bloody ribbons until they decide to behave. But this does not come easily to Cook, who is humane by nature. Rather, though he has the lash administered when necessary, he prefers to talk to the men and set an example that they can follow – constant, disciplined work. Ultimately, follow they do – over time the men see that Master Cook is different, not a class or two above them, but almost one of them; a solid, stolid and fair leader of men. They come to not only like him, but respect him, and with that the problems of ill-discipline start to fade.

What is also fading is France's military capacity in this part of the world, as it has been relentlessly ground down by the might of Britain over the last seven years, and the forces of Great Britain can soon lay claim to all of Canada, Nova Scotia, Cape Breton, Florida, Senegal, St Vincent, Tobago, Dominica and Grenada, as battles in the North American theatre draw to a close and the war looks set to end. In October 1762, the *Northumberland* is ordered home.

On arrival at Wapping, James Cook walks tall down the gangplank and, though he doesn't strut, as it is not in his nature, he has every right to. When he had left here, almost five years earlier, he had been little more than a modest Master of some skill, but he now returns as a master of surveying and chart-making. What is more, now discharged from his long term of duty, he has a handsome sum of money saved in his pocket – 291 pounds 19 shillings 3d – a substantial sum, when judged against his father's wage of two shillings a day.

Speaking of whom, it is time for James Cook to visit his parents in their humble cottage in Great Ayton, Yorkshire, and they are incredulous, and proud, to see their strapping 33-year-old son, no less than a Master in the Royal Navy, walk through their front door to their warm embrace. Certainly Cook's father must struggle to understand his son's consuming interest in a Greek mathematician from 300 BC. But James has little time to explain to his dear father, when even a simple explanation of the intricacies of Euclid are beyond that good man's education if not his natural intellect. Besides which, with typical commitment, James now wishes to start a family of his own, if only he can find a suitable wife back in the city. Yes, if only he can meet the right woman – one with high morals, strong character and wholesome ambitions, just like him – and if all goes well he will not tarry to marry.

Wonderfully, it doesn't take long.

Her name is Elizabeth Batts, and while he is renting lodgings in the port town of Stepney, just two miles East of central London, he meets, in an alehouse, this 'decent plump English-woman',[9] as no less than James Boswell will describe her, the very woman who the famous diarist and biographer will describe as a good match for 'Cook, a grave steady man'.[10]

Yes, though all of 13 years younger than him at 20, Miss Batts is just his speed and with just the right jib – reliable, steady, solidly middle-class. She is very close to the human equivalent of a Whitby cat – though without the thick waist and snub nose. She lives in the parish of Barking, in Essex, and is visiting her mother and stepfather at their inn, The Bell Alehouse in Wapping. This meeting with James Cook by mere chance makes it feel like fate or even divine providence that they are just meant to be together, for she is smitten from the first with this Warrant Officer of the Royal Navy. Indeed, there seems to be a magnetic force that continues to pull them together. They are content when together, and pining when apart – not ideal for a sailor in love, but there it is.

James Cook, the man of action, moves fast. He would like to make this black-eyed beauty with a shy smile and pleasing carriage an offer. They do not have time for the traditional posting of the banns – the notice of intent to marry – for Cook's intent is to marry now, with haste not hesitation.

But you can see them there, on this beautiful sun-dappled day of 21 December 1762. They are the couple walking deliriously happily hand in hand through the green meadows of Barking on their way to the parish church of St Margaret's where Vicar George Downing and a hastily assembled handful of guests, including Elizabeth's mother, await.

Not for James Cook and his bride, Elizabeth Batts, the horse and carriage, not for them the finery, and the big reception. All they want is each other. When the groom shortly afterwards tells his own parents, James and Grace Cook – together with his two sisters, Christiana and Margaret – they are surprised but not shocked. That is so like James. He is not a man for fuss, and will go a long way out of his way to avoid it.

And of course, beyond his mathematics and astronomy studies and quick courting of fair Elizabeth, his map-making continues – returning to Newfoundland just under six months after being married – and he is so aware of how important it is that his maps can be relied on that he even feels obliged to alert any reader, most particularly any future Captain, of any of the few weaknesses that might be found within them. And so he compiles all his survey work of the St Lawrence River and parts of the coasts of Newfoundland and Nova Scotia, all his draughts and observations and sends them to the Admiralty.

One of his maps of Quebec carries a precise, cautionary wording, which soon becomes a Cook hallmark:

> That part of this plan between the Pilgrims and Green Island is not so correct as I could wish as I had not the time to make sufficient observation there myself [I] have been obliged to collect those of others. With respect to the middle bank, which is the only danger in this passage, I find no person I have yet conversed with to have any true Idea either of its form or extent . . . I thought it proper to make the above remarks in order to point out what may be doubtful in this chart.[11]

Careful. Cautious. Honest to a fault, not that he has many. As precise as a Swiss watch. These are the hallmarks of both James Cook and his maritime charts. And it is coming from a mere Master, not a Captain. It is noticed. So stunning is Cook's output that his Captain from the *Northumberland*, the newly promoted Admiral Lord Colville, on the 30 December 1762, decides to compliment and complement Cook's valuable opus by writing a missive to my Lords of the Admiralty about this extraordinary young man in their ranks.

> I beg leave to inform their Lordships, that from my Experience of Mr Cook's Genius and Capacity, I think him well qualified for the Work he has performed, and for greater Undertakings of the same kind.[12]

A genius with extraordinary capacity.

Said of a nigh nameless sailor, a regular jack originating from the *lower orders?*

Admiral Colville goes on:

> These draughts being made under my own eye, I can venture to say they may be the means of directing many in the right way, but cannot mislead any.[13]

It is perilously close to un-British to record such glowing views about one who is not a gentleman born. But these are changing times, heady times, and James Cook finds himself working in an area that is on the cusp of major change. More and more, it is understood by the Admirals, thanks in large part to the insistence of Admiral George Anson, that good navigation could not only mean the difference between life and death for hundreds of your sailors at a time, but also death for *thousands* of your enemy. It means that those like James Cook who can master this esoteric art must be promoted even if they have no personal resources, have not been to a famous school and still speak with the mashed and bashed vowels of a Yorkshireman, one of the richest accents of some of the poorest people in England.

It is relatively straightforward thus, that when Captain Thomas Graves, the British governor of the newly won territory of Newfoundland and Labrador, is instructed by my Lords of the Admiralty to prepare and communicate 'Draughts of Coasts and Harbours', his first port of call is none other than the impressive Master James Cook, who he had met during the Seven Years' War and who is now back in London. To give the job to another would be absurd.

The Admiralty clearly feels the same way, for their approval is swift, and so it is that, in April 1763, Cook bids his newly pregnant wife, fair Elizabeth, a sad farewell and heads off across the Atlantic once more.

His most important task is to map the coastline and waters of Newfoundland – England's oldest colony, claimed for England and King

Henry VII in 1497 by John Cabot – an island bigger than Ireland. The task is as exacting as it is exhausting as it is . . . profitable. In recognition of his all but unique skill in the field, Cook is granted the handsome stipend of 10 shillings a day and – unlike the limited missions of a naval Captain – with a 'commission' that is as limitless as his ambition.

In short order, Captain Graves takes the crucial step of purchasing a separate vessel – the *Grenville* – that can be exclusively devoted to surveying, with plans to place in command none other than . . . Master James Cook.

After his first season in Newfoundland, Cook leaves the *Grenville* and heads back to London with a note from Captain Graves to the Admiralty saying the necessary charting for the season has been completed 'with indefatigable industry' by the talented Cook. 'As Mr Cook, whose pains and attention are beyond my description, can go no farther in surveying this year, I send him home in the *Tweed* in preference to keeping him on board, that he may have the more time to finish the difficult surveys already taken . . .'[14]

On arrival at Spithead, Cook takes a carriage straight home to Shadwell in London, to his dear Elizabeth and his new baby boy, just seven weeks old. They baptise him James.

That winter, James Cook *Senior*, if you please, every morning bids his wife and son fond farewell to take the horse bus from their newly purchased home by a reeking distillery on Mile End Road, some five miles to the Admiralty at Westminster, where he is ever and always absorbed until late in the evening drawing fair copies of his charts. Unsurprisingly, it does not take long before his presence becomes known to the likes of Admiralty Secretary Philip Stephens. For have you *seen* these charts?

Done by a fellow the name of . . . James Cook. A mere Master. We must give him extra scope.

As comfortable and rewarding as his current circumstances are, Cook wants more than simply to be England's greatest map-maker, living happily ever after on a handsome stipend. For rather than mapping what has already been discovered by others in known parts of the globe, rather than being at best the dutiful Master to an upper-class Commander . . . he wants to be a genuine Captain himself, and take his ship to parts of the globe where there is no map, where he could be both the discoverer of new lands, and the first one to map them.

None of which Cook broadcasts to superiors or colleagues, friends or family. A modest man, who is reserved to the point of appearing enigmatic and ... entirely closed off, he engages in little needless conversation. A humble visionary surrounded substantially by toffs, an enthusiast for the modern in the midst of purveyors of high tradition and passing the port to the left, it makes sense to keep himself to himself, to not make too much noise, and in any case that is precisely the way of the Quakers whose culture he had been immersed in during his teenage years.

Only to fair Elizabeth Batts does he reveal his true self – which to be fair is just a little up from the ultra modest façade he shows the world – and usually only with her, and for her, does he show that impulsive side of his nature.

13 February 1764, London, Banks robbery

Off into the wild night they go.

For Joseph Banks and his many dandy friends, London is their oyster tonight of all nights, for on this day just gone, Joseph has inherited his late father's considerable fortune.

My good man! Take us to the Athenian Club, and be on standby for after that we will likely go to Piccadilly, and after that, who knows?

A small fortune is spent this night on amusing Banks and his friends, not to mention the many women they meet, but what does it matter? Three years earlier his father, William, had died, leaving his vast inheritance – encompassing sprawling estates in Lincolnshire, Staffordshire, Derbyshire and Sussex, yielding a most impressive £6000 a year income – to his only son and heir, Joseph, held in trust until now, his 21st birthday.

Waiter! More cognac for my friends!

Eat, drink and be merry, for tomorrow I botanise!

For yes, from early adulthood onwards, Joseph had been studying at Oxford, where – beyond being as unfocused as ever on studying the classic staples of Greek and Latin – he has been able to indulge more than ever his fascination with studying the natural world.

Occasionally, Banks' passion has caused problems, to the amusement of his friends. On one occasion when a gentleman in a post-chaise had been robbed by a highwayman out Hounslow way, the aggrieved man and his driver set out in hot pursuit on their horses alone, when sure enough, they saw what they took to be the highwayman trying to hide under a hedge.

'Here he is!'[15] cried the driver, before they dragged him out from under the hedge by his ankles. It was in vain for Joseph Banks to protest that he was not a highwayman, that he was but a gentleman out botanising, looking for new plants, for they dragged him to Bow Street Magistrate's Court, and charged him with robbery before the famed magistrate Sir John Fielding. Of course it is all sorted out eventually and apologies presented, but no-one blames the gentleman in the post-chaise for the mistake. It is unbelievable that a real gentleman should be on his knees, with his head under a hedge! *Anyone* could have made such a mistake.

Banks doesn't care. Passionate for the natural world since he has been knee-high to a grasshopper – or, as he knows it, to a species of *Acridomorpha* – he is so obsessed with his passion he either wants to be engaging in it or at least learning about it and is soon doing exactly that at that great seat of learning, Oxford.

True, it is a small problem that Oxford has no botanist who could be classified as a leader in his field, but what cares a man like Banks? For the abundant wealth he now boasts comes complete with its own set of silky keys, capable of opening practically every door. To keep with his standard of only getting the best of the best of *la crème de la crème DE la crème*, the enterprising young Banks simply pops over to Cambridge and arranges for its leading botanical expert, one Israel Lyons, to come over to Oxford and give him private tutorials, all paid for out of his own pocket – which is as deep as it is elegant. Problem solved.

Indeed, the way Joseph treats Oxford is less like the bastion of classical book learning that it is, and more like one of Whitby's apprentice schools – working, often with his bare hands, on the craft of natural history: botanical, animal and mineral – just as James Cook had been taught the craft of sailing and all things sea life.

It is a happy circumstance for both men that they are entering their fields of endeavour at the time that both fields are taking great leaps forward in their capacity to make sense of the world. For yes, even as the science of maritime navigation is, ahem . . . finding its way, so too is the study of botany . . . blooming.

Each man positions himself at the forefront of the expanding frontier, and will be swept along by it.

In the case of Banks and botany, it is clear where the frontier lies – always with the latest work and theories of the leading botanist of Europe, the great Swedish naturalist Carl Linnaeus. He is no less than the 'Father of Taxonomy', the man who wrote the book in 1735, the first and last word on the subject – *Systema Naturae* – and whose system of identifying, naming and classifying organisms is quickly becoming universally accepted among men of science.

For you see, the entire natural world can be broken down into three basic kingdoms: animal, vegetable and mineral. They in turn are divided into *classes*, which can in turn be divided into *orders*, *genera* and *species*. Not for nothing would the Swede frequently say of himself, in the Latin language of science, '*Deus creavit, Linnaeus disposuit*, God created and Linnaeus organised.'[16]

The greatest breakthrough of Linnaeus is to institute his 'two-name naming system', whereby the first name identifies the genus, while the second name identifies the species of organism within a kingdom. Humans, for example, belong to the genus *Homo* and within this genus to the species *Homo sapiens*. The same system could be applied to plants – including the countless plants that remain unknown to Europeans; and, as he is the first to use the system, Carl Linnaeus simply gives the groups the names of his friends and esteemed colleagues. The genus of the flower known as Gardenia, for example, is named after the Scottish-born naturalist Dr Alexander Garden, while the Magnolia and Dahlia are named for French botanist Pierre Magnol and Swedish botanist Anders Dahl. It is a system which quickly takes hold and, as a system of classification, is in its golden dawn. It means there is a great deal to do – Linnaeus would himself name and catalogue an extraordinary 5600 plant specimens – as his disciples spread.

True, for Banks, it is slightly problematic that the great Swedish botanist writes in Latin, a language which Banks has never ceased all but ignoring, picking up only enough to just get by, but now that he sees that understanding Latin can be useful in learning about botany, he suddenly gets very interested indeed.

After all, botany is such a joy.

Never once since that day bouncing down the lane where he had seen the old woman with the herbs has his passion waned and, if anything, it has only increased. For beyond wanting to know about every flower, shrub and tree in Britain, he now wonders what plants and animals are out there on this vast globe, as yet undiscovered? Perhaps there might be species out there even beyond imagination?

Of course the tried and 'true Oxonians'[17] among his peers look askance at these strange, unscholarly, earthy enterprises of Banks and do not bother to hide their distaste for anything of this nature that involves getting your hands dirty in nature. Banks knows that attitude well. As a matter of fact, early on in his days at Oxford, he had wandered by happenstance into one of the old reading rooms – all rich mahogany, pompous portraits of wigged men with academic poise, and thousands of books – where his fellow Oxonians were earnestly discussing an ancient text when, as soon as he was spotted one of them looked up and let out a ready remark: 'Here is Banks, but he knows nothing of Greek.'[18]

It was their way of saying, yes, Banks may be a popular enough fellow, but he is not to be taken seriously. For he is no more steeped in the ancient languages than he is in the ancient texts.

Banks took it in good humour, just as he does when he hears the same remark several times afterwards, but quietly vows to himself, 'I shall very soon beat you all in a kind of knowledge I think infinitely more important.'[19]

For you can have your ancient language and ancient texts. I wish to make my mark in modern knowledge, do my bit in adding to it and make my name in doing so.

For all that, even Banks' most fierce critics have no doubt about his abilities in this new field of natural history, and whenever questions do arise among these classical men about this field the first response is always the same: 'We must go to Banks.'[20] And he is always found in the same place – somewhere out on the grounds 'botanising'.

Banks is always happy to help, though always on the grounds of adding to knowledge, rather than helping them with their marks. He cares as little for their marks as he does his own.

For many of his peers, the dream is to spend time after university doing a 'Grand Tour' of continental Europe and travelling the Mediterranean, but when they suggest such a trip to Banks, they get a curt reply: 'Every blockhead does that; my Grand Tour shall be one round the whole globe.'[21]

And yet even a global gallant gallivanter must have a firm base, and so he buys a three-storey-with-a-garret-and-basement-for-the-servants terrace house on London's New Burlington Street – a particularly fashionable part of the burgeoning metropolis called Mayfair. So modern are these houses, so fashionable is this part of the world, that New Burlington Street is the first in all of London to be numbered, with Banks living at number 14.

Joseph Banks also remains close to his widowed mother and his dear sister, Sarah, both now living happily in Turret House on Chelsea's Paradise Row. For years now he has loved going to visit, not just because of the pleasure of seeing them, but also because of the house's happy position, right next to the Society of Apothecaries' 'Physic Garden' – where herbs are grown and seed collected for use as medicines – which happens to be overseen by a very well credentialled botanist by the name of Philip Miller, whose impressive personal resume includes being a close friend of the legendary Carl Linnaeus. Oh, the happy hours, days, weeks, young Joseph spends in those gardens, talking to Miller and his offsiders, digging, clipping, harvesting – soaking up knowledge as he goes.

And although power and influence can also be found in this part of the world, in no-one are they found in such abundance as in the person of the long-time Banks' family friend, that debonair dasher of a man, John Montagu, no less than the fourth Earl of Sandwich.

Like Joseph Banks, the Earl is an Old Etonian, in his case 25 years older than Banks, but he takes quite a shine to the young man anyway, taking him under his wing and introducing him to the key people in Britain's upper echelons he knows well, which is very nearly everyone. As a man who has already twice served as First Lord of the Admiralty – the key politically appointed naval adviser to the Prime Minister – he is now in the British Cabinet as a Secretary of State. Beyond such important posts, however, Lord Sandwich has also been an active Fellow of the powerful Royal Society of London for Improving Natural Knowledge, that most august British institution popularly known as the 'Royal Society', which means he is fully briefed at all times on just where the frontiers of knowledge lie in a dozen fields at once, including botany, and Banks delights being in his company, and those of his Fellows. As Lord Sandwich is also something of an amateur botanist, the two often go on long rambling walks through the fens of Lincolnshire and elsewhere across England and Wales, collecting samples, fishing in the Thames and the Serpentine (Hyde Park's lake), all while trading gossip and knowledge. Helping to bind the two even further, despite the disparity in age, is a shared hedonistic streak whereby they delight in angling for other fine specimens most highly prized by men of their ilk . . . beautiful women.

Certainly Lord Sandwich is married, but in the first place that had never slowed him down as he had already been openly celebrated for taking the famous beauty and courtesan mentioned in Casanova's memoirs, 'the celebrated Miss Fanny Murray'[22] as his mistress – and open enough about it that he famously displayed a portrait of her, nude, in his London lodgings. And in the second place it is well known that Lord Sandwich's wife had long before descended into insanity.

At the moment Sandwich has moved on from Fanny Murray to a talented and gorgeous 17-year-old singer, Martha Ray, 28 years his junior, for whom he even finds a room in his lodgings. Word of his sexual proclivities get around and one oft-repeated anecdote among London's social set, celebrated ever afterwards, is an exchange Lord Sandwich had with the actor, Samuel Foote.

'Foote,' Sandwich is said to have declared in jest, 'I have often wondered what catastrophe would bring you to your end; but I think, that you must either die of the pox, or [the noose].'

'My lord,' replied Foote magnificently, 'that will depend upon one of two contingencies; whether I embrace your lordship's mistress, or your lordship's principles.'[23]

One of those principles is that sundown is not the signal for the end of the day's activities, but merely that things are about to warm up, and one of Sandwich's keenest nocturnal pursuits, beyond the obvious, is playing cards – betting big early and staying late, playing Lanterloo, Pope Joan and Ombre, among others – and he is usually so engrossed that he refuses to take pause for meals, instead ordering his servant to simply place his salted beef between two slices of bread. Soon, his gambling, grumbling acquaintances are habitually calling for 'the same as Sandwich!' as they try to stay with him in the gambling stakes.

Few attempt to compete with Sandwich when it comes to bedding women, but Joseph Banks is at least an intent student of the art, and a good starting point proves to be showing women his grand home. Against that, as magnificent and large as that home is, after Banks makes tours of England and Wales for weeks at a time, returning with an ever fresh collection of specimens, both flora and fauna, the house is soon groaning under the weight of them all, as every tabletop and unused room is filled up, giving it the appearance of a natural history museum. Fortunately, the women don't seem to mind, much, and nor does Banks' growing coterie of eminent friends, men of influence and women of grace, most introduced to him by – *Waiter! More bread and meat!* – Lord Sandwich.

Joseph Banks follows even more in the Lord's glorious wake, launching himself on the capital of the British Empire, quickly becoming a ubiquitous man about town, the centre of attention, the man with the best stories, the most beautiful women, and the biggest bar bill.

•

A reserved, self-contained man, James Cook does not make friends easily. Never garrulous by nature, since the time he became serious about learning all there was to learn about navigation, he has always preferred his studies to the tavern, his work to social occasions.

Beyond that, his rapid rise through the ranks, despite not being well born, has meant that he has left behind all those with whom he grew up, all those he first served on ships with. And among those fellow commanders he now mixes with, he is perpetually an outsider, not of their class, their background, their world. He is a man born to be before the mast, who has somehow made his way aft of the mast, and not only do some of them resent the rapidity of his promotion, but also the persistence, for he keeps vaulting higher.

James Cook does not care, particularly.

It is his happy circumstance that his dear wife, Elizabeth, is also his cherished friend, his closest confidante and the person with whom he most wishes to spend time. It means that, while his ambitions to conquer the world only grow, the one he wants at home is a very small one – not much more than Elizabeth and whatever children they might be blessed to have, all in their home on Mile End Road. And she feels the same.

And yet, as will ever happen in their life together, however happy Cook is at home, the coming of spring 1764 brings the call of the sea, where he continues to prosper. By the middle of April 1764 – superb with handling the men and the ship, and his mapping coming along at pace – he has been appointed by the Admiralty to command the *Grenville* from spring to autumn each year, travelling across the Atlantic from London to continue his methodical surveying work until it is complete.

He sets off once more to Newfoundland – excited to get there and see his old Captain and patron, Sir Hugh Palliser, who is the newly appointed Governor of Newfoundland.

Elizabeth, pregnant with their second child, farewells him and frets until his blessed return.

Every time he departs, Elizabeth is fearful that he will be hurt or drowned, and those fears are not unfounded, for on 6 August 1764 . . .

James Cook is on the Northern shore of Newfoundland out hunting for animals and birds, reloading his musket after a missed shot when it happens. He is just about to pour the powder from his horn (literally the horn of an ox that is used to hold gunpowder) into the pan when a spark near the touch hole ignites the powder . . . BOOOM! Unfortunately for James Cook the explosion shreds his right hand in a split second.

The entry in the *Grenville*'s log that afternoon will be written, not surprisingly, by another.

> 2p.m. Came on board the cutter with the Master who unfortunately
> had a large powder horn blown up and burst in his hand, which
> shattered it in a Terrible manner and one of the people that stood
> hard by suffered greatly by the same accident.[24]

As the *Grenville* has no Surgeon on board, a French doctor on a nearby
fishing vessel is sent for and must work vigorously to save the hand, most
particularly suturing the massive rip that extends from between Cook's
thumb and forefinger, across the palm, and right around to his wrist.

It will leave him with a massive and angry red weal of scar – and such
a sensitivity to it that for the rest of his life his right hand will, more often
than not, be either gloved or firmly planted in his right pocket. Others
might say they can read the future by gazing in the palm of their hands,
but James Cook wishes to hide his past by covering that hideous scar. In
any case, Elizabeth is at pains to assure him – as soon as he returns to
her own unblemished arms – it's no matter to her whatsoever, and that
is all that truly counts. He forgets the bulging scar, at least momentarily,
when he returns home that winter in his own vessel, the *Grenville*, and
holds his second beautiful baby boy, Nathaniel, in his arms.

Such a time of familial joy is tempered, however, when his mother,
Grace, dies in the family cottage on Bridge Street, Great Ayton, at the
age of 63, just before he must head off on his third season in 1765. Of
course he makes one of his infrequent returns to his childhood home for
the funeral, and while there returns briefly to his old stamping ground
at Whitby – and the word soon spreads to the likes of the Walkers,
Mr Sanderson, his old Captains, the old fishermen, the sailors, and those
still in the taverns, all these years on. They have aged, and no doubt
about it. But look at *him*. He has filled out, grown beyond six feet,
beyond Whitby. And a *Master* in the *Royal Navy* now, young James?

Well, come and share a pint, as in days of old.

Whitby is proud of him, and James Cook would be inclined to
stay longer but, as ever, he must away to the trumpet's blast from the
Admiralty, which he has been heeding for more than a decade.

In late July 1766 while commanding the *Grenville*, Master Cook
is doing what he does best when he finds himself in fog so thick that
pea soup would be envious – all on an unnamed and uncharted island
of the Burgeo Islands just off the South-west coast of Newfoundland.
After the 13th morning, on 5 August, the fog at last clears, and the sun
shines through, but . . .

But what is this?

Before Cook's very eyes, just as he had been hoping, an eclipse starts. Cook instantly brings his brass telescopic quadrant to bear, to scientifically observe what is occurring. (Typically, James Cook had not just studied Charles Leadbetter's astronomy text given to him by Captain Simcoe, and left it at that. No, after coming to realise the virtues of eclipses in solving riddles for Mariners, he had followed astronomical events closely since, had always known what was about to occur in the heavens, and done many observations to hone his skills, and practise his calculations. This latest event is not manna from heaven, it is his due.)

Accordingly, looking through his brass telescope quadrant, just a minute after a part of the sun starts to be eaten by a small black ball, he notes the time of the beginning and the end and then, comparing it with the times of the eclipse at other known meridians, most particularly the one in Greenwich – he has to consult his books – he calculates his own precise local longitude.

He goes back to his cabin to make his calculations and, after writing up several pages of his notes, he prepares to send them to a learned acquaintance back in London, Dr John Bevis.

Thereafter, Master Cook in Newfoundland completes his survey of the previously unnamed island, now marking it down as . . . let's see . . . 'Eclipse Island', before moving on to survey the next island along the coast. There's much to do, as ever, in the life of Master James Cook, and he is entirely unaware that the wheels of fate are starting to work in synchronicity, pushing his cause as never before.

For when, in London, Dr Bevis receives James Cook's eclipse observations he is in turn so taken with them he presents them as a formal paper under the name of James Cook to the Royal Society – that august and enlightened body of gentlemen scientists that embodies the age of enlightenment, hoping to use science to beat back the mystery that still surrounds much of the globe – on 30 April 1767:

> An Observation of An Eclipse of the Sun at the Island of New-found-land. Aug. 5 – 1766
>
> By Mr James Cook, with the Longitudes of the Place of Observation deduced from it.[25]

Good Lord!

A paper presented and well received at the *Royal Society*, from the notes of a mere Master in the Royal Navy? How could a relatively humble seaman make such observations? And then even make deductions from those observations himself? And he's not a proper astronomer, nor a mathematician of any repute? It is remarkable, *unheard of!*

It has much the same impact as Cook's charts had had on the Admiralty. Who can this fellow James Cook be?

Well, Dr Bevis is only too happy to give the answer, assuring the society that Mr Cook is 'a good mathematician, and very expert in his Business'.[26]

The episode provides just one more feather in the cap of one who is gathering at least his fair share. Just how far will Cook go?

A long way, most of his superiors agree, though none remotely approaches the truth of it.

•

Among those impressed by this unique paper by an obscure Navy man over in Newfoundland is none other than the fresh-faced Joseph Banks, who was elected as a member of the highly influential Royal Society just the year before, in 1766.

Of course he attends every meeting he can, apart from those many times when he is away on one of his many natural history expeditions through the wilds of England and Wales, returning to London with his many servants laden down with boxes of freshly pressed plants, newly stuffed birds and mammals that he has just captured and killed to add to his collection.

Due to the influence of Sandwich, in 1766 Banks had been afforded the wonderful opportunity to voyage across the Atlantic to Newfoundland and Labrador on HMS *Niger*, charged with studying the islands' natural history, documenting and cataloguing several newly discovered species of animal and vegetable. And though Mr Banks didn't get to meet this outstanding James Cook fellow that Governor Sir Hugh Palliser kept telling him about, he had brought home a number of fine and exotic plant species, which he hopes to use as the foundation for the grand 'herbarium' he plans to establish – essentially a storage and display facility for plant specimens.

Most importantly, he had brought back splendid memories and a passion even greater than before for going on more adventures. For, oh, what a time he'd had, some of the happiest of his life to date, seeing new sights every day, collecting samples and specimens in the outdoors from dawn to dusk, all of it in the company of adventurous, experienced officers. Yes, perhaps other high-born gentlemen would struggle with roughing it in such circumstances, but he had been so caught up in the fun of it all, he had barely noticed any of the trials visited upon them.

In the circles he now moves in – and is often dead centre of – he soon hears through his friends in the Royal Society stories about some plans to send a ship to the Pacific to observe the Transit of Venus . . .

Now *that* is the Grand Tour he has truly been looking for!

Most wonderfully, the dear Earl of Sandwich, as a member of the Society and a former First Lord of the Admiralty, knows all about it, and promises to help him get aboard.

Banks can think of little else, talk of little else and, one cold night in the winter of late 1767, is in full cry on the subject at the private home of a friend – enjoying another 'bibulous male dinner party'[27] – when the tubby fellow sitting across from him, jumps to his feet and declares in a light Nordic accent: 'I wish to come too!'[28]

Banks beams to hear it. For the tubby fellow is no less than the esteemed Swedish naturalist Dr Solander, the 'beloved pupil'[29] of Carl Linnaeus. Solander has spent most of the last decade in England bringing English naturalists up to speed on the master's taxonomy. He's been working at the British Museum since 1763, where he spends his days describing and cataloguing all manner of natural specimens – vegetable, animal and mineral.

He is the perfect teacher for Banks, 'for his polite and agreeable manners, as well as his great knowledge in most departments of Natural History'.[30]

Come, my good sir! We can botanise in lands unknown, it'll be a lark!

18 June 1767, somewhere in the Pacific Ocean, the Day of the *Dolphin*

Aboard the HMS *Dolphin*, Captain Samuel Wallis is feeling rather ill. Confined to his cabin, he suffers from a bilious disorder, a sign of the dreaded scurvy. Two of his senior officers are in the same condition. It had taken three months to bring the *Dolphin* from England West through the Straits of Magellan at the bottom of South America, and another two thereafter of sailing in the vast blue expanse of the Pacific Ocean, searching for *Terra Australis Incognita*, only to find . . . nothing. Not a single speck of land. Until now. A tiny island in the middle of the South Seas. And thank the heavens, they need it. Fresh water and food are severely depleted, and the men are beginning to drop like flies.

George Robertson, Master of the *Dolphin*, sends word to the Captain that the Master's Mate, John Gore, has had an unsuccessful venture ashore. Yes, he went ashore with a small party in search of fresh food and water, but he and his men were beaten off by Natives, fellows none too impressed with the intrusion. There was nothing else to do than fire above their heads before returning to the ship. They will try again.

Now, they are headed towards peaks on the horizon, not too far to the West. It looks to be a much larger island.

They will try their luck there.

24 June 1767, Tahiti, rue Brittania

Word spreads like fish darting away from a spear. The island the locals call 'Otaheite' is abuzz with the news. Something is coming. Something big, like we have never seen.

The warriors, their brown skin marked with intricate black lines, make ready for a fight, sharpening their spears and readying their fastest canoes. Sure enough, the rumours prove true, and it is not long before the giant canoe arrives on the coast, white apparitions billowing in the distance. The islanders crowd the beaches, staring in wonder at this strange visitation, following its course until it approaches Matavai Bay – home to a thriving community in the fertile valleys, which rise up to the old volcano's peak. Now the giant canoe slows and the Me'eti'a witness strange men – *are they men, they look so white?* – climb down into smaller canoes, of more recognisable mien. Instantly the brave Tahitian warriors are rowing out to meet these intruders now gathering beneath the *Dolphin*'s enormous hull.

They yell out, asking what they are doing, why are they here, what are their intentions? *This isn't your land!* They wave plantain branches to signal peaceful intentions. Everything will be fine as long as these white men leave these shores. Some men have different ideas, enterprising entrepreneurs bringing hogs, fowls and fruit, looking to trade for whatever these ghostly intruders might have brought with them. But the white men can only respond in their own strange tongue, a flowing litany of barking sounds that signify nothing. The language barrier between these disparate peoples will not be an easy one to overcome. Now the white men start to bring their hands to their mouths, making motions of eating and drinking. They begin to crow like chickens and snort like pigs.

Do they want our animals?

There's confusion all around as yet more canoes arrive and a full flotilla of Tahitian warriors begin to encircle the *Dolphin*. From one of these Native canoes now comes a rock, hurling through the air and landing with a thump in the white men's smaller canoe. The white men yell. More rocks, hitting the men in the cutter. As one, the white men pluck something from their sides and brandish them in the air – sticks that, amazingly, *shine* in the sun.

With a crack fiercer than lightning, one of the sticks lets out . . . fire!

•

Master's Mate John Gore has thought himself a hunter since he was a boy in his native Virginia, and he really is a good shot. When the rocks start hitting his men, he takes aim at the man in the canoe who had thrown the first stone . . . and *boom*, clean shot to the right shoulder. The islander screams in agony. Whatever he expected in return for throwing a stone, it wasn't . . . this. Whatever this hellish trickery is, something has wormed its way into his body and lies there burning. He bleeds.

The rest of the Natives can't begin to comprehend what has happened either, but they heard the noise and they have seen the blood. They jump, flying overboard and diving deep under the water. But the white men are not done. After fussing about what looks like a tilted, shiny black log, something amazing occurs. A much louder, harsher explosion suddenly bursts forth, followed by a geyser of water behind them suddenly reaching for the skies. The roar of the water reminds the Natives of the largest waves they have ever seen. What have these cursed white men brought to our shores?

Row! *Flee!*

Another blast like *patirihoainia*, thunder, though this time the hellish black ball flies into a canoe holding one of the chiefs. The flimsy wooden craft is no match for a nine-pound iron ball shot from an English cannon, and it turns to splinters before the sound of the explosion has stopped reverberating across the water. The men jump to safety, though within half an hour there is not a canoe to be seen in Matavai Bay.

Watching this extraordinary sight from a nearby hilltop is an exiled priest – a charismatic holy man and a proud, strong warrior in his own right, hailing from Raiatea. A high practitioner of the cult of the deity *Oro*, he has left his own island because it was invaded by warriors from neighbouring Bola Bola. His name is Tupia, and he continues to watch from relative safety as puffs of smoke start emerging from the side of the visitors' ship, followed by dirty balls of thunder rolling over the people, and trees crashing down and people being blown apart on the beach. Whoever these men are, whatever their magic is, it is clear to Tupia from the first that they are powerful and, as ever, his instinct is to get closer to this power, to understand it, and perhaps have some of it for himself. All he needs to do is to work out how it might be done.

•

The skirmishes continue for five days, with the Tahitians making constant darting attacks that are as quickly beaten off. On the sixth day the Tahitians launch another flotilla, larger than any the white men have seen before. These islanders have gathered some 4000 men, each one a fearsome warrior in his own right. A sea of menacing dark faces now surrounds the *Dolphin*. The tension is palpable as the Native men look above to the pale-skinned British sailors on deck.

And now, with a guttural cry from one of them, in the grandest canoe of all ... suddenly, stones begin to fly. It is a precise, concerted attack. They are simple weapons, but they are expertly wielded. Many of the white men duck for cover as the rocks whistle by, though more still are too slow. With blood pouring from wounds to their head, they fall to the deck and wait for the initial salvo to pass.

Now ...

Rising from behind the gunwale of the ship, some of the white men take aim with their long sticks, while others fuss around the shiny black logs. Thunder cracks out over the water, a volley of iron balls, small and large, crashes down upon the ocean and the men aboard the canoes. It is total carnage, and the ocean foam turns pink with lifeblood among the detritus of shattered canoes and floating bodies. But the white men are not done. Hurl stones at us, will you? Following the fleeing Tahitians back to the shore, the white men disembark and begin hacking at the canoes with their strange tools and weapons. Before long, 80 of the Tahitians' finest canoes have been destroyed.

The next time the Tahitians dare to approach the big canoe in their bay, they go with plantain branches.

And so peace takes hold as the white men begin to trade with the Tahitians. Beads, trinkets, curios, but most importantly *nails*. It is the most prized possession the white men have with them, and the

Tahitians will trade anything for them. Indeed they are so valuable, so priceless, that the first package of them is taken directly to the temple, where they are laid out as an offering to the gods. Some are even planted like seeds. Soon every man in the area is making his way towards this strange ship, bringing with him hogs, chickens, plantains, cocoa nuts and other fruits, before the Tahitians realise the best trade of all.

For you see, if you can believe it, these unusual white fellows have brought no women with them! Shortly thereafter, the Native men bring their women along with them, and it is not long before the white men – bellies full and carnal desires satisfied – decide that they have grown 'madly fond of shore'.[31]

Things get so out of hand so quickly that ere they have been in Tahiti for a month, the Carpenter gravely informs the Captain that 'every cleat in the ship is drawn and all the nails carried off',[32] even as the Bosun informs him that 'most of the hammock nails are drawn and two-thirds of the men obliged to lie on the deck for want of nails to hang their hammocks'.[33]

Another month again, and for the men at least, things become grimmer still when mere small nails can no longer satisfy the desires of 'the young girls . . . [who] raised their price for some days past [to big] nails . . . and some were so extravagant as to demand a seven or nine inch spike'.[34]

Of course, only a very few sailors are able to meet such requirements.

•

On 27 July 1767, Captain Wallis gives the order to weigh anchor. He is reluctant to do so as morale is higher than ever and the crew is as happy and manageable as a crew can be. And yet, even so, they must sail on to the Great Southern Land, or failing that, bring the ship home to England in one piece.

Before the wind picks up and the sails billow, Wallis finds the time to claim the land for England, naming it King George III's Island. The men of the *Dolphin* gather on the stern, each one of them lamenting the loss of the land they leave. It melts away into the distance, a paradise found, a paradise lost.

They pray they will return, though it seems terribly unlikely. As they leave, Master George Robertson writes that Tahiti boasts, 'the most beautiful appearance it is possible to imagine . . .'.[35]

•

Wait . . . what?

What?

How did he *do* these?

It is late 1767 and, for the first time, those in the higher echelons of the Admiralty have a chance to look at the charts of Newfoundland and Labrador composed by this fellow Master James Cook – and they are stunned. No-one has ever seen charts like them. They are minutely detailed, perfectly framed from the point of view of the needs of the Mariner, and show everything from the contours of the coast to the positions of reefs and shoals to the depth of the water at every point. And so too, now that they have a closer look at it, is the record of Master Cook as commander of the *Grenville* these past five years. Actually, when you look closer still, his entire record of 20 years at sea is something more than exemplary, nary a mark against his name.

Until one day, 10 November 1767. Master James Cook, returning from another summer season of surveying in Newfoundland, has just sailed the *Grenville* into the Thames Estuary and dropped anchor when a tempest descends. So violent is the storm that the *Grenville*'s anchors cannot hold her, and she is thrown into the shoals, and 'lay down on her larboard bilge',[36] only being saved by Cook and his men launching the ship's boats in the shrieking gale and pulling her upright and off. In the course of the tumult, a piece of far-flung foreign cargo comes loose and floats away. It is a Native canoe – a present from Governor Palliser of Newfoundland for Cook to present to a Mr Joseph Banks, whoever that might be, when he returns to London. Ah well, so close yet so far. Mr Cook is about to be back in London in a day or two, but where the canoe is nobody knows, up the Thames without a paddle, probably half the way to Essex by now for some surprised farmer to find. Mr Banks will have to do without his Native novelty and without meeting Master James Cook.

It is no more than a minor episode in Cook's very busy life. His only respite from frenzied activity is when he can finally get home to his dear Elizabeth, falling into her arms after months away, before being presented with another of his children that he has not met. Not a boy this time but a bonny baby girl, named after her mother and instantly just as beloved by her father – rocking her lightly even as his two young boys urgently grab at his pant legs, desperate for some attention of their own from their father who has been so sorely missed.

Governor Captain Sir Hugh Palliser, meanwhile, continues his generous patronage from Newfoundland. After the 1767 season, he writes to the Secretary of the Admiralty, praising Cook's work and seeking permission for Cook to publish his charts.

> I am of opinion [Master Cook's charts] will be a great encouragement to new adventurers in the fisheries upon these coasts, be pleased to move their Lordships to permit Mr Cook to publish the same . . .[37]

James Cook is a rising star. Appropriate really, as the next part of his fate is, if not quite written in the stars, at least manifestly guided by one rising star in particular.

CHAPTER THREE

THE RISING STAR

'Nullius in verba ...'
> The motto of the Royal Society, it translates to, 'On the word of no one'.[1]

Terra australis incognita, the unknown Southern land – or, more hopefully, nondum cognita, not yet known but in due course to be revealed: the brief words trail a long history, are aromatic with an old romance, as of great folios in ancient libraries, compassing all philosophical and geographical knowledge, with pages and double pages of maps whose very amplitude and pattern ravish the mind; and they present us with one of the great illusions.[2]
> J.C. Beaglehole, *The Life of Captain James Cook*, 1974

Then we plow'd the South Ocean, such land to discover
As amongst other nations has made such a pother
We found it, my boys, and with joy be it told,
For beauty such islands you ne'er did behold.
We've the pleasure ourselves the tidings to bring
As may welcome us home to our country and king.[3]
> 'The *Dolphin*'s Return', 1768, a Naval song
> to the tune of 'The Lilies of France'.

Early 1768, London, a fate written in the stars

It is the tiniest of cogs in the clockwork of the heavens, but like clockwork it is – if a little complicated.

Every 243 years, the 'Transit of Venus' occurs four times in a known pattern. The transits occur in pairs spaced roughly eight years apart. Then the cycle starts again.

Viewed from Earth, each transit lasts for around six hours as the closest planet to Earth, Venus, moves in front of the sun, showing up as a small black disk on its mighty face. Prima facie, it is not something to excite any of the sailors in His Majesty's Navy, nor her Captains, nor Masters, nor even most of the Admiralty, but that is of no account. What counts is that it means a great deal to the learned and powerful men of the Royal Society.

For these select men – the shining lights and brightest minds of the entire realm leading the most venerated and powerful scientific institution in the country, and perhaps the world, boasting all the finest scientists, across all the major disciplines, and officially in charge of the Greenwich observatory – it is *their* opinion which holds sway, and none more than the Society's well-connected and influential elderly president, the 14th Earl of Morton, Scotsman James Douglas, an astronomer.

Most importantly, the men are guided by the astronomically inclined ghost of Sir Edmund Halley. Before absconding from his earthly bonds in 1742, the legendary Astronomer Royal had realised the breakthrough that could be achieved by observing the same event at the same time from widely spaced locations on Earth. These transits would occur in 1761 and 1769, he said, and if they could be properly examined from geographically distinct areas at a precisely known relative time, then the distance from Earth to Venus could be calculated.

With that key distance established, so too could the dimensions of the rest of the solar system be calculated, including the precise distance between Earth and the sun, known to scientists as the Astronomical Unit – the fundamental yardstick of solar astronomy, by which they could begin to calculate everything else.

Sir Edmund had been so convinced that this was the golden key to unlock the mysteries of the solar system that he had left that key in a safe place for future generations, setting it all out, in Latin, the language of science, in his paper for the Royal Society, and his words have been treasured since:

> Venus's transit over the sun's disk, whose parallax, being almost 4 times greater than that of the sun, will cause very sensible differences between the times in which Venus shall seem to pass over the sun's disk in different parts of our earth. From these differences, duly observed, the sun's parallax may be determined . . .[4]

Oh, and take a tip from the grand master in this field:

> I would have several observations made of the same phenomenon in different parts [of the Earth], both for further confirmation, and lest a single observer should happen to be disappointed by

the intervention of clouds from seeing what I know not if those either of the present or following age shall ever see again; and upon which, the certain and adequate solution of the noblest, and otherwise most difficult problem depends. Therefore again and again, I recommend it to the curious strenuously to apply themselves to this observation . . .[5]

Brandishing Halley's golden key to the universe, the learned men of the Royal Society had approached the British government of 1760 to fund a voyage to St Helena to observe the eclipse for, 'the improvement of astronomy and the honour of this nation',[6] and it had been done, only for weather and other factors – including Halley's miscalculation of precise start times – to render most of the data unusable.

So now the 1769 transit is their last chance before . . . 1874. As early as 1766, the Royal Society's esteemed President, Lord Morton, recalled all the Society's astronomical instruments, 'for the purpose of putting them in proper order'.[7]

As the transit approaches, Lord Morton and the Royal Society make their formal approach to the King, writing a letter to His Majesty George III in February 1768 seeking support for the expedition:

To the King's Most Excellent Majesty. The Memorial of the President, Council and Fellows of the Royal Society of London for improving Natural Knowledge humbly showeth –

That the passage of the Planet Venus over the Disc of the Sun . . . on the 3rd of June in the year 1769 is a phenomenon that must, if the same be accurately observed in proper places, contribute greatly to the improvement of Astronomy on which Navigation so much depends . . .

That a correct Set of Observations made in the Southern latitudes would be of greater importance than many of those made in the Northern. But it would be necessary that the observers who are to pass the line, should take their departure from England early in the Spring; because it might be some time before they could fix upon a proper place for making the observations within the limits required.[8]

Mercifully, the Royal Society is blessed that their Sovereign, who is just shy of 30 at this time, is not shy of embracing science, for he is actually the first British Monarch to have studied the subject and it will be noted that, 'its study and advancement were always objects of his deep interest and solicitude'.[9]

On this project the Royal Society will have the full support of the most important Royal of all. In fact, His Majesty throws such support behind the whole enterprise that on 24 March 1768 Lord Morton informs the Royal Society council that the Treasury has already transferred £4000 to their coffers. The King further instructs my First Lord of the Admiralty, Sir Edward Hawke, to select and make ready a suitable ship, and to aid the Royal Society insofar as it is deemed appropriate.

In typical style, Hawke moves quickly and ere a month has passed, on 29 March, the Navy Board informs the Admiralty:

> We have purchased a cat-built Bark, in burthen 368 tons and of the age of three years and nine months, for conveying such persons as shall be thought proper, to the Southward for making observations of the passage of the planet Venus over the disk of the sun, and pray to be favoured with their Lordships' directions for fitting her for the service accordingly . . . And that we may also receive their commands by what name she shall be registered on the list of the Navy . . .[10]

They receive a swift reply, on 7 April: 'Ship purchased to be sheathed, filled and fitted for a voyage to the Southward. To be called *The Endeavour*[11] . . .'[12]

•

Now, as to where in the Southern Hemisphere the Royal Society should send their observation party, the Astronomer Royal, Dr Nevil Maskelyne, has already informed the King that it must be a place 'not exceeding 30 degrees of Southern latitude, and between the 140th and 180th degrees of longitude, West, from your Majesty's Royal Observatory in Greenwich Park'.[13] That is, somewhere in the South Pacific, but not too far South.

They are not long in looking, however, as there is one man of enthusiasm and influence who, though not a Fellow of the Royal Society, ingratiates himself into Society circles and makes it known that *he* has spent more time in the Southern Hemisphere and the South Seas than most of the Society men put together. It is Scottish geographer Alexander Dalrymple who positively quivers with excitement – and certitude of success – when he thinks of the voyage that is to be launched. He now becomes ever louder in voicing many views, the first of which is that the most appropriate Southern observation point in the South Pacific is most likely in the Marquesas or Tongan Islands.

Personally, Dalrymple can see the climax of his career just up ahead. For beyond the leap forward in science and power of the Royal Navy that such a trip will engender, it might also see his self-proclaimed position as England's leading 'Speculative Geographer' – the one who has long supported that centuries-old hypothesis about the existence of a Great Southern Land – elevated to England's finest geographer of all time.

No, not New Holland, for that enormous continent in the Southern climes is already known – or at least the Western end of it is, and substantially mapped, courtesy of the Dutch, who had been all over it since the early 1600s without settling on what appeared to them as barren wastelands. The Great Southern Land is another continent, one posited since the days of Aristotle and expanded by Ptolemy, the great Greek mathematician, astronomer and geographer, who believed it stands to reason that there will be a great land mass in the South to balance the giant land masses of Europe and the Americas in the North. Alexander Dalrymple agrees. For all of his adult life, the 31-year-old Dalrymple – all coiffed curls and a certain smarmy smugness – has been gathering historical hints about the existence of this place, every scrap of map, every oblique reference, and by putting them all together is convinced that it is no myth. Ptolemy's famous map had just been a mere starting point. However, the circumnavigation of the globe by Captain John Byron – known as 'Foulweather Jack' – in the *Dolphin* from June 1764 to May 1766 had turned up nothing. So Dalrymple's hopes are now pinned to Captain Philip Carteret and Captain Samuel Wallis, currently on the high seas in the ships *Swallow* and *Dolphin* respectively – the latter on its second trip around the globe – charged with instructions to search for the elusive land mass. And yet, Dalrymple sets little store in them finding it, for they lack the key thing – *him*.

And though the Royal Society men know nothing of his private plans to captain the ship and discover the mythical continent, and finally get the recognition he deserves, they see no problem recommending him to the Admiralty as a suitable person to join the expedition as the observer.

But Alexander Dalrymple won't stop there, particularly as he is sure that he is invaluable to the success of the endeavour and trusts that the Royal Society men will understand that a man of his own eminence, as he writes to the Society's secretary, 'can have no thought of undertaking this Voyage as a Passenger going out to make the Observations, or on any other footing than that of having the management of the Ship intended for service'.[14]

Indeed?

Indeed.

Yes, things are a little complicated by the fact he has never actually commanded a Royal Navy vessel before, and nor has he even been in the Royal Navy. It's hard to know whether he even knows the differences between a schooner and a collier. The Royal Society men tacitly support the idea, but the final decision is for the Admiralty.

And yet, how can the First Lord of the Admiralty, Sir Edward Hawke, put this?

No.

As a matter of fact, he writes to the Royal Society's President, Lord Morton, that such a notion is 'entirely repugnant to the regulations of the Navy'.[15]

The First Lord of the Admiralty goes even harder than that, declaring to his fellow Admirals, sitting upright in prim uniforms around the dark, ornate wooden table in the Admiralty boardroom: 'I would rather cut off my right hand than permit anyone but a King's Officer to command one of the ships of His Majesty's Navy.'[16]

Well, that's it, then.

Mr Dalrymple has given the Royal Navy his conditions, and if the First Lord will not agree to them, then they will not be getting Mr Dalrymple on their ship at all! They can get their own Captain, their own scientist, and good luck in finding any as brilliant as Mr Dalrymple! (And that is Alexander Dalrymple for you. Such tirades are very familiar to all who know him, and just as it is said of him that, 'not the least of his talents is a talent for jumping to conclusions',[17] today's conclusion – that the Admiralty are ingrates, and whoever is chosen ahead of him will be unworthy by comparison – is very much of the variety known as foregone.)

Nevertheless, as it turns out, there is another member of the Royal Society who is more than interested in going on a voyage of such astronomical significance, one who does not insist on the Captaincy being thrown in with it, that gay young blade of London Town, Joseph Banks, the gentleman with the peaches and cream complexion, curiously ever and always fronted by his perennially sunburned nose from his ceaseless outdoor ramblings. The exceedingly wealthy young Banks has two great passions and while one of them is indeed heavenly bodies, the ones in question are not zooming across the sky but ideally zooming towards his bed chamber. Yes, what Banks truly cares about are women and botany, with astronomy not figuring in any way, but now is his opportunity to seize the moment and do precisely what he told those blockheads he would do – gallivant around the globe! Yes, the Newfoundland journey had been a memorable tour, but this, *this*, journey to far corners of the map, and then beyond, would be an embarkation for the world itself. *The* Grand Tour. His mind reels to ponder the botanical realms that might open up to him on such a trip.

And, in smart contrast to that bloviating blow-hard Mr Dalrymple, Mr Banks understands that 'command' of this proposed voyage is neither here nor there – it is simply not important who formally gives the orders on the ship – for what truly counts is *control*. And one way to secure control? Buy it, of course. Committing his own money to the cause should be enough to not only secure him a position as naturalist on board, but also allow him to bring a suite of servants and scientists to help with the work that will come from all the botanising . . . like Dr Solander, for one. And his greyhounds, for two and three.

Hopefully it can even buy him some influence in deciding who the Captain – effectively the driver of their ocean carriage – should be. Quietly, Banks is told that he has the support of Lord Morton and the council of the Royal Society, as it is obvious that having a botanist of Banks' repute, together with his entourage of experts, can only add to the voyage's scientific clout – with the fact he will pay his own way, a singularly significant bonus. It is not yet pursued formally, however.

No matter, Joseph Banks, no more than 25 years old but with that swagger and confidence that goes with wealth as extreme as it is well connected, begins his private preparations for the journey regardless, ordering 'the making of special cases and boxes for the stowage of his specimens (plant and animal) and the ordering and purchasing of the equipment and material to meet the expected hazards and opportunities in a circumnavigation of not less than two years' duration'.[18]

•

Back in the U-shaped Admiralty building, around the dark wood ornate table, one name keeps coming up, a man backed by the highly regarded Captain Sir Hugh Palliser and the powerful Admiralty Secretary Philip Stephens – he is a great Mariner of greater promise who is not yet a Captain, but who has the desired qualifications to command the ship.

Perhaps, most importantly, this fellow has already demonstrated a proficiency in astronomical observations. You know the one, that fellow Master James Cook, the one who navigated the fleet up the St Lawrence to Quebec, who has been commanding a vessel and charting the coast-lines of Newfoundland and Labrador these past few years. He comes to the Admiralty each winter and has produced the most precise, exquisite charts we have ever seen. The same man who accurately observed the eclipse of the sun at Newfoundland a couple of years ago.

Good God . . . the *same man*?

Yes, Cook! He is surely perfect for the role!

After all, you can't ask for better than one who has maritime, carto-graphical *and* astronomical skills, while also having come from nothing and nowhere with no influential familial connections such as an imposing father-in-law or uncle, nor any sizeable inheritance with which to throw his weight around. The route from total obscurity to pre-eminence in a highly respected field has been a supremely difficult one, spreading across the globe and through all manner of shoals and reefs, but somehow this extraordinary navigator might just have found it?

In sum, when the Navy come up with their list of possible Captains for this venture it could be written on the back of a postage stamp, as it consists of just one name: James Cook.

Yes, there is the complication that Cook has not yet passed his exams to be a Lieutenant, let alone a Captain, but if he is willing to take on the role, that can be surely resolved . . .

5 May 1768, Council Room of the Royal Society, Crane Court, London, Oh Captain, our Captain

It had been no less than Sir Isaac Newton himself, the then President (and friend and colleague of Edmund Halley – the pair were viewed as the giants of their age), who had selected these grand premises for the Royal Society back in 1710, and also that great man who had begun the tradition we see on this very evening of 1768.

As evening falls, the old porter emerges onto Fleet Street from the Society's grand Crane Court premises, in a formal gown and bearing a staff displaying the arms of the Society in silver. On the end of the staff is a lit lantern, which the porter carefully places above the marble portico to indicate to the world that a meeting of the Royal Society is now in session.

Gazing intently at the building before him as he steps out of his carriage, a tall handsome fellow in a navy blue coat with gold trim worn open with white breeches and stockings that end in shiny black boots – the dress uniform of a warrant officer of the Royal Navy – takes pause. It is quite the moment.

The son of a farm labourer from the tiny village of Marton in Yorkshire, whose fate was in all likelihood to be a farm labourer from Marton, now summoned to meet the members of the mighty Royal Society – all Lords, Earls, Barons, Professors, eminent scientists and public intellectuals – at their premises of rather stately splendour, just off Fleet Street in London. Giving a rather . . . dull shilling to the coachman, James Cook makes his way through the many carriages in the courtyards with their personal coachmen waiting for the return of their masters, up the stairs through the portico columns and into the premises proper. In the foyer, he hands his peaked hat to a porter with a gracious nod.

He is neither 'greeted' nor 'welcomed', as both would imply warmth of reception, but he is certainly ushered silently upstairs to a wooden bench by a thick wooden door, where he is to await his summons to meet with the Society's council.

On the other side of the thick wooden door is a long, narrow, rather drab room with an ornately decorated ceiling. At one end, the august council members of the Society sit on wooden benches rising up in tiers on both sides of a long table covered in green cloth. At the far end of the table is another smaller table, where the President, James Douglas, the 14th Earl of Morton, sits with his back to the fireplace, facing the men gathered. On either side of him sit the Society's two secretaries, notes scattered before them.

Lying by Lord Morton's right hand is a small wooden mallet by which he can render the entire room silent with a single knock, while at the foot of his table lies a large silver-gilt mace, the symbol of his authority, placed so to show the council is in session – just as happens in the House of Commons.

Captain John Campbell stands to speak. He happens to be that rare breed of Royal Navy man and Royal Society man that the Admirals had sought for the South Seas voyage, unfortunately he is already commissioned as Captain of a ship and is unable to leave that post. Not that he seems to mind too much.

'James Cook,' he announces to his fellows, 'who is in attendance, will be appointed by the Admiralty to the command of the vessel destined for the observation in the Southern latitudes. He is a proper person to be one of the observers in the observation of the transit of Venus.'[19]

A murmur rumbles through the room as the Fellows speak among each other. 'Cook', his name is. That same fellow who observed the eclipse in Newfoundland. True, he's a fellow who has been to no grand school (*sniff*), is the offspring of no fine family (*sniff, sniff, what is that smell?*), but apparently – we are informed by Dr Bevis *and* Captain Campbell – he is more than worth his salt, and it is for very good reason he has already been appointed by the Admiralty to the role, and now he will be a leading observer of the transit, too.

With a few muttered words from Lord Morton, one of the secretaries at the head table looks up and imperiously calls to an orderly to show Mr Cook inside. The door opens with that agonised creak that is incumbent on all doors of such heavy constitution when their very nature is to remain closed, and, after a quick clip-clop of maritime boots on the wooden floor, a large figure is briefly silhouetted taking up just about the entire doorway, before a naval officer of notably robust bearing strides into the room.

The august Fellows cast a gimlet eye over this newcomer, this fellow of such plebeian nomenclature and background . . . but it seems he bears no resemblance to the plebeian archetype. He is a remarkably tall, solid fellow with a strong-featured visage unusual in one with no breeding.

Cook, with remarkable poise under unnerving circumstances, gazes back evenly, taking it all in.

Very well then.

We of the Royal Society, the instigators of this whole voyage, just want to be satisfied that he is capable, will follow our instructions regarding the observation and won't . . . rock the boat.

Cook listens carefully as the august Fellows outline the mission they have in mind for him, and speaks with even more discretion as he answers the questions put to him to the best of his abilities . . . which are clearly considerable. For in speaking about the science of navigation, about his tracking of the eclipse at Newfoundland, he is speaking the language of science, and the members of the Royal Society cannot help but be impressed.

Cook not only walks as a distinguished naval officer, he talks the language of the accomplished scientist.

The faces of Lord Morton, Captain Campbell and Astronomer Royal Nevil Maskelyne say it all. This wondrous James Cook is that rarest of things, a man who is truly both a sailor and a scientist, and is just the man to command the voyage.

And the most important thing for now is Cook's response when questioned about his own views.

Yes, he wishes to go on this venture. Yes, he is sure he is capable of making the calculations concerning the Transit of Venus. Yes, a Royal Society gift of £110 in addition to his naval pay of £20 per annum is quite acceptable.

And with nary another word needing to be spoken, Master James Cook turns on his shiny black-booted heel, and strides to the back of the room where he stands, back to the wall.

Next!

For with the Cook matter taken care of, the next man ushered into the grand room is another nervous Yorkshireman, Mr Charles Green, former assistant to the Astronomer Royal, Sir Nevil Maskelyne, the former nearly as experienced as the latter in spending his days keeping correct time at Greenwich and gazing at the heavens.

Green is a meticulous kind of fellow, but he is used to observing, not being observed and gazed at by the great, the good and the glaring, who are now all around him. Nervously he stands, blinking back at them, as formalities are read through inviting him to be the other official observer of the Transit of Venus on the coming expedition. Finally, he is invited to speak, regarding whether he agrees to the sum of £120 that the Royal Society has seen fit to equip him and this Captain Cook with to observe the transit.

'Do you agree to allowance aforesaid?'

Yes, yes he does.

'With a further gratuity to yourself of 200 guineas . . .' *200 guineas! Don't say yes now, wait till the man in the wig stops speaking . . .* 'for the voyage, and if the voyage should exceed two years, then at the rate of 100 guineas per annum?'[20]

Yes, Mr Green agrees to that as well. After all, he is not really being asked, and is rather more being told. One does not argue the toss with the Royal Society. It is an extraordinary privilege to be in their presence, let alone be given a mission by them.

Very well then, Mr Green, take your place by your fellow Yorkshireman, the one in Navy uniform, up the back on the left. Master James Cook keeps his own counsel and attention now turns to the equipment itself.

And so Master Cook is approved to be kitted out by the Royal Society, with his freshly secured astronomical instruments – telescopes, a sextant, a Journeyman clock and more.

Oh, and we shall also need such specialised instruments as a 'dipping needle', to measure the angle between the horizon and Earth's magnetic field, and an astronomical quadrant to measure the altitudes of celestial bodies, providing crucial data to calculate geographical position.

Once the meeting room is emptied, the secretary picks up the large silver-gilt mace from the floor and places it upon the table.

The Royal Society council is no longer in session.

Early morning, 20 May 1768, Aphrodite's Isle

Weary Captain Wallis sits in the Great Cabin of the *Dolphin*, dictating his final log entry to his clerk: 'The ship anchored safely in the Downs, it being just 637 days since her weighing anchor in Plymouth sound.'[21]

A short time later, he climbs down the rope ladder into a waiting Navy tender, which drops him at the dock and he is soon on his way to London and the Admiralty with the news of an island paradise he has discovered in the South Pacific, an island paradise by the native name of Tahiti,[22] now renamed King George III's Island.

•

Sure enough, just three weeks after meeting with the Royal Society, on 25 May, James Cook receives a letter from the Admiralty addressed to – Elizabeth, come quickly! – *Lieutenant* James Cook. He opens his first commission with a tremulous left hand, knowing it will be life-changing.

And indeed . . .

> . . . We have appointed you First Lieutenant of His Majesty's Bark, the *Endeavour*, now at Deptford, and intend that you shall command her during her present intended voyage . . . you are hereby required and directed to use the utmost despatch in getting her ready for the sea accordingly.
>
> Given etc., etc., 25th May 1768[23]

So it is done. James Cook has his commission as a Lieutenant and his preliminary instructions.

Yes, there will be surprise in some quarters that a newly promoted Lieutenant will be in charge of such an expedition, when the two previous

English expeditions to the Pacific had been conducted by Commodore Byron and Captain Wallis, but the Royal Navy is firm. Cook has precisely the credentials required, if not the expected rank, and that is all that counts.

Two days later, at dawn, Lieutenant James Cook leaves his Mile End home, crosses the Thames in a ferry and heads by carriage down to Deptford, where his very own ship awaits.

As to what kind of bark the *Endeavour* is, Captain James Cook – for he will be so addressed by his men as a matter of 'nautical courtesy' – could not be more delighted, and there is a very good reason that she feels like home the minute he sets foot upon her pine deck.

For yes, the *Endeavour* is none other than one of the old coal tubs he learnt to sail on and has come to adore, a Whitby cat. Built and launched on the high seas just under four years earlier, it is capacious enough to hold their stores and sturdy, reliable and clearly capable of getting them to the other side of the world, and back. With its flat bottom and snub nose, the *Endeavour* is perfect for getting in and out of all the new shallow coves, bays and estuaries they will surely discover.

Cook, meticulous as he is, has studied the Navy Yard's report on the *Endeavour* and knows it backwards: 'stern back, single bottom, full built . . . is a promising ship for sailing of this kind and fit to stow provisions and store as many as may be put on board her'.[24] He studies the statistics eagerly: '97-feet overall, 29-foot 3-inches beam, height between decks [an important consideration for a man of Cook's build] varying from 7 foot 11 inches to 7 foot 6 inches, with ample space for stores and provisions.'[25]

He is more than pleased with the choice, later writing, 'No consideration should be set in competitions with that of her being of a construction of the safest kind, in which the officers may, with the least hazard, venture upon a strange coast . . . These properties are not to be found in ships of war of forty guns, nor in frigates, nor in East India Company's ships, nor in large three-decked West India ships, as such are built for the coal trade, which are peculiarly adapted for this purpose.'[26]

And oh what a pleasure it is, as this man from such humble beginnings strides around his maritime equivalent of home and hearth – a Whitby cat. Here is the capstan, and there is the wheel with the binnacle containing the compasses, and when you take three steps to your left, of course here is the ship's bell, while there by the stairs leading to the quarter-deck is the copper bowl known as the 'pissdale', where officers could relieve themselves. All of them, Cook insists, even the pissdale, must be polished till they shine – ship-shape – as brightly as the brass buckles and buttons on the officers' uniforms.

With no little pride, 'Captain Cook' watches as a young tar – not so long ago, he used to be one of those, he muses – hauls on the rope to haul to the top of the masthead the *Endeavour*'s officially commissioned pennant, a cross of St George in the hoist and a white fly, dancing on the summer breeze.

But to work. No sooner is Cook aboard than he begins the task of fitting out his, *his*, ship, ensuring that everything is done just so. From long and sometimes bitter experience, Cook knows that proper preparation now can make all the difference to the success of the entire expedition and will very likely be the difference between life and death for many of the ship's company. Just a quick glance tells him that all five anchors are in perfect nick, which is to the good, while of the ship's three main boats, the long-boat, pinnace and yawl . . . the long-boat is not. The past command of this ship has allowed a simple coat of varnish to cover wood that has been eaten by worms and turned rotten. With a few sharp commands, Cook has the shipwrights from the yard start to strip it back, replace the wood and have it painted with white lead, which should do the trick to protect it in the tropics. These ship-boats are important for carrying out the myriad ferrying operations Cook and his men will need to go from ship to shore, and will also be crucial to acting as life-boats should the *Endeavour* ever founder. It is unthinkable they not begin the voyage in pristine shape.

From first light until that part of the dusk which no longer argues the toss with night as to who holds sway – and sometimes beyond, courtesy of lanterns – the sound of hammering, sawing and . . . cursing, comes from the *Endeavour*. Yes, it had been perfect for carrying coal, but to carry some 90 people with their attendant luggage and accoutrements, a third deck must be built into the hold, replete with cabins for the ship's warrant officers and Midshipmen, as well as a powder magazine for the cannon it will carry and many extra storerooms for the victuals that must last them as long as 18 months.

Now, in terms of protecting the hull, Captain Cook does not wish it to be copper-sheathed, as the Admiralty has ordered. A covering of copper had been used as an experiment on the *Dolphin*, but to Cook's mind had proved too easily damaged, impossible to repair far from home without a dry dock, and there had been issues of chemical reaction between the copper and the iron bolts in the hull as the copper caused the iron to corrode, making the ship 'nail-sick'.

No, he insists, her hull must be protected with an extra layer of thin oak planking over tarred felt, caulked with oakum – basically tarred fibre, produced by the painstaking unpicking of old tarred ropes, a task mainly undertaken by hapless prisoners lodged at prisons up and down the country – all of it to protect the precious hull from the borer worm known to plague ships in the tropics.

•

As to where specifically in the South Pacific the transit should be observed, Captain Wallis of the *Dolphin* has handed the Royal Society their answer on a silver platter, and right in time.

An island paradise perfectly positioned for their purposes. It is one that sounds so exotic that my Lords of the Admiralty can barely believe that the accounts they hear are true. The least of it is the formal geographical description: 'We have discovered a large, fertile and extremely populous island in the South Seas. The *Dolphin* came to anchor in a safe, spacious and commodious harbor.'[27]

Yes, this Otaheite, expressed in the English tongue as 'Tahiti' – is apparently like nothing ever discovered before, with the inhabitants extending extraordinary hospitality to their British visitors, and no more welcoming gestures more gratefully received than those extended by Tahiti's voluptuous brown-skinned women – who are so free with their sexual favours some of the sailors are reportedly *worn out.*

Generally, the Europeans are as much wonder to the Tahitians as the Tahitians are to them: 'From the behavior of the inhabitants, we had reason to believe she was the first and only ship they had ever seen.'[28]

What better place than this – a stable speck in the South Pacific, unclaimed by any other nation, with water, food, helpful men and beautiful women on call – to base the *Endeavour* for the transit?

Already the *Dolphin*'s Master's Mate, who sailed with both 'Foulweather Jack' Byron and Wallis – he is one of the few men in known history to have circumnavigated the globe twice – the 38-year-old American-born Mariner John Gore, has joined, and wants to get underway, and the sooner the better. No, really, can we get underway tomorrow?

And despite Captain Wallis swearing his men to secrecy about their discovery, already a shanty is doing the rounds of the inns and taverns dotted nearby the docks.

Ye bold British tars, who to glory are free,
Who dare venture your lives for your fortunes at sea,
Yourself for a while of your pleasures disrobe,
And attend to a tale of a voyage 'round the globe,

For the Dolphin's *return'd, and such tidings does bring*
As may welcome us home to our country and king . . .
Then we plow'd the South Ocean, such [land] to discover
As amongst other nations has made such a pother.
We found it, my boys, and with joy be it told.
For beauty such islands you ne'er did behold.
We've the pleasure ourselves the tidings to bring
As may welcome us home to our country and king.

For wood, water, fruit, and provision well stor'd
Such an isle as King George's the world can't afford,
For to each of these islands great Wallis gave name,
Which will e'er be recorded in annals of fame.
We'd the fortune to find them, and homeward to bring
The tidings a tribute to country and king.[29]

But can this magic land of 'Tahiti' actually be real? Some at the Admiralty remain incredulous.

And with good reason.

Foulweather Jack's raconteur Midshipman, Charlie Clerke, had come back to tell wild but believable stories of how they had encountered *a race of Giants* in Patagonia. A people no less than nine feet high! Actually, once Charlie had thought about it, and the story had taken off in the English press, he had decided over a bottle with friends that they were 11 feet high and the story had gained such legs it had been recorded in the Royal Society's journal *Philosophical Transactions*, complete with illustrations.

(One can only hope the editor remained philosophical when he learnt that he was having his leg pulled by a master of the art.)

But, yes, serious inquiries with Captain Wallis establish that Tahiti is real, ideal for the Society's purposes and so Tahiti it is.

All up it means that Lieutenant Cook is going to have little trouble filling out his crew roster. One of the first appointments is none other than Commodore Foulweather Jack's tall-tale-telling Midshipman, Charlie Clerke, who joins as one of two Master's Mates. There are six more sailors who had been on the *Dolphin* with Wallis and who have only been back in England a few weeks, and are now eager to return. There is the American-born John Gore, who had sailed with Foulweather Jack and Wallis, who soon receives his first King's commission to join the *Endeavour* as 3rd Lieutenant. (Yes, Gore is from the American colonies – and a notably charismatic, impetuous and independent kind of man to boot – but there are quite a few from New York, Virginia and the like serving with the British at this time.)

There is Dick Pickersgill, a 19-year-old Yorkshireman who is too fond of grog, like most sailors, but when sober has such a talent for surveying and chart-making that he knows *precisely* where he left his heart – back in Tahiti. He cannot sign up quickly enough, and is appointed as the other Master's Mate in spite of his youth.

Nor can Robert Molineux wait to get back to Aphrodite's Isle. Also a heavy drinker but three years older than Pickersgill, he is appointed as no less than the ship's Master – Captain Cook's usual role; while young Frank Wilkinson, a Welshman, and James Gray are soon on the muster roll as Able Seamen. James Magra, a 22-year-old fellow from the backwoods of the American colonies, who has been at sea since the age of 15, and fought in the Seven Years' War – a smooth man when sober, rare as that condition might be – is also signed on as a Midshipman. All of them are impatient to get started, to get back to Tahiti.

On a personal note, there are two young fellows that Cook is also quick to sign up. The first is his young servant from his last season on the *Grenville*, a 16-year-old London lad by the name of William Howson, who will fill the same role on the *Endeavour*. And at the behest of his dear wife, Elizabeth, Cook also signs up her cousin, 16-year-old Isaac Smith, who had also proved his worth aboard the *Grenville* as a sailor and amateur surveyor – and is, besides, the epitome of a 'likely lad', a fellow well liked by crew and officers alike.

The positions of the officers are quickly filled, with Cook the Commander, Captain and 1st Lieutenant. One Zachary Hicks is chosen as 2nd Lieutenant, Cook's second-in-command. Hicks is a 29-year-old of great experience, and Cook has liked the cut of his jib from the first.

•

Come mid-July, Captain Cook has a full muster of 70 sailors, all of whom, once hired, must provide their own uniform, together with a bowl, a spoon and a mug. His Majesty's Royal Navy will provide them with a sea chest so they may tightly and tidily stow their gear. Most of the sailors sport ponytails, that distinctive ribbon of hair that tells the tale that these are seafaring men, not dandies.

There are the ship's three 'standing warrant officers' – they don't hold a 'Commission' from the Crown but they do have a 'Warrant' from the Navy Board – the Carpenter John Satterly, the Gunner Stephen Forwood, and the Bosun John Gathray, as do the armourers, who are responsible for keeping all muskets and cannon in working order, while dealing with all things metal – and are the most engaged in its actual operation. Though risen from the ranks, the standing warrant officers have not risen that far – for they still mess and dine with the common herd of sailors. (As for herds that make a mess, the *Endeavour* will carry sheep, hogs and fowl as well as men. Their numbers will decrease as appetites increase, but the boat shall initially be a vessel of menagerie rather than botany.)

The most important of the warrant officers from Cook's point of view is the noted Navy Surgeon, William Monkhouse. He's the one over there – the fellow with the rheumy eyes and slightly sagging jowls of a sad hound-dog – forever taking a silver snuff box from his pocket and sniffing a pinch of the tobacco contained within. Cook already knows and respects Surgeon Monkhouse from their years in Newfoundland together. There are some Captains for whom the collective care of their sailors is neither here nor there, who accept a number of deaths per voyage as simply something that goes with the territory – but Cook is not one of them. From the beginning it will be a point of pride with him to keep as many of his men healthy and alive as possible, and with Surgeon Monkhouse on board, he is off to a good start.

By happy coincidence, Monkhouse not only also knows Joseph Banks Esq. well, but as the Surgeon on the *Niger* in Newfoundland, he had been credited with saving Banks' life when the naturalist fell gravely ill with ague and fever. So highly does Captain Cook regard Monkhouse that he also readily agrees to take on the Surgeon's younger brother, Jonathan, as a Midshipman. (The medical man is gratified, both for himself and for his brother. For one thing he personally needs to get away from his life in London . . . for private reasons he does not care to talk about right now . . . And for another thing, his brother Jonathan, though a fine young man, can be of sometimes impetuous disposition, and could do with some watching over.)

Cook is less pleased, and even angered by other appointments.

For just one glance at the frail old man the Admiralty has sent him to act as the *Endeavour*'s cook sees the Captain dash off a note to the Navy Board complaining that the cook assigned is 'a lame infirm man, and incapable of doing his Duty'.[30]

For once, the Navy Board reacts relatively quickly, withdrawing the old cook and sending a new one, a John Thompson, who comes down to the yards at Deptford, but cannot take Cook's proffered gloved right hand in welcome, for . . . Mr Thompson doesn't actually have anything more than a blunt stump. Yes, the Admiralty has sent him . . . a one-handed cook, to feed nearly a hundred men for the next two years.

Again Cook dashes off a note of protest, only to see his hopes dashed, for the Admiralty will neither budge nor fudge – working as a cook is one of the few occupations available to cripples or maimed men and if Captains don't like it, so be it.

In any case, Captain Cook's temper *is* tempered soon enough when he finds Thompson to be more than competent after all. (And of course, but for the grace of God and a good Surgeon all those years ago, the Captain himself would have been a one-handed Cook.)

As Cook's people shape up, so does his ship.

A set of 28 feet long sweeps – long oars – are brought on board so that if they are becalmed or even de-masted, they will still be able to have some propulsion in any direction they choose.

No less than eight tons of ballast – large rocks, together with slabs of pig iron – are carried aboard and placed in the bilge to keep the *Endeavour* stable in heavy seas. Now, against the possibility of their shipping water in such great quantities it might sink them, Cook also insists on four of the best possible pumps, known as Elm Tree Pumps, so called because they are made from hollowed out elm trees. When properly manned with two good men and true working the brake handle, the pumps are capable of moving an extraordinary amount of water out of the bilge – 25 gallons a minute – in what usually amounts to 15-minute lots before the men need to rest and be replaced by fresh men. Ideally, they will never have to face such a situation for they will not take water, but it is just Cook's way to try to cover every possibility, most particularly worst-case scenarios. These pumps can also be used to pump up seawater with which to scrub the decks, and also in case of fire.

It is as similar insurance against misadventure that Cook oversees the installation of a copper distilling apparatus, capable of making 42 gallons of fresh water from 56 gallons of seawater.

It all takes time, and care, but Cook has no doubt that it is worth it. And of course he makes sure to have the best navigational instruments – sextant, compass, and Nevil Maskelyne's *British Mariners' Guide* and *Nautical Almanac* (a rich new resource that charts the skies and will help Cook to calculate longitude). The astronomical tools and equipment given to him by the Royal Society are also safely brought on board, tested once more, and carefully stowed, all under the watchful eye of the Captain.

But wait. One last thing. Cook requests from Admiralty Secretary Philip Stephens a set of instruments 'in order to make surveys of such parts as His Majesty's Bark the *Endeavour* under my command may touch at'.[31]

On the list, of course, is a plane table and all the accoutrements, just the same as he had used for the first time almost 10 years ago to the day, when he met Lieutenant Samuel Holland at Louisburg.

There is also a ship's cat and a remarkably worldly goat that has already spent three years in the West Indies and circumnavigated the globe with the *Dolphin* under Captain Wallis – and is now bound to do the same again in a manner to make Dick Whittington's cat weep with jealousy. After all, this is no folly, given that a good goat fed on kitchen scraps can provide the handsome return of two quarts of milk a day to be served on the officers' table (or on this voyage, the Officer and Gentlemen's table). And as this particular goat is a champion proved to provide at least that amount and more, she can – *thank you, Ma'am, that will be a shilling* – go around the world for sixpence, *twice*.

Now, beyond goat milk, they need victuals enough to last them 18 months. James Cook oversees the purchase of such things as five tons of barrelled flour, 185 pounds of great Devonshire cheese, salt beef by the ton, seemingly endless biscuits – known as hard tack or sea biscuits by the jack tars who love to hate the things – and vinegar . . .

The list seems endless, but not unmanageable for a former grocer's apprentice like James Cook.

Cook receives instructions advising that 'His Majesty's Bark the *Endeavour* at Deptford being fitted out for a distant voyage . . . will afford an opportunity for a fair trial to be made of the efficacy of sauerkraut against the Scurvy (etc.) . . . a proportion for twelve months for seventy men will be sent at the rate of two pounds per man per week.'[32]

Cook is delighted, sure that the almost three and a half tons of sauerkraut will keep men in good kilter and the voyage on course.[33] Yes, there might be resistance from the sailors to eat that much fermented cabbage, but Cook has his own firm ideas how that can be overcome.

In addition, the Admiralty instructs Cook to purchase and serve the men malt wort, a dense liquid extracted from the mashed malt used to brew beer, which is thought to fend off the dreaded sailors' affliction.

For alcohol, 250 barrels of beer are rolled aboard, with 44 barrels of brandy and – *yo ho-ho* – 17 barrels of rum.

•

The next morning at Gallions Reach, Captain Cook watches from the quarter-deck as 10 four-pounder cannons and eight swivel guns – at two feet 10 inches long, they are more moveable than cannon and can even be taken onto the long-boat – along with all the gunner's stores, including barrels of powder, are brought on board. The sailors mount all eight swivel guns and six of the six-foot long cannon on the upper deck, while the other four cannon are taken below and stored in the hold.

The guns, mind, are not to defend the *Endeavour* from the French or the like, so much as to give her the firepower that might be necessary should they find in foreign climes that . . . the Natives are restless. And now everyone stand back as we manhandle the guns on board, even as the *Endeavour* sinks an inch lower in the water for the added weight of over seven tons.

•

On 22 July, Captain Cook receives orders from the Admiralty advising that, after conferring with the Royal Society, 'You are hereby required and directed to receive on board . . . Mr Charles Green and his servant and baggage, as also the said Joseph Banks Esq. and his suite consisting of eight persons with their baggage.'[34]

So begins the fantabulous tale of 'Mr Banks' Voyage', which spreads faster than a delicious rumour through the parlours of London.

Banks, naturalistly enough, has gone ahead and specially selected his entourage, led by the eminent Swedish naturalist, Dr Daniel Solander, who just a couple of weeks before was released from his duties at the British Museum. There is also artist Sydney Parkinson, a 22-year-old quiet Quaker from Edinburgh, with a particular aptitude for accurately drawing and painting flora and fauna – as he had already done spectacularly well with those specimens Banks had brought back from Newfoundland – while also being possessed of a certain resolution of purpose which Banks believes will stand them in good stead on the long voyage to come. In a similar vein, another artist, Alexander Buchan, a 24-year-old from Scotland, will draw landscapes and peoples. Yes, he is a physically infirm kind of man – he suffers from occasional fits that take over his whole body – but his art is so outstanding Banks just can't leave him behind.

To assist Mr Banks and Dr Solander in the scientific examination and cataloguing of whatever they find, they decide to bring Herman Sporing, a somewhat sombre fellow Swede who for the past two years has been Dr Solander's clerk, secretary and draughtsman at the British Museum.

All of them will be waited on by four personal servants. Peter Briscoe and John Roberts are tapped to come from Revesby Abbey, Banks' family estate, while two further black 'servants', Thomas Richmond and George Dorlton, are also hired. (In fact, those black servants, are little more than 'slaves' by another name.[35] Most likely born in Jamaica, they are among 10,000 slaves in England at the time, bought and paid for from slave-masters down at the West India Quay in the Thames, and thereafter obliged to work for whoever has bought them – in this case, Joseph Banks. Whatever the nomenclature of 'servants', possessing slaves at this time in London marks you as a man of means, and that is precisely what Joseph Banks is.)

Banks completes the entourage by bringing his two favourite greyhounds – the favoured dogs of the high-born since the days of the Pharaohs, and the only dogs mentioned in the Bible – for the simple pleasure of their company. They include his favourite bitch, 'Lady'.

As to where they will all sleep . . . Joseph Banks has ideas, and more importantly, he has the monetary means, and the weight of the Admiralty behind him, to make his ideas reality.

And so he prepares lengthy written instructions for refitting the *Endeavour*'s Great Cabin – a spacious central dining room known as the 'Gentlemen's Quarters' or 'Officers' mess', located directly under the quarter-deck, which usually has two cabins reserved for the Captain and his most senior officer. Under Banks' instructions it is to be refitted to accommodate science and the men who study it – first and foremost, one Joseph Banks Esquire, along with Mr Green, Dr Solander and Mr Sporing.

At Banks' insistence – for class *must* travel First Class – he personally will take the Captain's cabin on the starboard side, while Cook will sleep in the near identical one on the port side. Those cabins come complete with a small four-paned square window looking into the central mess. Mr Green, Dr Solander and Mr Sporing are to take the cabins that are to be built encircling the Gentlemen's Quarters, each with seven foot ceilings for plenty of comfort.

The cabins of Cook's officers, Lieutenants Gore and Hicks, are usurped as they are relegated to the much smaller cabins – just five feet, *bump-on-the-head*, from floor to ceiling and six feet across – that lie below the Great Cabin on the rear lower deck that surround the Mates' Mess. Yes, they will likely be miserably uncomfortable for a voyage around the entire world, but Captain Cook is firm in the face of their complaints: everything must be done to accommodate commodious accommodations as close to the class of the Banks' entourage as possible. Only the best for Banks!

Banks wishes the shared space in the Great Cabin to be luxuriously fitted out, stipulating green baize on the floor, a big table with comfortable leather chairs, and a total of six windows so there is plenty of light for them to work, and a great view – two windows on each side of the ship, and four bigger windows at the stern. Banks also wishes to have a transom seat installed below the four, round-topped stern windows set into rectangular openings, so they may sit and observe the fish, birds or other beasts that play in the ship's wake (not to mention a place where his beloved greyhounds may like to curl up for a long nap). And only the best quality for everything. Send me the bills, and they will be paid promptly.

The arrangements for Banks' entourage will see them travelling in relative great comfort, at least in comparison to the 70-odd sailors whose own living space on the lower decks is dark, cramped and smelly.

Mr Joseph Banks is informed that many of his suggested changes to the Great Cabin will indeed be made once the ship is at Plymouth, the real starting point for their voyage. As ever, through a combination of charm, powerful friends and inherited wealth, young Joseph gets precisely what he wants, spending so much it could drain several banks, with nothing to be left to chance. Indeed, so numerous is their equipment that it shocks Banks himself, who writes to a friend: 'I take also besides ourselves two men to draw & four more to Collect in the different branches of Natural

History & such a Collection of Bottles, Boxes, Baskets bags nets &c &c: as almost frighten me who have prepared them.'[36] And of course they must have bird cages in which to keep whatever exotic avian species they might find, and hundreds of quires of paper for pressing and drying of flowers, leaves and the like. (As paper is in such short supply in the 1760s they end up securing printer's proofs of Milton's *Paradise Lost* which would otherwise have been thrown out.)

Indeed, Banks' friend Mr Ellis writes a long letter to Carl Linnaeus *himself* enthusing on just how far the botanist's £10,000 has gone.

'No people ever went to sea better fitted out for the purpose of Natural History,' he writes. 'They have got a fine library of Natural History; they have all sorts of machines for catching and preserving insects; all kinds of nets, trawls, drags and hooks for coral fishing, they have even a curious contrivance of a telescope, by which, put into the water, you can see the bottom at a great depth, where it is clear . . .'[37]

On and on the unique list goes.

In time it is done, and all loaded in the holds of the *Endeavour*.

30 July 1768, Admiralty House, London, signed, secret and delivered

With practised flourish, Admiralty Secretary Philip Stephens signs at the bottom of the document that lies on the desk before him, just as he does dozens of times a week.

This particular document he has just authorised, however, is different.

These are the final instructions for Captain James Cook of His Majesty's Bark *Endeavour*, bound for Tahiti and beyond – and they are in two parts, sealed in separate envelopes, the second of which is to be opened only after the Transit of Venus. (And yes, such security is important. The Admiralty can't risk a jack of the legless and loquacious variety blabbing the beans on England's secret search for the mysterious Southern land to a Spanish spy in some port town alehouse . . . Britain must get there first!) The envelopes are handed to his clerk with instructions that they be delivered personally to the good Captain himself, and it is soon done.

Godspeed, Captain Cook.

Shortly afterwards, Captain Cook receives the envelopes from the humble clerk with a grace and gratitude to which the young fellow is not always accustomed, but it is Cook's way. He will not forget he is a man who has risen through the ranks, not a man born into one.

But yes, while of course in England every man's home is his castle, in this case it is his ship and now that he has the awaited instructions, the good Captain gives some firm if loving orders to his First Mate Elizabeth, now again heavy with child, and his eager crew of two young boys, Nathaniel and James Jnr, and his bonny baby girl, Elizabeth Jnr. You shall accompany me down to the *Endeavour* for a look-see, before the pilot and his crew takes it from Gallions Reach down to the Downs, navigating the lower Thames and the treacherous estuary, whence I will take back command from the Navy pilot and sail for Plymouth.

Aye, aye, Cap'n!

Sure enough, the boys are beside themselves with excitement, and it is only for care of the enormous First Mate that they all must move gently. At last though they are out the door and James Cook has his whole family with him as they take a carriage down to Gallions Reach. Oh how the lads' eyes widen to the size of tea saucers, filled with wonder, just as their father's had when he first dropped down into Whitby all those years ago to see the huge cats anchored in the port.

Which one is yours, Daddy! Which one is yours!

That one, right there!

That one!

Oh, how truly grand the *Endeavour* looks to wee lads who have little else to compare it to. All they know is that their father is a great man, and has command of this ship. And yes, he will soon be going away for a long time, which is sad, but he is with them today on this great adventure, and that is all that counts.

Taken out by a waiting tender, the Cook family boards the ship, and the boys run excitedly about and even climb a little way up the rigging before both parents sternly call them down. If Elizabeth is the sterner of the two, it is understandable. Exhausted, she is about to lose her husband to this very ship, a vessel that will take him to the other side of the world and, she prays, back to her again. Still, as the passive face is key to the success of a card sharp – or so Lord Sandwich insists – so too is stoicism the stock-in-trade of a good Navy Officer's wife. She is worried and wan, but does her best to hide both, the better to ease the passage of that boldest and most daring of men, her husband, Captain James Cook.

The main thing now is to enjoy, as a family, what little time they have left together before, inevitably a week later, he really must say goodbye to them all, and this time she cannot hold back as her tears flow and he puts his arms around both her and their baby inside her, even as the children crowd in for a final family embrace.

The carriage awaits outside, with his trunk already placed upon it.

Murmuring softly, affirming his love for them all, assuring Elizabeth he will stay safe and lovingly telling the boys they must look after their mother and help her with the coming baby, James Cook straightens himself – duty calls, as ever – and walks out the door.

This is the life he has chosen, and it has been very good to him so far. In a moment he is gone, on his way from their Mile End home, and soon enough headed down the Thames to the Downs, where the *Endeavour* now awaits his arrival just beyond the most difficult parts of the river.

7 August 1768, the Downs, England, ship shapes

They are not a chatty pair. Captain Cook is a man more often than not content with his thoughts, while Charles Green only truly comes alive at night when gazing at the stars – and even then his activities do not much lend themselves to conversation. Ah, but on this grey day, they are both at least light of spirit as they travel together in a carriage from London down the cobble-stoned roads to the Downs to board their awaiting ship – on their way at last, in service of science and England.

Following protocol, the tinny blast of a tin whistle reaches them as the Bosun's Mate summons the ship's company to form up on the deck to receive the Captain, before piping him aboard, with his best impression of a maritime martial tune. Cook makes his way to the top of the gangway thus, and is greeted by several dozen men, all offering a salute which the Yorkshireman returns.

Captain Cook – for the first time wearing the distinctive tricorn hat of the Captain – is nevertheless quick to climb down through the hatchway on the quarter-deck and make his way to his private room in the Great Cabin. Here he takes the Admiralty's sealed Secret Instructions from his breast pocket, only to be opened after observing the transit, and places the envelope in the Captain's strongbox, a solid oak box, ribbed with iron and chained to the floor of his private cabin – designed to thwart thieves, defy dilettantes and survive shipwrecks. He clicks the padlock shut and puts the key in the inside breast pocket of his jacket, safely on his person, where it shall stay for the duration of the voyage.

The next day, Cook gives the order, 'Take her out, Mr Molineux,'[38] which sees a series of cascading orders from there, until . . .

'Anchor aweigh!' comes the cry of the Bosun, John Gathray, some 10 minutes later – and so begins the journey down to the great British naval launching ground that is Plymouth Sound.

For all the excitement in the Royal Society over the coming expedition to these new worlds, there are some who have qualms, led by none other than their president, Lord Morton – and he has some real concerns.

Leading those concerns is the treatment of the Natives in these new worlds that the expedition will encounter. A Scot, a humanitarian both by nature and upbringing, a philosopher trained to take an overview of life on this planet, Lord Morton is a truly enlightened man. An intellectual colleague of Montesquieu and David Hume, he has thought long and hard on the subject of mankind and there are a few things he wants Captain Cook, Joseph Banks and Dr Daniel Solander to bear in mind as they take their leave.

Writing them a collective letter, he sets them out.

He begins with the most important point – that they:

> exercise the utmost patience and forbearance with respect to the Natives of the several Lands where the Ship may touch . . .
>
> To check the petulance of the Sailors and restrain the wanton use of Fire Arms.
>
> To have it still in view that shedding the blood of these people is a crime of the highest nature – They are human creatures, the work of the same omnipotent Author, equally under his care with

the most polished European, perhaps being less offensive, more entitled to his favour ...

They are the natural, and in the strictest sense of the word, the legal possessors of the several regions they inhabit.

No European nation has a right to occupy any part of their country or settle among them without their voluntary consent.

Conquest over such people can give no just title; because they could never be the aggressors.

They may naturally and justly attempt to repel intruders, whom they may apprehend are come to disturb them in the quiet possession of their country, whether that apprehension be well or ill founded.

Therefore should they in a hostile manner oppose a landing and kill some men in the attempt, even this would hardly justify firing among them, till every other gentle method had been tried ...

If a landing can be effected, whether with or without resistance, it might not be amiss to lay some few trinkets, particularly looking glasses, upon the shore ... Lastly, to form a vocabulary of the names given by the Natives to the several things and places which come under the inspection of the gentlemen.

The foregoing hints, hastily put together, and probably very incorrect, and however humbly submitted to the consideration of Captain Cook and the other gentlemen by their hearty well-wisher and most obedient servant,

Morton.
Chiswick
Wednesday 10th August 1768.[39]

At last finishing his wide-ranging 'Hints', Lord Morton places the quill back on its stand and, after placing the letter in an envelope, affixes his wax seal. As Cook is already aboard the ship down in Plymouth, Morton sends the letter off to Joseph Banks, who has not yet left London, with the request that he deliver it to the Captain.

•

Midshipman Jonathan Monkhouse, just 19 years old, could not be more pleased. At last, at last, after all the preparations, all the lead-up, Captain Cook and his men of the *Endeavour* have a tedious passage down the channel, but they finally arrive at Plymouth on 14 August, meaning they are now not far away from leaving. Of their arrival at Plymouth, the younger Monkhouse records, 'Got the ship into a proper berth betimes this morning . . . Captain Cook and I went ashore before breakfast to send an express to Mr Banks acquainting him of our arrival here. We found the postmistress extremely pert.'[40]

Monkhouse can barely contain himself. He is about to meet the fair maidens of Tahiti, women he has heard ever so much about . . . can the tales really be true?

As for Mr Banks, the letter he received from James Cook has requested his immediate presence in Plymouth.

Not that they are *quite* ready to sail, for at the Admiralty's Plymouth office the next day, Captain Cook receives instructions to increase the number of sailors to 85 and to receive aboard 12 Royal Marines, all of whom are armed and arriving soon. Furthermore, he is told, shipwrights will be coming aboard to make changes to the Great Cabin, so it may accommodate not only yourself, but also your entourage of gentlemen. For a high-born Navy Captain, such an arrangement may have been untenable, but for James Cook, whose first ship was hardship – sleeping under a shop counter with cockchafers and weevils nibbling him – it is fine.

Cook's men are busy loading the ship for the long voyage ahead. Fresh meat, bags of fresh bread, beer and water, the men are physically and mentally preparing for the trip of a lifetime when a boat approaches. The regular sailors pause in their important work to watch as 12 Marines[41] in shining red coats climb up the ship's ladder, stride by the sailors on deck and disappear through the hatch, bound for the lower decks. Captain Cook records in his log. 'Received on board a supply of Bread, Beer and Water. A Sergeant, Corporal, Drummer, and 9 Private Marines as part of the Complement.'[42]

They are a rough bunch to say the least, though at least at their head they have a Sergeant in John Edgcumbe who, in the words of Captain Cook is 'very much a gentleman',[43] and has a certain way with his men, in part built on a kind of running banter. Yes, he chides and barks at all his privates when the occasion requires, but at heart he is perpetually amused, never more so than when making a joke of one of his charges for the entertainment of the others. One such is a waifish lad by the name of William Greenslade, who can't be more than 16 and wears his fear on his face . . . always looking as scared as a lost child, which he essentially is. Never mind, Sergeant Edgcumbe will have some fun at his expense, and make him a man bit by bit.

The next day, work on the Great Cabin begins, Captain Cook recording in his log, 'Several shipwrights and joiners from the yard employed on board refitting the gentlemen's cabins and making a [exercise] platform over the tiller.'[44]

Yes, Captain Cook will make his men exercise when off duty and not sleeping; there can be no idleness on his ship.

15 August 1768, The King's Theatre, beaucoup de Blosset is not enough

For all of the loyal followers that Joseph Banks is taking with him, the cherished person most on his mind is the one he is leaving behind, his 20-year-old fiancée, dear *Mademoiselle* Harriet Blosset, a blue-eyed brunette with the delicate neck of a swan and the most perfect unblemished alabaster skin. An exquisite beauty, the perfect symmetry of her features contrasts with the mess of beautiful curls that surround her irresistibly pretty face.

Their romance has surprised many on quite a few grounds, not least of which is that Mademoiselle Blosset is French and cannot speak a word of English, while Banks, as a proud Englishman, cannot speak a word of French. Banks is not fussed. He and this woman he characterises as the 'fairest of the flowers',[45] speak the language of love, and that is all that counts.

He just wishes he had told her that he is about to depart, heading off around the world for three years. He had meant to many times, at least in sign language, but every time he had tried they had been distracted by . . . other things, and so he had kept putting it off. She will likely be upset when she finds out, which is a pity.

As it happens, the timing of his departure is a little awkward.

For on this evening of 15 August 1768, Banks is at The King's Theatre to see the opera *La Buona Figliola*, and is sitting with Harriet and Dr Solander when a message is passed to him, which has been written by Captain Cook only hours before, directing him to come to Plymouth directly, for the *Endeavour* is about to sail. As it happens, the geologist Horace de Saussure is at the Opera with them and will later recount how, at supper afterwards, while Joseph proceeds to get rip-roaring drunk, Mademoiselle Blosset – who is clearly deeply in love with him – proceeds oblivious, wondering only why her dear fiancé is calling for ever more – *waiter, if you please!* – bottles of wine.

And so it goes.

'Banks,' de Saussure will recount, 'drank freely to hide his feelings.'[46]

The amount of alcohol imbibed, or perhaps Banks' naturally loquacious nature, surely explains why, despite de Saussure having never met Banks before, the gay young blade boasts to him of how strong his connections are high up in the Admiralty and their 'secret instructions' whereby, 'after observing the passage they will endeavour to make discoveries in the Southern Ocean and return by the East Indies'.[47] Those instructions are now a little less secret than they were.

Either way, the next morning, Mademoiselle Blosset wakes to find herself unaccountably . . . alone. There is no Joseph, and no note, no clue as to *ou il est*.

Where can he be?

CHAPTER FOUR

LEAVING ENGLAND

'Endeavour: *Labour directed to some certain end.*'

Samuel Johnson, a Cook contemporary, and Banks'
acquaintance, in his dictionary, published in 1755.

Come, come, my jolly lads, the wind's abaft;
Brisk gales our sails shall crowd;
Then bustle, bustle, bustle boys, haul the boat;
The Boatswain's pipe aloud;
All hands on board our ship's unmoored;
The rising gale fills every sail;
Our ship's well-manned and stored.[1]

The farewell shanty, 'Sling the Flowing Bowl',
beloved by sailors in Cook's time

19 August 1768, Plymouth, all aboard! Regulation before navigation

A motley crew, yes, but still as healthy and certainly as well presented as they are likely to be at any time in the next two years, they stand some 85 strong, alongside the 12 strong Marines, in the sparkling morning light, gathered around Captain Cook as he prepares to read out the Articles of War – 36 clauses on discipline and punishment, the formidable rule book of the British Navy, which for every sailor is both Bible and law. As they know, this is a ritual that takes place before every ship of the Royal Navy leaves home port on a mission, and the men stand silent before their Captain, as he begins . . .

'One! All commanders, Captains, and officers, in or belonging to any of His Majesty's ships or vessels of war, shall cause the public worship of Almighty God, according to the liturgy of the Church of England . . . and the Lord's day be observed according to law.'[2]

The men gaze vacantly back, with vaguely respectful but infinitely bored faces that resemble a half-hungover congregation on a Sunday

81

morning. It is not out of lack of respect for the rules or for Cook himself, it is because they have heard this list *every month* since joining the Navy. They know it better than the Lord's Prayer, and regard it in much the same way: a great guide when under scrutiny, but otherwise to be ignored. In any case, as they have divined that Cook is not particularly religious and has not included a chaplain on this voyage, it means this particular edict carries little weight and it is Captain Cook himself who will have to do the honours when it comes to conducting services.

But onwards Cook must read:

'Two! All flag officers, and all persons in or belonging to His Majesty's ships or vessels of war, being guilty of profane oaths, cursings, execrations, drunkenness, uncleanness, or other scandalous actions, in derogation of God's honour, and corruption of good manners, shall incur such punishment as a court martial shall think fit to impose, and as the nature and degree of their offence shall deserve.'[3]

And on the list goes . . .

'There shall be no wasteful expense of any powder, shot, ammunition.

'If any person in the fleet shall commit the unnatural and detestable sin of buggery and sodomy with man or beast, he shall be punished with death by the sentence of a court martial.'[4]

These articles do not mince words. They spell out as precisely and sharply as a cat o'nine tails what waits for any man who breaks the code. Finally, Cook informs the men they are to now receive two months' pay in advance of their leaving the port.

This time they are listening.

'You are not to expect any additional pay for the performance of our voyage,'[5] he adds, scanning the sea of faces before him, which all appear more than happy with the arrangements.

'They were well satisfied,' Cook records in his journal that evening, 'and expressed great cheerfulness and readiness to prosecute the voyage.'[6]

25 August 1768, Plymouth Sound, Mr Banks, I presume?

On this auspicious afternoon, the ebullient figures being rowed out to the *Endeavour*, at anchor in Plymouth Sound, are of course none other than Joseph Banks Esq. and Dr Solander, who have journeyed from London courtesy of Banks' driver and carriage, then stayed in a hotel on shore while the Great Cabin was being refitted. Now their suite has preceded them on board, and as they approach, the last men to take their berths, they survey the scene before them with no little excitement. For here now is the shining ship the *Endeavour*, the King's pennant flying high atop the mainmast signalling that all persons should report on board as the vessel is about to proceed to sea. The hull and decks are all scrubbed down and the crew are scrubbed up for the occasion. A modest vessel, yes, it almost looks a little shy to be out there in the Sound, anchored among His Majesty's finest, largest, fastest and sleekest men-o'-war – what with her own diminutive length and unusually broad waist, a mark of her common birthright as a collier for the coal trade – but she is on a mission, to go where none of them has ever dared venture, and so holds her place. Around her in these last busy hours before departure a handful of small service craft are fussing like chicks around a brooding mother hen, darting back and forth as the last of fresh supplies are hauled up, the sailors from on high hauling hard as the final boxes and barrels are brought aboard.

It is a first day, like the first day at a new school, when old routines seem somehow new and a nervous energy flows through every greeting. It is the first day when all Navy crew and civilian passengers are assembled, a day of laconic lags tugging their forelocks to fresh-faced Midshipmen, even as day-old acquaintances are renewed and new friendships formed.

Two such strangers greet each other on the deck this very morn. *Mr Banks, I presume?* Captain Cook shakes the hand of Joseph Banks for the first time; two men whose lives have been leading to this moment, yet remarkably have never met until both are on the deck of the *Endeavour*. Life has dealt them entirely different cards, and they have played them in an entirely different fashion. And yet, somehow, fate has meant that not only has their ship come in, but they will go out on it, together.

Early the next afternoon, 26 August, with the last of the lashing South-west winds and rains passed, and with a mild, fresh wind veering Northerly, a single jack at the fore topmast, the sailors on watch scurrying around the decks, and Captain Cook surrounded by officers and gentlemen on the quarter-deck, he is at last able to give the command: 'Weigh anchor!'

The moment is recorded in Cook's HMS *Endeavour* log: 'At 2 p.m. got under sail and put to sea having on board 94 persons including officers, seamen, gentlemen and their servants, nearly 18 months provisions, 10 [cannon], 12 swivel [guns] with good store of ammunition and stores of all kinds.'[7]

As England starts to sink into the horizon, many of the men on board – most particularly those who are not sailors, among them, newly

engaged Surgeon's Mate, 21-year-old William Perry, for whom a disappearing England is an entirely new experience – crowd the stern. Also
among them is young Isaac Smith, the cousin of Captain Cook's wife,
Elizabeth. And yet, in the strictest of terms, young Isaac is not the only
one on the muster roll from Cook's family.

For, in fact, it also includes James and Nathaniel, Captain Cook's two
sons – aged five and six – and their salary will be paid. Of course, they are
not on board, and it is no more than a relative standard ruse employed
by naval Captains, to which the Lords of the Admiralty generally turn
a blind eye, as they often did much the same thing when they were
younger. By putting absent family members on the roster, you lift your
own salary and have a record that the young ones actually went to sea
this young, which marks them down as having much more experience
than they have, for when they actually enter the naval service.

Just along a little is Alex Weir, a married man in his mid-30s, a cheerful
if sensitive soul, though no less a sailor because of it. Hailing from Fife,
Scotland, he's been aboard ships since Adam first jumped on a floating
log, and is now excited that the expedition is truly underway. Still, as
always at this stage of a voyage, he is wondering if he will ever tread
upon the shores of his homeland again.

Two others wondering the same thing are Joseph Banks' two black
'servants', Thomas Richmond and George Dorlton – except this is *not*
their home shore and they are not free men. On the one hand, travelling
like this, free to move around as the servants of Mr Banks, feels like
luxury. But on the other, they are still a long way from their home of
Jamaica.

Meanwhile, the mood aboard is happy and relieved to get underway,
with Banks chronicling that 'we at last got a fair wind . . . and set sail,
all in excellent health and spirits perfectly prepared (in Mind at least)
to undergo with Cheerfulness any fatigues or dangers that may occur
in our intended Voyage'.[8]

While Banks and his fellow land-lubbers in his entourage must initially
struggle to overcome the effects of sea-sickness – for the first 12 hours
you are afraid you're going to die, in the next six hours you're afraid
you're not going to die – at least they take no little satisfaction in how
well prepared they are for the journey ahead.

•

With one last mighty push, and wail, it is done.

Elizabeth Cook is delivered of a wee baby boy, Joseph, the fourth child of James Cook, who set sail into the unknown just the day before. Drenched in sweat, her face as red as a radish, Elizabeth takes the swaddled bundle from the midwife and holds him tightly to her breast, saying a prayer that he be healthy.

If only James could be here!

But he is not, and she is resigned to it, something she had accepted would be her likely fate when she married that blessed man. She rights herself once more, and gets on with it, as she is ever wont to do.

•

The following morning already finds Banks and Dr Solander, afloat on a fresh natural world, beside themselves with enthusiasm, as they closely observe a shoal of playful porpoises in the English Channel, Banks chronicling: 'probably the *Delphinus Phocaena* of Linnaeus, as their noses are very blunt'.[9]

The other thing that is blunt, of course, and a little too blunt for Mr Banks – who is impatient to botanise in lands unknown – is the nose of the Whitby-built *Endeavour*. Just two days after leaving Plymouth, Banks finds the going too slow for his liking and realises that the Whitby cat will not be a fast ship, but a steady one 'much more calculated for stowage, than for sailing'.[10]

Of course, under the circumstances, Banks can hardly complain about the space given over to stowage, given that his own luggage, instruments, bottles and books are already taking up the majority of the stowage space. Already, however, his men are busy, with Banks and Dr Solander occupying themselves hauling creatures from the sea so that – the best he can – Sydney Parkinson can draw them. Alas, in these first days of the voyage when they are still in North Atlantic waters, off the coast of Spain, the weather proves to be so bad, and the ship rocks so violently, that the young artist 'could not set to his pencil'.[11] The following day Banks records it as being even worse.

'Wind still Foul, ship in violent motion,'[12] he writes, though as the evening settles so too does the ship and, finally, Banks' stomach.

It is only a short respite, however, as by 1 September 1768 even so seasoned a sailor as Cook notes in the log how foul the weather is, particularly to fowls:

Cook Log 1 September 1768
Thursday, September 1st. Very hard gales, with some heavy showers
of Rain, the most part of these 24 Hours, which brought us under
our two Courses, Broke one of our Main Topmast phuttock Plates,
washed overboard a small Boat belonging to the Boatswain, and
drowned between 3 and 4 Dozen of our Poultry, which was worst
of all.[13]

But when the sun comes out a couple of days later, and the winds calm,
Mr Banks and Dr Solander get back to executing their *raison d'être* on
this journey – discovering, collecting and classifying the natural world.
Of course, it is Banks' servants who do most of the grunt work, forever
traipsing behind the unencumbered gentlemen, lugging their equipment
or their collections, or both. (A gentleman does *not* lug, and certainly
never lugs luggage.)

Among their gatherings on this blessed day are two new kinds of
marine worm, which they name:

> *rostrata* and *strumosa* . . . only one of *rostrata* and two
> of *strumosa* were taken . . . It seems singular that no naturalist
> before this time should have taken notice of these animals as
> they abound so much where the ship now is, not twenty Leagues
> from the coast of Spain; from hence however great hopes may
> be formed, that the inhabitants of the deep have been but little
> examined, and as Dr Solander and myself shall have probably
> greater opportunity in the course of this voyage than any one has
> had before us, it is a very encouraging circumstance to hope that
> so large a field of natural history has remained almost untrod, even
> till this time, and that we may be able from this circumstance alone
> (almost unthought of when we embarked in the undertaking) to
> add considerable Light to the science which we so eagerly Pursue.[14]

Still, as the journey goes on and the winds start to blow stronger, the
Endeavour is sailing *so* well at the hands of such a skilled Captain and
crew that Banks has a *new* complaint, recorded on 7 September 1768 . . .

> The wind was now fair and we went very pleasantly on towards
> our destined port, though rather too fast for any natural Enquiries,
> for my own part I could well dispense with a much slower pace,
> but I fancy few in the ship, Dr Solander excepted, are of the same
> opinion.[15]

For the moment, Banks decides not to raise the subject with Captain Cook. For one thing he really does understand that their orders, to get to this new South Sea island paradise in time to set everything up to observe the Transit of Venus, must be closely followed. For another, Banks' regard for Captain Cook is growing daily. Though not particularly well versed in Banks' field of botany, there is no doubt that Cook's interest in, and knowledge of, matters of science is really quite extraordinary. The fact that he is eager to learn more and asks acute questions is impressive. And for his part, Cook is equally pleased to spend time with both Banks and Dr Solander as it is a rare pleasure, aboard a ship, to be able to keep company with men of such learning, who know so many things that he does not. In some ways it is like being back on the *Pembroke* a decade ago in Halifax with Captain Simcoe and Lieutenant Holland. It shouldn't be a problem sharing a confined space with these men for the next couple of years . . .

True, Mr Banks is not always the most generous of companions, invariably doing only what suits Mr Banks, but it is truly said of the portly Dr Solander that, 'He is exceedingly sober, well-behaved and very diligent . . . I can assure you the more he is known, the more he is liked.'[16]

On 10 September the *Endeavour*, pushing South, crosses an imaginary line that means they are no longer a tiny dot off the map of Europe but now, effectively, an even tinier dot off the much larger map of Africa. 'Today for the first time, we dined in Africa,' records Banks, with no little satisfaction. For the botanist, it prompts melancholy thoughts on how they are taking their 'leave of Europe for heaven alone knows how long, perhaps for Ever; that thought demands a sigh as a tribute due to the memory of friends left behind and they have it; but two cannot be spared, it would give more pain to the sigher, than pleasure to those sighed for'.[17]

14 September 1768, Madeira, at anchor and a man down

It is, of course, the way of shipboard life. So intense is the daily experience, so unrelenting, that you soon become intimate with the details of lives of men you had never met just a month ago. You dine with them, bathe with them, work with them, see them under pressure, when they're under the weather, when they're drunk, when they recover and within only a few short weeks you know them every bit as well as your childhood friends.

And what strange stories some of them have to tell. The snuff-sniffing Surgeon William Monkhouse, for example.

No, he still doesn't want to talk about it. But he told me on the quiet that just a few years ago his wife of a decade, Jane, had been arrested for stealing a cloak, been tried at the Old Bailey and transported in chains to North America to serve seven years' penal servitude. Oh, the humiliation. No wonder he wants to get away from it all, no wonder there is always sadness in his rheumy eyes.

Matching him in the slightly lugubrious stakes is the Scottish artist Sydney Parkinson. A man with the soul of an artist, born to a family of quiet Quakers that had never quite understood his passion for drawing, he had waited for his father to die before pursuing his dream of a life in art in London. There he had come across Joseph Banks – who had instantly recognised his phenomenal drawing ability, and, well, here he is.

Only *just* is he here though, as his bird-like physique – without an ounce of either fat or muscle, and complete with a beak nose – means it really looks as if he might blow away in the first squall. An intelligent, good man, yes, but oh so serious! He is the lone teetotalling Quaker aboard the *Endeavour*, which marks him out as a different kind of man from the start. (Abstinence is like celibacy for most of the rum-swilling, foul-mouthed sailors. They've heard of it, but don't like the sound of it, and certainly never witnessed it up close.) Still, with the right amount of jollying along, Sydney really can be good company, which is something no-one says about Richard Orton, Captain Cook's clerk. A cheat's cheat, a cur's cur, he is very open about the fact that he had once been a mighty purser in the Royal Navy before 'various roguery' had seen him savagely demoted to his current humble role. Here, as a contemporary, William Perry, would describe it, he, 'managed the victualing department with such a degree of cunning, as did not at all tend to whitewash his old and known character . . . He messed by himself, and had no man his friend. He gloried in recounting anecdotes of his own disgraces, and drunk or sober exhibited to the life a low-bred foul-mouthed black-guard.'[18]

These prove to be merely Perry's opening remarks.

How this wretch, Orton, should find himself in such close affiliation with the seemingly fastidious and principled Captain Cook is a mystery to Perry.

Far more popular is the Master, Robert Molineux, even if Cook has a constant struggle to keep him from losing himself to the bottle, giving him a constant round of tasks to keep him busy. (The only one on board who can keep pace with Master Molineux on the grog is the sail-maker, John Ravenhill, 70 years old if he's a day, who has had a lot more practice than anyone.)

Charles Green, the principal astronomer on board? When not serving his navigational calculations by 'shooting the sun' (so called because the astronomer looks like an archer as he sets his sextant aloft and aims it at his yellow target), mostly he pines quietly for his wife, Elizabeth, who he had married only six months earlier. So many nights of their married life, he had been at the observatory while she lay cold in her bed, while now he is to be away from her for perhaps 700 nights in *succession*. Is she all right? Will he be all right, and get back to see her again?

Pining. Pining. Pining away.

And so it goes, as the days pass and the men continue to get to know each other better.

Mr Banks, cordial but remote from the Captain, chats with Midshipman Charlie Clerke to while away his evening – the two men in their mid-20s sitting by the back of the stove, where an open fire is reserved for officers and gentlemen to warm themselves. Banks and Clerke are two of a kind in any case, both quick with wit and women. Clerke is one of the very few men who gets to tweak the lordly Mr Banks, joshing him about his wealth and ways with a roughish charm that makes Banks laugh and delight in his company. It is a fact Cook can't help but note; he and Banks are cordial colleagues at best, not friends. Neither would seek out the company of the other were they not confined to this floating small kingdom.

And yet, so too is the situation with all of the crew, as men from all parts of Britain, Ireland and North America are thrown together, to shinny up ratlines together, set sails together, and spend many long evenings talking together either in their quarters where their hammocks hang side by side, or in the 'mess' – six eating companions for every meal, huddled together, slurping their slop and talking of their lives, their loves, their problems and joys – and becoming ever closer. Meal over, those officers and sailors not on watch retire to their bunks for the former and hammocks for the latter, their respective quarters separated by the hammocks of the Marines whose principal job is to defend sailors when on shore, the ship from external attack and all other times to defend against mutiny, which is why two are on sentry duty outside Captain Cook's cabin for 24 hours a day, every day, while another defends the gunpowder stores, to ensure no-one gets close with a naked flame.

And so it goes. Every man has a role, and together the men are a living, breathing organism afloat on the high seas.

Overall, Captain Cook is happy with how things are proceeding. The crew is healthy, productive, and moving into the rhythm of ship life. They all seem happy enough, their demeanour never more chipper than when the sun is over the foreyard, meaning it's about 11 am, which is when the Bosun's Mate brings his trusty whistle to his lips and pipes the tune known to all sailors as 'up spirits'. Promptly, they all come a'running to receive their half pint of 'grog' – a concoction of one part rum to four parts water.

Not that there aren't some problems – mostly with outbursts of drunken rowdiness, where the worst offender is the man whose very job it is to stop such outbursts, Master Robert Molineux. As ever, so specialised are Master Molineux's abilities, severely punishing him is not an option. His very expertise demands he be given some leeway and – *pass the ale, young Isaac, and tell me if you hear the Captain coming* – the Master continues to use it to full effect.

After bringing the *Endeavour* into the picturesque Portuguese island port of Madeira and dropping anchor, Captain Cook faces the next rainy, squally morning with news that the heaviest anchor on the ship, the stream anchor, has not been properly secured and has detached completely from the ship.

Grumbling lightly – for even in the face of bad errors of this kind, Cook is calm by nature – he takes quick action. Fortunately they are in a sheltered port so, rain notwithstanding, the *Endeavour* itself is not at risk, and the anchor's rope and buoys can be seen some 50 feet off to show where the anchor, all 800-weight of it, lies on the bottom.

There is only one thing for it, some sailors must take the cutter and haul the anchor up so that it may be rowed and rebound to the *Endeavour*.

Cook gives the order to his experienced Scottish Quartermaster. 'Mr Weir, heave up the Anchor in the boat and carry it out to the Southward.'[19]

Aye, aye, sir.

Quartermaster Alex Weir had been anticipating this exact order and quickly has the cutter lowered with his best men on board. All else being equal, it should only take a few minutes. Like all of them, Weir is eager to get everything ship-shape with the *Endeavour* in harbour so they can go ashore and enjoy what Madeira has to offer. Cook watches from a distance as the cutter is rowed forth before the buoy is taken on board, the rope is secured, and all together now they begin to haul on the rope to make the anchor first break its bond with the harbour floor and then make its long ascent from the watery depths.

And heave!

And *heave!*

And HEAVE!

Yard by yard, the stream anchor rises, and the coil of watery rope in the cutter starts to get a little in the way of the men hauling. Stepping forward to move some of the rope, Alex Weir is right in the middle of the coils when one of the men hauling on the anchor slips, meaning that the others get a sudden surge of weight. It makes another man slip, and with a shout he must let go. And now they are all shouting and cursing as one after the other they slip and let go, until inevitably they all must release the rope or go over themselves and it plunges to the bottom, with . . .

With Alex Weir right behind! Oh no!

The Quartermaster had been in the coils and when they had tightened around his leg he had been dragged over the side in a split second, and is now heading to the bottom, 22 fathoms deep.

'*Heave to, heave to!*'

Cook yells from the *Endeavour* and every man on the cutter pulls the mighty cable, the thrice-bound rope whose fathom lengths now bind the anchor and poor Weir. Perhaps there is a chance that Weir might break free, that even now he struggles with the rope to free himself as they drag him to the surface, to air, to the land of the living . . .

Alas, alas. No.

By the time the frantically heaving men manage to bring the rope back up it is to find Weir – his leg still entangled – completely lifeless.

Pale, swollen, eyes and mouth wide open in petrified panic, and with that extraordinary gluggy looseness of limbs that marks the newly drowned, Mr Weir is brought back to the deck of the *Endeavour*, where his body is quickly sewn into part of an old sail – with tradition observed by putting the needle and twine through his nose, too, to eliminate any chance he is still alive. He is not, and somewhere in England his wife, Anne, is now a widow, and his children without a father.

This voyage of the *Endeavour* has suffered its first fatality and, as a dark shadow moves over nearly all in the ship's company, all are reminded that even with so careful a Captain as Cook, death may strike with the smallest slip. If you're not crushed by a falling yard-arm or left to drown after a slip from the mast into the sea as the ship sails on, something else might occur, as with poor Alex, to send you hurtling to your end in Davy Jones' locker.

And yet, even a moment after death, life must continue.

With a formality borne of trying to keep his heavy emotions in check, Cook crisply orders the cutter to stand by to receive the empty casks which must be taken ashore to be filled with wine. Yes, and the body of Mr Weir, now enshrouded in canvas and weighed down with a cannon-ball, must be put into the yawl and taken to deeper water, where he is consigned to the deep.

As ever, Captain Cook must record the day's events in the ship's log and does so with the deepest of sorrows, pausing before writing the worst words of all:

> Hove up the Anchor by the Ship as soon as possible, and found
> his Body entangled in the Buoy rope.[20]

Joseph Banks is not on board to witness the whole tragedy. He and Dr Solander are comfortably ensconced in the home of the English Consul, a Mr Cheap, whose abode is anything but cramped and damp; a wonderful change from the ship – particularly for Banks' greyhounds, which have revelled in being back on land. Even when Banks hears the news, the tragic loss of Alex Weir has not been significant enough in the life of the botanist to rate a mention in his journal, which instead concentrates on what has really attracted his attention on this day: the island's general particularities and botanical features.

'The season of the year was undoubtedly the worst for both plants and insects, being the height of the vintage, when nothing is green in the country but just on the verge of small brooks, by which these vines are watered . . .'[21]

At least here in port Captain Cook is able to move quickly to find a replacement. It is the American sailor John Thurman who is approached by yet another American – albeit one wearing a British naval uniform – Lieutenant Gore, only to be informed that he will be press-ganged into His Majesty's Navy! To wake up in the morning as a free Yankee and fall asleep that night under the orders of a Yorkshireman is a bitter day indeed. But America is a colony, not blessed with the freedom and sovereignty that would give its colonists any independent rights. For now, Mr Thurman is bound to the *Endeavour*.

16 September 1768, Madeira, If you don't eat your beef, you get lashes for pudding

In some ways it is like the old days back with Mr Sanderson. For once again James Cook is compiling a careful list of things that must be purchased, buying them, and then checking to the last penny that he has received full value. (He particularly does not want a shiny silver shilling to go missing.) It is all just a difference of quantity. For here in Madeira, Captain James Cook is buying victuals for the entire ship. As per his written instructions, he takes on board water and wine, but he also insists on buying as many green vegetables and as much fresh beef as he can, together with a load of freshly dug onions.

For Cook's view is that by far the most important defence against scurvy is his insistence that the men eat their greens – including whatever green things can be purchased, purloined or simply gathered at every port – as well as freshly slaughtered meat. Though he is not quite clear about the causes of scurvy, he has noticed that *freshness* and *greenness* seem to be the keys to avoiding it.

To compensate for the fact that on long sea journeys green freshness is not possible, he wants his men to go with the next best thing, which is to consume greens that have been preserved as fresh as possible, which is to say ... sauerkraut, which is to say finely chopped raw cabbage allowed to ferment for just the right amount of time before being put in tightly sealed barrels. So, too, are fresh supplies well received, with Captain Cook noting in his journal: 'Received on board fresh Beef and Greens for the Ship's Company.'[22]

It is Cook's way – at any new port, fresh supplies are the priority. The greener the vegetables and the more freshly slaughtered the meat the better.

The next day dawns fine, no sign of rain clouds ... but there's a different storm on the horizon.

Brutality is not in Cook's nature, violence not in his spirit. Though not a gentleman by birth, he is certainly a gentle man by nature and Quaker influences have helped to mould his soul. Most matters of discipline can be sorted out by having misbehaving sailors stand barefoot for hours on end in fair weather or foul with their toes between the seams of the planks on deck, known as 'toeing the line'. In other matters, however, he must be more harsh. Ordering lashes to be given gives him no pleasure, and yet doing his job properly requires a certain hardening of that soul, an embrace of the brutality needed to keep the men in line, and he knows he must oversee the whole operation.

Glowering, the seaman Henry Stevens and the Marine Thomas Dunster are brought from below, still in chains, and after their shirts are removed they are lashed to a grate placed vertical for the occasion, their arms above them, their backs entirely exposed as the ship's company follows Captain Cook's order – 'all hands on deck to witness punishment' – and gathers around, just forward the mizzen mast.

The charges are read out, and with a grim nod from Captain Cook, the Bosun's Mate, Thomas Hardman – as non-eponymous in nature as his Captain – to whom this kind of barbaric punishment does not come easily, though he knows it is his duty to administer it, gets to work. He steps forward. First is Thomas Dunster. Taking the cat o'nine tails – a whip with nine leather strands, with the end of each one having a small knot – from its red baize bag, he dips the implement into a bucket of seawater, withdraws it, brings his right arm back well behind him and then swings it forward.

There is a small hissing sound before a mighty crack rings out, a *thwack* on Dunster's back – the agonising kiss of nine salty electric eels – and on the instant angry red welts show up in strips across his pale skin.

On it goes for a dozen lashes, until Dunster is untied to slump to the deck, where a bucket of seawater is thrown over his wounds and he is carried down to his hammock, to be swiftly replaced by Henry Stevens to receive his lashings of fate on the grate.

Five minutes later the now bloody Stevens is untied to receive his own bucket of seawater.

Let that be a lesson to all.

This is what happens to those who refuse . . . to eat fresh meat.

Who knows why the meat would not appeal, but Cook is so obsessed with diet – with eating fresh food – that his men's refusal to do so has resulted in such a beating. Cook notes in his journal: 'Punished Henry Stevens, Seaman, and Thomas Dunster, Marine, with 12 lashes each, for refusing to take their allowance of Fresh Beef.'[23]

Others lashed include the new recruit Thurman for refusing to assist the old sail-maker – the ever drunk John Ravenhill; while on 1 December another two men are lashed for abusive language to an officer and an intent to desert. And yet, as Cook feels that the lasher, John Reading, boatswain's mate, has not put his heart into the lashes, he too gets a dozen lashes. With six men lashed in six weeks, the point is made – do not be deceived by the Captain's mild nature. He can still hand out lashes with the best of them.

As the *Endeavour* stays in port for re-supply and caulking under the watch of ship's Carpenter John Satterly, Mr Banks and Dr Solander are determined to make the most of it, even if it is not the ideal season. As Banks records, they rise at morning, ride out on horses supplied by the obliging Mr Cheap, collect specimens of unknown plant life, return at night, eat, sleep and repeat. One day Banks is aggrieved to find that the Governor of Madeira has requested the pleasure of his and Cook's company for luncheon. As a gentleman, of course, he must oblige, which means that he must waste an entire day that could otherwise be spent putting plants in bottles, which is his chief pleasure. As to the residents of Madeira, Banks is simply not interested in these well-heeled Englishmen, Spaniards and Portuguese who he meets at the Governor's table. For their species, their tribes, are known. Banks wishes to make his mark by discovering *unknown* people, *unknown* plants, *unknown* animals and *unknown* reptiles. It is the thrill of the new which excites his brilliant scientific mind and he has little time or patience for small talk with small folk of known origins and . . .

And, sorry, you were saying, Governor?

In the end, despite the unfavourable season, Mr Banks and Dr Solander prove industrious during their short stay on Madeira, collecting around 300 species of plants, from salvia to rosemary. The entire collection of plant specimens, together with 200 insects and 20 new species of fish – once they have them back in the Great Cabin and ready to get to work – is to be described, preserved, labelled and stored. Captain Cook is impressed by the endless series of new specimens that Mr Banks and Dr Solander return gleefully to the ship with each night.

For his part, during the five-day stay in Madeira, Captain Cook brings aboard 270 pounds of fresh meat that will fill the bellies of his men. And yet, on their way towards South America, the Captain learns from his cooks that while the fresh meat has gone down a treat, the men have been leaving their sauerkraut uneaten.

The Surgeon's Mate, young William Perry, takes it upon himself to approach his Captain, the prevention of scurvy being a special province of his own interests. He notes that the crew has been supplied with a quantity of onions, and boldly suggests an additional preventative supply of wort – one quart a day, perhaps?

Cook surveys the young medico with surprise. He is the Surgeon's *Mate*, not the actual Surgeon William Monkhouse, and it is not quite the place of the young man to make such a suggestion. Of course Captain Cook already knows all about wort, and has brought barrels of it with him. Happily, there will be no problem in getting the ship's company to down the malt drink, as they already relish the sweet flavour, which is a welcome change from tepid water.

But getting them to eat their sauerkraut is much more problematic as not only do they not like it, but they also do not take the threat of scurvy as seriously as they should, even though it's been the end of many a man and almost as many ships. Very well. Cook can hardly flog the entire crew, so he uses a ruse – one that will long be regarded as evidence of Cook's understanding of the makeup of the common sailors, for he used to be one.

With no fuss, Cook, instructs his hook-handed cook, John Thompson, to dress the sauerkraut every day and serve it at the Great Cabin's dining table. If the Captain and gentlemen eat it, surely the jacks will take note. He further permits, 'all the Officers, without exception, to make use of it, and left it to the option of the men either to take as much as they pleased or none at all'.[24]

Now let's see if the crew turn up their noses at it? Yes, though not quite an old salt, James Cook certainly displays uncommon common sense and is not without wiles. By hook or by crook, and with help from his cook with one hook, Captain Cook's men will eat their kraut.

The result is all but instantaneous, at least in the perspective of long voyages at sea.

'This practice,' Cook records, 'was not continued above a Week before I found it necessary to put everyone on board to an allowance; for such are the Tempers and disposition of Seamen in general that whatever you give them out of the common way – although it be ever so much for their good – it will not go down, and you will hear nothing but murmurings against the Man that first invented it; but the moment they see their superiors set a value upon it, it becomes the finest stuff in the world and the inventor an honest fellow.'[25]

Late September 1768, three days out from Madeira, of jaws and paws

See it there on the horizon? Way out in the distance!

It's the peak of Tenerife, the sailors insist to Mr Banks and Dr Solander, who can barely distinguish a mountain from a cloud.

If you say so.

Far more enchanting for Mr Banks are the dozens, if not hundreds, of flying fish that abound around the ship's stern, slipping through the wake and up into the air, where they soar for yards at a time. Mr Banks soon works out that watching them from his cabin window gives him the best vantage point, as he records: '[their] beauty especially when seen from the cabin windows is beyond imagination, their sides shining like burnished silver; when seen from the Deck they do not appear to such advantage as their backs are then presented to the view, which are dark coloured.'[26]

And so it goes as the men settle into the rhythm of ship-board life, setting out for the long haul South-west across the Atlantic. The officers bark orders, the jacks shinny up and down rigging and along yards, reefing or shaking out sails, all while John Thompson is as busy as a one-armed cook feeding three meals to 100 men every day, and the gentlemen tend to the wildlife – catching and categorising fish, sharks, birds, and anything else that crosses their path. For his part, Captain Cook is ever and always a calm presence on the quarter-deck, all-seeing, all-knowing, keeping one eye on the ship and the other on his men, and inspiring utmost confidence in every last man-jack aboard. Master Molineux, however, has quite the opposite effect. When the last of the beer runs out on 27 September – and they have to serve only wine thereafter – no-one is surprised. The Master has been drunk from the first day on board, and if any man could drink the ship dry, it is him.

On 28 September, Mr Banks and 'the Doctor' – as Dr Solander has become known to one and all – are thrilled to catch a small yellow swallow, of cheeky but affectionate disposition, which they name *Motacilla avida*, in accordance with Linnaeus's system. (Oh, and once they have properly examined him, they also name the bird louse found on his feathers *Acorus motacillae.)*

Once the windows and doors of the Great Cabin are tightly closed they allow the dear little thing to flutter-fly about and, its small 'accidents' notwithstanding – which the servants quickly clean up – it soon establishes a real bond with Mr Banks and his gentlemen. For yes, the swallow quickly makes itself quite at home, establishing favourite perches, hopping about Banks' writing bureau as he records the day's events in his journal, atop the piles of books – everywhere – and accepting the offering of crushed insects with a gracious nod of its head and nip of its beak, and even sitting quietly to have its portrait done by Sydney Parkinson. No small yellow wagtail bird has ever been treated to such luxury, ever travelled so far from home. (All the while watched by a single set of eyes, perpetually narrowing, waiting for the right moment.)

While the little bird is at one end of nature's spectrum of living creatures – tiny, harmless – Banks has at least as much interest in things at the other end, as on this day he looks out the cabin window to see a young shark swimming alongside the boat! By use of a baited hook it is quickly caught and hauled up onto the deck.

'He proved,' Banks records, 'to be the *Squalus Charcharias* of Linn[aeus] and assisted us in clearing up much confusion which almost all authors had made about that species.'[27]

The very species that will become known as the great white shark is impressive indeed, but inspires no camaraderie as the yellow swallow has done.

Instead, as Banks records, 'We made swift to have a part of him stewed for dinner, and very good meat he was, at least in the opinion of Dr Solander and myself, though some of the Seamen did not seem to be fond of him, probably from some prejudice founded on the species sometimes feeding on human flesh.'[28]

Indeed it is. The Mariners have long had a superstition against eating something that eats Mariners and nothing the gentlemen can say, no marinade the cook can make to hide it, will change their view. Captain Cook, with a foot planted in both worlds 'fore the mast and aft, does not engage, and is simply glad to eat his portion – silently.

One living being that has no qualms about eating another living being of any description is the ship's cat, who for weeks following the capturing and taming of the little yellow swallow, manoeuvres to do a little yellow swallow of its own.

For the key, you see, is to betray but little interest and simply engage in waiting . . . waiting . . . waiting . . .

NOW!

For, one moment on 21 October the little bird is flitting about happily and the next there is a *snap* – yellow swallow meets yellow swallow – and all that is left is a single yellow feather floating to the floor as the cat licks her paws and face clean.

Banks, upon discovering his small friend gone, writes a regretful obituary in his journal: 'He was hearty and in high health so that probably he might have lived a great while longer had fate been more kind.'[29]

As the *Endeavour* pushes ever further South, leaving behind the latitudes where the trade winds blow and now heading to tropical torpor, the pace slows, the mercury rises in keeping with the humidity and the steamy heat is interrupted only by regular squalls.

'I can liken it to nothing so much as April in England,' observes Mr Banks. 'When it is very showery, the weather is never certain for two hours.'[30]

At least, for Mr Banks and Dr Solander, the calms when they come are so calm that they are regularly able to go out in their small boat, bob about the *Endeavour* and haul in whatever fish they can, before taking them back to the Great Cabin where the real work begins. First the fish are measured, before being described in detail, with commonalities noted and entered into the books – 'a fish was taken which was described and called *Scomber serpens* . . .'[31] – even as Sydney Parkinson and Herman Sporing set about drawing them. Now they are dried, labelled and stored in specimen jars in a bid to preserve them, before most are stowed away. (Others however, if not of specific interest, are claimed by hungry sailors, cooked and wolfed down.)

On one such calm day in October, Joseph Banks takes in a haul of what the sailors tell him is called 'a Portuguese man-of-war', or what Linnaeus has called: *Holothuria physalis*. Banks can barely believe his eyes.

> The Holothuria proved to be one of the most beautiful sights I had ever seen, it consisted of a small bladder in shape much like the air bladder of fishes, from the bottom of which descended a number of strings of bright blue and red, some three or four feet in length which if touched stung the person who touched them in the same manner as nettles, only much stronger: on the top of this Bladder was a membrane which he turned either one way or the other as the wind blew to receive it, this was veined with pink in an uncommonly beautiful manner . . .[32]

It's all so exhilarating!

While that first summer collecting samples back at Revesby Abbey had been invigorating – when everything sparkled with the magic of newness and discovery – this is something else again, with everyone having a real sense of being right on the frontiers of science. Where they go, what they

100 • JAMES COOK

do, the frontiers are being pushed outwards, ever outwards. And still the air becomes heavier and hotter, as the *Endeavour* pushes South. The salty damp not only leaves its mark on the men, who display a listless laziness that never quite leaves them, but on the ship too, rusting every skerrick of iron that is exposed to the air – 'the knives in peoples pockets became almost useless and the razors in cases not free'.[33]

As torpor threatens, Captain Cook is as vigilant as ever in ensuring his people keep to the correct diet, he does not accept men being late to their watches, or swearing, or even looking anything other than spick, span and ship-shape at all times. *Repair that tear. Sew that button.* All men are supplied with thread, needles and buttons and are expected to present well.

So too must their hands be kept clean, and it is a regular occurrence for the men to line up on deck and place their hands palms up and then palms down before their Captain so he can ensure that nails are cut and fingers are not covered in muck. Cook firmly believes that while cleanliness is next to Godliness it is also very close to health, and by insisting on that cleanliness he is reducing the chances of them developing scurvy or other diseases. All those found to be not up to the mark on cleanliness have their daily allowance of grog cut, a very easy way to gather their full attention.

Pass the soap!

And open the portals!

Captain Cook is of the view that there are few problems of health that fresh air can't help, and he insists that the latticed gratings found on every deck be left uncovered at all times unless waves are bursting over the sides and the men risk being drenched – just as he prefers the *Endeavour*'s ventilation ports be kept open in calm weather.

Cook also orders everything to be swabbed with vinegar, a powerful tool for a Captain who takes cleanliness seriously, and has the armourers work twice as hard as usual on keeping the guns functional, and that's just the rust. For who could forget the problem of mould? Cook orders the hammocks be brought up to deck daily – twice daily if possible – to be bared and aired.

Of course, as is the way of these things, the people most affected are those with the most effects. Mr Banks records: 'still the damper every thing grew, this was perceivable even to the human body and very much so, but more remarkably upon all kinds of furniture ... All kinds of Leather became mouldy, Portfolios and trunks covered with black leather were almost white, soon after this mould adhered to almost every thing, all the books in my Library became mouldy so that they were obliged to be wiped to preserve them.'[34]

25 October 1768, the equator, zero degrees of latitude, but latitude for some

The hot dampness on board need not dampen the sailors' spirits on this sultry afternoon. Old salts who've done this many times before know the *Endeavour* is close to the invisible line known as 'the equator'.

For together with the hot weather come other tell-tale signs, such as pronounced calms being followed shortly thereafter with vicious squalls. Like a cranky, flustered dowager, not happy with the servants when she does awake, the weather stirs only to snarl, and then goes back to sleep. The most savvy sailors of all know that the key sign is in the heavens, where the sun has moved ever closer to being directly overhead, even as the night sky is presenting constellations many of the young ones have never seen before, while Earth's closest planetary neighbour, Venus, known as the 'Evening Star' or the 'Morning Star' depending on its time of rising and setting, is also rising higher in the sky.

And today it happens, the moment that those who have sailed over the zero parallel before have been waiting for . . .

From his position on the quarter-deck, Captain Cook puts down his sextant and dip circle, which he had been using to measure, to 'shoot the sun', and gives them the cherished word around 8 am, right now they are actually crossing the equator. (Yes, as it is Captain Cook doing the calculations and the shooting of the sun, it is even more precise than that – as they haven't crossed the equator *per se*, so much as the 'Aequinoctial line . . .'.[35])

A wave of excitement moves through the ship, as an ancient and cherished tradition acknowledged by all seafaring nations gets underway. Known as 'the equatorial baptism', it will see nearly all those 'crossing the line' for the first time paying their respects to the Lord of the Seas, King Neptune, to gain his acceptance and be initiated into his Court.

An important part of the age-old rite of passage is that the whole affair is under the command of the sailors and junior officers, and not the Captain. Though they will need his permission, of course.

Sure enough, as the buzz moves around the ship while the Captain and gentlemen are enjoying their midday meal – as ever, Cook is at the head of the table and there in the middle of the table, taking pride of place, sits the dressed sauerkraut – Cook's clerk, Richard Orton, brings to him a list of every living being on the ship. It includes dogs and cats and affixed to the list is 'a petition, signed "the ship's company", desiring leave to examine every body in that List that it might be known whether or not they had crossed the line before'.[36]

And no, of course Captain Cook will not suffer the indignity of being dunked in the ocean, even though it is his first time, but for the privilege of remaining dry with those on the 'Black List' he must hand over a bottle of rum. Cook says for the ship's company to enjoy it, which is why the buzz is even stronger now as the men guzzle their tankards. When it comes to you, Joseph Banks, as you also wish your entire retinue to be spared, including your dogs, the penalty will be much stronger as in your case we will take many bottles of brandy – and one bottle of rum for each of your two dogs!

'Permission is granted,'[37] Captain Cook says to his clerk with a rare wry smile.

It's on! With no little glee, one of the Midshipmen is soon tramping through the cramped, damp corridors of the lower decks, calling out for all ship's company to assemble on the quarter-deck. There's a stampede of sailors' feet along the wooden decks and up the ladders to the deck, where, for some, a surprise awaits. The brandy, Mr Banks sees, is already being handed out and things appear set to get merrier still.

By traditional maritime law it is the right of all those who have crossed the line before, the 'shellbacks' as they are known, to perform a dunking of all those 'griffins' who are doing it for the first time.

Bosun John Gathray is the commanding 'Lieutenant' of this ritual, and so steps forward, blowing his whistle for attention.

Now, the Lieutenant calls out the names and asks the men to provide 'proof' that they have previously crossed the line, and if not, to confess it now.

Suddenly, a breakthrough.

The 16-year-old Isaac Smith, the cousin of Captain Cook's wife, confesses that this is his first time. A roar goes up.

Now if Isaac chooses, he can escape the dunking by giving up four days of his allowance of wine, and having it handed out to the others right now but, no, he is not willing to do that, and so must pay the price. A rope has already been put through a pulley secured to the main yard on high – and out over the ocean – with one end of the rope now in the hands of some of the strongest of the crew. The other end of the rope has three cross struts of wood tied into it, each about a yard apart.

Now Isaac loops his legs over the bottom strut and is securely tied onto it, while he can hold the second strut for stability. The third strut is above his head and is simply there so that when we haul him up, he can't come flying out and hit his head on the pulley.

Once all is ready, the air of delicious expectation reaches its near climax as the Bosun, *ahem*, 'Lieutenant' Gathray, blows his whistle again and Isaac is immediately hauled as high as the highest cross-piece allows. And now they let the rope go, as he in turn roars down to the ocean with a massive splash and the cheer of the crew crowding the quarter-deck goes up. Three times the process is repeated before, now inducted, he is hauled up once more and a cross rope brings him back to the deck, all gasps and splutters, with the water still pouring off him.

Welcome to the Court of King Neptune!

Next let us go to the youngest Marine on board – for even His Majesty's Marines must take part in the sailors' ritual and bow to King Neptune – that painfully shy and sensitive young fellow, William Greenslade. Of the Marines he is the least swaggering, the least verbose, far and away the least inclined to even imply he has any authority over the sailors. To the sailors, he appears to be just a simple soul, and a silent simple soul at that, something that has occasionally earned him the rancour of his barking Marine commander, Sergeant John Edgcumbe, who is forever goading the young man, trying to toughen him, to make a man out of him so he can be a swaggering Marine just like them. But it has simply had no effect on the young fellow. He is as silent, and just as quivering, as ever he was.

Right now, that natural quiver turns to outright trembling as his name is called out by 'Lieutenant' Gathray and he makes a hesitant step forward. And another. And one more until he has the ropes put around him, at which point as the mob roars he is strung high up in the air, now shaking with fear as he awaits the drop . . .

And there he goes, with a satisfying splash as the cry goes up, the rum goes down and morale lifts even further. William Greenslade emerges, gasping for air but at least momentarily glad to be fully immersed with the ship's company, not just the odd one out. The well-born gentleman from the American colonies, Midshipman James Magra, knocks back the rum with the best of them and is just one of many roaring in this matey and macabre ritual. It is typical of him to be right in the middle of it, a popular figure among the sailors for his worldliness, and among the Midshipmen for his sheer intelligence.

Despite having been the one to hand Captain Cook the list, it is equally typical of Richard Orton to decline to have anything to do with the event itself. Yes, he wants to drink. But he doesn't need to put himself in the middle of this mob to do it. He is the clerk to the *Captain*, don't you know, and is ever and always a man apart.

And so it goes.

Twenty more times the process is repeated as the drinking and dunking goes on – one after another of the sailors emerging from the sea, mostly grinning and shaking their heads vigorously to shed the water, their long ponytails flying about like wet whips – with the whole thing finishing just as night falls.

'Sufficiently diverting it certainly was,' Mr Banks chronicles, 'to see the different faces that were made on this occasion, some grinning and exulting in their hardiness whilst others were almost suffocated and came up ready enough to have compounded after the first or second duck, had such proceeding been allowable.'[38]

Captain Cook watches on, the slightly upturned corners of his mouth belying his amusement, though he declines the brandy bottle as it passes by. He is a man of moderation, especially when in view of his men, but that's not to say he doesn't enjoy the spectacle, and, climbing back through the hatchway, down to the Great Cabin, he lets a broad smile blossom on his face.

But, back to work, chronicling their journey: 'We crossed the Line in the Longitude of 29 degrees 29 minutes West from Greenwich. We also try'd the Dipping Needle belonging to the Royal Society, and found the North point to Dip 26 degrees below the Horizon . . .'[39]

29 October 1768, South of the equator, flashes of light to break the night

Oh, the sheer pleasure of it.

Certainly seafaring can have its challenges, but on a night like tonight, as the *Endeavour* sails serenely through her aquatic realm, the moonbeams shining brightly upon the delightful phosphorescence in her wake, Banks has reason to wax lyrical in his journal.

'This Evening the sea appeared uncommonly beautiful, flashes of light coming from it perfectly resembling small flashes of lightning, and these so frequent that sometimes eight or ten were visible at the same moment . . .'[40]

Ever and always scientifically curious, Banks and his cohort ask the seamen the cause of this extraordinary light show, only to find them divided. They are seafarers, not scientists, and have long accepted the things they see and experience the way a dog accepts its tail – that is just the way it is, the way it has always been, and the way it always will be. But yes, seeing as you scientific gentlemen ask, there have long been stories about what causes it.

'Fish make the light by agitating the salt water when darting at their prey,'[41] one sailor offers an answer.

Mr Banks likes the theory, which encourages another sailor to add, 'We often seen them and knew them to be nothing but Medusas [a kind of jelly fish].'[42]

Banks, of course, is eager to get to the bottom of it, to find the scientific answer rather than mere stories, and sets about at least catching some of the Medusas to test the theory, and, within a short while, by casting his net, has indeed brought some of the creatures on board.

'They proved,' Banks records carefully, advancing the frontiers of science just a few inches, 'to be a species of Medusa which when brought on board appeared like metal violently heated, emitting a white light.'[43]

6 November 1768, far Western Atlantic Ocean, we go to Rio

Having now crossed most of the Atlantic Ocean, Captain Cook takes stock, only to find those stocks are starting to run quite low, and they are in need of water, fresh meat and vegetables, and other stores. Yes, they could last a few more weeks without getting fresh supplies and likely make it to their next port of call at Porto Alegre, or further South at the Falkland Islands, but, ever careful – insuring themselves against unforeseen circumstances – he decides to call in at the Portuguese port of Rio de Janeiro, where, 'from the reception former Ships had met with here I doubted not but we should be well received'.[44]

Very well then. By now, the men of the *Endeavour* understand things better. If Captain Cook has no doubts, all should be smooth sailing.

They will go to Rio.

De Janeiro.

13 November 1768, Rio de Janeiro, harbouring suspicions

Finally, nearly three months after leaving England, the sailors on the *Endeavour* spot finch-like birds with flashing wings gliding majestically over the waters to them, a sure indication that they are close to land. And on 12 November, they spot Cape Frio, and the 'high and mountainous'[45] silhouette of South America's Eastern coastline.

It's the Portuguese colony of Brazil. After a few days sailing South by West, marvelling at the brilliant, impossibly white sandy beaches off their starboard – 'the whitest colour I ever saw',[46] records Banks – Captain Cook spots the rocky islands that sit just off the heads of a fine, well-protected harbour, on the banks of which lies the famed city of Rio de Janeiro.

For now, those sailors not on watch gravitate towards the bow of the *Endeavour* as it blow-bobs forward on a light breeze at their South-east, through the narrow entrance, gazing closely at the stone fortifications that sit atop each rocky headland – the Northern side sporting the largest fort, known as Santa Cruz – their cannon looking out over the sea like rusty iron sentinels, even as the gaping maws of the capacious harbour of Rio de Janeiro reach out to swallow the *Endeavour* whole.

As they carefully sail past the several tiny islands dotted around the harbour, the men's attention is drawn West by a massive conical mountain, looming over half a mile high and garbed in green but for a flat, brown, bare top and steep cliffs on each side. 'Pão de Açucar', the Portuguese call it, meaning 'Sugarloaf', after the conical moulds made of clay used to transport sugar on ships. It towers over the whole bay, a brooding presence that says you have arrived in a strange land, where most things are out of all proportion to what you might have seen in other lands. Majestic vessels, of classic Portuguese design, pass by the *Endeavour*, filled with swarthy looking sailors and merchants gazing at them with a slightly menacing curiosity.

At least it is good to have made port.

With a nod from Captain Cook, Master Molineux takes matters in hand, giving the orders that see the tars scampering every which way.

'*Shorten sail,*' and the *Endeavour* begins to slow, as the sails are furled.

'*Head to wind,*' and the *Endeavour* actually comes to a halt as the wind falls from those sails.

'*Let go the anchor.*'

'*Take in all sail.*'

'Lieutenant Hicks,' Captain Cook says, turning to his 2nd Lieutenant.

Yes, Captain?

'Take the pinnace ahead to the city and acquaint the Vice-Roy that we wish to procure water and other necessities.'

'Aye, aye,' says Lieutenant Hicks, nodding in acknowledgement.

'And desire the assistance of a pilot to bring us into proper anchoring ground,'[47] instructs Captain Cook.

Protocol dictates that when entering a foreign harbour, one must gain permission from the presiding authority before anyone may go ashore – and sending a pilot is little more than a matter of the locals knowing the harbour better than any foreign commander could, and so lending a courteous hand. For a vessel of the British Royal Navy visiting the port of a friendly European country, this should be no more than a formality. Lieutenant Hicks is accompanied on this errand by Master's Mate Charlie Clerke. As they leave, Captain Cook gives the order to drop the anchor – 'Make the anchor ready for letting go,' comes the cry – and nudges the *Endeavour* around to the Northern side of a small island, *Ilha das Cobras*, the island of cobras, atop which 'is the chief fortification that defends the town',[48] to the calm bay right at the foot of the thriving colonial settlement. Cook is going through the list of things he hopes to buy in Rio, when he looks up from his work and is shocked to see the pinnace returning to the ship without the familiar figure of Lieutenant Hicks standing sternly at the stern.

Where is he?

The answer is provided by the rather shocked coxswain, next to whom stands a Portuguese subaltern bristling with disdainful officiousness.

'The Lieutenant is detained on shore,'[49] the coxswain calls up for all the ship's company to hear.

No sooner had they landed, he reports, and gone to Rio's Customs House, *alfândega*, to present their papers than Lieutenant Hicks and the petty officer had been led off by Portuguese soldiers on the direct orders of the Vice-Roy, His Excellency Dom Antonio Rolim de Moura Tavares – the leading Portuguese official in this colony, a man of keen eye and deeply forbidding aspect. Hicks will remain detained until Captain Cook turns up *in person* to claim him.

What? Cook's second-in-command, the strong and able young Hicks, a Lieutenant in His Majesty's Navy, has been frogmarched off somewhere at the orders of this *impertinent* Vice-Roy? Cook admires Hicks, a solid sailor who has risen through the ranks on the back of his vigour and intelligence alone. The Captain knows that Lieutenant Hicks will be livid to be so mistreated by Portuguese officials, but is thankful that he is also proven to be quick-witted and prudent in an emergency. Cook can picture it now, Lieutenant Hicks' face puckered, his lips pursed in stern frustration, but holding himself in. Frankly, there is no better representative from the *Endeavour* to be detained like this. He isn't alone either, the dependable Charlie Clerke has also been confined. Two of his best men. Well, at least the two will surely put up a diplomatic but forceful front.

Captain Cook seethes at this particular affront and gets a hurry-on – this is outrageous! – and after the anchor is finally dropped, he is about to ready himself to go ashore when, *hulloa!*, what's this?

Coming from the shore towards them is a Portuguese ten-oared vessel bearing 14 armed soldiers – all bristling bayonets and menacing machismo – who have no sooner reached the English vessel than they row around it, clearly getting a good look so they can report back. First Cook and now Banks hale them from the deck of the *Endeavour*, politely inquiring: 'What is your business?'[50]

'We have orders from His Excellency to permit nobody from this ship to go on shore but the *Capitão*. And to hinder anyone from coming on board your ship unless they have particular leave to do so.'[51]

Cook makes further inquiries . . . There is no reply, bar glowering glares.

Joseph Banks, an English gentleman whose opinion has always mattered, has never been so blatantly ignored in his entire life. He stands exasperated, watching the indifferent Portuguese row defiantly in the water below.

Another boat now arrives bearing an officious-looking Portuguese Colonel, who informs Captain Cook – in a tone which makes clear that he is demanding not asking – that he wishes to come aboard.

Captain Cook obliges.

As soon as they are on deck the questions start – 'many and varied particular questions',[52] Cook records, all of which he answers in typical fashion, 'with the utmost candour and precision'.[53]

The senior officer then assures Cook: 'Your Lieutenant has not been confined; he has been detained. It is our constant custom to detain anyone who comes ashore from a ship until a boat from His Excellency has visited the ship. Your Officer will be sent on board as soon as I go back on shore.'[54]

Captain Cook is so shocked he can only think there must be some kind of mistake. *Surely?* The alternative is unthinkable. For the moment the important thing is to retain his diplomatic demeanour and so he wishes them well on their way as they climb back down the ladder to their boat and make for shore. Still, as Captain Cook watches them row away, his thick brows are knitted with concern. Something is not right.

•

On shore, in custody, Lieutenant Hicks continues to make no headway with the Vice-Roy, a man who considers himself just one down from the King – in Portugal. But here in Brazil, he is KING, and don't you forget it, Lieutenant Hicks.

Yes, a pompous, officious man of high noble birth, the Vice-Roy is in no doubt that his own importance is only matched by the lack of importance of his interlocutor, and it is in vain for Hicks to insist that they really are on an expedition of science.

For His Excellency, *Sua Excelência*, the *Governo*, snorts unpleasantly. He has heard many tales in his six decades, but this one is among the most preposterous. As if *os Bretões* would send a ship of the Royal Navy with 100 men aboard, including some gentlemen civilian scientists, just to *go and look at the sun!* Ludicrous. The Vice-Roy will not be so easily fooled. Why, take a look at the ship itself! Is that a standard vessel of His British Majesty? Of course not, insists the *Vice-Rei*. Who has *ever* seen a ship like that? There is something off, something different about this suspicious vessel bobbing about in the Brazilian bay.

And I don't much like the look of the crew either!

In the words of Lieutenant John Gore, once those on the *Endeavour* realise what this is all about, 'one suspicion of us among many others is that our ship is a trading spy and that Mr Banks and the Doctor are both supercargoes and engineers and not naturalists, for the business of such being so very abstruse and unprofitable that they cannot believe gentlemen would come as far as Brazil on that account only'.[55]

Exactly.

Well, they have come up against the wrong man. But for now, you may go back to your ship, Lieutenant Hicks.

Still aboard the ship, Joseph Banks is beside himself with rage.

He has come all this way, risking his life and spending his fortune to collect plants, and he is now forbidden by Portuguese (*sniff*) 'authorities' to even land on their shores, and take his greyhounds for much needed walks, let alone explore for plants? It is unconscionable.

•

Determined to sort out the mess himself, Captain Cook is quick to go on shore to try to explain to a highly sceptical Vice-Roy what exactly a 'Transit of Venus' is. It proves, however, to be tough going, 'for he Certainly did not believe a word about our being bound to the Southward to observe the Transit of Venus, but looked upon it only as an invented story to cover some other design we must be upon, for he could form no other Idea of that Phenomenon (after I had explained it to him), than the North Star Passing through the South Pole; these were his own words'.[56]

The Vice-Roy in turn struggles to explain to Captain Cook how things are going to be, but he means every word of it regardless. Your so-called 'botanist', *Senhor* Banks, will not be allowed on shore while in Rio, along with the rest of the so-called supernumeraries, and you, *Capitão*, will only be allowed when accompanied by OUR armed attendant for every step you take, including on your own boat when being ferried to shore, presented 'as a compliment'[57] – which Cook knows instantly means 'a portable jailer'. Oh, and you may not buy your own provisions directly – you must employ a representative from the port town to buy the necessary things, which will inevitably both slow everything down and make everything rise in price.

What is not slow to rise is Cook's anger – which for once does not dissipate quickly.

Not this time.

Though he bites his tongue, his mind swirls.

It is an outrage. A slight on my command. An insult to the Royal Navy and to Great Britain. How can I tamely submit to such a Custom, which, when practised in its full force, must bring disgrace to the British Flag? On the other hand, I must resist entering into such disputes, seeing how much I am likely to be delayed and embarrassed in getting the supplies I want. What to do? What to DO?

After a number of days languishing under this tyranny of tedium by the Vice-Roy and two further attempts to remonstrate, Captain Cook decides that enough is enough.

'I resolved, rather than be made a Prisoner in my own Boat, not to go any more ashore unless I could do it *without* having a Soldier put into the Boat, as had hitherto been done; and thinking that the Vice Roy might lay under some Mistake, which on proper Application might be cleared up.'[58]

With that in mind, the ever patient Cook takes a quill in hand and writes a long letter to the Vice-Roy, putting forth his 'whole case'.[59]

Which is fine for Captain Cook.

Personally Joseph Banks has lost all pretence of patience and is beside himself, as he gazes longingly at the fresh South American continent before him, the verdant hills behind Rio surely home to all manner of unknown vegetables, animals and minerals, just waiting to be 'discovered' by him. Oh, yes, the locals likely know all the various species and types, and even have names for them, but this is different. If Banks can just get his hands on them, he will be bringing a scientific eye to them for the first time, and that is what truly counts. For four days, it has been a torture to be denied permission to land, to get amongst it, and so now the botanist decides to take matters into his own hands.

Yes, it is time to tell the Vice-Roy just who he is dealing with – a gentleman of great pedigree just like him. Taking his own quill in hand, thus, the botanist begs to bring it to the Vice-Roy's attention: 'Disagreeable as it is for any man to declare his own rank and consequence, my situation makes it necessary. I am a Gentleman, and one of fortune sufficient to have at my own expense fitted out that part of this expedition under my direction which is intended to examine the Natural History of the Countries where we shall touch . . . I ask, therefore, leave to go on shore, taking with me proper People who may assist me in collecting and examining such Trees, Shrubs, Plants, Birds, Beasts, Fishes and Insects as I may meet with.'[60]

Captain Cook sends off both missives together, and it does not take long for the Vice-Roy to reply, writing back that very afternoon with a terse few sentences for them both:

No, to you, *Capitão*, and your so-called naturalist 'Gentleman' on board.

He adds, as Cook relays to his fellow officers with a rare wry scoff: 'that if I think it hard submitting to the Customs of this Port I may leave it when I please'.[61]

In other words, 'Take your strangely built and unusually fitted out British ship with your nefarious purposes, your ludicrous stories of mapping the stars across the sun from some speck of land in the Pacific, and become someone else's problem, for we will not help you.'

Captain Cook is exasperated. Joseph Banks Esquire is furious.

'And thus a Paper War commenced between me and His Excellency,' Cook records, 'wherein I had no other Advantage than the racking [of] his invention to find reasons for treating us in the manner he did, for he never would relax the least from any one point.'[62]

The next day, Cook decides it is time to force the issue, so he sends an understandably nervous Lieutenant Hicks to the shore once more with a letter from his Captain, backed by the full weight of Cook's Commission from King George III (proffered for his Excellency's approval and intimidation).

In his grand Vice-Regal residence, positioned at right angles to a great square skirting the beach off which the *Endeavour* is anchored, His Excellency Don Antonio Rolim de Moura Tavares is impressed with this English *Capitão's* sheer tenacity, as seemingly every knock on the door brings another insistent missive, like . . .

Like now.

For again comes the anxious knock, as if its lightness might somehow lessen the unwelcome intrusion.

'*Vice-Rei?*' breathes a timid servant.

'*Si?*'

Another letter from the troublesome *Endeavour* Captain, Vice-Roy. He is now refusing to have a man guard him or any of his men.

The Vice-Roy is unmoved.

No.

And tell the *Senhor* Lieutenant he will be only allowed back to your ship if he is accompanied by *um guarda Português*, a Portuguese guard.

The servant passes on the message to the waiting Lieutenant Hicks.

I refuse, Hicks replies.

Very well, then you are under arrest. As are all of your crew.

Beside himself with fury when he hears the latest news, Cook sends one of his petty officers on shore, with another letter, insisting that Lieutenant Hicks, the crew and the pinnace be released immediately, and demanding the reason for their detention in the first place.

'*Vice-Rei?*' interrupts the timid servant once more.

This time, at least the Vice-Roy allows the petty officer to return to the *Endeavour* without being arrested, albeit with his ears still ringing from the Vice-Roy's verbal salvo fired right at him.

Climbing up the steps to the deck, the petty officer makes his way past all the sailors, hammering, sawing, sewing sails and caulking seams – getting the ship ready for what will hopefully be departure soon, but who knows? – and reports directly to Captain Cook.

The Vice-Roy is not happy. Lieutenant Hicks and the men are still on shore, under arrest. And for more formal communication from the Vice-Roy, 'An answer will be sent tomorrow.'[63]

•

It is a dark and stormy night.

After the troubling events of the day, ship-board life has continued as before regardless, with the sounds of industry ceasing at sundown as ever, and after their evening meal most of the men taking their daily allowance of grog – one gallon – before retiring to their hammocks. But there will be little sleep for Captain Cook. What troubles him is not merely the Vice-Roy's venality, nor even the unfairness of it. (Just this afternoon he has seen a Spanish ship come into harbour and be received with courtesy. Yes, the Spanish. Can you imagine? The *Spanish*, the natural enemy of the Portuguese are being given permissions not granted to us English.)

No, far more troubling is just how stormy the weather is. Dangerously stormy. After midnight, the wind from the South becomes so violent that the ship is tossed about while at anchor and even hit by big harbour waves, one so big that it carries away Banks' small boat, which had been tethered to the stern of the long-boat – the latter holding a precious cargo of four pipes of rum!

It means that the following morning, 20 November, Captain Cook must send Master's Mate Charlie Clerke with a note to the Vice-Roy rather different from the one he was intending. Ah . . . Vice-Roy, we need your help. Specifically, the English Captain now 'desires leave and the Assistance of a Shore Boat to look after her'.[64]

For once there is co-operation from the Vice-Roy, orders are given and by the end of the day the long-boat has been retrieved from the shore upon which it has washed up, and returned to the *Endeavour*, with the rum still inside. If that is not miracle enough, so too are Lieutenant Hicks, his boat's crew and their pinnace brought back to the *Endeavour*.

Could it be that the Vice-Roy is sending them a message: anything, if you will just *VAI!*, GO!

No.

For the following morning, comes another missive from the Vice-Roy, this time putting forward his view that the *Endeavour* is a smuggling vessel – for what else could explain its unusual, capacious build, which has so bothered him from the start? She is simply made up to look like a British ship.

Yes, *Capitão* Cook has a convincing commission, but many smugglers are convincing forgers. The Vice-Roy will not be fooled by a piece of paper, a cock and bull story about watching Venus or a 'Navy' ship full of uppity gentlemen sent to collect ferns. Pull the other one, English.

Joseph Banks reads the latest missive incredulously.

'The viceroys answer to the Captain's last memorial came on board in which the Captain is accused of smuggling, which made us all angry but our venting our spleen against the Viceroy will be of very little service to us.'[65]

But seriously. *Cook* as the pirate Captain of a league of smugglers, with Banks the head of his band of brigands?

There are so many levels of absurdity to this that it is hard to keep track. Meanwhile, James Cook does the best he can to have men on shore procure the provisions he requires to get out of this port as fast as he can.

26 November 1768, Rio de Janeiro, botany bandits commit leafy larceny

Joseph Banks, meanwhile, has come to fancy the Vice-Roy's idea – Joseph Banks Esquire, the leader of a band of brigands. It has a certain something to it.

That is why, before dawn the next morning, he smuggles his black servants to shore on the reckoning they will blend in best with the locals, some two-thirds of whom are black.

By the time the sun is shining brightly that morning, the men are collecting plants and insects on the outskirts of the city, working towards Mr Banks' goal, even as Captain Cook – entirely unaware of the botanist's antics – is exasperated to receive yet another missive accusing him and his men of smuggling.

Deeply frustrated now, he records in his journal that the Vice-Roy, 'still keeps up his Doubts that she is not a King's Ship, and accuseth my people of Smuggling, a thing I am very Certain they were not guilty of, and for which his Excellency could produce no proof'.[66]

And even as the good Captain denies it outright, Banks sends his servants ashore again the next morning – so bountiful had their collection been the previous day, to his utter delight! – even as he maintains that the very *idea* that he and his men would engage in something illegal like smuggling – sneaking about, no doubt under the cover of darkness – is preposterous!

•

Sneaking about, under the cover of darkness, it is time for Joseph Banks to earn his pirate's equivalent of stripes and by stealth and by wealth go ashore illegally himself . . .

It is midnight when he, Dr Solander, Sydney Parkinson and the servants climb out of the Great Cabin window, slip down the rope that drops them into their own little boat that waits below, and let the current carry them away from the ship before rowing softly – *softly*, I said, no more of even the tiniest of splashes – to an 'unfrequented part of the shore',[67] where they land and begin their excursion up into the country.

Madness? Risking your life and liberty for some pedestrian plant fetching? Risking the entire voyage and the reputation of Captain Cook? Yes, but also pure Joseph Banks. A lark. A jape. In this case, it is in the service of science. The only thing that could make it better would be if it somehow involved bedding a woman, but for the moment, this will do. A wonderful time ensues.

Meeting with some of the inhabitants, they are delighted to be well received, even going into their houses, then head into the countryside, which positively 'abounded with a vast variety of Plants and animals'.[68]

Most important to Banks is that these specimens are nearly all unknown, and at the very least undocumented, he notes, because so few naturalists 'have had an opportunity of coming here; indeed no one that I know of even tolerably curious has been here since Marcgrave and Piso about the year 1640'.[69]

And yes, of course everything they see is already well known to the local 'Indians' – the generic term, together with 'Natives', applied by most of the British to non-Europeans in foreign parts – and has been known for millennia as well as the qualities thereof. Perhaps they have even written some of the names and the qualities, who knows?

What counts to Banks is that none of that knowledge has yet been effectively colonised by his own scientific world, meaning he and his entourage may do the honours themselves. Yes, it is all fresh for them to gather, examine, catalogue, give names to and put their own English stamp upon. Such joy!

Well after darkness has settled in, Joseph Banks, Dr Solander and the rest steal back to the boat on the shore to smuggle themselves and their bursting collection back to the *Endeavour*.

•

Quill in hand, Cook fires off his latest salvo in the paper war, responding to the renewed allegation that he and his men might actually be a band of smugglers.

> If my Commission should be counterfeited it follows of course that every other Officer's Commissions & Warrants are counterfeits, that all other papers in the ship tending to the same end are counterfeits, that the Officers & Marines uniforms are counterfeited and lastly the letters of credit I brought with me from Madeira are counterfeits. Was this true, Your Excellency must agree with me in declaring it to be the most Strange, the most daring & the most Public piece of Forgery that was ever committed in the Whole world.[70]

Cook is exasperated.

Banks is less . . . ah, shocked.

'We heard it said in town,' the botanist overhears the breathless petty officer telling Captain Cook, 'that people were sent out in search of some of our people who were ashore without leave.'[71]

Yes, well.

'[The circumstances,]' Banks will record, 'made it necessary for us to go no more ashore while we stayed.'[72]

Banks feels as though he has taken leave of his senses and walked into a daydream. Tropical plants abound in these climes, each one more fascinating than the last.

From 8 am to 2 pm every day, Banks and his men work on in the Grand Cabin – among other things, retrieving each blossom, every leaf, and placing them upon pieces of unfixed blotting paper, which are then encased in more sheets before folding for preservation. Mr Banks has already recorded the joy of such a scene with typical whimsy in his journal:

> Now do I wish that our friends in England could by the assistance of some magical spying glass take a peep at our situation: Dr Solander sits at the Cabin table describing, myself at my Bureau Journalizing, between us hangs a large bunch of sea weed, upon the

table lays the wood and barnacles; they would see that notwithstanding our different occupations our lips move very often . . . [73]

In the meantime, as November draws to a close, the ongoing paper war
of attrition – a clash of wills via a clash of quills – sees the pugnacious
Vice-Roy tire first. If the only way Cook and his ship will leave is with
full supplies, then so be it. The most important thing is that they leave
him in peace.

On 1 December the final supplies – a large quantity of fresh beef,
greens, yams and fresh fruit including lemons – are brought aboard
by the still glowering Portuguese soldiers, with Banks pleased to note:
'This Morn thank God we have got all we want from these illiterate
impolite gentry.'[74]

Once more the *Endeavour* is a heaving hive of activity, seeming chaos
to those who don't understand, but brilliantly regimented rituals to those
who do. Yes, of course smugglers creep away in the dead of night, but we
are His Majesty's Royal Navy and we take our leave in all-guns-blazing-
daylight, displaying pomp and precision, pluck and daring, and . . .

And, Lord no!

Just as they are about to leave, one of the sailors, Peter Flower, loses
his footing from high in the main shrouds, and hits the water so hard it
seems to knock him unconscious. He drowns before anyone can reach
him. Two ports; two men lost.

And this last one, who had sailed with Captain Cook as far back as
the Newfoundland days on the *Grenville*, hits the Yorkshireman particularly hard. 'A good hardy seaman and had sailed with me above five
years,'[75] he sorrowfully records.

By the time the drowned Flower is retrieved, sewn up in a canvas
shroud and 'buried at sea', the wind has changed once more. And so
they must sit out the day, before an ill-wind, beneath a pall of gloom,
and continue their face-off with the Vice-Roy's residence across the
water. At least the calm gives Cook a chance to replace his lost sailor
with a young Portuguese jack, while also buying boxes and barrels of
fresh supplies . . .

At last, they are ready to go, ready to leave this infernal place.

CHAPTER FIVE

ROUNDING CAPE HORN

Consider the first hollow trunk of an oak, in which, perhaps, the shepherd could scarce venture to cross a brook swelled with a shower, enlarged at last into a ship of war, attacking fortresses, terrifying nations, setting storms and billows at defiance, and visiting the remotest parts of the globe.[1]

Samuel Johnson, *The Rambler*, 1750

Dawn, 5 December 1768, Rio, allaying the Harbour of Suspicions

At last the wind blows fair and true. Away from Rio. It is with great relief that Captain Cook orders the *Endeavour*'s anchor to be weighed, turns her stern to Rio and moves towards the harbour's mouth. That feeling of freedom that comes to every born sailor when beckoned by the open sea is now upon him.

In fact, however, from a distance of almost half a mile, O *Commandante* of the Santa Cruz Fort that guards the harbour from the Eastern headland has the *Endeavour* locked squarely in his sights and is making estimates as to range, wind direction, and speed of the English vessel.

With some urgency now, the Commandant – distinguished by the silver braid on both his black tricorn hat and the shoulders of his black coat – gives his orders, finishing with the order that those manning the particular 32-pounder cannon they've primed and aimed have all been waiting for:

'*Fogo!*'

Instantly, the officer commanding the gun crew brings a slowly burning piece of rope held in a special device which allows him to do it at arm's length, and brings it quickly to the open vent connecting to the gunpowder. There is a fizz, a flash, and, as all of the Portuguese military men, including O *Commandante*, put their fingers in their ears, awaiting the explosion . . .

118

•

Aboard the *Endeavour*, the mood is light, the sea-breeze fresh, and all is right with the world when . . .

When off to larboard comes the unmistakable boom of a cannon! The roar of the big gun rolls over the *Endeavour* like a ball of dirty thunder at much the same time as the whizzing sound of the cannonball itself is heard, and an angry splash rises up, some 100 yards forward and off to starboard.

First stupefied, then horrified, then infuriated – all in the space of a couple of seconds – Cook and company turn to see where the shot has come from. It is, of course, Fort Santa Cruz, which stands guard over the harbour entrance. No ship may enter or leave without coming under the sight of its guns.

Still, Captain Cook does not waver: *Steady as she goes, Mr Hicks. We shall call their bluff.*

And now, a second shot!

This one goes straight over their mainmast, and lands even closer to them! The message is clear.

Turn back immediately, or be blown out of the water.

Steady as she goes? No.

Now none is steady, and a steady course would merely present an easier target for Portuguese cannon that are puffing, but surely not bluffing.

How *can* this be? The same Vice-Roy, who has spent the best part of a week urging them to leave, is now preventing their departure by cannonball?

Dropping anchor, Cook sends a cutter one and three-quarter miles to the fort and is informed by O *Commandante* that he has no orders to allow the *Endeavour* to pass, and therefore the *Endeavour não passará.*

'This surprised me not a little,' Cook chronicles, 'as I had but this very morning received a very Polite Letter from the Vice-Roy (in answer to one I had wrote some days ago), wherein he wishes me a good voyage.'[2]

At 6 am, Cook pens and despatches a final missive, causing a now familiar scene a few hours later.

'Vice-Roy?'

'*SI?*'

Another letter from *Capitão* James Cook. He wants to know when they can leave.

This time, the answer is surprising, and Master's Mate Charlie Clerke returns three hours later to the *Endeavour* with the news.

You have His Excellency's apologies, Captain. As it happens, a letter was written by him several days ago, instructing *O Commandante* to let the *Endeavour* pass but, as Cook will note after Clerke reports back, 'either by Design or neglect [it] had not been sent'.[3]

At least that letter has firmly gone to the fort now, and the *Endeavour* is free to go, except . . .

Except – well, this is awkward – the wretched anchor proves to be stuck in the muck, somewhere between a rock and a hard place. For no matter how much the men strain on the capstan, it will not budge and Cook is reduced to – *Mr Clerke!* – sending another note to an acidly amused Vice-Roy advising how the anchor 'got hold of a Rock, where it held fast in spite of all our endeavours . . .'.[4]

The men heave, the men strain, the men groan as they exert every ounce of their combined power to shift the anchor. Well, nearly their combined power. Even as the men haul on the capstan, Mr Banks and Dr Solander charge around the deck with nets, capturing a fluttering, cluttering horde of beautiful butterflies that has suddenly descended upon them.

From the balcony, looking out to the bay, the Vice-Roy is afforded one of the more absurd spectacles in his career – all seen through his telescope – as the grim-faced Cook oversees his sweating charges getting precisely nowhere, all while the uppity botanist and his underling charge about on deck and up the rigging with their nets, like giddy schoolchildren.

His Excellency is moved to mirth, but nothing moves the anchor. As night falls even Cook must bow to reality and the efforts are stopped. They will have to wait another night in this accursed port before finally escaping the next day, but escape they finally do – though it is not until mid-afternoon the next day, thanks to a conspiracy of the tide, the wind, the collective cursing of the men, the roars from the officers and the grace of Christ Almighty himself, that Providence at last dislodges the anchor from its rocky prison.

Three weeks and two days after arriving in this infernal place, the *Endeavour* is floating free once more. True, they all steel themselves as they once more pass by the Santa Cruz Fortress on the Eastern headland, but this time they are able to make their way to the open sea without incident.

Cook feels a relief and a general lift in mood that not only extends into the night and all of the next day as they continue to push down the South American South-eastern coast towards the dreaded Cape Horn, but in fact goes until Christmas – a rowdy day on board, as the mostly sober Captain records of the ship's complement, 'being Christmas Day the people were none of the soberest'[5] – and well into the new year, despite the shrieking gales that get ever stronger, the further South they go.

One particularly vicious gale, on the night of 6 January 1769 is so violent that all of Mr Banks' books and his bureau are knocked over, but . . . . . . that lifts the collective mood more than anything else. For beyond the quiet pleasure of seeing the blessed Banks brought low for once, what truly gladdens the sailors' hearts is how well the *Endeavour*, the humble Whitby cat, is able to handle the shattering battering, without problem, something that surely bodes well for the trials to come – getting around Cape Horn, though there will be at least some respite on land before they must face it.

Mid-January 1769, Bottom of the World, less an ill-wind than a chill wind

The more Southerly the latitude, the more howling the winds, the bigger the waves, and the colder the temperature. Just a week into the new year every tar is issued with a pair of thick trousers and a fearnought jacket – thick, tightly woven woollen jackets familiar to all those, like James Cook himself, who have spent freezing winters in the North Sea off the English coast. The men are going to need them in the coming weeks as they attempt to round Cape Horn. (For Joseph Banks and his entourage of course have no need, as the two servants simply retrieve from stowage the stylishly cut thick flannel jackets, waistcoats and trousers that have been purchased for all of them, with no need of government issue – as if – for them.)

And now as the *Endeavour* continues to plough Southwards, ever Southwards, they can see out to starboard across the white-capped waves the towering white-capped mountains of Tierra del Fuego, the archipelago off the Southern Patagonia tip of South America. Navigating closer to the coast, and within three leagues of the slate-strewn shoreline, Cook at last sees precisely what he has been looking for – the tell-tale signs of its native population, the reason Ferdinand Magellan, the 16th century Portuguese explorer, called the area the 'Land of Fire'.

'Saw some of the Natives,' Cook records in the log, 'who made smoke in several places, which must have been done as a Signal to us as they did not continue it after we passed.'[6]

On 15 January 1769 Cook guides the *Endeavour* to anchor in nine fathoms at the Bay of Good Success, just inside the Le Maire Strait, and which looks like a fine spot to 'wood and water' – gather the same, with wood for the stoves now being in particularly short supply – before attempting to get around the dreaded Cape Horn into the Pacific.

It is an icy, wind-blown place, but at least the anchorage is sheltered enough from the elements for Cook's men to have some respite. This is the very spot to dive deep into the eternal well of tasks that characterise the life of a sailor even in port; scrubbing the decks, mending the sails, airing the hammocks and doing whatever else the officers order, singing sea shanties all the while:

> 'All hands on board!' our Bosun cries, his voice like thunder roaring;
> 'All hands on board!' his mates reply, before all sing together:
>
> Tis the signal for unmooring.
> Then your messenger bring to,
> Heave your anchor to the bow,
> And we'll think on those girls when we're far, far away
> And we'll think on those girls when we're far, far away.[7]

The sounds of their chanty sea-shanty floats to Captain Cook over the waves as he is rowed to the shore by half-a-dozen Marines, accompanied by the ever restless Mr Banks and Dr Solander. And look there!

Just as the pinnace approaches the rugged shore, a handful of Fuegian Natives, all men, emerge from the forest, seemingly friendly. As the bow of the boat crunches onto the rocky beach, Cook disembarks first, and, wearing a broad smile, opens his hands wide to indicate that he is unarmed and comes in peace.

The Fuegians clearly take him at his word, and gestures, for mere moments after Cook, Banks, the Doctor and the Marines have landed they are tightly surrounded by some 30 or 40 Natives, including women. They are a curious-looking bunch – with neatly made bows strung diagonally across their torsos, and their wild eyes peering out from horizontal stripes of black and red painted across their animated faces – and they seem to be all chattering rapidly in words that are completely unintelligible, although not Portuguese. Most of the words are rubbery and round – and sound as though they might bounce on a hard surface, although others, Mr Banks notes, 'seem to express much as an Englishman when he hawks to clear his throat'.[8] Even while chattering madly, the Natives gesture and prod at these strange white men dressed in strange, colourful garb.

In response Cook continues to smile and nod, while quietly ordering the Marines to do the same. In a situation like this, if things turn ugly – and it is always a chance, in a strange world when you are outnumbered like this, no matter how many muskets you have – they will be perilously close to helpless to save themselves if the Natives feel threatened and get their attack in first.

And yet, mercifully, despite the growing numbers of Natives, and their poking, the mood doesn't change and all remains friendly. Cook allows himself to get a closer look at the Natives, to observe, rather than to watch warily. There is no doubt they are a handsome-looking people. Their skin is a dark copper colour and they are hard and muscled. No, they are nowhere near as big as the nine-foot-tall race of Patagonian giants that exists in the mind of credulous Londoners, but they are formidable-looking men, most of them bigger than the English visitors. Some of them appearing to be able to ward off the crippling cold simply by coating their bodies in oil they have extracted from animals and fish, streaked across their skin. While the women wear 'a piece of skin over their privy parts', the men, as the battoned-down-buttoned-up Cook records, 'observe no such decency'.[9]

The less robust among them are wearing either llama or seal skins draped loosely from their shoulders and hanging down to their knees, fur side out.

Some of them, Cook notes, have in their possession, 'European things . . . such as rings, buttons, cloth, canvas, etc, which I think proves that they must sometimes travel to the Northward, as we know of no Ship that hath been in these parts for many Years'.[10]

Some of the Native men bring their beads right up to his face, pointing and gesturing at them, saying over and over, 'Nalleca, Nalleca',[11] making Cook assume that is the Native word for 'beads'. For some reason they are entirely besotted with this simple curio, so much so that when Mr Banks and the Doctor start handing out beads and ribbons from a stash they have with them, the Natives whoop with joy, particularly when one of a particular colour is produced.

'They are Extremely fond of any Red thing,' Cook observes in his log, 'and seemed to set more Value on Beads than anything we could give them; in this Consists their whole Pride, few, either Men or Women, are without a Necklace or String of Beads made of Small Shells or bones about their Necks.'[12]

(Indeed, while most colours abound in these parts, most particularly in their birdlife, red is in rather short supply and is the colour of peace, making it very highly valued.)

Soon enough comes further proof that the Natives are familiar with the ways of Europeans when the man who appears to be their Chief carefully points to Cook's pistol, before pointing his hand to a bird flying overhead and letting out a sound like a roar, followed by a squeal. At once all the Natives around him start babbling, jumping up and down, and making the same gestures – pointing to the skies and making their best imitations of the sound of a shot.

Use your guns! Use your guns!

(Perhaps a surprising thing for a people who, historically, have suffered because of such guns – the Portuguese had first colonised Brazil in 1532

ROUTE OF THE *ENDEAVOUR* THROUGH LE MAIRE STRAIT 1769

MAGELLAN STRAIT

TIERRA DEL FUEGO

LE MAIRE STRAIT

– but on the other hand, this part of the world had been judged as so cold and worthless they had declined to settle here, leaving it for the Ona, Yaghan and Alacalufe Indians, the traditional owners.)

For James Cook the key thing is that the Natives are friendly.

Joseph Banks beams to be here and is like one suddenly let free from the botanical prison of Rio into this wilderness wonderland of Tierra del Fuego with fresh delights in every direction. The young Englishman is determined to explore everything he can on his botanical odyssey to beat them all, in this geographical oddity like none he's ever seen – with lush ferns all around them here, standing in strict contrast to the snow they can see atop nearby hills. That snow, Banks is sure, must be left there from last winter, in high enough citadels that it never melts.

Alpine plants, generally, fascinate him – most particularly their capacity to flourish despite extremes of weather, and, having already gathered and brought back to England alpine plants on a trip to Iceland, he is now, as he chronicles, 'eager to arrive at [the bare rock mountaintop] expecting there to find alpine plants of a country so curious'.[13]

Most wonderfully, in terms of exploring this land and doing their botanising, there will be no problem with the locals, as there had been in Rio.

So it is that while Cook intends to spend all of 16 January on shore overseeing the replenishment of their wood and water supplies, he is not surprised when Mr Banks rises 'very early',[14] and informs him that he will be taking his entourage with him to gather fresh plants and animals and sketch fresh landscapes. He does not ask Captain Cook's permission for such an exercise. On matters botanical, Banks is in charge. (Not to forget, Joseph Banks has spent £10,000 to outfit this voyage before it even left England, and James Cook is being paid by the Admiralty a mere . . . well, five of His Majesty's shillings a day – none of them shiny. It would be against nature, not to mention centuries of the English class structure, for Mr Banks to seek the blessing of Captain Cook to go on such an expedition and it does not occur to either man.)

So it is that when Captain Cook emerges on deck he sees Banks in the cutter with his full retinue – Dr Solander, Mr Sporing, Mr Green, Surgeon Monkhouse, Mr Buchan to draw the sights, two seamen and Banks' four servants to bag, cut, cook, fetch and carry – heading to the shore in merry expectation. The devil-may-care dozen are due to return before dark.

Banks' plan, as he will chronicle, is to 'try to penetrate into the country as far as we could, and if possible gain the tops of the hills where alone we saw places not overgrown with trees'.[15] They leave Cook's sight via a small sandy beach and yet, when the jaunty crew try to follow rough paths through the thickets, it is to find as the thickets get thicker and the paths disappear, their jauntiness disappears very quickly – particularly because they are 'always going up hill'.[16] Still they press on the best they can, the branches tearing at their skin and their clothes, and by 3 pm – after a solid eight hours of pushing higher – it is not that they have got anywhere in particular, but at least as the irrepressible Banks records, they have 'a near view of the places we intended to go to'.[17]

Yes, the men are generally tired, and yet Banks – *bloody Banks, will he never slow down?* – is so full of enthusiasm and youth he is like a young pony, a show-pony perhaps, who has learnt to gallop for the first time.

Onwards!

Not back to the, ah, ship, Mr Banks, before it starts to get too dark?

No. Onwards!

Banks notes chirpily that 'the weather had all this time been vastly fine much like a sunshiney day in May, so that neither heat nor cold was troublesome to us nor were there any insects to molest us'.[18]

They take time to shoot at birds, taking particular satisfaction in bringing down a vulture who had swooped too low on the possibility they might be lunch. The whole of the dead bird is trussed up and now strapped on the back of one of the servants before they move on, at least the best they can.

For in short order they are confronted by 'low bushes of birch about reaching a man's middle',[19] that are so thick and stubborn they refuse to bend to the will of men, instead forcing Banks and his men to bend to nature's will. It is painful, painstaking progress, with every step a ritual of lifting your foot up and over a tangled thicket and then placing it down on unseen earth where pungent mud slurps it whole, letting out a satisfied burp followed by a long squelch as you withdraw it again, to do the whole thing again.

Even Banks must now concede that, 'no traveling could possibly be worse than this', which still doesn't mean he is ready to turn back, however much the bloodshot, rolling eyes of his men might plead for him to do so. Still they go for another mile, Banks, like a hound on the hunt, determined to determine what alpine plants manage to get such a foothold and so thrive in this unique highland where surely no other explorer, let alone another botanist, has been.

Banks insists that, 'Our people, though rather fatigued were yet in good spirits, so we pushed on intending to rest ourselves as soon as we should arrive at plain ground.'[20]

After all, they are so close now to the peaks they have been struggling towards all day that it would be madness to turn back now, like swimming halfway to an island before giving up and turning back. Already his fingers are itching to pluck all kinds of exotic plants that are surely there.

But what now?

About two-thirds of the way through the birch barrier, before their very eyes, Mr Buchan falls to the ground, rolls on his back, and starts shaking, from his toe tips to the tip of his head. His eyes roll back, his jaw sags and a thin, sickly stream of dribble rolls down his chin.

An epileptic fit, known as 'the falling sickness'. As they continue to stare, aghast, Buchan continues to writhe, his possessed body contorted into a grotesque tangle like the birch underfoot, a white foam now spilling from between his twitching lips, small, frightening gasps for air . . . or is it pain? Surgeon Monkhouse moves first (well, a quick sniff of snuff first). As a trained apothecary of vast experience, he knows that fits like this can quickly turn fatal unless prompt action is taken.

A fire, men, and be quick about it!

We must bring Buchan back from the brink, and some basic warmth should help. It is so urgent that even Mr Banks himself is seen to help, as they all fan out, awkwardly forcing their way through the birch thicket, and breaking off the driest twigs and branches they can find as they go, all while Monkhouse clears a patch of *tierra*. Once the men return with their twigs and branches they all huddle around as protection from the howling gale, and light a fire for the patient, which flickers, nearly dies and . . . suddenly takes hold!

Before long the poor fellow is laid close to the life-sustaining warmth and seems to slowly come back to himself, to realise that most of the men are staring at him anxiously, while some are making ready to . . . depart?

Despite the fit, Mr Banks insists on pushing on. All those who are most tired may remain behind, declares Banks magnanimously. Dr Solander, Mr Green, Surgeon Monkhouse and myself will advance for the alp.

And how about 'near dead', can I stay behind, too?

The shattered Buchan, with seven others, stays by the fire, while the rest of the Banks party heads off.

The Lord alps those who alp themselves and Banks and his men do just that when they arrive at the peaks in the late afternoon, helping themselves to whatever exotic alpine plants they can find. Banks loses himself in the novelty of collecting samples and specimens at the bottom of the world. There is, however, one slightly troubling distraction: the plummeting temperature with the waning sun, even as the rising wind whistles with chilling menace. To make matters worse, it started to snow, quickly and with surprising ferocity.

'The air was here very cold and we had frequent snow blasts,'[21] Banks will chronicle.

Only now, with the rush of discovery past, does Banks realise their predicament. There's no chance they can get back to the safety of the ship before dark, and the best they can hope for is to descend far enough from these freezing altitudes that they can make the woods and build some kind of 'wigwam'[22] just like the Natives, which should keep them warm enough to get through the night. Certainly, they cannot be as hardy as the Fuegian Natives, and will pass a dreadful night, but the challenge right now is not to be comfortable, it is to live.

Mr Green and Surgeon Monkhouse are sent back forthwith to retrieve Buchan and the others from their spot in the thick of the thicket, while Banks, after pointing out the particular lower hill he desires them to rendezvous on, goes a different route, dropping into an adjacent valley where the short birch appears less hostile. Alas, as the sun continues to wane the cold waxes, creeping through their skin into their bones, sapping them and slowing them. By the time Monkhouse and Green have regathered the others and joined Banks at the rendezvous spot, it is 8 pm, with only languishing light left to get through the rest of the birch to a place suitable to make camp.

Quickly now, men.

'I undertake to bring up the rear and see that no one is left behind,'[23] Banks declares in a sudden if belated burst of concern for the welfare of his party. No, really.

And by the way, Mr Buchan, how are you?

The answer, in Banks' assessment, is, 'stronger than we could have expected'.[24] Which is good. But Banks now also starts to realise that this full day of intense exertion, little food, high drama, higher altitude and now *intense, bone-shattering* cold has made the rest of the men weaker than expected. And the first to falter is not Buchan at all, but Banks' most faithful companion of all, the good Doctor. Yes, despite being a

Swede, raised in such conditions, Daniel Solander is beyond battered by the conditions.

'Banks, I can not go any farther, I must lay down,'[25] he groans.

What? *Lay down?*

Why, Dr Solander, you of all people must understand stopping now in this manner is madness, as the ground is covered with snow and will freeze you to the bone! The Doctor doesn't care. Or he can't care. A frozen soul has a frozen will and whatever he might want to do, whatever might make sense, his legs simply buckle beneath him and he slumps to the ground in a crumpled heap, as the wind continues to howl and the snow blasts begin to cover him.

Alarmingly, Dr Solander is not the only one, for now Richmond, one of Banks' two black manservants, also makes clear that he wishes to stop. This, at least, is a little easier to deal with, as Banks orders him to keep going. Alas, even the English class system has its limits and soon enough Richmond is disobedient enough to be 'much in the same way as the Doctor'.[26]

Annoyed, as this really is very inconvenient, and likely even dangerous, Banks sends five of the party forward to establish a camp and get a fire going, while he will stay behind with the laggards, bringing them on slowly. Who should lead the faster group? Ironically it is none other than Mr Buchan who, braced by the night air and recovered from his fit, is the strongest among them, and leads them off, down the valley. Now, for Banks and the four reasonably fit men with him, the task is to coax the Doctor and Richmond forward. But still Solander and Richmond lie in the snow, fallen snow angels that will soon become real angels on high if they do not get up and get moving! Dr Solander, I implore you! *All you have to do is get up, and finish crossing the birch, it is but half a mile and then we shall be safe and you will be warm! Richmond, dammit, get up and get moving. If you stay here you will surely freeze to death!*

Through a combination of honeyed persuasion and barked snark, Banks at last has both men on their feet and moving slowly, making it through the worst of the birch until both men once again collapse in the snow. Banks cannot believe it.

'Sir,' says Richmond, 'I cannot go any further.'

'If you do not, you must be froze to death!' snaps Banks.

'I will lie and die,'[27] says Richmond, with – fie – poetry that chills Banks more than the weather. Truly, this is madness, these men have lost not just the use of their limbs, but their whole reason. Banks then begs Dr Solander to set an example and to save his own life. *Get up, man!*

'I must sleep a little before I can go on,'[28] replies the Doctor as he nestles in a bed of snow that clearly risks being his deathbed. Unbelievable. But still he lies . . , in a frozen, perhaps deathly slumber for all of 15 minutes, Banks, by his side, is lost in concern for his friend until one of the seamen returns from the advance party to tell Banks in a weak voice: 'A fire is lit about a quarter of a mile ahead, Sir.'[29]

Solander, do you hear?

Banks shakes his dear friend awake.

Just a few hundred yards up ahead, there is a fire, and you can be saved! Wake up!

With a groan Solander ascends from the deep lair of Morpheus and stirs, and with great relief Banks lifts him to his feet. For his part, Richmond still refuses to budge, so Banks leaves the two men who seem least affected with cold to look after him.

'I will send two to relieve you as soon as I reach the fire,'[30] he assures them. Half dragging, half carrying his friend, Banks keeps Solander staggering forward through the falling snow that's collecting quickly on the ground, towards the faint glimmering of a fire – real or imagined – they can see up ahead. It is that flicker, that promise of warmth that keeps them going, through the sucking slush and brutal birch. At last, nearing 10 pm, Banks drags Solander to the fire, and sinks down gratefully to it himself.

Just as soon as his pale fingers have enough feeling so that he can control them once more, Banks decides to open the bottle of rum they had brought with them, only to remember that . . .

Good Lord! He has left it in the knapsack of one of the two men left higher up. Slumping in disappointment, it is a good minute before he can gather himself to send two men back up the hill to rouse Richmond, aid the two men posted there, and bring them all back . . . *and* the rum, too, don't forget!

Just 30 minutes later those same two men return.

'We have been all round the place,' one of them says, 'shouting and hallowing but could not get any answer.'[31]

Banks' worst fears start to crystallise.

They are missing?

'They must have drunk immoderately and slept like Richmond,'[32] he thinks out loud, echoing the thoughts of all around the fire.

Could they survive?

After all, this is no nippy night that follows a 'sunshiney day in May'[33] in England, this is full-blown snowstorm, high in the Southern South American alps, and the poor men will likely be completely covered come midnight, buried by the wee hours and frozen solid by morning.

Nearing midnight, however, the howl of the wind brings with it the howl of a man, and it is with great joy that Banks and four of the men immediately go out to find him.

There!

It proves to be one of the seamen who'd been left with Richmond, his ice-covered form barely distinguishable in the hazy abyss, now half insensible with cold, and the other half insensible with alcohol; they had smelt him before they had seen him.

The freezing rascal is led to the fire, and as the flames thaw him Banks roars urgent questions at him. *Where are the others? Where lies Richmond? Can you find your way back? Can you direct those who might?*

Through chattering teeth, the wretch gives answers enough that Banks himself, accompanied by two men, go out to find the lost men. Smashing through the snow, ascending, and regularly yelling, they finally hear an answer from an unexpected source. For it is the voice of Richmond and they soon find him. To Banks' amazement, though groggy, he can stand, which is something – though he cannot walk. As to the third man, Dorlton, he is alive, which though something, is not much when he is prone on the ground, still and mute as stone. He will be his own frozen tombstone unless he rises.

Banks returns to the fire. All hands on deck. We need help. All together then, they do their best to bring the men down. Alas, the snow is so thick and swirling, the wind so strong, the night so darkly pressing and the path so impassable that for every five yards they descend one or other of them falls badly, frequently resulting in injury. It is all they can do to find one another, let alone try to drag near-corpses who are refusing to budge. It is impossible. Should they light a fire? If only they could.

With a heavy heart and a kind of shocked disbelief that this can really be happening, the 25-year-old Joseph Banks realises there is every chance that he is about to freeze to death, that his life is going to end within hours on this wretched mountain. In the meantime, they must look after those most at risk first, and he now instructs his men to lay boughs on the ground and put the two men on top so they have at least some insulation from the icy earth. And now they cover their friends with yet more boughs, saying silent prayers and begging for mercy upon these two wretches.

And so they stumble about for half an hour, only wishing that they were numbed with cold, but in fact feeling it with every frozen fibre of their beings, as the snow just keeps swirling about them, dancing on their misery.

Finally it is done, and 'thus we left them hopeless of ever seeing them again alive'.[34] Stumbling on towards the fire, one of Banks' servants, Peter Briscoe, tells his master through chattering, shattering teeth that h-h-h-he f-f-f-f-eels s-s-s-strange . . . and indeed is soon hardly able to crawl. Still Banks stays with him, and onwards they push, Banks coaxing forth the last bit of energy the poor man has in him, to get him to the fire as Briscoe is now 'almost dead with cold'.[35]

To say the least, their situation is dire, as Banks will faithfully record in his journal: 'Now might our situation truly be called terrible: of twelve, our original number, two were already past all hopes, one more was so ill that though he was with us I had little hopes of his being able to walk in the morning, and another very likely to relapse into his fits either before we set out or in the course of our journey: we were distant from the ship we did not know how far, we knew only that we had been the greatest part of a day in walking it through pathless woods: provision we had none but one vulture which had been shot while we were out, and at the shortest allowance could not furnish half a meal: and to complete our misfortunes we were caught in a snow storm in a climate we were utterly unacquainted.'[36]

It had all happened so quickly.

They had set out in fine weather, simply to search for some alpine plants, and now, here they are in the night, lost, and very close to dying in a snowstorm.

After all, Banks defensively notes, 'it was very little after midsummer',[37] and to experience such sudden, brutal change is 'a circumstance unheard of in Europe for even in Norway or Lapland snow is never known to fall in the summer'.[38]

Alas, Banks is all too aware now, but all he can do is snatch what sleep he can before finding out who lives at dawn.

With that dawn – a slight lessening in the sheer blackness of the pounding whiteness that keeps going until Banks can see nothing but 'the earth covered with snow as well as all the tops of the trees, nor were the snow squalls at all less frequent . . . we had no hopes now but of staying here as long as the snow lasted and how long that would be God alone knew'.[39]

At 6 am the sun peeks through the squalls, the sole glimmer of light in the Stygian gloom, and, 'we immediately thought of sending to see whether the poor wretches we had been so anxious about last night were yet alive, three of our people went but soon returned with the melancholy news of their being both dead'.[40]

Yes, Banks' two black servants, Thomas Richmond and George Dorlton, are dead. The boughs meant to save them will now act as their wooden tombs, cemented together only with the snow. Born in Jamaica after their parents had been forcibly taken from Africa, sold into slavery in England, die on a mountain in Brazil.

At least the wind has stopped, and huddled together around the fire, the remaining 10 men can do nothing but wait. In the mid-morning the snowfall eases, the sun manages to send small splinters through the thick clouds and the breeze that has picked up makes the snow fall in clumps from atop the trees. A thaw, thinks Banks.

There is even a stirring from the most ill of Banks' companions, Peter Briscoe, who after a while – though still extremely ill, his face a deadly grey – is able to declare, 'I think myself able to walk.'[41]

Thank Christ!

Let us have breakfast to sustain us, and then make through the snow for the *Endeavour*. Irony of ironies, the only thing for breakfast is the vulture they had caught the previous day, when all was well and the devil-may-care dozen was still whole. Yes, the near dead will now eat the dead bird that had hoped to prey on their corpses. Oh – and those ancient superstitions about not eating the flesh of creatures that might have eaten human flesh – as they had had the luxury of doing with the shark Banks once served them? Those really were just silly superstitions. Indeed, the men salivate as the vulture is dressed by Banks' remaining servant and 'skinned and cut into ten equal shares, every man cooking his own share which furnished about 3 mouthfuls of hot meat'.[42] It is the first food they have had since a cold lunch yesterday and 'all we were to expect till we should come to the ship'.[43]

And if not, well then, the vultures will soon have their revenge served cold, the just deserts, of the English, for dessert.

It is around 10 am when Banks leads the party off and notes, as amazed as he is thrilled and relieved, that, 'after a march of about 3 hours [we] arrived at the beach, fortunate in having met with much better roads in our return than we did in going out, as well as in being nearer to the ship than we had any reason to hope'.[44]

Fortune at last has favoured the foolhardy.

The ship, they can see the ship. The boat they had left here yesterday will be just here along the shore.

•

Captain Cook, I can see them!

It is a short while after noon, and Sydney Parkinson is one of many who has been looking out anxiously for the missing men since dawn. He is at last rewarded by the vision of them coming out of the thick forest and walking down towards the sandy beach.

Infinitely relieved, Cook goes up on deck in time to see the cutter approaching . . . . . . strangely, looking a little thin in numbers?

Yes, once they are aboard he is apprised of the terrible news. Two men have been lost, and their frozen corpses remain high on the mountain. Seriously saddened for them and deeply disappointed for himself – the loss of every man under his command is a reflection on that command – still Cook also evinces another emotion in the immediate aftermath. He is shocked by the behaviour of one man: Joseph Banks. They all are.

No, Cook makes no criticism of the results of the tragic expedition. No-one could have predicted such freakish weather. But it is Banks' behaviour immediately after returning from a trip where two good men have been lost, and indeed Banks had become perilously close to losing his own life. As Master Molineux notes incredulously in his private journal: 'As soon as they came on board they refreshed themselves and were put into warm beds. The only exception was Banks, who on hearing that they would soon be sailing away from this bay, after the briefest pause and with undiminished enthusiasm, began combing about the ship with his [boat]'[45] dragging a fishing net.

Yes, it is said that some aristocrats have ice water in their veins, that they are different from the common folk, but here is the embodiment. Deaths shatter Cook, while Banks pays little regard regardless. His own survival simply means he is able to collect more flowers, plants, animals, birds and fish – and he does not intend to waste a moment. His is a fierce fascination that bemuses Cook, and he simply does not understand how Banks can be *so* passionate for his collection. So much so that Cook observes in his journal that Banks' beloved gatherings are, 'unknown in Europe and in that alone consisted their whole value'.[46]

When poor weather keeps the *Endeavour* at anchor for another day Cook takes the time to complete his survey of the bay, but this man of the Royal Society simply takes his boat and his retinue ashore, to search for more specimens, none of which are as exotic, or as oft wild, as the one they return with.

Josephus Banksia, a unique species indeed.

At last, on 21 January, the wind blows fair and the *Endeavour* is able to head South once more, bound for that turbulent sea on the Southern tip of this archipelago where the Atlantic, Pacific and Southern Oceans fight a daily duel for supremacy that continues through the night, every night and on into the next day.

Cook and the old salts only know what to expect from what they have read in reports or heard at dock or around the mess table. Even the seven men on board who circumnavigated the globe aboard the *Dolphin*, those with actual experience sailing in these wild Southern latitudes have not, in fact, rounded the Horn itself, instead they had gone through the Strait of Magellan further to the North – named for the pioneering Portuguese Captain who first navigated the route – and which is thought to be the easier of the two passages.

And so, as Lieutenant Gore and that great yarn-spinner, Midshipman Charlie Clerke, and Master Robert Molineux and the others tell them, though none of us have been South of the Cape, the Straits of Magellan were bad enough, and there are wild stories from those very few men who have been South of the Cape and lived to tell the tale. Let us tell you . . .

Consequently the rumours soon circulating among the lower decks are so compelling they are shared all over the ship; between swinging sailors high up in the riggings, tarrying tars down in the bilge, and even at the dining table of the gentlemen and officers in the Great Cabin. With Charlie Clerke at his best, the tall tales become taller still, nearly as tall as the Patagonian giants, and certainly ever more dire with every re-telling as the men sail South.

For you already know the heart of the matter!

The waters off Cape Horn are the most infamous sailors' graveyard on the planet, born of the stormiest patch of sea on Earth with the most horrific gales and tempests, the most savagely unpredictable currents and the biggest waves – some of which are monsters suddenly coming from unexpected directions.

My friend, in those parts the winds are so wild they could blow a dog off a chain and a man from the mast unless he is lashed on. The same with the rain and snow – so torrential and blizzard-like that they can sweep a man from the deck and into the ocean afore his mates know he's gone.

And the *currents*. My God, the currents are so strong to the East, swirling around the Horn, that many a time when we were with Captain Wallis we would sail to the West for days on end, only to check our bearings and find that we had gone backwards as the currents and mountainous seas pushed the ship further to the East. Oh yes, those waves are sometimes higher than the mizzen mast and if just one of them hits you broadside, it is certain death for everyone on board within seconds. They can swallow you whole, and not even burp, and you head for Davy Jones' locker.

And in those wild parts, South of the Horn, there are so many whales that, altogether they near tipped Commodore 'Foulweather Jack' Byron's ship over! Facing such obstacles, it had taken Byron just under two months to get through the Strait. Wallis had an even harder time, taking four months to battle the contrary currents, winds and storms that hit during this mere 350-mile passage, not to mention losing his fellow ship, the *Swallow*, for the duration of the voyage.

Yes, the ship's company of the *Endeavour* – from Captain to Gentlemen to Crew – have heard it all. It is for good reason the old sailing saying runs that, 'below 40 degrees latitude, there is no law; below 50, there is no God' . . . and the tip of Cape Horn is thought to sit at 56 degrees South.

For you see, feeding the apprehension even further is that Cook is under strict instruction to eschew the Strait of Magellan and go around Cape Horn itself, to keep as far South as possible – that is, in the *unexplored* part of the Pacific Ocean. Both Byron and Wallis had found it difficult to sail West from the Pacific exit of the Strait against the prevailing Westerlies. But by rounding the South American continent further South – tracking the coast South-west, descending to a latitude of roughly 60 degrees South, which is safely below the tip of Cape Horn – Cook's *Endeavour* will enter the Pacific at a more Southerly latitude, and though he too will be sailing straight into the teeth of what are usually howling gales, he will be in an unexplored tract of the ocean, before tracking North-west to Tahiti.

Ah yes . . . Tahiti. For when it comes to the mountainous seas to come, the greatest balms to the sailors' qualms are psalms to the palms of the island of their destination, and the beautiful bare-breasted women who wait beneath them. These are women who want nothing more – *I am telling you, boys!* – than to lie with an English sailor!

We just have to get through the trial that awaits . . .

In preparation for it, in a manner that would have done Honey James proud all those years ago – hitting the books into the wee hours – Captain James Cook starts studying. In precisely the manner of his mentor, Captain Simcoe – who had shown him what a scientific Captain's cabin could look like – he sits at the head of the table in the Great Cabin at every spare moment, surrounded by books and papers, poring over everything he can get his hands on.

'As I have never been in those Straits,' he notes in his log, 'I can only form my Judgement on a Careful Comparison of the Different Ships' Journals that have passed them, and those that have sailed round Cape Horn.'[47]

Reading and rereading the journals and logs of Admiral George Anson, 'Foulweather Jack' Byron, and Wallis, he also studies the translated accounts of 'the Dutch Squadron commanded by Hermites',[48] who sailed around the Horn in 1624. This is not simply an exercise in seamanship, but in intellect and knowledge – and as is typical of him, Cook intends to be no less than learned on the topic before facing the actuality.

In the meantime, as is also his wont and forte, he builds upon their works, roughly charting the coastlines as best he can without doing proper surveys, noting bays for safe anchorage or water and wood as they continue down the coast. The resultant charts he is coming up with are imperfect, but far better than existed heretofore, as Cook notes: 'It was the Vice Admiral Chapenham, of [the Dutch Squadron commanded by Hermites], who first discovered that the land of Cape Horn . . . consisted of a Number of Islands, but the account they have given of those parts is very short and imperfect, and that of Schouton and Le Maire still worse, that it is no wonder that the Charts hitherto published should be found incorrect.'[49]

Even as they get closer to the turn to the West, Banks, the Doctor and their suite are every bit as busy as Cook, categorically categorising the newly gathered specimens, before stowing them away, ultimately to be taken all the way back to England. Everyone is busy, but no-one more than Banks, who flits between his personal work bureau and the big table where his people sit at every hour, describing, classifying and storing their finds from the Bay of Success. Every now and then, one of Banks' two greyhounds, who lie curled up under the table, opens a sleepy eye to check that its master is still in the room before the ship's rocking sends it to sleep again.

On 25 January, after four days of surprisingly fast sailing on fair winds and relatively calm conditions out of the Bay of Success, Captain Cook is on the quarter-deck enjoying a rare glimpse of clear skies when he sees it. It is the infamous Cape itself.

'It appeared not unlike an Island with a very high round Hummock upon it; this I believe to be Cape Horn, for after we had stood about 3 Leagues the weather cleared up for about a quarter of an hour, which gave us a sight of the land bearing West-South-West, but we could see no land to the Southward or Westward of it, and therefore conclude that it must be the Cape . . .'[50]

As do so many of the sailors on deck who also see that round hummock, and spread the word – *the Cape, the Cape, the Cape, we are close to it right now!*

The excitement is short-lived, however, replaced by another emotion as fog rolls in on a fresh and fierce Westerly wind and for the first time they are exposed to swells that have come across an entire ocean, with no barrier of land to break them up or break them down and . . .

And BOOOOOOOM, they are hit by one of the biggest waves since leaving England.

And now another.

And another still.

Here we go, lads, here we gooooo . . .

The wind howls. The waves rise. The bow of the *Endeavour* starts climbing up and over huge swells before crashing down the other side.

The sailors look at each other with weary, wary, eyes as the walls of black icy water keep rolling towards them. With every crash over the *Endeavour*'s bow their own bowels loosen a little and, if they're lucky, only salty spray blows into their faces. Unlucky, and there is so much water cascading over the deck they can be knocked over, and must tie ropes around their midriffs to make sure they are not swept away.

And so the terror begins. Still, Captain Cook is in his element on the quarter-deck, confident of his mighty Whitby cat.

As each wave hits the *Endeavour*, with the top of it often breaking over the ship's bow, there is a long shudder as she tries to shake it off, to settle herself for the next one. The shrieking Westerly winds lift a shriek angrier still, hissing through the rigging and tearing at the sails, even as the skies darken and regularly unleash tempest. Had this been mankind's experience when first he went to sea, he would have stayed ashore.

Above decks, the men of the *Endeavour* man their posts the best they can, a frozen band of brothers following the Master's orders to tack ship, out the maintop sails and the foretops, even as their mouths curse and their frozen fingers falter and fumble as they stand 40 feet above the swaying deck trying to untie knots that have frozen stiff and the very marrow of their souls turns to ice.

Below decks they sleep in their violently swaying hammocks in the time before their next watch, or huddle around the fire in the galley as the BOOOOOM of the waves on the bow and their sodden berths conspire to keep them awake most of the night.

Onwards they go, ever further into this endless maelstrom of appalling weather. Those coming off their four-hour watch bear a cold in them that will not cede no matter how close they huddle to the smoky fire. For the damp and cold has been seeping into everything, their fellow sailors, their meals, the decks, their bunks and hammocks, their beings. What started as a sliver of a shiver in their souls has now frozen their entire beings solid.

And yet, just as the very 'morning star' that is *the* morning star, and it must cross Cook's mind THAT THERE IT IS, *the* MORNING STAR, the thing they are going to observe the eclipse of.

Come the dawn, the dawn, the blessed dawn, when they are up and moving once more, there is some reward for their punishment. For they can see it! It is a glorious view of the barren Cape. Few Mariners have seen it this close and lived to tell the tale, and they can at least take their place among the former. The challenge will be to avoid taking their place among the latter, too. But Captain Cook's main concern now is to help to tame the Cape for future Mariners by recording its precise co-ordinates, so he and Mr Green are on deck all morning, afternoon and into the night, taking as many observations as they can.

'The Longitude of Cape Horn being deduced from no less than 24 Observations taken at no very great distance from the Cape, and on both sides of it, and when the Sun was both to the East and West of the Moon; for in this case the Errors arising from the Observations are most likely to Correct one another.'[51]

And onwards they sail, making 70 odd miles a day – on one day over 100 miles – a feat almost unheard of in these parts, where it is more common to have some days when you are blown backwards. It is the last day of January and the *Endeavour* is only 10 days out from the Bay of Success when Cook turns the ship towards the North-west. He is heading to the South Seas for the first time in his 40 years, those same seas depicted on the shilling he had taken from Mr Sanderson's till as a lad.

To the delight of Banks, particularly, curious whales appear in ever greater abundance, as do myriad seals and penguins, even as enormous albatrosses with wing-spans of up to eight feet start to swirl about, emitting their curious call, a long, high-pitched bray interspersed with low, nasal grunts.

So huge! So majestic! So many of them, gliding among the masts as they follow the ship's progress ... Loading his musket with bird-shot Banks manages – commendably without tearing holes in the sails – to bring a couple of the birds down on the deck and not in the sea. It is not long before Cook and the officers are dining on albatross and 'eat heartily' of it, so delicious – much tastier than vulture, Banks and the Doctor concur – that many reach for this avian delicacy even when there is pork left on the table, proving that the desire for fresh meat trumps idle superstition. For those who might wonder, or even follow in their wake, Banks includes his recipe for a good albatross dinner:

> The way of dressing them is thus: Skin them overnight and soak their carcases in Salt water till morn, then parboil them and throw away the water, then stew them well with very little water and when sufficiently tender serve them up with Savoury sauce.[52]

Onwards!

By 13 February, once he has confirmed they are 'now advanced about 12 degrees to the Westward of the Strait of Magellan, and 3½ degrees to the Northward of it',[53] Cook can relax a little and even feel a little pride in his ship, his men and his achievement. What had taken Wallis three months had taken Cook's mighty Whitby cat just 33 days.

Proud on the quarter-deck, he orders the men to continue the North-west course, straight through the Pacific Ocean to their destination, Tahiti.

Late February to late March 1769, the Pacific Ocean, Melancollier

Oh, the mighty Pacific!

How sweetly the sun shines, how blue is the ocean, how superb has the sailing been for nearly all of it since they had rounded Cape Horn and headed to the North-west following a straight course. Day after day, Captain Cook delights in standing on the quarter-deck and looking out at the vast expanse stretching before him, a glittering, endless plain of vast blueness.

The Pacific is . . . pacified.

Yes, the drinking water is growing stale and the men yearn for a fresh piece of fruit, but at least they have been making headway in remarkably calm waters.

Not until today, 26 February has the weather turned foul, but sure enough, here she comes as strong gales, squalls and buckets of rain batter the *Endeavour* and its crew, who slish-slosh about the deck, forever swaying in the opposite way to the natural motion of the ship and so riding it like a wild steed galloping along with the 'white horses' of the wave-tops coming from all directions. Soon, however, the wind is so strong that not even the most experienced sailors can stay erect.

'Close-reef the main topsail!'[54] Captain Cook yells through the howling winds to his Master.

The order is passed to the fore, and in no time at all agile young tars are scurrying up the ratlines – now swaying like the pendulum of a grandfather clock – to reduce the area of canvas being filled by the squalls and threatening to knock the ship over.

But then, after just two days, all returns to as it was before – clear weather and smooth waters. It is an episode that has piqued the perspicacious Captain's inquiring mind. He writes on the last day of February, 'little wind and fine clear weather; the Air full as warm as in the same Degree of North Latitude at the Correspondent Season of the Year. The South-West swells still keep up, notwithstanding the Gale hath been over about 30 Hours, a proof that there is no land near in that Quarter.'[55]

Yes, Alexander Dalrymple believes the Great Southern Land likely lies in that very quarter. Yet James Cook, with years of finely honed seafaring instincts coming into play, is becoming ever more sure that Mr Dalrymple is – how to say this quietly? – *wrong*.

As a seafarer of vast experience, he knows the clues of when a large land mass is close in a particular direction – and when there is no such land mass nearby at all. When it is close, you can tell by the types of seaweed and birds you observe. If you see a crow, raven or rook at sea, then land must be within 30 miles, as they don't cross the open seas. And even from a great distance the shape of the swell coming your way is a sure sign of what does and doesn't lie as far as a hundred horizons away. If there is a long slow swell – with broad and evenly spaced waves, then there is almost certainly no large land mass in the direction from which the swell is coming. And that is precisely what he notes now, coming from the West – the direction that Mr Dalrymple's Great Southern Land is said to lie, but of which Captain Cook can see no sign.

> March 1769 . . . we have had no Current that hath Affected the Ship since we came into these Seas. This must be a great Sign that we have been near no land of any extent, because near land are generally found Currents. I can see no reason why Currents should not be found in this Sea, supposing a Continent or lands lay not far West from us, as some have imagined, and if such land was ever seen we cannot be far from it, as we are now 560 leagues West of the Coast of Chili.[56]

For yes, Mr Dalrymple, for all your clever theories, gathered from ivory towers across the land, James Cook is rather more hands-on when it comes to understanding the world – he simply goes to see for himself – and the further they go on this voyage, the more convinced he is that no such Great Southern Land exists.

Onwards the *Endeavour* sails, the seas grow still calmer and the weather still warmer. Joseph Banks, as the senior representative of the Royal Society, is sure to note in his journal on 11 March: 'Though it had blown a steady breeze of wind these three days no sea at all was up, from whence we began to conclude that we passed the Line drawn between the Great South Sea and the Pacific ocean by the Council of the Royal Society, notwithstanding we are not yet within the tropics.'[57]

Onwards they sail in clear weather, the crew contentedly going about their work without complaint, which is no small feat for a Naval Captain commanding a hundred-odd men. Yes, Captain Cook is popular with his sailors. Yes, he commands them, and occasionally loses his temper, and very occasionally has them flogged. But in many ways he is of them, of their class, speaks like them and understands their needs. All of the things they do, he has done and sometimes even knows how to do it better. He clearly cares for them. There is no chance anyone on the ship would ever do him harm, or that there would be the rumblings of a mutiny.

Nevertheless, such is the way the Royal Navy works that there must always be a Marine on guard outside the Captain's door, right around the clock, and on this day it falls to the shy young Marine William

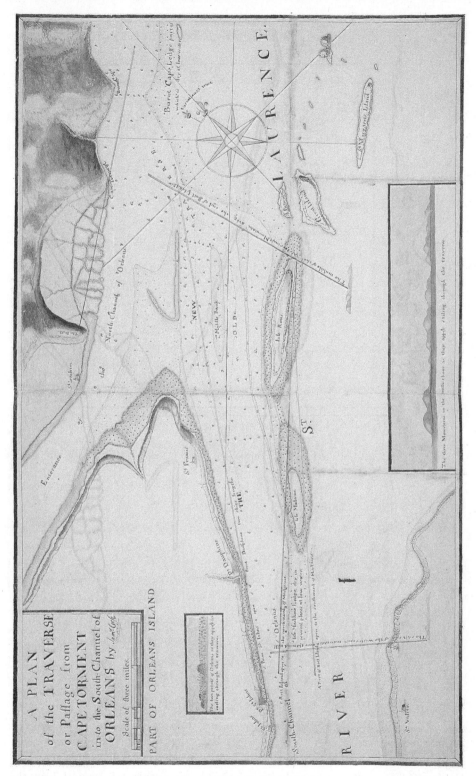

'A plan of the traverse or passage from Cape Torment into the South-Channel of Orleans' by James Cook c1759.

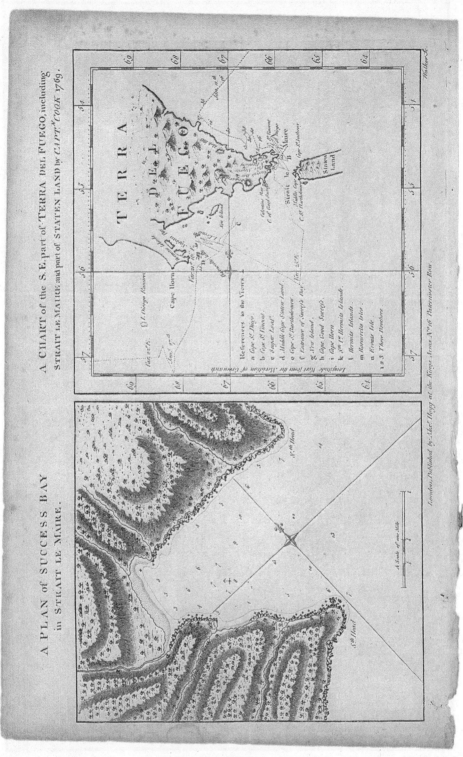

'A plan of Success Bay in Strait le Maire' and 'A chart of the S.E. part of Terra del Fuego, including Strait le Maire and part of Staten Land' by James Cook 1769.

Original held at the National Library of Australia.

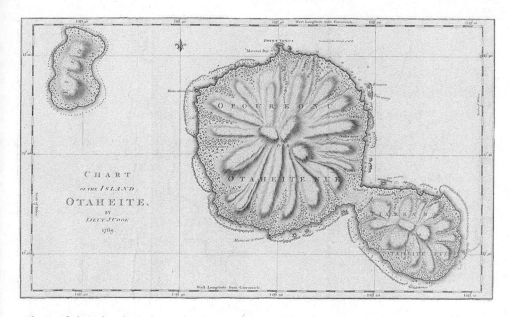

'Chart of the Island Otaheite' by James Cook 1769.

Original held at the National Maritime Museum, Greenwich, London.

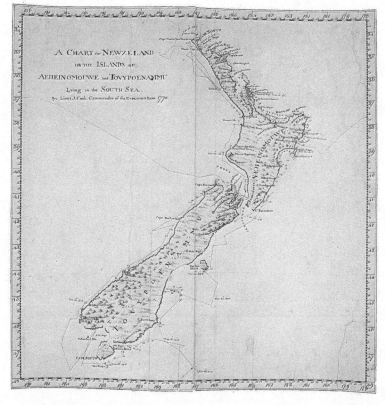

'A Chart of
New Zeland'
by James Cook,
surveyor and
Isaac Smith,
draughtsman.

Original held at the
British Library.

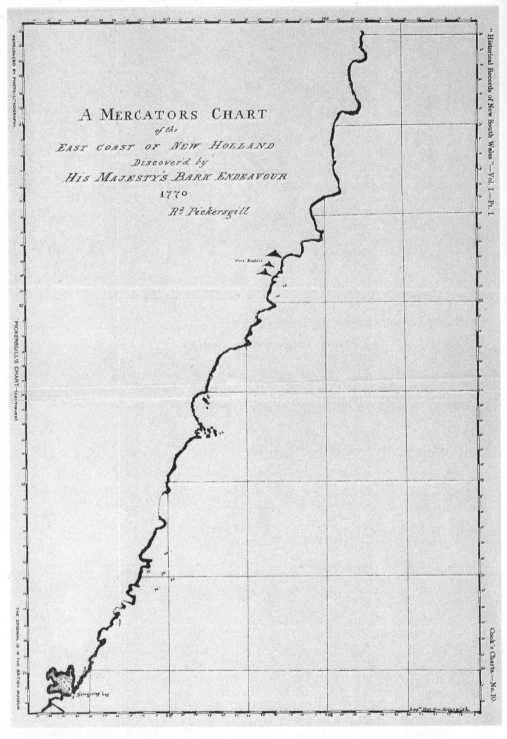

'A mercators chart [of part] of the East Coast of New Holland' by Richard Pickersgill 1770.

Published by Charles Potter, Government Printer 1893.

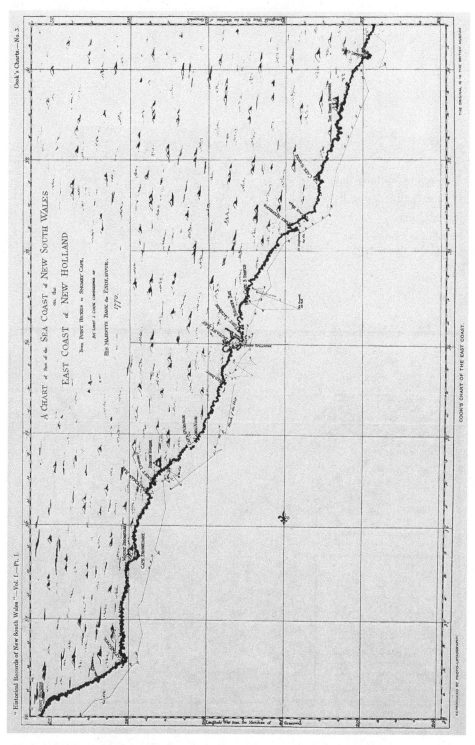

'A chart of part of the Sea Coast of New South Wales on the East Coast of New Holland from Point Hickes to Smoaky Cape' by James Cook 1770.

Published by Charles Potter, Government Printer 1893.

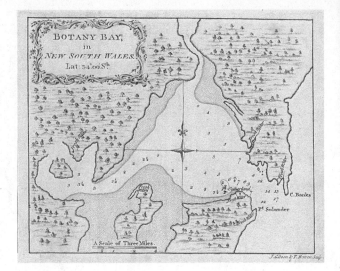

A sketch of 'Botany Bay in New South Wales' by James Cook.

Published by Charles Potter, Government Printer 1893.

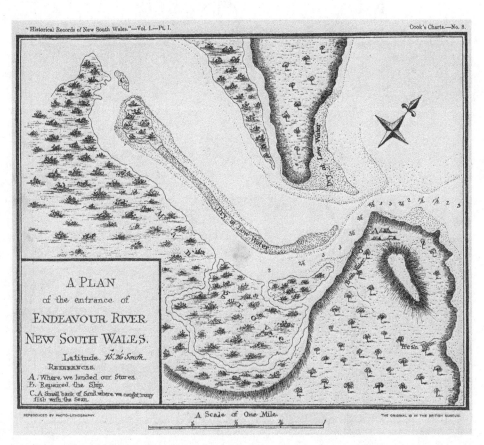

'A plan of the entrance of Endeavour River New South Wales: latitude 15°26' south' by James Cook.

Published by Charles Potter, Government Printer 1893.

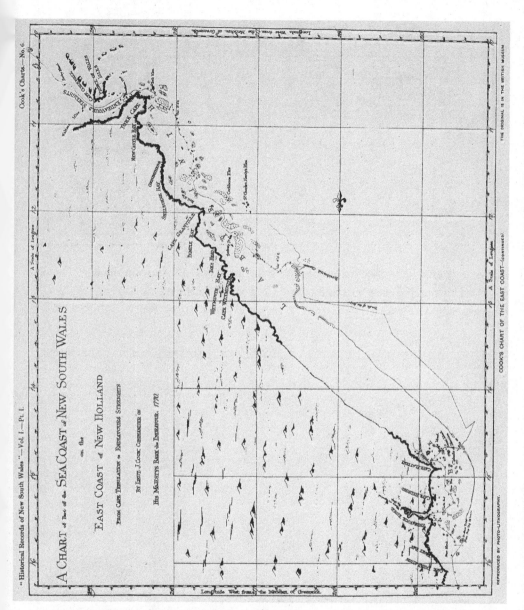

'A chart of part of the sea coast of New South Wales on the East Coast of New Holland from Cape Tribulation to Endeavours Streights' by James Cook 1770.

Published by Charles Potter, Government Printer 1893.

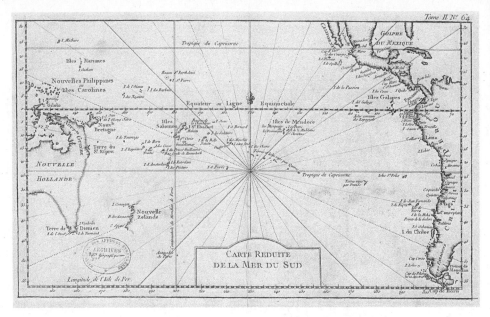

'Carte réduite de la Mer du Sud' by Nicholas Bellin c1753 showing the coastline of New Holland and New Zealand before Cook's visit to the region.

Original held at the Bibliothèque de France.

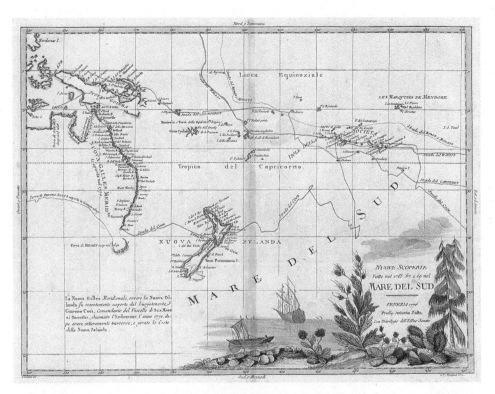

'Nuove scoperte fatte nel 1765, 67, e 69 nel Mare del Sud' by Antonio Zatta. Published in 1785 and taking into account Cook's mapping of the area.

Courtesy of Alamy.

Greenslade, that diligent and sensitive fellow who has only recently started to overcome his shyness and get into the rhythm of ship-board life. Yes, though not really given to guns or marching, or even talking, he had nevertheless joined the Marines and been the pride of the Greenslade family when he sometimes returned home on furlough, always arriving in full uniform.

So smart, William! So spick! So span!

And yet for all the excitement of going away, of being a Marine, there are few things more tedious than defending a door that no-one wishes to attack. To pass the time, young William chats idly to one of Cook's servants, William Howson, who is with great skill working on a piece of oiled sealskin, carefully cutting it up and then sewing it with twine to make tobacco pouches for several of the sailors. It is skilled work, and William admires the elegant if rustic results. Perhaps the servant might make him one?

No, William Howson will not.

But, please?

No, I shan't. These are for my sailor friends.

It is good-natured banter, no more, concluding with Greenslade remarking in jest, 'Since you refuse me so trifling a thing, I would if I could steal one from you!'[58]

At this very moment Howson is called away to do an errand for the Captain, and he leaves the sealskin in the care of William. Well, the opportunity for one of those little jokes that leaven ship-board life is too good to miss and, after looking left and right to see that he is not observed, Greenslade cuts off a small piece of sealskin to make a pouch of his own.

Alas, when William Howson returns he does not take it in good humour at all, and as a matter of fact is furious, snatching back the remaining leather and the purloined piece, but declaring, 'I will not complain to the officers for so trifling a cause.'[59]

Mortified, yet taking heart that at least he won't be reported, that would appear to be the end of the matter for young William Greenslade.

And yet, for William's fellow Marines, nearly all of whom are older than him, the opportunity is too good to miss.

Are we all in?

We are all in!

A joke? They chide young William. No, a Marine stealing is no joke. You have violated 'the honour of our Core'.[60]

The Marines don't let up on their painfully sensitive young comrade. Oh, they go on with it all right, giving him hell for leather.

'They drove the young fellow almost mad,' Banks will note, 'by representing his crime in the blackest colours as a breach of trust of the worst consequence: a theft committed by a sentry upon duty they made him think an inexcusable crime, especially when the thing stole was given into his charge.'[61]

No, no joke, boyo. It is the Sergeant of the Marines, John Edgcumbe, who – with a wink to the others when the young unfortunate is not looking – leads the attack in the Marine quarters, aft.

'If the person aggrieved will not complain,' Edgcumbe says roundly, 'I will! For the Marines should not suffer scandal from the ill behaviour of *one*.'[62]

What will Captain Cook do? A flogging? Of course.

By now, William is a shambling wreck, begging leave to retire to his hammock. The sergeant gruffly agrees, but allows him only a few minutes respite before he goes to where William is silently weeping and barks: 'Mr Greenslade, follow me up on deck!'[63]

The other Marines can barely hold it all in, as the sergeant solemnly heads above deck, followed by the quaking Greenslade looking like a beaten dog on a tight leash behind its master. A few minutes later the sergeant returns alone, and asks, 'Where is Greenslade?'[64]

But he was with you, Sergeant?

Yes, but once we got up on deck, I looked around and he was gone. He was simply not there.

. . .

. . .

. . .

It is one of the cleverer Marines who comes up with the solution.

'I think he has gone to the head!'[65]

Laughter.

Of course.

The privy – the 'seat of ease' on the bow, a double plank with a hole cut in it, extending over the side of the ship – where else would he be? The lad's literally shitting himself with fear.

. . .

They wait.

. . .

. . .

And wait.

. . .

. . .

. . .

But when, after 10 minutes, young William does not return, it is obvious that something is amiss. Perhaps he has gone into a dead faint somewhere?

The deck is quickly searched, for no result. Below deck is searched, no William Greenslade.

The search continues for half an hour, as one by one all the nooks and crannies on the ship are eliminated, with a dreadful fear starting to crystallise and now grow to an undeniable conviction. If he is not on this ship, he must have . . . jumped to his death. It is the only explanation. He preferred suicide to the horror of facing the consequences of the 'dishonour' he has brought to his uniform and to his family.

The shaken Marines – it was a joke! – can scarcely believe it. With great sorrow, but an eye to pointing out his own blamelessness, Captain Cook records in his log, 'I was neither made acquainted with the Theft or the Circumstances attending it, until the Man was gone.'[66]

Cook records the death as having occurred, 'by accident or design'.[67] It is a calculated ambiguity. Yes, as suicide is a mortal sin, it is clearly kinder to his memory and to his family to note the possibility that the death was caused by an accident.

Banks is affected badly, sadly writing young Greenslade's epitaph in his journal: 'He was a very young man scarce 21 years of age, remarkably quiet and industrious, and to make his exit the more melancholy was drove to the rash resolution by an accident so trifling that it must appear incredible to everybody who is not well acquainted with the powerful effects that *shame* can work upon young minds.'[68]

In fact, not just shame, but the effects of long months in a confined space at sea, where as well as the threat of scurvy to the body there is the menace of madness to the mind in some measure, worn down by dull routine interspersed with stormy terror; with eating stinking salty sea biscuits that never quell their hunger but only make them thirsty; with drinking stale water that never slakes their thirst; with sharing their hammocks with lice that feast on them as they try to sleep, with rodents that scuttle and scurry around the lower decks.

Even the up spirits tune from the Bosun's whistle can barely lift the unoccupied jacks out of their hammocks to receive their half-pint, let alone lift them out of their gloom.

Yes, the sooner they reach Tahiti and leave the mental crucible of a ship at sea the better . . .

Late March 1769, approaching Tahiti, sweet birds of paradise

On such long hauls, Captain Cook, as ever, ensures that his men are kept so busy that the tropical torpor cannot seep into their bones. There will be no laxness on his watch, and he is indeed watching all the time, even when you think he's not. Cleanliness! Ventilation! Air the hammocks! Scrub the decks! And prepare for gun drills!

And so they do, with the ship's company at least encouraged when those who had visited Tahiti before note flocks of what they call 'Egg Birds' fly by, a very distinctive kind of bird they had noted on their previous trip there. They must be getting close!

•

Again, Master Molineux, *again*!

In the face of the Master's wretched propensity for drunkenness – particularly in these benign times, where the weather lends itself to torpor once more, and both officers and men have many more hours in the day than duties – Captain Cook is eager to keep them all, and Master Molineux in particular, as busy as possible.

Which is why this day, as many days, the tropical torpor is regularly shattered by the sound of both small arms fire, and the boom of cannon. Against the possibility of encountering Natives who do not understand the expectation upon them to cede territory and resources without a fight, both sailors and Marines must practise priming, loading and firing their muskets.

As the orders ring out, the men move with martial rhythm.

Prime and load. Taking their cartridges – paper tubes filled with a measure of gunpowder and a musket ball – they place it in the barrel.

Make ready. Using their ramrod, they push the contents tightly together at the bottom of the barrel. Now the firing pan on top of the barrel is opened, and more gunpowder poured into it.

Present. They 'cock the piece', pulling back the hammer so that when they pull the trigger, it will fall, and the flint upon it will strike the frizzen, causing the spark to ignite the gunpowder. They aim, looking down the barrel.

Fire! They pull the trigger, and the musket is fired. Occasionally, the powder simply burns off, without firing the ball, an event known as a 'flash in the pan'.

And now, under the command of Gunner Stephen Forwood, the men move into their nominated gun crews to also fire the cannon. No. 1 is usually one of the Midshipmen, in command of the gun, who aims it by looking along the barrel before barking out orders. No. 2 is the sponge man, whose duty is to scrub the inside of the barrel before and after each shot, to damp out burning embers. No. 3 loads the cannon by placing a bag of gunpowder and the cannonball in the barrel then ramming them down it. Through the touch hole (which is at the opposite end to the barrel's mouth) the No. 4 pricks the bag that the No. 3 has placed in the barrel. He now pours a measure of powder into the touch hole. And now upon the command of No. 1, the No. 5 lights the match and brings it to the touch hole where the gunpowder explodes, propelling the ball out of the barrel at about 1400 feet a second.

And so the result.

Momentarily, from a distance, the *Endeavour* looks and sounds on a sunny day like a ghost ship lost from Sir Francis Drake's flotilla, firing upon a vision of the Spanish Armada that only it can see. Puffs of smoke sprout from its side, as volleys ring out and out to starboard and port, enormous splashes rise as the cannonballs hit.

The *Endeavour* sails on, supreme, the ghosts of the Spanish Armada quelled for another day. Master Molineux reaches for a drink.

•

As for deterring the dreaded scurvy, Cook is continuing to closely follow the Admiralty's dietary instructions. In early April, not far from their destination – the much-anticipated Tahiti – Cook records with pride: 'The Ship's company had in general been very healthy, owing in a great measure to the Sauerkraut, Portable Soup and Malt . . . By this means, and the Care and Vigilance of Mr. Monkhouse, the Surgeon, this disease was prevented from getting a footing in the Ship.'[69]

The Care and Vigilance of Surgeon's Mate William Perry, however, is not recorded, despite the young man's keen observations and attention to several of the poorly, as proudly recorded by Perry himself, 'At Terra del Fuego we collected wild celery, and every morning our breakfast was made of this herb and ground wheat and portable soup. January, 1769, we passed Cape Horn, all our men as free from scurvy as on our sailing from Plymouth.'[70]

There is a notable exception, alas. When Joseph Banks develops pimples on the inside of his mouth, and swollen gums, he quickly moves to have no less than six ounces of lemon juice added to every kind of liquor he drinks. 'The effect of this was surprising,' Banks records. 'In less than a week my gums became as firm as ever and at this time I am troubled with nothing but a few pimples on my face which have not deterred me from leaving off the juice entirely.'[71]

•

Tell us again, Master's Mate Charlie Clerke!

The closer the *Endeavour* gets to Tahiti, the better and more lurid the stories of buxom Tahitian princesses. Their *breasts*, lads! Their *skills*! And they're all just there, waiting for us. Midshipman James Magra – more often than not drunk – joins in, his American accent lingering over the more lascivious of the words used. And of course the two biggest drinkers on the ship – Master Molineux and the old sailmaker John Ravenhill – while engaged in their nightly battle to see who can drink who under the table, also contribute raunchy reminiscences.

James Cook has no interest in this aspect of Tahiti. All he cares about is executing his orders from the Admiralty efficiently, and doing all he can now to prepare for their arrival on the island. To this end, he invites Lieutenant Gore and Master Molineux to the Great Cabin, asking them one last time to tell all they know about their destination.

Beyond the produce they may find – 'the bread-fruit and apple trees were planted in rows on the declivity of the hills, and the cocoa nut and plantain, which require more moisture, on the level ground'[72] – Gore explains – the quality of the anchorage and the wood and watering arrangements used by Captain Wallis, they tell of one old Tahitian man in particular, a man by the name of Owhaa.

'He was of service to us,'[73] says Lieutenant Gore to his earnest Captain, who sits at the head of the table, nodding in silence, taking it all in but offering no response. Gore tells of an expedition he made into the inland, guided by Owhaa.

'As soon as I got onshore, I called upon our old man and took him with us,'[74] Lieutenant Gore goes on. He tells his Captain that when they were startled by a group of Tahitians who appeared shouting, looking down on them from a hilltop, they made for their weapons, but, he explains, 'our old man, seeing us rise hastily, and look to our arms, beckoned us to sit still, and immediately went up to the people who had surprised us'.[75]

Captain Cook nods, but again says nothing. Sometimes, Lieutenant Gore can tell such stories in a way that seem to almost lord it over the Captain for the fact that he, the American, has already circumnavigated the world *twice*, with many a story to tell, and though he does not have the rank of James Cook, he certainly has the personality which draws men to him and makes them want to follow him. Captain Cook is slightly wary of him, and even resentful.

'As soon as he joined them they were silent,' Gore continues, 'and soon after disappeared; in a short time, however, they returned and brought with them a large hog ready roasted, with plenty of bread-fruit, yams, and other refreshments, which they gave to the old man, who distributed them among our people. In return for this treat, I gave them some nails, buttons, and other things, with which they were greatly delighted.'[76]

Captain Cook smiles and nods once more. With any luck, they will meet this man again.

On 11 April, sailing on a calm sea at sunset, the sky streaked with brilliant pinks and oranges, the men get their first look at Tahiti, or what Wallis called King George III's Island. Banks records, 'at sunset Georges Land appeared plain though we had not neared it much: since the clouds went from the tops of the hills it appeared less high than it did though it certainly is very high'.[77] He takes a moment to rejoice, adding: 'I am now on the brink of going ashore after a long passage thank god in as good health as man can be.'[78]

Now that the vision of their destination is before their very eyes, and given the rumours and restlessness of his men, eager to meet these fabled sirens of the Pacific, James Cook takes a moment to not just honour the 'Hints' given him by the Royal Society's president, James Douglas, the Earl of Morton (though Cook knows not that Morton had died six months earlier), but to make sure their supply of beads and nails, which they will need to conserve to conduct ongoing trade throughout their stay on the island, does not deteriorate too rapidly. As he notes in his journal, demonstrating his grasp of economic supply and demand well before it is even articulated by Adam Smith: 'I thought it very necessary that some order should be observed in [trading] with the

Natives, that such Merchandize as we had on board for that purpose might continue to bear a proper value, and not leave it to everyone's own particular fancy, which could not fail to bring on Confusion and Quarrels between us and the Natives, and would infallibly lessen the value of such Articles as we had to [trade] with.'[79]

And so Cook writes, and posts on the mast, formal rules of behaviour for the men while on Tahiti:

> Rules to be observed by every person in or belonging to His Majesty's Bark the Endeavour . . .
> 1. To endeavour by every fair means to Cultivate a Friendship with the Natives, and to treat them with all imaginable humanity.
> 2. No Officer or Seaman or other person belonging to the Ship, excepting such as are so appointed, shall Trade or offer to Trade for any sort of Provisions, Fruit or other Productions of the Earth, unless they have my leave so to do.
> 3. Every Person employed on shore on any duty whatsoever is strictly to attend to the same, and if by neglect he looses any of His Arms or working Tools, or suffers them to be stole, the full value thereof will be charged against his pay . . . and he shall receive such further punishment as the nature of the Offence may deserve.
> 4. The same Penalty will be inflicted upon every person who is found to Embezzle, Trade, or Offer to Trade with any of the Ship's Stores of what Nature so ever.
> 5. No sort of Iron or anything that is made of Iron, or any sort of Cloth or other useful or necessary Articles, are to be given in Exchange for anything but Provisions.
>
> J.C.[80]

CHAPTER SIX

ARRIVING IN TAHITI

The country has the most delightful and romantic appearance that can be imagined.[1]

Captain Samuel Wallis, the first European to visit
Tahiti, aboard the *Dolphin*, June 1767

I have nowhere seen such elegant women as those of Otaheite. Such the Grecians were from whose model the Venus of Medici was copied undistorted by bandages, nature has full liberty the growing form in whatever direction she pleases and amply does she repay this indulgence in producing such forms as exist here only in marble or canvas . . .[2]

Joseph Banks, 1773

Late afternoon, 12 April 1769, Tahiti, the Garden of Eden with many Eves, by the sea

Land ho!

From the West, the rays of the setting sun paint the cloud that wraps the peak of a soaring mountain. First a yellow tinge, then orange, pink and finally a vivid red – while below it all sits an unchanging emerald green. Ten leagues off and closing, Captain Cook orders the Master, Robert Molineux – as badly hungover from his heavy drinking as ever – to sound the depths as the deep Pacific blue of the ocean gives way to crystalline turquoise waters and brilliant coral reefs all around . . .

Tahiti! An island that time forgot, in a timeless ocean. Beyond the sparkling translucence, the white waves break onto the reef, before lapping onto the sands of the beach, even as the palm trees lining the beach wave a verdant welcome and, beyond them again, the darker green valleys and ridges rise up and up to volcanic peaks. With his artist's eyes, the waifish Scot Sydney Parkinson surveys the splendid scene, jotting in his notepad: 'The land appeared as uneven as a piece of crumpled paper, being irregularly divided into hills and valleys; but a beautiful verdure covered both, even to the tops of the highest peaks.'[3]

They are a few leagues from the island when they spot the first canoes cutting through the water towards the *Endeavour* as she nudges into Matavai Bay.

As expertly carved as they are handled, these vessels are the product of aeons of ancestral knowledge, of which these Natives – their white teeth gleaming, their brown bodies covered with beautifully arranged black markings – are simply the latest recipients. The bottoms of their boats are heavy with cocoa nuts and plantains, and a few papaya, ready for trade.

Every man not occupied furling the *Endeavour*'s sails pushes to the bow as it in turn pushes the cascading clear waters to either side to get a better look. For this, they have been told by the likes of Lieutenant John Gore, Master Robert Molineux and Master's Mate Dick Pickersgill, is a land like nowhere else on Earth, a sailor's fancy, a heaven made real by some divine happenstance. *And here. It. Is!*

Within half a mile of the shore, Captain Cook gives his nod.

'Let go the anchor!' comes the Bosun's cry.

The men release the anchor with a resounding splash, followed by the familiar whirr of the unfurling rope, a coarse hessian snake chasing the metal shank down to the bottom.

The idlers among the jack tars, meanwhile – those not on watch – continue to crowd the gunwale, staring in sheer slack-jaw awe at the first few canoes coming towards them from the shore, filled to bursting with laughing, chattering, black-marked Tahitians, men and women – *glorious* women – who stand swaying in their vessels like they were born on them, waving the broad green fronds of the plantain tree.

Standing right beside Captain Cook, Lieutenant John Gore is bemused to note a rare show of emotion from their Commander; he's actually smiling broadly as he takes in the marvellous scene. They have come a long way, faced many trials, but here they are and, as a beginning, it is everything they could ever have hoped for. For once, just for once, the Captain lets go of his modest upbringing, his moderate nature, his Quaker immersion, his by-the-book, steady-as-she-goes, Royal Navy manner, and displays something close to joy as he contemplates the sheer aching beauty of this place. All those years ago, when he had swapped his dull shilling for his master's shiny South Sea shilling, he could never have dreamt that the actuality would be *this* beautiful.

The jewel of the South Pacific shines before him, its inhabitants bartering their goods, and he would not trade the moment for anything in the world.

He is here at last. Here they will crane their necks and stare to the heavens.

The Transit of Venus approaches.

•

They are coming!

~~Va'a tele~~! ~~Huge canoes~~!

The canoes are beautifully constructed, carved from Tahitian chestnut, with proud ornamental prows like the tips of the goddess Nike's wings, moving so fast through the water that the feathers of red – the colour of the deities, employed to symbolise the impersonal otherworldly power, the *mana*, of the Gods – hanging from those prows are nigh horizontal in the wind as the 20 Natives in each canoe thrust their oars in the water in synchronised strokes, surging forward with every splash from the flash of their efforts.

Riding in the wake of each large craft are smaller canoes – some simple, some double-hulled, some with sails and clever wooden out-rigging. All are managed expertly by their broad-chested handlers, to the apparent delight of the bare-chested women sprinkled among their complement.

Within moments, there are swarms of these flying vessels! Like an armada of eager seagulls, coming at them across the water, with the paddles flashing high and brightly in the sun before hurtling down and splashing water along the side of their canoes.

'*Tyos?*'[4] those in the first canoes shout up at the incredulous sailors.

Lieutenant Gore, who has spent a little over a month here on his last voyage, translates. *Tyos* means *friends*!

Yes, friends!

After all, how could you not want to be friends with these bare-breasted beauties, these lithe, gorgeous, voluptuous maidens smiling up at them – even more gorgeous than the sailors had dared to imagine.

Typically, while James Cook focuses on what clothing the Tahitians wear – 'a Piece of Cloth or Matting wrapped 2 or 3 times round their waist, and hangs down below their Knees, both behind and before, like a Petticoat'[5] – Joseph Banks is more interested in what the 'soft sex'[6] do not wear. He compares the Tahitian women before him with the women he is used to courting back in England: 'not squeezed as our women are by a cincture which scarce less tenacious than Iron at best but imitates an exaggerated smallness of waist, an artificial beauty not founded at all on the principles of nature . . .'.[7]

No, these are natural beauties with dresses to show off the same: 'Such Dresses are universally to be seen in antique Statues and gems and in the work of the best Italian Painters who . . . Clothed their goddesses and angels in loose folds of Cloth not shaped to their bodies exactly as the Otahiteans now wear theirs.'[8]

Venus de Medicis all.

After more calling and gesticulating between the deck and the canoes, it is established that the newcomers are from the same kingdom as their first visitor, Captain Wallis, from *Pretanie* – and not the second visitor who arrived some eight moons later, in ships commanded by the one called Bougainville, from *Fransa*, France. (Not that the men of the *Endeavour* know about the latter's visit at all.)

And so the white men begin to trade, the Natives whooping with glee when they produce the item that appears to most attract their fancy; as Cook chronicles, 'beads, particularly white cut glass beads'.[9]

Joseph Banks is struck by the civility of this sun-kissed folk who 'traded very quietly and civilly for beads chiefly, in exchange for which they gave Cocoa nuts Bread fruit both roasted and raw some small fish and apples'.[10]

Resplendent in tricorn hat and gold trim navy coat, Captain Cook steps forward. It is imperative to show the Natives that he is the Chief of this ship. He motions to the eldest man among the Natives, the man with the flowing white beard, whose name is Owhaa.

Come aboard.

Climbing up the ladder and onto the quarter-deck the dignified old Native embraces Lieutenant Gore in the manner of an old friend, as they even exchange words in a strange, lyrical language beyond most of the *Endeavour* crew's remotest comprehension.

Cook is eager to ingratiate himself with Owhaa, 'thinking he might on some occasions be of use to us'.[11] All is going well until they hear a spot of yelling and disagreement elsewhere on the ship. Those Natives who haven't been welcomed aboard don't seem to care too much about getting an invite. The boldest of the men on the canoes have begun to climb the newly taut ropes mooring the ship in place, clambering up with a grace and dexterity that the white men could never dream of.

Hey! Get offa there, you buggers!

The Natives are not dissuaded by all the shouting and carry on, and soon find themselves standing aboard the great hulk of the *Endeavour*, a far cry from the sleek vessels they have floating below.

Soon enough the *Endeavour* is positively swarming with incorrigible yet friendly Natives, poking and prodding at the strange objects scattered around the deck. They pinch and pull at the skin of these strange white men, curious how anybody could be so very pale. But where are the women? Oh. You don't have any with you? Just like the last lot of white men. Poor men. *Strange* men.

Just *look* at them. These ghostly beings swarm with lice, have fewer teeth than fingers – with survivors rotting and black – their strange skin is covered in pock-marks, and they smell like . . . like . . . Well, frankly, there's nothing the Tahitians have to compare it to for, as a people who bathe three times daily, they just aren't capable of smells like that. These are men whelped and whipped in cold slums, icy hells next to the Arcadia they find themselves in now. Cook's men can hardly contain themselves when the Tahitian women reach out to touch their strange white skin and the curious shape of their noses. Encouraged, feeling a little bolder, the men respond in kind and begin to touch the women, with a particular focus on their breasts. Shockingly, their hands are not slapped away!

Watching on, Joseph Banks' alabaster complexion turns as red as the feathers on the prows of the Tahitian canoes. Has he found Arcadia?

•

As trading between Cook's men and the Natives goes on – a veritable floating market engulfing the *Endeavour*, Natives hooting at the sight of every bead produced from the white men's pockets – the ship's boats are hoisted from their position on deck, and lowered to the busy water below.

Taking old man Owhaa along with them, Captain Cook, Lieutenant Gore, Joseph Banks, Dr Solander and their retinue, including all 11 armed Marines, are rowed towards the shore. As they leave, Lieutenant Gore notices some of the sailors – their eyes like saucers, clearly contemplating just how good it will taste, roasted – haggling over the price of a succulent-looking pig. How much?

Well, how about a nice hatchet, made of sturdy iron and good for cutting down whatever you like? The Natives seem impressed and the deal is all but done before Lieutenant Gore intercedes.

'They will never lower their price,'[12] Gore calls to them, so set the bar low and set that hatchet down.

Cook and company row to a spot indicated by the old man, where dozens of Natives, mostly men, have gathered on the beach.

Captain Cook records, 'No one of the Natives made the least opposition at our landing, but came to us with all imaginable Marks of Friendship and Submission.'[13]

One Native comes graciously forward and offers a green plantain frond to the Captain.

'It is a token of peace,'[14] Gore tells them.

Following Lieutenant Gore's suggestions, Cook accepts the frond, puts his hand on his chest and says, 'Tyos' – before every one of the visiting Englishmen follows the Natives in gathering up a green frond of his own.

Owhaa leads them up the beach, the Native man barefooted, moving with ease while the Captain and his men are constrained to a stilted gait, their shiny black shoes sinking into the bleached white sand with every step. Arriving at a clearing in the trees behind the beach, the Tahitians scrape the ground clean of all small plants that grow upon it, and then throw their fronds down, indicating that the white men should do the same.

Captain Cook has the Marines lead the way, marching in formation to drop their fronds atop the Tahitians', followed by the rest of the *Endeavour*'s men on shore.

'And thus,' Banks notes simply, 'peace was concluded.'[15]

Now, James Cook looks to Owhaa and makes a drinking signal by bringing his thumb to his mouth.

Water. We need water. Owhaa understands and leads them off to the place where Wallis had watered in 1767. Cook nods in approval, and directs his men to follow the old man into the woods. As they move, Cook and his men realise their jaunt has become quite the parade, with a number of joyous Natives following in their wake. 'In this manner,' Banks chronicles, 'we walked for 4 or 5 miles under groves of Cocoa nut and bread-fruit trees loaded with a profusion of fruit and giving the most grateful shade I have ever experienced, under these were the habitations of the people most of them without walls.'[16]

Joseph Banks is stunned! In all of his years spent studying the natural world, never has he seen such luxuriant surrounds, such exotic plantations. Just look at this bread-fruit! Bread growing from a tree! It's no wonder the Tahitians smile so broadly, exemplars of fine health.

And the women. So forthcoming . . . so amorous!

Lieutenant Gore – with the slightly superior and worldly wise air of one who has seen it all before – enjoys watching the gentlemen's faces light up as they move through the country, receiving attention from women, a wondrous glee written into their expressions. Ah, but they have seen nothing yet!

14 April 1769, Matavai Bay, Tahiti, I spy with my fiery eye

Just one day and the *Endeavour* and her people are transformed. Welcome to Tahiti. The ship's company are helping themselves with great enthusiasm to the luscious delights of Tahiti brought to the ship in their dozens. (Not to forget some of the fruit these delights carry with them.)

James Cook wakes early, and climbs up to the quarter-deck. The first suggestions of daylight have reached the night sky, faint blue flecks on the horizon are heralding the approaching dawn. As the sun rises, he glances to the West to see another armada of canoes filled with Natives who are soon swarming over the *Endeavour*. Two Chiefs among them invite Captain Cook to join them on a trip to shore.

So Cook gives the order for the ship's boats to be lowered and, accompanied by a retinue of gentlemen and their cadre of Marines, he is rowed Westward, whence their latest lot of visitors had appeared, landing at a place Wallis had marked on his chart as 'Canoe Harbour'.

James Cook has barely put his toe on the shore when he is surrounded by eager and friendly Natives. They have apparently lost their reservations of the previous day, and are so familiar as to reach into the white men's pockets and help themselves to the contents. It takes an extended brouhaha of confused conversation and gesticulation from the white men to have their items returned before the two Chiefs lead them up the beach, through the trees to a 'long house'.[17] They are conducted inside, where they must go through the greeting ceremony with the plantain fronds that attend every fresh acquaintance. With friendship established, Banks records, 'Mats were spread and we were desired to set down fronting an old man who we had not before seen.'[18]

The man before them is older than the rest. Older, but nonetheless strong; a huge and handsome man of great bearing, he sits straight backed, his arms covered in the intricate black images of their culture.

In a deep, rumbling voice that sounds like menacing thunder, this new Chief gives an order to one of his servants, who returns with a cock and a hen, which are presented to James Cook and Joseph Banks, who sits eagerly alongside the Captain, wishing his own important pedigree to be acknowledged even in these far-off lands. How frustrating it is that the Royal Navy has uniforms to indicate rank, but Mr Banks has only fine cloth and finer manners to advertise his superiority. The Tahitian women have already noted Joseph Banks' good looks and have correctly guessed that Banks would much rather attend to matters that require no uniform whatsoever.

Banks records the scene: 'Then a piece of Cloth was presented to each of us perfumed after their manner not disagreeably which they took great pains to make us understand.'[19]

A young woman helps Mr Banks to unfurl his gift, all 11 by two yards of it. In return, Banks unties his laced silk neckcloth, plucks the linen handkerchief from his breast pocket and offers her both, cupped in two open palms.

'After this ceremony was over,' Banks chronicles delicately, 'we walked freely about several large houses attended by the ladies who showed us all kind of civilities our situation could admit of, but as there were no places of retirement, the houses being entirely without walls, we had not an opportunity of putting their politeness to every test that maybe some of us would not have failed to have done had circumstances been more favourable . . .'[20]

It is really quite breath-taking. These gorgeous, voluptuous women are actually pointing to the mats, suggesting the men lie down with them and even 'sometimes by force seating themselves and us upon them they plainly showed that they were much less jealous of observation than we were'.[21]

Surely not even Arcadia boasted such available favours? Is there another place on Earth where the sun shines so bright, but the fresh water flows so crystal clear and freely? Where the fruit is so rich, the juice so sweet, and the maidens so free and *available* with their charms? Right to the point of making love in daylight?

'In short the scene we saw was the truest picture of an Arcadia of which we were going to be kings that the imagination can form.'[22]

A meal is offered with another Chief and they are soon cross-legged on the ground, along with the Captain and the Chief – sitting side by side – when arrives a parade of delectable foods – 'broiled fish, Cocoa Nuts'[23] and more, all served with 'great hospitality'.[24]

Following the Chief's lead, James Cook allows one of the Native women to sit by him. Pulling a steaming piece of fish from the bounty before them, she dips it into a cocoa-nut shell filled with saltwater, the Tahitian dressing of choice. Slowly, she brings the dripping fish up to the Captain's lips, lips he parts only just enough to accept the morsel. Surely Elizabeth wouldn't mind this, a gesture so benign?

Now, as Cook follows the Chief's example, so too do the men follow his and eagerly permit the Native women to take up seats near them. Yes, these generous ladies intend to hand-feed the crew no differently to the Chief. Not like this back home, was it? Banks is already swallowing a mouthful when he feels a hovering presence. Looming almost, and soon enough squatting right next to him.

'Our chief's own wife (ugly enough in conscience),' he realises. And just as he is reckoning what to do with the Chief's wife, who clearly wants them to be more than mere *tyos*, he spots 'among the common crowd a very pretty girl with a fire in her eyes'.[25]

That's the girl for him. Not the Chief's, ahem, less attractive wife, who is currently writhing gently next to him as she raises fish to his mouth.

'Unconscious of the dignity of my companion,' Banks writes in his journal, 'I beckoned to the other who after some entreaties came and sat on the other side of me: I was then desirous of getting rid of my former companion so I ceased to attend to her and loaded my pretty girl with beads and every present I could think pleasing to her.'[26]

The Chief's wife stands up in a display of great disgust and deep offence . . . only to sit back down just as quickly, this time even closer to Joseph Banks. She doubles her efforts and expressions of lust, feeding Banks even more fish and pouring sweet cocoa-nut milk directly into his mouth.

Alas, alas, just when Banks is on the point of spiriting the fiery one away, Dr Solander cries out, '*My spyglass!*'

His spyglass is missing. *Stolen!*

Uproar . . .

Thieves! Curs!

The feast erupts in a frenzy of explanations, justifications and lost translations.

In all the excitement, Surgeon Monkhouse finds himself craving a sniff of snuff, and defying his Captain's orders reaches into his pocket . . . only to find his snuff box missing.

The Chief orders his men to go at once in pursuit of anything that might be missing, reaching forward and grabbing a cocoa nut as he speaks in the Tahitian tongue. The Natives, seeing their Chief reaching for something that could easily be thrown in their direction, turn in unison and flee into the woods, post-haste. All that remain are 'only the chief his three wives and two or three better dressed than the rest'.[27]

'The chief,' Cook records, 'seemed very much concerned for what had happened, and by way of recompense offered us but everything that was in his House; but we refused to accept of anything, and made signs to him that we only wanted the things again.'[28]

Soon enough, the Chief's men return with one of the stolen articles. William Monkhouse lets out a heavy sigh, as he opens the box; it's still full. An addict reunited with his vice, Monkhouse brings the tobacco powder to his nose and takes a sharp sniff. Ahhhh. Much better. The Natives look on in bewilderment. What is *that*?

The Chief moves on to the Doctor, as Banks records: 'The Cloth was as resolutely forced upon Dr Solander as a recompense for his loss.'[29] They have not recovered his spyglass.

There is a polite back and forth followed by endless offers of compensatory gifts, yes, yes thank you, but if they cannot return the spyglass, then it is surely time to leave.

The Captain, his gentlemen and their Marines trudge along the beach back to their boat, all the while thinking up English names for the Chiefs. (They had not thought to learn their real names.) The first Chief, the taller one, had such a commanding presence, he was such an imposing fellow ... *Hercules*, he would be, after that semi-divine Greek hero. And the other, his sense of justice! A just soul through and through. *Lycurgus* seemed fitting, after the lawgiver of ancient Sparta.

The whole experience has a mythic feel to it, as though they have stumbled upon a legendary peoples hitherto undiscovered by the rest of the world.

'We returned to the ship,' Joseph Banks records, 'admiring a policy at least equal to any we had seen in civilised countries, exercised by people who have never had any advantage but mere natural instinct uninstructed by the example of any civilised country.'[30]

As for James Cook, he is invigorated, or as he records with typical reserve, 'about six o'clock in the evening we returned on board, very well satisfied with our little Excursion'.[31]

15 April 1769, the *Endeavour*, line in the sand, death in the sun

Hercules and Lycurgus come aboard with the dawn, bearing hogs, breadfruit, plantains and more. Cook responds in kind: hatchets, linen and beautiful glass beads, all of them among England's finest. Their friendly trades complete, the Chiefs row back towards the West, both parties richer for having met.

After ordering wood and water parties to head ashore and the rest of the crew to scrub the decks, mend the sails and tend the ship, Captain Cook, Mr Green, Mr Banks, Dr Solander and the Marines are rowed ashore. A sandy spit, Cook supposes, will be the ideal spot to observe the Transit of Venus.

Cook and his men climb up from the beach to the flat piece of land on the point, known to the Tahitians as *Te Auroa*. As they rise higher, their view widens and Cook finds he was correct. It *is* ideal. Satisfied, Cook writes, 'I therefore, without delay, resolved to pitch upon some spot upon the North-East point of the Bay, properly situated for observing the Transit of Venus, and at the same time under the command of the Ship's Guns, and there to throw up a small fort for our defence.'[32]

For yes, despite the Royal welcome they have received, he is taking no chances.

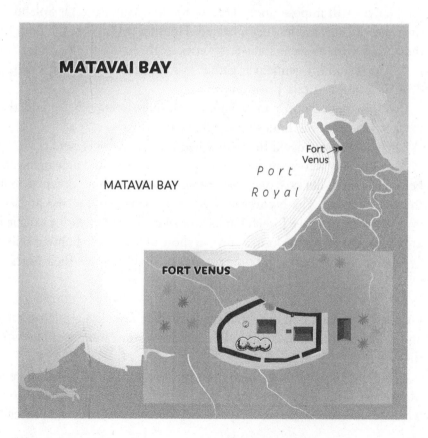

•

After pitching the tent, Joseph Banks brings his musket to bear. Turning it upside down, he uses the butt for yet another purpose, bending down to draw a literal line in the sand. Hundreds of Natives have gathered. What is he doing with the thunder-stick? According to Tahitian lore, the Tahitian people have been here for countless moons, likely centuries, and these English for only a couple of days, but this line asserts that you Tahitians are no longer allowed to set foot beyond this line on this point, which goes right across, from beach to beach – or you risk facing the angry end of this musket.

Owhaa translates and, as Banks notes, 'They obeyed instantly and not a man attempted to set a foot within it, above two hours were spent so and not the least disorder being committed.'[33]

Encouraged, Captain Cook decides to go for a stroll in the woods. He was surprised yesterday to learn that Lieutenant Hicks had been forbidden from venturing so far and is now curious to find out what limits the Natives will impose upon *him*. As for Mr Banks and Dr Solander, their motivations are less complicated. Hunting enthusiasts the both of them, they wish to see if some stray hogs might be roaming around . . .

As Cook and his gentlemen gather in readiness to head off, Owhaa does his utmost to talk them out of it.

But Cook cares not, and orders his Marines to stay and guard the marked land that the English have claimed as theirs.

They have just crossed the river when . . . a shot rings out.

The Tahitians accompanying Cook's party hit the ground only moments before . . . three ducks – one, two, three – come crashing down with a thud, not far off. The Natives stay close to the ground, terror in their eyes. Cook turns to see Joseph Banks lowering his musket with a satisfied grin. He'd got all his ducks in a row – a show of his superb hunting skills.

Cook nods in approval, hoping such skills will impress their hosts.

•

On the North-east point of Matavai Bay, there now lies a pitched tent and a line in the sand. The Englishmen are having some trouble with the latter.

A milling group of Natives approaches the line. The English threats of violence don't seem to be having an effect. Don't the Natives know what these sticks we carry are capable of? Can't you Natives comprehend it? We've set down a border, a barrier, a boundary. A line, you hear us? Do you not understand? To the Natives, it is exactly that. A line. In the sand. That will disappear with the next breeze. The notion of such a scratching in the ground having any control over a man is beyond ridiculous. Before long, one Native is eager enough to test the power of the line's meaning, sprinting forward and pushing one of the sentinels off balance. He is so quick there is no time to stop him, and in the blink of an eye the Native has grabbed a musket, waving the weapon around like a freshly caught fish. The line has been crossed.

Well, what can the exceedingly young Midshipman, Jonathan Monkhouse, do?

'Fire!'[34] he yells to his command of Marines.

It all happens so quickly.

The Marines bring their thunder-sticks to bear on the flying mass of tattooed Tahitian torsos, trying to distinguish the musket thief among them.

Run . . . RUN!

A volley of shots. Tahitians hit the ground – *one, two, three*. Two get up to stumble forward and hobble on, burning hot lead buried in their flesh. As for the poor foolhardy soul who stole the musket, knowing not what he brought upon himself? He falls to the ground, dead. The white men retrieve their weapon from his lifeless hands. Innocent men have been shot, but British justice has been done.

•

Cook, Banks and his companions are just closing in on some promising hogs when they hear shots in the distance.

Instantly, old Owhaa calls the other Tahitians to him and quickly has them disperse. Cook sprints back to the Marines with the gentlemen in tow, but they have no sooner crossed the river than they see a Tahitian man lying, unmoving, face-down in the sand. Dead.

Shaken, after he'd ordered soldiers to fire on fleeing and unarmed men, Midshipman Jonathan Monkhouse's voice cracks as he speaks.

A Native . . . grabbed a musket and started to run away . . . I had to do something, Captain.

Oh, he has done something all right, and it is up to the Captain and Mr Banks to explain to the Natives as best they can the 'justice' that has been meted out. Owhaa gathers some 20 Tahitians, each of them emerging cautiously from the cover of the woods to enter the splendid tent. They sit on the sandy ground and try in earnest to decipher the words of these strange visitors, killers who have come to their shores. It is Banks whose voice now cuts above the rabble: 'the man who suffered was guilty of a crime deserving of death'[35] he says, sure he can make these Natives understand that in the English world, the civilised world, when it came to the act of thievery, outright murder was quite normal, necessary actually. Surely they could understand that?

Cook now points to Owhaa and back to himself, and says out loud, '*Tyo*' to affirm they are still friends. Banks does the same.

It takes some time, but presently the old Native steps out of the tent and comes back with some younger Natives, all of them bearing the symbol of peace – branches of plantain trees.

Clapping their hands to their breasts, they slowly approach, crying '*Tyo*'.[36]

Carefully – for they are still not entirely confident they are not about to be shot – they sit with the white men, and send young ones to bring them cocoa nuts, so they all may drink the milk together, as friends at peace. Little by little, confidence returns, and the Natives even start to laugh, as Parkinson notes, 'more so than could have been expected, considering what they had suffered in the late skirmish. Have we not reason to conclude, that their dispositions are very flexible, and that resentment, with them, is a short-lived passion?'[37]

All's well that ends well, so to speak.

'At sunset they left us seemingly satisfied,' Cook will recount, 'and we struck our Tent and went on board.'[38]

'We retired to the ship not well pleased with the day's expedition,' records Joseph Banks, who further notes in his journal that, as a group, he and his British brethren had been 'guilty no doubt in some measure of the death of a man who the most severe laws of equity would not have condemned to so severe a punishment',[39] despite his insistence to the Natives that it was a crime punishable by death, a threat which had caused the blood to drain from their shocked faces.

'If we quarreled with those Indians,' Mr Banks notes to the quiet Quaker Sydney Parkinson, 'we should not agree with angels.'[40]

For his part, Parkinson is simply appalled by the whole thing, noting that, no matter how trivial the offence was, once the boy of a Midshipman had given the orders to fire, the soldiers with him, 'obeyed with the greatest glee imaginable, as if they had been shooting at wild ducks . . .

What a pity, that such brutality should be exercised by civilized people upon unarmed ignorant Indians!'[41]

As for the young Midshipman, Jonathan Monkhouse, the man who gave the order, he feels the sting and the shame from both Captain Cook and Mr Banks. Diplomacy has mended things with the Tahitians but will not mend Cook's opinion of him. *Rash, intemperate, foolish* . . . Again and again Monkhouse sees his Captain's eyes turn away from his. He has little doubt what Captain Cook's verdict shall be on him when they return to England. As for what Mr Banks' opinion is, he can see that just by looking at him. Mr Banks and his party view him as a careless murderer. His brother offers counsel and soothing words, but Surgeon Monkhouse cannot cure a reputation. That nigh impossible task is left for Midshipman Monkhouse to brood upon.

•

Cook wakes early, heads up on deck and sees . . . nothing. There is not a single canoe in the bright blue water below the *Endeavour*'s hull. It seems that after yesterday's ahem . . . *misunderstanding*, the Natives are keeping their distance.

Cook orders the ship brought closer to the shore, so it can be within range and have cannon trained on 'Point Venus', the name the *Endeavour*'s men have called the spit of land on which they plan to build the fort.

Friendly or unfriendly, the Captain will complete his mission.

•

It really *is* one of those things.

On the night when 17 April meets 18 April 1769, at two in the morning, the unfortunate artist Mr Alexander Buchan – who back in Tierra del Fuego had suffered the epileptic fit which had so debilitated him – is struck down by another fit.

Buchan's eyes roll back leaving only the whites visible, even as his tongue lolls out, and his whole body shakes. The last time this happened, it had stopped after he was warmed by a fire. But now it just gets worse and worse and . . . worse still. It is as though poor Buchan is possessed of an evil spirit that simply will not let him go until it has completely shaken the life out of him. From shaking violently Buchan weakens to the point he can only shudder weakly until at last he lies . . . still.

It is over.

'I sincerely regret him as an ingenious and good young man,' Banks chronicles, 'but his Loss to me is irretrievable . . .'[42]

No, not because they are friends, and not because of Buchan's service of science, but for rather more selfish Banksian reasons.

'My airy dreams of entertaining my friends in England with the scenes that I am to see here are vanished. No account of the figures and dresses of men can be satisfactory unless illustrated with figures: had providence spared him a month longer what an advantage would it have been to my undertaking but I must submit.'[43]

Yes, Banks must reflect as they commit Buchan to the deep for all eternity, life can be cruel. Why couldn't Mr Buchan have the decency to drop dead 30 days from now? So inconvenient; good help is hard to find. Thankfully, Buchan is not the end of the line, and Banks shortly passes his duties on to the grieving Mr Parkinson. Yes, yes, I know you're here to draw and paint plants, but you can surely find some time to turn your hand towards people as well.

Yes, sir, Mr Banks, cold fish that you are.

•

Every man, from the Captain to the lowest mess-hand, tries to decipher the riddles of the Tahitian way of life. The white men are yet to fathom the finer details of the Tahitian justice system, but they know there are complex and enforced rules in place, even if there is no written legal code. 'Certain penalties, from long usage and ancient custom,' records Midshipman James Magra, '[apply] to certain crimes or misdemeanours . . . for example, those who steal clothes or arms are commonly put to death, either by hanging or drowning in the sea; but those who steal provisions [are punished by such things as having the soles of their feet caned]. By this practice they wisely vary the punishment of the same crime, when committed from different motives, judging perhaps, that he who steals cloth and arms, steals because he is either idle or avaricious, qualities which probably will always continue with the offender, to the disturbance of society, but he who steals from hunger is impelled by one of the most importunate desires of nature, and will not offend again, unless the same impulse recurs, which it is not likely will happen.'[44] In some ways, thus, their legal system is more advanced than the English one, as it actually takes into account the motive for the crime.

In England justice is blind and proud of it. In Tahiti it has both eyes open, wanting to work out why someone has misbehaved. Their religion is similarly gentle, and Joseph Banks is bemused to learn a Tahitian belief concerning the afterlife, which is typically sunny. For you see, for them, even hell is fairly wonderful! It's just not quite so wonderful as heaven.

'Heaven they describe as a place of Great happiness and hell is only a place enjoying less of the luxuries of life . . .'[45]

18 April 1769, Point Venus, work and play, night and day

Now ordinarily, when you needed men to work like navvies, Navy navvies were among the best. With no means of escape on a ship, operating under the Articles of War, which would see them lashed if they disobeyed an order to work hard, you could count on them to set to with a will.

But here on Tahiti, five days after they have arrived, when most of the men are relaxing, bathing, eating, drinking and making love to Tahitian maidens, rounding enough of them up to begin building the fort – to put walls and obstacles where the lines had been marked around the tent – is not quite as easy. And nor, once they are set to work, do they go at it with much enthusiasm.

'Some were employed in throwing up entrenchment,' James Cook records, 'while others was cutting fascines, Picquets, etc.'[46]

To Cook's surprise, rather than protest from the Natives on this first afternoon of building, they are more than happy to lend some elbow grease and great grunt, lugging materials and provisions out of the forest and up to the construction site.

Cook interrupts the work of his men, already dripping with sweat despite the early morning hour, to reiterate:

No tree may be cut down without getting permission from the Natives first.

The men nod, grunt, and wipe the perspiration from their brows. They understand, though it does seem very odd to care about what the Natives think. They continue digging, sawing, lugging and hammering.

Meanwhile, the armourer and his mates set up the forge not far from the fort's construction site, and begin the work of repairing all the ship's ironwork. Axes are honed, attracting a crowd of Natives who watch the sparks fly in wonder.

As to the design of the fort, Cook orders his men to dig a deep, wide moat around the Northern, Western and Southern sides of the building. The Eastern side is to be bordered by the river.

The point of the exercise is to guarantee a completely tranquil and secure environment in which the precious astronomical instruments can be set up to record the Transit of Venus, which is now just six weeks away. It is effectively a secure compound, plenty of space for tents, a kitchen and pens for the sheep and goat – able to sustain and support the *Endeavour* cohort whose job it will be to mind the fort.

'My tents were got up before night,' Mr Banks chronicles, 'and I slept ashore in them for the first time. The lines were guarded round by many Sentries but no Indian attempted to come near them during the whole night.'[47] Well, no Indian men anyway. Mr Banks welcomes visitors of the fairer sex, who the sentinels allow into the construction area no questions asked.

•

As it happens, there is no shortage of volunteers to live and work on the island, and for very good reason as, as Cook will later note, the local women are 'so very liberal with their favours',[48] that it is worth working all day, if you can enjoy their charms all night.

Why are these women so available?

The sailors have no clue . . . and no time to ask.

Again?

Again.

The women are riddles to which there is no answer. But what glorious, stunning riddles they are.

Back home, to get a good woman into bed with you required a commitment of marriage, together with a good 10 minutes to get her corsets and all the rest off, while women of more . . . ill repute could be got into bed for two shillings.

But here in Tahiti, they're all just good women ready to be bad at a moment's notice, ready, willing, and amazingly able – as a matter of fact far abler than the tars themselves. Indeed, quietly, the Tahitian women suspect these white men have no women among their own kind – for if they did, why on earth would they sail the seas without them? Whoever heard of such a thing? That would explain, among other things, their complete ignorance of carnal pleasures.

So the women take it upon themselves to take control, slowing these randy white men down from their absurd, desperate, percussive, hammering rhythm into the way it was all meant to be done, the way a palm tree sways back and forth in a very light breeze, slowly, sensually, like a flowing dance, with lightly swaying hips, a flowing dance, and . . . well, the men have never felt anything like it.[49]

Again?

Again!

Nearly all of the *Endeavour*'s officers and gentlemen are equally enamoured of the local delights, and partake heavily, except for Richard Orton, the much-hated personal clerk of Captain Cook, who, as William Perry will recount, displays 'some presentiment of evil . . . from a consciousness of universal hatred [extended towards him]; for, whilst at an anchor during our long stay at Tahiti, when the Captain and better half the ship's company were ashore, he was always afraid to sleep in the great cabin alone'.[50]

Not that Captain Cook is ever ashore for anything other than proper purposes. He has no experience at all with the local women. Happily married to dear Elizabeth, waiting for him back in England with their four children, that is all he cares for himself. Beyond everything else, even if he were disposed to be unfaithful, Cook is mindful of the delicate art of diplomacy. If he sleeps with one Chief's wife, then all the other Chief's wives would . . . well, that is a challenge Mr Banks can meet if he pleases. But James Cook's faithfulness to his wife places him in a tiny minority, as Sydney Parkinson will note.

> Most of our ship's company procured temporary wives amongst
> the Natives, with whom they occasionally cohabited; an indulgence
> which even many reputed virtuous Europeans allow themselves,
> in uncivilized parts of the world, with impunity; as if a change
> of place altered the moral turpitude of fornication: and what is a
> sin in Europe, is only a simple innocent gratification in America;
> which is to suppose, that the obligation to chastity is local, and
> restricted only to particular parts of the globe.[51]

Joseph Banks' 'flame'[52] of the month is Teatea, 'a fine Grecian girl'.[53] Lieutenant John Gore is head over heels and more for Mrs Toaro, Master Molineux cannot get enough of Tiari, while Charlie Clerke spends every available minute with Hautai, and Sydney Parkinson does the same with Piari'i.[54] (Yes, even devout Quakers like Sydney Parkinson cannot resist the lures of the flesh in Tahiti.)

Charles Green? Yes, he has been mournful over dear Elizabeth, his new bride he has left behind in London, but he has found solace with Tuarua – sometimes twice a night, and occasionally in the afternoon. Of the officers and gentlemen, it is really only Surgeon Monkhouse who sleeps alone, just him and his snuff box, though not from choice. There is just something about his droopy jowl and sad hound-dog features that the Native women find ... unattractive, and it means he couldn't find a root in a mangrove swamp.

As for Captain Cook, he is quietly appalled by his men's sexual proclivities with the Tahitian women, knowing what shameful distemper it could unleash among all who partake. Being noisily appalled would be beside the point, because trying to stop what is going on would be like trying to hold back a king tide by standing on the beach and putting his hands out – he would have as much success in this regard as had King Canute. All he can really do is register his disapproval, so at least the Admiralty will know what lies in wait for future expeditions to these parts.

'One amusement or custom more I must mention ...' he writes. 'Both sexes express the most indecent ideas in conversation without the least emotion, and they delight in such conversation beyond any other. Chastity, indeed, is but little valued, especially among the middle people — if a Wife is found guilty of a breach of it her only punishment is a beating from her husband. The Men will very readily offer the Young Women to Strangers, even their own Daughters, and think it very strange if you refuse them; but this is done merely for the sake of gain.'[55]

Joseph Banks has no such qualms.

Quite the reverse, he records his own learned scientific opinion with an entirely different tone.

'I have nowhere seen,' he writes in his journal, 'such elegant women as those of Tahiti.'[56]

And if Captain Cook takes that attitude, well, Joseph Banks is so happy to help himself to the humble Yorkshireman's share and more, in fact he likely sets new records for congress. For yes, though already handsomely educated at all of Harrow, Eton and Oxford, his Doctorate in Love takes place on Tahiti and he applies himself to his studies as never before, thankful for the heavy practical component with a lot of outdoor activity.

Yes, Joseph Banks, now living ashore each night, has plenty to learn and is dedicated to the methodical, practical study of such charms by turning his tent into the Tahitian equivalent of his Chelsea home back in London, hosting gatherings, only his tent is more ... intimate.

Soon enough, the Chief Lycurgus and his wives move from the Western side of Matavai Bay closer to where the whites are building their fort, 'bringing with them all their household furniture and even houses to be erected in our neighbourhood'.[57]

Banks becomes ever more intimate with them every day.

'Lycurgus dined with us,' he chronicles on 20 April, 'he imitates our manners in every instance already holding a knife and fork more handily than a Frenchman could learn to do in years.'[58]

And so the white men on shore fall into a routine. Bouncing between the ship and the half-constructed fort, they share meals and trade sexual favours with the Natives in the evening, only to rise the next morning to trade food and tools. Lieutenant Gore superintends relations with the Natives out at the ship, while Banks is in charge at the Fort. A nail for a fish? Yes, thank you. How about a single bead for a bread-fruit? Done.

The terms of trade spring up even in paradise, as an amused Sydney Parkinson notes of the new 'iron age': 'The rates, or terms, on which we trafficked with the natives, were a spike for a small pig; a smaller for a fowl; a hatchet for a hog; and twenty cocoa nuts, or bread-fruit, for a middling-sized nail.'[59] But, as ever, Mr Banks focuses on the broader picture and on beauty . . .

'In the Island of Tahiti,' Joseph Banks opines, 'where love is the chief occupation, the favourite, nay almost the sole luxury of the inhabitants; both the bodies and souls of the women are modeled in the utmost perfection for that soft science . . .'[60]

Helping them achieve that perfection is a plant known to the Tahitians as *tiare*.[61] It is a gorgeous white flower that grows only in the highlands and is used to infuse cocoa-nut oil for use in lovemaking. Banks comes across it one night when, lying naked and spent by his current Tahitian flame, his own flame flickering on the edge of exhaustion, she reaches into the special cocoa-nut shell she keeps by her mat and soon draws her dripping fingers over his shuddering body. For yes, just a few drops of this fragrant oil somehow makes him shake and shiver, just as the stroke of her oily hands makes him relax as he breathes deep of this potent perfume and . . . his strength returns and rises once more . . .

Afterwards, he realises her purpose has been not just his reinvigoration but, just as it is for all the Tahitian women, the oil is the best way to mask the overpowering smell of the dirty white men! Either way, for Joseph Banks it is heaven in a cocoa-nut shell, combining his twin passions, with a blessed plant enhancing his sexual experience.

Surgeon Monkhouse has become irritated watching his former chum Banks dedicating every spare moment to swaggering around the beach with the prettiest ladies, hips thrust forward and positively *reeking* of the love potion. Surgeon Monkhouse knows that Banks has no time for him. But why does *he* get all the girls? The Surgeon longs to be anointed with the oil, and every day he is not, his resentment grows, and his face becomes even droopier.

•

By 22 April, just five days after starting, Captain Cook's observatory on Point Venus, which the men christen 'Fort Venus', is shaping up enough that more tents can be erected inside.

'This day,' Cook records proudly, 'we mounted 6 Swivels at the Fort, which was now nearly finished. This struck the Natives with some fear, and some fishermen who lived upon the point moved farther off.'[62]

By about now, there are some 45 sailors, Marines, Midshipmen and officers sleeping at Fort Venus, about half the ship's company.

Using a mish-mash of sign language and charades, Captain Cook does his best to explain to Owhaa and the gathering group that he has come from beyond the horizon, all the way from Britain, '*Pretanie*' – *points over the ocean towards the Eastern horizon.*

To observe – *points at his eyes.*

Venus – *points to the sky. Venus, do you know Venus?*

Of course they know Venus, the brightest object in the Southern night sky. She is '*Ta'urua-nui*', named for the beautiful eldest daughter of the mother of all the stars, *Atea* herself, the sun. Cook is fascinated as the Tahitians teach him something of their own astronomical knowledge.

> They compute time by the Moon, which they call *Malama*, reckoning 30 days to each moon, 2 of which they say the moon is *Mattee*, that is, dead, and this is at the time of the new moon, when she cannot be seen. The day they divide into smaller Portions not less than 2 Hours. Their computations is by units, tens, and scores, up to ten score, or 200, etc. In counting they generally take hold on their fingers one by one, Shifting from one hand to the other, until they come to the number they want to express; but if it be a high number, instead of their fingers they use pieces of Leaves, etc.[63]

But what do you want from *Ta'urua-nui*? Cook does his best, but there is simply no hope of explaining the upcoming transit, though they do grasp it is something to do with *Atea*, the sun.

The Tahitians, meanwhile, are making headway in distinguishing the white men from each other – at first, all the white men, at least those wearing the same rough uniform, all looked remarkably alike. As to the different names of the whites, as Mr Banks notes, 'The Indians find so much difficulty in pronouncing them that we are forced to indulge them in calling us what they please, or rather what they say when they attempt to pronounce them.'[64]

Captain Cook becomes *Toote*, Banks is *Tapáne*, Dr Solander becomes *Torano*, Lieutenant Hicks is *Hete*, Gore is *Mr Toaro*, Surgeon Monkhouse becomes *Mato*, and Master Molineux is called *Boba*, 'from his Christian name Robert'.[65]

'In this manner,' Banks writes, 'they have names for almost every man in the ship.'[66]

And, of course, the array of extraordinary characters the crew meet in this wonderful place continues to grow. On the morning of 28 April, Captain Cook is busily filling out his log in the Great Cabin when Master Molineux knocks and enters with a tall, fair-skinned Tahitian woman crowned with a dramatic headdress. It is, he will come to learn, a *Tomou*, six long strands of threaded human hair, anchored to her own that if laid out would go for almost a mile long. The whole extraordinary ensemble is wrapped in the finest cloth Cook has yet seen on the island. *Who* is this?

'This is the *Dolphin*'s "Queen Oberea",'[67] the Master announces rather grandly, at which Cook stands and goes through the appropriate motions when meeting a Queen. Her reputation has preceded *him*. For this, of course is the great Queen spoken of so highly by the *Dolphin*'s men. The Captain begins with a special gift, presenting Queen Oberea with a child's doll that she is soon coo-ing over, almost as if it were her own baby.

'She appeared to be about 40,' Banks writes, noting her 'tall and very lusty, her skin white and her eyes full of meaning, she might have been handsome when young but now few or no traces of it were left.'[68]

Cook and Queen Oberea are taken ashore, where this once great Queen tells the visiting Captain she has presents waiting.

'A hog and several bunches of plantains. These she caused to be carried from her canoes up to the fort in a kind of procession, she and I bringing up the rear.'[69]

As the ceremonies and rites roll on, Oberea beams to find herself the centre of attention once more, just as in days of yore. It lasts until the glowering King Tootaha (Hercules) arrives 'midst his flanking flotilla of canoes. Walking ashore, surrounded by his warriors, he grandly approaches the fort and stops just shy of the gathered crowd, though there is nothing shy in the way he looks at Oberea. It is a glare that transcends language barriers.

Oberea – still buoyed by the high regard these white men have bathed her in – shows Tootaha the child's doll with a flirtatious flash of the eyes, a gesture which only makes him stand taller, his face angrier than ever. Cook, ever the diplomat, despatches a man to the ship to retrieve another child's doll, a gift the Captain then hands to the Chief. He appears placated . . . mildly. Crisis averted, but Cook is beginning to understand how it works around here. Whatever 'Queen' Oberea once was, she is no longer.

'She is head or chief of her own family or Tribe,' he records, 'but to all appearance hath no Authority over the rest of the Inhabitants, whatever she might have had when the *Dolphin* was here.'[70]

Oberea, the Queen that was.

And King Tootaha, the real power in this land.

'Hercules,' Cook records for the Admiralty, 'whose real Name is Tootaha, is, to all appearance, the Chief Man of the Island.'[71]

Cook and Banks come to understand that Arcadia is in fact two realms or districts, each ruled by a Chief of Chiefs – an *Eare dehi* in Tahitian, or a Queen or King as the British prefer to think of it. Each of these realms is divided into smaller districts, or *Whennuas* as the Tahitians call them, and at the head of each is a Chief, or *Eare*.

Mysteries abound in this strange land, though what is what, who is who, and how it all works is at least slowly becoming apparent.

29 April 1769, Matavai Bay, more lashings of leather

Chief Tubourai (Lycurgus) is aggrieved. The ship's butcher, Henry Jeffs, has threatened to cut the throat of the Chief's wife, Tomio, with a hatchet. He tells Joseph Banks, who, upon seeing guilt writ large in the butcher's demeanour, is appalled, and promises that he will see Jeffs punished.

As good as his word, Banks tells Captain Cook, who is *very* aggrieved.

The firmest rule he has while in Tahiti is for his men to treat the Natives well – it is at the top of the list of rules hanging on the mainmast for goodness sake.

'To endeavour by every fair means to Cultivate a Friendship with the Natives, and to treat them with all imaginable humanity.'[72]

Those who flout that rule must face the consequences, and be *seen* to face the consequences in front of the offended Natives.

That is why, once Cook is satisfied the accusation is sound, Jeffs is placed in chains below, and now – without giving the Chief and his wife any warning of what awaits – the Captain has invited them on to the *Endeavour*.

Once they are in place, aft, sitting by Joseph Banks, and all the ship's company are assembled, as for every flogging, Jeffs is hauled up through the hatchway, blinking in the sunlight and after his shirt is removed, tied to the rigging so his back is exposed.

After Captain Cook makes a quick speech explaining how the rules are as clear as the consequences for those who broke them, he gives the nod.

Mr Gathray, if you please.

Expertly, Gathray draws the cat o'nine tails out of its red bag, steps forward, brings the cat back behind his head, and whistles it forward.

At the first explosion of leather against the butcher's skin, there is a cry, but it comes not from the recalcitrant sailor, but the Chief's wife, Tomio.

'The woman,' Master Molineux chronicles, 'was in the greatest agonies, and strongly interceded for him.'[73]

So too her husband, the Chief. Both had been upset, but not so upset that they wished to see such cruelty.

Which is regrettable, but it changes nothing.

The two go on, Banks chronicles, 'begging the punishment might cease, a request which the Captain would not comply with'.[74]

How strange are these white beings?

They shoot a man who crosses a line in the sand, yet whip a man who stands still.

Strange indeed.

•

For his part, Captain Cook is thrilled with the fort. Perhaps the Natives struggled with the line Cook's men had drawn in the sand, but surely they would understand *this*. With guns in place and all in working order. On the afternoon of 1 May, he and Mr Green bring ashore the astronomical equipment, including the quadrant – consisting of a telescope and a heavy metal quarter-circle arc – still packed safely in its case since England, and other instruments like telescopes, looking glasses and the astronomical clock.

With enormous care, the clock is placed at one end of a larger tent facing the observatory, with its wooden base dug into the earth to make sure it is absolutely stable. Exactly 12 feet away, in the observatory and facing the clock, a large cask is filled with wet sand to make it equally unmoving, and upon this, when the time comes, will be placed the quadrant.

The essence of the observatory is quickly set up, with the larger instruments placed on stable foundations in a locked-off environment. With the Transit of Venus just a little over four weeks away, Captain Cook has every right to be satisfied.

'I now thought myself perfectly secure,' he records.[75]

•

Captain Cook is eager to at last bring the observatory up to working order. There is but one thing left to do. Moving from the great tent to the smaller round one only 12 feet away, Cook and his men walk up to the feature in the middle of the room. It is the heavy cask fixed to the ground, filled to overflowing with heavy wet sand. In order to keep it stable, they will affix the astronomical quadrant to this cask, fast and firm and . . .

And hold on . . . Captain, the case feels too light!

Where is the quadrant?

Cook is appalled. His one quadrant is missing. How can this be? How can something so precious, so big, packed up in a box inside its case and held under armed guard, a sentinel not five yards away from this tent, in there for less than a day now be . . . yes, stolen? Without it, no observations of the transit of any worth may be made, and they all will have wasted two years of their lives for naught.

Cook wastes no time in placing a bounty on the missing object and word soon arrives from the fort by way of Oberea that the quadrant has been taken Eastward! It was taken in the night, taken by a Native under the cover of darkness.

Mr Banks and Mr Green arm themselves with muskets and go to find Chief Tubourai, who they meet on the riverbank, coming to them with news. He picks up three small twigs and arranges them into a triangle shape, resting on his palm . . .

Yes! The quadrant's tripod! Tubourai knows where the quadrant is!

No time to waste, Banks tells Tubourai: 'he must instantly go with me to the place where it was'.[76]

And so Tubourai joins them in the hunt.

As they pass homes and abodes, Tubourai draws the panting white men to a halt, inquiring after the thief by name.

'Moroameah!'[77] Where is he?

Every Native they pass points the party Eastward.

The search races on, until Tubourai halts the procession and motions to a hill some three miles away. The white men are told: 'you are not to expect the instrument till we get there'.[78] Banks can't help but note that there are 'no arms among us but a pair of pocket pistols which I always carried, going at least 7 miles from our fort where the Indians might not be quite so submissive as at home, going also to take from them a prize for which they had ventured their lives'.[79]

Banks sends back the Midshipman, to inform the Captain and request some assistance – armed.

•

Cook turns to Lieutenant Hicks – there are to be no more canoes leaving the bay, and if anyone so much as attempts it, detain them. Understood?

Yes, Captain. But with one caveat: 'If Tootaha comes either to the ship or the fort he is not to be detained.'[80]

The Marines and the Captain move off into the woods.

•

Tubourai turns to stone. The great Chief has been striding through the island like a titan, though just as quickly he is still, an instant statue.

He has heard something.

His arm raises slowly, deliberately. *There.* Banks sees over Tubourai's shoulder a Native man, polished metal shining in his hands. *The missing quadrant!*

A rapid report of pistol fire cracks out from Banks, and the Natives scatter far and wide. Then, using the butt of the very same gun, he marks a circle in the dirt beneath him. This, *this* is my space. You lot, keep to yourselves. The Natives need not be told twice, and respect his wishes.

'They behaved with all the order imaginable,' Banks records, 'though we quickly had some hundreds surrounding a ring we had marked out.'[81]

Only after receiving permission thus, does one of Tubourai's warriors carefully cross the line and carefully place a packing box at the feet of Mr Banks.

Mr Green rushes to open it, only to find, as Sydney Parkinson records, 'Some of the Natives had taken it to pieces.'[82] And Mr Green is infinitely relieved to inform Banks that they do indeed have the most crucial parts, and what is missing can be fashioned in the forge of the armourer. Their mission survives.

'So,' records a triumphant Joseph Banks, 'we packed all up in grass as well as we could and proceeded homewards.'[83]

•

An affray in the bay.

How dare they?

Restrained and escorted by armed guards under the command of Lieutenant Gore, the outraged King Tootaha is being led up the beach towards the fort. This sort of treatment is an affront to his *mana*, his power and prestige.

Lieutenant Gore brings the King to Lieutenant Hicks, who is . . . perplexed. Can the always headstrong and hasty Gore really have detained the King *despite* Captain Cook's specific instructions forbidding any such action. Well, Lieutenant Gore?

Gore explains in muted tones so as not to raise any further alarm. He had sent the yawl, filled with sailors, in hot pursuit of a double canoe that was busy trying to escape the bay. Bosun John Gathray had led the furious chase, only to find that when they came alongside the fleeing canoe, every one of the Natives had dived overboard. And there, among the messy mass of Tahitians swimming back to shore, the Bosun had squinted to see . . . *King Tootaha!* Well, what else was there to do but take the man back to shore?

So acted John Gathray, and thus Tootaha had come into Lieutenant Gore's custody, and as a result he had thought it the prudent thing to bring him back to the fort, to you . . . Lieutenant Hicks.

He was my problem. Now he is *our* problem.

And very soon he will be Captain Cook's problem, too, for he is on his way.

•

What is going on?

Captain Cook and his Marines, now in the company of Mr Banks, Mr Green and Tubourai with whom they have met up – all happy that the quadrant has been retrieved – have no sooner come within sight of the fort than they can hear wailing. And it is getting louder now, more agonised with every step closer they take. Actual *screams*. Wrenching sobs.

What *is* going on?

It is a mourning mob massed in front of the fort gate. Cook strides in to find the distressed King Tootaha, sitting on his haunches. King Tubourai follows Cook, and – quite touchingly it must be said – the two Tahitian Kings immediately fall into each other's arms.

'They wept over each other for some time,' Cook records. 'As for [Tootaha], he was so far prepossessed with the thought that he was to be killed that he could not be made sensible.' Even news that he is to be released is not enough to console him. Cook quickly orders King Tootaha returned to his people and he is 'carried out of the Fort to the people, many of whom Expressed their joy by embracing'.[84]

'After all,' Cook chronicles, 'he would not go away until he had given us two Hogs, notwithstanding we did all in our power to hinder him, for it is very certain that the Treatment he had met with from us did not merit such a reward. However, we had it in our power to make him a present of equal value whenever we pleased.'[85]

Gore explains himself to his furious Captain – not remotely with the level of apology needed in the Englishman's view – but either way the damage is done, both to the dignity of Tootaha and to James Cook's opinion of Lieutenant Gore. It is a wound that will linger.

•

The Englishmen have been working these past five days without a peep from the Natives. No spectators, no visitors, no lovely ladies coming by to distract the men of the *Endeavour*. Captain Cook knows instinctively that the kidnapping of Tootaha has done precisely the damage he feared it would do. To shoot one of the men who had stolen a gun, that was one thing, and seemingly something the Natives had begrudgingly tolerated. But to kidnap their King, to dishonour and disrespect Tootaha, a man who had been so good to them . . . Yes, the Tahitians are now reluctant to spend time near any white men, refusing to bring their produce to the fort or ship.

Cook catches neither sight nor sound of Tubourai, much less Tootaha. But in the void that has formed in the time since the King's kidnapping, one Tahitian sees his chance. Tupia, a tall older gentleman and right-hand man to the pretender Queen Oberea, begins to spend his time around the fort. He is seemingly the only Native on the island unfazed by the kidnapping of Tootaha. A charismatic fellow and a bridge between the British and the Natives, Tupia could not have come into the picture at a better time.

Tupia soon becomes a key figure in the circle of Banks' intimates, advising Banks on the properties of plants and herbs, and showing Surgeon Monkhouse ancient local remedies of startling effectiveness, showing Sydney Parkinson the Tahitian manner of art, from sculpture to making paper from bark – *tapa*, as it is called – to the use of dyes for painting and tattoo. Parkinson is so impressed by the priest's skills, he begins to teach Tupia how to draw in the European fashion. It isn't long before Tupia's name and face are known by every man on the *Endeavour*. He seems to be a friend to everybody, this good priest Tupia.

Not least among his new-found companions is James Cook, who recognises with surprise and delight that Tupia is a navigator not just of boast but of knowledge, a man who can draw islands Cook has seen and, tantalisingly, ones he has not, with a confidence and consistency that simply amazes the Captain.

Perhaps King Tootaha is a little concerned with just how Tupia's influence is growing, and resolves to reach a peaceful accord with the English lest his own standing fall too far. A feast then, a great banquet in honour of resuming their relationship, and followed by a public wrestling match no less!

With peace comes trade, and the morning after the feast, everyone is bleary-eyed from a long night of revelry – and no-one more, Cook notes, than Master Molineux, a glutton for food, drink and women. With everything back to normal the men of the *Endeavour* breathe a collective sigh of relief.

Paradise continues and Venus awaits.

CHAPTER SEVEN

TRANSIT OF VENUS

Not a Cloud was to be seen the whole day, and the Air was perfectly Clear, so that we had every advantage we could desire in observing the whole of the Passage of the planet Venus over 'the Sun's Disk.[1]

James Cook, 3 June 1769

10 May 1769, Matavai Bay, Oh Tahiti

The Natives who watch Captain Cook are two parts mesmerised to three parts confused.

What is Toote doing?

Actual physical labour? Yes.

Extraordinary.

Their own Chiefs are so disinclined to exert themselves, they have servants to feed them their meals. But here is Toote with a shovel in his hands, labouring away and planting seeds, which he has brought, bottled up, all the way from Mile End, London.

With every swing of the hoe, the soil loosens. Cook stoops to place a single seed in each small divot . . . a tamarind tree here, an orange tree there.

Again, the Tahitians are confused, for they lack nothing in the way of fruit or trees, but Cook insists. If the measure of a good man is to plant a tree under which he knows he will never sit in the shade of, the Englishman surely qualifies as in this case he goes one better, wanting the Tahitians to enjoy the fruits of his labours, even though he will be very unlikely to eat those fruits with them.

Very well, *Toote*, let us see what we reap from the seeds you sow.

•

Oh Tahiti, how the *Endeavour* men love thee!

It is another typical mid-May day in Paradise and it looks like it will be another night there too for Joseph Banks, accompanied by a rather

181

excessive number of young ladies – at least to the mind of Surgeon Monkhouse. To the medico's considerable chagrin, the botanist has managed to make a constant flame of Oberea's pretty handmaiden, the delicious Teatea for two-two, and still – STILL! – the botanist is receiving constant overtures from the lusty Queen! Why, *dammit*, and *how*, does bloody Banks get all these ladies to himself? Can he not perhaps share or guide a lovely creature towards say . . . Surgeon Monkhouse? But no, Mr Banks is not inclined to share beauty. Physician heal thyself! Mr Banks is busy with the busty and the lusty and not in the giving vein today. As for the astronomer Mr Charles Green, he finds that beer, rum and rum help soothe his guilt about his adultery and, well, help inspire more of it. It is a vicious circle, but it's not the seventh circle of Hell, it's an enjoyable one.

28 May 1769, Matavai Bay, heavens above, *heivas* below

Joseph Banks has received an intriguing offer from Queen Oberea that he may sleep in her canoe if he wishes. Mr Banks, the Captain and the Doctor are sleeping for the night on the other side of the bay where they have feasted on hogs with King Tootaha and the former Queen.

'I acquainted my fellow travelers with my good fortune and wishing them as good took my leave,'[2] records Banks.

Arriving at the former Queen's communal sleeping canoe, Banks strips off his coat and waistcoat, his shoes, socks, shirt and breeches . . . the lot, until he can feel the air on his skin.

The night is balmy, calm and carefree. The warmth in the air is liberating, freeing. The botanist will sleep naked tonight. And why shouldn't he?

The Queen now requests Banks' clothes, she assures him she will keep them safe. Good, one fewer thing to worry about on this peaceful night.

'Otherwise they will certainly be stolen,'[3] she warns Mr Banks.

Very well, then.

'I readily submitted and laid down to sleep with all imaginable tranquility.'[4]

Banks wakes to relieve himself in the middle of the night. The night is so dark, it must be near that hour when the sun can make no impression from either end of the day – the most wee of all wee hours, which is what he needs to do right now. Rolling over to where Oberea had placed his clothes, Banks fumbles in the inky darkness for his trousers and belt, only to find . . . nothing. Not his trousers, not his coat, not even his pistols and powder horn.

'Oberea!' He roars then sees her familiar figure sit bolt upright with a start, a yard further down the canoe.

'Where are my clothes?'[5]

Banks begins a barrage of complaints and accusations, carrying along loudly enough to wake Tootaha sleeping in the next canoe along. Rising simultaneously is Tupia, the charismatic priest moving to Banks' side shortly after waking. Tupia's loyalty is without question.

Queen Oberea calls for firelight before disappearing into the night with Tootaha in tow. They are determined to find the missing robes. Feeling rather vulnerable and *naked*, Banks checks for his musket, eager for some reminder of his rank and position, something to signify who he is, who he thought he was when he fell asleep. He finds the firearm, gripping the handle tightly, thank God. Only . . . it's empty. Banks has forgotten to load it, and it is far too late and dark to find anybody and bother them for ammunition. Banks is defenceless. All he can do now, is wait. And wait. And wait some more, silent in the darkness.

Oberea and Tootaha return within the hour, bearing . . . absolutely nothing. *Dammit!*

If everything is going to go belly-up anyway, the botanist thinks it better to lie down and sleep. Wiser that than worrying endlessly in the middle of the night. Only sleep is impossible, as no sooner does Banks rest his head than he hears the sound of what must be music. Faint, but definitely the rhythm and tempo of the islanders' music. How odd.

Rising again, Joseph Banks sees light in the distance, not just one but many. More than many, it is a glowing flock of brightness, brilliant pinpricks of light moving far off in the distance. Settling for a modest strip of cloth that Oberea has so generously provided in absence of decent clothes, Mr Banks walks towards the light . . .

Drawing up on the perimeter of a glowing circle, Banks realises much of the light he could see is the Natives' torches, the same familiar nut kernels on stakes filled with burning oil. Within the burning ring are three men beating drums and a quartet of flautists. Though to say that the woodwinds and percussion instruments are a far cry from Banks' native British orchestras would be a laughable understatement. The drums are 'made of a hollow block of wood covered with Shark's Skin'[6] and are beaten not with padded drumsticks but the great black hands of the Native men. Meanwhile the flutes are 'made of hollow Bamboo about 15 inches long, in which are 3 Holes'[7] far less complicated looking than their Western counterparts. And yet the way they are played seems more complex than anything Banks knows, and he has to look twice to confirm what Cook will later record: 'they blow with one Nostril, stopping the other with the thumb of the left hand, the other 2 Holes they stop and unstop with their fingers, and by this means produce 4 Notes, of which they have made one Tune'.[8]

But the wonders do not stop at the instruments, as Banks' eyes are drawn to a group of eight young women, dancing and writhing in a rhythmic fashion that remind Banks of things he'd rather be doing. He is transfixed by these sirens who sway and moan in the flickering light, moving to the sound of these strange instruments, when suddenly he spies a pair of less lustful eyes on the other side of the circle. The Captain sits in silence, watching the spectacle before him and betraying no emotion.

What else can Banks do but walk over and recount his pitiful tale?

'Oberea took charge of my things, and yet they were stolen from her,'[9] he cries as James Cook listens patiently. Far from being reprimanded, Banks is relieved to hear that the Captain is no stranger to situations like these, and Cook commiserates as he says, 'For my own part I had my Stockings taken from under my head, and yet I am certain that I was not a Sleep the whole time.'[10]

Banks looks down to the Captain's feet, thinking on the Captain's story. He can't help but notice the Captain's legs are exposed to the night, two hairy white limbs that the botanist has not before seen. The Captain responds with a subtle shrug, a rare display of amusement. There is a shared understanding between the two, a camaraderie that belies their situation and exists in spite of the fundamental differences between James and Joseph. They turn their heads away from one another and back to the illuminating performance in front of them. A 'Heiva', the locals call it.

From his observations, Cook has come to the conclusion that these musicians, 'go about from House to House and play, and are always received and rewarded by the Master of the family, who gives them a Piece of Cloth or whatever he can spare, for which they will stay 3 or 4 hours, during which time his house will be crowded full, for the people are extravagantly fond of this diversion'.[11]

As for the young girls *dancing*. Well. He can give them no points for modesty or common decency, but credit where it is due, their knack for rhythm is incredible. He notes for the Admiralty that they sing, 'most indecent songs and using most indecent actions, in the practice of which they are brought up from their earliest childhood; in doing this they keep time to a great nicety'.[12]

By the dim light of the perpetual flame common to most Tahitian communities – its wick made of rolled bark cloth and secreted from the wind – the midnight mystery concert draws to an end. Hairy-legged Cook and the near-nude Banks agree there's little to be done to recover their items tonight, and head back to their respective sleeping places.

And yet, the light of the risen sun reveals no trace, nor even news of the missing items. The men walk back to their waiting pinnace and are soon rowing North for Matavai Bay, carrying with them Captain and botanist both shattered from exhaustion, an unusually chipper Dr Solander – for he has had a full night's slumber in a quiet hut some half a mile distant from last night's festivities – and last but not least, a hog.

All of them are lost in their own thoughts when they happen upon . . . happen upon . . . well, *what is it*? It is mass of lithe Tahitians in the water right where the surf is breaking onto the beach, but what in the name of God are they doing, if not risking their lives with every breaking wave? As the pinnace goes by, well clear of the breaking swell, Banks is able to take a closer look, writing later that night:

> In our return to the boat we saw the Indians amuse or exercise themselves in a manner truly surprising. It was in a place where the shore was not guarded by a reef as is usually the case, consequently a high surf fell upon the shore, a more dreadful one I have not often seen: no European boat could have landed in it and I think no European who had by any means got into [it] could possibly have saved his life, as the shore was covered with pebbles and large stones. In the midst of these breakers 10 or 12 Indians were swimming who whenever a surf broke near them dived under it with infinite ease, rising up on the other side; but their chief amusement was carried on by the stern of an old canoe, with this before them they swam out as far as the outermost breach, then one or two would get into it and opposing the blunt end to the breaking wave were hurried in with incredible swiftness. Sometimes they were carried almost ashore but generally the wave broke over them before they were half way, in which case they dived and quickly rose on the other side with the canoe in their hands, which was towed out again and the same method repeated. We stood admiring this very wonderful scene for full half an hour, in

which time no one of the actors attempted to come ashore but all seemed most highly entertained with their strange diversion.[13]

Joseph Banks has become the first man to record what will come to be called 'surfing'. Like tattooing, it is a local curiosity that surely will not catch on . . .

Early June 1769, Matavai Bay, when the stars align

After consulting with Tupia, Captain Cook decides upon two additional observation points: a small island named Eimeo, some 20 miles to the West and another on the Eastern coast of Tahiti.

'We are now very busy in preparing our Instruments, etc., for the Observations,' Cook records on 29 May ahead of the 3 June transit, 'and Instructing such Gentlemen in the use of them, as I intend to send to other parts to observe, for fear we should fail here.'[14]

So it goes that on 1 June, Captain Cook and Mr Green bid farewell to Lieutenant Gore, Mr Banks and the good Surgeon Monkhouse as they are all rowed off in the long-boat to Eimeo. For his part Lieutenant Hicks is headed to the other location to the East.

'Fix upon some Convenient situation . . .' Cook orders, 'and there Observe the Transit.'[15]

Captain Cook and Mr Green remain, pacing in and out of the tent to check the skies are clear, as the single chance in 200 years to solve the mysteries of the heavens draws near.

3 June 1769, Point Venus, heavens above

The day dawns, crisp and clear.

Gazing to the Eastern sky, and then above, Captain Cook is infinitely relieved. All this time he has been keenly aware that it is quite possible to journey to the other side of the planet for a specific purpose, have prepared *everything* possible to make it a success and . . . see the whole thing come undone simply because it might be a cloudy day.

Mercifully, however, the sky is 'as favourable to our purpose as we could wish',[16] though Cook finds himself distracted. The big clock, its base buried at the end of the tent, ticks ever closer to the time Venus will first appear against the sun: 9.21 am. The Captain can scarcely draw his attention away. So long they have waited, such a journey it has already been.

Tick. Tick. Tick.

Yes, his reflecting telescope and that of Charles Green – with a magnifying power of 140 times that of the eye – is in readiness, positioned with the lenses pointing directly towards the sun.

And yes, the white screen is positioned behind the telescopes so, as the light of the sun streams through, the men will be able to closely observe the reflected images and record the exact times that the black dot of Venus enters and exits the image of the sun, represented by the white circle of light. The screens have been situated at a distance the men deem optimum for their requirements, which give a small image with sharp resolution. This is important, because we must be careful to try to discern between Venus's limb and its blurred penumbra, the lighter shading of shadow that hangs upon the outskirts of a darker shadow. And we also must be completely focused throughout the day to re-aiming our telescopes to keep track of the sun. We are ready, and only anxious now to get started.

The day is already intolerably hot, which seems to make the clock tick more slowly as they wait for the big event . . .

And there it is!

Green first notices the small black dot showing up on the periphery of the sun – 'Light thus on the sun's limb' – at 9.21 am and 45 seconds.

Five seconds later, Cook makes his own initial observation – 'The first visible appearance of Venus on the Sun's limb' – at 9.21 am and 50 seconds.

And so begins the next six hours of very tight observation, with each moment of significance – 'Penumbra and Sun's limb in contact . . . Small thread of light seen below the penumbra'[17] – faithfully recorded by each man. No matter that the temperature in the tent keeps climbing, as the perspiration pours from them, still they keep to their posts, eyes on the screen, pencils to paper.

Still the mercury climbs, as Venus transits, with the temperature at one point nudging 119 degrees Fahrenheit (48.3 degrees Celsius), and still the observers barely blink. They have come a long way to get this exactly right, and there can be no distractions.

As the transit comes to its close, Green notes last contact between Venus and the sun's limb at 3.31 pm and 28 seconds, while Cook records it as having finished six seconds earlier, at 3.31 pm and 22 seconds.

Immediately, Cook and Green compare their observations, disappointed to find they differ quite markedly.

When they check the figures of Dr Solander, who has also been observing from the fort with an even more powerful telescope, his timings differ further from both theirs, and as Cook glumly records, all of their observations vary by 'much more than could be expected'.[18]

What has gone wrong?

There is less consensus among the three observers' data than a truly accurate reading would demand, though one oddity rings true for all of them. There was a dark shadow, 'an Atmosphere or Dusky shade round the body of the planet',[19] that appeared moments after contacts were observed.

Such clear conditions, so perfect for an observation, all compromised by this dark and mysterious blur! Cook records his frustrations with the whims of the cosmos, stating it 'very much disturbed the times of the Contact, particularly the two internal ones'.[20]

In the meantime, the mood of Joseph Banks over on the island of Eimeo is decidedly upbeat. Having little interest in the whole Transit of Venus affair, he has instead busied himself observing the transit of three mortal Venuses at sunset, recording his joy in his journal:

> 3 hansome [sic] girls came off in a canoe to see us . . . they chatted with us very freely and with very little persuasion agreed to send away their carriage and sleep in [the] tent, a proof of confidence which I have not before met with upon so short an acquaintance.[21]

Oh yes! It was for good reason that the men of the *Dolphin* had crowned this place Aphrodite's Isle, and now there is a new Greek god: Joseph Banks Esq. is the mighty Adonis.

And so, as Captain Cook through the night focuses on the movements of heavenly bodies, so too does Banks. Each man is satisfied he has performed to the best of his abilities, but only Banks is confident his abilities are so fine that there are requests for yet more encores, noting in the morning: 'We prepared ourselves to depart, in spite of the entreaties of our fair companions who persuaded us much to stay.'[22]

In the meantime, others on the *Endeavour* have been so eager to have their own share of the charms of the Tahitian women that, as Banks chronicles on the day after the transit, we 'heard the melancholy news that a large part of our stock of Nails had been purloined by some of the ships company during the time of the Observation, when every body was ashore who had any degree of command'.[23]

It is a gross breach of one of the specific orders that Captain Cook had posted on the mainmast before arriving in Tahiti – 'No sort of Iron or anything that is made of Iron, or any sort of Cloth or other useful or necessary Articles, are to be given in Exchange for anything but Provisions'[24] – and in reaction to such wanton misuse of nails for females, Cook reacts quickly, and without mercy.

In short order, the culprit is detected and quivering seaman Archibald Wolf is strapped to the grating, before the entire ship's company realises the 'cat is let out of the bag'. That is, the cat o'nine tails is taken out of the red baize bag where it hangs in the mess deck, and brought upstairs, where Wolf eyes it with terror pure before being given two dozen lashes.

The crew wince with every whipping blow. It is a cruel thing to lead them to this nirvana bursting with beautiful women and nature, only to be told that if they let nature take its course, a bleeding back will be their reward.

•

The transit now behind them, Captain Cook retires to his private cabin, takes the key from his inside breast pocket, sits on his haunches and clicks open the thick padlock on the strongbox chained to the floor. For yes, it is time to open his sealed instructions from the Admiralty. Only now does he formally find out the second part of his mission, though he has long had a fair idea of it.

Taking his paper knife to the red wax of the Admiralty seal, he carefully opens the thick white envelope to reveal the single sheet of paper that contains his instructions.

> <u>Secret Additional Instructions for Lt James Cook,</u>
> You are to proceed to the Southward in order to make discovery of the [Unknown Southern] Continent . . . until you arrive in the Latitude of 40° . . . But not having discovered it or any Evident sign of it . . . you are to proceed in search of it to the Westward between the Latitude aforementioned and the Latitude of 35° until you discover it, or fall in with the Eastern side of the Land discovered by Tasman and now called New Zealand.

The Admiralty instructs him

> to observe the Nature of the Soil, and the Products thereof; the Beasts and Fowls that inhabit or frequent it, the Fishes that are

> to be found ... and in Case you find any Mines, Minerals, or
> valuable Stones you are to bring home Specimens of each, as also
> such Specimens of the Seeds of the Trees, Fruits and Grains as you
> may be able to collect ...

The Admiralty further instructs James Cook

> to observe the Genius, Temper, Disposition and Number of the
> Natives, if there be any, and endeavour by all proper means to
> cultivate a Friendship and Alliance with them, making them
> presents of such Trifles as they may Value inviting them to Traffic,
> and Showing them every kind of Civility and Regard; taking Care
> however not to suffer yourself to be surprised by them.

Yes, these are wide-ranging instructions, not least of which are the next
lines Cook reads:

> You are also with the Consent of the Natives to take Possession
> of Convenient Situations in the Country in the Name of the King
> of Great Britain.

'Take possession' of the land? If my Lords say so. Captain Cook has
previously done his best to take possession of a French ship of war, and
even a French city. At least there, there were people to claim possession
from. What if, in this case, you find the place uninhabited? My Lords
have thought of that.

In that case,

> take Possession for his Majesty by setting up Proper Marks and
> Inscriptions, as first discoverers and possessors.

If you don't find the continent at all, you will head towards New Zealand
and

> carefully observe the Latitude and Longitude in which that Land
> is situated and explore as much of the Coast as the Condition of
> the Bark, the health of her Crew, and the State of your Provisions
> will admit of ...[25]

A long journey on the unknown open ocean awaits. James Cook, whose
eye has been cast beyond the known horizon ever since he was a lad, and
whose ambition has brought him to the brink of just such a journey of
discovery, can hardly wait. It is nothing less than his long-time dream

coming true, sailing off into unknown territory. The last English Captains given the task – 'Foulweather Jack' Byron and Captain Wallis – had declined to go too far South without knowing what they may find in terms of safe harbour and supplies. But this Mariner has no hesitation.

He will indeed go South, and he gets straight to the business of victualling and preparing the *Endeavour* for its next leg: the first real exploring in unknown waters they are to embark upon. Within hours the 'Knights of the tar-brush', as the tars are sometimes jocularly referred to, are using the substance for which they have been named, as they ladle boiling hot tar from the kettle, mix it with oakum and force the lot into the ship's seams.

Early June 1769, Matavai Bay, untempered distemper

Oh dear.

There is a problem, Captain.

Yes?

The 'venereal distemper' has 'spread itself over the greatest part of the Ship's company',[26] reports Surgeon Monkhouse regretfully (his own appendage burning in his breeches; perhaps he shouldn't have striven to emulate Banks' example).

The pox, sir – chancres on the genitals, oozing pus, bouts of burning, stints of scratching. Many of the Tahitian women are displaying the symptoms, too.

The good news is that after three months of fresh fruit, fresh greens, newly slaughtered meat and bountiful clean water, there is no further trace of scurvy among any of the crew.

The bad news is that many of the crew are 'pissing razor-blades', as the expression goes.

'Call the Bosun there,' orders Captain Cook.

'Mr Gathray, pipe all hands to the Doctor.'[27]

Again, the sailors effectively move to the tune of the whistle and within minutes are silently if sullenly lined up in front of Surgeon's Mate, William Perry, who looks carefully askance at both Captain Cook and Surgeon William Monkhouse, who have asked him to do this lowest of all low medical tasks. (Actually, it does not surprise him that Surgeon Monkhouse should assign him this task. Mr Perry feels that Monkhouse is often jealous of his abilities, and can often be a bit of a prick when he feels like it. Speaking of which . . .) For he in turn now places his hands, very carefully, on all the sailors and officers. Every man must undo his fly and pull out his penis, at which point Perry – who in recent times has been assiduously studying *An Introduction to Physiology* by Malcolm Flemyng MD, the medical book he has brought with him that covers this procedure – places one hand on the base of the penis, and with the thumb and forefinger of the other hand delicately placed, moves it down the shaft of the penis to see if there is any emission of pus.

Finally it is done, and Perry's verdict is swift: 'All alike.'[28]

Every man-jack of those tested has the jack!

Captain Cook is appalled that it has spread so quickly. The first reports had occurred soon after arrival, and given there had been no such reports of anything like that happening to the crew of the *Dolphin*, under Captain Wallis, or at least none that he had heard, Cook can only draw one conclusion.

'To think that we had brought it along with us,' Captain Cook writes, 'gave me no small uneasiness.'[29]

He has done all in his power to prevent the disease progressing further, insisting that his men abstain from further congress.

Alas, it is a losing battle, his powers too feeble a match for the allure of buxom, expert women, which he readily acknowledges: 'the Women were so very liberal with their favours — or else Nails, Shirts, etc., were temptations that they could not withstand'.[30]

Yet Cook is soon relieved to find that the plague afflicting his men and the islanders is not of his doing. The Natives speak of a visit perhaps a year earlier, two ships that docked in a harbour to the East – which fits with the odd European tools they have come across that are not of British construction. The disease predates our arrival does it? Well, who else could be responsible but those earlier European arrivals? Happily, Cook records, 'I have the satisfaction to find that the Natives all agree that we did not bring it here.'[31]

Some of the *Endeavour*'s officers have their suspicions as to which nation these sexually filthy ships came from . . . After all, syphilis is not called by the English sailors 'the French disease' for nothing.

Merde!

For his part, however, Mr Banks suspects another nation, recording on 8 June, 'Fresh proofs of the Spanish ships every day in thing[s] of theirs which have been left here, among the rest a course shirt and a woolen jacket both of manufacture different from any English.'[32]

19 June 1769, Matavai Bay, a mad Monkhouse

Surgeon Monkhouse has finally got there.

He finally has a woman to call his own! And not just *any* woman, she is a handmaiden to the once Queen Oberea no less! How do you like that Mr Banks? Isn't she beautiful?

Mr Banks agrees.

So much so, in fact, that later that night Surgeon Monkhouse, looking for his love, hears a familiar giggle and realises . . . with that shattering shudder reserved for those who are humiliated, frustrated and angered all in the one overpowering jealous jolt . . . that she is in Banks' tent!

BANKS!

In an instant, Monkhouse is bursting into the tent of the rakish botanist, accusations at him and lamentations at her flying free.

'You should not sleep in here!'[33] he roars to the Tahitian woman, before trying to drag her out. The night is filled with curses, screams, confusion and anger.

The surgeon's intrusion into the tent kills the mood entirely, and soon all but one of my fair ladies in Mr Banks' tent rush out. The remaining woman is too alarmed, too frightened of this crude Mr Monkhouse to move at all. She wails as Banks sees to her, calming and reassuring the woman that everything will be all right. Banks leads her out, only to be greeted by a confused gaggle of Tahitian women and a very, *very* upset Surgeon Monkhouse.

'Mr Monkhouse and Mr Banks,' Parkinson will recount, 'had very high words, and I expected they would have decided it by a duel, which, however, they prudently avoided. Oberea, and her retinue, had gone to their canoe, and would not return; but Mr Banks went and stayed with them all night.'[34]

Surgeon Monkhouse is alone again. He reaches into his breast pocket for his snuff box, his only worldly comfort, it seems.

26 June 1769, Tahiti, sacred sojourn

The men of the *Endeavour* prepare for departure. Drying gunpowder on the deck while the sun is out, filling the water casks, rowing provisions to the ship, hauling everything onto the deck and stowing it in the hold – there is no shortage of work to be done, an endless litany of tasks that must be seen to before the ship is heading off into the great blue. Meanwhile, accompanied by Mr Banks, Captain Cook sets out in the pinnace at first light to fulfil his remaining instructions concerning Tahiti – to fully circumnavigate this, the principal island in the archipelago, and chart it, particularly noting where its best harbours lie.

Their days at sea pass idly, the weather clear, the temperature agreeable, and the ship content. Yet, neither Cook nor Banks takes rest from their tasks, the Captain observing, sketching and recording the coastline; the botanist keeping his eyes on fish, seabirds and distant plants. As they reach the Southern-most part of the island, Banks is amused to spy a rather familiar bird, one he has not seen since he was last home. A good ol' British goose! None of the men have seen fowl at Matavai Bay, but they know Captain Wallis had left behind some of the distinctly British birds. It seems as though one of Tahiti's Chiefs now keeps them as pets. The wonders of the British Empire!

Unfortunately, the novelty of the geese soon becomes a reminder of just how hungry they are. They had been hoping to find bread-fruit along the journey as it had been curiously absent from Matavai, a fact that seems to ring true elsewhere on the island. Where was that wonder food that had filled their bellies so many times before!

'We found the season for that fruit wholly over,' Cook records, 'and not one to be seen on the Trees, and all other fruit and roots were scarce.'[35]

It is the season of scarcity, another good reason to set sail.

The next few days entail an arduous journey, tracking the Western shoreline Northwards, to the home of their friend Oberea. On the final evening of their sojourn, they land in Oberea's district of *Papárra*, in the North-west of the island. The two propose to sleep the night at this place, however, they find Oberea absent, having gone to visit them at Matavai Bay. They settle matters with her father before proceeding to where they are told they may find a grand *marae*, the Tahitian version of a church or a temple, as the Englishmen tend to think of it – a built place of worship like a flattened wide pyramid without a peak, covered with ornate carvings, and upon and around which the Tahitians make sacrifices to their gods.

Captain and botanist are chatting idly, being careful of their step, when they suddenly stop dead in their tracks.

For here before them is the most monumental *marae* they have ever seen. Certainly they have seen several *maraes* before, around Matavai Bay, but they are little more than piles of rubble, even if they are important, revered piles of rubble. But not this *marae*. This is the great *marae* of Mahaiatea.

'It appeared to have been built many Years, and was in a State of decay,' Cook notes. 'From this it would seem that this Island hath been in a more Flourishing state than it is at present, or that Religious Customs are (like most other Nations) by these people less observed.'[36]

Banks is stunned by the workmanship, and has no doubt this is 'certainly the masterpiece of Indian architecture in this island . . . its size and workmanship almost exceed belief'.[37]

Cook takes it in, silently impressed, his surveyor's mind ticking rapidly to record the size of this man-made wonder: 'It is a long square of Stonework built Pyramidically; its base is 267 feet by 87 feet; at the Top it is 250 feet by 8 feet.'[38]

It is not just the structure's size, but also its beauty, the decorous adornments. Still what most captures the wonder of Mr Banks is its proportions.

'It is almost beyond belief,' he writes admiringly in his journal, 'that Indians could raise so large a structure without the assistance of Iron tools to shape their stones or mortar to join them, which last appears almost essential as the most of them are round; it is done though, and almost as firmly as a European workman would have done it . . . The labour of the work is prodigious . . .'[39]

The Captain and the great natural historian circle the perimeter of the building, finding to the West 'another court or paved area in which were several *ewhattas*, a kind of altars raised on wooden pillars about 7 feet high'.[40]

One wonders what those altars were used for, specifically . . . ?

Cook and Banks suddenly stiffen as they notice bones, *many* bones, on the edges of these suddenly macabre ruins. For yes, as they soon come to learn, these pillars had been used for a ghoulish purpose, where 'they offer meat of all kinds to the gods; we have seen large Hogs offered and here were the Skulls of above 50 of them besides those of dogs'.[41]

Oh, but their discomfort does not abate. For while making their silent way back to the boat, the two Englishmen cannot help but notice bones they had previously given no attention – bones that look strangely . . . familiar?

Good . . . *God*, these are *human bones*, especially ribs and vertebrae, scattered around like the leftovers of a great feast!

What is this place to which chance had brought them?

Where has this extraordinary altar of worship come from?

Myriad questions jostling in their minds, Cook and Banks proceed homewards to Matavai Bay looking for the one man who should be able to provide answers.

Tupia does not mince his words in response.

Yes, yes, animals are sacrificed here, great hogs and large birds. And yes . . . *we also sacrifice people.*

Doing his best to make the white men understand, Tupia describes a terrible war that took place only a year ago. Prior to the bloodshed, this grand *marae* belonged to Queen Oberea and another Chief named Oamo. But it was not to last, as Banks records the essence of Tupia's message:

'The greatest pride of an inhabitant of Tahiti is to have a grand *Marae*, in this particular our friends far exceed any one in the Island, and in the *Dolphin*'s time the first of them exceeded every one else in riches and respect as much.'[42]

As is so often the case, peace reigned until it was no longer convenient for one of the sides involved. That side was the Southern district, who concocted a terrible ambush, descending on Oberea's people and killing many of them, with their bones now the very powder beneath our feet. The Queen herself? She was forced to retreat to the safety of the mountains, an exile in her own lands.

'The Conquerors burnt all the houses which were very large and took away all the hogs etc.'

(Cook and Banks can only conclude 'the jaw bones which we saw hung up in Oamo's house . . . had been carried away as trophies and are used by the Indians here in exactly the same manner as the North Americans do scalps.'[43])

5 July 1769, Matavai Bay, stick, poke, scream, bleed, repeat

On this day, Joseph Banks, ever the astute observer with the scientific bent, finally gets to watch that most curious practice, a permanent marking of the body, undertaken by all on Tahiti. It is called a 'tattoo'. The white men have seen several different tattoos since arriving on the island, from 'ill-designed figures of men, birds, or dogs'[44] to 'Circles, Crescents, etc., which they have on their Arms and Legs'[45] to the figure Z that the women have 'simply on every joint of their fingers and Toes'[46] (in fact, many of the jacks now sport their own tattoos). For all the variation, all of the Tahitians 'agree in having their buttocks covered with a Deep black. Over this Most have Arches drawn one over another as high as their short ribs, which are near a Quarter of an inch broad. These Arches seem to be their great pride, as both men and Women show them with great pleasure.'[47]

And so it is performed today by a man upon the buttocks of a 12-year-old girl, who is held down by two women upon a mat, as with furrowed brow he breaks her skin with a 'very thin flat piece of bone'.[48] The bone is a little shorter than an index finger and an inch broad, with a handle at one end, and 30 razor-sharp pointed teeth stuck into the other end. And watch now as this highly skilled artisan, this tattooist dips the razor-sharp teeth into a 'lamp black'[49] substance – 'prepared from the Smoke of a Kind of Oily nut, used by them instead of Candles'[50] – and places it on the girl's buttock before delivering a series of short sharp blows from a stick to the handle of the instrument, which drives the black substance below the surface of the sweating girl's skin, every blow from the stick drawing a fresh stream of lightly spurting blood.

The effete Englishman winces with every blow.

'The patient bore this for about ¼ of an hour with most stoical resolution,' Joseph Banks chronicles, 'by that time however the pain began to operate too strongly to be peaceably endured, she began to complain and soon burst out into loud lamentations and would fain have persuaded the operator to cease; she was however held down by two women who sometimes scolded, sometimes beat, and at others coaxed her.'[51]

The process goes on for an hour, by end of which that particular buttock indeed has an impressive swirling Tahitian design upon it to match her other buttock, which had obviously undergone the same process some time before. And yet there remains work to do.

'The arches upon the loins upon which they value themselves much were not yet done, the doing of which they told caused more pain than what I had seen.'[52]

•

The men of the *Endeavour* continue to labour mightily to prepare their ship – even as Fort Venus is slowly dismantled, with all that is not local brought back on board. But as their date of departure draws near, some of the men grow reluctant to leave. After all, do they *really* want to leave this paradise? What can the rest of the world offer that Tahiti cannot? Marines Webb and Gibson certainly don't remember any Tahitian women with beautiful bodies back on the streets of England. Frankly, they don't remember much of anything before Tahiti, this heaven is simply too good to bid farewell to. Thinking on it some, the two make their decision and on the night of 9 July, which they know is the eve of the Captain ordering everyone back to the ship, the privates dash to the hills with their new wives. Having received an offer from one Chief regarding both land *and* servants, Webb and Gibson have decided to embrace the Tahitian way the way they embrace their women – with everything they have in them – and are now brothers in everything. A beautiful and free life in a boundless paradise awaits them.

To Cook, such desertions cannot be tolerated. Diplomacy be damned, desertion cannot be tolerated. Cook orders a dozen Chiefs, including King Tootaha, to be held as hostages. (With the transit now recorded, holding Tootaha no longer puts their whole operation at risk as it had been when Lieutenant Gore had done it.)

The dramatic gesture succeeds as all Tahiti races to return the miscreants and the two Marines return to the *Endeavour*, where their dashes are met with lashes – chained to a post and given a truly terrible 24 strokes each, until their backs are little more than a mess of red ribbons.

There is no shortage of sheepish faces among the witnesses, jack tars who may have been thinking of their own mad run for the mountains as well.

They aren't anymore.

12 July 1769, Tahiti, take Tupia from Utopia

Tupia is no longer as popular as he once was among the Chiefs. Assisting that dastardly Chief-napping Captain *Toote* has given many of the Tahitian elders reason to detest him, none more so than the humiliated King Tootaha. If Tupia knows anything, it's which way the wind is blowing, and he is now as eager to leave as Webb and Gibson were to stay.

Say, Mr Banks, why not take me with you?

In fact, Tupia doesn't ask so much as he states in a quiet but solid voice that he is 'resolved to go with you to England'.[53] Curious about the world beyond him, Tupia wishes to learn the white man's language and understand the source of their power – ideally to learn how to harness it himself, to return to his own island and rid it of his enemies. Not only that, he has been promised by the *Endeavour*'s men that *Pretanie* is only 10 moons sail from here. That is not too many moons, and should allow him to arrive back to his homeland with the knowledge he needs, and fit enough, and young enough, to claim back his island.

Mr Banks?

Banks, ever a fan of an odd plan, thinks it is a wonderful idea.

'He is certainly a most proper man,' Banks records, 'well born, chief Tahowa or priest of this Island, consequently skilled in the mysteries of their religion; but what makes him more than anything else desirable is his experience in the navigation of these people and knowledge of the Islands in these seas; he has told us the names of above 70, the most of which he has himself been at.'[54]

For while it is one thing for them to have the know-how, means and instrumentation to add to their knowledge of this world, it is quite another to have an extremely learned man who is happy to share what he knows – effectively sharing with them the knowledge that the Tahitian people have built up over the centuries. It is this last point he will belabour to convince the Captain.

'I will go ashore and return in the evening,' Tupia tells Banks, with seemingly no trace of doubt in his mind. 'I will make a signal for a boat to be sent off for me.'[55]

Banks agrees, somewhat amused at Tupia's confidence.

•

Banks approaches Captain Cook.

Why not take Tupia back to England with them?

For Cook the answer is easy – *No.*

For one thing, he is sure that the Lords would take a very dim view of having to support the Tahitian priest once they arrive back in England.

'The government will never in all probability take any notice of him,'[56] Cook tries to make his zealous gentleman friend understand. And then what do you propose, Mr Banks?

But Captain, their Captain, Tupia knows these waters for hundreds of miles around, and he can tell us the names of new lands, show us their safe harbours, help us commune with the Natives.

Captain Cook's brow furrows in thought; he is more interested, but still, fearing for Tupia's ultimate fate, says in the manner of a concerned father . . . no, Mr Banks.

Very well then. If the Captain does not wish to take him 'on his own account',[57] Mr Banks is happy to charge to another account . . . And so plays the card that has worked best throughout his life – his wealth.

Will Captain Cook agree to take Tupia if I, Joseph Banks of New Burlington Street, Mayfair, personally pay all of the Tahitian's future expenses and undertake to take care of him? (Beyond the joy of showing

Tupia off in London – *he will be the hit of the season!* – it will be of genuine scientific interest to see how the Tahitian will react and interact with English life and European ways. Banks records in his journal, 'Thank heaven I have a sufficiency and I do not know why I may not keep him as a curiosity, as well as some of my neighbours do lions and tigers at a larger expense than he will probably ever put me to.'[58])

The reluctant Cook agrees, and also allows Tupia to bring his servant boy, Tayeto, a lad of some 12 years old, for it is unthinkable that a man of Tupia's caste be obliged to wash his own clothes, prepare his own meals and bathe without an attendant.

13 July 1769, Tupia torn, Tahiti mourned

At last the day has come.

After three glorious months in this emerald Eden in the azure sea, it is time to bid farewell. As regretful as the moment is to most of the sailors, who have lived a life they could never have even dreamt of over these last 12 weeks – filled with food, drink, sunshine and voluptuous women of sweet disposition – it seems equally to be a matter of deep regret to the Tahitians that the men of the *Endeavour* are leaving them. Oberea is brought out on a canoe to farewell them, and she is surrounded by at least another hundred canoes, filled with waving, weeping Tahitians, many women among them.

Just before noon, Captain Cook gives the orders.

Weigh the anchor!

Some sailors man the capstan to haul up the anchor while others scramble across the spars, as swathes of heavy canvas unfurl and snap to attention, filling with the light Easterly breeze, perfect for the occasion.

The *Endeavour* starts to move, the sailors not on watch crowd the gunwales, waving to their swaying lovers and friends.

'On our leaving the shore,' Sydney Parkinson chronicles, 'the people in the canoes set up their woeful cry, *Awai, Awai*; and the young women wept very much. Some of the canoes came up to the side of the ship, while she was under sail, and brought us many cocoas.'[59]

Cook reflects on their time on Tahiti as the ship gathers speed:

> Some few differences have now and then happened owing partly
> to the want of rightly understanding each other, and partly to their
> natural thievish disposition, which we could not at all times bear
> with or guard against; but these have been attended with no ill

consequence to either side except the first, in which one of them was killed, and this I was very sorry for, because from what had happened to them by the *Dolphin* I thought it would have been no hard matter to have got and keep a footing with them without bloodshed.[60]

Two men on the *Endeavour* can see better than anyone. Joseph Banks and Tupia, who have climbed into the crow's nest, the lookout point on the highest spar of the topmast. For Banks this island has delivered the most extraordinary time of his life. For Tupia this had become his home, farewelled perhaps forevermore.

As Banks waves his hand in his delicate, limited, excruciatingly English manner, he watches the Tahitians on the shore and in the canoes swaying in a rhythmic farewell that beckons as much as it says goodbye. What sort of fools are they to leave this paradise?

Banks is also deeply moved to notice Tupia trying to hide his tears. Of course, it must be a deeply wrenching thing for the man to leave behind all he holds so dear, to wonder when next he will return. But Banks has little doubt of just how useful he will be to *them*.

A solitary night in his bed, lying pristine in the moonlight for the first time in many months beckons. Before dousing the lantern, Banks writes in his journal:

'We again launched out into the ocean in search of what chance and Tupia might direct us to.'[61]

16 July 1769, North of Tahiti, Tupia awes and draws

Only seconds after they weigh anchor in the small harbour of this island, Huaheine, the Natives – all dressed, tattooed and speaking in the manner of Tahitians – come out to the ship in canoes. They remain shy of coming aboard however, until they see Tupia, after which they all come aboard, the King and all. Captain Cook, accompanied by Mr Banks, Doctor Solander and Surgeon Monkhouse, head to shore with Tupia and this King, upon which they are treated to a grand ceremony led by . . . Tupia. The priest wastes no time in disrobing to the waist.

'He then sat down before a great number of the Natives that were collected together in a large Shed,' records James Cook '. . . the rest of us, by his own desire, standing behind.'[62]

Tupia moves through the crowd like a messiah of sorts, handing beads, handkerchiefs, bunches of feathers and even a black silk neckcloth to the parishioners before him. That seen to, Tupia heads off to the nearby *marae*, 'to pay his Oblations' as Cook records.[63]

Upon leaving, Captain Cook presents the leading Chief with a small plate inscribed with the words: 'His Britannic Majesty's Ship, *Endeavour*, Lieutenant Cook, Commander, 16th July, 1769, Huaheine'[64] and with that, the *Endeavour* men, along with Tupia, take their leave, weighing anchor and sailing South-west on their way to Tupia's original home island, Raiatea, the place from which he was exiled.

'The first thing done was the performing of Tupia's ceremony in all respects as at Huaheine. I then hoisted an English jack, and took possession of the Island and those adjacent in the name of His Britannic Majesty, calling them by the same names as the Natives do,'[65] Cook records.

As they arrive at the next island, the ritual is repeated and at each successive island Tupia performs his ceremony and Cook claims possession in the King's name. Simple as that.

However, Tupia finds himself just as busy when aboard the *Endeavour*, answering a relentless onslaught of questions from Captain Cook. What shape is the island? How far is it from the last one? What type of bay does it have? Indeed, the more the two men talk with one another – Tupia has his own litany of questions – the more the English Mariner comes to appreciate the sophistication of this Native priest and the level of their knowledge. No, the island folk do not have the huge vessels of the Europeans, nor the instrumentation, nor the books. But they have their own school of thought, their own systems, developed and honed over generations. Cook records that in their longer voyages, the South Sea islanders 'steer by the sun in the day, and in the night by the stars; all of which they distinguish separately by names, and know in what part of the heavens they will appear in any of the months during which they are visible in their horizon; they also know the time of their annual appearing and disappearing with more precision than will easily be believed by a European astronomer'.[66]

Cook is scarcely able to believe what the Natives are capable of 'their wonderful sagacity in foretelling the weather, at least the quarter from which the wind shall blow at a future time'.[67] Tupia is proud to show off his methods of weather divining, but one strikes Cook as particularly genius. 'They say that the Milky-way is always curved laterally; but sometimes in one direction, and sometimes in another: and that this curvature is the effect of its being already acted upon by the wind ...

so that, if the same curvature continues a night, a corresponding wind certainly blows the next day.'[68]

There can be no question of Tupia's talent, his value to the ship.

'Of their rules,' Cook writes, 'I shall not pretend to judge; but I know that, by whatever means, they can predict the weather, at least the wind, with much greater certainty than we can . . .'[69]

Joseph Banks, however, is not as convinced of Tupia's genius. For Tupia is becoming a fast favourite among the crew of the *Endeavour* for his 'wind spell':

Yes, he can bring the wind, just by chanting for it, I swear.

Look now, as he raises his arms to the heavens above, turns his face skywards, and begins his chant, with a refrain meaning, *Oh Tane, bring me a fair wind!*

'*O Tane, ara mai matai, ora mai matai.*

'*O Tane, ara mai matai, ora mai matai.*

'*O Tane, ara mai matai, ora mai matai.*'[70]

Sure enough, within mere minutes the sails flap and then fill, and the *Endeavour* starts to surge.

It is Tupia *magic*, I tell you!

Banks is far less impressed as he notes in his journal that when it comes to casting his spell, Tupia 'never began until he saw a breeze so near the ship that it generally reached her before his prayer was finished'.[71]

But Tupia's popularity leads to pride, which quickly leads to a fall . . . in his popularity. As sailor James Magra would recount: 'Tupia . . . was a man of real genius, a priest of the first order, and an excellent artist: he was, however, by no means beloved by the *Endeavour*'s crew, being looked upon as proud and austere, extorting homage, which the sailor who thought themselves degraded by bending to an Indian, were very unwilling to pay . . .'[72]

However the white men regard him, Tupia must simply adapt the best he can to the rhythm of life aboard the *Endeavour*, the discipline, the eternal maintenance, the periodic furl and unfurl of sails. He spends his time with the Captain, trying to understand the ways of the white men, particularly the way they keep a calendar and measure months the way he measures moons, always with an eye to the promise that they will get to England within 10 moons.

Moving like an exotic fish through a coral reef, darting from one spot to another, Tupia pops up all over the ship, a silent observer. He is fascinated by the riggings, the ropes, the routine with which the sailors move about, how they can manoeuvre so great a vessel through so capricious a sea, how they sound the depths and measure the speed, how they record shapes and sizes of islands, their distance and direction from each other, and how important such charts are to them. Would Captain Cook like his help in making his chart of Tahiti and its surrounds, detailing all of the holy man's own knowledge of the islands in these parts? Yes, Captain Cook would. The chance to create such a map – giving the visitors the benefit of these centuries of accrued knowledge, in just a short time – is an extraordinary one.

Excited, James Cook quickly turns the Great Cabin into a supremely scientific space. At one end of the table sits Mr Banks, the Doctor and Sydney Parkinson, all three learned men discussing and dissecting flora and fauna, which genus is this, what species is that, and what precisely shall we call it?

At the other end, Captain Cook and Tupia stand over maps and charts, tracing coastlines with their fingers and sketching islands with pencils. Scattered throughout the room and captivated by both ends of the table, the *Endeavour*'s senior officers and Midshipmen are in awe, knowing that this is a time to listen rather than speak.

Very occasionally, when Captain Cook is so engrossed in the task at hand that he will barely notice – his heavy brow deeply furrowed in concentration – Tupia leaves Cook's side and flits to Banks' end of the table, eager to paint and draw under the watchful eye of Sydney Parkinson who has begun to teach him.

For the most part, though, Tupia stands right there as Cook, with an expert's practised hand, places the charting paper upon the table and as Tupia uses his finger to trace the shape of Tahiti, the island at the centre of his own world, Cook's pencil carefully traces behind. Sometimes, Tupia will stop him as the shape that is emerging has an error and does not conform to the shape the priest has in his head, at which point Captain Cook rubs it out and redraws it. Bit by bit, however, the coastline contours of Tahiti emerge, at which point Tupia moves on to the next island he is eager to visit, Raiatea; its place is marked, its path is traced, and another piece of Tupia's archipelago emerges before Cook's eyes have even seen it.

•

As the *Endeavour* hops from South Sea island to South Sea island, the charts form. And after each island is drawn, Tupia tells Cook whether, 'it was either larger or smaller than Tahiti, and likewise whether it was high or low, whether it was peopled or not, adding now and then some curious accounts relative to some of them'.[73] Yes, Tupia even recounts the characteristics of the tribes that live on the islands and knows the names of the many Chiefs. And of course, Cook also marks down the name of each island, trying to record with European phonetics the local nomenclature.

Tupia does not measure distance by degree of latitude or longitude of course, nor by nautical miles or leagues, but simply how many days sail one is from another, and in which broad direction, which helps Cook determine a rough positioning of each island. And so it goes, through a combination of Cook's European knowledge surveying and chart-making, and Tupia's ancestral knowledge, passed down from father to son for nigh on a millennium, a singularly valuable chart is made, recording the outlines, positions and names of no fewer than 70 islands.

Tupia himself displays such a singularly impressive amount of knowledge that Cook himself is stunned. Years later, one who talked to Cook of it on a later voyage, Johann Forster, would recount that Tupia 'must have been the most intelligent man that ever was met with by any European navigator in these isles'.[74]

Which is a good thing for the task ahead.

Now early August, the *Endeavour* is about to turn South, soon to sail into unexplored waters, the endless unknown of the great blue before them. Alexander Dalrymple is convinced that somewhere in that direction lies the Great Southern Land. Cook does not believe it, but suddenly it occurs to him that he is with someone who might know!

Say, Tupia, is there . . . is there, perhaps . . . a large land mass, a VERY big island somewhere . . . to our South?

Tupia considers it for no longer than a heartbeat.

Of course not. If there was, we would know about it. There is nothing of significance to the South.

Very well then.

Captain Cook is, frankly, not surprised. But he has his orders and follows them – ordering the *Endeavour* South on 9 August.

Late August 1769, somewhere in the South Seas, comet and ka mate cometh

One night at the end of August, there's a faint streak of light in the night sky, which Mr Green quickly identifies as *Comet Nebulus*, though

Tupia's understanding differs wildly. Standing on the swaying deck, as still as a statue in the moonlight, Tupia recognises the faint streak for what it obviously is – a sign from the gods. He is aghast, capable only of whispering to his servant boy, Tayeto, whose eyes widen in horror as he gazes towards the heavens. The comet brings ill portents. The Bola Bola people will soon kill the people of Raiatea. So it is known. Despite this news, Tayeto steels himself. They are far from Raiatea, and Tupia has not failed him yet. Tupia and Tayeto contemplate their fates in silence, though are each comforted by the presence of the other – two beings from the sweet tropical islands, so very, very far from home and getting farther away all the time.

The *Endeavour* sails on. The winds blow ever colder. There is no sign of any Great Southern Land – just endless horizons of hazy oceans.

●

Putting down all his navigational equipment after once more 'shooting the sun', Captain Cook does his calculations and records that on this day of 2 September, the *Endeavour* has indeed reached the latitude of 40 degrees South.

Here the weather deteriorates considerably and Captain Cook decides to alter course to the Northward, noting in his journal, 'but as the weather was so very tempestuous I laid aside this design, and thought it more advisable to stand to the Northward into better weather lest we should receive such Damage to our Sails and Rigging as might hinder further Prosecution of the Voyage'.[75]

As their journey continued, Cook observed an interesting phenomenon. 'Note, while we [were] between the Latitude of 37 and 40 degrees we had constantly blowing tempestuous weather, but since we have been to the Northward of 37 degrees, the weather hath been very moderate.'[76]

And Banks later wrote: 'The Captn told me that he has during this whole vo[y]age observd that between the degrees of 40 and 37 South latitude the Weather becomes suddenly milder in a very great degree, not only in the temperature of the air but in the Strenght and frequency of the gales of wind, which increase very much in going towards 40 and decrease in the same proportion as you approach 37.'[77] This weather pattern was later dubbed the roaring forties.

●

With still no continent in sight, they now head to the place named by the Dutch in the mid-1600s, *Nova Zealandia*, after Holland's province of Zeeland, and referred to by the English as New Zealand.

It was first discovered by Europeans back in 1642, when the Dutch maritime explorer Abel Tasman – sent by the Dutch East India Company to find what lay East of the Dutch East Indies, centred on their Javanese capital of Batavia, and whether Native peoples might have anything worth . . . stealing – had turned North-east from Van Diemen's Land and discovered what he thought to be a large land mass at latitude 42° 17' and longitude 171° 14'. Never one to sail blind, Cook has read everything written about Abel Tasman's landing on this large piece of land in the South Pacific. It had not gone well . . .

Approaching the shore, the Dutchmen had been met with threatening warriors in canoes, who only retreated when Tasman fired a cannon. Alas, the warriors returned, chanted, and dragged four Dutch sailors overboard before clubbing them to death. Not for nothing would Tasman name his sole, brief contact point in New Zealand *Moordenaersbay*[78] ('Murderer's Bay'), and the closest his men had come to landing were the four bodies on the seabed, just offshore.

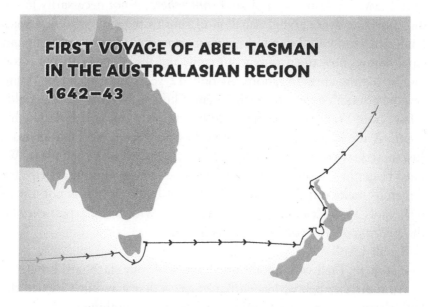

FIRST VOYAGE OF ABEL TASMAN IN THE AUSTRALASIAN REGION 1642–43

After meeting the fearsome locals, Tasman did not linger longer to explore the land's contours, and so the Royal Society now wishes to know . . . was it perhaps the start of the Great Southern Land's coast?

They will, of course, find out in due course – *South-west, at six knots, steady as she goes if you please, Mr Molineux* – and in the interim engage in the usual ship-board activities. One of these is musket and cannon drills, which take place under a cloudy sky as the gun crews again fire their great guns into the vastness of the ocean. When it comes to the small arms, the Marines, petty officers and seamen are put through their paces as ever, though this time with a particularly interested observer. It is Tupia, eager to learn everything he can about this strange power the white men possess, against the day he will need such power to retake his home island of Raiatea from the heathens. Before long he, too, is bringing a musket to his shoulder, squeezing the trigger and having the satisfaction of seeing a splash just a few yards in front of the white top he had been aiming at.

•

It is but an occasional occurrence that those who make their mark on the map are of low rank and common birth. And yet . . .

On 24 September, something is drifting along the surface of the water. Not a fish, nor a bird. Green, brown, long tendrils and spooling loops of it. Seaweed! A sure sign of land *somewhere*, if not necessarily in the direction they were going. A gallon of rum to the man who first spies land! The land you find will bear your name from here on in! Captain Cook knows how to encourage his crew, and the promise of rum is too terrific for the crew to ignore. At only 12 years old, Nicholas Young certainly doesn't expect to be that man. Though, like any boy, he holds a faint hope that it will be him, that he can prove his worth despite his youth. A week goes by, and nothing has been seen. No land anyway. Just more seaweed. More seaweed. More . . . driftwood? Land birds? We must be getting closer! Finally, on 6 October, the conditions are ripe for a man to make out the faintest glimmer of land. Only it is not a man who spots New Zealand. It is a boy. A boy with the sharpest eyes on the *Endeavour*, the young Nicholas Young.

'Land! LAND!'[79]

It is there, I tell you, about nine leagues off our starboard bow.

From directly below, Joseph Banks gazes that way but – denied the lad's sharp eyes and height above deck – can see nothing.

No matter.

'Within a few minutes,' Banks will recount, 'the cry circulated and up came all hands . . .'[80]

Still none of them down low can see anything, and for a better view, one by one – led by Captain Cook and Mr Banks – they clamber up the mast, each anxious that their eyes can spy what might be, no, what Joseph Banks particularly is convinced *must* be, the Great Southern Land.

Captain Cook, of course, does not believe it – but is fairly sure that it will be part of New Zealand.

Abel Tasman had charted some of its West coast. This will be simply the East coast of New Zealand, he is sure. The first step, of course, is to name what has just been sighted by European eyes for the first time.

For perpetuity let it be known on atlases of the world as 'Young Nick's Head' in honour of the boy who first saw it. The lad beams red with pleasure, a little like a summer sunrise. A bonus is the gallon of rum he is given for his reward, to be consumed entirely by his 12-year-old self.

For his part, Joseph Banks bubbles with enthusiasm as he dashes down his first impressions in his journal, his mere hopes crystallising into solid facts with every slashing stroke of his pen:

> Land still distant 7 or 8 leagues, appears larger than ever, in many parts 3, 4 and 5 ranges of hills are seen one over the other and a chain of Mountains over all, some of which appear enormously high. Much difference of opinion and many conjectures about Islands, rivers, inlets etc., but all hands seem to agree that this is certainly the Continent we are in search of.[81]

Well, at least all hands that shake Banks' hand. In the Captain's mind, whether or not this is indeed the Great Southern Land will emerge in due course. What is most important for the moment is what he sees through his telescope in a large bay a couple of days later as they move along the coast – this land is inhabited.

'We saw in the Bay several Canoes, People upon the Shore, and some houses in the Country.'[82]

Ideally, the Natives will be friendly. For now, Cook orders his men to bring the ship into the bay while he begins the first accurate map of a land that until now has been a few uncertain lines and a smattering of rough co-ordinates ...

CHAPTER EIGHT
REVEALING NEW ZEALAND

They eat their enemies Slain in Battle – this seems to come from custom and not from a Savage disposition, this they cannot be charged with.[1]

Captain Cook, 1770

Our friends here, do not seem to feel the want of such places as we have not yet seen the least appearance of cultivation, I suppose they live entirely upon fish, dogs and Enemies ...[2]

Joseph Banks on a Tribe of Māori Natives
specific to Queen Charlotte Sound, 1770[3]

Their faces are the most remarkable, on them they by some art unknown to me dig furrows in their faces a line deep at least and as broad, the edges of which are often again indented and most perfectly black ... always different spirals ... all these finished with a masterly taste and execution, for of a hundred which at first sight you would judge to be exactly the same, on a close examination no two will prove alike; nor do I remember to have seen any two alike, for their wild imaginations scorn to copy as appears in almost all their works.[4]

Joseph Banks on the New Zealand Natives, 1770

8 October 1769, North Shore of Tūranganui-a-Kiwa, first contact for all, final contact for one

And ... stroke.

And ... stroke.

And ... stroke.

On this perfect afternoon, a soft breeze caresses the English sailors, helping to cool them from their exertions as they draw closer to this strange shore.

Armed and primed in the pinnace, their nerves tingling with alertness, the Marines feel they are ready for whatever this land may throw at them, once they set foot on the beach. In the yawl, right behind them, Captain Cook, Joseph Banks and his gentlemen are being rowed by four young jacks. With his eye for coastal detail, the Captain notes that the land rises high up from the shore in chalky white cliffs, not unlike those in Dover. Yet as high as those cliffs reach, the middle is 'low land with hills gradually rising behind one another to the chain of high mountains inland'.[5]

With nerves tingling ever more, they now see many individual plumes of smoke, some by the bay's edge, others far inland, but so very many and so widespread that the men agree with something less than ardour: 'this is surely a most populous country'.[6]

Not long after the bows of the boats nudge onto the fine sandy shore on the East side of a small river mouth, Cook spies some Natives on the opposite bank – muscular brown torsos with black markings, jet black hair in a knot atop their heads – and, eager to talk with them, decides to take a chance.

'Carry us over,' he orders the four sailors in the yawl before turning to the posse in the pinnace. 'Lay at the entrance,'[7] he orders them, in case they need a rapid escape.

Alas, as soon as the Natives see the yawl crossing the river, they fade back into the bush. Undaunted, Cook has the yawl come into the shallows and stay there, held by two of his men knee-deep in the water, as he, Banks and the Doctor clamber ashore with weaponry in hand and walk apprehensively up the beach to the edge of the bush, hoping to see Natives. Peering through the trees and scrub, the Captain can make out homes and huts, the dwellings of the Natives. But nary a soul to greet them . . .

•

From the pinnace, lying at the river entrance, the Marines are watching closely, first noting the yawl landing on the West bank, then the Captain and his two companions walking towards the huts back in the trees.

Good *God*!

Look! Four Natives have emerged from the bushes on the Eastern side of the river, further upstream and are stalking towards the unwitting sailors waiting with the yawl, as their own attention lingers on the Captain and the gentlemen heading in the other direction.

'Drop downstream!'[8] one of the Marines shouts to the four oblivious lads, who turn their heads, wondering what the trouble might be. The Marines are motioning wildly, frantically trying to make them see . . . what?

Four stalking Natives, each one now knee-deep in the river, each one with a long spear. The boys pile into the yawl and push off downstream. Stroke. Stroke! STROKE! But the agile Natives bound through the shallows in swift pursuit. The Marines shout and scream, some begin to run upstream along the river along the bank, but the Natives continue to advance on the yawl, spears foremost in the sunlight. Even from this distance, they look as serious as a hole in the hull.

In an instant the morning stillness is shattered by the blast from the musket of the coxswain in the pinnace, enough to bring Captain Cook, Banks and the Doctor running back towards the river.

Curiously, at the sound of the shot, the Natives merely turn their heads towards the Marines at the river mouth, then keep on charging nimbly forward.

Another blast shatters the air.

This time, the Natives take no notice of the musket's report and keep moving forward. Why should they, they have never heard such a noise. It holds no fear for them.

And what now?

In the startled skip of a heartbeat, they raise their long spears, pointy ends towards the white men, and *charge the yawl* . . . . before, with the crack of a single shot, the lead Native goes down in a bloody splash.

Time hangs suspended.

The four sailors are the first to understand what has happened.

The Marine's musket ball has flown straight and true, through the heart of the enormous man who'd been about to thrust the first spear. He is Te Maro, the great-grandson of Chief Rakaiatane, fearless Chief-to-be of the *Te Aitanga-a-Hauiti* people.[9] He falls with his spear still in hand, his arm still crooked above his head, his body bobbing up and down as crimson first blurts and then spurts, weeps and then seeps from his chest into the crystal water. He is dead within 30 seconds, his spear falling from his lifeless hand and settling on the bed of the river shallows.

The other three Natives, stunned by the devastation wrought by a single clap of thunder, stand stock-still. Their faces betray their shock, their horror that so great and noble a Chief could fall so quickly, so unceremoniously.

They had been about to attack these pasty white figures from another world when thunder had come from the river mouth, where the other white figures stand, and then the mighty Chief had fallen down dead, at their feet.

His body is swaying slightly with the flowing water, a vibrant red feather comes loose from his thick dark hair and begins its own journey downstream as the stiff Native cloth of his garments flutters gracefully in the current. Having departed to join their sacred ancestors, he takes with him an ancient understanding of the land, the sea, the gods – now lost for all time in the space of a final gushed heartbeat. At least, to these warriors, the greatest honour is to die in battle, and he has done exactly that, at the head of his warriors, defending his land.

The sailors in the yawl stare down at the fallen man, too. His face holds no expression beyond the vague, unfocused mask of the recently dead. But the carvings and tattoos that mark his face? Not even death can take those. Deep canals marked with what looks like black ink run up and down his face, regular whirls and spirals, each one unique and telling a story and signifying the stature, achievements and tribe of the man who lay beneath them.

For no less than two minutes, an *eternity*, neither the Natives nor the boy sailors move – each group petrified. The Marines are motionless, too, like figures in a tableau.

Are we about to be slaughtered by spears? the sailors wonder. *One move, and it may be our hearts pierced through, our lifeless bodies swaying in the river's flow.*

Who will be the next to fall by thunder? the Natives wonder. *Who will be the next to die by magic? Don't move!*

But one man *is* moving and shouting. It is Captain Cook, musket in hand, running towards them, closely followed by Banks and the Doctor. The Natives are jolted out of their stunned state and quickly begin dragging the body of Te Maro up the riverbank, a smear of blood in his wake. But he is too heavy! They only get him a few yards before they give up the uneven struggle, letting their Chief's crumpled body slump to the muddy ground before they flee into the bush.

From the safety of the woods, the Natives see the tall one, the leader, with the younger one beside him, look down on their slain Chief.

Cook and Banks examine the body curiously: 'He was a middle sized man tattooed in the face on one cheek only in spiral lines very regularly formed; he was covered with a fine cloth of a manufacture totally new to us . . . his complexion brown but not very dark.'[10]

The body is left where it lies. Cook and his party row back to the *Endeavour* in an uneasy silence.

The night will be even more uneasy as Banks records: 'Soon after we came on board we heard the people ashore very distinctly talking very loud no doubt, as they were not less than two miles distant from us, consulting probably what is to be done tomorrow.'[11]

Those voices are a mix of mass misery and rage, a high keening, an unworldly sound to make all those aboard the *Endeavour* feel as far from home as ever they have been in their lives – which is in fact the geographical truth. On the morrow, both the Englishmen and the Natives will be ready for each other, if not at all sure what the other will do. Captain Cook doubles the guard on deck this night, against the chance that the Natives might make a nocturnal attack.

At dawn, Captain Cook and Mr Banks bring their spyglasses to bear and scan the shoreline near the river mouth. They spot the Natives immediately. A group of some 50 men, gathered on the Western bank of the river.

All are dressed the same, adorned in what must be the Native equivalent of a uniform. A piece of cloth hangs from each waist, and from each head grows a thick mass of dark hair, knotted and woven with red feathers. But most striking are their faces. Each one is fiercer than the last, lavishly adorned with tattoos of spirals and swirls, a black web of menace. Peering closer, Cook wonders if these markings are the same as those he saw in Tahiti. Their lips are certainly tattooed in the Tahitian fashion, a simple blackening of the skin, but the markings on their cheeks are so much deeper, so much darker than those he has seen before. It is almost as though . . .

No. Surely not. But yes, these are not just tattoos, but also scars!

Four spears rise above the throng of warriors, the rest hold smaller club-like weapons. Mercifully, there appears to be no mass army formed as the Englishmen had feared.

Captain Cook must go ashore. The ship's company is in desperate need of fresh water. Non-co-operative Natives or no, terrifying tattoos or no, James Cook will not be deterred. Ordering the pinnace and yawl back into the water, Cook fills the boats with Marines and the sturdiest, burliest and most menacing of his sailors.

Tupia is eager to come too. The last few weeks, particularly, have been wretched for him, trapped in this realm of cramped spaces, sweaty sailors, stale food and a chill that does not abate, a freezing of their very souls like he and Tayeto have never experienced, with their only recourse having been to dress in the absurdly cumbersome European garments that the sailors had lent them. So, yes, Tupia has had enough of the hulking wooden ship and is desperate for a break, for the chance to again feel solid earth beneath his feet, see trees, smell bush, gaze upon birds and watch animals. He will go too.

And . . . stroke.

And . . . stroke.

And . . . stroke.

And . . . now they surge forward with a rush as the breaking waves catch their boat and hurtle them towards the beach, where the Natives await. It is as though the gods of this land are anxious to see what will happen when the two parties make contact, though whether the result will be blood on the white sands or an embrace of peace, nobody is sure. The waves pound on the Eastern side of the river, crashing down with a frantic force before receding and rallying, ready to do it all over again. It is a compelling vision, but pales in comparison to what takes place on the *Western* bank. Some 50 men have gathered there, and now sit patiently, prepared for the arrival of these strangely pasty-faced visitors in their amazingly large vessel.

Eager for peace, even at his own risk, Cook orders all the men, including the armed Marines, to stay on board and take the vessels back out beyond the breakers, while he, Banks, Solander and Tupia are dropped to shore during a lull in the menacing shore break.

Keep an eye on us, I will give the signal to land if needed, the Captain tells Sergeant Edgcumbe.

Very cautiously now, the three Englishmen and the Tahitian approach the edge of the river, unsure of how to proceed. Perhaps the Natives will be familiar with the Tahitian tongue? Surely it must be closer than English. Tupia calls out to them.

All 50-odd Natives rise up at once.

'Every man produced either a long pike or a small weapon of well-polished stone about a foot long and thick enough to weigh 4 or 5 pounds,'[12] records Joseph Banks.

Arms at the ready, some of the Natives call back to Tupia in their own tongue, their words unknown.

I teie nei!

Neither Tupia nor the white men can make sense of the language, it is foreign to their ears. But the tone, the timbre of their tongues? That is far more recognisable.

Leave. Right now.

There can be no misinterpreting this message, yet Cook is not one to turn his heel on the orders of a rabble of Natives. Yes, he and his men will stay put, though their resolve is rattled somewhat when the Natives take their next step.

Suddenly, they move into some kind of formation, with several rows of them standing behind one large Native, who crouches as if he is about to pounce forth like a big cat.

Behind him, the 50 warriors also crouch. Shining muscles ripple in the sunshine. Tattooed visages scowl at the white men with wide-eyed grimaces and snaking poked-out tongues that would make a cannon quake, a newly launched ship slip *back* up the slipway.

In the distance, there is the cry of a bird. Around the white men, insects buzz. Waves crash on the beach. The rhythmic thudding may be distant drums, or their own hearts, they can't be sure.

The lead Native gives out an ear-piercing yell.

The 50 warriors give out an ear-piercing yell in response.

What follows is an extraordinary chanting dance, 'a dancing war song',[13] as Lieutenant Gore describes it from his vantage point on the yawl. It is filled with synchronised moves of vibrating violence and it is 'calculated in my opinion to cheer each other and intimidate their enemies'[14] – a mesmerising rhythm of rage that seems to come not just from 50 yards away across a river, but from ages past.

At first the cadence is slow and the shouts are no more than rolling thunder in the distance. But soon that thunder is overhead and the pace is a race, the shouts are booms and the moves ever more violent, until the full-blown storm breaks upon the white men.

And though the Englishmen cannot understand the words, there is no doubt as to their broad thrust:

We are very disposed to kill you. We do not want you on this land. Go. And go now. Leave the field. Go!

Their entire bodies now are a blur of movement, their heads are thrown back as they roar their rage – still in perfect cadence – 'distorting their mouths, lolling up their tongues and turning up the whites of their eyes',[15] even as the thrusting movements of their twisting hands and shaking fists demonstrate their desire to *hurt*. Their eyes widen, their pupils roll back and they make grimaces of such grotesque contortions it is as if they are channelling spirits from the underworld where their ancients dwell.

The Natives intersperse their war dance with terrifying pauses, the silence almost more menacing than the staggering staccato of yells and movements – shouting when the leader shouts, stomping when he stomps, and slapping their thighs when he slaps.

Cook, Banks, the Doctor – and their companions out in the boats – watch, mesmerised, never having seen anything like it in their lives, a verbal and visual violence as they have never experienced. No missile is yet thrown, no blood yet shed, but the white men still feel as though a battle is just breaking upon them. Are these Natives about to attack, Captain Cook wonders, and takes his musket from the sling around his shoulder, levels it, and almost without thinking runs his thumb over the flint to ensure that it had been knapped to a sharp edge, the best to create a spark when the flint hits the flat metal of the frizzen. Satisfied he pulls the cock back, even as the Natives become ever more threatening.

As it all builds to a climax, it is as if they have been possessed *en masse* by evil spirits, as they finish in one last shattering howl before falling silent, their hands dropping back to their thighs in unison, their snaking tongues finally rolled back to their mouths, their pupils returning from rolled-back eyes.

Well, if there's one thing these Natives will have to respect, no, *fear*, it is the power of muskets. Cook raises his musket, levels it at this dance of war, and squeezes the trigger. A crack, and the shot is whistling through the air, flying closer . . . closer . . . only to fall *deliberately* short, striking the water with a spraying burst of foam. A warning shot.

It is heeded. The Natives take a cautious step back, then another, frightened yet resolute that they will not fully retreat.

Very well then. Still eager for peace, Cook orders his own men to retreat from the river's edge back down towards the river mouth. They move slowly, calmly, facing the grimacing Natives, even as Cook waves his hand, signalling for the Marines to land. Within minutes the pinnace comes flying – propelled by a large wave that delivers it right on to the beach, unscathed. The Marines with weaponry and ammunition loaded down, are soon piling out and forming up.

Under Captain Cook's lightly uttered orders, Sergeant Edgcumbe unfurls the Union Jack. Flying it high atop a flagpole they have brought for this very purpose, the Marines slowly march up the beach, conscious of the tentative peace they have with the Natives. As a further gesture of peace, Cook leads the procession 200 yards ahead of the Marines and is soon back by the river's edge with Mr Monkhouse, Mr Green and the gentlemen all. These elegant men are now backed by His Majesty's Marines, muskets ready and loaded, each man holding fast in his formation.

Great Britain, in the form of all the King's men, has arrived.

The Natives remain in a looser war dance formation, eyes popping, heads rolling, weapons waving. Cook's warning shot may have rattled them, but not nearly enough to take the menace out of their presence. These are truly fierce warriors, and this pre-battle ritual is *terrifying*.

For his part, James Cook has no desire to see more violence or death as had happened the day before to the Native Chief whose body he can see still lying up on the muddy riverbank where it was left. He is also cognisant of his instructions from the Admiralty, which he repeats often to his own men: to 'endeavour by all proper means to cultivate a Friendship and Alliance'[16] with the Natives. In lieu of friendship, peace will suffice. That is all they need in order to fill their water casks, restock their wood supplies and take . . . their leave.

Cook gives Tupia a nod. His moment has arrived – he takes a few steps forward, his feet in the river's muddy shallows, and hails the Natives across the water.

'Hello!'[17]

And now a cry comes back.

'Come over . . . ! We are friends!'[18]

Tupia understands it! And they had understood him!

Extraordinary.

Though separated by time and tide – not to mention 4000 miles of ocean – these Natives share a language, or at least enough words, with the Tahitians to be intelligible!

'It was,' Cook will record, 'an agreeable surprise to us to find that they perfectly understood him.'[19]

And now that they can understand each other, Tupia dares hope they might be able to come to an understanding.

'We want provisions!' Tupia calls again. 'And Water! We will give you iron in exchange!'[20]

The call comes back. Yes, the white men may have food and water.

Encouraged, Tupia goes on:

'I desire you to lay down your arms!'[21]

This request is less well received.

Lay down our weapons? It would be easier to lay down our heads. We are warriors. These weapons are part of our birthright, practically part of our bodies.

The hair on the back of Tupia's neck rises, even as he stiffens. Be careful. This is not going the way we want it to go. Translating the tension he feels radiating off the Natives, Tupia warns his party to be ready for treachery at any moment.

These men are not your friends!

At least one part of the problem is that the iron and beads the white men are offering seem to have little purchase with these Natives.

'They seemed to set little value upon either,' Banks notes, 'but especially upon the iron the use of which they were totally ignorant of.'[22]

'*Kāo!*' No.

Tupia pleads in vain.

Again and again, he makes the request, imploring them to put down their spears and clubs for their own safety. But they will not cede. To the contrary, they start to brandish their weapons once more.

Anxious, Tupia warns Cook and the others, again and again: 'Be upon your guard! They are not your friends! Be upon your guard!'[23]

Cook, nevertheless, remains confident that they can collectively keep the peace – and now signals for the Natives to swim across the river to them. The Natives respond by signalling to Cook that he and his men should instead swim the river to meet them on their own side.

'At last however,' as Banks records, 'an Indian stripped himself and swam over without arms.'[24]

Surely this is a sign of peace, thinks James Cook.

And when the first Native swimmer arrives on the opposite riverbank and is neither beaten nor killed, when the cracking thunder of yesterday is not heard, when he is given something by the white men, two more Natives come across the river, and then some 30 of them – but the crowd all bring their arms with them. And so now both the Englishmen and the Natives are standing face to face, both parties armed, two worlds set to collide.

Captain Cook, Banks and their party get their first close-up look at the New Zealand Native weaponry – including many a *patu*, a foot-long club of well-polished stone or wood, and many a *taiaha*, a five-foot-long spear of heavy wood – just as the Natives are able to get a close-up look at the English thunder-sticks, trying to determine how such a small and *hauarea*, insignificant-looking thing could make such a noise and kill at such a distance. Does it unleash bad spirits, do you suppose? And why do you suppose that these men are wearing such strange garb? One of them has a shining blue coat with alluring bursts of gold light coming from it, while others have red coats and white trousers, and still others have a strange kind of knee-length garment that floats about their legs as they walk.

Eager to take the Natives' minds off weaponry, and move their interaction off fighting and killing, Cook busies himself overseeing the giving of presents to them – iron and beads – something that has worked so well so far in their journey.

Alas, alas . . .

They care not for the proffered items.

No, what the Natives truly want is obvious – those thunder-sticks.

And they are happy to trade for them.

Will you take this *patu* for that musket?

Given that Marines and sailors have been hanged for less, the answer is a very firm no, indicated by grimacing and furiously shaking their heads. The Natives, however, are not sure what the head-shaking signifies and after several of them try to grab the muskets, Cook shouts to Tupia to make clear what the dreadful consequences will be if they persist.

'They must kill you if you snatch anything from them!'[25] Tupia calls frantically.

Is that understood?

Not really.

Captain Cook sees his men grip their muskets with intent, even as they narrow their eyes. The Natives in turn tighten their hands around spears and ready themselves in the sand. The tension swells, a pregnant promise of pandemonium to come, though neither side is yet ready to act.

Within a minute of the warning, one enormous Native, a Chief by the name of Te Rakau, has grabbed a 'hanger' – a short sword worn at the waist – from the astronomer Mr Green, and is so pleased he lets out 'a cry of exultation' before waving it triumphantly above his head as he retreats 'gently',[26] entirely unaware of the danger he is in.

For, oddly, the one who is most affected by the theft is neither Green himself, nor any of the Marines, but one Joseph Banks who, flushing with two parts fear to one part anger, speaks sternly to Cook.

'It now appears necessary for our safety that so daring an act should be instantly punished,'[27] Banks declares, while shaping his musket, loaded with small shot, to shoot at the thief, who is no more than 15 feet away.

'Fire,' orders Captain Cook.

A flash from Mr Banks' musket – never before has he shot at another man – a puff of smoke, an almighty blast and, on the instant, angry red splotches appear all over the Native's back, haunches and thighs. And yes, the Native's cries of exultation cease but, somehow, he is still able to wave Mr Green's hanger defiantly above his head.

The white men stare, truly stunned. The men of this land are true warriors like they've never seen before, displaying the most unheard of bravery they've ever *heard* of! The thief writhes in pain as the small shot nestles deep into his flesh, yet still he stands, fierce in the face of this foreign incursion. Still, the other Natives are not foolhardy, and so move to the middle of the river, taking the higher ground upon a great rock.

Taking matters into his own hands, Surgeon Monkhouse momentarily sets aside his sacred Hippocratic Oath – 'First do no harm' – and decides to do a great deal of harm indeed.

He aims his pistol, loaded with a lead ball and not mere bird-shot, at the staggering yet somehow still swaggering Native and fires. The warrior swaggers no more. The hanger drops from his limp hand, landing with a sandy splash on the river's edge. The Native groans and falls beside it – stone, motherless, *dead*. Horrified, angered, uncomprehending all at once, two other Natives come down from the rock and try to get to him to check the body and grab the sword, but Dr Monkhouse is too quick and runs to grab the sword first.

The remaining Natives descend, whooping, howling cries of violent vengeance as they fly towards the invaders. The Marines turn their rifles as Cook, the Doctor and Tupia level their own.

'*Kaoure Horomai!*'[28] 'Do not come here!' Tupia screams, his message lost in the melee.

They brace . . . take position . . . aim . . . and fire. Clearly they hit their mark, as three of the Natives fall wounded, 'one seemingly a good deal hurt',[29] and the rest of the Natives must retrieve the wounded and drag them safely back across the river.

Cook gives the word to his men that it is time to return to the *Endeavour*. All of them are exultant.

A battle! A real, genuine battle, and we are victors!

This is the adventure they have yearned for, the promise of noble battles with savages fulfilled. Once on the boats, however, and pulling away from the shore, the mood starts to turn sombre and even dark. Have they really just killed two men, and wounded three others since arriving not one day ago?

Captain Cook himself looks back with horror at the two dead bodies, piles of prone, lifeless flesh where warriors once stood proud. Their deaths are on his conscience.

A shame there had been no recourse, no option that avoided bloodshed. Both James Cook and Joseph Banks are visibly affected, the weight of their actions hanging heavily. Banks' was the first shot, the catalyst for the murderous mayhem that followed.

For now though, the men are thankful for the distraction of the water, the focus of this entire endeavour. The river proves too silty and salty to be potable, and thus their search must continue. Later that night, the men of the *Endeavour* row to the North, heading for the uppermost point of the bay.

Captain Cook and Joseph Banks continue to reflect on how badly everything has gone thus far, while the Marines still ride high on the afterglow of a battle won, adrenaline a fresh memory. All are lost in thought until coming nearer the shore. How on *earth* are they supposed to land there? The waves are monsters, great falling walls beating into the sand and exploding with white fury. Suddenly, they spy a Native watercraft, moving through the surf as though it were no trouble. A canoe with a sail! No. *Two* canoes!

The second canoe has no sail and upon seeing the ship, makes for shore.

The sailing canoe, however, keeps coming straight for them.

Have they not seen us? It appears not.

Cook orders his men to row towards the canoe.

When it is close enough, Sydney Parkinson gets a good look at the vessel which is 'thirty feet long, made of planks sewed together, and had a lug-sail made of matting'.[30]

The hooks, lines, nets and spears make clear its purpose. They are fishermen returning with the morning's catch ... completely unaware that James Cook has designs to catch *them*.

After all, the small lighter spears they carry are designed for fish, not men. These are the perfect Natives to capture as there will be no question of more violent conflict.

Surely they can be safely approached and shown that, despite the unfortunate deaths so far, the Natives have nothing to fear from the visitors.

Tupia?

The indispensable holy man calls out to those in the canoes, encouraging them to come aboard peacefully. It's safe! No really! For their part, the Natives are now acutely aware of the white men in their bay, and it is clear by their expressions they are desperate to be rid of them.

'Come alongside!' Tupia calls to them regardless. 'We will not hurt you!'[31]

The startled fishermen are not disposed to find out. Furiously paddling, the Natives pull away from the *Endeavour*'s boats, as Banks notes, 'the fishing canoe she outran our boat'.[32]

Very well then. It is time for that most ancient but still most reliable of English remedies: a whiff of the grape.

'Fire a Musket over their heads,'[33] orders Cook, in the hope that the shattering noise will 'either make them surrender, or jump overboard'.[34]

No chance.

Far from the fire cowing them, it fires them up. Yes, they stop paddling, but only to lift up their paddles in defiance; from fishermen to warriors in a flash.

The moment the white men come alongside, the Natives unleash upon them a barrage of blows with their paddles, followed by a deluge of hurled and accurately aimed rocks . . .

In the next moment, there are shattering blasts. Screams fill the air, blood bursts forth, teeth fly, several Natives fall into the water, others leap.

After the deadly volley, four of the seven fearless fishermen turned warriors are bobbing in the bloodied water, face-down. The three other Natives are trying to swim away!

A couple of the Natives are scooped up by the brawny sailors, significantly easier to catch than the fish they had preyed upon. They are but boys, one no more than 10 or 12 years old and the other not much his senior. Now aboard, the third Native must be seen to. He is a skilled swimmer cutting through the water, away from the pursuing boat. Yet no swimmer can outrun a modern yawl, and it quickly pulls up beside the aquatic escapee. Plucked out of the water like his friends before him, the third boy does his utmost to fight back, writhing and thrashing like an eel out of water, making 'every effort in his power to prevent being taken into the boat',[35] but losing in the end.

James Cook sees that all three are no more than shivering, fearful boys who, having been captured by an enemy, look like they are awaiting their imminent execution. They all seem to squat, with their heads bowed, and to the eyes of the white men it looks as if they are submitting to their fate.

But the killing blow never comes. Whatever these white men want, the boys are more valuable than fish. The first of the boys to realise these strange visitors will not hurt them – or at least feel his curiosity outweigh his quite reasonable fear – steals a glance away from the floor of the yawl towards the foul-smelling white men in front of them. The others join in. Coming now into the shadow of the biggest canoe any of them have ever seen, the lads grow wide-eyed with wonder, shocked at its sheer size and still reeling from what they thought was certain death.

On deck, they are treated well, given clothes to wear – delightedly, the lads try on torn breeches and stained shirts, laughing to see each other so robed – along with beads and nails to marvel at, bread to eat and plenty of water, which they gulp by the gallon, likely having not had a drop since going out fishing early that morning.

Recognising they won't be killed (today, at least), the lads begin to bombard Tupia with endless questions. The lads, remarkably, seem to 'recover their spirits in a very short time'.[36]

Which is more than can be said for Joseph Banks and Cook.

Cook, a man with Quaker roots and a father of four wee bairns himself, who often thinks of them, and misses them desperately, is keenly aware that in all likelihood there are wee bairns in a Native village nearby who will shortly hear that their fathers will never return to them. And he, James Cook, has been the cause of that tragedy.

But did he have a choice?

With one eye on the Admiralty and one on history, he records in the ship's log his distress, his regret and, most importantly, his justification for what has happened:

> I am aware that most Humane men who have not experienced things of this nature will Censure my Conduct in firing upon the People in their Boat, nor do I myself think that the reason I had for seizing upon her will at all justify me; and had I thought that they would have made the Least Resistance I would not have come near them; but as they did, I was not to stand still and suffer either myself or those that were with me to be knocked on the head.[37]

Even Joseph Banks, who has been able to meet the death of English sailors and companions with something that – if you catch it at just the right angle, with the sun shining from behind – looked perilously like a shrug, finds himself deeply affected. After all, the other deaths had not been caused directly *by* him. They had simply occurred. But today he had been the man who had fired a musket at a man. Yes, it had only had small shot, but then Monkhouse had followed up with an actual lead ball. It means he, Joseph Banks, had begun the murderous melee that ended with four fishermen fallen.

'Thus ended,' he finishes his journal account this evening, 'the most disagreeable day my life has yet seen, black be the mark for it and heaven send that such may never return to embitter future reflection.'[38]

The only relief for Captain Cook and Joseph Banks is to see that the Native boys are now calm and happy. Cook going so far as to remark, they 'seemed much less concerned at what had happened than I was myself'.[39] They appear to bear their captors no ill-will, which is an unexpected relief. Tupia relates to the white men the identities of their catch. Taáhourange there, he is 18. He was the great swimmer who tried to elude you. Koikerange is his brother, the middle boy at 15 years old. Finally the little one, his name is Maragooete and he is only 10 years old. The lads spend a warm day and evening on the *Endeavour*. This meeting of worlds is not without its troubling moments, however.

One such moment comes in the mess at lunch, when a freshly slaughtered lamb is served and the Native lads wonder if, perhaps, this is *human* flesh?

No . . . . . . *why?*

Because the only animal this large in our land is human.

But *do you eat humans?*

'They . . . seemed ashamed of the custom,' Banks chronicles, 'saying that the tribe to which they belonged did not use it but that another very near did.'[40]

Tupia is among the most shocked, having never heard of such a thing, and insists to the boys that such a thing is *very, very wicked*. Yes, in Tahiti and its surrounding islands, human sacrifice is practised as a part of religious ceremonies, but actually eating humans is disgusting to him.

Still, they talk of many other things too, on much happier subjects – even as they tuck into generous helpings of salt pork served for dinner with nearly as much enthusiasm as they wolf down enormous slabs of bread – and keep talking until the midnight watch is about to head up on deck, whereupon, the boys are invited to bed down for the night upon the long transom seats beneath the Great Cabin's stern windows, whereupon 'they laid down to sleep with all seeming content imaginable'.[41]

On the shore, however, there is no such content. Late at night, Cook awakes to the sound of angry voices drifting through the Great Cabin's open windows from the shore. The Natives' rage-filled discourse is heard through the night.

While Cook spends an uneasy night tossing and turning, unable to properly get back to sleep, Joseph Banks is – strangely – awoken by a lullaby. Emerging from the land of nod he can, yes, hear not just singing, but something of a *choir*. What on earth can it be? Finding his slippers, he pads up towards the deck, the singing getting clearer with every step.

Oh.

He emerges from the hatchway to find that it is Tupia, with the three Native boys and his own servant lad, Tayeto, who is about the same age as the youngest captive. They had woken in fear and Tupia – intent on looking after them – had encouraged them to start singing a soft song they all know. The lads sing, and Tupia nods his encouragement.

Delighted, Banks chronicles it as, 'a song of their own . . . and contained many notes and semitones; they sung it in parts which gives us no indifferent idea of their taste as well as skill in music'.[42]

Through Tupia, the three lads are happy to talk with the white man, each of them learning from one another's culture. They continue to the wee hours of the morning, at which point Banks has had enough and must retreat to his bed.

•

Captain Cook emerges on deck at first light to find his three guests dressed and ornamented with bracelets, anklets and necklaces after their own fashion and in remarkably good spirits. Which is as well, for the Cap'n has a very simple plan for the day which relies on exactly that. 'I intended to put our 3 Prisoners ashore, and stay here the day to see what effect it might have upon the other Natives.'[43]

As the young captives heartily wolf down their breakfast – the only souls on board who look at sea biscuits with such enthusiasm – Cook sends a party of men accompanied by Marines on shore to collect wood. They are all under strict instructions to land on the Eastern side of the river and to have no contact with the Natives. There can be no repeat of the disasters of the previous two days. Once they are despatched, Cook, Banks, the Doctor, Tupia and the three satiated Native lads head to shore, too, this time landing on the West side of the river where the Natives had formed and performed their terrifying war dance. It is also where, Cook can't help but notice, the victims of their two previous meetings still lie on the Eastern bank. Those corpses are a terrible reminder of their failures up until this point.

Landing the pinnace on the sandy beach, James Cook, Banks and Tupia all encourage the lads to go, to join their people . . . and yet . . .

'They were very unwilling to leave us,' Cook chronicles, 'pretending that they should fall into the hands of their Enemies, who would kill and Eat them.'[44]

But the Captain insists. They cannot stay in the company of the white men any longer. Regardless of their reluctance, the boys now drag themselves up the beach, seemingly sorry to say goodbye to the white men and fearful of what may await them here on the shore. Whatever fate may befall them, Cook is distracted now by the approach of men in the distance.

Yes, there are a handful of large Natives now coming their way, holding . . . Hold on, it is actually a lot more than a handful. It's a large mass of Natives emerging onto the beach, a way off but approaching with intent. Quickly, Cook and his party ford the river, joining the party of sailors and Marines, who have come down from the woods and are gathered on the Eastern bank. Taking stock of his men, Cook notices the three Native lads among their number. Nothing Cook or Tupia can signal or say will persuade them to leave and, in any case, there is no time to tarry, as a bristling mob of 200 Natives are gathering on the other side of the river, all of them armed, all of them looking aggrieved.

'Tupia,' Cook chronicles, 'now began to Parley with them.'[45]

When Tupia's efforts appear foiled, and the Natives across the river seem only angrier than before, to Cook's great amazement, Koikerange, the middle lad, steps forward, takes the beads and nails and handkerchiefs he has received from the white men and carefully places them on the body of the man that Banks and Dr Monkhouse had shot and killed the day before.

The presents and Tupia's pleading seem to do the trick.

For now, one Native tentatively crosses the river, while the rest sit down on the sand, carefully watching.

Cook and his men crowd around the lone Native and shower him with gifts, as do the three Native boys, who pass on some of their own presents, while saying what must be soothing words to him. Cook invites the Native man to join them on the ship, but he refuses and the conversation appears ended. No, it is not quite peace that reigns. But at least it is not attack unleashed.

With that small triumph achieved, and the dozens upon dozens of New Zealand Natives still sitting peacefully enough on the opposite riverbank, Cook decides to take all his men back to the *Endeavour*: 'I now thought proper to take everybody on board, to prevent any more Quarrels, and with us came the 3 Natives, whom we could not prevail upon to stay behind.'[46]

Rowing away, the white men watch the sole Native man go up to the edge of the woods, where he picks up a green bough.

'With this in his hand,' Joseph Banks notes, 'he approached the body with great ceremony, walking sideways, he then threw the bough towards it and returned to his companions who immediately sat down round him and remained above an hour, hearing probably what he said without taking the least notice of us.'[47]

Back on deck, Tupia explains, this is an act of mourning. Cook and Banks can see through their spyglasses that the Natives have at last decided to carry off the body by the river, though it can't be forgotten that they have left the corpse of the Chief Te Maro, killed on the first day. It *still* lies on the Eastern bank. For what reason it must remain, the white men cannot guess, but they do presume that the other body must have been taken as a 'ratification of peace',[48] a sign that the battle is over.

After dinner, Cook summons his translator. 'Tupia, ask the boys if they now have any objection to going ashore at the same place.'[49]

Tupia and the boys confer. Any objection?

'*Kahore he whakahe.*' 'We have not,'[50] the boys chorus. Cook sends two Midshipmen in the yawl to row the three boys ashore, with strict instructions, 'to leave them so they *are* left'.[51]

From the quarter-deck, Cook and Banks watch closely, with rising tension, as the boys approach the riverbank. Are they to be welcomed back as prodigal sons, or struck down as tribal traitors for having broken bread with the white warriors? And here now is a Native man in a catamaran – a remarkably sophisticated looking double-canoe, with sleekly designed and decorated hulls, and a flat platform between from which a sail billows – coming out from the shore.

This Native, at least, seems to greet the boys well as he takes them on board, and takes them back to the river. Once ashore no fewer than 50 Native men emerge, embrace the lads, and they all sit and talk until the sun starts to set – whereupon the men stand, and the lads run back to the shore and wave their hands to those watching them from the *Endeavour*. Whether it is in joy or sorrow, or even a simple farewell, it is not possible to determine. But they have certainly got through the day unharmed, which is a good start.

'We therefore hope that no harm will happen to them,' Banks notes, 'especially as they had still the clothes which we gave them on.'[52]

The sense that the boys are fine and are perhaps even speaking up for the white visitors grows as eventide descends and animated but not angry voices float across the waters to the *Endeavour*.

Cook decides to move the *Endeavour* a little further from the shore, just for added safety. At dawn, he orders the anchor weighed and sails out of this place, which he has decided to call 'Poverty Bay' for the simple reason, 'it afforded us no one thing we wanted'.[53] (Even the inimitable specimen-collecting naturalist, Joseph Banks, leaves more empty-handed than he would like, recording that they set sail with 'not above 40 species of Plants in our boxes, which is not to be wondered at as we were so little ashore and always upon the same spot'.[54])

What is next?

'My intention is to follow the direction of the Coast to the Southward,' Cook writes, 'as far as the Latitude of 40 or 41 degrees, and then to return to the Northward, in case we meet with nothing to encourage us to proceed farther.'[55]

11 October 1769, Poverty Bay, the *Endeavour* gains three

South of Poverty Bay the following afternoon, the *Endeavour* finds itself at a small island. They are still close enough to shore to be quickly surrounded by an armada of vessels, at the prow of each is 'carved the head of a man with an enormous tongue reaching out of his mouth'.[56]

It is unlike anything the white men have seen, Mr Banks recording, 'These grotesque figures were some at least very well executed, some had eyes inlaid of something that shone very much; the whole served to give us an Idea of their taste as well as ingenuity in execution, much superior to any thing we have yet seen.'[57]

The trained eye of Sydney Parkinson takes it all in, soaking up the detail for his later drawing: 'The bottom of their canoes was made out of a single tree; and the upper part was formed of two planks, sewed together, narrowed both at head and stern. The former was very long, having a carved head at the end of it painted red, and the stern ended in a flat beak. They had thwarts to sit on, and their paddles were curiously stained with a red colour, disposed into various strange figures; and the whole together was no contemptible workmanship.'[58]

All of the vessels are filled with seemingly friendly Natives, though to a man they are . . . just that. All male.

Sydney Parkinson looks very closely, and winces: 'They tie their foreskins to their girdle with a string, and have holes pierced in their ears . . .'[59]

But where are the women?

After the joys of the flesh that had been experienced in Tahiti, the sailors and a good number of the officers and gentlemen are eager to see just what kind of women this strange land has and whether they might be . . . available.

The Natives make clear they wish to clamber aboard and get whatever presents the white men have to give. What on earth has happened to change the whole attitude of the Natives?

Cook soon has his answer, after Tupia interprets. 'The people in this boat had heard of the Treatment those had met with we had had on board before, and therefore came on board without hesitation.'[60]

While pleased at the way things are turning, Joseph Banks for one is more than a little sceptical that their troubles in this strange land are over. He does not doubt the sudden friendliness of the New Zealand Natives, but doubts whether this will be true throughout the land. 'God send that we may not there have the same tragedy to act over again as we so lately perpetrated,' he writes in his journal, 'the country is certainly divided into many small principalities so we cannot hope that an account of our weapons and management of them can be conveyed as far as we in all probability must go and this I am well convinced of, that till these warlike people have severely felt our superiority in the art of war, they will never behave to us in a friendly manner.'[61]

For the moment, however, there can be no doubting the friendliness of the Natives on board. When Cook, through Tupia, explains that the *Endeavour* will shortly be sailing South to look for other harbours as this place provides little of what they need, they make a singular request. Given that Cook has brought Tupia from Tahiti, perhaps Cook could take three Natives with him, just as the *Endeavour* had already taken the three boys on board?

Their logic, Tupia explains, is that if Cook takes three with him, they will be able to eventually return to tell the rest where the *Endeavour*, this extraordinary vessel, is now! It will likely be for just a few days,

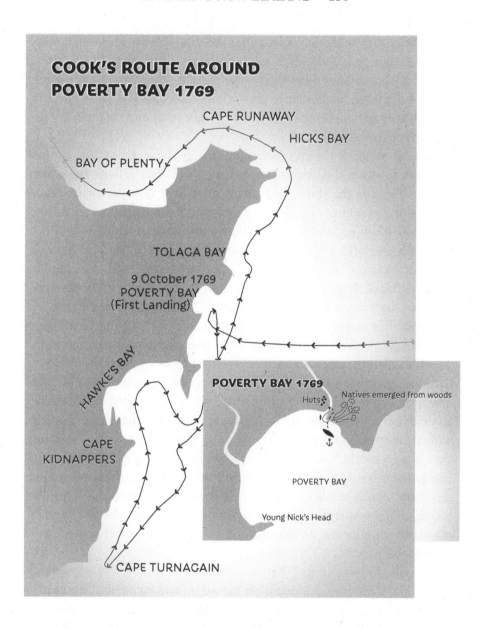

COOK'S ROUTE AROUND POVERTY BAY 1769

CAPE RUNAWAY

HICKS BAY

BAY OF PLENTY

TOLAGA BAY

9 October 1769
POVERTY BAY
(First Landing)

HAWKE'S BAY

CAPE KIDNAPPERS

POVERTY BAY 1769

Huts

Natives emerged from woods

POVERTY BAY

Young Nick's Head

CAPE TURNAGAIN

and they might be useful for telling other Natives that there is nothing to be afraid of with the white men. Amused, Cook agrees.

The *Endeavour* sails South with three proud Native men aboard, waving goodbye to their people and promising to return with news of their adventure. Alas, during the night the wind blows so strong, and the

Endeavour sails with such speed that the three Natives begin to weep, thinking that they will never see land again. With the aid of Tupia, Cook tries to reassure them that in the morning they will still be within sight of the land, as they have gone along the coast not away from it, but still they remain tense until the morning comes and they can see for themselves the blessed land.

As well as land, the next morning brings the sight of two canoes paddling towards the ship in the morning sun. Friends! As the canoe comes alongside the ship, the Natives see that it is more than a trade procession, as one of the canoes contains an old man dressed in fine *kākahu* or clothing, and he is carrying a *patu* made of whale bone, both signs of high status and power, or *mana* to the Native. A Chief! After a brief conversation with the white men and the Native men, the old man takes his leave. In tow are all three Natives, shinnying down the rope and back onto the canoe, 'much to our as well as their satisfaction'.[62]

Slowly but surely, the *Endeavour* sails South along the East coast, stopping occasionally whenever the crew spies curious Natives in canoes. Tupia, as always, greets every new party with his characteristic charm, each time meeting with various levels of success. Sometimes the Natives dare not come within a quarter mile, other times spitting distance. Sometimes they come aboard to trade and talk, other times they threaten with their spears and *patus*. The latter is always met with a warning shot from a musket, which is always enough to force a hasty retreat.

Southwards ever Southwards the *Endeavour* sails on, the wind getting still more chilly, while the white cliffs give way to fertile green hills, before giving way again to unruly, swampy lowlands. This is a land of many differing scenes, an extraordinary array of unexpected aspects.

For look now . . .

'In sailing along shore,' Banks notes, 'we could clearly see several spots of land cultivated, some fresh turned up and laying in furrows like ploughed land, others with plants growing upon them some younger and some older; we also saw in two places high rails upon the Ridges of hills, but could only guess that they belong to some superstition as they were in lines not enclosing anything.'[63]

On 15 October, just as high and regal mountains crowned with tips of white become visible off to their distant starboard, the *Endeavour* shortens sail as it arrives off the Southern headland of a gloriously vast and sweeping bay, which Cook decides to christen Hawke's Bay, in honour of Sir Edward Hawke, First Lord of the Admiralty.

Not long after they drop anchor just abreast of the South-west point of the bay, canoes filled with Natives come out, presenting an amazingly colourful spectacle that pleases the eye of Sydney Parkinson, as he notes: 'Their spears were not unlike our sheriffs' halberts, having red and yellow tassels tied to them. In one of their canoes we saw a hatchet, made of the green stone, in shape like those of Tahiti.'[64] (The ever-searching eyes of Mr Banks too are quick to spot the green stone, noting: 'some of our people imagined it to be a Jewel, myself thought it no more than the green stone of which most of their tools and ornaments are made'.[65] The Natives of New Zealand seem to prize it.)

Each canoe is between 50 and 60 feet long, has around 20 warriors aboard with 18 paddles, and each one is a work of art in itself.

Sydney Parkinson studies the craft in detail. '[They] were adorned with fine heads made out of a thick board, cut through like filigree-work, in spirals of very curious workmanship. At the end of this was a head, with two large eyes of mother-of-pearl, and a large heart-shaped tongue. This figure went round the bottom of the board, and had feet and hands carved upon it very neatly, and painted red: they had also high-peaked sterns, wrought in filigree, and adorned with feathers, from the top of which depended two long streamers, made of feathers, which almost reached the water.'[66]

Typically, Parkinson cannot wait to do a drawing of them, and with Tupia closely watching his method, immediately begins sketching, even as the Natives themselves pull alongside and do two of their versions of a *Heiva*, or is it a war dance? The white men aren't sure.

'They beat time with their paddles, and ended all at once with the word *Epaah*; at the same instant striking their paddles on the thwarts: all which afforded a truly comic act.'[67]

As for trade, a bemused Banks records, 'they sometimes cheated us by bargaining for one thing and sending up another when they had got their prize'.[68]

And so the bartering continues. A basket of fish for a mirror. An armful of *kumara* – a kind of sweet potato – for a piece of cloth.

Captain Cook himself seeks to make an exchange for a kind of coat being worn by one of the warriors, which to his eyes, looks to be 'something like a Bear Skin, which I was desirous of having that I might be a better judge what sort of an Animal the first Owner was'.[69]

Would the Native give it to him in exchange for a piece of red baize?

'He seemed to jump at [it] by immediately putting off the Skin and holding it up to us, but would not part with it until he had the Cloth in his possession . . .'[70]

And that is where the trouble starts.

For as an amused Joseph Banks chronicles, 'no sooner had the man got hold of it than he began with amazing coolness to pack up both it and his fur jacket in a basket, entirely deaf to the Captains Demands . . .'[71]

The other Natives are suddenly seemingly deaf to the King's English, for all together, they paddle furiously away.

Well, it is only a piece of red cloth and Cook thinks it a lesson cheaply learnt. He is not alarmed when a short time later another canoe approaches, this time with Natives offering fish.

This time, after consultation with the officers, a combination of looking glasses and tomahawks is enough to have the Natives agree to part with their whole canoe! (For the men of the *Endeavour*, what a sensation it would make, and how interested the people would be, once they got it back to London!) They are about to get a line around the head of the canoe, hoping to haul her on board the way they would an anchor, when it happens.

Tayeto, known to the jacks as 'Tupiah's little boy',[72] happens to be 'in the main chains', standing on one of the platforms by the side of the ship at the bow, from where the sailors 'swing the lead', and as the Natives in the canoe come alongside, one of the warriors stands up, grabs the boy and pulls him into the canoe before they too are paddling furiously away!

The cry goes up, and many muskets – always kept loaded, primed and at hand when Natives are about – are brought to bear, aimed at those Natives farthest away from Tayeto . . .

And . . . fire!

The muskets roar. In the canoe, three Natives suddenly slump, falling back on the men behind them. In the chaos, Tayeto is able to break free from the Native holding him, jump overboard and start swimming back towards the *Endeavour*.

'Lower the pinnace!'

'And fire the cannon!'

Yes, for good measure sending some cannonballs the way of the Natives will make the point that the white men are not to be trifled with.

It is done within the minute as the orders ring out – 'Bear a hand! Bear a hand!' Before the Natives can gather themselves, the pinnace is launched, the cannon creates further havoc, and Tayeto has been gathered up, all while the Natives beat – in time, despite the pandemonium – a hasty retreat.

Tayeto climbs the rope slower than the jacks have ever seen him move. There is a weariness in his movement, a lad who, having given the last ounce of energy he has to fear, now has little left to give to anything, not even relief. Compounding his exhaustion are his drenched clothes, thick and heavy, impeding his every move.[73] Reaching the deck, he falls to the wooden floor with a thud, shivering from the cold, unable to lift even his head. Yet by the same token, he is also relatively quick to recover and it is not long before the Tayeto they all know and love has returned to them. A bounce back in his step, Joseph Banks watches as the boy walks over to retrieve something from a pail by the mizzen.

He then approaches his master, Tupia, bearing what Banks sees is a fine fish that had been previously traded for.

'I intend,' Tayeto tells the priest, 'to offer this to *Eatua* or God in gratitude for my escape.'

'I approve,' Tupia says heartily. 'You must throw it into the sea.'[74]

The two walk together to the gunwale, where Tayeto goes ahead with his offering. The fish flies over the side, a lucky escapee released by one and the same, returning whence it came.

'This affair,' Captain Cook chronicles that night, 'occasioned my giving this point of land the name of Cape Kidnapper.'[75]

17 October 1769, South-west of Hawke's Bay, hawk's eye view

A *skua* bird would see it perfectly from on high – a strange thing, never observed in these parts before.

It is a great canoe sprouting billowing white, coming to a halt off a large bay – at which point the billowing white sags loosely – before the enormous vessel turns, heading back into the eddying remains of its own wake.

Interested, the bird sways and swirls in the breeze, following it along, tracking its journey past Cape Kidnapper, past Hawke's Bay, past Poverty Bay.

Wherever it comes to rest, it is quickly met with a flotilla of tiny trading vessels, throwing off sparkling water on both sides. Sometimes their meetings lead to peace, bartering trade and friendly relationships. Other times, they end in a thunderous roar followed by hurried and harried paddling away. Conversation, commerce, or conflict, the white above the great canoe soon starts to billow once more and it again moves on.

Late October 1769, East Coast New Zealand, where the line goes, nobody knows . . .

The Captain sits at the oak bureau in his private cabin, pondering the charts spread before him. His eyes are drawn with no little pride to the nascent first chart of New Zealand's East, or at least, the first drawn by a European. Lingering a moment, James Cook pinpoints the position of the *Endeavour*'s about face a couple of days prior and names it 'Cape Turnagain'.

As for the weathered white cliff he had seen this late afternoon, the one that so resembled the gable of a house, he names it Gable End Foreland. And there the line on his chart stops abruptly, as it must until the morrow when Cook will start again, observing the coast, sounding the depths, marking the newly discovered contours of this unknown land, all in the hope of making some important discoveries, by way of harbours, major rivers or the like. Perhaps, they are even now circumnavigating the Great Southern Land? Cook does not believe so, but keeps his counsel, while Joseph Banks is openly convinced that they are already sailing on the Eastern edge of Dalrymple's geographical dream, they only need to keep on sailing to confirm its extraordinary size.

Cook folds up the chart and places it safely in the top drawer of the bureau. He disrobes and snuffs out the light in the room, a fine candle. It is a near-nightly ritual in his rigorously disciplined life.

In the morning, Captain Cook spies two bays and orders Master Molineux to bring her in to the Northern-most one, where they anchor in seven fathoms on a black sandy bottom in the forenoon of 20 October 1769.

This time the Natives who paddle out to the ship seem friendly without reservation, and Cook is able to invite them aboard and ply them with gifts, for he wants no repeat of the events at Poverty Bay.

The Natives respond in kind, readily answering the queries of where the men of the *Endeavour* could secure fresh water, and Captain Cook sends men ashore with barrels with orders to fill them. The work is slow, owing to a high surf upon the shore, but it is done.

The following day, Mr Banks and the Doctor take the opportunity to make their own landing at this place called Tegadoo to gather specimens and make observations, and Banks is soon impressed beyond measure by a particular discovery.

For here now are the loveliest forms that nature has to offer – women! No, not bare-breasted like the Tahitian maidens, but alluring and certainly a vital force in this impressive community. Men, women and children gather as one to form a welcoming party, bestowing an air of normality on proceedings.

Banks is impressed with the settlement laid out before him.

'One piece of cleanliness in these people I cannot omit as I believe it is almost unexampled among Indians,' he chronicles. 'Every house or small knot of 3 or 4 has a regular necessary house where every one repairs and consequently the neighbourhood is kept clean which was by no means the case at Tahiti. They have also a regular dunghill upon which all their offals of food etc, are heaped up and which probably they use for manure.'[76]

Outhouses! Compost heaps!

This is an advanced people and they meet with the white men on the basis of presumed equality. When the white men visit people in their villages, and go into houses, 'Men women and children received us, no one showed the least signs of fear.'[77]

Now when it comes to the Native women, it is not as if they do not have their charms – far from it – but Banks' key wish, as with many men of the *Endeavour*, is that they would *not* paint their faces with red ochre and oil as it is generally still 'fresh and wet upon their cheeks and foreheads, [and therefore] easily transferrable to the noses of any one who should attempt to kiss them'.[78]

Not for nothing are sailors often showing up back at the *Endeavour* with red noses.

For the main thing remains that the women are generally available.

'[While] more modest in their carriage and decent in their Conversation than the Islanders . . . if the consent of their relations was asked and the Question accompanied with a proper present it was seldom refused.'[79]

Such presents include cloth, beads and ribbons, but even then, 'the strictest decency must be kept up towards the young lady or she might baulk the lover after all'.[80]

The English sailors learn as they go along. When one of the Midshipmen approaches a Native family 'of the better sort'[81] – for there really are strata of classes among them, most readily discernible by the quality of their garments – seeking the favours of one of the daughters, Banks records the response of the family matriarch.

'Any of these young ladies will think themselves honoured by your addresses,' he is told firmly, 'but you must first make me a proper present and must come and sleep with us ashore, for daylight should by no means be a witness of such proceedings.'[82]

To help things along, they are sure to take Tupia with them on every journey ashore, as he has proven himself an indispensable bridge between two worlds, the best chance they have of both sides going back and forth without losing their lives. He is capable of enabling both the passage of goodwill, and – more importantly – translating to the Natives the supreme, otherworldly power of the Europeans. (In fact, more than that, he is picking up European skills, delighting no less than the quiet Quaker Sydney Parkinson one evening with his rendering of Mr Banks' trading with the New Zealand Natives. *Fabulous, Tupia!* The Scottish artist is delighted to see his pupil coming along so quickly, creating works full of salient detail *and* tolerably pleasing to the eye.)

All through the capes and inlets of the North Island, Tupia's name has travelled, his prestige preceding him. *Tupia has come.* His legend has grown to the point that when the *Endeavour* drops anchor, the canoes of Natives will come out and ask for him by name.

The Tahitian holy man explains their reasons for coming, and that, 'We will neither hurt nor molest you, if you behave in the same peaceable manner to us.'[83]

Helpfully, the Natives even speak of a location to the South, a lovely little bay with good anchorage and accessible water – Tolago. Tolago. *Tolago.*

The Natives will not cease repeating the name, though it means little to the white men. Thankfully, Tupia can confirm that this is their name for bay, and so it is one of those rare occasions where the Native name for a feature is actually marked on the Captain's map.

A short time after the *Endeavour* arrives – busying themselves by gathering wild celery and 'scurvy grass', which is welcomed by the Captain and served to the men forthwith – the locals lead Tupia to a sacred cave of notably high arch, high on a hill, and inform him that it is his.

Recognising the enormous honour that has been accorded to him, Tupia gravely accepts the gift, and in the course of the *Endeavour*'s time there – six days – receives many visitors in his cave, where he is almost drowned with even more gifts, draped with precious cloaks and welcomed as an honoured guest among the *whare wanaga*. There, in the fleeting light of the village's perpetual flame, which has been carried upon a flax wick up the meandering path to the cave, Tupia speaks long and strong with the local priests of spirits, gods, and the land where their ancestors live. As it happens, both parties are in agreement on questions of religion.

'Tupia was a great favourite with our fathers,' the locals will say thereafter, 'so much so, that to gratify him, several children who were born in the village, during his sojourn with us, were named after him.'[84]

That cave will ever after be known as *Rua a Tupia*, Tupia's cave.

Of course, the Native names for geographical features often amuse the white men but on a trip ashore at Tolago Bay, Mr Banks and the Doctor hear about one that will amuse them for years to come.

That splendid rock formation for example, that tight, circular cavern that leads through a large rock to the sea.

To the impressed eyes of Joseph Banks it is an 'extraordinary natural curiosity . . . a most noble arch . . . certainly the most magnificent surprize I have ever met with'.[85]

The locals, however, are less fussed.

They refer to it in rather less glowing terms as *Te Kotore o te Whenua* 'The Anus of the Land'.[86]

Charmed, they're sure.

Sydney Parkinson meanwhile, is genuinely charmed, though not with strange Native names. No, Mr Parkinson is transfixed with the beautiful parrots that fly around this place, bursts of chirruping colour that fly and flit about like tiny rainbows. Yet he can't help but notice the absence of more substantial land creatures, he records that the only quadrupeds in these parts are dogs.

Cook also notices the birds, recording that there are 'plenty of wild fowl in these parts, such as shags, ducks, curlews and crows'.[87] He also records of their time at Tolago Bay, 'We saw no 4 footed Animals, either Tame or Wild, or signs of any, except Dogs and Rats, and these were very Scarce, especially the latter. The flesh of the former they eat, and ornament their clothing with their skins as we do ours with furs.'[88]

In terms of trading with the Natives, Cook is insistent that his men behave well, for both the sake of decency, and replenishment: 'I suffer'd every body to purchase what ever they pleased without limitation; for by this means I knew that the Natives would not only sell but get a good Price for every thing they brought. This I thought would induce them to bring to Market whatever the Country afforded, and I have great reason to think that they did.'[89]

•

The Captain and his men continue to sail East along the coast, the cartographers happily and constantly charting, chatting and noting everything they see. Everything from small rocky islands to great towering cliffs and tiny inlets are recorded in exquisite detail.

(True, not a lot of creative time is spent on the naming exercise – it is simply a matter of ignoring whatever the local population might have called it for centuries and planting some kind of literary flag of the King's English upon these ancient land forms, and any will do.)

Reaching a North-east-facing cape, which Captain Cook believes is the coast's most Easterly point, the *Endeavour* passes to its Westward side and Cook names it after Lieutenant Zachary Hicks, who was the first to spot it, then 'Cape Runaway', so named for the Natives there who flee from the *Endeavour*'s cannons thundering forth grapeshot, before dipping to the South-west into a bay that affords them not only safe anchorage, but will for good reason be named the Bay of Plenty.

'We saw,' Cook notes, 'a great deal of Cultivated land laid out in regular enclosures, a sure sign that the Country is both fertile and well inhabited.'[90]

Even more happily, the waters around abound with the fruits of the ocean – fat lobsters, mussels, succulent oysters, even eels – and the Natives prove to be more than willing to trade in return for nails, beads and cloth, a thrilling development for the crew, leading to sumptuous seafood feasts.

When occasionally, warlike parties do approach, Tupia takes matters in hand, telling them that the power of the white man is not of their world, it is like nothing they have ever seen, and that is why he wants them to watch as a cannon is first fired, while they gaze to yonder trees.

. . .

Timmmmmmmmmber!

. . .

Do they *really* want to be on the wrong end of such power?

. . .

They do not.

CHAPTER NINE

THE CIRCUMNAVIGATION

The man who does no more than carry out his instructions will never get very far in discovery.[1]

Captain Cook, 1775

The Southern Continent having been seen on the West-side, by Tasman, in 1642 and on the East by Juan Fernandes, above half a century before, and by others after him, in different latitudes from 64 degrees to 40 degrees South, it is impossible for any one at this time to discover it . . . although the land has been seen, and once visited, yet to open an intercourse with its inhabitants, is a task still to be performed.[2]

Alexander Dalrymple, 1770

3 November 1769, Te-Whanganui-a-Hei, white sails in the great bay

From the shore of this land of *Aoteaora*, the *Ngāti Hei* tribe of this area of *Whitianga*, watch, mesmerised. This spot is not their main base, just one of several spots they move to from time to time throughout the year so as not to exhaust the natural food in one particular area, and also, as one among them would explain, so 'that our fire might be kept alight on each block, so that it might not be taken from us by some other tribe'.[3]

Yes, they have travelled far in this land, and seen many things. But never have they seen anything like this enormous vessel with its billowing white sails, now dropping something with wings from one end that goes into the water with a splash, trailing a rope behind it.

As ever, the younger ones look to their *Kaumātua*, their elders.

What is this? What is happening?

The old men are firm,

'The vessel is a *tupua*, a god, and the people on board are strange beings.'[4] The latter is confirmed once small boats splash down by the *tupua* ship and start to make their way to the shore. For look there!

The people on board have their backs to us, but are making straight to the shore.

'Yes, it is so,' say the old ones, 'these people are [*tupua*], goblins; their eyes are at the back of their heads; they pull on shore with their backs to the land to which they are going.'[5]

Yes, these visitors are '*tangata tupua*', goblin people, while the Natives regard themselves as '*tangata Māori*', normal people. Once the goblins have landed, all of the women and children, including a very little boy by the name of Te Horeta te Taniwha, run into the forest, leaving the warriors alone to face them.

•

'All hands bring ship to anchor!'[6] comes the Master's cry.

It is the afternoon of 3 November, and the *Endeavour* is safely anchored in a fine inlet, albeit one as yet unnamed by white men. Cook hopes for a peaceful relationship with the Natives, hardly desirous of any further conflict or disagreement. If they could just allow us to stay for a few days without interference then this would be the perfect place to observe the Transit of Mercury, soon to occur, on 9 November. And on that note, what better name for the bay? It is six days before the transit even occurs, but by the time it takes place, *Te-Whanganui-a-Hei*, the great bay of Hei, will have been rechristened as Mercury Bay.

'If we be so fortunate as to obtain this observation,' he records that night, 'the Longitude of this place and Country will thereby be very accurately determined.'[7]

Before long, however, and not for the first time, nor for the last time, the *Endeavour* finds itself positively swarmed by lesser watercraft. Natives in canoes abound, each of them speaking 'very civilly' with Tupia.[8] Trade and talks take place at the typical pace and fashion until suddenly one of the jacks fires a shot. A few paces off, a bird drops dead in the water. Initially shocked but recovering quickly, a canoe of Natives retrieves the dead bird and follow instructions by tying the bird to 'a fishing line that was towing astern for which they were rewarded with a piece of cloth'.[9]

The *Endeavour* and her men are happy for the peaceful presence of these Natives, though perhaps they are *too* at ease around the white men. As Banks describes, the Natives grew 'very saucy'[10] and lingered by the ship all night, 'singing their song of Defiance and attempting to tow away the buoy of the anchor'.[11]

The men on watch fire three musket shots, which only further riles the Natives who row off into the inky night shouting promises of retribution when daylight returns – 'We will return with more men and kill you all!'[12]

If you say so. But we will be ready.

True to their word, the Natives return at dawn '150 men in 10 or 12 Canoes all armed with pikes, [spears] and stones'.[13]

After much conversation that oscillates wildly, one moment the Natives are trading, the next the white men are firing musket balls through the canoe of a man trying to escape with purloined cloth, even while another poor Native is getting sprayed with small shot. The *Endeavour* men establish such a superiority of arms that the Natives go back ashore and remain, from this time, 'neither friends nor foes' – they are a mercurial lot these Natives – and much to the white men's liking, they exhibit 'much fear whenever our boats approached them'.[14]

The *Endeavour* plans to restock while anchored in this bay, eager to replenish their supplies for the days ahead, and the men cast their fishing nets wide in the shallows – alas, without success. In time, some of the braver Natives paddle back out to the *Endeavour*, each canoe laden with the wealth of the sea: cockles, clams, mussels and salty dried fish. There is more than enough for everyone on board, and the men are delighted. Banks, for one, is as happy as the clam he sups on.

In the meantime, he and the good Doctor are able to venture inland, up hill and down dale to botanise and naturalise with, as Banks records, 'good success which could not be doubted in a country so totally new'. The hilltops around the bay are populated exclusively by a 'very large fern', curious for its silver undersurface, and 'the roots of which [the Natives] had got together in large quantities as they said to carry away with them'.[15] Banks cuts away a sample from one of the ferns, filing it away for a closer inspection. *Ponga* he hears from behind him. *Ponga*. One of the locals is gesturing towards the fern. *Ponga!* Well, that name might be fine for these Natives, but it hardly follows scientific naming conventions, does it? The friendly Native has succeeded in passing on the name for this plant, though the language barrier proves too great for him to explain the special place that this silver fern, this *Ponga*, holds in Native society, a symbol of strength, endurance and power.

In the meantime, Cook paces the shore, gazing at the sky and clouds above him. Here? No, here. Picking the best vantage point to observe the transit – as open as possible and yet with shelter – is an absolute imperative. Time must be taken to get everything right. Once he has selected the right spot, the Captain gives the order, and the *Endeavour* is brought further into the bay, just off the Southern tip and a place that will soon take on the name 'Cook's Cove'. And so the preparations continue. The men chop wood, build fires, collect wild foodstuffs and even dig a freshwater spring with the help of Tupia. The Natives are quick to dub it *Te Wai Keri a Tupaia*, 'the well dug by Tupia'.[16]

Finally, on the seventh day?

Cook orders the men to heel and scrub the ship – first moving all the ballast and cannon to one side of the ship's hold to savagely tilt it, exposing much of the hull to be scrubbed clean of molluscs and the like, before shifting it all to the other side and doing the same again.

It is loathsome, tiring work and a far cry from where they'd rather be. However all is not terrible, as the Natives happen that day to bring out a haul of freshly caught mackerel and offer it to the crew. Every man falls asleep that night with a belly full of tasty white fish meat.

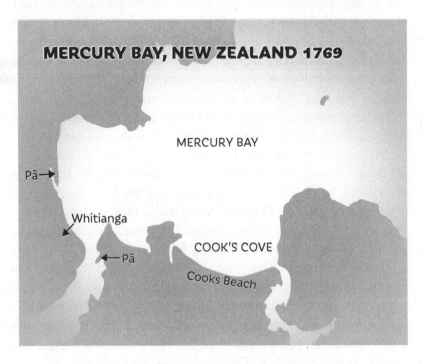

Early November, Whitianga, gobbling goblins

'But,' as Te Horeta te Taniwha will later recount, 'as the goblins stayed some time, and did not do any evil to our braves, we came back one by one, and gazed at them, and we stroked their garments with our hands, and we were pleased with the whiteness of their skins and the blue eyes of some of them.'[17]

As the goblins start to gather oysters the Natives give some *kumara*, fish and fern-root to them, which they gratefully accept.

'And as we saw that these goblins were eating *kumara*, fish, and cockles, we were startled, and said, "Perhaps they are not goblins like the Māori [goblins]."'[18]

But what now? Some of the goblins go into the forest and start to climb the hill to the Native *pā* – their fortified village, protected by trenches, ramparts and stockades – to gaze at the land and the ocean, and they even make drawings on white sheets. While there, they collect grasses from the cliffs, and when they descend to the beach they keep knocking stones together, placing some in their bags along with shells and coral (observing the instructions from the Admiralty to 'carefully . . . observe the Nature of the Soil and . . . in Case you find any Mines, Minerals, or valuable Stones you are to bring home Specimens of each').[19]

It is mystifying.

'Why,' the Natives ask, 'are these acts done by these goblins?'[20]

If it is grass and stone they want, so be it. And so the women and children are set to gathering stones and grass of all sorts to give to the goblins to see what pleases them.

'Some of the stones they liked, and put them into their bags, the rest they threw away; and when we gave them the grass and branches of trees they stood and talked to us, or they uttered the words of their language. Perhaps they were asking questions, and, as we did not know their language, we laughed, and these goblins also laughed, so we were pleased. The warriors and old men of our tribe sat in silence and gazed at these goblins . . . then we went up the Whitianga River with them.'[21]

But what now?

The Natives have noticed that the goblins have walking sticks with them which they carry over their shoulders, rather than use them as support on the ground, which seems strange. But stranger still is what happens when they get to the trees where the shags do their nesting. For now the goblins point their walking sticks at the birds, and just a short time later, 'thunder was heard to crash and a flash of lightning was seen, and a shag fell from the trees; and we children were terrified, and fled, and rushed into the forest, and left the goblins all alone. They laughed, and waved their hands to us, and in a short time the bravest of us went back to where the goblins were, and handled the bird, and saw that it was dead. But what had killed it?'[22]

The old people are more suspicious now and not at all sure what to make of the visitors, whether they can be friends or not. They walk back to the shore and for the first time the goblins give them some of their own food.

'Some of this food was very hard, but it was sweet. Some of our old people said it was *punga-punga* from the land from which these goblins came.'[23]

Inevitably, with more contact between the Natives and the goblins, the less fear there is on both sides, and there is even a certain amount of friendliness. Those who have most contact with the goblins – which are those Natives who have actually been on their massive canoe – are the most loquacious of all about the wondrous things they have seen.

'When they came on shore,' Te Horeta te Taniwha will recount, 'they gave our people an account of what they had seen. This made many of us desirous to go and see the home of the goblins. I went with the others; but I was a very little fellow in those days, so some of us boys went in the company of the warriors.'[24]

Wide-eyed, Te Horeta te Taniwha climbs the rope ladder that hangs down the side of the canoe, and emerges on the deck proper, goggle-eyed at the many pathways meandering around the great canoe, the strange structures adorning the boat itself, and the tall logs planted in wood, that have such a tangle of ropes coming from them.

And yet as fascinated as Te Horeta te Taniwha and the others are, it seems the goblins are even more entranced by the small lads, the first time they have seen children up close. As soon as the wee ones are sitting on the deck, the goblins come over and coo over them, stroking their hair and [woven] mats, while 'at the same time they made much gabbling noise in talking, which we thought was questions regarding our mats and the sharks' teeth we wore in our ears, and the *hei-tiki* we wore suspended on our chests; but as we could not understand them we laughed, and they laughed also'.[25]

In short order there is an exchange of certain items of English clothing for Native clothing.

'Ka pai,'[26] say the Natives, meaning 'very fine'. When the goblins repeat the words in their strange garbled way, the Natives laugh, which makes the goblins laugh in turn.

9 November 1769, Mercury Bay, blood and Gore

As Mercury approaches the rising sun, Captain Cook and Mr Green, accompanied by Lieutenant Hicks, head ashore with their instruments. They are ready. The morning is bright and clear, the precursors of a successful observation.

In their absence, aboard the *Endeavour*, it all happens so quickly.

Five canoe-loads of Natives paddle out to the ship carrying a fresh haul of mackerel for these strange white beings who collect 'shells, flowers, tree blossoms and stones'.[27]

In the absence of Captain Cook and Lieutenant Hicks, the Commanding Officer in charge is Lieutenant John Gore, who – far from staying removed from the fray, as befitting the man in command – engages in vigorous bartering with the Natives. At one point he comes to an agreement with one of the Natives by the name of Otirreeoònooe, to exchange some of his own cloth for the warrior's and trustingly passes it down to him – at which point it seems Gore is betrayed. For instead of passing up his mat, Otirreeoònooe and his companions immediately push away from the *Endeavour*, and shake their paddles in triumph. Fooled you!

Even as the Natives furiously paddle away, 'they immediately began to sing their war song as if to defy any revenge those on board might choose to take . . .'.[28]

Alas, the Natives have defied the wrong goblin.

For now, reaching for one of the muskets, Lieutenant Gore walks to the stern of the ship to get as close as possible, takes careful aim and . . . squeezes the trigger.

There is a flash, a roar, a puff of smoke and at a distance of 50 yards the thieving Native sprouts a bloody red hole in his back . . .

In an instant, all the other canoes race away from the *Endeavour*.

As the canoe bearing Otirreeoònooe arrives on the shore, eight of the Native men in it jump out, only to note that the thief 'sat still with his dog-skin mat and the garment of the [white man] under his feet'.[29]

His companions call to him, to come quickly.

'Otirreeoònooe! Otirreeoònooe! Otirreeoònooe!'

Alas, Otirreeoònooe, does not answer.

'One of them went and shook him, and the thief fell back into the hold of the canoe, and blood was seen on his clothing and a hole in his back.'[30]

Otirreeoònooe is no more, his spirit diving into the underworld, the realm of his ancestors.

Aboard the *Endeavour*, there is immediate consternation. Really? It has come to this?

'What a severe punishment of a crime committed,'[31] Sydney Parkinson chronicles in his diary, the Quaker disgusted once more at the savagery of Lieutenant Gore's justice.

•

In the forest, Banks and his entourage, accompanied by the usual gathering of Natives, hear the gunfire. Soon after, a distressed Native arrives, who imparts the devastating tidings. Otirreeoònooe has been killed by one of the white men with his thunder-stick.

There is an immediate stirring among the Natives, a mixture of grief, anger, and fear.

As quickly as the procession of Natives hounding Banks had come together, it now melts away. One moment they are chattering and nattering and carrying on, the next they are ghosts, fading back into the bush whence they came.

'In a little time however,' Banks records, 'they returned on their own accords and acknowledged that the dead man deserved his punishment.'[32]

As it happens, the Natives are far more forgiving than Captain Cook who, with Mr Green, has successfully observed the Transit of Mercury; or Banks, who, as Banks notes, are appalled, thinking the Native's fate:

> severe, knowing as we did that small shot would have had almost or quite as good an effect with little danger to his life, which tho forfeited to the laws of England we could not but wish to spare if it could be done without subjecting ourselves to the derision and consequently to the attacks of these people, which we have now but learnt to fear not least they should kill us, but least we should be reduced to the necessity of killing a number of them which must be the case should they ever in reality attack us.[33]

As for Cook, he can feel fury rising within.

It is rare for Cook to lose his temper completely, particularly with officers, but in this case he is appalled at the wanton slaughter of a Native over a mere trifle and gives full vent to his rage, upbraiding Gore in front of gentlemen and officers alike. The arrogant American's burst of anger has threatened their entire discourse with the Natives in these parts, and made it virtually impossible for Cook and his men to fulfil their charter from the Admiralty to 'cultivate a Friendship and Alliance with them . . .'.[34]

In response to Cook's anger, Lieutenant Gore comes perilously close to arguing with a senior officer, maintaining he was entirely justified in punishing the thief.

Their dispute is loud enough that it is within earshot of other senior people on the *Endeavour*, with some of them thinking that there is more to Cook's anger than just the killing, it is everything about the American Gore that rankles.

'Cook was jealous of [Gore] . . .' Solander will recount. 'Gore had a sort of separate command in the vessel . . . which gave him super-intendence over all the transactions with the Indians. He made use of this sometimes to disobey Cook; & therefore they hate each other. Gore always blamed severity [on] the Indians & yet by a sudden emotion shot the man who cheated . . .'[35]

Such an unmitigated disaster. And yet James Cook is also cognisant of the need for official calm, and when he comes to his journal to record the events of the day, he writes in a totally dispassionate tone.

'I must own,' Cook notes, with much more mildness than he had displayed with Lieutenant Gore in person, 'it did not meet with my approbation, because I thought the Punishment a little too severe for the Crime, and we had now been long Enough acquainted with these People to know how to Chastise Trifling faults like this without taking away their Lives'.[36]

And yet while Cook regains his equanimity quickly, the same cannot be said for the American.

Profoundly shaken, Lieutenant Gore will neither forgive Captain Cook for so upbraiding him, nor get over the horror of having taken the life of a man, all by his burst of anger that he has always had trouble controlling. Dr Solander notes that the American, 'did not recover for 12 days of the shock it gave him'.[37]

•

And yet, whatever the *Ngāti Hei* think of Lieutenant Gore at the time, one small Native boy, Te Horeta te Taniwha, and his friends have a great opinion of one of the white 'goblins' who visit their shores. The memory of James Cook will stay with them for their whole lives and be remarkably passed on to posterity.

'There was one supreme man in that ship,' Te Horeta te Taniwha will recount many years later. 'We knew that he was the lord of the whole by his perfect gentlemanly and noble demeanour. He seldom spoke, but some of the goblins spoke much. But this man did not utter many words: all that he did was to handle our mats and hold our *mere*, spears, and *wahaika*, and touch the hair of our heads. He was a very good man, and came to us – the children – and patted our cheeks, and gently touched our heads.'[38]

Perhaps it is because he misses his own children James, Nathaniel, and precious little Elizabeth, who James Cook reflects, must be six, five, and two years old now. They, too, must be about this size, or perhaps even a bit bigger. He misses them, their innocent looks, their tender love, their simple worlds; a far cry from their father's, but he will be home with them soon enough. And of course dear Elizabeth had been pregnant when he had left, so that little one must be a year old now. Oh, how he *aches* to see them all again, and to meet his new child.

What few words he says to the children have a curious 'hissing sound, and the words he spoke were not understood by us in the least'.[39]

In any case his attention has now turned to the warriors, as he clearly wants some information from them. The speech 'the lord of these goblins' makes to the warriors is translated by the one among them who speaks the Native language.

Taking a piece of charcoal, Cook makes a wavy line on the deck of the ship, before pointing to the nearby shore and then looking meaningfully at the warriors.

It is one of the old Native Chiefs who divines his meaning first.

'He is asking for an outline of this land,'[40] he says. Well, the answer to that is very easy, and that old man himself takes the proffered charcoal and draws the outline they all know of the land, including all the bays, inlets, rivers, cliffs and rocky outcrops. With Tupia translating, the old Chief explains to the Chief goblin, the best he can, the meaning of all the marks that go beyond just the contours of the shoreline, while everyone else on deck watches them closely, listening.

'After some time the chief goblin took some white stuff, on which he made a copy of what the old chief had made on the deck, and then spoke to the old chief.'[41]

Te Horeta te Taniwha takes it all in, still stunned at everything he is seeing and hearing.

'I and my two boy-companions did not walk about on board of the ship – we were afraid lest we should be bewitched by the goblins; and we sat still and looked at everything we saw at the home of these goblins.'[42]

And now here is the Chief goblin again, coming their way!

As before, he smiles and ruffles the hair of the boy and his two young friends. They are gentle children. He then proffers his hand to Te Horeta te Taniwha, offering special nails that he has brought as a gift. Te Horeta te Taniwha's companions aren't so sure, afraid to take these strange trinkets. But when Te Horeta laughs, the Chief goblin gives the nail to him.

'*Ka pai,*' the young fellow says in response, meaning fine.

'Kah pie . . .' the Chief goblin repeats slowly, before again affectionately patting their heads with his hand, and then going away.[43]

'This is the leader of the ship,' the other two boys say to Te Horeta te Taniwha, 'which is proved by his kindness to us; and also he is so very fond of children. A noble man – one of noble birth – cannot be lost in a crowd.'[44]

Te Horeta te Taniwha will treasure the nail like a goblin might treasure a gold ring, the most precious thing he owns.

•

The *Endeavour* continues its journey, first tracking North-west then following the coastline to the North-east, Captain Cook pencilling its contours and geographical quirks into his chart each night and soon noting another quirky though familiar contour, in parts where they are not so warmly welcomed (and of parts that are certainly warm but rarely welcomed up close) . . .

For sometimes, when they are passing close enough to the coast to observe the Natives, he can see them, lined up on cliffs with their backs to them only to . . . only to . . . oh dear, only to bend over and bare their buttocks.

Te Kotore o te Whenua, the Anus of the Land, indeed. Look, if the exact meaning is unclear, certainly the sentiment is unmistakable . . .

21 November 1769, Tupia lectures, Cook learns

While Lieutenant Gore remains shell-shocked by the Captain's public dressing-down, Tupia is blooming before the Captain's eyes, a revered figure wherever they go.

Wherever they drop anchor, the Natives who approach ask for Tupia by name and either seek his help with trade, or at least his help translating their threats. That news of the *Endeavour*'s visit can travel so far so fast across such distance is evidence of co-operation and communication between a cornucopia of varied tribes and peoples scattered across the land. To the white men, it is another foreign land, full of strange sounds, smells and sights. To Tupia it is strange as well, though not unlike Tahiti and her own necklace of islands. He is now a man of many worlds, at one with and apart from the white men, the New Zealand Natives, and his Tahitian homeland – which is no small thing as he continues to pine for his homeland, and count the moons until they can get back to Britain and soon afterwards, he hopes, begin the journey home once more.

And so, he is constantly busy. On 18 November, when they drop anchor just outside 'the Firth of Thames', or so the white men will come to call it, they have only just finished naming it when some of its traditional inhabitants arrive.

'Come ashore and we will kill you all,' shouts one Native, being 'very saucy' indeed.[45]

'Well,' replies Tupia evenly, 'while we are *at sea* you have no manner of business with us, the sea is *our* property as much as *yours!*'

Banks – whose own grasp of the language has improved enough that he can follow and record the exchange – is stunned.

'Such reasoning from an Indian who had not had the smallest hint from any of us surprised me much and the more as these were sentiments I never had before heard him give a hint about in his own case.'[46]

Yes, bit by bit, both Mr Banks and Captain Cook are lifting their estimation of Tupia's capacities and, with it, the abilities of his whole race. No, not the equal of white men they are sure, but still . . . they really can use deductive logic, and have an instinctive grasp of even such sophisticated concepts as that of sovereignty. In his journal, Banks is clear: 'That these people have a larger share of ingenuity than usually falls to the lot of nations who had so little or indeed no commerce with any others appears at first sight. Their boats, the better sort of them at least, shew it most evidently.'[47]

To Banks' own surprise, he even finds himself admiring their *art*, a field in which he had initially thought that Europeans were the last word: 'For the beauty of their carving in general I fain would say something more about it but find myself much inferior to the task.'

Sydney Parkinson is equally impressed, and also fascinated by their use of spirals.

> The men have a particular taste for carving: their boats, paddles, boards to put on their houses, tops of walking sticks, and even their boats . . . are carved in a variety of flourishes, turnings and windings, that are unbroken; but their favourite figure seems to be a volute, or spiral, which they vary many ways, single, double, and triple, and with as much truth as if done from mathematical draughts: yet the only instruments we have seen are a chisel, and an axe made of stone. Their fancy, indeed, is very wild and extravagant.[48]

Yet it is more than the artistic talent of the Native carvers that impress the men. It is their more practical endeavours – what they use these beautifully carved canoes *for* – that so fascinates the men.

Fishing?

'Nets for fishing they make in the same manner as ours,' Banks records, 'of an amazing size . . . Besides this they have fish pots and baskets worked with twigs, and another kind of net which they most generally make use of that I have never seen in any country but this. They are circular and about 7 or 8 feet in diameter and 2 or 3 deep; they are stretched by two or three hoops and open at the top for near but not quite their whole extent; on the bottom is fastened the bait, a little basket containing the guts etc. of fish and sea ears which are tied to different parts of the net. This is let down to the bottom where fish are and when enough are supposed to be gathered together are drawn up with a very gentle motion by which means the fish are insensibly lifted from the bottom; in this manner I have seen them take vast numbers of fish and indeed it is a most general way of fishing all over the coast.'[49]

More than ever now both Cook and Banks are glad that they have Tupia with them to not only translate words, but also interpret Native actions so they can better understand them.

Looking at the trees that grow in these parts, Cook is also stunned.

Their *straightness*.

Their *height*.

Taking his quadrant, he carefully measures the height of one with his usual precision.

'I found its length from the root to the first branch to be 89 feet; it was as Straight as an Arrow and Tapered but very little in proportion

254 • JAMES COOK

to its length, so that I judged that there was 356 Solid feet of timber in this Tree.'[50]

Banks is similarly impressed, most particularly noting, like Cook, the lack of taper: 'I dare venture to affirm that the top where the lowest branch took its rise was not a foot less in diameter than where we measured, which was about 8 feet from the ground. We cut down a young one of these trees; the wood proved heavy and solid, too much so for mast but would make the finest Plank in the world.'[51]

There is no doubt about it, this New Zealand is a place filled with resources that would have enormous value back in Europe.

26 November 1769, Cape Brett, North Island, once more into his breech

'They have heard of us,'[52] Tupia tells Captain Cook, as they both peer over the gunwale at the seven canoes carrying some 200-odd Natives in the small open bay where they are anchored.

Word of the goblins' largesse, and gullibility, has preceded them yet again.

Thankfully, the Natives of the area are eager traders, happily brandishing their offerings: fish and oysters not clubs, spears, nor menacing tongues. (They do bare their buttocks, though not with any aim to offend, and each cheek, down to a man, is marked with a black spiral. Many have 'their thighs almost entirely black, small lines only being left untouched so that they looked like striped breeches'.[53])

And so the bartering begins.

My fish for your knife?

No. (The jacks have been enjoying their fishing rods, hauling in loads by the pail. What type of fish is it? Well, frankly, the lads are really fishing for the fun of it, but now that you ask, Mr Banks . . . sea bream they are. Yes, sir, that's what Tupia told us. Banks makes a note of it as the sailors continue to cast their lines into the water, catching so many fish that they no longer need to rely on the Natives for them. Cook takes notice as well, and always on the lookout for the impetus for a good name, decides that the cove will be called 'Bream Bay'[54] from this day forth.)

Perhaps then, my whale rib for your 'old pair of black breeches?'[55]

Yes.

Everything goes well enough and the journey continues unabated over the next two days – notwithstanding a few warning shots towards some pesky Natives – until they find themselves once again trading with a litter of canoes. Yes, here you are, I'll give you this if you give me . . . Oh. This old trick. It is not the first time that a Native has taken his half of the trade without providing something in return, and the crew have become familiar with it. Familiar, but no less infuriated. On this occasion the Midshipman gathers the nearest weapon at hand, a fishing line with a cruel hook on the end, and 'heaves the lead', at the retreating Native thief.

A bite!

Well, not quite a bite, but that is what it feels like to the recalcitrant Native, as the hook really does bite deep into his backside, right in the eye of his spiral tattoo, when the Midshipman yanks on the line with all his might.

That is for all your brothers, who have been showing their bottoms to us!

The Midshipman keeps pulling with all his might, the Native yelping in agony, until the shank breaks leaving the bend and pointed barb implanted in the Native's bottom.

And that's one in the brown-eye for you.

'No very agreeable legacy,'[56] Mr Banks notes wryly as the *Endeavour* crew fall about laughing.

The Natives are considerably less amused, and yet, while it is no doubt a terrible pain in the posterior for the thief, it is so much better than the trigger-happy, gun-totin' American Lieutenant Gore shooting you dead.

The encounter, however, appears to have poisoned relations and the next day the Natives reappear under the guise of trade only to start hurling stones at all those on the *Endeavour*, 'with more courage than any boats we had seen'.[57]

Captain Cook will suffer it no longer.

He climbs up to the poop deck, a shiny white beacon for the rock-hurling Natives who soon send a barrage his way.

Captain Cook draws his musket loaded with small shot, he aims it at one of the Natives who is poised to throw a stone and . . . pulls the trigger.

A second later the Native is thrown back into his canoe, and as Banks records, 'He sunk down so immediately into the Canoe that we suspected he was materially hurt.'[58]

Does this stop the rest of them?

It does not.

Another *waka taua*, war canoe, filled with many Natives, all clearly about to throw stones, sallies forth. Captain Cook allows them to get within a range of 50 yards – calculated to be that distance whereby they can't hurt him with stones, but he can hurt them with small shot – and again fires, whereupon they quickly retreat.

It is becoming ever more apparent, and worryingly so, that these New Zealand Natives will not be as pliant as the tractable Tahitians had been. Even when outnumbered and out-gunned, they are warriors by nature and won't surrender without a fight. On occasion they might relent and retreat, but only as a means to regroup and fight again. Sailing deeper into the Bay of Islands, Cook writes: 'I was obliged to pepper 2 or 3 fellows with small Shott, after which they retired, and the wind coming at North-West we stood off to Sea.'[59]

Firing his musket at Natives does not come easily to him, as it does to Lieutenant Gore, but sometimes it simply has to be done.

29 November 1769, Bay of Islands, cannon to the left of them, celery to the right of them

Natives!

A handful of curious sailors of the *Endeavour* have only just landed on the beach, when they realise the mass of bold Natives who had been floating about the ship moments earlier have followed them to shore and are about to land . . . on them – running across the sands with frightening speed, while brandishing weapons as fearsome as their faces. A squalling, skirmishing scrum of Englishmen and Māori takes place. The result? The Englishmen give ground and are bloodily beaten back into the sea. Instead of the shore, they have come up with a new destination: wherever these ferocious Natives aren't. Unfortunately they neglect to report their brief battle to Captain Cook, who, in the company of some Marines and the ever botanising Banks, is even now approaching this same landing spot in the yawl . . .

It is, thus, no sooner than the bow of their boat hits the shore – about three-quarters of a mile from where the ship lies – than they see Natives coming at them in canoes, even as others come rushing along the beach. Still others, as Banks describes, 'appeared on the tops of the hills and numbers from behind each head of the Cove so that we were in a moment surrounded by . . . 200 of them'.[60]

Cook is born for this moment. A man given to drama would act dramatically – and dangerously. But it is not in his steady-as-she-goes-if-you-please nature, which is precisely what is required. He motions for Mr Banks to follow him and strides confidently towards the bulk of the Natives on the beach.

The Natives jostle to get a look at the white men coming towards them, each with his spear lifted, and yet, for the moment, their curiosity seems to quell their truculence and no-one moves to strike.

Just what manner of beings are these, who show no fear though completely outnumbered by heavily armed warriors?

Captain Cook waves at the Natives, beckoning them to follow him back to the major party of sailors and Marines. They do so, walking at a wary distance behind the two white emissaries and stopping well short of the main group, watching as some of the white goblins come forward and draw a line in the sand with their strange sticks, and make clear to the Natives that they are not to pass over it.

Stunned, the Natives appear to agree . . . before another group of Natives comes from the other end of the beach and, with no such line, are soon mingling with the white men when a cry rings out, immediately taken up and repeated by other baleful voices, as they all go into a crouch.

> *Whiti whiti*
> *Toa*
> *Whiti whiti*
> *Toa*
> *Ka eke i te wiwī*
> *Ka eke i te wawā*
> *Ka eke i te papārahua i Rangitumu*
> *Huia i Ka Eke i Ka Eke*
> *Kāea: Wēku . . . Wēku, Wēku, Wēku mai te whiore hī*
> *Rōpū: Toa*
> *Ko roto koe taku puta . . . a*
> *He puta aha te puta . . . a*
> *He puta tohi te puta . . . a*
> *E rua nei ko te puta . . . a*
> *Hī*[61]

Captain Cook and his men watch warily, but make no move until three Natives suddenly break from the pack, wade into the shallow waters and try to drag the pinnace and the yawl onto the beach.

With things turning dramatic, it is time to take dramatic action.

Captain Cook snaps the orders and those whose muskets are loaded with small shot fire in the Natives' direction, which for the moment succeeds in driving them back.

But wait!

One Native, braver than the rest, attempts to rally his friends and makes great charges forward, waving his *patu* club.

It is the Doctor – whose gun is still loaded with small shot for he had declined to fire in the first volley – who must do the honours. It is a strange thing for a man of bookish bent to find himself on the other side of the world pointing a loaded gun at a human being, but he feels he has no choice.

When the brave man is just 20 yards from them, he fires, and, on the instant, the man, with specks of blood suddenly appearing all over his torso, stops, turns and runs, retreating with the rest to higher ground where they regroup, preparing for another sally . . . Something stronger is called for, and aboard the *Endeavour* – where the confrontation is being watched very closely by Lieutenants Hicks and Gore, through their spyglasses – they have just the thing.

Hicks gives the order to prepare for fire.

Five of the cannon are primed, loaded and await only the signal from Lieutenant Hicks, who now lifts his sword in readiness.

Hicks drops his sword.

Fire!

For the Natives on the hill, it is extraordinary.

One moment they are preparing to charge down upon the white devils, and the next, the tops of the magnificent Kanuka trees behind them are entirely shattered, as trunks split and branches come tumbling down, just before bursts of thunder roll over them on this clear day.

The Natives look behind them as the trees fall. *If this is what the goblins can do to trees, what might they be able to do to us if we continue our attack?*

White man black magic. It is too strong for them. They decide to retreat after all.

'They went off,' Banks records, 'and at last left us our cove quite to ourselves, so that the muskets were laid down upon the ground and all hands employed in gathering Celery.'[62]

9 December 1769, off Rangaunu Bay, Tupia tricks the truth

As happens so often, on this morning the bay floods with canoes. Yet this time, the greetings of the Natives are hesitant at best, and maybe even fearful. They are clearly reluctant to stray too near. For yes, the word has spread along the forest pathways and by canoes across the bay:

these visitors have great black tubes on their vessel that can unleash the power to fell a tree as far as you could throw a spear 40 times, and blow as many warriors apart with a single blow if it just hit them once. The apprehension that might otherwise have developed into a delicate stalemate is quickly dissolved thanks to Tupia convincing the Natives that no, no, don't worry, there is nothing to fear from these white men. In short order, the Natives row beneath the stern and begin to trade cloth and fish.

Now, amid the cacophony of tongues and trades, Tupia begins to delve into the history of these islanders, desperate for information that could help their journey.

'Do you know of any countries besides this or ever been to any?'[63] he asks.

'No,' the Natives reply, before pointing to the North-west, 'but our ancestors have talked of a large country [in that direction] to which some people had sailed in a very large canoe, which passage took them up to a month. From this expedition a part only returned who told our countrymen that they had seen a country where the people eat hogs, for which animal they used the same name (Booah) as is used in the Islands.'[64]

'And have you no hogs among you?'[65] asks Tupia.

'No,' comes the firm reply.

'And did your ancestors bring none back with them?'[66] inquires Tupia once more.

'No.'

'You must be a parcel of *liars*!' barks Tupia 'Your story is a great lie, for your ancestors would *never* have been such fools as to come back without them.'[67]

Either way both Captain Cook and Banks are convinced these New Zealanders must be great sailors and navigators to have come this far, even if their skills transporting hogs is not up to the high mark set by Tupia and his people.

With the assistance of Master Molineux and his Mates, Captain Cook sets out to survey this new bay, finding it 'to all appearance nothing but white sand thrown up in low irregular hills, lying in Narrow ridges parallel with the shore'.[68] Seeing nothing more significant than the endless empty white of the beach, Cook names it Sandy Bay and moves to the more important task of divining just where this bay lies in relation to the world around it. While it is Banks who has come this far to look at plants, Cook is no stranger to turning to flora for further information.

Tracing the lay of the land with his eyes and resting on the greenery he can see in the distance, Cook notices, 'The first ridge behind the Sea beach is partly covered with Shrubs, Plants, etc., but the second ridge hath hardly any green thing upon it, which induced me to think that it lies open to the Western Sea.'[69]

Who needs a botanist?

Days later, Captain Cook's calculations prove correct when they see there, on the horizon, the Northernmost point of visible land. Being both in the North, and a Cape, the Captain dubs it North Cape, and records its location to be 'in the Latitude of 34 degrees 22 minutes South and Longitude 186 degrees 55 minutes West from Greenwich'.[70]

'Saw land bearing South-West being the same North-Westernmost land we have seen before,' he records in the log, 'and which I take to be the Northern Extremity of this Country, as we have now a large swell rolling in from the Westward which could not well be, was we covered by any land on that point of the Compass.'[71]

It is further evidence that the Great Southern Land does not exist at all . . . but it puts the sailors on their guard as sails rip and the men work around the clock to manoeuvre the *Endeavour* Southward. For the next fortnight or so, the *Endeavour* battles a strong Easterly current and mercurial winds off North Cape, finally falling in with what appears to be New Zealand's North-western shore on 23 December and following it South-east.

On Christmas Eve Banks shoots some geese. One notable tradition, thus, is observed, even though at the other end of the Earth.

'As it was the humour of the ship to keep Christmas in the old fashioned way,' Joseph Banks notes, 'it was resolved of them to make a Goose pie for tomorrow's dinner.'[72]

And so it is done, gone the sun.

'Christmas day: Our Goose pie was eat with great approbation and in the Evening all hands were as Drunk as our forefathers used to be upon the like occasion.'[73]

In fact, so much do they drink that on the following day an even more established, if not so cherished, tradition is observed: 'This morn all heads ached with yesterday's debauch.'[74]

All heads, in fact, except that of the moderate Captain Cook, who on this day recognises a small island to the North-west of their position, which he takes 'to be the 3 Kings discovered by Tasman'.[75] They are on the same stretch of coast charted by Abel Tasman!

Onward they sail, fighting stiff on-shore winds and roiling seas such as they did not encounter on the Eastern side of the cape, the jacks forever striking, repairing and replacing their sails, attempting to stand in to shore when the weather calms, but mostly standing at least three leagues out to sea, and pushing Southward as much as conditions allow.

As the sands of the hourglass start to drift, and even tremble, as a new decade begins to tumble over, a slow battle is taking place aboard the *Endeavour* – no less than a battle for a continent. Or at least, it is a battle over whether New Zealand is but an island, or a solitary series of islands, or the beginning of the Great Southern Continent. The further they go, the more Cook is convinced that New Zealand is an island, or a series of islands, and is intent on proving this beyond all doubt by circumnavigating it. Banks on the other hand – and he has the unanimous support of his own party, and a fair measure of the crew – is convinced that New Zealand is but the start of the Great Southern Land, and this dip South is but temporary. Either way, the fact that Cook is now pushing his mighty Whitby cat to prowl further means that they will soon have the answer, in the form of the map that continues to form under Cook's precise hand, even as Banks shoots birds, hooks fishes, gathers plants when they go ashore, and continues to expand his now groaning catalogue. While each is content for the other to focus on his own field of duties, Banks does have a growing frustration at just how careful Cook is with his mapping, as it means the *Endeavour* must move so slowly.

Still, just as ugliness begets distemper, so too doth beauty soothe souls, and both men continue to be impressed by the sheer natural wonder of everything they are seeing from sunrise to sunset every blessed day. This is clearly a land that is strikingly pretty, green and fertile from East to West and North to South. From the deck, they can see snow-capped mountains, white beaches, green bushes and luscious fields, all boasting a lyrical loveliness that is completely bewitching.

14 January 1770, entering Cook's Strait, a full-bodied meal

No less than 400 miles down the West side of New Zealand, the same stretch sailed and roughly charted 128 years ago by the Dutchman Abel Tasman, exploration too close to shore remains dangerous. The coast continues trending Southerly but to what end? The question is answered soon enough. For on this day, Captain Cook sees two things of great significance. The first is *land* to their south! And the second thing, to their

East, the wide opening of what he supposes is a large bay, or perhaps it is what Tasman marked on his chart as *Zeehaen's Bight.*

Bight or bay, the inlet seems to call to them like a siren song, beckoning them into her calm waters.

The following morning, after they have proceeded a little further into it and can see more clearly, Cook notes in his log that rather than a bight or bay – a seafarer's cul-de-sac – this broad opening has a strong current pushing to the East, strongly suggesting it is a strait and that there is an outlet at the other end. Proceeding further into the broad inlet to confirm it, the opening narrows as they go, though the current becomes still stronger as they note a complex series of bays, coves and points on the land that appears to their South. If this is a strait they are in, this Southern shore is perhaps of another large island?

'The Shore,' Cook notes in an upbeat mood, 'seems to form several Bays, into one of which I intend to go with the Ship in order to Careen her (she being very foul) and to repair some few defects, recruit our Stock, Wood, Water, etc . . .'[76]

Despite the danger, the *Endeavour*'s venture into these waters is greeted by a friendly, if unfamiliar face. Surfacing from the water from time to time with black saucer eyes, long grey whiskers and smelling a lot like fish, is a male sea lion. Resplendent and regal with a shaggy mane, the lion seems pleased with the visitors to his realm, keeping a watchful but friendly eye on the *Endeavour*. He is the king of these parts, but not a despot, and they are welcome. Others of the locals feel differently however, as some eight miles in the men spot a canoe full of Natives crossing a small bay but keeping a wide berth from the white men. The Natives on the canoe disembark on the beach of a small island before they climb up to a small dwelling on its highest point. If only all their interactions with the locals could be as agreeable as with the sea lion.

On 16 January, Cook finds a wide and bountiful inlet, and soon, a cove in which to anchor after several weeks under constant sail.

From their anchorage, in what Cook describes as 'a very Snug Cove', they look out upon a fertile landscape, well forested and well watered for the purposes of refilling a ship. The jacks are aching for the stability of shore after weeks of hard travelling and violent waters. What they most want are fresh fish, and their wish is granted shortly after the seine is hauled. Better than a land of milk and honey, this is a land of fish, and hundreds of pounds of them are procured in an instant.

And yet, even in a place of such moving beauty, they come across the strangest of things, well beyond anything in their previous experience.

After dinner one evening, they decide to go for a pleasant row in the yawl to land on a nearby cove and stretch their legs when they come across . . . what is this floating on the water?

A dead seal?

No.

A dead woman, and so bloated and rotted is her body it is clear she has been dead for some time.

Shocked, they arrive on shore to find a small family of Natives so afraid they initially run up the beach and take shelter in the woods, but who return to tell Tupia that, 'the woman was a relation of ours and that instead of burying our dead our custom is to tie a stone to them and throw them into the sea'.[77]

Clearly, Banks surmises, the 'stone [must] have been unloosed by some accident'.[78]

Very well then, the morbid mystery has been solved. With great hospitality, the family welcome Cook and Banks to dine with them, eager to share a roast meal. Roast dog, which is already cooking deep in the ground. The Englishmen are famished, and are much obliged. Banks, curious as always, snatches a quick glance in their 'many provision baskets' as so 'by accident observed 2 bones, pretty clean picked, which as appeared upon examination were undoubtedly . . . human bones'.[79]

Good God!

Sharp as can be, Occam's razor tells Banks what this must mean; but still he cannot quite fathom what he is seeing and the implications. Reeling from his revelation, he is only just able to maintain his mask of steely indifference. His stomach lurches as his eyes dart to this otherwise friendly family who are hosting them. *This* family are cannibals? And are we visitors possibly intended to be the next meal? Must we be on our guard for an attack? Horror after horror, after grisly thought after grisly thought keep whirling around, as Banks feels decidedly ill. It is one thing to hear tales of it, to imagine a religious rite of solemnity, it is quite another to see bodies in a basket as a family sits calmly readying its evening meal.

'Though we had from the first of our arrival upon the coast constantly heard the Indians acknowledge the custom of eating their enemies we had never before had a proof of it, but this amounted almost to demonstration: the bones were clearly human, upon them were evident marks of their having been dressed on the fire, the meat was not entirely picked off from them and on the grisly ends which were gnawed were evident marks of teeth.'[80]

With Tupia translating, the Englishman wants to know more.

'What bones are these?' Banks begins carefully.

'The bones of a man,' they reply, perhaps a little bemused at his interest.

'And have you eaten the flesh?'[81]

'Yes.'

'Have you none of it left?'

'No.'

'Why did not you eat the woman who we saw today in the water?'[82] inquires Banks, morbidly interested now.

'She was our relation,' comes the answer. Apparently one must draw the line somewhere.

'Who then is it that you do eat?' Banks continues.

'Those who are killed in war.'

In war?

'And who was the man whose bones these are?'

Again, by Banks' detailed account, the reply comes . . .

'Five days ago a boat of our enemies came into this bay and of them we killed seven, of whom the owner of these bones was one.'[83]

The Natives seem extraordinarily matter of fact about what appears to be an ancient custom, but the English sailors cannot help themselves . . .

'The horror that appeared in the countenances of the seamen on hearing this discourse which was immediately translated for the good of the company,' Banks chronicles, 'is better conceived than described.'[84]

When it comes to Banks however, his fascination to be able to document such an extraordinary practice helps him overcome his horror – at least to the point that he can dissemble it enough that the Natives will continue to talk openly to him. While quietly stunned, the social scientist in him is 'pleased at having so strong a proof of a custom which human nature holds in too great abhorrence to give easy credit to'.[85]

Captain Cook is every bit as confronted.

'It is hard to account for what we have everywhere been told, of their eating their enemies killed in battle,' he writes, 'which they most certainly do; circumstances enough we have seen to convince us of the truth of this. Tupia, who holds this custom in great aversion, has very often argued with them against it, but they have always as strenuously supported it, and never would own that it was wrong.'[86]

Tupia is horrified, but eager to question the Natives about their carnivorous practices. He has seen so much, more than most men, Native or otherwise, and yet still he cannot bring himself to believe that the Natives can eat each other.

'But where are the skulls?' Tupia asks the old man. 'Do you eat them? Bring them and we shall then be convinced that these are men whose bones we have seen!'[87]

'We do not eat the heads,' answers an old warrior, Topaa, paramount Chief of these, the Motuara people. 'But we do the brains and tomorrow I will bring one and show you.'[88]

Very well then.

20 January 1770, Queen Charlotte's Sound, Banks gets ahead

Not for nothing will the crew informally christen this place as 'Cannibal Bay'.[89]

As good as his word, a couple of days later, the old man is back, bringing with him . . . four severed heads.

One is the head of a lad about '14 or 15 years of age, and evidently showed by the contusions on one side of it that it had received many violent blows which had chipped off a part of the skull'.[90]

They are, Banks records, 'preserved with the flesh and hair on and kept I suppose as trophies, as possibly scalps were by the North Americans before the Europeans came among them; the brains were however taken out as we had been told, maybe they are a delicacy here. The flesh and skin upon these heads were soft but they were somehow preserved so as not to stink at all.'[91]

While Captain Cook looks on, quietly appalled, Joseph Banks proceeds at once to try to make a trade for that particular head, offering in exchange a pair of splendid, albeit slightly used, pair of linen drawers he happens to have with him.

The old man, though taken with the drawers, remains reluctant to part with his head, until Joseph Banks pulls out his musket, points it towards the other man, and the deal is done.

To clear their own . . . heads, Mr Banks and the Doctor head off on another excursion, tramping through the mostly thick undergrowth. They are interested to note the topography of the land is so hilly that there is barely enough of a flat patch to host a potato garden, even if they had wanted to tend one.

'Our friends here,' Banks notes, 'do not seem to feel the want of such places as we have not yet seen the least appearance of cultivation, I suppose they live entirely upon fish, dogs and Enemies . . .'[92]

The horrors and mysteries of Cannibal Bay now a secondary concern, Captain Cook's mind turns to pressing matters. The *Endeavour* is anchored 20 miles from the head of the inlet, but the Captain's goal is to formulate a plan from which to proceed. He must now discover an elevated vantage point from where he can map the way forward.

23 January 1770, Queen Charlotte's Sound, sea seen, passage proclaimed

Captain Cook, Joseph Banks and the Doctor climb the nearest hill, no easy thing given how heavily wooded it is. At the summit, they pause to survey the inlet and realise the way forward will not be so easy. They are hindered by higher hills in the way, followed by impenetrable woods that make further advancement impossible. And yet what is that to the East? Turning his head further in that billowing wind nearly always found at the top of such hills, Captain Cook sees sea, the wide open blue stretching out, unbroken from here on the hill to the horizon . . . It is wonderful news, though not yet confirmed that there will be passage through possible reefs and shallows to get there.

So on the last day of January 1770, Cook tries again, climbing to the peak of the highest hill in the whole area, where the view is unencumbered. And there it is! To the East he can see the full, glorious passage. Cook is quick to descend, eager to raise the anchor, put to sea and get through. Clearly now, what lies to their North is no more than a small island, and not the Great Southern Land. Cook won't dare state it as a certainty yet, but privately his thoughts are clear: 'I had some Conjectures that the lands to the South-West of this Strait (which we are now at) was an Island, and not a Continent.'[93]

Attempting to ignore the rather disconcerting four human skulls an old Native man has brought aboard – their empty eye sockets seem to stare accusingly – Cook buries his disgust for the macabre trophies and asks, 'Is there a strait or passage into the Eastern sea?'[94]

'Yes, there is a passage . . .'[95]

Before Cook leaves this land, he wishes to claim it for King George and erect wooden markers should any Frenchman or Spaniard follow with similar imperial ideas.

With that in mind, Captain Cook, Surgeon Monkhouse and Tupia travel to speak to Native Chiefs on a nearby island to advertise their intent to put up these posts with, by his account, a happy result: 'They not only gave their free Consent to set it up, but promised never to pull it down.'[96]

The English Captain confers with the Chief of the Motuara people, Topaa. While they are setting up the post, Cook questions the old man about the lands to the South-west. Topaa tells him of the South Island on which they stand, *Te Wai Pounamu* – The Water of the Greenstone – which 'would take up a great many Moons to sail round'.[97]

(Lost in translation for the moment is how these lands were actually formed. As all the tribes know, as it has been handed down through the generations, told around the fires and intoned in the sacred places: the South island is the *Te Waka a Māui*, the canoe of Māui, and the North island is *Te Ika-a-Maui*, 'the fish of Māui'. The demigod, Maui, stood upon the canoe to haul up the fish, and so *Aotearoa* was formed.)

As always, gifts are in order, the free exchange of rare and obscure items a well-proven path towards peace. Cook offers '3 penny pieces dated 1763 and spike nails with the King's Broad Arrow cut deep in them'.[98] Safe passage essentially bought and paid for, Cook orders his men to take a post to the highest point of the island, where the Union Jack is to be hoisted. An entire island, for nowt but pennies and nails.

'I dignified this Inlet with the name of Queen Charlotte's Sound, and took formal possession of it and adjacent lands in the name and for the use of His Majesty.'[99]

With both the literary and actual flag of the British now firmly planted in the name of King George upon this new territory, Captain Cook and his men toast His Majesty's health with a bottle of wine. Eager to include the Natives in their celebration, Cook's officers offer the bottle to Topaa, though not before having drained it of every last drop of wine.

A message in a bottle if ever there was one . . .

3 February 1770, Queen Charlotte's Sound, sod's law

Surgeon Monkhouse is ropable.[100]

'The Natives,' he advises Joseph Banks, 'are given to the detestable vice of Sodomy.'[101]

Do tell?

Yes, Monkhouse recounts between sniffs of snuff, he had been with a family of Natives and 'paid a price for leave to make my addresses to any one young woman they should pitch upon for me. One was chose and I willingly retired with her but on examination "she" proved to be a boy! On returning and complaining of this another was sent who turned out to be a boy likewise! On my second complaint I could get no redress but was laughed at by the Indians.'[102]

As it turns out, not just the Natives. For in truth, Banks is highly amused himself as, with barely muted glee and the quick flick of his sharpened quill, he once again consigns the passions of Surgeon Monkhouse to where they belong – in the doghouse.

'Far be it from me to attempt saying that that Vice is not practised here,' he notes in his journal, 'however I must say that in my humble opinion this story proves no more than that our gentleman was fairly tricked out of his cloth, which none of the young ladies chose to accept of on his terms, and the master of the family did not choose to part with.'[103]

In any case, it is time to weigh anchor and they are soon underway once more, when . . .

When just 20 miles from the Eastern entrance of Queen Charlotte's Sound, as they are attempting to sail the rest of the strait that bears South-east, the ripping tide suddenly carries them towards an outcrop of perilously rocky islands, too quick for the men to change course. A great roar begins to rise, suddenly Cook and his crew are among the breakers!

'It made a very great ripping,' Sydney Parkinson records, 'especially near the islands, where the water running in heaps, bears and whirl-pools, made a very great noise in its passage.'[104]

With no other options, Captain Cook barks his commands and the *Endeavour* quickly drops anchor amidst the breakers, the heavy iron crashing down through white sea foam. The sailors watch as the coils of heavy cable on the deck continue to unfurl with a metallic whirr and snake up and over the side and ever downward into the depths for what feels like an age as they get ever closer to hitting the rocks! At last however, after full 150 fathoms of cable have unfurled the anchor hits bottom, the cable is pulled tight and the *Endeavour* holds! They are within spitting distance of the rocks.

It is a near thing, but so long as the anchor holds steady, they will be safe and the *Endeavour* will make it through the night.

The dawn brings an ebbing tide, and Cook is more than happy to follow it through the strait.

8 February 1770, Leaving the strait and narrow, an aye for an island, bye to a continent

After the *Endeavour* finally sails clear of – let's see – 'Cook's Strait', they turn North, to sail up the Eastern side of New Zealand's Northern island to finally put to bed any ongoing speculation aboard that the land may extend South-east between Cape Turnagain and Cape Palliser, leading to the Great Southern Continent.

Yes, I'm gazing intently at you, Lieutenant Gore, as I have heard your loud speculations on this matter.

Of course, Captain Cook personally has no doubt but is still 'resolved to clear up every doubt that might Arise on so important an Object'.[105]

The next morning they sight Cape Turnagain and prepare to . . . turn again, again. The circumnavigation of what Captain Cook has discovered to be the Northern island of New Zealand is complete, and Cook formally calls the officers up on deck to officially ask them – particularly you, Lieutenant Gore – if they are *now* satisfied that further exploration is not required in this direction.

'They answered in the affirmative,' he chronicles, 'and we hauled our wind to the eastward . . .'[106]

Within minutes they have fully turned and are heading South to explore the coastline of New Zealand's Southern land mass.

•

It never ends.

James Cook is almost certain he is on his way to proving that there is no Great Southern Land, there is a New Zealand made of two islands. But for some on board, the dream never dies. Joseph Banks is one of these and he reports the fresh 'news' with excitement in his journal, 'In the morn early Mr Gore imagined he saw land to the S. Eastward.'[107]

'Imagined' is precisely right in the opinion of Captain Cook. The matter is settled, by science, by maps, not by the imaginings of Lieutenants.

There can be no land mass in that direction, you must have been mistaken, Lieutenant Gore. Gore bristles at the correction, nay the rebuke. He has sailed in the South Pacific before, he is no gentleman dandy, he is an officer.

Lieutenant Gore knows why Cook does not believe him; he is jealous. Jealous of Gore's command of the men, jealous of his ability to speak the Polynesian tongues, jealous of the trust earned by experience that the crew of the *Endeavour* give to him.

It really is, as Dr Solander observed, 'a sort of separate command'[108] that Lieutenant Gore has and now he commands that Cook pay attention to him. Speaking of separate commands and people who think they know better, Mr Joseph Banks is most interested in this new imagined land and he encourages Lieutenant Gore to bring it up once more.

And so Lieutenant Gore waits until he has an audience of gentlemen and officers on the quarter-deck, as Joseph Banks watches and Captain Cook approaches, Lieutenant Gore, with the minimum of respect, makes an announcement in his light American accent.

'I am of the opinion that what I saw yesterday might be land,' he says. Cook knows precisely what he is doing. This is a public announcement of disagreement, to be noted and reported, to be delighted over by Dalrymple and all those armchair Continentalists who wish to declare Cook incompetent, to declare there is a land there unlooked for, passed over by a hasty Yorkshireman. But Cook knows when to call a bluff. *Mr Gore imagines a land? And imagines it publicly?* Very well then, we shall all waste the next couple of days searching for a figment. Gore is taken aback when Cook orders him to direct the *Endeavour* towards his imagining. Cook now makes his own declaration, loudly, publicly, for all those listening to record and remember: 'I resolve that nobody shall say that I have left land behind unsought for. Lt. Gore, steer the ship South East.'[109]

Yes, other captains have a dictum of no man left behind, for Cook it is no land left behind. Two days of searching take place with ... precisely no result. Which is precisely what Captain Cook knew would happen. Lieutenant Gore's cheeks flush red from embarrassment and anger. He has been made to look a fool, a time-wasting fool. His pride is hurt. He has been outwitted by James Cook. Oh, you, Lieutenant Gore might be experienced with the South Pacific, but James Cook has also been sailing for the better part of his life, and understands both intellectually and intuitively – on both counts much better than the American – how the wind, water and land interact in such a way that they give strong clues as to what lies over the horizon. In this case, *nothing*. The 'Continentalists' will think twice before they speak of their imaginings again, for they know the Captain will destroy their beliefs with a most devastating method; he will listen to them.

24 February 1770, off the East coast of the South Island, a duo of dreamers

When evening falls on this blowy day in late February, the *Endeavour* veers West, following the coastline . . . and when the sun returns in the morning, it reveals a vast empty ocean ahead! Even Banks has to concede just how few people there are on board who maintain the faith that New Zealand is the start of the Great Southern Land, not simply a group of islands. As a matter of fact, he can count his support on the fingers of two fingers . . .

'. . . Sorry I am to say that in the ship my party is so small that I firmly believe that there are no more heartily of it than myself and one poor midshipman, the rest begin to sigh for roast beef.'[110]

Indeed, the mood grows ever stronger. There is no Great Southern Land, at least not in these parts. Let us return to England, the land of beef and gravy!

All they need to do, it seems to many of the men, is complete the circumnavigation of this Southern land mass, and they should be free to go.

5 March 1770, New Zealand, Continental breakfast

As the days pass, the mood of Joseph Banks is in sync with the coastline before him. As it falls away, veering to the West, so does his mood fall as it seems more likely they are circumnavigating a mere island rather than the Great Southern Land itself. But as it reappears, and the likelihood of a continent increases, so does he feel stronger.

So it is on this morning when, as the mist clears and they can see the smoke from last night's fires on land still trailing in the sky . . . it is obvious that the shore is trailing away to the West.

This, Banks notes, is 'supposed by the no Continents the end of the land; towards even[ing] however it cleared up and we Continents had the pleasure to see more land to the Southward'.[111]

Rarely, if ever, has Captain Cook been so focused on a chart as now. From sun-up to sundown, there is the Captain, gazing at the shore through his spyglass, measuring his angles, making his notations, checking his calculations – then checking both his angles and his calculations again and again and again. He must be thorough, there must be no doubt.

For this is not just another shore. This is a shore that Mr Alexander Dalrymple and his fellows of the 'Continent' Club will be minutely examining, on the lookout for any ambiguity, any error which might indicate that there could be a continent there after all.

And he will not be gainsaid on exactly how the land lies. When at one point Banks is so intemperate to express his view that land is dangerously near and that the Captain must pull the *Endeavour* back, Cook carefully explains, Mr Banks, that what you are seeing is a low-lying cloud.

Alas for Banks and for the great 'speculative geographer', Alexander Dalrymple, on 10 March 1770, the *Endeavour* rounds the Southern point of a small island lying just off the mainland. He calls the point 'South Cape', the farthest point South of the South Island. Here Banks accepts that these islands stand alone – as islands. Reluctantly, if gracefully – at least in his private journal – he notes that Captain James Cook has by his own endeavours single-handedly destroyed an entire imaginary continent – or at least established it not in this area where Mr Dalrymple had supposed it to be. Banks concedes defeat: 'Blew fresh all day but carried us round the Point to the total demolition of our aerial fabric called continent.'[112]

Yes, what Captain Cook had thought instinctively since leaving Cape Horn more than a year ago, has now been accepted by the gentry on board. It had been all very well for Joseph Banks to dwell on his 'aerial fabric', his geographical castle in the air – the Great Southern Land – but Captain Cook's knowledge of the elements, his experience in the ocean, his careful map-making has blown it away, at least for now.

Now heading North, along the Western side of the South Island, the *Endeavour* cuts through something that is no less than a long white cloud, a damp fog that nestles on the water with just enough gaps that they can glimpse where they are going, and the land they are outflanking. High above, off to starboard, Cook spies a number of snow-capped mountains, their peaks rising from the haze like icy giants. Impressed by the sheer jagged grandeur of this place, its rugged contours, he notes how the land 'rises into hills directly from the sea'.[113]

In the meantime, bit by bit, Joseph Banks is grasping more of the nuances of the Natives' language, in part thanks to tutoring by Tupia and Tayeto. While in Tahiti, his progress in the basics had been rapid as it had been a part of his daily intercourse, here in New Zealand his exposure to the Natives' way of speaking has been less regular – the South Island appears sparsely populated compared to the North – but still a few key things are becoming clear.

'The Genius of the Language especially in the Southern parts,' he notes in his journal, 'is to add some particle before a noun as we do "the" or "a"; "the" was generally *He*, or *Ko*; they also often add to the end of any word, especially if it is in answer to a question, the word *Oeia* which signifies yes, really, or certainly.'[114]

With the dawning of this understanding comes the realisation that the geographical Native names they have been recording for various places around New Zealand have been inaccurate – and too long.

'In the Bay of Islands,' he notes by way of example, 'a very remarkable Island was called by the Natives *Motu Aro*: some of our gentlemen asked the name of this from one of the Natives, Who answered I suppose as usual *Kemotu aro*; the Gentleman not hearing well the word repeated his question, on which the Indian again repeated his answer, adding Oeia to the end of the name which made it *Kemotuarooeia*: this way at least and no other can I account for that Island being called in the Log book etc. *Cumattiwarroweia*.'[115]

On the Southern island of New Zealand the word for 'the' is 'To' or 'Ta', hence why they have recorded many Native names there beginning with that article.

It seems obvious to Captain Cook that the Natives of New Zealand and those of Tahiti are the one people, and he postulates: 'They have the same Notions of the Creation of the World, Mankind, etc., as the people of the South Seas have, indeed, many of their notions and Customs are the very same. But nothing is so great a proof of their having had one source as their Language, which differ but in a very few words the one from the other.'[116]

Finally, after circumnavigating the entire South Island of New Zealand, on 23 March, Cook farewells its North-westernmost point, later mulling over the name, for perhaps three seconds, in a manner that as ever will not drain his creative reserves.

Cape Farewell perhaps? Cape Farewell it is.

Before Cook orders the *Endeavour* to the West, away from New Zealand to explore the ocean once more, the coastal winds have other ideas, blowing from the East in a fierce gale, 'right in the teeth' as Banks records. Forced to grin and bear it, he continues, 'The sea is certainly an excellent school for patience.'[117]

As Cook's journal records: 'As we have now Circumnavigated the whole of this country, it is time for me to think of quitting it . . .'[118]

31 March 1770, Admiralty Bay, a continent curtailed

There is no Great Southern Land in these parts. James Cook is now absolutely certain of it.

But perhaps it lies elsewhere?

Cook is already forming his thoughts for another expedition to find exactly that, as he carefully notes in his journal.

'. . . our own Voyage [has] set aside the most, if not all, the Arguments and proofs that have been advanced by different Authors to prove that there must be a Southern Continent; I mean to the Northward of 40 degrees South'.[119]

He adds, 'Thus I have given my Opinion freely and without prejudice, not with any View to discourage any future attempts being made towards discovering the Southern Continent; on the Contrary, as I think this Voyage will evidently make it appear that there is left but a small space to the Northward of 40 degrees where the grand object can lay. I think it would be a great pity that this thing, which at times has been the Object of many Ages and Nations, should not now be wholly be cleared up; which might very Easily be done in one Voyage . . .'[120]

Another grand voyage of exploration, to finally settle the existence or otherwise of the Great Southern Land, lies in the future. What they have just achieved is a cause of great satisfaction. Beyond proving what does *not* lie in these parts, they have precisely captured what *does*, having transformed what had been no more than a couple of squiggles on a map left by Abel Tasman 130 years before into a highly detailed map of a magnificent land, populated by a singularly hardy and impressive people.

Open parenthesis. In fact, the accuracy of the map of New Zealand will make contemporaries reel. It is so good, that three years later when surveying Cook's work, even French navigator Julien Marie Crozet is moved to offer a paean of praise. 'I found it of an exactitude and of a thoroughness of detail which astonished me beyond all powers of expression, and I doubt much whether the charts of our own French coasts are laid down with greater precision.'[121] Close parenthesis.

But where to now?

Straight back to England as the vast majority of the ship's company want?

No. That is not the Captain Cook way. That would be the easy option. Rather, Cook wishes to find a way of 'returning home by such a route as might Conduce most to the Advantage of the Service I am upon',[122] and again consults with his officers and gentlemen. All else being equal he would like to return home by way of the Cape of Good Hope by a route as far South as possible, so as to exclude the possibility of the Great Southern Land being there, too.

But everything is not equal.

For one thing, as he notes in his journal, 'in the very Depth of Winter . . . the Condition of the Ship, in every respect, was not thought sufficient for such an undertaking. For the same reason the thoughts of proceeding directly to the Cape of Good Hope was laid aside, especially as no discovery of any Moment could be hoped for in that rout.'[123]

And so the solution beckons. Instead of heading straight to the Cape of Good Hope, by going South of New Holland, the better way would be 'upon Leaving this Coast to steer to the Westward until we fall in with the East Coast of New Holland, and then to follow the direction of that Coast to the Northward . . . until we arrive at its Northern extremity'.[124]

Again, there is agreement from the officers, while Banks – excited by setting foot on an entirely new part of the world – is enthusiastic, with one qualification.

'Although we hoped to make discoveries more interesting to trade at least than any we had yet made,' he records, 'we were obliged entirely to give up our first grand object, the Southern Continent: this for my own part I confess I could not do without much regret. That a Southern Continent really exists, I firmly believe; but if asked why I believe so, I confess my reasons are weak; yet I have a [predisposition] in favour of the fact which I find it difficult to account for.'[125]

For his part, Tupia has no care for a Southern Continent and no particular interest in new things. He has joined this expedition to get to England to try to understand and then harness the power of the white man, not to visit yet more lands. New Zealand had been fine enough, but the first he has heard of visiting New Holland is now and as it is something that will add yet more time till they get to England he is openly against it. Beyond everything else, as they have entered these Southern climes, the falling temperature has seen his own resilience plummet, and he has been complaining to Surgeon's Mate, William Perry, of a pain in his stomach and general lethargy. The good Mate does his best to make him comfortable, though the Tahitian priest eschews any medicines, his only concession to his health being to try to keep himself out of the wind. Loyal Tayeto, also feeling the chill in the air, is by his side and will see to his needs.

CHAPTER TEN

NEW HOLLAND

All they seemed to want was for us to be gone . . .[1]

Captain Cook on the 'Natives' of New Holland, in his log, 30 April 1770

That they are a very pusillanimous people we had reason to suppose from every part of their conduct in every place where we were except Sting Rays Bay, and there only the instance of the two people who opposed the Landing of our two boats full of men for near a quarter of an hour and were not to be drove away till several times wounded with small shot, which we were obliged to do as at that time we suspected their [spears] to be poisoned from the quantity of gum which was about their points; but upon every other occasion both there and every where else they behaved alike, shunning us and giving up any part of the country which we landed upon at once.[2]

Joseph Banks, 26 August 1770

6 am, 19 April 1770, land sighted, unwelcome to country

First come the tell-tale birds and marine life. Now gulls perched atop floating, tangled clumps of a long brown seaweed like mermaid tresses. And presently an enigmatic smudge appears on the distant Western horizon, slowly revealing itself by the rays of the rising sun, creeping forth.

What appears to be little more than a low-lying shadow or cloud becomes ever more apparent.

Land ho!

The call comes from Lieutenant Hicks, positioned on the quarter-deck, and is greeted with great excitement by most aboard the *Endeavour*. (And so Lieutenant Hicks earns himself the good Captain's distinction for first land-peepers: the first place name on Cook's map of New Holland – 'Point Hicks' – and a gallon of rum. Yo ho!)

A howling Southerly wind with heavy swells the day before has pushed them North of their intended course, and the Captain calculates that they shall see land never seen by another; they are far indeed from Abel Tasman's old explorations. They've also been contending with a strong Northerly current since leaving New Zealand, so it's no surprise that, comparing charts and readings, Captain Cook surmises that Van Diemen's Land must be somewhere to the South, into the great unknown. Joseph Banks is not so convinced by the information coming from the Captain and his Master, noting: 'we got fast on to the Westward but the Compass showed that the hearts of our people hanging that way caused a considerable North variation which was sensibly felt by our navigators, who called it a current as they usually do every thing which makes their reckonings and observations disagree'.[3]

Mistake or intention, what lies ahead is a dream for both Captain Cook and Mr Banks, unlikely a duo as they make; an uncharted, unexplored land where no European has ever ventured.

By the time the sun has risen in the sky enough to mark mid-morning, shining brightly on the land before them, lending it a dusty halo, they are close enough for Joseph Banks to observe the topography, and something else besides.

> The Land was . . . covered in Part with trees or bushes, but interspersed with large tracts of sand. At Noon . . . we were called upon deck to see three water spouts, which at the same time made their appearance in different places but all between us and the land.[4]

Extraordinary. For these spouts are not from whales, but are like mini tornadoes, whirling white dervishes of wildness, dancing across the waters with no apparent rhyme or reason.

While two remain distant, the third roars down upon them and storms about them for all of 15 minutes, allowing Banks to observe it with a scientific eye. It is about the thickness of a mast and goes from a smoke-coloured cloud above, to a distance about two-thirds of the way down to the sea itself. Right beneath it,

> the sea appeared to be much troubled for a considerable space and from the whole of that space arose a dark coloured thick mist which reached to the bottom of the pipe. When it was at its greatest distance from the water the pipe itself was perfectly transparent and much resembled a tube of glass or a Column of water.[5]

It expands, it contracts, it sways and dances around, seeming to generate tiny baby spouts all around that attempt to rise from the waves and join their mother, only to fall back defeated. Finally, one baby grows into a hell of a mother, terrifying in its sudden strength and whirling threat, until Mother Nature sags and the wind curiously whips it down to a child once more, before it gradually disappears altogether.

The spirits of this land have spoken to them. You have come to a strange shore, filled with strange things. You will see things here you have never seen before.

Now, at a 'Latitude of 38°. 0' S and in the Longitude of 211°. 07"[6] it is clear that this land lies due North of the East coast of Van Diemen's Land. Could it be a continuous coastline from there to here? Bringing his spyglass to bear and gazing closely, the Captain doubts it, as the coast here seems to veer away to the South-west. James Cook is growing doubtful as to whether 'they are one land or no'.[7]

In any case, Captain Cook now sets his sails to the North, hopeful of finding a bay or harbour where they can drop anchor, collect fresh food and water, and perhaps even inspect the bottom of the hull.

For the moment, as they proceed North at the rough speed of five knots, there is no sign of any human habitation, but on the following day, as they continue North up the coast of what they are now sure is the Eastern coast of New Holland, tell-tale thin streams of smoke coming from the land, spiralling high into the shimmering blue sky, tell a different story.

Where there are such smoky columns in the sky, there must be humans at the base, and all those on the *Endeavour* now gaze expectantly to the shore, hoping to see some sign.

The next day again, the smoke from five separate fires is seen as they sail along this remarkably green and bushy coastline, protected only by long, pristine beaches interspersed with regular crops of craggy cliffs, when they see it . . .

Movement on the shore!

From the deck of the *Endeavour*, as they continue to plough North-north-east up the coast, pushed along by a gentle breeze from the South-west, they can suddenly see on this fresh morning silhouetted figures on the impossibly white sands.

'They appeared to be of a very dark or black Colour,' Captain Cook chronicles of the figures, 'but whether this was the real Colour of their skins or the Clothes they might have on I know not.'[8]

Banks is less circumspect: 'In the morn we stood in with the land near enough to discern 5 people who appeared through our glasses to be enormously black: so far did the prejudices which we had built on Dampier's account influence us that we fancied we could see their Colour when we could scarce distinguish whether or not they were men.'[9]

Captain Cook is more eager than ever to get the *Endeavour* close enough to the shore so that they can explore this bushy country and hopefully make contact with the Natives but, alas, no harbour appears, and the thunderous white waves pounding on the shoreline make clear the danger for any vessel that gets too close.

The surf, in fact, is so rough that Captain Cook doubts that 'there was even security for a Boat to land'.[10]

For just under a week they continue to make their way up this beautiful coastline, noting ever more smoke plumes from the shore, and occasional flitting black figures, until, on 28 April 1770, they see four Natives on the shore, carrying a canoe.

Are they, perhaps, hopefully, about to put to sea, to make contact with the *Endeavour*? Alas, no. For not long after they appear, they disappear once more. Perhaps they might be encouraged to come forth to a less imposing vessel? It is with that in mind that Cook gives the order to drop the anchor, and he is soon in the yawl with Mr Banks, Dr Solander, Tupia and four Marines, heading to the shore two miles away, to the spot where they can now see a handful of coal-black Natives, sitting on rocks, right by their four canoes.

To Banks' eyes it looks as if the Natives are 'expecting us'[11] and the visitors might at last be about to make genuine contact.

Alas, once more as soon as they get close to the breakers, 'when we came within about a quarter of a mile they ran away hastily into the country'.[12] Even more aggravating is that Captain Cook dare not risk traversing those massive breakers, and, as Cook will recount, 'we nowhere could effect a landing by reason of the great Surf which beat everywhere upon the shore'.[13]

There is nothing for the visitors to do but to row back to the *Endeavour*, the disappointed Banks noting how they were 'obliged to content ourselves with gazing from the boat at the productions of nature which we so much wished to enjoy a nearer acquaintance with. The trees were not very large and stood separate from each other without the least underwood; among them we could discern many cabbage trees but nothing else which we could call by any name.'[14] An unknown botanical wonderland, holding promise of the novel and the new, the two perpetual desires of this old Etonian.

To the eyes of Sydney Parkinson, 'the country looked very pleasant and fertile, and the trees, quite free from underwood, appeared like plantations in a gentlemen's park'.[15]

Back to the *Endeavour* for now.

•

Really, it is the most extraordinary thing . . .

Aboard the good ship HMS *Endeavour*, the eager men strain forward. Some kind of bay has been spotted Nor' by Nor'east and Captain Cook has given the orders. *Shorten the sails, prepare to loosen the anchor*, as the ship nudges towards the gap between the North and South headlands.

•

We are the Gweagal people of the Eora nation and we have been here since the Dreamtime. Our people are of this land to the river in the South, and to the mountains to the West, while the Gadigal people are from the Northern shore to the North.

The Gweagal sit in their *nawis* – lightweight canoes made from the stringy paperbark tree, about 14 feet in length, bound tightly at both ends and kept open in the middle by a thwart of sticks. The Gweagal float gently, softly, atop the surface of the water, blending in with the scene around them as though they are not in man-made canoes, but extensions of nature itself. Paddling easily towards the shore, a few of the Gweagal men abandon their fishing, disembark and hide their slender crafts among the scrub at the top of the beach. Taking their impressive fishing spears and haul of *wallumai*, the Gweagal fade into the bush, soon indistinguishable in the verdant blur.

They must deliver a message, they must warn the others.

Do not look for long now. But some visitation from the spirit world is approaching. They will know more soon, but for now the key is not to engage with these spirits in any way, for there might be terrible spiritual consequences.

The men remaining in the *nawis* continue with their fishing, stealing only the tiniest of glances towards the headlands.

For it is a very strange thing that is happening, something well beyond their experience, though it may be explained by a visitation from the spirit world. For, there, a great spirit, a billowing white cloud has lumbered across the ocean to visit them. It is entering the *Kamay*, the sacred bay in which they thrive. Through the headlands, closer to shore, it is . . .

'a big bird [with] something like possums running up and down about [its] legs and wings'.[16]

Yes, a very big bird indeed, with its huge white wings tucked in like a duck's as it makes its way across the waters, and you can tell that the strange white things running all over it might be possums, by the tails they have running down their backs.

Only a short time later, the great spirit bird comes to a halt. A sound rings out across the bay, something like rumbling thunder. There is a loud splash and suddenly they can see that the spirit is releasing a long grey tail into the water. The tail sinks and sinks before suddenly growing rigid. What on *earth* is this thing? Small *nawis* appear from the sides of the bird, tiny floating children of the great spirit that birthed them. Into each *nawi* there seem to be . . . men? Men with pallid skin, untouched by the sun and each one covered in strange and colourful garb.

They are *Berewalgal*, yes, *strange men from far away*.[17]

As the Gweagal men move deeper into the bush, the women and children rise from their crouching positions and they descend from the rocky headland – there are pools and beds full of plump oysters to forage, but they must wait for now.

The women fade into the bush after the men, returning to their camp. There, the elders and youngest children will be preparing to find shelter elsewhere for now.

Though on edge and watching developments closely, the Gweagal are not unduly alarmed by this strange visitation beyond their previous experience. Their world is populated by spirits, who created and guide this world still, and will do so for eternity. Mostly they are unseen, but if this one has chosen to appear, then so be it. Some of the Gweagal are so calm they choose to stay by the shore, tending the daily needs of their family, just as they always do at this time of day.

Something must be done, though quite what they *can* do remains unclear. They do not fear it, though they know they would be fools not to keep a watchful eye on it. What might it want? What does it bring here? Some purpose beyond their comprehension? They will wait and see.

•

Nudging Westwards, with the narrow jaws of the headlands reaching out to embrace them, those on board the *Endeavour* suddenly see people. Black people, holding spears and leaning out of their canoes; the men are staring intently into the water looking for exactly the right moment to strike the apparently bountiful fish-life beneath. Even as the sailors watch, there are several sudden jerks of the arms, the spears thrust down and emerge with a fish on the other end.

The most extraordinary thing?

Here the British sailors are, aboard a vessel some thousand times the size of the Natives' canoes, visitors from another world, and the men with the spears don't seem to care.

As the *Endeavour* passes, no more than 300 yards away, the men on deck look closer, ever more flabbergasted that the Natives neither wave, nor shake their fists, nor make with all possible speed to the shore. They . . . just . . . keep . . . fishing, with no more interest in them than they might have had with a floating log drifting on past. This lack of reaction stuns Joseph Banks, who records in his diary that the Native men '. . . scarce lifted their eyes from their employment . . . They were totally unmoved by us . . .'[18]

Perhaps, it is that the noise of the surf and their intense focus means that the Natives have not seen the visitors?

But, no . . .

As the *Endeavour* comes so close that the Natives are practically in its shadow and they *still* don't look up, it is apparent that theirs really is either genuine or studied indifference, but not accidental ignorance.

It really seems as if the fish they have been hunting for millennia are of more interest to them than this visitation from another world that . . . just might be hunting them.

As the *Endeavour* continues to move slowly into the bay, Tupia draws the scene, sketching the fishermen who have no eye for them.

Beyond the Natives in canoes, they can see on the Northern shore a few more Natives round a fire. 'Both men and wo-men were quite naked, very lean and raw-boned; their complexion was dark, their hair black and frizzled, their heads unadorned, and the beards of the men bushy.'[19]

The *Endeavour* moves on, her crew standing at the gunwale stupefied by the indifferent welcome and, well, a little disappointed. It seems that, unlike their time in Tahiti, there will be no bare-breasted women heading their way any time soon.

Captain Cook gives the order close to the Southern shore of the bay, just inside the lip of the Southern heads. The Bosun pipes his whistle, and the anchor is soon falling to the bottom.

Less than 1000 yards off, up on the tree line, they can see close a 'village', or perhaps just a smattering of a scattering of dwellings, about half-a-dozen rough habitations, appearing to be little more than bark lean-tos, the like of which the Englishmen have never seen.

The village appears to be empty, but even as they are gazing upon it: 'an old woman followed by three children came out of the wood; she carried several pieces of stick and the children also had their little burdens; when she came to the houses 3 more younger children came out of one of them to meet her'.[20]

And again, watching her, the British sailors are stunned.

'She often looked at the ship but expressed neither surprise nor concern.'[21]

And nor do the children who, so young they are clearly incapable of artifice of any kind, clearly, genuinely, don't care.

Can you believe it?

For the life of them, the British visitors cannot work it out.

True, after a while, some of the Natives deign to shake weapons at them – which is the smallest of signs that they care at all. But still most of them can't be bothered to look at all and those who do, in the face of the biggest man-made thing they have ever seen by a factor of a thousand, look the human manifestation of a bored yawn.

Now the old woman lights a fire, which sees those in the canoes who had so resolutely ignored the *Endeavour* men return to the shore with their catch, and drag their canoes from the water, whereupon they all 'began to dress their dinner to all appearance totally unmoved at us, though we were within a little more than ½ a mile of them'.[22]

In Patagonia, Tierra del Fuego, Tahiti, New Zealand, and every other far-flung land the *Endeavour* has visited, the sheer size of the ship had either amazed, intimidated or angered their hosts, but here in New Holland the locals appear not to care.

An odd people.

And odder still, for something else Banks notices through his spyglass.

'Of all these people we had seen so distinctly through our glasses we had not been able to observe the least signs of clothing: myself to the best of my judgement plainly discerned that the woman did not copy our mother Eve even in the fig leaf.'[23]

Is this an Eden so divine that it will not even acknowledge the serpent that enters it?

Captain Cook is curious to find out with a proper landing at last. And where better than this grouping of indifferent spectators, 'hoping that as they regarded the ships coming in to the bay so little they would as little regard our landing'.[24]

Still, there will be no chances taken, and Cook gives orders for the pinnace, the yawl and the long-boat to be filled with armed Marines and sailors, 40 men in all, for this crucial first landing on this side of New Holland.

In the yawl are Cook, Banks, Tupia, Sydney Parkinson with drawing materials, Dr Solander, and the 17-year-old cousin of Cook's wife, Elizabeth, Isaac Smith, with the Captain's vessel heading off in the lead. When they near the shore it seems as well that they are so numerous and so well armed, for the closer they get to actually setting foot on the beach the more it becomes apparent that they will be opposed. For the Natives, allowing this thing into this bay is one thing.

But the *Berewalgal* setting foot on this land?

Kabeeno. No.

As the boats are approaching the rocks, two brave Native warriors suddenly come down upon them, each man bearing a 10-foot spear in one hand and some kind of implement in the other which, Joseph Banks is sharp enough to surmise, is 'a machine to throw the [spear]'.[25]

(A small shaft with a kind of cup on one end to hold the blunt end of the spear, it allows the thrower with a few steps forward to put the full force of his body behind the spear as he hurls it.)

And their words and actions seem every bit as threatening.

'They called to us,' Banks will recount, 'very loud in a harsh sounding Language of which neither us or Tupia understood a word, shaking their [spears] and menacing, in all appearance resolved to dispute our landing to the utmost though they were but two and we 30 or 40 at least.'[26]

These are, no doubt about it, brave men.

Within their clan, there has been no little confusion about these visitors, and not just because of the colour of their skin, their coverings, their general lack of beards and the means by which they arrive. It is their total lack of ceremony, their failure to seek a spiritual blessing from the Gweagal people to pass through their land, if that is indeed what they are doing. They must be challenged and the two most senior men of the clan have been sent forth.

Sydney Parkinson observes them very carefully, noting the intricate piercings and markings on the warriors, how 'some of whom were painted white, having a streak round their thighs, two below their knees, one like a sash over their shoulders, which ran diagonally downwards, and another across their foreheads'.[27]

(Far from mere decorations, such markings and piercings are actually part of their intricate culture, bespeaking their status within the clan, their spiritual education, their seniority.)

'*Warra warra wai!*' the warriors yell at them.

'*Warra warra wai!*'

'*WARRA WARRA WAI!*'[28]

If the exact translation is not apparent, at least the meaning is:

Leave!

Leave our land!

Leave us!

Resolutely, hoping to indicate that they come in peace, Cook and Tupia yell back their salutations in English and Tahitian respectively – none of which calms the locals. The two Natives still insist that the new people must return whence they came, and clearly indicate that the visitors will face a fight if they try to land.

'*Warra warra wai!*'

'*Warra warra wai!*'

'*WARRA WARRA WAI!*'[29]

'Their countenance bespoke displeasure,' Sydney Parkinson records, 'they threatened us, and discovered hostile intentions . . .'[30]

'*WARRA WARRA WAI!*'

We mean it. We are not backing off.

'*WARRA WARRA WAI!*'[31]

But the white men won't go away, and try, in their own language and gestures, to make clear that they come in peace.

'In this manner,' Banks chronicles, 'we parleyed with them for about a quarter of an hour, they waving to us to be gone, we again signing that we wanted water and that we meant them no harm.'[32]

Still there is no sign of the Natives ceding a single step.

Perhaps they could be cajoled into giving way?

It is with this in mind that, as Captain Cook will recount, they resolve to 'throw them some nails, beads, etc., ashore, which they took up, and seemed not ill pleased with . . .'[33]

The Natives' actions at this point are not clear, but momentarily they are encouraging enough that, as Cook records, 'I thought that they beckoned to us to come ashore . . .'[34]

Sure . . . sure . . . surely they will lower their spears and step away, allowing a landing?

But no. Cook is mistaken.

'For as soon as we put the boat in they again came to oppose us.'[35]

After 15 minutes, the Captain becomes impatient. This cannot go on all afternoon. They *need* to land. These warriors are blocking their way. They *have* to be moved on so the shore can be made safe for Englishmen.

Lieutenant Gore's impatience has a different angle – it is tightly focused on his Captain. For these men on the shore are armed and dangerous savages, needlessly putting at risk every civilised man on this English boat. The Captain might be taking the stance of the Quakers – the first blow shall not be theirs – but that puts us all at risk! Surely we must get our retaliation in first? In New Zealand, they shot a man who sneakily crept up behind their Captain on the shore. In New Holland, are they to sit in a boat and simply wait to be speared?

Gore is in no mood for speculation on the distance that a spear might fly. But James Cook is torn. What did New Zealand teach them if not the folly of lives unnecessarily lost? Diplomacy is preferable. But there is no avenue to pursue it, as there is no shared tongue, no understanding. Truly the only message that has so far crossed the language divide has been a very clear 'we do not want you here' from the Native men. These are warriors, not diplomats, and the duo urge departure with unmistakable and unrelenting vigour. Something must be done, a decision must be made. James Cook is lost in a struggle between caution and common sense.

Lieutenant Gore – the first white man to shoot a Native in both Tahiti and New Zealand – stands off one shoulder, *willing* him to shoot, while Banks stands at the other, understanding why the Captain hesitates.

The agitation on the shore grows and grows.

Something must be done.

Lieutenant Gore looks to his Captain.

Mr Banks looks to Lieutenant Gore.

Gore's look is clear.

Do you want one of us to die by the hand of a Native? *Shoot!*

Finally Cook decides he must take the matter into his own hands – specifically, a musket. Carefully, he brings it to bear, aiming right between the two men and gently . . . . . . squeezes the trigger. There is a flash, an acrid puff of smoke, a God almighty roar and in that frozen moment the youngest of the two warriors drops his 'bundle of [spears], on the rock, at the instant in which he heard the report', something which appears to bring a sharp rebuke from the older warrior – for the younger man just as quickly regathers them and the two are as they were once more. Threatening. Blocking. *Willing* for a fight.[36, 37]

They do more than that, the elder man picks up a stone and hurls it.[38]

As it whistles past Cook's ear, he comes to a key decision.

If he and his men are not to be received hospitably, voluntarily, it will have to be insisted upon . . . by force.

Again he brings what he will describe as 'a Second Musquet, load with small Shott'[39] to bear and takes careful aim. But this time, instead of aiming it between the warriors, he aims it at the legs of the older warrior who has hurled the rock at him and . . . . . . squeezes the trigger.

His intention is not to kill, but to 'sting' and so 'frighten them into the woods'.[40]

Nevertheless, it is, effectively, a shot that will ring through history, as the commander of the first English troupe – and even troops – to arrive on the Australian continent visits violence on a people who've been there for 60,000 years . . . even before he has set foot on the land.

For again there is a roar, but this time instead of the shot flying harmlessly, it indeed hits the elder man in the legs, bringing up angry red splotches on his black skin. Though stunned, and stung, glaring down at these splotches which have come from nowhere, but are somehow connected to these extraordinary white-skinned visitors with their thunder-sticks, still the old warrior and his younger companion stand their ground.

Isaac Smith, not unreasonably under the circumstances, hesitates long enough that Captain Cook follows up with the order: '*Jump out, Isaac!*'[41]

But Captain . . . ?

The warriors? The spears?

Very well then.

Putting his best foot forward, that foot comes down on soft sand, and Isaac Smith becomes the first European to walk on the land of the Gweagal people.

Immediately behind Smith comes Captain Cook and Joseph Banks, both hopeful that the previous unpleasantness with the warriors will have seen them disappear, but . . . no.

For now, here they are again.

Despite being vastly outnumbered – they are just two men against 30 or 40 men in two vessels – and despite the fact that the invaders have thunder-sticks capable of hurting them at a great distance, what had appeared to the white men to be the retreat of the Natives was not that. They had merely gone to get their biggest weaponry – long spears, some 15 feet in length, with cruelly sharpened points. One of them also has, Sydney Parkinson notes, 'a shield, of an oval figure, painted white in the middle, with two holes in it to see through, and also a wooden sword'.[42]

The warriors, who have been hurling spears since they were knee-high to an emu, now run at the intruders, and hurl their pointed wooden shafts from a distance of perhaps 40 yards. The spears arc through the air towards the freshly landed men of the *Endeavour*, occasioning a mad scramble to jump out of the way in time. The spears, Banks notes, 'fell among the thickest of us but hurt nobody'.[43]

(Not counting, perhaps, Sydney Parkinson's sense of equanimity – and perhaps even his drawers – as he records, 'After we had landed, they threw two of their [spears] at us; one of which fell between my feet.'[44])

Captain Cook fires a third musket shot.

Now, as two more shots follow up, the elder of the two Natives holds his ground long enough to hurl one more spear, which bears the same result. He has the satisfaction of seeing the white men scurry out of the way, but that is all – his shield has been hit, and dropped.

'*Hala, Hala mae!*' the warriors call repeatedly, imploring support from their fellows. '*Hala, Hala mae!*'[45]

Alas, no support arrives.

Reluctantly, the two defenders of their land at last retreat.

Now, and only now, do Cook and his men advance, scooping up the shield as they go – for it might be useful. Banks yells out a warning: 'The [spears] are poisoned!'[46]

This, Cook will note, 'made me cautious as to how I advanced into the Woods',[47] but advance they all do, heading up the hill into the bush to the 'houses', curious 'small huts made of the Bark of Trees'.[48]

With a practical bent, Midshipman James Magra has a close look at how they are constructed and records them as, 'Very simple structures, being made from bark enfolding one side or half the trunk of a tree which they had tied together at each end by a kind of flexible . . . twig, and spread and separated in the middle by pieces of wood placed across from side to side.'[49]

At first, it seems that all of the Natives have gone, but no . . .

For, as Sydney Parkinson notes, with some distress, the 'wives and children set up a most horrid howl'.[50]

Where are they?

'We went up to the houses,' Banks records, 'in one of which we found the children hid behind the shield and a piece of bark in one of the houses.'[51]

They see no wives, but there are four or five very small children there, seemingly left in a kind of bark stall which hides them, and makes it difficult for the intruders to get a full view of them.

Cook is unsettled. What to do with these? Cook only decides after talking to Banks.

'We were conscious from the distance the people had been from us when we fired that the shot could have done them no material harm; we therefore resolved to leave the children on the spot without even opening their shelter.'[52] After all, as soon as the white men return to the *Endeavour* the children's people will return and they will be cared for. The most important thing now is to try to win back the Natives, to convince them that, despite now having fired on them no fewer than three times, the boat visitors really have come in peace. Perhaps some baubles, which have worked such wonders in the other isles of the Pacific, might do the trick?

'We therefore,' Banks will recount, 'threw into the house to them some beads, ribbons, cloths etc. as presents and went away.'[53]

Oh. And as a precaution against having a repetition of the previous unpleasantness, Banks notes they do one other thing.

'We however thought it no improper measure to take away with us all the [spears] which we could find about the houses, amounting in number to forty or fifty. They were of various lengths, from 15 to 6 feet in length; both those which were thrown at us and all we found except one had 4 prongs headed with very sharp fish bones.'[54]

Banks is still worried that some 'greenish coloured gum'[55] on the tip of the spears may be poison, but Cook thinks that these are fishing spears, nothing more. His reasoning? Well, surely the fact that each of them has seaweed stuck in their four prongs is a clue?

Returning to the shore, where their vessels have been left under guard, Cook takes the opportunity to get a closer look at the three Native canoes that have been left nearby and pronounces them, 'the worst I think I ever saw . . .'.[56]

Now, one last thing before they leave. Look for a supply of fresh water. There obviously must be plenty nearby to sustain the Natives, but for the moment none is found 'except a little in a Small hole dug in the Sand'.[57]

Very well then.

And now it is time for them all to head across to the other side of the bay, where they had seen people on the way in, stopping off briefly at the *Endeavour* to offload the spears.

Upon reaching the Northern bank, however, they find there are no Natives to be seen and though Cook finds rockpools full of fresh water, it is too hard to get at to try to water the ship with any efficiency. As they pull away from the shore and re-embark the ship, Captain Cook has much to contemplate.

Yes, they have made a landing, and established contact with the Natives, but the fact that he had personally fired his musket upon them is distressing. As night falls, and the *Endeavour* men gaze on the shore, it is to see many lights all around the bay, small flickering fires that indicate night fishing, just as they had seen in Tahiti. These people, however, seem very unlike the Polynesians who populate the rest of the South Pacific. They appear to be a breed apart. Joseph Banks, from a scientific point of view, records his detailed impressions of these strange new people in his journal before dropping off to sleep:

> The people were blacker than any we have seen in the Voyage though by no means negroes; their beards were thick and bushy and they seemed to have a redundancy of hair upon those parts of the body where it commonly grows; the hair of their heads was bushy and thick but by no means woolly like that of a Negro; they were of a common size, lean and seemed active and nimble; their voices were coarse and strong.[58]

•

By a fire well back in the bush from the strange encounter of this day, there is deep discussion among this tribe of the Gweagal people as to what it all means. The two warriors who have come closest to the strangers are intensely questioned, and the strange wounds of the elder one across his thighs and buttocks closely examined. Both warriors agree. While it had been thought that these beings had been *guwinjwulawal*, spirits returning from the after-life, or possibly enormous possums, that is not the case.

The intruders are powerful, and dangerous – but they are men, after all. And the enormous thing still floating in – amazingly – exactly the same spot is some kind of *barangga*, big vessel or floating island, and not a big bird or a low-lying cloud.

In all their years, they have never heard tell of such a spirit. And it is tens of thousands of moons that the clans of the Eora nation have lived in harmony with the great spirits and the land, prospering, *thriving* off this copious coast, this bountiful bay. The Eora are a massive mob, spread out across the harbour's rivers and coves, each one acting as a natural divider between clans that – at least for the most part – get on with each other.

Of course, from time to time there are disputes, spears fly thick and fast when there is a call for it, though that day is not today. For now, they work in co-operation. The Eora have never seen anything quite like it, nothing so large or so imposing.

Racing like a great wildfire, word of the billowing spirit spreads throughout the Gweagal clan's territory, the Southern end of the majestic *Kamay*. Transmitted by tongue, word reaches over the river to the Bidgigal clan, then jumps again over the next river to the Kameygal on the Northern end.

Before long, it approaches the banks of *Birrabirragal* – that extra-ordinarily grand harbour, just a day or two's walk North from *Kameygal* bay. The waters are calm, while the shores teem with activity. Since the beginning of the Dreamtime the Gadigal people of the Eora nation have thrived on the Southern shores of this expanse. Gadigal women launch their *nawi* from the Southern banks while the men spear fish from the shore, and women with children forage on the rocks, venturing at low tide to a point of sheer exquisite beauty known as *Tybowgule*, covered in white shells. For yes, it is here that the oyster beds brim with plump bounty, and the shells are shimmering. The Gadigal often perform cere-monies and feasts on this tongue of land that protrudes out into the harbour, being sure to come back before the tide turns and rises, trans-forming the point into an island once more. Many clans live around the munificent harbour, its inlets and rivers acting as natural boundaries between the Gadigal clan and such clans as the Gweagal to their South and the Gorualgal across the water to the North. To the West, are the Wangal people of the *Burramatta* River that feeds *Birrabirragal* from the West.

By the shores of *Burramatta* on this day a very young lad, *Woollarawarre Bennelong*, who is newly proud to have at last outgrown the spot of toddlers, squished between his mother's knees as she fishes from her *nawi*, is now walking the shoreline himself, spearing *wallumai* (snapper) with his *muting*, a pronged fishing spear. One day soon, he hopes, he will be able to use his *mogo* – a stone axe – to cut sheets of bark from trees, and so build his own *nawi*, and guide it out into the deeper waters, to fish like his elders. But now what? There is a stirring among his elders. Stories pass along. It seems that strange-looking men with pallid skin and ornate dress, *Berewalgal*, have arrived at *Kameygal*, coming and going as if apparitions. Young Bennelong listens closely, as his people try to fathom what it means.

•

Bizarre. Befuddling. James Cook enters the abandoned camp on the Southern shore and looks inside the hut where the children had been the day before. They are gone but the beads, ribbons and cloth are still scattered about the ground. Captain Cook stares in momentary disbelief. How many times have the Natives of other lands fallen over themselves to gain hold of things as simple as an iron nail? These Natives have been handed a glut of goodies the likes of which they have never seen, and they respond with . . . ingratitude? No, that isn't quite right. It is not disrespect, it is something simpler. It is straightforward indifference. For whatever reason, they just do not care for these small valuable things the white men have brought to their shores.

Extraordinary.

All that Captain Cook can presume is that, 'probably the Natives were afraid to take them away'.[59]

Very well then.

We will be here for at least a few days. Lieutenant Hicks have the animals brought to shore to graze, and get together a watering party.

A small stream has been found close by the shore and if we make a small dam, it will be sufficient to water the ship.

For his part, Captain Cook goes in active search of the disappeared Natives, taking the pinnace to, 'explore the Bay, in the doing of which I saw some of the Natives; but they all fled at my approach. I landed in 2 places, one of which the people had but just left, as there were small fires and fresh mussels broiling upon them; here likewise lay vast heaps of the largest Oyster Shells I ever saw.'[60]

Only a minute or so after Cook's party get back in their vessels to be rowed back to the *Endeavour*, the Natives magically re-appear on the shore. They walk right past the water casks that the white men have left, take their own canoes and paddle off.

Cook and his men shift uncomfortably on their planks. They had gone to the shore to observe the Natives. But now it is clear that *they* have been under close observation the whole time.

Late that afternoon, the watering party of a dozen sailors under the command of Lieutenant Zachary Hicks go to shore back at their original landing place and are going about their business, rolling casks up the beach and digging to increase the stream's flow, when a group of 15 Natives 'all armed with [spears] and wooden swords',[61] approach to within a hundred yards – meaning the sailors instantly bring their muskets to bear, in case of attack.

They stop. When just two of the warriors come forward, the sailors do the same, and send two of their own forward to meet them, bearing some of the trinkets they have brought with them.

'But it was to no purpose, all they seemed to want was for us to be gone. After staying a short time they went away.'[62]

It is becoming ever more clear. All the Natives want is for the white men to go, to leave them in peace. They do not want gifts beyond the greatest gift of all – to be left alone.

After dinner, Captain Cook goes to shore to raise the English colours, the Union Jack soon flapping a little listlessly from a temporary flagpole – a sharpened staff – then oversees an important ritual. An inscription is cut into a tree near the watering place, setting forth the ship's name, the date and that it had landed here on a mission for 'King George III, under the command of Captain James Cook'.[63] Some of the men continue to gather water, as the Captain heads out with some jacks to sound the bay. As it turns out, plumbing the depths provides an extraordinary bounty as, while swinging the lead, they also do some fishing and in a cove on the North shore, pull out an extraordinary 300 pounds of fish. Typical of Captain Cook, he orders Cook Thompson to divide the bounty equally among the ship's company with nothing extra for the Captain, officers, or gentlemen. With few fresh fish in recent times, it is most welcome.

Joseph Banks, the Doctor and Mr Banks' favourite greyhound, Lady, meanwhile, start carefully tramping through the fascinating bush – always on the lookout for dangerous Natives – and are immediately stunned by the array of fresh wonders that greet their every step. With each new discovery, they carefully cut the flower, or leaves, or stems, and place them in the vasculums – wooden vessels, specifically designed to store botanical items. So stunning is the array of new botanical items – trees, flowers, bushes, grasses – that the vasculums quickly fill and Mr Banks has to send for more.

The flora is flabbergasting. Joseph Banks runs his fingers through the thin green leaves of *Acacia longifolia*, marvelling at the vibrant yellow of this coastal wattle and excising several black and gold seeds from the twisted pods growing along it. My God, what a specimen!

The good Doctor is busy as well, though he hasn't the time or the eyeline to notice the wattles. His eyes are trained upon the ground, where he spots a small shrub of *Boronia paviflora*. Such a very hurried and harried looking shrub, though among the sharp triangular leaves hide tiny delicate petals. A pale, precious pink, they are each less than an inch long and more beautiful than a chrysanthemum in spring. He feels like a prospector who has suddenly stumbled upon dozens of diamonds in the rough, but reminds himself to take a step back. Slowly, slowly, Doctor. All care must be exercised; every precaution must be taken.

Carefully gathering each of his specimens and accounting for everything, Solander moves excitedly, if deliberately, through the bushy undergrowth.

For his part, Captain Cook, exploring parts of the bay in the pinnace, is stunned by the number of sting rays he spies. Great grey diamonds glide through the water, ghostly shapes that move in harmony with the water. They are enormous creatures, one of them all black and measuring two yards across by nearly five yards long, including the sting in the tail.

'They tasted very much like the European rays,' Sydney Parkinson records, 'and the viscera had an agreeable flavour, not unlike stewed turtle. These rays, and shell-fish, are the Natives chief food.'[64]

•

Carefully, the Gweagal observe the white intruders. They see them walking on their land, fishing in the bay, walking with those bizarre animals that look like long and tall dingoes with big snouts, a group of men with nets and curious cutting and digging implements poking around among the long grass and the *waratah* bushes, sometimes cutting pieces off and, mysteriously, putting them in the bags they carry, before carrying them away. Others walk along the shore, prising off oysters from rocks, while still others are rolling something that looks round and wooden towards the small stream, where the water trickles just enough they can fill the round wooden things, filling them to the top then closing up with loud banging upon more wood, and then they roll it back to their big *nawis* waiting on the shoreline.

From the looks of them, the white men seem very frustrated at the lack of water they collect which makes them appear very stupid. It seems amazing that they don't know how easy it is to get fresh water whenever you need it. Everyone knows that, far easier than getting water from the tiny stream, or by digging holes in the sand as some of the white men are now doing, you simply follow the signs – the rivers, creeks, rock wells, lakes, lagoons, seas and springs – left by the ancestral spirits who created the sources of water in the first place, and still guide its ongoing supply. As the Gweagal have learnt since they could first walk, you simply need to watch the flight of the birds, track the rhythms of the movements of animals, or even heed the signs left by other Gweagal – artworks upon a tree trunk or a pile of oyster shells. The signs, natural and man-made, are *everywhere* as to which way the water-filled rock holes, creeks and springs lie. And if ever those sources did not provide, everyone knows the roots of certain trees only have to be tapped before they burst open, water flowing freely.

But these ignorant visitors clearly know less than a three-year-old about any of such basic know-how. If only the strange white men looked. If only they hunted *silently*, again and again, with a spear or a boomerang, as many times as you or your family need. Yes, those thunder-sticks give them a power which it is hard to understand, but in every other way they seem so . . . *primitive*.

Perhaps they will go, as quickly and as mysteriously as they have come?

It seems not. At one point they are even seen to have some kind of ceremony of their own, as they stand around in a circle, and plant a piece of fabric – red, white and blue, in crosses – on the end of a stick and put it in the ground. Might it be that they plan to stay? It couldn't be, surely. Visitors never stay in these parts. They sometimes pass through, yes, but only after following a strict protocol, where the visitors – like those of the Bidgigal clan on the opposite shore – hover on the edge of Gweagal land, often on the very shores, until they are approached and welcomed to country.

But the intruders have done none of these things.

It is all very confusing.

•

The next day there is yet another odd interaction.

While Joseph Banks, his dogs and the Doctor head off into the bush, a troop of grass-cutters head off to some nearby grassy terrain to gather grass for the sheep. While they are so engaged with their scythes,

> towards them came 14 or 15 Indians having in their hands sticks that shone (said the Sergeant of Marines) like a musket. The officer on seeing them gathered his people together: the hay cutters coming to the main body appeared like a flight so the Indians pursued them, however but a very short way, for they never came nearer than just to shout to each other, maybe a furlong. At night they came again in the same manner and acted over again the same half pursuit.[65]

Half pursuit?

Yes, exactly that.

The Natives want to chase them away. They don't actually want a full fight, rather just to warn them off – just as the English don't want a battle themselves, they just want contact.

As time goes on, this strange half pursuit half dance continues, to the growing frustration of the intruders.

'Myself in the evening,' Banks records for 30 April, 'landed on a small Island on the Northern side of the bay to search for shells; in going I saw six Indians on the main who shouted to us but ran away into the woods before the boat was within half a mile of them, although she did not even go towards them.'[66]

This is not first contact – it is first ignoring . . .

30 April 1770, Botany Bay, Cook explores alone, no takers . . .

All up, Captain Cook is impressed with this strange landscape, and the possibilities for some kind of European outpost. They have enough fresh water, while wood for fuel abounds all around.

Some of the trees, he notes approvingly, 'are as large or larger than our Oaks in England, and grow a good deal like them' providing a highly valuable kind of hard wood, while another sort of tree, 'grows tall and Straight something like Pines . . . The Country is woody, low, and flat as far in as we could see, and I believe that the Soil is in general sandy. In the Wood are a variety of very beautiful birds, such as Cockatoos, Lorikeets, Parrots, etc., and crows, [the last] exactly like those we have in England.'[67]

Evening is falling at the end of the kind of gloriously sunny day that this land seems to have such a bountiful supply of and, as Cook stands on the deck of the *Endeavour* gazing at the shore – as ever, trying for the life of him to work out what kind of a people the Natives are – he looks again, but more closely. For there they are! About 10 of them have suddenly appeared on the shore, near the spot where the visitors have been able to successfully dig for fresh water.

Now, Cook is not an impulsive man.

Most of the moves he makes could be taken straight from Royal Navy Captain's Textbook for Proper Behaviour. Anything that strays from that is usually deeply reflected on.

But just this once?

Just this once he acts on instinct and moves quickly. With no weaponry at all, he has himself rowed ashore. He wants to meet with the Natives face to face, man to men. He is trusting that they won't attack him. And he wishes to earn their trust, to demonstrate that he has no desire to attack them. Yes, he was the man a few days ago who had fired his musket at them, but he hopes that they won't be holding a grudge. And so he stands at the front of the boat, arms wide to show he comes in peace, as it nudges towards the shore where they are grouped.

But this is not going to be easy.

For when he is only 50 yards off, the Natives move away from the beach and melt away.

Undaunted, Cook alights on the shore and – despite the aghast looks of his men, who cannot quite believe what their Captain is doing – pursues the Natives, into the bush, entirely alone.

'But,' as Cook will recount, 'they would not stop . . . These were armed in the same manner as those that came Yesterday.'[68]

Carefully, not sure if this is madness or not, Cook scrunches along the sandy shore following them – a lone English Captain, who has himself caused injury just days ago to one of the most respected of the Gweagal warriors. Yes, come to think of it, this is madness. And yet still he goes on.

For now Cook sees the Natives up ahead again. Are they waiting for him? Expecting him?

He is not sure. But they are just there, perhaps a hundred yards ahead, and he must make a decision. Advance or retreat?

A little way off, the bush is filled with extraordinary sounds of the falling evening. Insects hum. Birds chirrup. In the distance there is the sound of twigs breaking as some large animal moves through the thick undergrowth.

Alone. All alone. Just 20 minutes ago, he was safe on the deck of the *Endeavour*, surrounded by men with guns, bayonets and cannon. And now, of his own volition, unarmed, unaccompanied and quite possibly unhinged, now that he comes to think of it, he is isolated on a foreign shore with armed warriors – out of range of those on the *Endeavour*, even now looking through their spyglasses for some sign of him.

It is getting darker still. Back on the beach his men await, but they have no idea where he is. If the Natives were to rush him now, he would be dead within seconds. But what an opportunity! It was his original intent to show trust in them and meet them, man to men, and so gain their trust. And here they now are, waiting for him.

What to do?

The crickets roar.

Captain Cook, observing prudence, turns on his heel and quickly walks back along the shore to where his infinitely relieved men quickly whisk him away.

•

The discussion among the Gweagal people continues, with many stories offered to explain this spirit and these strange men.

But still it is a mystery for the Gweagal people, who must try nevertheless to carry out 'their spiritual duty to Country by protecting Country',[69] only allowing strangers to pass through their land with the clan's consent, which can only be granted after spiritual communication and ceremony.

Perhaps they will go, as quickly and as mysteriously as they have come?

It seems not.

1 May 1770, Sutherland Point, Sleeping shores, and glassy bays . . .[70]

Captain Cook wakes on this first day of May to terrible news. One of the sailors, Forby Sutherland, who has been suffering for some time from tuberculosis and has been under the care of Surgeon Monkhouse, has died overnight. With some ceremony, Forby's body is wrapped in canvas and taken on deck, where Captain Cook calls the company together and says prayers over his body. Thereafter the young man's body is 'buried ashore at the watering place, which,' the Captain records, 'occasioned my calling the south point of this bay after his name'.[71]

Yes, this will be Sutherland Point for a fine sailor, the first Briton to lie at rest on Gweagal land. So Forby Sutherland becomes far more famous in death than in life, his body in a far more foreign land than any Scotsman has seen. His body to lie forever in a land he never set foot upon.

After some quiet reflection, Cook heads into the woods to investigate the discovery of some more Native huts, this time leaving a different combination of trinkets which he hopes might please them, consisting of, 'Cloth, Looking Glasses, Coombs, Beads, Nails, etc'.[72]

That accomplished, and now in the company of Mr Banks, Dr Solander, and 10 armed sailors, Captain Cook heads North, making 'an excursion into the country, which we found diversified with Woods, Lawns, and Marshes. The woods are free from underwood of every kind, and the trees are at such a distance from one another that the whole country, or at least great part of it, might be cultivated without being obliged to cut down a single tree.'[73]

Which is the good news. The bad news is that there seems a good reason there is not a lot of undergrowth, as noted by Joseph Banks: 'The Soil wherever we saw it consisted of either swamps or light sandy soil on which grew very few species of trees.'[74]

Establishing a colony here, capable of feeding itself through its own agricultural endeavours might be possible, but in terms of the fertility of the soil, this part of the coast is not like Tahiti, where you could plant a toothpick and grow a pine tree, plant a nail and grow a crowbar.

But oh, the bursting nature of the nature here!

Traipsing through the thick bush – the whirr of crickets ringing in their ears – they also find 'the dung of a large animal that had fed on grass which much resembled that of a Stag; also the footsteps of an animal clawed like a dog or wolf and as large as the latter; and of a small animal whose feet were like those of a polecat or weasel'.[75]

Banks and Solander are ecstatic. What a glorious change from New Zealand, where, despite its glorious birdlife, the seeming pinnacle of the animal kingdom had been . . . the dog, followed by the only other quadruped to be found on those islands, the rat. But New Holland? In one short excursion, they have seen one unknown creature and the prints of three more. In the air, whole flocks of strange birds fly by in such extraordinary numbers, and of such diversity – colourful birds, crested birds, clamorous birds; birds that Banks affirms he has never seen before – that the Englishman himself is all aflutter, even as his heart soars on high.

As for the new plants they are finding it is nothing less than extraordinary, unprecedented, and barely of this world. Seemingly with every step they find a new one, so many in fact that Mr Banks and Dr Solander decide that they must split up, so they can cover more area, snipping new specimens at a rate unknown to both of them, in fact unknown in the history of this burgeoning glorious science of botany. One way or another, it is clear that this is botanising heaven in a way they could never have imagined.

It becomes equally clear, as they move through the bushland, that the Natives do not live by hunting and fishing alone. Clearly, agriculture – or at least a partial taming of the bush – also helps to provide some of their food.

'I saw some Trees,' Cook notes, 'that had been cut down by the Natives with some sort of a blunt instrument, and several trees that were barqued, the bark of which had been cut by the same instrument; in many of the Trees, especially the Palms, were cut steps of about 3 or 4 feet asunder.'[76] For his part Joseph Banks is intrigued by these notches in the tree trunks, which lead up to the canopy, and agrees with the Captain that they must be to help the locals climb up . . . But to what end, exactly? To throw their spears from the treetops? Or to sneak up upon birds, though that seems unlikely.

James Cook supposes there is much more to these people than meets the eye. If only he could actually meet with them, sit down, look them in the eye and make them understand that the English have not come to hurt them. But for the moment, they remain fleeting, flitting figures in the distance, and the closest encounter he has on this morning is seeing the black back and flashing white soles of a lone Native, fleeing.

Lieutenant Gore's experience this morning is quite the opposite. On an excursion to the shore with a Midshipman to gather up the succulent oysters that abound in these parts, Gore brashly decides to send the boat away. Yes, that's right, we will walk back through the bush, along the Native paths, just the two of us, to the watering place at the South head. We can signal you from there to come and pick us up, so keep a lookout.

After all, it's not far, and we are . . .

Not alone.

Whirling around, Lieutenant Gore and the Midshipman see a couple of dozen Natives following them with remarkable stealth from a distance of just 20 yards. They are heavily armed with spears and, upon being spotted, begin constantly 'parleying but never daring to attack'.[77]

Shortly after this encounter, Lieutenant Gore and the Midshipman run into Dr Solander, Surgeon Monkhouse and two others about a half mile from the watering place, whereupon unfolds an extraordinary *pas de deux* between the white men and the black men in the teeming, whirring bush, each fascinated by the other, yet fearful of what might happen. When Lieutenant Gore and three others, 'more curious perhaps than prudent',[78] approach the Natives, they get close enough to see individual facial features, their bodies 'lean and raw-boned, their chests adorned with white paint'.[79] It is at this point that some of the Natives pretend to be afraid and start to run – perhaps in the hope of luring the white men further forward – only for the Natives who remain to suddenly fling four spears, which go an extraordinary 40 yards, landing just beyond Lieutenant Gore and his men.

It is almost as if the Natives want to scare, but not hurt them? Like a shot across the bow . . . ?

That done, the Natives gather up their spears and, 'the Indians retired slowly'.[80]

Or so it seems.

Arriving back at the watering place in the mid-afternoon, Lieutenant Gore informs Captain Cook in his light American lilt what happened. The Captain is fascinated and, losing not a moment, sets out with the Doctor and Tupia, in hot pursuit of the Natives, hoping to make contact.

And yet, as before, once they try to come close, the Natives appear to simply melt into the bush and disappear. It is not that they retreat, or run away – for there is neither any sense of great activity, or of fear. It is just that they are here . . . and now they are gone. It is as if they are of the land, not merely on it, and can become one with it as they like.

As before, Cook gives up pursuing. The episode is every bit as remarkable as it is remarkably frustrating.

The longer they spend in this strange, strange land filled with extraordinary plants, animals, fish and Natives, the clearer it becomes that it is not just men with white skin the Natives want nothing to do with, for, as Banks chronicles his adventures that evening: 'Tupia who strayed from us in pursuit of Parrots, of which he shot several, told us on his return that he had seen nine Indians who ran from him as soon as they perceived him.'[81]

Everything here is different, sort of front-to-back, turvy-topsy and upside-down-down-under.

In New Zealand, Tupia had been celebrated as a near demigod. Here in New Holland, he is every bit as much a pariah as Cook and all the other white men. With no adulation to lift his spirits, he appears to sink ever lower, with only Tayeto able to comfort him.

3 May 1770, Botany Bay, Cook and Banks try, try again . . .

This morning Captain Cook sits at the back of the pinnace, with Mr Banks and the Doctor up the front, while they are rowed to the head of the bay. Today they intend to make a landing with the specific purpose of meeting with Natives and exploring the country. As they glide across the sparkling blue water – the eddying calm peace occasionally disturbed by the ripples of what Dr Solander identifies as a breeching sting ray – they pass by a dozen Natives in a dozen canoes with their spears poised . . .

. . . over darting schools of fish.

Now, just a few days ago, Natives like this had barely blinked even as something the size of the *Endeavour* had passed by. Back then, they had not decided what to make of the visitors, thinking them a visitation from the spirit world, here to visit and go. So they had just kept on doing what they had been doing. Now, they scarper at the first approach of the strangers.

And so Cook and his men proceed, the sailors bending to their oars, the officers and gentlemen tending to their chores – drawing, sketching rough maps, observing, taking notes, then landing at the head of the bay and walking inland, gazing in wonder at the many strange and exotic plants, stopping at the call of new birds – two loud types the Naturalists call 'Lorikeets'[82] and 'Cockatoos'[83] – always busy discussing all they see, collecting samples, sniffing, touching, occasionally tasting, but overall *reeling* from the sheer volume of new nature! Once again, these lands look promising for England, and Natural History! (With his musket – the shooting of which he has continued to practise – Tupia brings down several of the birds so they can be more closely inspected. When one of the lorikeets proves to be only lightly winged, the peripatetic priest claims it as a pet, allowing Sydney Parkinson to capture even more perfectly its 'beautiful plumage'.[84] It can be kept in one of the cages Mr Banks has brought for this very purpose, and even allowed to flutter around the Great Cabin when the windows and doors are all closed – and the ship's *cat* is put outside.)

Captain James Cook, by
Nathaniel Dance, 1776.
Image © National Maritime
Museum, Greenwich, London,
Greenwich Hospital Collection.

Engraving of Joseph Banks
by William Dickinson, after
Joshua Reynolds, 1774.
Collection: National Portrait Gallery,
Canberra.

A portrait of Solander, Hawkesworth, Cook, Banks and Lord Sandwich by John Hamilton Mortimer, 1771. Courtesy of the National Library of Australia.

The Bar, *Earl of Pembroke*, later *Endeavour*, leaving Whitby in 1768, by Thomas Luny. Courtesy of the National Library of Australia.

Portrait of Surgeon William Brougham Monkhouse, c1768. Courtesy of the National Library of Australia.

Portrait of Elizabeth Cook in her later years, by William Henderson. Courtesy of the State Library of NSW.

'A Representation of the Surrender of the Island of Otaheite to Captain Wallis by the Supposed Queen Oberea', from Vol. 1 of Hawkesworth's *An Account of the Voyages Undertaken by the Order of His Present Majesty for Making Discoveries in the Southern Hemisphere*, 1773. Courtesy of the National Library of Australia.

'Venus Fort, erected by the *Endeavour*'s people, to secure themselves during the Observation of the Transit of Venus, at Otaheite', by Sydney Parkinson. Courtesy of the National Library of Australia.

Drawing of a tent observatory by Robert Bernard, from the French edition of Cook's second voyage. Wikimedia Commons.

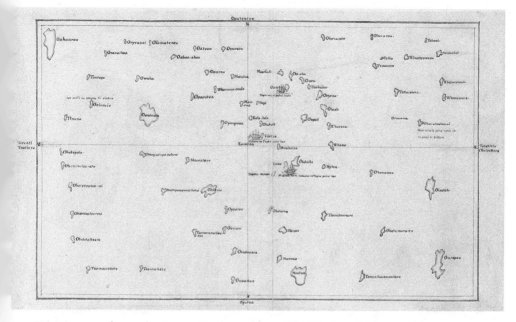

Tupia's map, drawn by James Cook as directed by Tupia. Courtesy of the British Library.

'A War Canoe of New Zealand', by Sydney Parkinson. Courtesy of the National Library of Australia.

Tupia's drawing of trading between Joseph Banks and the Natives, 1769.
Courtesy of the British Library.

Tupia's drawing of Indigenous fishermen seen upon entering Botany Bay, 1770.
Courtesy of the National Library of Australia.

'The Lad Tayeto, Native of Otaheite, in the Dress of his Country', by Sydney Parkinson.
Courtesy of the State Library of NSW.

'The Head of a Chief of New Zealand, the face curiously [tattooed], or mark'd according to their Manner', by Sydney Parkinson.
Courtesy of the State Library of NSW.

'Oberea Enchantress', by Philippe Jacques de Loutherbourg, 1785.
Courtesy of the National Library of Australia.

A pā, or Māori fort, on the coast between Poverty Bay and Cape Turnagain, by Sydney Parkinson. Courtesy of iStock.

'Two of the Natives of New Holland Advancing to Combat', by Sydney Parkinson. Courtesy of the State Library of NSW.

One of two sketches Sydney Parkinson made of a 'gangurru', 1770. Original held in the National History Museum.

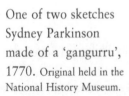

'We found the face of the Country much the same as I have before described,' Cook notes, 'but the land much richer for instead of sand I found in many places a deep black soil, which we thought was capable of producing any kind of grain. At present it produces, besides timber, as fine Meadow as ever was seen . . . The stone is sandy, and very proper for building, etc.'[85]

As they are rowed back towards the *Endeavour*, Captain Cook sees something of interest.

Look. Over there!

It is thin plumes of smoke coming from fires on a far beach which, on closer inspection, has six Native canoes pulled up just beyond the water's edge. Perfect. As eager as ever to make contact with these Natives of New Holland, James Cook orders the men to row over. Alas, just as he has now come to expect, the Natives disappear well before the bow of the boat nudges onto the soft white sand. Alighting anyway, the Englishmen find themselves just in time for a meal to which they have not been invited. Each of the six disappeared Native men had made their own small fire to cook their fish, but the shellfish remain broiling on the coals, perfectly cooked and ready for the slurping. Captain Cook decides to enjoy the repast regardless.

'We tasted of their Cheer, and left them in return strings of beads, etc. The day being now far spent, we set out on our return to the Ship.'[86]

Back on board the *Endeavour*, Mr Banks and the Doctor bring their latest discoveries to the Great Cabin whose cup of fresh discoveries now does runneth over! One by one, Banks and his entourage pull new and strange things from their collecting containers and place them at their own end of the huge table. For yes, while Captain Cook and his officers are charting an overview of the world at one end of the table, the Banks brigade are at the other, on the *prow* of charting the world up *close*, recording its natural history. They truly have found it all here in this fine bay – everything from the fish and boundless sting rays to the mussels, parrots and quail – and particularly interesting to Banks, a tree bearing a fruit that resembles cherries. After observing the Natives eat them, so too do the sailors, which pleases Captain Cook as, whatever else, they are fresh and should help against the scurvy.

When it comes to plants generally, there are so many that Banks' key worry is that they will spoil before being properly catalogued and preserved.

The solution, he decides, lies by way of a spare sail. With sailors lending a hand, they take a staggering 5000 specimens of flowers to the shore, where, on this calm, warm day, they begin to lie them out on a sail to further dry in the sun. It is an exacting process to lie them all out and then remove the top sheet of paper to further expose them to the sun's rays, but by mid-morning it is done and for the rest of the day the moisture which risks rotting them on the journey back to England is gently burned from them as they are regularly turned over.

Once again, while Banks and his men are going about their business, a dozen or so Native canoes come near, fishing.

'We soon saw that the people in them were employed in striking fish; they came within about ½ a mile of us intent on their own employments and not at all regarding us.'[87]

How could it be that these strange beings are not fascinated by a young Englishman drying plants? What is wrong with them?

Well, the main thing is that the whole process is uninterrupted and, as the sun starts to wane, all the specimens are gathered once more and carefully pressed back into their quires, before being loaded back into the folders.

'By this means,' Banks chronicles, 'they came on board at night in very good condition.'[88]

With the plant specimens now secured, Banks is more keen than ever to gather yet more, and is ashore again the following day collecting more specimens in the bush, where again the local Natives ignore them. By this time Banks declares himself, 'quite void of fear as our neighbours have turned out such rank cowards',[89] rather than the brave, cunning, poison-spear wielding Natives he had first supposed.

Captain Cook and the other crew members do not take such a bold view and continue to treat the Natives with a great deal of caution, and many of them believe the lack of desire for interaction they show is nothing to do with cowardice and everything to do with the unique manner and being of this people. How can the *Endeavour* sail next to a canoe and a fisherman not even glance up? They are unique, and to a man like Joseph Banks, used to categorising and labelling all of nature and man, they are an enigma he simply cannot get to the bottom of. It eats at the Englishman. It defies reason.

Still, at least one interaction the next day, 4 May, is of particular note.

One of the Midshipmen who'd been straggling a long way behind a party that had been sent out by Captain Cook to try to form a connection with the Natives, suddenly comes across something that few from the *Endeavour* have seen to this point close-up. It is a . . . . . . woman.

Yes, the crew had been disappointed early on that this was clearly going to be no Tahiti, no sexual free-for-all. And at least in New Zealand they had seen women up close, and a few lucky sailors had been able to have congress with them. Here, so far, the women have steered a wide berth around the visitors.

The Midshipman has been following a foot path through the bush and come around a corner when he happens upon a very old man and very old woman – the man with great bushy grey hair and long beard, the woman's hair tightly cropped, both of them with wrinkled countenances and sagging flesh – sitting together under a tree minding some very young children. Though startled themselves, and clearly fearful, perhaps they can sense the young Englishman's fear too, which reassures them that he is not likely to attack them.

In fact, fascinated to be so close to them, he offers them the only gift he can muster – some of the parrots he has just shot. Taking a couple of them, he tries to place them in their hands, only to see them pull their hands back, 'in token either of extreme fear or disgust'.[90]

The young Englishman is interested by the encounter and will tell Mr Banks all about it, but for now, conscious that there are many men in canoes fishing nearby who might quickly come ashore if they see him, he decides it is better to bid them adieu and quickly join the others.

Dr Monkhouse's own experience on this day is less benign.

In the company of a Midshipman, he is following a path when, after emerging from a part of the bush with many thick thickets, they look up to see six Native warriors just up ahead. Deciding to approach them, the ship's Surgeon takes a few short steps towards them when – far from melting away, as he had expected – one of the six suddenly shouts a single command and seemingly from out of nowhere, for they make no aggressive move, a *spear* lands right by the medico!

Though shocked, neither Monkhouse nor the Midshipman with him retreat.

This seems to shock the Natives even more, for it is they who now do precisely that, at some pace, leaving behind a young lad in the tree who it seems had thrown the spear on the Native elder's command. This lad, too, however, is extraordinary for the speed with which he now descends and disappears.

Has the Surgeon just survived an attempted ambush?

Dr Monkhouse is not sure.

There is, of course, no way of knowing. But, all up, it proves to be the last interaction anyone on the *Endeavour* has with the Natives while they are here. The next day Cook goes in search of them again, trekking inland and going around the shore – still eager to earn their trust and fulfil his orders from the Admiralty – but can find neither hide nor hair of them. Not that the day has been without some reward.

'In the evening,' Captain Cook records, 'the Yawl returned from fishing, having Caught 2 Sting rays weighing near 600 pounds. The great quantity of this sort of fish found in this place occasioned my giving it the name of Sting-Ray Harbour.'[91]

But now Cook pauses for a moment. There is one thing that has been more impressive here than the sting rays and Mr Banks and Dr Solander have been extraordinary in their endeavours to gather them. With that in mind, Captain Cook draws a line through his words, and adds new, small words above, so the sentence reads: 'the great quantity of ˄New Plants &Ca Mr Banks & Dr Solander collected of this sort of fish found in this place occasioned my giveing it the name of Sting-Ray Harbour Botan˄yist Bay'.[92]

Yes, that's it. Not Sting-Ray Harbour. And not Botanist Bay. But Botany Bay. It just has a great ring to it, and is the right name.

After all, in even the brief time they have been here, just a little over a week, Mr Banks and his entourage have discovered no fewer than 132 plant species previously unknown to the scientific world. And in the end, the bay's sheer number of extraordinarily diverse plant types is marginally more impressive than the size and number of its sting rays.

6 May 1770, Botany Bay, pass the port and miss the marvel

As magical as it all is, now that Captain Cook is confident that they have 'seen everything this place afforded',[93] it is time to move on. The wood has been gathered, the water barrels filled, and the ship scrubbed clean from top to bottom. In terms of replenishing some of their supplies, they have caught a great deal of fish – one which the crew call 'leather jackets' – together with the sting rays they've caught and a great number of birds . . .

Edible plant life has been much harder to come by – certainly nothing like the array of fruit they'd had in Tahiti – but that is no surprise. Nothing but Tahiti could be like Tahiti. Move on.

And so, just after dawn on this bright day, the *Endeavour* men weigh anchor and put to sea, harnessing the light breeze from the North-west to move through the heads of Botany Bay before picking up a Southerly which pushes them easily North up the coast of New Holland.

Now, in terms of mapping the coastline, things are different on this coast from the way they had been in New Zealand. There, it had been important to chart every nook and cranny, explore every indent, just in case the Great Southern Land was attempting to hide from them. But here, a partial map of this land already exists, courtesy of the Dutch, and all Cook needs to do is to track the basic contours of the East coast. There is no imperative to document every indent because this coastline is clearly not the Great Southern Land that Mr Dalrymple is certain of, with its fabled mountains and rivers and fertile plains teeming with people; this is the completion of an old continent, not the discovery of a new one.

So yes, although only three hours after setting sail Cook notes the grand entrance to a very likely grand harbour, just 20 miles North of the entrance to the rather more modest heads of Botany Bay, it is no more than something of passing interest.

'We were by observation in the Latitude of 33 degrees 50 minutes South, about 2 or 3 Miles from the Land, and abreast of a Bay, wherein there appear'd to be safe Anchorage, which I called Port Jackson.'[94]

(Yes, as a man raised in the Royal Navy, he has long been taught to pass the port to the left, but this is . . . unfortunate.)

Banks, who is below cataloguing his plants, misses it entirely, merely noting: 'The land we sailed past during the whole forenoon appeared broken and likely for harbours; in the afternoon again woody and very pleasant.'[95]

The opening Banks and Cook simply sailed past, two or three miles out, is actually a rather grand . . . harbour. It will one day be named Sydney Harbour. It is the great non-discovery of Cook's life, an irony that he will never know.

CHAPTER ELEVEN

ESCAPADES ON THE EAST COAST

These people may truly be said to be in the pure state of Nature, and may appear to some to be the most wretched upon Earth: but in reality they are far more happier than we Europeans, being wholly unacquainted . . . with the superfluous but also the necessary conveniences so much sought after in Europe they are happy in not knowing the use of them. They live [in a Tranquillity] which is not disturbed by the inequality of condition, the Earth and Sea of their own accord furnishes them with all things necessary for life; they covet not Magnificent Houses Household-stuff & c. they sleep as sound in a small hovel or even in the open as the King in His Palace on a Bed of Down . . .[1]

Captain Cook, upon his return from New Holland,
to his former captain, John Walker, 1771

Conversing with any but the most uncivilized savages perhaps in the world.[2]

Joseph Banks on the Indigenous peoples of New Holland, 1770

15 May 1770, 'A tolerable high point of land bore North West by West distant 3 Miles – this point I named Cape Byron . . .'[3]

The *Endeavour* cuts through the beauty of the blue coastal sea, sweeping past a foreign coastline full of high sandstone cliffs, jagged, crooked rocks that hang and jut in startlingly new yet still ancient patterns. Each novelty is carefully noted, as Captain Cook charts and Mr Banks catalogues. And yet the hope for a satisfactory encounter with its Natives starts to fade.

On 15 May 1770, they see a new group of Natives on the shore – about 20 strong, 'each of which carried upon his back a large bundle of something which we conjectured to be palm leaves for covering their houses'[4] – and yet Banks despairingly notes the same stunning shunning, their refusal to acknowledge what, to them, must be an extraordinary spectacle:

'We observed them with glasses for near an hour … Not one was once observed to stop and look towards the ship; they pursued their way in all appearance entirely unmoved by the neighbourhood of so remarkable an object as a ship must necessarily be to people who have never seen one.'[5]

Not one! Could you train 20 of His Majesty's Marines so well that in the course of an hour, not *one* would turn his head *once* to gaze upon something thousands of times bigger than they have ever seen before? Unlikely. But for these Natives of New Holland it doesn't even seem to be a matter of discipline. They genuinely appear uninterested.

By 20 May, the weather has demonstrably warmed as the *Endeavour* has come so far up the East coast that the Tropic of Capricorn beckons just 400 miles to the North. Captain Cook again sees so many Natives crowded onto a headland – about 20 in all – that he names it Indian Head, to mark the occasion. As ever, the Natives do not care to become excited by the appearance of the *Endeavour*.

Three days later, the *Endeavour* drops anchor off Sandy Cape, having passed Hervey Bay, so that Mr Banks and his people may go botanising – and Captain Cook too, wishes to examine the hinterland. Not long after they have disappeared into the thick scrub, those aboard the *Endeavour* see 20 Natives appear on the beach and, for once, look their way for a short time before disappearing again.

Having seen the smoke from several fires in the distance, Captain Cook and Mr Banks approach one, and though the fire is burning when they arrive, all the Natives are gone. It affords the Europeans at least the opportunity to get some idea of how the Natives hereabouts live. Nearby are 'several vessels of bark which we conceived were intended for water buckets, several shells and fish bones, the remainder I suppose of their last meal'.[6] And in fact instead of one small fire, they see many small ones, just as they had seen on the beach at Botany Bay – one fire per man – all built in the lee of a bark barricade on its windward side, and by each one is a piece of upturned soft bark, perfect for a makeshift bed.

'The whole was in a thicket of close trees, defended by them from the wind; whether it was really or not the place of their abode we can only guess. We saw no signs of a house or any thing like the ruins of an old one, and from the ground being much trod we concluded that they had for some time remained in that place.'[7]

Is this a village? Do these people *have* villages? Cook is uncertain but Tupia has a more definitive verdict.

'*Taata Eno*'s,'[8] he says to Captain Cook and the gentlemen with a look of pity. The white men know by now that means: 'poor people', naked as they are, sleeping exposed.

Yes, to some on the *Endeavour* the Natives are 'savages', and yet it is not as if those on the ship don't have their own fair share of actually savage people.

On the night of 22 May 1770, an episode occurs which rather demonstrates it.

Richard Orton, Captain Cook's clerk, responsible for maintaining the muster, victualling and related duties, had been drinking with shipmates during some time off, and had indulged in such liberation of the libation that two things had happened.

Firstly, he had fallen nearly insensible.

And the second thing becomes apparent the following morning when Captain Cook's personal servant, William Howson, has to take only one look at him lying drunk in his bunk that he races off to fetch the Surgeon's Mate, William Perry.

That gentleman arrives to look closely and confirm the truth of it: Mr Orton, his head completely covered in caked blood, has had a big chunk from both his ears sliced off in the night! It looks like he has been on the losing end of a wild dogfight.

Shaking him awake from the abysmal depths of his all but comatose drunken slumber, Surgeon's Mate Perry tells the fiercely complaining man that he has lost his ears.

I SAID YOU HAVE LOST YOUR EARS.

His mind still marinating in rum, Orton refuses to believe it until Perry takes his looking glass and holds it up for him. Through his bleary eyes so weary, mere slits, Orton focuses just long enough to see the rather more damaging kind of slits that have been made where his whole ears used to be, and . . .

Shouts!

'Magra!'[9]

Yes, Orton has no doubt from the first who has done this to him – James Magra, the New Yorker Midshipman, with whom he has not only had a long-running enmity, but has quarrelled with the night before.

Sensation on the ship!

Captain Cook is called for, as is Surgeon William Monkhouse, to bind Orton's wounds. Upon arrival, the commander of the *Endeavour*, deeply aggrieved at this, 'the greatest insult that could be offered to my Authority in this Ship',[10] starts to ask questions.

What is clear from the first is that Orton had been heavily drinking on deck the night before, a calm night, and had quarrelled with several others. While he was staggering back to the hatchway to get to his bunk, on one dark part of the deck, Captain Cook concludes, 'some Malicious person or persons in the Ship took Advantage of his being Drunk, and cut off all the Clothes from off his back; not being satisfied with this, they some time after went into his Cabin and cut off a part of both his Ears as he lay a Sleep in his Bed'.[11]

James Cook, of course, is appalled by the sheer bloody brutality of the act, but is reluctant to believe that Orton is correct in his accusation that the guilty man is indeed Midshipman James Magra. Yes, he had been with Orton on the evening and yes, they had quarrelled, but . . . a *Midshipman* cutting off a large chunk of a clerk's *ears*? It is unthinkable – even if in England it used to be the punishment for a person spreading malicious rumours. Only in the backwoods of the American colonies is it still practised, which . . . come to think of it is where Magra is from . . . but . . .

But Captain Cook, a decent and mostly gentle man himself, has trouble believing in other officers being capable of this kind of viciousness, despite there being no doubt that *someone* had done it.

Further inquiry, however, establishes that not only has Magra been inclined to cut off his own clothes when on one of his 'drunken frolics . . . [but had] been heard to say (as I was told) that if it was not for the Law he would Murder [Orton]'.[12]

Well then.

'These things considered, induced me to think that Magra was not Altogether innocent . . .'[13]

For the moment, thus, Captain Cook dismisses him from the quarter-deck, and suspends him from further duties. Magra is, in any case, the kind of gentleman 'one of those Gentlemen frequently found on board King's Ships that can very well be spared [and] besides, it was necessary in me to show my immediate resentment against the person on whom the suspicion fell, lest they should not have stopped here'.[14]

As to you, Mr Orton, I say . . . AS TO YOU, MR ORTON – as you take down your commander's dictation once more – Captain Cook concedes, 'he is a man not without faults, yet from all the inquiry I could make, it evidently appeared to me that so far from deserving such Treatment, he had not designedly injured any person in the Ship; so that I do – and shall always – look upon him as an injured man'.[15]

For his part, Banks does not mention a thing in his journal about the whole curious affair. Had someone shorn the twigs off one of his shrubs there would undoubtedly have been outrage on his part and a page or more in his journal but, as Orton is not a rare plant, his pruning is of no interest to one Joseph Banks Esq.

Banks aside, the gossip, rumblings and rumours on the ship – the *scandal* of it, a violent *crime* committed on His Majesty's vessel! – goes on for days. It is given another surge when, upon deeper consideration, the Captain decides that, as there were no witnesses to the attack, and as – as recounted by William Perry – 'it being evident that a person wallowing in liquor, unconscious of hurt or pain, and ignorant (until told) of his own loss, could not possibly say *who had assaulted him*',[16] Captain Cook relents.

Midshipman James Magra is no longer under arrest, until such times as there is a confession, or a witness might come forward.

Getting someone to betray the butcher will not be easy however, as 'Everyone despised the poor suffering wretch, and the Captain, who probably made private enquiries, at the end of a week, knew no more than at the first moment of our Surgeon's report.'[17]

Perhaps a reward might help loosen lips?

The Captain puts up 10 guineas of his own money and is pleased when his Lieutenant Zachary Hicks offers five guineas of his own for the cause.

Lieutenant John Gore, however, who has a particular detestation for Orton, and knows more than most about his 'criminal excesses and blasphemous sallies',[18] as his own cabin adjoins the clerk's, declines to add any money and is blunt about it.

'Sir,' says he to Captain Cook, 'it will be my duty to report whatever I may be told relating to transactions amiss on board; with respect to your mutilated clerk, I hope never to hear aught, and I will not give *sixpence* to encourage informers.'[19]

Master Robert Molineux, momentarily sober, is flattered to be asked, and gives a little, while Surgeon Monkhouse does the right thing and also puts in a few guineas of his own. In sum, a total of 15 guineas – more than a year's salary for an ordinary sailor – and 15 gallons of arrack[20] is offered as reward for someone to come forward and bear witness, for 'whatever information might lead to fix and prove the guilt'[21] of Magra or another.

For the moment, that is where the matter rests. Orton resumes his duties, interspersed with heavy glaring at James Magra whenever they cross paths, and the *Endeavour* sails on as before – though certainly few of the ship's company are disposed to spread rumours about Mr Magra.

Fine man, and I won't hear a word against him.

Or repeat that word . . .

1 June 1770, on the topic of the Tropic of Capricorn

Scurvy is not one of those medical conditions that strikes suddenly. There is a reason why the French call it *la grosse maladie*. There is no instant pain, no waking up to find a horrible rash that has appeared overnight, no casual affliction. Rather, it creeps from the inside out, slowly corrupting the body. It first surfaces with a man who realises he has been feeling off-colour lately, with a sore mouth to boot, complains . . .

'I have swollen gums,' Tupia complains this evening as Cook turns quiet. 'I have had a sore mouth for nearly a fortnight.'[22]

It is a real worry, and it deepens when Sydney Parkinson is also taken ill with similarly worrying symptoms.

Though New Holland has been a great provider of fresh fare in terms of fish, birds and animals, it has provided little in the way of fresh greens – with the exception of the small cherry-like fruit they found at Botany Bay – and the sauerkraut has only been able to keep the scurvy at bay for so long.

And now Tupia has had these symptoms of scurvy for a fortnight without saying anything, only letting the condition take ever greater hold?

An experienced sailor would have known the significance much more quickly than that, and Cook and his officers berate themselves for not having noticed Tupia's suffering sooner. All that can be done for the moment is to consult the Surgeon, who 'immediately put him upon taking extract of Lemons in all his drink'.[23]

In the meantime, Captain Cook concentrates on continuing up the coast of this extraordinary land, and is particularly impressed by the sheltered waters through which they are now travelling.

This passage I have named Whitsundays Passage, as it was discovered on the day the Church commemorates that Festival

... It is formed by the Main on the West, and by Islands on the East ... Our Depth of Water in running thro' was between 25 and 20 fathoms; everywhere good Anchorage; indeed the whole passage in one Continued safe Harbour.[24]

At one point a small group of Natives is spotted in the distance, but they show the usual interest in the *Endeavour* – none at all. The one thing Cook does know is that the *Endeavour* will have to stop soon, somewhere, to replenish their supply of fresh water. Having crossed the Tropic of Capricorn just today it is not only hot, but getting hotter every day. If they can't find any water, they may have to gather and live off cocoa-nut milk.

•

A week later, in the afternoon, they see some Natives and canoes on a nearby island, which appears to have cocoa-nut trees. Lieutenant Hicks is despatched to investigate the possibility of replenishing water barrels, or at least getting some cocoa nuts, and Joseph Banks and the Doctor take the opportunity to accompany him, to gather specimens.

Alas, when they return in the evening, it is with the usual news: they had seen no Natives, and only heard them once, when they were pulling away from the shore. The Natives' ability to disappear at will, even on a small island, appears to be almost in the realms of magic. Worse, there was no fresh water, and what were thought to be cocoa-nut trees proved to be nothing more than cabbage palms, milk-less and useless to the *Endeavour* men.

9 June 1770, off Cape Grafton, a novelty noticed

It is a group of Natives actually showing *curiosity* in their visitors.

Joseph Banks, particularly, is delighted to observe and be observed at last: 'In the morn we passed within ¼ of a mile of a small Islet or rock on which we saw with our glasses about 30 men women and children standing all together and looking attentively at us, the first people we have seen shew any signs of curiosity at the sight of the ship.'[25]

It is something.

But Captain Cook, not wanting a repeat of the previous episode, where they had lost a day looking for Natives and water for no result, decides they will sail on, looking for a better place to drop anchor. The fact that the Natives appear more populous on this part of the coastline, and the foliage is so green, means there must be fresh water nearby.

11 June 1770, North of Cape Grafton, between a rock and a hard place

All quiet on the quarter-deck. All quiet below.

The *Endeavour* surges through the bright ocean on this 'clear Moon light Night',[26] the moonbeams shining brightly upon the delightful phosphorescence in her wake.

An hour before midnight, it only needs 14 men, under the command of the officer of the watch, to keep the *Endeavour* on course, some six or seven leagues from the shore and heading North-east with 'a fine breeze of wind',[27] Captain Cook having altered course slightly to avoid islands he'd seen dead ahead in the last of the daylight. As a precaution against hitting shoals or shallow reef in the middle of the night, standard procedure is followed, with a sailor placed at the bow swinging a sounding lead – with a 12-pound piece of lead on one end, at the base of which is some sticky tallow – to determine both the depth of the seabed, and even whether it is shale, sand or weed. At the moment it is 20 fathoms, so nothing to worry about, particularly as their speed is only moderate.

As everything is ship-shape and calm, Captain Cook – as is his wont – ensures that the watch is in place and alert, and retires for the night, pausing only to give his usual instructions that he be awakened for even the most minor of issues.

Yes, sir. Good night, sir.

After many months at sea with no opportunity to scrape barnacles and growth from her hull, there is a drag, meaning the ship is only managing about four knots with this good breeze. All is almost eerily calm. Beyond the odd murmurs of the sailors to each other and the odd muttered order by the lieutenant – *The breeze is freshening, Mr Molineux, be ready to shorten sail* – there is little sound heard bar the three pine masts creaking happily under the light strain as pine masts do in such benign conditions, the odd snap of the sails, the swish of the water, the lap of the waves hitting her starboard side, and . . .

And what is that?

A cry from the bow . . .

Is it a cry from the goat, perhaps?

I don't think so.

Perhaps a sailor then, measuring the depths and shouting a warning?

The sound of waves breaking . . . !

There is no time to alter course. The *Endeavour* is a fully loaded vessel weighing well over 400 tons, under full sail, and travelling at four knots. It has a momentum all its own, and, given that it would take 15 minutes to take in all sail, stopping quickly is simply not remotely possible. Directly beneath the poop deck, in the Great Cabin, Joseph Banks is just lying his head upon his pillow.

In his own room, beyond the vestibule separating them in the Great Cabin, Captain Cook is already sound asleep. Around and about him, for'ard in the hold, about 60 crew are slumbering in their hammocks, rock-a-bye-byed by the endlessly comforting side to side motion of the ship rolling on the sudden swell, and . . .

And now, from completely out of nowhere for most of those on board, comes a massive physical shock as four knots goes to nothing in a split second. Sailors tumble from their hammocks and everything not tied down lurches forward – including the sheep, chooks, pigs and the goat, all of whom squeal and squawk in protest. The air fills with the clang and crash of the crockery smashing on the wooden floor, the breaking of wood, the crunch of cannon breaking their moorings and hurtling into masts, followed near instantly by a shattering cacophony of oaths, cries of dismay and, from above, the thunder of furiously flapping sails going nowhere.

What has just happened?

The bow of the *Endeavour* has suddenly run into, and up and over, a reef . . . for a reef it is.

On deck, toppled sailors rise back to their feet, filling the sea-sprayed air with the shouting and cursing native to the sailor's tongue. Somewhere down below there is the angry yowling of a cat.

Among the sailors and Marines on the lower deck there are grunts, groans, curses and sheer terror.

The sails are like the jacks: all angry impotence, furiously flapping in the wind to no effect.

In the Great Cabin, the shock has been severe, and Joseph Banks has been awoken violently, before being 'called up with the alarming news of the ship being fast ashore upon a rock which she in a few moments convinced us of by beating very violently against the rocks'.[28]

Cook has been similarly awoken, and gathering himself, is quick to throw on his boots, and gets topside, to see most of the sailors pouring out the hatchway amidships. Some of those sailors pause to see the Captain still in only his drawers – the undergarments in which he sleeps – but there is no time to reflect as he starts barking orders.

Take in all sail!

Launch the boats!

Mr Satterly, below to check the damage to the hull . . .

For many of the men have no sooner emerged from below decks than they are knocked over by the shaking of the ship, as another wave crashes into the side. Captain Cook sees that the *Endeavour* is stuck fast on the coral, so it can neither rise nor fall with the swell, but only rock violently, as the bigger waves wash over the sides, and push jagged coral barbs ever deeper into the ship's hull. The sailors can hear the agony of the ship with every buffeting, *feel* it through the soles of their feet, the rip'n'roar of waves and rock compete in their terrors, each sound signalling a doom surely measured in moments.

They are in desperate trouble.

As the old salts know, the naturally abrasive nature of coral means that it is much worse than rock as it is like a grinding machine that can splinter and smash even the stoutest hull in minutes. Their best hope is to be lifted off by the rising tide, but within 30 minutes, as more of the reef they are stuck on is revealed, it becomes clear they had hit at high tide and are definitively and definitely stuck – high and dry – though at least the last of the sails have been taken down, which helps lessen the flapping.

Captain Cook, however, is not flapping at all. Yes, a brilliant navigator, maker of charts, and no doubt a more than able seaman. But above all he is a leader of men, and the best chance they have to survive a crisis is through calm resolution.

Master Molineux, he says calmly, even above the roar of the waves and the violent rocking of the *Endeavour*, *lower the yawl to take soundings around her.*

Master Molineux, with the aid of four good men, equally calm, does exactly as bidden and is soon in the yawl with a lantern, being rowed about the stricken hull of the *Endeavour* to get a close-up look at just how it is stuck fast, and what precisely it is stuck fast upon, and to sound the depths, to see where the deepest exit route lies.

'All this time,' Joseph Banks will note, 'she continued to beat very much so that we could hardly keep our legs upon the Quarter deck; by the light of the moon we could see her sheathing boards etc. floating thick round her.'[29]

They are in serious trouble. Their hull is being shredded to bits on the sharp reef and all their collections, their celestial discoveries, their new charts, all the knowledge accrued over two years, looks every bit as doomed as their *lives* to be destroyed.

Gasping from exertion, Master Molineux climbs back up on deck with the news, all of it bad: a large outcrop of coral has penetrated the starboard bow of the *Endeavour*. If they do break free, the risk, or rather the perilous probability, is that they will leave a chunk of the hull on that reef, leaving a large hole for the water to pour through and sink them.

For the moment, nothing can be done until the tide rises once more. At least, as the tide continues to drop, the *Endeavour* stabilises on the reef, and ceases to rock so violently, but as rests go it is a notably uneasy one. And so, as Banks notes, all they can all do is wait in the dark, listening as the coral continues 'grating her bottom making a noise very plainly to be heard in the fore store rooms; this we doubted not would make a hole in her bottom, we only hoped that it might not let in more water than we could clear with our pumps'.[30]

The stream anchor is carried out to starboard with the coasting anchor and cable, and both are soon taking the strain as the sailors turn the capstan and the windlass. All to no avail. They are stuck fast, and the water is gaining on the ship.

In extremis, Captain Cook gives further orders.

Jettison everything we can that is not absolutely needed, starting with the heavy cannons. We have a little under 12 hours until the next high tide and when it comes the Endeavour *must be light enough that it lifts off the reef on which it is impaled.*

Aye, aye, Cap'n!

It takes a great deal of grimacing, grunting and groaning, but they are finally able to bring four of the six cannon they have on deck to the edge of the gangway and push them over, watching as they plummet to the shallow waters below. (Typically, Captain Cook has insisted each cannon have a rope and buoy attached so that, if all goes very well, they might be able to retrieve the cannon and get on with the journey, as well armed as previously, but no-one – not even Cook – believes that the fates will be so kind to them. It is obvious to all that the cannon will lie there forever and a day.) Following them just minutes later are the stone and iron ballast, the firewood, the pig iron, casks and hoop staves, together with all 'decayed stores'[31] and the cannonballs. No less than 40 tons are thrown overboard.

'All this time,' Banks notes, 'the Seamen worked with surprising cheerfulness and alacrity; no grumbling or growling was to be heard throughout the ship, no not even an oath (though the ship in general was as well furnished with them as most in His Majesty's Service).'[32]

Despite jettisoning the excess weight, the ship continues to take on water, and soon enough the level increases to as much as two pumps can handle. The men push and pull the pumps' levers, which are on the top deck right by the mainmast, with elm-tree tubes leading down to the bilge. The sailors are put on tight shifts manning the pumps to keep the water at bay and where it belongs – back in the bay.

Despite the grimness of their situation, there is no panic at all as, 'the officers . . . behaved with inimitable coolness void of all hurry and confusion'.[33] *Keep pumping!*

Not only is Cook demonstrating calm leadership, but the ship's company he has formed over the last 22 months is behaving with admirable and even extraordinary poise.

Joseph Banks, on the other hand, is far more realistic, deeply and obviously concerned . . . first and foremost for . . . Joseph Banks.

'Now in my own opinion I entirely gave up the ship and packing up what I thought I might save prepared myself for the worst.'[34]

For though it seems likely they will soon be free of the reef as the coral outcrops start to thin, the fact remains 'she leaked so fast that with all our pumps we could just keep her free'.[35]

The most likely thing thus is that once free, 'she must sink and we well knew that our boats were not capable of carrying us all ashore, so that some, probably the most of us, must be drowned'.[36]

Still the calm of the crew endures through the long night and even beyond the dawn, when for the first time they can see that there is no island nearby and their North-eastern path has led them now 24 miles offshore – not remotely swimmable for those who don't get in the boats. And what would be the fate for those who *do* get to shore? Nobody from England knows where they are. Yes, there is a map of the shore they would land upon, but as it is the one that has just been made by James Cook, and is with them on the *Endeavour*, it is all rather beside the point.

Well, if it did not prove to be a fatal shore, Banks concludes that even if those who made it there 'met with good usage from the Natives and food to support them, [they would still be] debarred from a hope of ever again seeing their Native country or conversing with any but the most uncivilized savages perhaps in the world'.[37]

Mr Banks is not at all sure whether it might not be better to drown in the first place. What is clear to all is that if they are to survive this it will come from their own efforts right now – and that there is only one hope. All eyes and ears – bar the two missing ones – remain on the Captain.

Expecting the next high tide to peak at 11 am, they wait, doggedly preparing for the right moment. Slowly the sea starts to rise up the ship's sides, until . . .

Until it rises no more.

'To our great surprise,' Captain Cook records, 'the tide did not rise high enough to accomplish this by a near two feet.'[38]

At least as the tide once more begins to ebb, it gives them the time they need to further lighten the load, as more heavy things surplus to survival are hoicked overboard, including two more cannon.

Pump, men! Pump!

They work the pumps harder than ever. True, there is a good deal of swearing when it is realised that the wood of one of the pumps has rotted through and it is useless – but all they can do is work the other pumps more vigorously. The problem is, the lower the ship sinks, the more the water rushes in. What is more, at noon, in the wake of the disappointing tide, the whole vessel is listing – let's see – 'three strakes keel to starboard',[39] as in, it is three lateral planks deeper on the starboard side. The list is not yet so pronounced that the men slip over on the deck, but it would not want to go much further.

At 5 pm the tide once more starts to rise, and the water begins to increase upon the ship so much that the third pump must be put to work and it is far from clear whether it will be able to keep up.

'This was an alarming and, I may say, terrible circumstance,' Captain Cook will chronicle, 'and threatened immediate destruction to us.'[40]

It is all a far cry from his prior most dire disaster as a commander, when his ship, *Grenville*, hit a shoal in the Thames Estuary – and he was home by dinner-time regardless. That was child's play compared to this.

On the reckoning that extreme circumstances require extreme action, that to do nothing is to guarantee their eventual destruction, Captain Cook now orders all five bow anchors to be dropped behind the ship in the hope they can haul themselves off the coral.[41] The sailors scramble and the ship's boats are quickly lowered, bearing the anchors with attached heavy cables.

'I resolved to risk all,' Cook will recount, 'and heave her off in case it was practical, and accordingly turned as many hands to the Capstan and Windlass as could be spared from the Pumps.'[42]

Banks writes with trepidation as they await their fate, 'The dreadful time approached and the anxiety in everybody's countenance was visible enough.'[43]

But there is *no* choice. Between certain death and likely death, a sane man must take action and vigorously pursue likely death.

So while some men continue to man the pumps, those in the boats take up their oars and row out to deploy the anchors on the starboard bow and quarter. The cables are pulled taut and all remaining take the strain on the capstan and windlass and begin to turn.

The strain on ropes, however severe, is more than matched by the strain on the men's faces, not merely from physical exertion, but because all realise they are likely either minutes from being shags on a rock, men clinging to a reef as their ship sinks . . . or possible salvation, and every turn of the wheel brings them closer to their fate. Will they be saved, or will their whole expedition end as an obscure scientific voyage that left Tahiti, only to disappear somewhere in the vast Pacific?

For Joseph Banks there appears no hope at all that the ship can be repaired, only that it can be kept afloat long enough that they can get it ashore, whereupon, 'out of her materials we might build a vessel large enough to carry us to the East Indies'.[44]

And pump! And *pump*! And PUMP!

And stroke! And *stroke*! And STROKE!

And heave! And *heave*! And HEAVE!

The cables continue to strain to the point of breaking. Something has to give, and they can only hope it will be the ship coming off the reef, intact. With every ounce of strength they have left, the men continue to haul on the windlass and capstan, until . . .

At about 20 minutes past ten, 'neath a benevolent moon, there is a lurch, a groaning of timbers, another lurch . . . and . . . the ship is suddenly moving, floating free!

Well, if not quite free, it is at least off the reef, and groggily, heavily, bobbing in the ocean, a water-soaked log that moves slightly up and down with the swell, rather than on it.

As quick as they can now, those in the boats continue to pull on their oars, to get the *Endeavour* away from the reef – the Midshipmen ready to quickly detach the ropes at their end in case she goes straight to the bottom.

But she doesn't.

She floats!

After a fashion . . . in a manner.

'To our great satisfaction,' Banks notes, 'she made no more water than she had done, which was indeed full as much as we could manage . . .'[45]

His fears somewhat abated, Banks takes the opportunity to lie down on his bunk – the first opportunity in the last 24 hours since they had hit the reef – and rest. Alas, only a very short time after the head of Joseph Banks hits the silken pillow he has brought for the voyage, it happens.

Sir! SIR! *MR BANKS!*

Banks is shaken awake to hear 'alarming news'.[46]

'The ship has gained so much upon the Pump, she has four feet of water in the hold!'[47]

Good God!

Four *feet*! That can only mean they will all be heading six feet under, and more, within *minutes*. To make matters even more perilous, Mr Banks is gravely informed by a panicked Midshipman that the wind is blowing strongly from the nearest land 'so that all hopes of running her ashore were totally cut off'.[48]

Against that, the curious feature of the way Englishmen generally react to a completely hopeless situation now comes into play. For yes, the news could not be worse. But . . .

'This however acted upon everybody like a charm: rest was no more thought of but the pumps went with unwearied vigour.'[49]

All hands on deck, and both hands on the pump – with the only exception being John Thompson, the one-handed cook. Everyone else, from officers to boys, from gentlemen dandies to grizzled salts, works the pumps in a frenzy. By God, they might be about to drown, but as a point of honour, they want it to be in their own sweat before the sea has a chance to get to them. In this life-or-death situation, class divisions and ranks are forgotten. In the face of their Maker, fighting to live, they are just men, and the only rank that counts is the physical strength needed to keep going.

As Banks' dear friend Samuel Johnson observes, 'When a man knows he is to be hanged in a fortnight, it concentrates his mind wonderfully.'[50]

As it happens, when he faces death at dawn unless he gets this right, the level of concentration is even more remarkable – for the prospect of sinking immediately has concentrated all limbs in a frenzy of magnificent movement.

Even Captain Cook is now showing signs of . . . concern.

The reckoning is that with another foot and a half of water the ship will no longer float and they will have to abandon her. If only they had a physically strong Yorkshireman here, perhaps the son of a day-labourer, raised doing physical tasks. Wait a moment . . .

They do!

For now Captain Cook himself is removing his jacket, rolling up his sleeves and taking his place on the pump.

How desperate is the situation?

Even more desperate than needing Captain Cook, it is so desperate that – can you believe it, lads? – that is Mr Joseph Banks *himself* now lending a hand.

So exhausting is the work that few men can keep hauling on the levers of the pumps for any longer than 15 minutes before, in an endless rotation, they must be relieved by the next man. Everybody on board – from Captain to Clerke – takes their turn. And yes, friends, the final measure of their desperation is that even the thin-as-a-leaf astronomer Charles Green is required to take his turns – no matter that he has biceps like peanuts and legs so skinny they would shame a pigeon.

The only exceptions to the rule are Sydney Parkinson and Tupia, the former extremely ill in his bunk and unable to move, while the latter is even sicker but is at least attended by the ever faithful Tayeto.

None rest, none stop, not for a moment, and then a miracle occurs 'the water was all out'! *Four feet dispelled? How is it possible?* Not only that it was 'done in a much shorter time than was expected'.[51]

Something is amiss here and, sure enough, 'upon examination it was found that she never had half so much water in her as was thought, the Carpenter having made a mistake in sounding the pumps.'[52]

God bless the bloody Carpenter, and may he make plenty *more* mistakes like that, for their collected vigour has the *Endeavour* free upon the sea, she floats and she may sail yet!

As Cook will record in his log, the man initially sent to read the depth of water was relieved by another who was ignorant of the manner in which the first man had sounded. So the Carpenter '. . . took the Depth of water from the outside plank, the difference being 16 or 18 inches, and made it appear that the leak had gained this upon the pumps in a short time'.[53]

All delight in the joy of the mistake, and the thrill of survival. But can they keep going at this pace? Is it possible to continually fight off the water that even now begins to test their pumps anew? That rush of muscle power that comes from desperation pure cannot last forever. The pitiless sea, however, can and will.

Soon enough, every man-jack on the ship is both exhausted and ever more relieved to be relieved by the next shift as the pumping goes on (and no-one more than Mr Banks, who is, as he puts it so 'unused to labour',[54] he has done the first sustained heavy physical work of his life!), as the ship, very sluggishly, starts moving back towards the coast.

But can it go on? Can they keep pumping at this rate, and survive long enough to get back to the coast?

As the men tire, the pumps fall behind and – this time there is no miraculous mistake – the *Endeavour* starts to settle ever deeper into the water, increasing the seepage. With every inch of freeboard that disappears as the ship goes lower and slower the feeling of gloom on the ship also starts to deepen once more.

But now a nervous young man, the 19-year-old Midshipman Jonathan Monkhouse, slowly approaches Captain Cook and begs leave to tell him a story.

Very well. At once and in haste. Out with it, man!

Sir, I was once aboard a ship that left Virginia and smashed a hole in its hull so large that that let in four feet of water in a single hour. But by use of a thing they called 'fothering', the Captain was able to sail that seemingly hopeless ship all the way to London!

Cook, like many of the sailors, has heard of the obscure practice of fothering, but like everyone else – with the exception of young Monkhouse – has never seen it done. So, do go on?

Young Monkhouse explains. It sounds like a miraculous method, which is useful, as all know that it will take a miracle for the *Endeavour* to remain afloat. So what do they have to lose? Captain Cook puts young Monkhouse in charge of the operation. (Young Monkhouse is overcome with joy – and tension. Since that slipshod shooting in Tahiti he has been all too aware that the warmth of the Captain's affection for him could not keep a mouse from freezing. And yet here is a chance for redemption – if it *works*. What is more Monkhouse might prove the salvation of every soul on board the boat.)

No matter his comparative lack of rank, young Monkhouse is to have total command over all, as the five sailors he is given to assist must jump to his instructions.

We begin by mixing together a large quantity of oakum chopped fine with strands of wool, so we have the basic material that might help plug the leak.

Oh, and to this we must add sheep dung or whatever filth we can find – the more fibrous the better. And small stones are also very important so let's throw these ones we have here into the mix.

In his own way, young Monkhouse might do the witches of Macbeth proud as he mixes his hasty potion:

> *Double, double, toil and trouble;*
> *Fire burn, and cauldron bubble.*
> *Fillet of a fenny snake,*
> *In the cauldron boil and bake . . .*[55]

Now take a spare sail, spread it out on the deck and, as loosely as possible place fist-sized bundles of our mixture on the sail, in rows so that each bundle is just three or four inches from the next. As the sailors work, all around are aware just what is at stake, as the ship becomes ever more sluggish and even starts to list. Mr Banks notes that the worsening situation makes 'all hands impatient for the trial'.[56]

Stand back! Everyone back!

Now a rope is fastened to each corner of the sail and, with infinite care, the whole thing is lowered over the bow of the ship – with the globs of oakum and wool topmost – before the ropes are drawn back so that the sail will come directly over the damaged part of the hull, still with the ropes holding it tightly to the hull.

'Where ever the leak is,' young Monkhouse explains to Banks, 'must be a great suction which will probably catch hold of one or other of these lumps of Oakum and wool and drawing it in either partly or entirely stop up the hole.'[57]

In the meantime, keep pumping!

For his part, Captain Cook takes advantage of a change in the wind direction – it is now pushing them towards land – and, as sluggish as she is, begins steering the *Endeavour* to the West.

Or . . . is she so sluggish after all?

She seems to be moving . . . faster?

Lifting a little in the ocean?

Yes, she is.

It is working, it is working!

'In about ½ an hour,' as Banks records, 'to our great surprise the ship was pumped dry and upon letting the pumps stand she was found to make very little water, so much beyond our most sanguine expectations had this singular expedient succeeded.'[58]

Rejoice, rejoice, rejoice for we are saved, at least for the moment, and it is for good reason that young Monkhouse practically skips along the deck, for he is no less than the man of the moment, and very likely the man of the whole voyage!

For the actual moment, as darkness falls, Cook has the anchors dropped as the ship approaches close enough to the coast to hear the surf in the far distance. On the morrow they will look for a safe harbour, a place 'where we might lay her ashore and repair her'.[59]

Mr Banks, for one, is stunned at how successful the whole thing is, and how everyone has co-operated to make it happen.

> During the whole time of this distress I must say for the credit of our people that I believe every man exerted his utmost for the preservation of the ship, contrary to what I have universally heard to be the behaviour of sea men who have commonly as soon as a ship is in a desperate situation began to plunder and refuse all command. This was no doubt owing entirely to the cool and steady conduct of the officers, who during the whole time never gave an order which did not shew them to be perfectly composed and unmoved by the circumstances howsoever dreadful they might appear.[60]

In fact, with little bothering, the fothering holds not only for the 24 miles back to shore, but for the following three days while Cook looks for a suitable harbour in which to beach his ship – his Master and Midshipmen ceaselessly searching for that very spot in their smaller boats. In the meantime, Captain Cook still must take extraordinary care, and his time, as they must dodge the endless shoals and outcrops of coral that form a veritable great barrier of reefs between them and the coastline. To get through them in a sluggish ship, all while encountering changing winds and swirling currents, is supremely difficult. And so

James Cook proceeds with utmost prudence. Finally, Master Molineux sends a report back that he has found a suitable spot to bring the ship to shore, a large river mouth, some five miles leeward of their current position. The news is manna from heaven for a ship's company keenly aware that, as things are, as Banks chronicles, there is 'nothing but a lock of Wool between us and destruction'.[61]

Though the weather has turned foul with howling gales, Cook carefully brings his ship closer to the position described and, sure enough, finds the river mouth with not only a deep enough entrance to accommodate the *Endeavour*, but, most usefully, sandy shores on both sides. It is the perfect place in which they can lay the *Endeavour* ashore – grounding her at high tide. The next step will be to 'heave her down', careening – that is, tip her over a tad to get at the damaged hull.

Waiting for the seas to calm – for the weather is too tempestuous for the moment to risk trying to enter the river mouth – the botanist spies a fire on the shore at night. There must be Natives here! Perhaps, at last, they might make a genuine acquaintance with these most elusive people, instead of just seeing them as flitting figures in the distance.

Captain Cook wishes for the same.

But for now he must exclusively devote himself to the key task at hand: to, effectively, strand his ship on the sands like a beached whale at high tide so it can come to rest, have repair work undertaken at low tide, and then later be floated off at high tide.

It is a tricky operation, from first to last, and will require all of James Cook's expertise, judgement and luck.

On 17 June – a full three days after the Master had advised of the existence of the river mouth – the weather has sufficiently calmed to make the attempt.

Master Molineux has taken soundings in the river entrance – looking for a deep enough route that the *Endeavour* will be able to navigate through without grounding on a shoal. It is such an important exercise that Captain Cook himself now goes forth and supervises the laying of 'buoys' – empty water casks anchored by ropes attached to rocks they drop over the side – just as he had in the St Lawrence River, when he was a Master all those years ago.

It is a tricky operation, and as it is out of the question to sail the *Endeavour* into such a narrow space as the river mouth – with no possibility of tacking, and no suitable on-shore winds pushing it from behind – they must slowly 'warp' the ship in, a technique which sees them send the long-boat forward with a stream anchor, which is dropped as far as 600 feet ahead and then, by hauling on the capstan, the ship is pulled forward.

Such an exercise, in strange waters, with disaster swirling all around, including potentially hostile Natives secreted in the trees over yonder, would be a nightmare for most naval officers on most ships. But Captain Cook is in his element. This is precisely the kind of thing for which the mighty Whitby cat was designed, getting through narrow river entrances and on and off the tidal flats and sandbars of the East coast of England, loading and unloading coal.

Which is as well, for within 60 minutes of weighing anchor and setting sail at 7 am, the *Endeavour*, with a gravelly and grinding groan, nudges into a sandbar, with many a sailor thrown off his feet and the greyhounds yelping in alarm.

Two hours later, by use of the anchors and the capstan, the men are able to back the ship off the bar, only to shortly thereafter come too close into the opposite shore, where she is grounded again. The process is repeated and so it goes.

'At 1 p.m. the Ship floated,' Cook records in his journal, 'and we warped her into the Harbour, and moored her alongside of a Steep Beach on the South side; got the Anchors, Cables, and all the Hawsers ashore . . .'[62]

Captain Cook's relief is palpable. Neither for the first, or last, time he is thankful for the kind of ship chosen for this venture, the flat-bottomed girl, the snub-nosed Whitby collier – as any other kind of ship would have foundered on the reef, and been impossible to beach in this fashion. It is directly due to the mighty Whitby cat and all her unfashionable qualities 'that those on board owed their preservation; and hence we were enabled to prosecute discoveries in those seas so much longer than any ship ever did, or could do'.[63]

Any of the grander ships of regular design – built for beauty, too – would very likely already be on the bottom of the ocean right now. But the Whitby cat had not only been able to withstand the impact of the reef and be pulled off without losing a part of her hull, but had managed to limp to the shore.

With the *Endeavour* now secure they use what long timber they have in storage to make a 'stage', from ship to shore – effectively a bridge from the deck to the steep bank, so that they can easily lighten the ship further by carrying everything in the hold straight across the bridge to dry land.

In the meantime, two tents are pitched on the shore, one to hold those crew members who have been sick and the second to hold what is still in the hold – the empty barrels, and provisions, the remaining cannon and spare anchors. (Among the sick carried ashore is the ill Tupia, who is now also dismayed by what has happened. In a hundred long voyages he had never hit a reef like the white men have. It stuns him that they have, and he must, once again, take down a notch or two his estimation of their powers. On Tahiti they had seemed all powerful. On the water, they can seem . . . primitive.)

Every day yet more ballast and stores are taken ashore (at least providing a good chance to stocktake and air things out), until after several days all that is left is a very little ballast in the stern of the ship, while the bow – which is where the coral has pierced the hull – is empty.

Patience persists in the *Endeavour*'s endeavours until four o'clock on the afternoon of 21 June, when the moment they have all been working towards arrives and they are able to warp her further along the inlet until she is nudging the Southern shore of the river. Having rendered the bow of the ship as light as possible, they employ the capstan and windlass, with their cables attached to strong trees on the shore to heave her forward at high tide, and so leave her high and dry on the sand when the tide falls.

22 June 1770, Endeavour River, he sees sea shell in the starboard

The tide recedes at 2 am and all remaining water drains from the *Endeavour*, her bow high on the beach. For the first time, at dawn, Captain Cook can stand on the sandy, stony shore right by the forward part of the hull to get a close look at the damage and . . .

And did someone just walk over his grave, or is the shudder that moves through him, followed by the wave of incredulity, simply a natural reaction – as Captain Cook realises the one in a thousand chance that has saved his ship from complete catastrophe.

For there it is right before him. There are holes in the hull on both the starboard and larboard sides. And filling the principal hole, the one that would have sunk her, is something resembling a miracle.

'A large piece of Coral rock was sticking in one Hole, and several pieces of the Fothering, small stones, etc., had made its way in, and lodged between the Timbers, which had stopped the Water from forcing its way in in great Quantities.'[64] His blessing and his curse, his peril and his path to salvation right there before him.

In Cook's whole naval career, he has never heard of such a thing happening, but it has happened to them, and *saved* them.

Examining it even more closely, Cook realises what has happened. The coral had pierced through the outer planks like a hot knife through butter, and would have continued to cut her open bar one thing. Providence had also seen the coral penetrate the hull right where one of the hardwood hull timbers that form the skeleton of the ship is positioned. The coral has gone deep enough that it looks to have been hacked with an axe, but it has not broken through. As they had rocked the ship from side to side and up and down to get it off the reef it must have been touch and go, sink or swim, live or die, as to whether the coral or the hardwood would break first. But in the end the coral had broken off, *inside*, saving a hundred families in England and several from the Americas and assorted European countries from being bereaved.

Very well then.

It is time for the ship's Carpenter, John Satterly, with the aid of his assistants, to get to work and so they do – starting at 9 am and going hard for the rest of the day, cutting away the broken wood and very carefully starting to shape the planks that can slot in to replace them, then all of it caulked to seal it off. When the tide goes out later in the day they are able to examine the mid-section of the hull on the starboard side, but mercifully find only minimal damage, so it is decided that no further action is required.

After finishing the repair of the starboard side of the bow, the ship is heeled over on to the other side by readjusting the strain on the hawsers linked to strong trees, and pulled back just a couple of feet towards the water for fear of neaping – being stuck on land. The men now begin work on the larboard bow as this side, too, has been damaged by the coral and is dangerously compromised.

In the meantime, Captain Cook chronicles, 'the Armourers were busy making Bolts, Nails, etc.'.[65]

Exploring the area a little, on the lookout for fresh and interesting specimens, Joseph Banks comes across empty Native 'huts' and burnt-out fires, though it is not easy to determine when anyone was last here. Still, such solid-looking human habitation means there must be a good supply of fresh water nearby, and so it proves when Captain Cook finds plentiful spring water. For a ship's company that has been right on the edge of oblivion it is good news. Water means life, means they will at least likely survive in the short term, whether the *Endeavour* sails again or not.

With their length of stay uncertain, Cook ensures that supplies of food are distributed according to a strict rule.

'Whatever refreshment we got that would bear a division,' he will proudly note, 'I caused to be equally divided amongst the whole company generally by weight, the meanest person in the Ship had an equal share with myself or any one on board.'[66] (Thinking of you, James Magra.)

It is James Cook's way. He is no better than these men, and demands no special privileges. It is possible, just possible, that Mr Banks does not take the same view. But the quartermaster and cook answer to the Captain, not him.

Either way, diminishing ship stored rations make everyone more than usually interested in finding what food they can while here, and a vigorous plan for hunting and fishing is put in place.

•

Strange and extraordinary creatures abound in these parts. The redoubtable Midshipman James Magra is out hunting when he sees a wild dog, resembling a smaller version of a wolf, 'perfectly he said like those he had seen in America; he shot at it but did not kill it'.[67] There are also enormous black bats, with reddish-brown fur and a wing-span bigger than a yard.

'A Seaman who had been out on duty on his return declared that he had seen an animal about the size of and much like a one-gallon keg. It was, says he, as black as the Devil and had wings, indeed I took it for the Devil or I might easily have caught it, for it crawled very slowly through the grass. After taking some pains I found out that the animal he had seen was no other than the Large Bat.'[68]

Out on the reef just offshore there are clams so enormous that, as Banks records, 'One of [them] was more than 2 men could eat. Many indeed were larger; the Cockswain of the Boat a little man declared that he saw on the reef a dead shell of one so large that he got into it and it fairly held him.'[69]

Amazing. The truth of it is that there are things to see in this extraordinary place that are true, that rival the stories Charlie Clerke used to make up about Patagonia!

Meantime, others of the ship's company who have been sent to the far shore on a pigeon-hunting expedition have a curious experience.

They are just firing at passing birds, gathering what they can and moving deeper and deeper into the bush, when one of the men sees something in a fleeting, fleeing moment.

Before him is one of the most extraordinary-looking animals he's ever seen, and quite unlike any he's ever seen. It is, as he will describe it to Mr Banks and Captain Cook a short time later 'an animal as large as a grey hound, of a mouse colour and very swift . . .'.[70]

Swift?

Yes. It sort of . . . *bounded* . . . away.

It is all so, so, so very *unworldly*, the fellow can't even be quite sure what exactly he had seen.

It is intriguing enough, however, that Cook and Banks wish to know more, and the following morning Captain Cook is on his own expedition a little into the bush when he, too, must take pause.

There!

Where?

There! Its head coming out of the tall grass!

It was just as the sailor had described to him the previous afternoon, and, as Captain Cook will recount, 'I should have taken it for a wild dog but for its walking or running, in which it jumped like a Hare or Deer.'[71] Cook cannot see the bottom of the creature, it is hidden by the grass, but others get a clearer view of this oddity. One sailor says that it has 'very small Legs, and the print of the Feet like that of a Goat'.[72]

This is a strange land indeed, with a strange people, a strange and treacherous landscape and seascape, and very strange creatures. One way or another, however, they will hopefully shortly be leaving it, as the carpenters and armourers go on with their work and, slowly but surely, a brand-new piece of hull takes shape, while the rest of the hull is at least scrubbed down to remove barnacles, seaweed and the like.

For the first time they can start to contemplate the next problem beyond surviving . . .

Leaving.

CHAPTER TWELVE

ENDEAVOURING TO LEAVE

I likewise sent some of the Young Gentlemen to take a plan of the Harbour, and went myself upon the hill, which is near the South point to take a view of the Sea. At this time it was low water, and I saw what gave me no small uneasiness, which were a Number of Sand Banks and Shoals laying all along the Coast; the innermost lay about 3 or 4 Miles from the Shore, and the outermost extended off to Sea as far as I could see without my glass . . .[1]

Captain James Cook, 30 June 1770

Late June 1770, *Gungarde*, the Guugu Yimithirr, the spiritual matters

The Guugu Yimithirr people only build small fires. You burn simply what you need to stay warm, or to cook what you have hunted, but no more than that. On this evening, as they have their evening meal around the fire, they discuss the strange spirit and ghostly men who arrived at *Wahalumbaal birri*, the river mouth of their land. The intruders are indeed strange and troubling. For they gorge on the fruits of this land, trample its grasses, disrespect its sacred sites and take more fish and turtles than they can possibly need. And they don't move on.

What is happening? Are these pale-skinned intruders *wangarr*, spirits of our long dead ancestors? Or are they *bama*, people – and if so, are they *yarrga*, men, or *ngandhu*, women? Their strange garb covers their groins so the Guugu Yimithirr cannot tell for sure.

On the one hand they have no facial hair. On the other hand, they have no sign of breasts. Only by stripping one down will they get to the bottom and more of it . . . But dare they go close?

The discussion goes well into the starry night as they keep feeding the fire just what it needs, and no more. Must we of the Guugu Yimithirr ignore their presence, challenge it, or welcome it?

For the moment they are not sure, having never faced anything like this before, nor even heard mention of such spirits in their ancestors' stories. For now, the elders caution patience. *Let us watch and wait.*

30 June 1770, New Holland, a great barrier is sighted . . .

It is 20 days since they hit the reef, and nine days since they managed to beach the *Endeavour*.

Cook and Banks, struggling to the top of the hill on this fine morning, barely speak, despite – or perhaps because of – having spent nearly every hour of nearly every day for the last 22 months within 10 yards of each other. It is not that they have little left to say, or actively dislike each other. It is simply that, for the most part, their interactions are on matters of direct import to the expedition, and on this morning the most important thing is to get to the top of this steep hill.

As they come upon the peak, it all lies before them. To the Western interior of this land they see, with poetical spirit, the vision splendid of a sunburnt country stretching for a hundred horizons. It looks forbidding for any people who would try to cross it. But out to sea, to the East, it seems even worse than they feared – a succession of reefs, stretching out as far as the eye can see. It is a great barrier, reef defending this continent from the open ocean and it seems a wonder that they were able to make their way through it in the first place. For yes, while it had been one thing to have the *Endeavour* almost seaworthy once more, it is clearly going to be something else entirely to guide it safely out to the open ocean once more, through the maze of shoals and reefs, some exposed, some hiding just below the surface waiting to hole them once more.

'The Prospect was indeed melancholy . . .' Banks records, 'and no prospect of any straight passage out. To return as we came was impossible, the trade wind blew directly in our teeth; most dangerous then our navigation must be among unknown dangers. How soon might we again be reduced to the misfortune we had so lately escaped! Escaped indeed we had not till we were again in an open sea.'[2]

The walk back down the hill is even more silent, each man alone with his troubled thoughts.

1 July 1770, Endeavour River, Eat your pease . . .

As for the men, they are a happy band. Against all odds, they have survived and are on firm land with plenty of fresh water *and* fresh food. The ship's boats keep returning laden with dozens of fish, while the fertile land in these parts grows small amounts of a type of edible green foliage that Banks calls 'West Indian Kale', which Cook orders to be prepared 'to be boiled among the peas, [to] make a very good Mess, which, together with the fish, is a great refreshment to the people'.[3]

For his part, Tupia finds 'coccos', a taro plant, the roots of which he personally roasts to serve to the men.

•

The waves low and the tide even lower, on the morning of 3 July, Captain Cook gives orders for the men to heave the *Endeavour* afloat, and they busy themselves making preparations. They must lash empty casks to the ship's bow, the collective buoyancy hopefully enough to float the *Endeavour* when the high tide comes in. Alas, the men are not quick enough, and fail to finish before the ocean has reached high water and is beginning to drop once more. They must try again come tomorrow's high tide.

So it comes to pass the next day, as all hands apply themselves to trimming her while she floats at even keel. Cook hopes to lay the great ship ashore once more, as the hull could do with an inspection under the larboard main chains. They warp the ship over to the long sandbank snaking parallel to the south bank of the river, and beach her once more. The inspection reveals that indeed there is damage to the hull. Nevertheless Captain Cook records Carpenter John Satterly's view that the impact on seaworthiness is 'of little consequence; and as I found that it would be difficult, if not impractical, for us to get under her bottom to repair it, I resolved to spend no more time about it'.[4]

Yes, good news for all. Some among the ship's gentlemen, however, led by the sniff-snuffing-turned-snivelling Surgeon Monkhouse, resent both Captain Cook's clear deep respect for the view of a mere Carpenter, *and* the said Carpenter's unseemly swagger because of it. Surgeon Monkhouse's view is supported by Surgeon's Mate William Perry, who also notes that the Captain is only interested in those that can heal sick ships, not sick men. Where is the respect for them?

Nevertheless, for the moment, Satterly is the sage, and all the medical men can do is work on a cure for their wounded pride.

Unhappily for the backs of her sailors, the ship must be floated anew. With grunts and oaths, urged on by the fearsome yells of Midshipmen and the grins of their shipmates standing on deck, the *Endeavour* is pushed by the sailors on shore as all three ship's boats tug her out with straining rowers and wary officers watching the mighty vessel sitting stubbornly on the sandbank. In the end, it is like the birth of a poddy calf as, after a *terrible* strain, everything suddenly comes with a rush and the *Endeavour* floats freely once more. Captain Cook watches the successful operation with pleasure then orders the crew to moor the *Endeavour* alongside the beach where the stores lie, and prepare to bring them aboard to be stowed.

•

The gun in Tupia's hands weighs more than its mass. It is a heavy burden, a terrifying power, but one he must get used to. It is 5 July 1770 on the white man's calendar . . .

A rustle. In the undergrowth, somewhere near. Tupia and his gun disappear into the scrub, under the watchful – if a little bemused – eye of Joseph Banks. It has been a fortnight now since the beaching of the *Endeavour*, and while the Englishman and Tupia are supposed to be busy botanising, the Tahitian man seems far more concerned with prey, suddenly eager to use the ungainly metal monster in his hands. Tupia stalks through the bush, winding through the harsh Native scrub like a silent predator, crawling over rocks, sliding through the gaps in the trees. He creeps over a rise now, searching for . . . well, not for men. And yet that is precisely what Tupia has found, two Natives, 'digging in the ground for some kind of roots; on seeing him they ran away with great precipitation'.[5] Two Natives peacefully collecting bush tucker as Tupia stands above them, gun brandished.

There *are* Natives in these parts!

Tupia continues apace with his hunting. Again and again he fires. Again and again and again, unseen by him, many sets of eyes in the bushes gaze in wonder. How can this be happening? The Guugu Yimithirr people are mystified. The brown man holds the thunder-stick to his shoulder, squints his eyes, and, after a puff of smoke emerges from one end, comes the shattering noise and then sometimes a distant bird will fall from the flock.

7 July 1770, Endeavour River, who roo?

Joseph Banks is transfixed.

While on a brief camping trip upriver to explore some of the inland, he and his companions have hauled the craft up on to the banks to explore a little when they see the most extraordinary thing. It *must* be the strange animal the others have talked about.

There are four of them, perched on their back legs, with their massive tails, and clearly they are aware they are being watched, that there are strangers in their territory. They lift their heads from eating grass, twitch their ears, shake their heads from side to side, have a little hop and . . .

And now they're off! Leaping away, nay, LEAPING away.

'We observed much to our surprise,' Banks will chronicle, 'that instead of going upon all fours this animal went only upon two legs, making vast bounds . . .'[6]

It is like nothing Joseph Banks and his companions have ever seen before. They stand staring in awe as these extraordinary animals take effortless, massive jumps which eat up yards of ground at a time. Eager to bring one down so as to be able to examine it, Banks unleashes his lightning-fast hound, Lady. *Run the beasts down!* With a yelp, Lady is on her way. When the four bounding animals split up into two pairs, the greyhound picks the closest pair and is closing fast . . . until they hit a patch of thick grass.

The hound is immediately slowed, while the bouncing animals bound . . . a big HOP . . . soaring over the top and far, far away!

The running English greyhound outpaced by the bounding New Holland greyhound! No, really. Overhead, a flock of colourful birds affirm it is the funniest thing they have ever seen, laughing till they can laugh no more at the very *idea* that a visitor to these shores could get the better of one of them. Lady limps back to her master, completely and utterly beaten by the local.

Never in all their born days have Mr Banks or the Doctor seen anything like it. Examining the tracks the hopping animals have left behind and pacing it out, Banks finds that they take, '7 or 8 feet at each hop'.[7]

Extraordinary!

For now, continuing up the river, the waterway narrows to the point that it is only a brook and so the men begin to make camp for the evening when Mr Banks sees smoke curling upwards in the late afternoon light from a spot not far upriver. The Natives are obviously there and as the men of the *Endeavour* are yet to see any up close, and are travelling in such a small, unintimidating group, this might be the perfect opportunity to show the Natives that they need have no fear.

Alas, it is less the visitors' reputation that precedes them than their sound and even *smell* – and when they arrive there is little to see beyond the small fire, 'in an old tree of touchwood', spindly and tinder-dry, some rough kind of shelters, scattered tree branches and, hauntingly, footprints, 'upon the sand below the high tide mark [which] proved that they had very lately been there'.[8]

And they really have. For look here, near the fire, is the evening meal they had perhaps been about to eat, including, 'shells of a kind of Clam and roots of a wild Yam which had been cooked in it'.[9]

It is a strange thing to have stumbled upon such an intimate thing – perhaps like they are intruding? – and yet there is nothing for it. These are people of such 'unaccountable timidity',[10] matched only by their skill in evasion, that if they don't want to be seen up close they won't be. In any case, it is getting dark and so it is time for the intruders to return to their own camp, where their own evening meal – of considerably more refinement – is nearly ready and their beds of plantain leaves and pillows of grass are laid out on the sandbank, ready for the night's slumber. Mr Banks reminds the men there's no need for more shelter, or any worry about attack. Unlike in New Zealand, here in New Holland the Natives never feel like a threat.

8 July 1770, Far North Coast New Holland, a land lost in time

The languid air hangs hot and heavy with the mingled odours of distant smoke and surrounding hibiscus. This bush of New Holland teems with life. Insects buzz and drone; birds caw and cackle; stunning snakes sun themselves on the riverbanks, and enormous lizards with long tails take fright at their presence and run up trees!

The water is alive, too. Regular flashing flurries of fish dart back and forth beneath the *Endeavour*'s bow, and strange insects whirr just above the water's surface, lowering themselves for a sip or a dip, leaving vanishing patterns when they take flight.

Everywhere the Englishmen turn in this extraordinary land, they see things they scarce could have imagined.

The next morning, Banks and the camping party are heading back down the river when from the mangroves comes crawling a reptilian beast straight from antiquity . . . a seven-foot-long crocodile, with massive jaws and gleaming pointed teeth.

Row on!

And stroke and stroke and stroke!

The sailors in the yawl put their whole bodies into every haul on the oar, leaving the gargantuan crocodile in their wake. Returning to the

Endeavour, Mr Banks is informed that while those in the pinnace have not been able to find a navigable route out of the great barrier of reefs, by simply dangling a boat hook from their stern they have managed to catch three delicious turtles – weighing 791 pounds in total! It is becoming clear that, in terms of the diversity and richness of their diet, they are more blessed here than any other place they have visited.

'The promise of such plenty of good provisions made our situation appear much less dreadful; were we obliged to wait here for another season of the year when the winds might alter we could do it without fear of wanting Provisions: this thought alone put everybody in vast spirits.'[11]

Come what may, Captain Cook must prepare for the prospect of imminent departure, and orders the seamen to begin bringing the ballast back on board.

9 July 1770, Upon the Reef, Banks meets his Master

Say *what*, Master Molineux?

I said 'No', Mr Banks.

And he means it.

The sun glares down on the two men glaring at each other, as they stand on a rocky crop on a coral land far out to sea. In England, Mr Banks' superior class would crush Master Molineux like a scurrying cockroach. But right here, right now, it is not so clear.

For while Mr Banks may have an esteemed position on the *Endeavour*, even there he is in no position to order the Master to do anything. And on this reef, in a party under the command of Master Molineux – who has taken the long-boat, towing Banks' small boat, to explore one of the reefs just a little offshore – Mr Banks can't order him to hitch his trousers up, let alone go after yet more turtles. Master Molineux had reluctantly taken Mr Banks along, but he will be *damned* if he is going to take orders from him – particularly when they already have more than enough turtles.

For his part, Joseph Banks is deeply frustrated. For despite his will to command and his anger that he can't, he has no recourse. He is reduced to sitting there impotent and in a red rage until – after a brief time examining the 'large cockles'[12] and gathering shells and the like – he returns to the *Endeavour* in his small boat, leaving Master Molineux and his men out there. A furious Joseph Banks finds Captain Cook and gives him, 'a Very bad account of our Turtlecatchers'.[13]

It is against *nature*, that he should have no such power.

At dawn the next day, after Captain Cook sends Lieutenant Gore forth to order the return of Master Molineux and his men, the ship's company note in the near distance, on the sandy spit on the North point of the harbour, four Natives in canoes with outriggers, using their spears to fish.

Captain Cook, perhaps *this* is our opportunity to make contact?

But the Captain has a better tactic. It is one he has learnt here in New Holland.

'Leave them alone,' he orders the men who are eager to row over and attempt contact, 'without seeming to take any notice of them . . .'[14]

So, instead of pursuing the Natives and perpetually being frustrated by their powers of evasion, the white men are ignoring *them*.

And sure enough, just 15 minutes later . . .

It is working.

It is *working*.

The Natives are suddenly interested, and two of them are now approaching!

As those on deck watch closely, still trying not to seem *too* interested, the two Natives in their simple bark canoe, which barely sits above the water, come close enough to the towering *Endeavour* that the men are able to throw a couple of shiny baubles down, which clearly please the two Natives well enough that they soon go away, to soon return with the other two men in the second canoe, this time coming closer and . . .

And what now?

They have stopped, just the distance of a long musket shot away and, in their incomprehensible language, are talking very loudly. Joseph Banks and many of his entourage, together with some of the sailors, call back to them and make signs that they should come closer . . . *come closer!*

And they do!

Little by little, the Natives paddle forward until they are right along-side, in the shadow of the *Endeavour*. But careful . . . Still they brandish their spears as if, Mr Banks notes, 'to show us that if we used them ill they had weapons and would return our attack'.[15]

Yes, yes, yes.

Some gifts, perhaps?

In short order, the men of the *Endeavour* are handing down to the Natives everything from cloth, to nails, to pieces of paper and beads, none of which seem to interest them remotely. Yes, they dutifully put them in their canoe, but there is barely a flicker of interest from them until . . .

Until, by accident, a small fish, recently caught, is thrown down to them, whereupon, as Joseph Banks records, 'they expressed the greatest joy imaginable and instantly putting off from the ship made signs that they would bring over their comrades'.[16]

All for a small fish, something they already appear to have in abundance!

This is indeed a strange people.

But, sure enough, the two soon return with their companions, although all have their spears with them and their throwing sticks. The Englishmen and the Natives both make their way to the nearest shore to parley, meaning it is time for Tupia – who has recovered just enough, now they are eating fresh food – to work his magic.

As ever, his dark skin alone has some power to soothe, although the Natives do begin by raising their spears to him, and make as if they might throw them, he is able to use his sign language to such effect that they lay down their arms and come and sit next to the Tahitian holy man.

It is safe. The Native men trust him. (Not so the women, who stay on the far shore and are notable for the 'feathers stuck on the crown of their heads' and their lack of any clothing whatsoever – 'they do not so much as cover their privates', records the Captain a tad disapprovingly – though 'they wear as Ornaments, Necklaces made of Shells [and] Bracelets'.[17] Later, Cook would elaborate for the Admiralty that each of the women they see are 'naked as ever she was born; even those parts which I always before now thought Nature would have taught a woman to Conceal were uncovered'.[18] Quite.)

And even after Captain Cook lands with some of his officers and Marines, still the Natives remain calm and receive presents, 'which they took and soon became very easy, only Jealous if anyone attempted to go between them and their arms'.[19]

For the first time Cook is able to get a close look at them.

While one of the Natives appears to be in his thirties or thereabouts, the other three can't be older than their late teens. They are lithe, athletic men, none of them taller than five foot six, and all of them entirely naked, with 'skins the colour of wood soot, and this seemed to be their natural colour. Their hair was black, lank, and cropped short, and neither woolly nor frizzelled.'[20]

And look closer now, at their physiques.

'Their bones were so small,' Sydney Parkinson notes, 'that I could more than span their ankles; and their arms too, above the elbow joint.'[21]

Like the Tahitians and the New Zealanders, they have all gone through some kind of ritual on their way to adulthood, which has left its peculiar mark: 'On their breasts and hips were corresponding marks like ridges, or seams, raised above the rest of the flesh, which looked like the cicatrices of ill-healed wounds.'[22]

(As it happens, the Guugu Yimithirr call their territory *Gungarde*, from the word *gun-gaar* – from the very distinctive kind of crystal quartz found in the area, perfect for forming the sharp edges they need to cut their chest skin for initiation ceremonies.)

And look closer still.

'Some . . . had a small hair-rope about their loins, and one about an arm, made of human hair. They had also a bag that hung by their necks, which they carried shell-fish in . . . Some of them had necklaces made of oval pieces of bright shells, which lay imbricated over one another, and linked together by two strings.'[23]

To Captain Cook's surprise, none of them appears to be missing their front teeth, a feature previously noted by William Dampier in his meetings with the Natives on the Western side of the country. They do appear to have some kind of red paint daubed over parts of their bodies, while one of them has 'his upper lip and breast painted with streaks of white, which he called "carbanda". Their features were far from being disagreeable; their voices were soft and tuneable, and they could easily repeat any word after us, but neither us nor Tupia could understand one word they said.'[24]

After which, as Captain Cook recounts, 'most of us went to them, made them again some presents, and stayed by them until dinner time [approached].'[25]

No matter, there has been such warmth in the exchanges that Captain Cook, reluctant to break off their seeming entente, even asks if the Natives would perhaps like to join them for a meal upon the ship?

'But this they declined,' Captain Cook records, 'and as soon as we left them they went away in their Canoe.'[26]

Still, it is a start, a real start.

For the first time Captain Cook feels they have had a genuine exchange with the Natives and though it is hardly a diplomatic success it is at least more than spying fleeting, flitting figures and flashing white soles in the distance, no sooner seen than they disappear.

11 July 1770, Endeavour River, fishing with compliments

Extraordinary.

The next sparkly winter morning as the men move about the ship, storing barrels of water in the hold, airing the bread on the foredeck, Joseph Banks is on the quarter-deck, scanning the surrounds when four Natives appear, as if from nowhere!

Three of them had come the day before, but the other is a stranger. And in the nose of the stranger is . . . a bone as thick as a sailor's finger.

Banks gets a welcome close look at them, noting how in fact, 'they all had the septum or inner part of the nose bored through with a very large hole, in which one of them had stuck the bone of a bird . . . 5 or 6 inches long, an ornament no doubt, though to us it appeared rather an uncouth one'.[27] Oddly, Cook notes, all of the women also have holes in their ears, but no ornaments hanging from them.

The Natives have come today with a specific purpose – to give the white men a fish, in return for the fish that they were so pleased to receive the day before. They do not wish to be beholden to anyone, and every kindness must be reciprocated.

'Their stay was but short,' Joseph Banks records, 'for some of our gentlemen being rather too curious in examining their canoe they went directly to it and pushing it off went away without saying a word.'[28]

There is an innate dignity about these people that Mr Banks had not previously understood, but is now slowly recognising.

In the distance now he can see the ship's yawl returning after its visit to the reef to hunt turtle. They have achieved a good haul – three more of them!

•

The next day the three Natives are back with three companions, all of whom are formally introduced by name, one of which was Yaparico. As they eat some of the fish that has been prepared for them – the rest of the fish they give to one of the greyhounds, as these big dogs fascinate them – Joseph Banks, along with an enthusiastic Sydney Parkinson, does his best to learn some of their language, and begins to make a list of Native words. They use the method they had perfected in Tahiti – pointing to various things and having the Natives say their word for it.

After all, the President of the Royal Society, James Douglas, the 14th Earl of Morton, had specifically told the Captain and Gentlemen not only to 'exercise the utmost patience and forbearance' when dealing with the local people, exhorting the voyage leaders to remind the crew of this same moral duty at every opportunity, but, in the event that relations are established, he asked them 'to form a vocabulary of the names given by the Natives to the several things and places which come under the inspection of the gentlemen',[29] and here is their first opportunity in New Holland to do exactly that.

Typically, Banks does not just trust his own ear, or his interlocutor, but asks Mr Parkinson and a couple of other men to ask different Natives about the same objects to make sure he has it absolutely right. Bit by bit, a list of words in the local language is built up.

Wageegee the head
Meanang Fire
Melcea the ears
Bonjoo the Nose
Unjar the tongue
Wallar the Beard
Ngalan the Sun
Tapool bone in nose[30]

Oh, and there is one thing in particular, something that Mr Banks can't point at but he can show the Natives the sketch by Mr Parkinson, the curious hopping creature?

'*Gangurru,*'[31] replies the Native they ask.

'Kangooroo,'[32] is carefully recorded.

'Their language was totally different from that of the Islanders,' Banks notes. 'It sounded more like English in its degree of harshness though it could not be called harsh neither. They almost continually made use of the *Chircau,* which we conceived to be a term of Admiration as they still used it whenever they saw any thing new; also "*Cherr, tut tut tut tut tut*" which probably have the same signification.'[33]

So too do the people of this part of New Holland often add an *urr,* thus '*tut tut urr, tut tut urr*',[34] which seemed to register astonishment, while they 'often whistled when they were surprised'.[35]

Among the sailors there is an English version of '*Cherr, tut tut tut tut tut.*'[36]

After the sexual delights of Tahiti and, to a lesser extent, New Zealand – despite the tut-tuts of their own Captain – there had been some hope that New Holland might provide the same, but what happens now is really the first time they have seen a young maiden in all her glory – and there is not the slightest possibility of taking it further. Not only is she accompanied by two Native men, but she has not the slightest aspect of come-hither about her. Whatever her charms, they will not be for the white man's enjoyment.

Joseph Banks is disappointed but too distracted to mull. For the most extraordinary thing unfolds before his eyes.

Taking one stick, about eight inches long, one of the Natives sharpens it at one end with a sharp rock and then places the stick between his hands with the sharp end sitting in a small bed of dry grass that sits atop a piece of soft wood placed on the ground below. By moving his hands back and forth, he makes the stick twist and spin both ways, back and forth, the sharp end boring into the soft wood below. Twisting, twisting, twisting . . . onwards he goes, as if warming his hands on a very cold winter's day in the highlands of Scotland rather than on this sunny day in the northern reaches of New Holland. Bemused, Banks continues watching closely when it happens. From below the pointed end of the stick, sparks suddenly start to fly spasmodically momentarily . . . *twist, twist, twist,* and *more* sparks begin to fly . . . and now the little bed of dry grass catches alight! A solid flame is soon flaring which in turn begins to devour the soft piece of wood below. Two minutes, a fire from nothing.

But now look. For one Native, with a great sense of fun, runs along the beach, to their eyes carrying nothing and yet . . .

Grinning, the fellow runs back and forth, and has no sooner bent down to a pile of wood than it starts to spiral smoke, and then burst into flames! Fire magic! The white men whoop their appreciation, even as they stare in amused disbelief – it is as if hands can shoot flame! So popular is the trick that it is repeated again and again for the pleasure of the laughing English and beaming Natives.

Beat *that,* you white men!

How is it done? The scientific side of Joseph Banks insists on finding out. Firstly it relies, he discovers, on 'the infinite readiness with which every kind of rubbish, sticks, withered leaves or dry grass already almost dried to tinder by the heat of the sun and dryness of the season would take fire'.[37]

So dry, just a spark will see each clump burst into flame! But how to provide that spark?

It seems that he does it by carrying in his fist a tight ball of smouldering grass that only needs air to be ablaze, and he then breaks off bits of it as he runs, expertly placing each blazing fraction on the part of the clump most likely to ignite!

'In this manner proceeding as long as he thought proper.'[38]

Mr Banks also notes how fire is used by the Natives to keep their hair, facial and otherwise, in trim: 'That they had no sharp instruments among them we ventured to guess from the circumstance of an old man who came to us one day with a beard rather larger than his fellows: the next day he came again, his beard was then almost cropped close to his chin and upon examination we found the ends of the hairs all burned so that he had certainly singed it off.'[39]

14 July 1770, Endeavour River, Lieutenant Gore on the hop

Hunting for meat in these parts – shooting the animals and birds – has not been easy for the white men. Clearly it is no problem for the Natives as they have methods all their own. For one, Joseph Banks finally understands the reason for the notches they had seen cut out of the trees at Botany Bay, 'notches which they had everywhere cut in the Bark of large trees, which certainly served to make climbing more easy to them, might be intended for the ascending these trees in order either to watch for any animal who unwarily passing under them they might pierce with their [spears], or for the taking of birds who at night might Roost in them'.[40]

Those Natives also have a natural way of moving through the bush as if they are of the bush.

Lieutenant Gore is not of the New Holland bush. He is originally from Virginia, before moving to New York, and he is on the hunt, when . . .

When he sees it.

Up ahead at a distance of about 70 yards, it's a *gangurru* that has, miraculously, not heard him or smelt him. Time is of the essence. Lieutenant Gore brings his musket to bear. He is not proud, particularly, to have been the first man to shoot a Tahitian and the first man to shoot a New Zealander, but, by God, he just knows he is *born* to be the first man to shoot a kangaroo. He pulls the trigger. The blast sends flocks of cockatoos as far as a mile away flapping skyward, screeching their alarm – but Lieutenant Gore has the satisfaction of seeing the kangaroo fall. For once, just for *once*, Mr Gore has shot something that will please his Captain.

Bending over the creature, he sees it twitching, its lifeblood flowing from the wound in its side. But it is soon still, and a couple of Lieutenant

Gore's men are able to sling it from a stiff pole and carry it back to the *Endeavour*, where even the carpenters still busily working on the hull take momentary pause to get a good look at it.

Indeed, it is like nothing they have ever seen, though this one is smaller than many of the others that have been spotted. Properly gutted to aid in its preservation, Mr Banks and his men find it weighs no more than 28 pounds. Even Captain Cook is so fascinated, he takes up the role of naturalist and begins some detailed notes on its form.

'It was hair lipped, and the head and ears were most like a hare's of any Animal I know; the tail was nearly as long as the body, thick next the rump, and tapering towards the end; the forelegs were 8 inches long, and the hind 22 . . . It bears no sort of resemblance to any European animal I ever saw.'[41]

So, in the end, aside from being faster than a greyhound, the kangaroo looks nothing like a greyhound either.

Sydney Parkinson couldn't agree more, and with pencil in hand tries to capture it. It is not easy. When drawing a man, or a dog or a bird, their form simply pours from his pencil as he is more than familiar with the basic contours and must only alter the shapes so as to properly capture the beak or the nose, the chin, the lines of the forehead etc. But here, he must first struggle to get even the basic contours right, before even getting to the detail.

Yes, he notes, it has 'a head like a fawn's; lips and ears, which it throws back, like a hare's . . . The tail, which is carried like a greyhounds, was almost as long as the body, and tapered gradually to the end. The chief bulk of this animal is behind; the belly being largest, and the back rising toward the posteriors. The whole body is covered with short ash-coloured hair . . .'[42]

All up, Joseph Banks is more than pleased with Lieutenant Gore's feat in bringing down, and then bringing back, the animal, and even more pleased the next day when, 'dressed for our dinners [it] proved excellent meat'.[43]

By now, as hunting expeditions continue to replenish their food supplies, all are feeling more confident about the immediate future and relieved that their days of being on a starvation diet may be over. This feeling grows even more on this evening when the yawl brings, to everyone's delight, another four turtles, each one between 200 and 300 pounds, 'so we may now be said to swim in Plenty'.[44]

And it is not just the quantity, but the quality.

'Our Turtles,' Banks notes, 'are certainly far preferable to any I have eat in England' where, slaughtered in captivity, after being fed on 'unnatural food', they do not give, 'so delicious a flavour as it is in their wild state'.[45]

So delicious are the turtles, and likely so good for the men's health, that Captain Cook decides to take some with them, alive – in tubs filled with water – so they can be eaten at the crew's leisure.

●

Among the Guugu Yimithirr people there is growing dismay, and unrest. Today these strange white visitors have taken *three more* enormous *maamiingu*, female green turtles, aboard their enormous vessel.

Why?

How can this be?

And how many of such turtles can be left for them?

In a community where the only things that are captured and killed are those needed to fulfil immediate needs, there is alarm, and outrage, at such a rapid depletion of such a valuable resource.

How long will these strange visitors stay?

17 July 1770, Endeavour River, no contact, Sir Joseph . . .

Even with a skiff, a boat with which he had little previous experience, Tupia is able to master it quickly, and move upon the water with such fluidity that he is a pleasure to watch. On this occasion, he rows back to the *Endeavour* from the shore, and once back on deck reports to Captain Cook that he had met with three Natives who had been friendly and given him some longish roots to eat.

Cook, Banks and Solander are so eager to meet the Natives that Tupia agrees to accompany them back to the shore, where they meet four Natives who happily receive beads offered as gifts, before taking their leave.

'We attempted to follow them,' Banks chronicles, 'hoping that they would lead us to their fellows where we might have an opportunity of seeing their Women; they however by signs made us understand that they did not desire our company.'[46]

●

What is to be done about these ghostly men on the shores of Guugu Yimithirr country?

They behave with such greed, with no thought for the natural world around them. They also don't appear to be moving on anytime soon. Something must be done. Would it not be wise to go aboard the hulking canoe themselves? Surely our turtles are somewhere aboard, and if not, then we can communicate with these men and find out more. Ah, but in order to be invited aboard, we must play along with their customs. We shall accept their trinkets, trades, and even eat with them. We will not go unarmed, though we cannot afford to show any menace or have them think we mean harm. Once we have their trust, we will climb aboard the great canoe, and from there we will learn the truth of what happened to the turtles.

18 July 1770, the Natives invade British territory

What has gotten into them?

In Banks' eyes, the Natives appear 'to have lost all fear of us and became quite familiar',[47] coming out to the ship as casually as if they were heading out fishing. One of them agrees to demonstrate his prowess with his spear, which is about eight feet long.

'It flew with a degree of swiftness and steadiness that really surprised me,' Banks notes, 'never being above four feet from the ground and stuck deep in at the distance of 50 paces.'[48]

As demonstrations go, even Joseph Banks is impressed. And, for the first time in New Holland, even a little intimidated.

How long would he and the rest of the ship's company last in the face of a mass attack by the Natives? From the look of this demonstration, not long. It seems to underline the point – of a sharpened spear – that the reason none of them have yet lost their lives to the Natives in their whole time in New Holland is because the Natives have chosen *not* to kill them, rather than lacking the capacity to do so. It comes as a shock and no-one is more shaken than Mr Banks, who had concluded that the locals posed no threat . . . only to find them fully possessed of dangerous weaponry of their own making and more than proficient in the art of battle.

Either way, today is a happy day and some of the Natives accept the invitation to come on board the *Endeavour*.

Surely, *this time*, they will be wide-eyed and seriously impressed with the grandeur of the vessel on which they are privileged to set foot. Surely, as men who are used to canoes, they will be like a man from a small thatched cottage setting foot in a cathedral for the first time, as they gaze at the towering masts high above, at the shimmering furled sails?

Actually . . . no.

Somehow, the Natives could not be less interested in the ship itself. But they are interested in the caged birds they see on deck, including Tupia's lorikeet.

'*Cherr, tut tut tut tut tut!*'[49]

Yes, new.

But that is not their gist. They are, in fact, appalled, and begin animatedly discussing the lorikeet when one of them darts forward and tries to wrench apart the thick strands of wire that form the bars of the cage before, as birds squawk and the crew shout, he is fallen upon even as other Natives cry out and try to do the same.

The birds must be freed to fly! And so must the turtles to swim and roam!

It takes some time, but the ruckus does eventually die down – even if the birds remain in their cages – and more peaceful, curious interactions ensue. Now more confident that the Natives will not make trouble, Captain Cook turns his attention to that which truly concerns him, getting away from this place hopefully within just a few days, and with that in mind, even while the Natives are still on board, he orders Master Molineux to take some men and the pinnace out to the Northward to seek out a channel among the shoals. The Captain and Mr Banks also head North, crossing to the opposite side of the river and make slightly inland, walking some six miles, up to the peak of another hill, and look Northward – their intended direction if they can find a navigable route – to see what obstacles lie between the *Endeavour* and the open sea. As before, the great barrier of reefs – as impossibly beautiful and colourful and positively magical as it is – provides 'a melancholy prospect of the difficulties we are to encounter, for in whatever direction we looked it was covered with Shoals as far as the Eye could see'.[50]

The two trudge back to the ship in near silence, arriving to find several more Natives on board.

As it turns out, the attention of these Natives is no longer on the caged birds, nor even the fact that one of the more sullen of the white men seems to be missing most of both of his *ears*. (That must be some strange white, tribal ritual.)

No, they are mesmerised by something else entirely.

They have found the turtles . . . clambering about on the wooden deck. Perhaps it is impressive to have caught so many, but why do the white men *need* that many? Is there no end to their greed?

The Natives soon leave, still concerned.

19 July 1770, Endeavour River, fire at will

From high on the deck, Joseph Banks spies something on the beach, something curious. Several Natives come out of the bush, bringing 'with them a larger quantity of [spears] than they had ever done before'.[51]

The Natives' weapons are carefully 'laid up in a tree leaving a man and a boy to take care of them'[52] while 10 Native men drag their bark canoes to the water's edge, hop in and paddle swiftly to the English ship. Captain Cook joins Banks at the gunwale and watches as the Natives approach. He can see six or seven Native women standing in the distance on the shore, too, watching. The English have never seen such a large grouping before. *Why?* Something is up. The Natives are welcomed on board, but it is clear by their faces that they are no longer in a mood to be welcomed.

The sole reason for their visit is soon made clear. The turtles. They want the turtles back. Now.

The Natives can see the dozen turtles lolling about the deck of the white men's ship. They also know the ship is intending to leave. But it will not leave with their turtles: 'They first by signs asked for One,'[53] records Mr Banks.

No, replies Captain Cook. The man who has been told no shows what can only be 'great marks of resentment'.[54]

He stamps his foot and shoves Joseph Banks out of his path, 'with a countenance full of disdain',[55] and asks another sailor for the turtles, but again they are told no.

At this point things become perilously close to getting out of hand as two of the Natives become angered at the refusal and the Captain barks commands for them to be hauled down the gangway and off the ship.

The other Natives, now getting angered themselves, 'grew a little Troublesome, and were for throwing every thing overboard they could lay their hands upon'.[56]

James Cook tries to pacify the Natives by offering them some English bread which 'they rejected with Scorn, as I believe they would have done anything else excepting Turtle'.[57]

Time after time, the Natives attempt to grab and rescue the turtles, *their* turtles – only to be thwarted every time by the Englishmen. Finally, it becomes clear to them that they will not succeed in this venture, at least not right now, and with a grunted command from the oldest of the men, suddenly they 'all in an instant leaped into their Canoe and went ashore'.[58]

They are deeply affronted.

While there is a great culture of give and take between tribes, whereby a tribe blessed with a sudden bounty of food will give to a tribe without that bounty, it is very much a reciprocal arrangement. All that the white men have done so far is take. And these turtles are *not* theirs *to* take! The key food of the Guugu Yimithirr people, it is outrageous for these strange men to just come in, help themselves, and take away *their* turtles. The *maamiingu*, female green turtles, are a sacred part of this world, a key food source that must only be captured and killed in season with great care, so they will continue to collectively thrive and feed the clan. Everyone knows that. Taking so many is against nature and an offence to the law of this land.

And so they go.

In the yawl, as it happens, Captain Cook and Mr Banks are not far behind them as Banks is desirous of doing one last round of plant gathering, while Cook in turn wishes to confirm that none of the *Endeavour*'s equipment has been left on shore. As the two Englishmen are about to land they are pleased to see many of the sailors doing no less than 'taking in the washing' – gathering the linen that has just been washed in the river and dried on tree branches – as well as striking the tents, all in preparation for their departure.

It is a peaceful scene, with no hint of trouble, until . . .

Until just a few minutes after they land, suddenly a group of armed Natives appear, approach and press around the fire where some of the men have a kettle boiling, ready to ply the seams of the *Endeavour* with boiling pitch.

What on *earth* are they doing?

It all happens so quickly there is barely time to comprehend it.

It is the . . . fire magic!

But this time it is being used as a weapon against them.

A Native's hands brush near the earth and fire springs up, each quick touch quickly sparking terror as well as flame. The Native's palm is cupped, the flame concealed and kept alive by his stoic refusal to feel its heat, and though the Englishmen have seen this 'trick' before, only now do they see the danger of the magic. It is no parlour trick; it is a death-trap. For now, the Natives run, spreading fire and panic in a succession of terrifying instants.

Too late, Captain Cook and Mr Banks realise that the tall grass that surrounds them is a deadly potential weapon, and watch in stupefied horror as one running Native 'began to set fire to the grass to wind-ward of the few things we had left ashore with surprizing dexterity and quickness; the grass which was 4 or 5 feet high and as dry as stubble burnt with vast fury'.[59]

Most shocking is the speed with which the fire takes hold.

It has gone from nothing to leaping flames in just a few seconds, and the resulting billowing smoke and sense of all-engulfing inferno is overwhelming. The white men had had no idea just how quickly the grass and bush of New Holland could burn.

As Cook notes, it was so swift that, 'before we well knew what he was going [on] about he made a larger Circuit round about us, and set fire to the grass in his way, and in an instant the whole place was in flames'.[60] (He's momentarily transported back to that late night on the St Lawrence River, when he had awoken to see the flaming French fleet drifting towards him.)

In every direction bar the sea there is a raging fire, meaning the newly arrived white men must do precisely what the Natives want – leave, get on their vessels and *go*.

While nearly all eyes look to Captain Cook for what to do, Joseph Banks – as is ever his wont – moves on his own account. Snapping orders at four sailors, even though he has no formal authority over them, he is soon on his way back to the *Endeavour* at all speed to get armed reinforcements. On the other side of those flames they have men, not to mention clothes, linen, fishing nets, the forge. All of them must be rescued. None can be left to the Natives, and least of all the men.

But there is a more important matter still – first and foremost, we must save the botanist's tent, placed there for the benefit of Tupia. The men row with all their might, as Banks' fury grows. The men still standing on shore, in the closing horseshoe of flames, the Captain at their head, hear the sudden squeal of a panicked piglet which had been let off the ship to graze. It is caught on the other side of the flames, which soon burn the piglet to death as it tries to run through.

Once there is the smallest break in the inferno, Captain Cook makes a mad dash to get through the raging wall and over to his men further down the beach, who are washing linen, and are as yet not surrounded by fire. A man of action, as he had been at St Lawrence. And yet, even as he runs towards them – making heavy weather of it as his black boots sink into the sand – he can see that Natives are unleashing precisely the same fire magic around these men. Like fire demons, these manic magicians run along belching flame with every thrust of their hands. The flames are spreading around his men, just as they had back near the landing spot.

With an anger that rises with equal ferocity to the still rising flames, Captain Cook roars for the Natives to stop, his gestures acting as exclamation marks for his words – his meaning is clear – but, 'no threats or signs would make them desist'.[61] In desperation, thus, Cook decides he must fire a gun at 'their new friends, who are friendly no more'.[62] But the Captain has no gun on his person.

Running back to where Mr Banks and his reinforcements in the yawl have landed and are dragging Banks' tent to safety, the Captain grabs a loaded musket from the botanist. Seeing how desperate the situation is, Mr Banks takes another musket and joins Cook as they both now run along the shore, the civilian and the naval commander yelling in unison for the sailors to run back to the pinnace and for the Natives to stop trying to burn them alive.

Still the Natives persist and so Captain Cook takes his desperate action. Taking up his already primed musket, he drops to one knee, and takes aim at the leading Native with fire in his hand, before pulling the trigger. Yes, the small puff of smoke that the musket emits is as nothing to the billowing smoke from the fires, but it is enough. For at this point, as Banks notes, the Captain's target, 'dropped his fire and ran nimbly to his comrades who all ran off pretty fast'.[63]

Cook himself pursues the fleeing men, noting drops of blood on the ground from the wounded man.

Captain Cook again loads his musket and fires into the mangroves the Natives have run into, to make the point, as the approving Banks notes, 'that they were not yet out of our reach'.[64]

It works.

'They ran on quickening their pace on hearing the ball and we soon lost sight of them.'[65]

Captain Cook and Mr Banks return to their landing spot, where Cook is pleased to see 'the people who were ashore had got the fire under [control]'.[66]

But now in the near distance, raised Native voices. Over in the mangroves where some of the sailors had been doing washing.

Anxious that more trouble is afoot, Cook grabs a party of four men, along with Banks, and starts running towards the voices.

There they are!

It is a dozen Native warriors, each carrying four spears. And despite the fact that James Cook and his men have muskets, and brandish them, the warriors do not draw back. Nor do they make an aggressive move. For now, all is deadly quiet. Maybe a little . . . *too* quiet? Birds have taken wing and the air is so still that the lazy wisps of smoke trailing through the branches barely disperse. All is uncertain. If a full-pitched battle breaks out, each side can do major damage, but it is just not clear if that is the intent.

What is happening?

No-one is sure.

And yet now the Natives have turned and are beginning to walk away, almost as if on a leisurely stroll.

Cook and Banks watch as the Natives go, noticing that a number of them have dropped their spears. Thinking it better to be on the safe side, the Captain and his men follow the Natives, seizing half a dozen of the spears as they go. Hostages. This terrifies the Natives who look over their shoulders to see it happen and they immediately take flight.

Wary, Captain Cook and Mr Banks follow the retreating warriors 'for near a mile, then meeting with some rocks from whence we might observe their motions we sat down and they did so too about 100 yards from us'.[67]

But now what?

One of the Natives stands and is coming towards them.

And he has something in his hand!

A spear?

A spear!

Hands fly to muskets.

It very well might be an attack, but . . .

But, wait.

They look closer, as the figure tentatively comes closer still. It is a little old man,[68] as Joseph Banks describes him, and what he is carrying is a deliberately broken spear, its once dangerous spearhead now lying at a limp right angle to the main shaft.

Several times he stops. But, encouraged by the white men beckoning him forward, he always starts approaching again, until he stands before them, still holding his broken spear.

This man, a deeply respected tribal elder by the name of Ngamu Yarrbarigu, speaks to them.

'*Ngahthaan gadaai thawun maa naa thi hu,*'[69] he says. 'We come to make friends.'

But of course none of the *Endeavour* men can understand a word. Nevertheless, it is clear that his gesture of having broken his spear is a gesture of peace. The man goes on to explain in his curious sign language what he wants. He uses a curious mannerism that includes, as described by Joseph Banks, 'drawing moisture from under his armpits [and] blowing the sweat on his hands into the air'.[70]

Unknown to the white men, he is performing a ritual known as '*ngaala ngan daamal mal,* my sweat from me sent to you',[71] a call for calm.

For Captain Cook and the ship's company have been extremely fortunate to land in a sacred part of the Guugu Yimithirr's *bubu* land, the place of the Waymburr clan, a place of peace where marriage and initiation ceremonies are performed, women come to give birth, celebrations are held and conflicts are resolved – a place where it is strictly forbidden for warring tribes and clans to spill blood.

The 'little old man' is making a gesture of peace, and in so doing is asking the white men to respect the lore and law of this sacred place.

As a Guugu Yimithirr elder of the clans, it is the duty of Ngamu Yarrbarigu to try to stop further desecration at Waymburr, and having identified Captain Cook as the elder of this intruding clan, he is asking him to stop further desecration of the area by spilling blood in a conflict.

Clearly, the reaction he receives from the white men now – the smiles, their warmth and, perhaps most importantly, the fact that he has been unmolested – is a clear sign that the white men, too, want peace.

For now, he turns and calls to the other Natives to come forward, clearly telling them to leave their spears. In the soft sunlight, throwing dappled shadows on their forms, they are seen to lay their spears beside a tree, before approaching, and joining the little old man. The Native men and white men stand gazing at each other.

What now?

'We now returned the [spears] we had taken from them,' Cook will recount, 'which reconciled everything.'[72]

Yes, reconciliation in our time . . .

Relations so improve that the Natives put forth an earnest request: 'We have three men with us who want to see the ship.'[73]

They want to see the ship? So the fire battle is over?

Oh yes, they explain, 'The man who was shot at is gone.'[74]

Very well then, bring them forward . . .

Some words are shouted in their curiously fluid language, and within a minute three Natives emerge from the bushes, and are given such trinkets as Mr Banks and Lieutenant Gore have with them, whereupon the newcomers are escorted to the ship. The mood is friendly, with the Natives communicating through sign language that they would no longer set fire to the grass, and the Englishmen in turn distributing musket balls among them and through their own sign language trying to explain a little how they work.

And here is the *Endeavour*, a mighty structure right by the shore, towering over Banks, Gore and their guests.

Would the three Natives like to come aboard?

No.

And nothing will convince them to try it. They don't quite know what it is, but they know they don't like it. Very well then. Mr Banks and Lieutenant Gore are quite content to leave 'them to their contemplations; they stayed about two hours and then departed'.[75]

•

The Guugu Yimithirr people approach the English one last time.

'They all came along with us abreast of the Ship,' Captain Cook notes, 'where they stayed a short time, and then went away . . .'[76]

Yes, very strange, but the *Endeavour* men have grown used to such strangeness. You never quite know what the Natives will do next. They don't react like white men. They seem to know the white men are soon to depart, but there is no sense of ceremony about it, no goodbye and . . . and . . . now what?

This is no ordinary fire, no beach brush lit by the fire magic, or just a few trees set alight. Oh no, this is much grander than that, awesome in its beauty and its terror. For the Natives have, as Captain Cook records, 'set the woods on fire'.[77] The massive conflagration rises and roars with dangerous beauty 'about a Mile and a half or two Miles from us'.[78]

Mesmerising and terrifying, it is an inferno reaching into the night sky. Now the wind shifts and the smoke all but engulfs them as the ship's company, with stinging eyes, start coughing, even as they hold whatever fabric they can to their mouth and nose to help with breathing. Even through the swirling smoke, however, they can still clearly see the inferno in the distance. It is clearly no accident, but is it a tribute or a warning? Have they friends on shore or an enemy revealed? Captain Cook broods on the tactical meaning as Banks absorbs the aesthetics.

'All the hills about us for many miles were on fire,' Banks records, 'and at night made the most beautiful appearance imaginable.'[79]

It is unnerving, and they can't help but wonder if the fires are the prelude to an attack of some kind, despite the broken spear of the previous day. Men stay on keen watch through the night – with their muskets loaded and primed – but no attack eventuates. The following morning Captain Cook is at least feeling confident enough to send men ashore to make contact with the Natives, but none are to be found in or around the still smouldering bush.

Evening, 19 July 1770, Endeavour River, she sails, ship sails, by the seashore

It is time to start looking to the sea once more, preparing to face new dangers of finding open passage to the ocean free.

The remaining stores are taken aboard the ship, which is re-berthed, and Cook gives the order to 'let her swing with the tide'.[80]

And yet, even though the *Endeavour* is now repaired, their water barrels filled, the cook's store room full of freshly slaughtered meat and fish, and live turtles tied up on the deck ready to slaughter, it is not a simple matter of just setting to sea.

For, sure enough, 'in the night the Master returned with the Pinnace, and reported that there was no safe Passage for the Ship to the Northward at low water'.[81]

Very well then. At sun-up, it is none other than James Cook himself, the master of Masters, the seer of sandbars, who takes some men to take his own soundings of those sandbars and finds that, sure enough, it is exactly as Master Molineux reported.

'To windward was impossible, to leeward was a Labyrinth of Shoals.'[82]

It will take more than a few days to be fully ready in any case. They now need to make further repairs to the ship's hull – ironically, it is discovered the *Endeavour* has actually suffered a little damage while being on shore being repaired! Without a cushion of water, wood warps and cracks swiftly in this harsh New Holland sun.

A new wait begins.

23 July 1770, Endeavour River, gathering greenery, unexpected scenery

It all happens so quickly.

One moment the young sailor that Captain Cook has sent into the country to gather edible greens is just walking along, and the next he has stumbled upon four Natives in long grass having a sumptuous meal of roast cockatoo and kangaroo, the uneaten portions of which are hanging from the tree by their side.

He is one, with no weaponry bar a small knife.

They are four, with spears.

To run would be to invite acquaintance with those spears, and so, with no little presence of mind, he simply sits with them.

Pleased to meet you.

And they are clearly pleased to meet him.

Still nervous, the young man offers the Natives his knife as a gift. They examine it closely, passing it between them before they hand it back.

What they really want to examine is *him* . . . or *her*. For they remain unsure, and now is finally their moment to find out. Taking the young sailor's *mangal*, hand, in theirs they look closely, seeing how the palm and fingers are exactly the same as their own. And now they wish to look at other parts of his body, indicating they would like him to strip down. Again, they clearly have genuine but not threatening interest as they poke and prod him in various parts.

The young sailor, at length, pulls down his pants to reveal . . . it's a *yarrga*!

The whole meeting has taken some 30 minutes. Yes, everything seems to be pretty similar to their own, if only a different colour, and all appears in working order – before he is encouraged to dress again.

At this point, an incredulous Captain Cook will record, 'they suffered him to go away without offering the least insult, and perceiving that he did not go right for the Ship they directed him which way to go'.[83]

Banks, too, is fascinated by the sailor's account, less about the Natives' anatomical curiosity but their supper. He wonders in his journal: 'How they had been clever enough to take these animals is almost beyond my conception, as both of them are most shy especially the Cockatoos.'[84]

Later in the day, while botanising on, Banks follows a track and suddenly there is something completely unexpected. It is a relatively neat pile of all the clothes the white men have been giving the Natives!

Yes, there they are, 'left all in a heap together, doubtless as lumber not worth carriage. Maybe had we looked farther we should have found our other trinkets, for they seemed to set no value upon any thing we had except our turtle, which of all things we were the least able to spare them.'[85]

This is, indeed, a strange people.

Early August, Endeavour River, the leaving of the boat people

On 3 August, Captain Cook makes two attempts to sail into the teeth of the on-shore wind to get the *Endeavour* to sea, only for the wind to blow them back to the shore both times. But the late afternoon brings a blessing; the wind abates and swings around, blowing lightly offshore. Captain Cook orders the coasting anchor and cable to be laid outside the sandbar in readiness. Should the wind be fair on the morrow, they can move quickly and . . .

And sure enough. With all still calm at 5 am the next day Captain Cook orders all hands to the capstan, and within minutes the cables are springing up from the water with a healthy twang, spraying water on all sides as the men take the strain. It is a long and arduous process to first get out into the channel once more, then to gather in the cables and anchors and finally to set the sails, but by 7 am, with a 'light Air from the Land'[86] they are, sure enough, slowly heading towards the barrier of reefs; their next obstacle to the open sea. The pinnace leads the way, sounding continually, lest they run afoul once more.

4 August 1770, Leaving Endeavour River, against a sea of troubles

It is time to take pause. Sometimes in sea life there is indeed the quick and the dead, but in this situation long experience has taught Captain Cook that the quick die. After anchoring in 15 fathoms in the channel, he sends Master Molineux on his way to try to find the way through, and in the meantime he wishes to wait until low tide so he can see for himself from the masthead the lie of the reef at low tide. If there proves to be no safe passage to the East or North, he will slowly sail to the South, 'around all the shoals'[87] to skirt them on the Eastern side. The only thing he knows for sure is that as they had got the ship in here, there must indeed be a way out.

But Robert Molineux returns with the news – there might be a way!

He hasn't quite seen the Promised Land, but, far more importantly, he has found a path to the open sea – first heading East, then North, then East again through all the shallows, till they get to a half-mile break in the reefs he has found.

That afternoon, from the crow's nest, Captain Cook can see for himself exactly what the Master has reported. By heading in exactly the directions he has suggested they will come out just beyond the spot where they have been catching all the turtles, called – let's see – Turtle Reef.

The next morning, at mid-tide, the crew weigh anchors again. That light offshore wind soon freshens however, and as it is coming from the South-east, Cook must proceed with infinite care, the pinnace going ahead to make many soundings.

And so it goes. With painful precaution, they proceed until nightfall, before dropping anchor to start again the next day. For yes, each night from now on they must stop, as it is too dangerous to proceed in the dark. But it is not as if the danger stops even then.

The problem is that the anchors sometimes will not hold. On the night of 6 August, in fact, Joseph Banks wakes to the sound of shouts being added to the shrieking wind that has been buffeting the *Endeavour* for hours. Captain Cook, of course, is already on deck, his wise brown eyes darting to every corner of his vessel, keeping track of her hardware and sailors, dispensing orders – as calm as ever, but also fiercely focused.

For this time the reef is not a bump in the night, but a looming peril – in every direction. Somehow the ship has shifted in such a way that there are breakers in every direction coming at them, meaning they must be all but surrounded by submerged reefs. The menacing curling white of the enormous waves betrays the clear if still hidden dangers that lurk and smirk at the fat wooden prey now drifting towards destruction.

Quickly, Cook has the men in the pinnace out, taking soundings in the direction the ship is drifting and yelling out how many fathoms of safety they have.

The short answer in the still shrieking wind is . . . not much, and getting less all the time. And they are getting closer and closer to a reef. Captain Cook barks commands to Midshipmen and swabs alike, in the hope that the *Endeavour* will be transformed into a mere bobbing cork, which the anchors will thereafter be strong enough to hold in place, keeping them off the reef. The men bob too, each so full of nerves that he cannot stand still, shifting more than the ship does, each hoping to see something that other eyes have missed, some passage unmarked, some break in the breakers that will signal safety. They look in vain.

Alas, while in a harbour this would have surely worked, in the open sea the forces upon the *Endeavour* are just too strong and with lurch after lurch they continue to move.

By dawn of 7 August, when they can fully see the peril they are in, they realise that overnight the anchor has dragged, they have moved no less than a league from where they had dropped it at dusk! All up it is extraordinary that they had moved that far and yet not finished up on one of the shoals that threaten them from all around – including the one dead astern that the wind and tide seem now intent on casting them upon!

Mr Molineux, see to a kedge anchor if you please.

But it is having no effect!

With every passing minute, they are being driven closer and closer to destruction, and it seems nothing will be able to save them.

Like Lord Sandwich in the wee hours, however, Captain Cook has one last card to play, and he plays it now: *'Sheet anchor to the fos'cle. Man the windlass.'*

It is the anchor of last resort, the largest anchor on board, kept amidships for emergencies. So heavy it can only be dropped by a chain it will take a good dozen of the crew to get it attached to the chain and over the side.

Mercifully, however, even before that order can be executed, all of the previous moves seem to combine, and – 'Belay that command!' – as Banks will recount, 'the ship stopped and held fast, to our great joy'.[88]

Captain Cook does not join in the general celebration, aware as he is that they have likely just received a stay of execution, not a reprieve.

For now, as the tide goes out, they can see even more terrors than before as ever more shoals are exposed in every direction.

Once again Captain Cook climbs the mast to get a better take on the overall situation.

'After having well viewed our situation from the Mast Head, I saw that we were surrounded on every side with Dangers, in so much that I was quite at a loss which way to steer when the weather will permit us to get under sail.'[89]

Master Molineux is insistent. Once the weather breaks their way, they must beat back to the South-east whence they came. But Captain Cook, after consideration, is even more insistent.

'[It] would be an endless piece of work, as the winds blow constantly from that quarter, and very strong, without hardly any intermission.'[90]

And even if they could get through it would put them on the wrong side of this barrier, having to face it once more. If instead they steer to the North-east, yes there will be shoals to dodge, but at least they have some chance of breaking through the barrier and leaving it behind them. (By the by, sailing North-east they will mostly be 'sailing large', with the wind astern, while doing zig-zags through the reefs will see them sailing into the wind a bit too, 'by the wind'. In order to escape, thus, they will have to sail 'by and large', as the jacks say.)

Oh! These are the times of battering days, and shattering nights, as the next three sunrises still see unfavourable winds and roaring waves coming at them from varying angles. Every sundown in turn sees them beginning to pray that their anchors will hold to the dawn as it will not be possible to take corrective action until that time, should they start to slip. At least in the day the pinnace goes ahead and they slowly, cautiously by use of anchors, and light sail occasionally, make their way through what appear to be the deepest, safest waters.

On the morning of 11 August, they spy three islands up ahead, each dominated by a large hill, which is exactly what they need. Taking the pinnace, Captain Cook and Mr Banks go to the Northernmost and largest of the islands and climb the hill – with many lizards dashing out of their way as they go, hence the name Captain Cook gives it, 'Lizard Island' – anxious to get as close as they can to a bird's-eye view of the reefs that surround them, and find a way out.

'The Island itself was high,' Banks' journal on 11 August 1770 reads. 'We ascended the hill and when we were at the top saw plainly the Grand Reef still extending itself parallel with the shore at about the distance of 3 leagues from us or 8 from the main; through it were several channels exactly similar to those we had seen in the Islands.'[91]

As always, the view reveals grim prospects. But it is possible, and after carefully noting the position of those channels, Cook and Banks descend from the hill to sleep overnight on the island before rowing back to the *Endeavour* the next morning. Cook is quick to give Master Molineux his rough map of where the paths to redemption through these reefs lie, and commands him to send the pinnace forth.

Really, Captain Cook?

The Master is highly reluctant, pointing out just how many shoals and reefs there are that are visible, let alone unseen ones. He is highly pessimistic about their chances of getting free without coming to grief. Cook, while more than aware of the dangers, insists that every choice from here is dangerous, so they must do their best anyway to progress.

See to it, if you please, Mr Molineux.

•

Yes, most of those on board the *Endeavour* are now feeling grim, including the artist Sydney Parkinson, whose name is now on the daily sick list. But none appears to be feeling grimmer than . . . Tupia. With an unrelenting moroseness now riding dark sentinel to his ever ailing health, he has become an ever more troubling presence on the *Endeavour*, with what little energy he does have too often devoted to querulousness. He had been firmly told it would take 10 moons to get to Britain, and has counted them down ever since. When those 10 moons had at last passed, they had been still in New Holland, and his dismay and depression has deepened ever since. Does this magical place of Britain even *exist*?

'Your account about Britain being the ship's country is a mere story,' he says morosely to William Perry. 'In fact, you have risen from the bottom of the Sea.'[92]

The Surgeon's Mate smiles broadly.

'Which of the many strange sailing canoes you have seen at Tahiti, have you known to grow in the Sea?'[93]

The question gives Tupia pause. It is a good point. But he is vexed. Nothing changes their wretched situation.

'If not so,' he finishes, 'you have however lost your way and can never find . . . Britain again.'[94]

This time it is William Perry who takes pause.

'This last opinion of Tupia,' he will note, 'had more force than he was aware of, for, at the time I speak of, my own expectation of ever returning to England was very faint . . .'[95]

•

Gathered around the fire, the Guugu Yimithirr talk long of these strange visitations, these ghostly men who landed at the river mouth and, with no ceremony at all, no observation of respectful requests to pass through, or to stay, gorged themselves on the land's precious bounty, trampled her plants, frightened many of the animals and caused them to flee with the noise they make and, most disturbingly, stole many of the ancient totem, the turtle . . . before finally, blessedly, leaving on their great spirit bird.

The fire magic has worked. The *wangarr*, spirits of dead Guugu Yimithirr ancestors are gone.

All that remains is for the elders to weave accounts of this troubling event, these strange spirits, into the sacred stories that have been passed down to them from their own ancestors, the very tales of all the spirits that have created and sustained their world through the ages; the very lore the young ones around the fire will one day tell to their own children.

'Then finally one day they watched the ship sail out of the *Wahalumbaal birri* . . . and away from our Guugu Yimithirr land . . . We called them *wangarr*, spirits of our dead ancestors . . . And that name is still used to this day.'[96]

Such is the Dreaming.

CHAPTER THIRTEEN

OUTWARD BOUND

For the first time these three months we were this day out of sight of Land to our no small satisfaction: that very ocean which had formerly been looked upon with terror by (maybe) all of us was now the asylum we had long wished for and at last found. Satisfaction was clearly painted in every man's face.[1]

Joseph Banks, 14 August 1770

Batavia, formerly called Jocatra, is situated in a very large open bay, in which is a great number of low islands. It is walled round, and has many canals cut through it . . .[2]

Sydney Parkinson, 1770

Batavia is certainly a place that Europeans need not covet to go to; but if necessity obliges them, they will do well to make their stay as short as possible, otherwise they will soon feel the effects of the unwholesome air of Batavia, which, I firmly believe, is the Death of more Europeans than any other place upon the Globe of the same extent.[3]

Captain Cook, 'Description of Batavia', 26 December 1770

15 August 1770, HMS *Endeavour*, the open sea

In his entire 23 years at sea, Captain Cook has never seen the like. Yes, the day before they had at last found passage through the reef before tacking to the North, and had soon left the long line of shoals in their wake. But now that dawn has risen on the new day?

Captain Cook gasps just to see it – dead ahead and stretching forever. Yet *more* reef.

Truly, James Cook cannot believe how vast this thing is:

> . . . we saw a reef, between us and the land, extending away to the
> Southward, and, as we thought, terminated here to the Northward

abreast of us; but this was only an opening, for soon after we saw it extend away to the Northward as far as we could distinguish anything.[4]

With infinite care, thus, Cook sets a Northerly course and continues until the night closes in, whereupon he tacks and stands to the Southeast – fearing getting too close to the reef in a night as black as pitch. After some two miles, the night air falls still as a tomb and the *Endeavour* is becalmed in water so deep a 140 fathom line can't find the bottom. The best they can do is hope that they are far enough away from the reefs to get through the night without being cast upon them, only . . .

Only for Captain Cook to wake with a start at 4 am to the unmistakable sound of roiling surf breaking on what must be a not-so-distant reef!

Cook paces the deck, straining both his eyes and his ears for a clue about the level of danger. It's loud, so it's likely dangerous. As his vision extends for no more than a few yards of the deck, his key hope is that the terrifying roaring sound of the breakers on the reefs will grow fainter.

Alas, alas, it does not and all sailors with him on deck know it. Rarely have they felt so far from home as now. At any second, it seems, they might hit yet another crop of coral down here in the unexplored South Seas, far beyond the edges of the known world . . . and that would be that, their fates a mystery to those at home forever, their bodies sacrificed on the altar of the reef, their *Endeavour* and their endeavour lost, all for naught.

As the black sky lifts a little to grey, Captain Cook makes out 'vast foaming breakers',[5] crashing down on, yes, a very nearby reef. 'Not a mile from us,' records the Captain. And every surge of the swell is carrying them ever closer to it.

Drop the anchors?

If only they could.

'We had at this time not an air of wind,' Captain Cook chronicles, 'and the depth of the water was unfathomable so that there was not a possibility of Anchoring.'[6]

'In this distressed Situation we had nothing but Providence,'[7] records the Captain, invoking the Lord's divine protection for the first time since they had sailed from England. On the chance that God won't help, however, he also has another plan.

Bosun, see to your oarsmen and launch the long-boat and yawl.

The pinnace, alas, is currently under repair, with a plank missing from its hull. But they will likely need it. Captain Cook barks orders to start repairing the pinnace, *now*.

With a rush, the first of the two boats is lowered, while a flurry of sawing and hammering breaks out around the pinnace.

In the meantime, as chronicled by Banks, 'Two large Oars or sweeps were got out at the stern ports to pull the ships head round the other way in hopes that might delay till the boats were out.'[8]

In the absence of rudder-steerage, it is the only hope they have of turning the ship away from danger. Yes, these are desperate times, requiring desperate measures. Redoubling their efforts, the rest of the crew soon have the yawl and the long-boat out before the bow, a long cable strung from each and fastened securely to the ship.

In a few minutes, they'll know if they will live or die – And stroke! And *stroke*! And STROKE!

Row, row, row your 400-ton ship merrily away from the reef . . .

Their red-faced, grunting efforts indeed slow the *Endeavour*'s approach to the reef, but it does not arrest it and by 6 am she is 'not above 80 or 100 yards from the breakers'.[9]

And still the men sounding the depths cannot feel the bottom.

The air is filled with salt-spray, another wave lifts the *Endeavour* high and surges her forward to the reef, dropping the ship just before it is surely dashed to splinters.

And the next wave surges towards them, sure as night and day . . . STROKE, MEN! STROKKKKKE!

'The same sea that washed the side of the ship rose in a breaker prodigiously high the very next time it did rise,' Cook chronicles, 'so that between us and destruction was only a dismal valley, the breadth of one wave, and even now no ground could be felt with 120 fathoms.'[10]

For the first time in his life, despite his projection of calm, Captain Cook is quietly convinced the battle is lost, any moment now they could very likely drown like rats.

'Yet in this Truly Terrible Situation,' he will chronicle proudly, 'not one man ceased to do his utmost, and that with as much calmness as if no danger had been near. All the dangers we had escaped were little in comparison . . .'[11]

Captain Cook is not alone in his gloomy forecast. Every man-jack among them feels the same, starting with Joseph Banks. 'A speedy death was all we had to hope for and that from the vastness of the Breakers which must quickly dash the ship all to pieces was scarce to be doubted.'[12]

But they are not quite done for yet.

Stand by to lower the pinnace!

Normally under such circumstances a newly repaired boat would be lowered first with one or two men only, to see if it floats. But there is no time. It is lowered with a full crew on the reckoning that it must float and go to the assistance of the other boats, or all is lost anyway.

And it does float!

The men row ahead to where they join the jacks in the other two boats, heaving with all their might to get the ship clear of the breakers.

Still the rollers surge upon the reef, each one lifting up His Majesty's ship, carrying her a few yards forward, and depositing her in the valley between waves, closer to doom. The 30 men in the three small vessels continue to haul with everything they have, making no headway, until . . . It happens.

Is it . . . ?

Yes!

A breath of *wind*!

It is, as Joseph Banks notes, 'so small that at any other time in a calm we should not have observed it',[13] but at this time it is more than merely observed, it is hailed as a miracle, as it is the only chance they have to live. Could it be Providence, after all?

Make sail! Make sail, Mr Molineux!

Make sail they do, the jack tars following the Master's orders – 'Sharp up to starboard!' 'Be ready to right the helm!' – to get as much canvas up as possible to capture the breath of God.

In less than a minute, the result is obvious. It is working! The wind has checked their progress towards catastrophe and the ship is now moving a very little, on slanting direction, away from the breakers. Alas, alas, as wonderful as the small breeze is, after just 10 minutes it falls away to such a point that a strong debate breaks out about which direction exactly the minute wind is now currently blowing in. Banks watches in disbelief as Cook throws small pieces of paper overboard to see where the tiny breeze might take them, or if any evidence of a breeze can be seen. It cannot.

Once more destruction beckons . . . when again God lightly whistles a hymn in their direction for, as Banks records, 'Our little friendly Breeze now visited us again and lasted about as long as before, thrusting us possibly 100 yards farther from the breakers: we were still however in the very jaws of destruction.'[14]

And yet perhaps the Lord might visit one more miracle upon them? For there it is!

About a furlong up ahead, they suddenly see an exceedingly small opening in the reef, so narrow it is only a little wider than their ship is long. By one measure it is madness to think they could get their ship through it. On the other hand, they have no choice – and if they can get through it, they can already see the calm waters that wait on the other side.

'The fear of Death is Bitter,' Banks records. 'The prospect we now had before us of saving our lives [made] my heart set much lighter on its throne, and I suppose there were none but what felt the same sensations.'[15]

Now the yawl and the pinnace are set in different directions, no longer trying in unison to pull the *Endeavour* out of the breaking swell, but instead, in opposition to one another, each tug correcting the course bit by bit, trying to make the mighty ship veer towards the tiny gap in the reef.

There is one exception to the all-in straining or at least furious focus from the gunwales. For in a display so very typical of him, the astronomer Charles Green chooses this time to 'shoot the sun' and calculate their longitude. After all, if they are about to die, they may as well know *where* they are dying!

'These observations were very good,' Green will record blithely, 'the limbs of sun and moon very distinct, and a good horizon. We were about 100 yards from the reef, where we expected the ship to strike every minute . . . the swell heaving us right on.'[16]

Lieutenant Hicks, meanwhile, orders the men in the pinnace to row alongside the ship, where he calls up to the quarter-deck: 'Captain, the opening is narrow, but it is a good anchorage and there is a passage quite free from shoals.'[17]

For all of Lieutenant Hicks' optimism, and all of their prayers, it still does not seem very likely. And yet, perhaps the Lord is watching over them after all, for now all of the tides, their comrades hauling oars in the boats and Providence itself seem to be with them as they indeed nudge towards this propitious opening.

But it is not to be. Instead, an ebbing tide proves the solution, gushing outward through the opening in the reef, it carries the *Endeavour* in the

opposite direction intended, but nevertheless they are out of the breakers
. . . into a new kind of hell. Around noon Captain Cook records, 'We had
got an Offing of 1 1/2 or 2 Miles, yet we could hardly flatter ourselves
with hopes of getting Clear, even if a breeze should Spring up, as we
were by this time embayed by the Reef, and the Ship, in Spite of our
Endeavours, driving before the Sea into the bight. The Ebb had been
in our favour, and we had reason to Suppose the flood which was now
made would be against us.'[18]

Yes, ebb and flow, give and take, by and large the incoming tide
will undoubtedly drive them back towards mortal peril. In desperation,
Captain Cook climbs the mast to look for any option that *doesn't* look
like certain destruction . . .

There?

It is another deep opening in the reef, a mile to the Westward.
Lieutenant Hicks is immediately sent forth to examine the possibilities,
and he returns soon with his views. Narrow, yes. Dangerous, certainly.
But without doubt it is their only hope, and so they try, their efforts
being met with a blessing: 'A light breeze soon after sprung up at East-
North-East, with which, the help of our Boats, and a flood tide, we
soon entered the opening, and was hurried through in a short time by
a rapid tide like a mill race, which kept us from driving against either
side, though the channel was not more than a 1/4 of a mile broad.'[19]

Having entered a kind of coral harbour, Banks notes the irony of
their situation: 'two days [ago] our utmost wishes were crowned by
getting without the reef and today we were made again happy by getting
within it'.[20]

For now Captain Cook has the men drop anchor to secure the ship
for the moment. But their ordeal is far from over.

Right now, the key problem is to continue to survive, and Captain
Cook is under no further illusions. He has learnt his lesson . . . twice . . .
and now he must change course. Given that 10 leagues off the shores of
New Holland in these parts there appears to be an all but impenetrable
maze of reefs, which extend South to North for a distance unknown,
the only way to lift their chances of survival is to stay squarely to the
West of those reefs, and sail North in the calmer passage of water that
lies between the reef and the mainland. At least, this way, if they get
into trouble again, and the ship is lost, they might be able to get some of
the men safely on land. Captain Cook further decides to make no more

landings on this coast other than for water. They must get to Batavia, the key port of the Dutch East Indies, to treat the growing number of sick men, and to rest.

Although no reasonable man could disagree with this course of action, Captain Cook remains all too aware that an unreasonable man named Alexander Dalrymple awaits in London, likely all too ready to criticise him, and so he includes a rare piece of explanation and reflection in the log about the pressures, pleasures and problems of the leader 'employed as a discoverer'.[21]

Is it worth it? And what will armchair critics say of the perils undergone and foregone? Captain Cook has little doubt.

'People will hardly admit of an excuse for a Man leaving a Coast unexplored he has once discovered.'[22]

After all, he is here on a voyage of discovery.

'If dangers are his excuse,' the Captain opines, 'he is then charged with Timorousness and want of Perseverance, and at once pronounced to be the most unfit man in the world to be employed as a discoverer; if, on the other hand, he boldly encounters all the dangers and Obstacles he meets with, and is unfortunate enough not to succeed, he is then charged with Temerity, and, perhaps, want of Conduct.'[23]

It seems he can't win either way. Observe the dangers, you are a coward. Ignore the dangers, and fall foul, you are a fallen fool.

'The former of these aspersions, I am confident, can never be laid to my charge, and if I am fortunate to surmount all the dangers we meet with, the latter will never be brought in question; although I must own that I have engaged more among the islands and shoals upon this Coast than perhaps in prudence I ought to have done with a single Ship.'[24]

His reasoning chronicled, his defence put in place against whatever charge Mr Dalrymple might lay against him, Captain Cook keeps the *Endeavour* moving up the East coast of New Holland, always on the lookout for the coastline to finally fall away (oh, and reefs, of course), and, ideally, a passage to the West to be revealed.

For yes, it really is time to now get home.

22 August 1770, Possession Island, in the name of His British Majesty

They first see it on 21 August. The North-trending coast falls away to the West, just as James Cook had hoped.

Looking through his spyglass from the crow's nest, it is clear that he and his men have at last reached the Northernmost tip of New Holland, and there is indeed what appears to be a Westward passage.

The next morning, 22 August 1770, the *Endeavour* drops anchor beside an island just to the West of what Captain Cook has named 'Cape York', and he is shortly being rowed ashore by 10 Marines in the company of Mr Banks, the Doctor and Mr Green, whereupon, as flitting black figures recede in the distance, the four of them climb to the top of the island's highest hill – barely three times the height of the *Endeavour*'s mastheads – and Captain Cook turns his spyglass West.

With expert eyes, scanning back and forth – with the others watching him earnestly, seeking a sign about whether the gods are with them or agin them – it does not take long. Cook finally smiles, a rare enough event to be worthy of remark. It bodes well.

There *is* a way through 'a strait, at least as far as we could see, without any obstruction',[25] which, from appearances, should get them out of deep trouble and into deep water.

Hurrah!

It is the difference between being able to go fairly directly West to the Dutch colony of Batavia, or being forced to turn back and go all the way around the top of New Guinea – a difference of many weeks, and likely of life and death for many of the exhausted, ailing crew.

And now, after descending the hill to rejoin the Marines, all in their rather tattered and faded red coats and tricorn hats – for they have been ordered to dress as formally as they can for the occasion – it is time to perform a particular ceremony, which is the second reason that Cook has come ashore.[26]

Now, ideally, Captain Cook could follow instructions from Admiralty to the letter and, 'with the Consent of the Natives . . . take Possession of Convenient Situations in the Country in the Name of the King of Great Britain'.[27]

But, under the circumstances, claiming possession 'with the Consent of the Natives' is simply not possible. The Natives parley with the white men when *they* want, not the other way around, for they are the masters of this domain. And, as ever in New Holland, they had simply melted away as soon as the white spirit-people had set ghostly feet upon this small island, leaving no-one in the vicinity who could consent.

First the Union Jack is taken from its pack, attached to a flagpole, and lifted high. Now taking the Letters Patent from his inside pocket, Captain Cook reads:

> George by the grace of God, King of England . . . Know ye that of our especial grace, certain science and mere motion, we have given and granted . . . free liberty and licence from time to time, and at all times for ever hereafter, to discover, find, search out, and view such remote, heathen and barbarous lands, countries and territories not actually possessed of any Christian prince or people, as to [King George], his heirs . . . and to every or any of them, shall seem good: and . . . to have, hold, occupy and enjoy to him, his heirs . . . for ever, with all commodities, jurisdictions, and royalties both by sea and land and . . . our heirs and successors, shall go and travel thither, to inhabit or remain there, to build and fortify at [our] discretion . . .[28]

And so, in the name of King George III, Captain Cook does hereby claim for Great Britain 'the Eastern Coast [of New Holland] from the Latitude of 38 degrees South down to this place'.[29]

At the conclusion of his words, the Marines, with their muskets pointed to the sky, follow the barked commands of Sergeant Edgcumbe and fire off three volleys. They are answered by three joyous volleys from the ship.

It is done. From the point of view of Great Britain, this land is now the sovereign territory of Great Britain. The ancient land itself does not blink, just as her ancient people have not the tiniest awareness of the significance of what has occurred.

And in fact, for Captain Cook personally, it is not of particular note, being accorded just a scant few lines in his journal, while Joseph Banks doesn't even give it that. It is no more than a small task, as ordered by the Admiralty, ticked off at the last possible moment. Once accomplished, it will be for the wise heads of London, much later, to decide what weight to give it.

But what to call this Eastern side of New Holland of which he has just taken possession? It is no Great Southern Land, but at least it can be a southern *something*.

After some consideration, Cook writes it down in his log, 'South Wales' – on the grounds that much of the topography of this coast reminds him of that place. Yes, that's it.

(Later he will remember there is already a place near Ontario named New Wales, so with a couple of strokes of his pen, just as he had modified the name of Sting Ray Bay to Botany Bay, he will change it to 'New South Wales'.[30])

For Banks' part, aware that they are finally leaving New Holland, or New Wales, he takes the opportunity to record his own reflections on the country and its inhabitants.

'Upon the whole New Holland, though in every respect the most barren country I have seen, is not so bad but that between the productions of sea and Land a company of People who should have the misfortune of being shipwrecked upon it might support themselves, even by the resources that we have seen.'[31]

A place to start a colony, perhaps? Joseph Banks does not even raise the possibility. And yet his next words at least make clear that if Britain does pursue that path, resistance from the locals – in strict contrast to the situation in New Zealand[32] – will likely be minimal at best.

'This immense tract of Land, the largest known which does not bear the name of a continent, as it is considerably larger than all Europe, is thinly inhabited even to admiration, at least that part of it that we saw: we never but once saw so many as thirty Indians together and that was a family.'[33]

Perhaps there might be a large population inland?

No, Joseph Banks is sure the inland is 'totally uninhabited'.[34]

As a matter of fact, Banks notes that New Holland has 'a soil so barren and at the same time entirely void of the help derived from cultivation could not be supposed to yield much towards the support of man'.[35]

And now for one of the most puzzling things about the Natives. In the simple way they live, these people don't seem to want anything and they don't steal!

The virtues of such a simple life are obvious to Banks.

'From them appear how small are the real wants of human nature, which we Europeans have increased to an excess which would certainly appear incredible to these people could they be told it. Nor shall we cease to increase them as long as Luxuries can be invented and riches found for the purchase of them; and how soon these Luxuries degenerate into necessaries may be sufficiently evinced by the universal use of strong liquors, Tobacco, spices, Tea etc. etc.'[36]

Captain Cook's own thoughts run along similar lines. 'These people may truly be said to be in the pure state of Nature,' he will note, 'and may appear to some to be the most wretched upon Earth: but in reality they are far more happier than we Europeans, being wholly unacquainted not only with the superfluous but also of the necessary conveniences so much sought after in Europe they are happy in not knowing the use of them. They live [in a Tranquillity] which is not disturbed by the inequality of condition, the Earth and Sea of their own accord furnishes them with all things necessary for life; they covert not Magnificent Houses Household-stuff & c. they sleep as sound in a small hovel or even in the open as the King in His Palace on a Bed of Down.'[37]

The *Endeavour*'s crew weigh anchor, set the sails and follow the sun as she falls towards yonder horizon.

17 September 1770, Savu, a rum Rajah and a Dutch treat

As close as the *Endeavour* is now drawing to Batavia, its crew is closer still to running out of supplies. Scurvy also stalks close, sending newly ill sailors to Surgeon Monkhouse almost daily.

Almost all of the renewed supplies from New Holland have been eaten. There is no salted beef left. Nor sea biscuit. Certainly no vegetables, they've not eaten vegetables in weeks. They can barely remember what fruit tastes like. They simply must stop for supplies at the nearest port, which proves to be the small island of Savu, where as Cook rhapsodises, 'we saw Houses, Cocoa Nut Trees, and a Flock of Cattle grazing; these were Temptations hardly to be withstood by people in our situation'.[38]

Lieutenant Gore is sent ashore as emissary for Captain Cook and is most surprised to find himself greeted outside the gates of the Rajah's palace by a curiously rag-tag yet charming kind of dark man in a sarong and coat who turns out to be the Rajah of Savu himself.

In a welcome change, the Rajah – the leader of the Native population, under the yoke of the Dutch – proves entirely open to all of Lieutenant Gore's requests. Fruit? Livestock? Wine, water, whatever you like! Of course we here in Savu can help you poor Britishers, we would be simply delighted! Lieutenant Gore beams, relieved that their storerooms and bellies will be empty no more.

But there is just one thing . . .

The only complication is they must involve a representative from the Dutch East India Company, you understand? Of course. That representative, another rather rag-tag fellow, though indeed a Dutchman – Johan

Lange – arrives a few hours later, and proves as eager to trade with the *Endeavour* as it is with him.

Wonderful! Cook and his crew are saved and the market is open. Although, there is just one thing . . .

The Rajah and Mr Lange would love – if it's not too much trouble of course – to come aboard the *Endeavour* and dine with them. Well yes, sure, but we are a little low on supplies . . .

Nevertheless, the Rajah's excitement and insistence prove irresistible, and it is a bemused if confused Captain Cook who that day welcomes the Rajah and *Meneer* Lange, and their surprisingly large retinue, aboard for lunch.

Of course, for such an occasion, they must empty the last of the cellar's wines, and have the next-to-last of their ship's animals slaughtered. At the first taste of the wine the Rajah seems most gratified, even commenting, 'I do not imagine that you, who are white men, would suffer me, who is black to sit down in your company.'[39]

Taken aback, Cook assures him that their ship and table is made all the more resplendent with his presence. Everyone assembled begins to drink and in short order the remainder of the *Endeavour*'s food is brought out. The Rajah has never eaten such delicacies. This? What is this? *Mutton.* What does it come from? *Sheep.*

'I desire to have an *English* sheep,'[40] the Rajah suddenly says, with the barest trace of menace as to what will happen if he does not get it. Captain Cook hesitates, as there is but a single sheep left. Yet trade is their only avenue, their only path forward, and if their last sheep must be sacrificed, it is a small price to pay. Hand it over, men. So be it, now can we get on with the trade . . .

'I desire an English dog!' now cries the Rajah, a single four-legged beast not quite enough for him.

Ah. Ah, well Mr Banks has a dog, a beautiful one at that. Two even! Surely he could part with one? A terribly reluctant Mr Banks considers the proposition though ultimately presents one of his greyhounds as a *present* for the Rajah. There you are, sir, take good care of him, won't you? The Rajah is ecstatic and brings an end to the lunch and his requests by assuring the assembled company that tomorrow morning, at the beach, they will have, 'buffaloes, sheep, hogs, and fowls!'[41]

The Rajah is seen off with a three-gun salute, the sound almost drowned out by the cheers from the men as he is rowed back ashore.

The ship's company all sleep well that night, dreaming of the breakfast they have secured for themselves tomorrow morning.

The sun rises to reveal the beach full of . . . nothing. Sand and seaweed aplenty, a little driftwood, but no buffaloes, no hogs, no Natives, no coolies driving their flocks and herds forward. Underwhelmed, but careful not to jump to conclusions, Captain Cook and Mr Banks go ashore to the 'grand palace', which, now that they look at it for themselves, is not so 'grand' at all. Some questioning reveals that it is a public assembly room, not a palace.

Captain Cook can feel a prickling sensation rising to a flushed heat. And yet, as the Captain feels his temper rising within, suddenly, a miracle . . .

Here comes the Rajah now!

Gentlemen! A terrible misunderstanding has taken place, a mistake that must be fixed. Yes, yes, everything we promised will be here, but not today. It will all be here tomorrow.

Captain Cook and Joseph Banks are reticent. And yet, despite their suspicions, the Rajah soon has the Captain, the botanist and the majority of the crew in a large house sitting before an excellent meal of dripping, succulent pork and ruby-red wine that is being 'passed briskly about',[42] when Mr Lange appears suddenly with a letter in hand. Bad news.

It's from the Governor of Timor, the Rajah explains, and you'll find that it says: *we can't trade with you.* The livestock is ready, so are the vegetables and fruits, but a Dutch ship is due in port this day, and the Governor has already promised them supplies as well. It just wouldn't be proper to trade with the Englishmen before the next visitors arrive. No matter, says Lange, he will sort it out himself, if only the Captain will afford him some more time. James Cook is tired of these delays, but once again finds himself without an alternative. Fine, Lange, go and sort it out.

Lange returns with a result, claiming he has secured a bevy of buffalo for the Englishmen to collect this very evening. We shouldn't worry about such things, not when the sun is high in the sky and wine flows freely, so feels the representative of the Dutch East India Trading Company. The lunch drags on to the evening, at which point the crew – well-fed and watered – stumble back to the ship, eager to see the fresh produce Lange has left them on the shore. Approaching the beach, a sense of *déjà vu* grips the crew. For the second time today, the beach is bare. Captain Cook sends a message as quickly as he can, demanding to know the meaning of this. Lange responds that it is no more than another misunderstanding, a hiccup really. Lange insists that he understands the Captain's frustrations, that he is also upset, but truly, what can he do? He is no more than a middleman. Maybe if they try again tomorrow, the Governor of Timor may be able to smooth things over with another letter? Oh and on that note, the Natives would prefer gold to bartering, perhaps you Englishmen should bring gold with you. Though they are entirely sheepless, the Captain and his gentlemen are quite certain that they have been fleeced.

Cook has had it. Tomorrow will be different.

The next morning, James Cook wakes to see great brown shapes lumbering about the beach. Buffaloes. Finally, the trade they have been promised is within sight, though precious little does it calm the Captain's frustrations. He is too wise to think that everything will continue unabated, and rows ashore with his guard up, their boats laden with gold and muskets. This time, the well-travelled and Dutch-speaking Dr Solander is in tow, ready to interpret and cut through any potential language barriers. The first Native is approached.

How about three guineas for a buffalo? No sale.

All right then, a musket for a buffalo? No, thank you.

Dr Solander inquires as to why they won't trade.

Mr Lange has told us not to. He takes a cash commission on each and every purchase and he has left specific instructions to ask five guineas per buffalo. Not only that, but the 'Rajah' is in on it as well, he skims off the top the same as Lange. A protection racket, here at the end of the Earth. Furious that three precious days have been wasted entertaining charlatans and cheats, Cook decides to introduce some good old-fashioned free market capitalism.

Why bow down to these meddling middlemen? Five guineas for the first buffalo, and a musket for each one thereafter! Say, you Natives wouldn't mind a few firearms, would you? In a matter of moments, literal herds of buffalo are brought onto the beach and the Englishmen are given their pick of the litter. Just don't tell Johan or that Rajah, there's no reason for them to find out.

The *Endeavour* stocks up with a mass of supplies as Banks records '8 buffalos, 30 dozen of fowls, 6 sheep, 3 hogs, some few but very few limes and cocoa nuts, a little garlic, a good many eggs . . . an immense quantity of Syrup which was bought for trifles, several hundred gallons at least – upon the whole more than live-stock enough to carry us to Batavia'.[43]

Now fully stocked with chooks cheek by beak and all the rest squashed in together, all prepared for the journey ahead, Cook is delighted with what proves to be the cherry on top. It is Johan Lange, sprinting in an ungainly fashion across the beach. By the time he reaches the white men, he is out of breath.

Captain Cook, I'm terribly sorry, there seems to have been another *misunder* . . .

All that Cook understands is that Johan Lange is too late. Oh yes, his voice is now 'all sweetness and softness' when in the past it had been 'as sour as verjuice' but the damage has been done. Lange prattles on about riches untold if 'we might come ashore the next day',[44] but the proverbial ship has sailed in much the same way the real one is about to. As Banks tells it 'Our business was quite done'[45] and he is as thrilled as the Captain to sail away from the scams of Savu and its so-called 'Rajah'. At least the men now have plenty of fresh greens and meat to help restore their health in relatively short time.

7 October 1770, Batavia, port of death

There is always a fraught moment when European ships arrive in foreign colonies after a long time spent at sea with no contact. Has, perchance, war been declared between the ship's home country and the colonial power whose port this is? Are soldiers about to storm aboard to take the crew and the ship into custody?

But no, as the *Endeavour* arrives in the Dutch port of Batavia on this day, all seems sleepy and calm. A lone Dutch ship does indeed come out to block their approach, but instead of soldiers and Marines forcing their way on board, it gives birth only to a small long-boat with a large Dutch pennant, from which steps a rather scrawny Dutch official with several even more scrawny underlings and sundry sailors asking them their purpose in these parts, how long they intend to stay and so forth.

As the Dutchman speaks, the men of the *Endeavour* keep staring at the Dutch entourage.

For *look* at this official and his men.

'Both himself and his people were almost as Spectres,' Joseph Banks notes, 'no good omen of the healthiness of the country we were arrived at; our people however who truly might be called rosy and plump for we had not a sick man among us, Jeered and flouted much at their brother seamen's white faces'.[46]

Captain Cook himself is no less than proud of the health of his men, pointing out for the Admiralty that, 'Lieut. Hicks, Mr. Green, and Tupia were the only people that had any complaints occasioned by a long continuance at Sea'.[47]

But yes, noting the sickly pallor of the Batavia officials, with the only colour coming from the greenness of their gills, Cook resolves to move as swiftly as possible to get his men back on the open sea again as soon as it can be done.

Indeed, if not for the mishap and near shipwreck on the reef, they would have been able to bypass Batavia entirely. But the *Endeavour* needs full repairs that only a European outpost can provide in order to journey back across the world to England.

At noon on 9 October, Captain Cook receives permission to enter the port from the Dutch officials and sails the *Endeavour* towards the harbour, at length, standing in Batavia Road.

'I sent Lieutenant Hicks ashore,' Captain Cook chronicles, 'to acquaint the Governor of our Arrival, and to make an excuse for not Saluting; as we could only do it with 3 Guns I thought it was better let alone.'[48]

Next, Captain Cook summons his Carpenter, Mr Satterly, to deliver his list of the ship's deficiencies.

> The Defects of His Majesty's Bark Endeavour . . .
> The Ship very leaky (as she makes from 12 to 6 Inches water per hour), occasioned by her Main Keel being wounded in many places . . . The false Keel gone beyond the Midships (from Forward and perhaps further), as I had no opportunity of seeing for the water when hauled ashore for repair. Wounded on her Starboard side under the Main Chains, where I imagine is the greatest leaks (but could not come at it for the water). One pump on the Starboard side useless, the others decayed within 1 1/2 Inch of the bore, otherwise Masts, Yards, Boats, and Hull in pretty good condition. Dated in Batavia Road, this 10th of October, 1770.
> J. SATTERLY.[49]

In the meantime, Dutch carpenters take a look at the ship, too. They gravely inform Captain Cook that the repairs required for the *Endeavour* are even *more* extensive and expensive than first thought.

First things first, at precisely 5 pm on Friday, 12 October, the smiling James Cook is 'introduced to the Governor-General, who received me very politely and told me that I should have everything I wanted'.[50]

And yet that very evening something happens which is almost a symbol of how potentially dangerous this place is, how disaster might strike at any moment, any of them, and it is only for the gods to decide who they will smite.

In the middle of a fierce storm, lightning strikes and destroys instantly the two mainmasts of the Dutch ship standing next to the *Endeavour* in port. Cook, a man of science, regards it with interest as a lesson:

> She [the Dutch ship] had had an Iron Spindle at the Main Topgallant Masthead which had first attracted the Lightning. The ship lay about 2 Cable lengths from us, and we were struck with the Thunder at the same time, and in all probability we should have shared the same fate as the Dutchman, had it not been for the Electrical Chain which we had but just before got up; this carried the Lightning or Electrical matter over the side clear of the Ship. The Shock was so great as to shake the whole ship very sensibly. This instance alone is sufficient to recommend these Chains to all Ships whatever, and that of the Dutchman ought to Caution people from having Iron Spindles at their Mast heads.[51]

(Typically, for James Cook, it is not enough that disaster has been averted. As conscientious as ever, he must do what he can so others can also be spared.)

As to how Captain Cook will pay for the repairs and victuals, he discovers no private means whereby an advance of money could be sought to cover the *Endeavour*'s repair, and so he pens a formal epistle to the Governor:

> Lieutenant James Cook, Commander of His Britannic Majesty's Bark the *Endeavour*, begs leave to represent to His Excellency the Right Honourable Petrus Albertus Van der Parra, Governor-General, etc., etc., That he will be in want of a Sum or Sums of Money in order to defray the Charge he will be at in repairing and refitting His Britannic Majesty's Ship at this place; which sum or sums of money he is directed by his Instructions, and empowered by his commission, to give Bills of Exchange on the respective Offices which Superintend His Britannic Majesty's Navy.

The said Lieutenant James Cook Requests of His Excellency,
That he will be pleased to order him to be supplied with such
sum or sums of money, either out of the Company's Treasure, or
permit such private persons to do it as may be willing to advance
money for Bills of Exchange on the Honourable and Principal
Officers and Commissioners of His Britannic Majesty's Navy,
the Commissioners for Victualling His Majesty's Navy, and the
Commissioners for taking care of the Sick and Hurt.

Dated on board His Britannic Majesty's Bark the *Endeavour*, in
Batavia Road, the 16th of October, 1770.

JAMES COOK[52]

•

On 18 October, the *Endeavour* is anchored off Cooper's Isle, lying off
the mainland in the Western side of the bay – a 10-acre patch of land
where the Dutch keep much of their spices in long warehouses that
lie parallel to each other – while Cook arranges for some space to be
allotted to land the ship's stores. After several days, the necessary orders
are in place, and on 23 October they land the stores. Here is where the
hard work begins. William Perry writes: '. . . the vessel was hauled up,
and lashed head and stern, alongside the jetty or wharf, immediately
dismantled, her stores all lodged ashore . . .'[53]

Divested of her finery, the ship's hull is then kept in readiness for
warping over to the nearby island of Onrust for careening and repairs.[54]

A caretaker crew is brought aboard, most of the ship's company are
able to pitch tents on Cooper's Isle[55] – in the shade 'neath a grove of
trees, by a wharf, a perfect place to take their rest, idly watching the
coolies constantly unloading some ships of spices, while loading others.

Captain Cook's servants erect a large marquee in which the Captain
may work in airy comfort, and a tent for him to sleep in.

Sydney Parkinson, meanwhile, free from all ship-related duties, strolls
around the city, writing enthusiastically of the scene, 'The roads which
lead from the city are many, and as good as ours in England; they
extend a long way into the country, and are so many avenues, planted
with Tamarind, Cocoa, Pisang, Bread-fruit, Jacca, Duriam, and Allango,
trees, which render them very pleasant. There is a great number of villas
all along these roads, many of which have a magnificent appearance.
In brief, the whole country looks like a garden, divided into different

plantations by hedge-rows of trees and canals which are so convenient and enrich the views of the country.'[56]

For Joseph Banks, the time of restoration in a European port will be spent in his usual way, leisure and pleasure. (As much as either can prove possible in a place like Batavia.)

Having spent the first few days exploring this European outpost, Banks is feeling a little more assured, though still with certain misgivings, 'Being now a little settled I hired a small house next door to the hotel on the Left hand for which I paid 10 Rix 2£/ a month; here Our books etc. were lodged but here we were far from private, Every Dutchman almost that came by running in and asking what we had to sell, for it seems that Hardly any individual had ever been at Batavia before who had not something or other to sell.'[57]

It is time to send for Tupia, who has remained on board the ship owing to his bilious illness.

Frail and pale, the Tahitian steps from the *Endeavour* long-boat onto the Batavia dock and looks around in sheer astonishment, as does young Tayeto, who has come with him. *The streets! The houses! The lanterns in the middle of the night!*

It is an astonishment that only grows in Tupia and Tayeto as they slowly follow Banks' servant, young John Roberts, through the port town.

Yes, of course the white men have previously told them stories about streets – wide pathways covered so completely with flat rocks that they are hard all over, free from any soft dirt. And they have equally told the Tahitians about houses that are entirely made out of flat rocks called 'bricks'.

But nothing could have prepared them for the wonder of what they see now. The brightly coloured clothing of all the people! Tigers in cages! The huge stone walls of the fort, with scampering monkeys atop! A bridge that lifts up so ships can pass by! The grand houses, higher than 10 huts! The carriages, drawn by these extraordinary beasts called – how do you say it? – *horses!* Rivers built by men that run absolutely straight, which they call canals.

Tupia and Tayeto are every bit as enchanted with the Dutch stronghold as the Englishmen had been with the Arcadian wonder of Tahiti.

Everything fascinates them.

Tupia's own presence is less remarked upon by the locals in regarding him, as there really *are* people here from all over the world. Though the Dutch are masters, the greater part of the inhabitants serving the company are Germans, Danes, Swedes and Hungarians, all with their own style of dress, most of it colourful.

'The men are dressed excessively gay,' Sydney Parkinson observes, 'having silk and velvet garments, richly laced and embroidered, with laced hats, and finely-dressed wigs.'[58]

Not that any of the Europeans or Natives seem to do much hard work.

That is reserved for the ubiquitous Chinese, who, the way Banks sees it, are remarkable for both their work ethic and lack of ethics generally. 'There is nothing,' he notes, 'be it of what nature it will, clean or dirty, honest or dishonest . . . which a Chinese will not readily do for money; they work diligently and laboriously . . . loath to lose sight of their main point, money getting. No sooner do they leave off work than they begin to game, either at Cards, dice or some one of the thousand games they have which are unknown to us in Europe . . . In short it is as extraordinary a sight to see a China man Idle, as it is to see a Dutchman or Indian at work.'[59]

All up, it is an extraordinarily cosmopolitan settlement, with so many people from so many lands, and, in that case, Tupia says, he no longer wishes to wear the suit of the English sailor. He is a proud Tahitian man, and wishes to dress like a Tahitian.

Very well then.

'South Sea cloth was sent for on board,' Banks notes, 'and he clothed himself according to his taste.'[60]

The simple fact of being back on land, once more in his native dress, seems to act as a tonic for Tupia, and he even agrees to do something that Banks has been begging him to do for weeks – eat. For there are plantains, bread-fruit, cocoa nuts; foods that Tupia is more accustomed to and scarfs down heartily, and so his health improves as the days pass by.

Captain Cook is relieved at Tupia's seeming recovery. On the general subject of health, Captain Cook recorded a very noteworthy thing which he had neglected to put in his log upon arrival, but now wished to bring to the Admiralty's attention: 'I had forgot to mention, that upon our arrival here I had not one man upon the Sick List.'[61]

And yet, despite their early impressions of Batavia being an outpost of sunny civilisation, a place for recovery and restoration, they come to understand it is also a place where illness and death are so commonplace they are barely remarked upon.

'It is hardly a piece of news,' Banks notes, 'to tell any one of the death of another unless the dead man is of high rank or somehow concerned in money matters with the other.'[62]

With everyone else, there is little more than a tired shrug or an expressed regret that they hadn't got from him the money he owed, before he died.

After all, it is a very bad, sad sign that – as Mr Banks notices while passing – the local graveyard has a series of fresh graves already dug, in the sure knowledge that they would soon be filled, like a macabre beach waiting for the inevitable tide of death to come in and leave its weekly wash-up of the damned.

It is the quintessential Port of Death.

The quiet Quaker Sydney Parkinson has his own ideas, tending to lay blame for the various fluxes in great measure on effluvia. With good reason, he suspects it's the city's picturesque canals that are the problem, '. . . in the dry season, they stagnate, be-come putrid, and, being exhaled by the sun, the air is charged with noxious vapours . . .'[63]

It is these 'vapours', the pestilent, stinking airs that rise from the city's stagnant and festering canals, coming complete with buzzing, biting insects, that bring typhus and malaria, which do all the damage.

And yet, due to the care of the men taken by Captain Cook over the last two years – his insistence on hygiene, sauerkraut, gathering greens – he is confident that his own men will withstand the local fevers and fluxes.

His ship's company are not thin, sickly skeletons with death's head grimaces like the Batavia residents – they are hale and hearty sailors.

The locals know better, and say so, telling Captain Cook, Banks and the senior men that it is *because* of the men's health and heartiness the plague will most heartily attack them. Banks, for one, does not believe it, noting that, 'This threat however we did not much regard thinking ourselves too well seasoned to [a] variety of Climates to fear any . . .'[64]

•

Camping on Cooper's Isle, many of the ship's company are beginning to ail. This is no easy place to be, and the weather is infernal, as Surgeon's Mate Perry records, 'Now and then we had a thunder-storm, and about once a week or oftener, there fell heavy rain. Hardly one evening shut in without some kind of lightning in view. During the showers our tent let water through wholesale, and, on such occasions, we get fairly washed out.'[65]

Compounding the problem is a pack of wild dogs that roam the island, though the men are soon able to fix that problem . . .

As summer approaches and the days get warmer and wetter, the tropical torpor of the place, not to mention the sheer stench, starts to weigh on them all.

For in truth, the place actually starts to stink like a dead dog in a rancid, stagnant sewage canal, rotting in the blistering afternoon sun – and for very good reason. There are dozens of such canals, with many dozens of such dead dogs lying in pools of human excrement, and for newcomers like Cook's men, uninitiated to it, it can hit you in the head like a dead dog rotting . . . in a pool of shit. Look, it wouldn't be so bad if the contents of the canal stayed put. But when the torrential rain comes at night the canals then overflow, throwing the mud and dogs into the street, whereupon the locals pile it all up *in the middle of the street* to dry!

'Every now and then,' a stupefied Banks chronicles while holding a silk handkerchief to his nose, 'a dead horse or hog stranded in the shallow parts of the [canals appears], a nuisance which as I was informed no particular person was appointed to remove, which account I am inclined to believe, as I remember a Dead Buffalo laying in one of the principal streets of thoroughfare for more than a week, which was at last carried away by a flood'.[66]

The result, as the men of the *Endeavour* are told by the locals, is that for every 'hundred soldiers who arrive here from Europe it is a rare thing for 50 to outlive the first year, and of those 50, half will at that time be in the hospitals, and of the [other] half, not 10 in perfect health.'[67]

The Captain himself will lament the 'unwholesome air of Batavia, which, I firmly believe, is the Death of more Europeans than any other place upon the Globe'.[68]

They must take care, as the spectre looms of having survived the entire perilous voyage through storms, reefs and battling Natives, only to be struck down at one of the last ports, and a European port at that.

Mid-October 1770, Batavia, monkey business

Joseph Banks, as ever, is still eager to experience everything he can that is novel and new, something that they just won't believe once he gets back to London and can hold court once more.

Having a meal of *roasted monkeys*?

Banks accepts the invitation from a friendly Dutchman immediately, as do Captain Cook and Dr Solander; the voyage has truly turned out to be an endeavour of culinary discovery. There is one problem, however. As they cross the courtyard to the house where they will dine, Banks sees 'half a dozen of those poor little devils'[69] – clearly of the genus *Macaca* – lying helpless on their backs, their little arms tied tightly to cross sticks behind their backs. They make a high-pitched crying sound – *Kera! Kera! Kera!* – as they lie there, looking up at the prospective diners beseechingly. Clearly, these are the ones who are about to be slaughtered to make their meal.

'Now,' Banks will later recount, 'as I love all sorts of animals I walked up to them and in consequence of their plaintive chattering and piteous looks I could not resist cutting the strings by which they were bound and they immediately scampered off so that we lost our monkey dinner.'[70]

Banks tells nobody about his soft-hearted monkey business, especially not their host, who is left to wonder about the extraordinary dexterity of these tasty escapees. At least the conversation over the dinner is good and Mr Banks hears an amazing story he will long treasure. For it turns out that the French navigator Louis Antoine de Bougainville, commanding the French expeditionary ships *La Boudeuse* and *Etoile*, had indeed been the European vessels that had visited a different part of Tahiti after the *Dolphin* and before the *Endeavour*, but here is the best part . . . For don't you know that *Capitaine* de Bougainville's head botanist, Philbert de Commerson – oh, how Mr Banks loves this – had had his mistress on board with him, as his assistant botanist! Jeanne Baret had kept her identity hidden from the crew for half the voyage – in part by binding her breasts tightly flat with bandages – and had only been exposed in Tahiti, when the Tahitians had worked it out within minutes!

A priceless story, which sets the envious Banks to thinking . . .

In the meantime, the Dutch are eager to get as many Englishmen as possible into much safer accommodation. And yet the half-annoyed, half-amused Joseph Banks notes the ceaseless Batavian 'generosity' comes at a very heavy price, most particularly when he and his entourage move into a private home. The fee for a place to sleep is not just steep, it is a sheer cliff: all five of them must pay, each, two Rix dollars in the local currency, the equivalent of eight shillings per day. Every visitor that dines at their table must pay, 'one Rix dollar 4 shillings for dinner, and another for supper and bed if he stayed ashore'.[71]

This, Banks discovers, is 'more than double the common charges of Boarding and lodging in the town',[72] but those rates only apply to those who have a choice, and the men of the *Endeavour* don't. There seems to be a tacit understanding among the Dutch that the British are to be treated like fat turkeys with their feet caught in a trap – to be first plucked and then eaten at will. When they squeal, it's just a bonus.

And if they don't pay up beforehand there is to be no co-operation at all.

This Dutch way with the English is, as the resigned 20-year-old Mr Leigth, the only Englishman who lives on the island, explains 'the method of living in Batavia'.[73]

It is all so *wretched*. Captain Cook used to hold the Dutch people in such high regard. After all, it had been Captain Samuel Holland, one of their number, who had been his teacher in how to survey and draw perfect maps. He had been generous to a fault, and caring. But *these* Dutchmen use their instruments to draw up perfectly ridiculous bills.

Still, it can't be avoided.

In the end, even this far from home and hearth, James Cook must observe some words of resignation from his Yorkshire childhood, 'There's nowt to do but wait!'

And so it goes.

Nevertheless, he is unsure how to use this time of enforced 'leisure'. So in typically industrious fashion, and, with the help of his newly trimmed clerk, Richard Orton, he busies himself with making a copy of his journals and important maps thus far and sends them to the Admiralty Secretary Mr Stephens on the next ship to depart Batavia. Cook is sure to put a note with it that is not only modest but also seeks to head off possible criticism. After all, the Transit of Venus measurements vary to a distressing degree, and there has been no sign of the Great Southern Land he had been sent to find:

> Although the discoveries made in this Voyage are not great, yet I flatter myself they are such as may merit the attention of their Lordships; and although I have failed in discovering the so much talked of Southern Continent (which perhaps [does] not exist), and which I myself had much at heart, yet I am confident that no part of the failure of such discovery can be laid to my charge. Had we been so fortunate not to have run ashore much more would have been done in the latter part of the Voyage than what was; but as it is, I presume this Voyage will be found as complete as any before made to the South Seas on the same account.[74]

For let the record show – and this time he cannot help but let his pride show through – 'I have the satisfaction to say that I have not lost one Man by sickness during the whole Voyage.'[75]

Ah, but how long can that last, Captain Cook?

For as the days pass, searing October turning to stinking-hot November, it is clear that sickness is indeed starting to take the men of the *Endeavour*, one by one, then two by two, and now whole swathes go down. Some rally after a few days. Others continue their descent. In the latter group, one man in particular of the *Endeavour* who – despite his original invigoration at the sight of Batavia – has quickly taken ill once more, but in an even worse fashion. Refusing to take medicine, because he simply doesn't trust any remedy, or food, that he has not seen before, is . . . Tupia.

'He grew worse and worse every day,' Banks chronicles. 'Then Tayeto his boy was attacked by a cold and inflammation on his lungs; then my Servants Peter and James and myself had Intermitting fevers and Dr Solander a constant nervous one.'[76]

Among those who remain on Cooper's Isle, one young man who has just taken violently ill, and is of particular interest to Captain Cook because he knows his father, is Isaac Manley. Perhaps, Cook floats the idea to William Perry, we should summon a local doctor from nearby Onrust Island – a doctor who could also be consulted in the case of Charles Clerke, who lately has begun suffering an agonising pain in one eye.

Quietly, Surgeon's Mate Perry thinks not. For one, he is fairly sure that his own left elbow knows more about medicine than any of the local fraternity. And when it comes to Mr Clerke, he already has him well in hand, persevering with a course of bleeding that has only seen him faint once . . .

Nevertheless, Captain Cook will not be denied, and eventually a doctor is summoned, who diagnoses Clerke's complaint and prescribes – as there is no cure – '*opium* to make death easy'.[77]

'So much for medical help from Onrust,' writes Perry.[78]

Before long, however, just about everyone on shore and most of those still on board are ill, with a variety of fevers and illnesses. Even Banks' health begins to spiral dangerously downwards and he suffers a 'series of fits . . . which were so violent as to deprive me entirely of my senses and leave me so weak as scarcely to be able to crawl down stairs'.[79]

His servants Peter and James are just as bad, as is the Doctor. Banks, however, as always using his own ingenuity, begins a regime of imbibing a tincture of Peruvian bark, with the aim of keeping the dreaded disease at bay. He remains the exception to the rule. When astronomer Charles Green starts to fall ill, he makes no alterations to his daily regime, and continues to saunter the streets of Batavia, oblivious to all but the night-time stars.

But worst of all is Surgeon Monkhouse, who is confined to his bed with a fever. So bad is the Surgeon that he barely reaches for his snuff box anymore.

Even the bastion of health, Captain Cook, also begins to ail.

It is now so difficult to find a healthy Englishman on the island that they take turns as doctor and patient. 'In the first month [in Batavia],' Surgeon's Mate William Perry writes, 'every man, two or three excepted, had been alternately the nurse or the nursling of his messmate. As weeks ran on, I found that we grew more prone to disease; the changes of the moon had very sensible effects, and even the flood-tide constantly rendered fever or local pains more severe . . . We struggled on, whilst death was making quicker progress at Batavia.'[80]

Unfortunately for Captain Cook and the crew of the *Endeavour*, the first man to die is the one they can least afford to lose, as chronicled by the Captain.

'Wednesday, 7 November 1770. Employed getting ready to heave down in the P.M. We had the misfortune to lose Mr. Monkhouse, the Surgeon, who died at Batavia of a Fever after a short illness, of which disease and others several of our people are daily taken ill.'[81]

Surgeon Monkhouse has sniffed his last, his life light snuffed out forever.

While young Jonathan Monkhouse grieves over his elder brother, Captain Cook goes to find William Perry at Cooper's Isle, formally advising him of his informal appointment to the more senior role. And yes, it has to remain informal because, as Perry will recount, 'our Captain now discovered, if not sooner, that his commission, though conferring command of the Vessel and her crew, did not contain any delegated power to fill up vacancies. Such was a strange omission of the Admiralty . . .'[82]

Captain Cook does, nevertheless, present Perry with a Warrant of Surgeon, a letter confirming his appointment that will hopefully be formalised and recognised by the Admiralty on their return. He, further-more, as Perry will note, 'said some handsome things, the more flattering from him who was endued by nature very sparingly with courteous and complimentary manners'.[83]

Captain Cook charges Perry with looking after all the sick, and treats him with something like elaborate respect, all the more notable for Perry because, 'up to the ship's arrival at Batavia, Hunger and Health had held both Doctor and Doctor's Mate as persons of very little use: in particular myself the Captain seemed to consider as one of the King's hard bargains, an eternal Idler, and like a 5th wheel to a coach, of much the same service to a ship . . .'.[84]

Ah, but look at him now!

Not only is he dealing with matters of life and death, but his own ministrations are now regarded as the difference between the two. It is strange, he reflects, how things turn.

For yes, while John Satterly's carpentry skills had made him a hero after they had hit the great reef of New Holland, here at Batavia, awash in Dutch carpenters, well, just how can he put this . . . ?

'The Carpenter, from being the Great Man, from being all in all, sunk into comparative insignificance, while little Bolus . . . Pill-monger, and Clyster-pipe arose into the by-gone Greatness . . . of our Mr Satterly, in seriousness a most worthy and respectable man.'[85]

So it is that even as the *Endeavour* is being restored to relatively robust good health, her crew is daily ravaged and ruined. Aware that it is their surroundings that are likely taking them down, two of the few who are not sick, Master's Mate Dick Pickersgill and Midshipman John Bootie, do a little exploring in their small boat and are taken by the charms of the nearby island of Parmarant. Yes, there is the fact that it has a leper's colony, but they are starting from such a low base that everything looks like up to them. Alas, while there they feast upon the nuts of a certain shrub, *Jatropha curcas* – the physic nut – toxic to humans and stock animals alike, and the results are devastating.

'Messrs Pickersgill and Booty made free with the kernels without clearing the skins away,' Perry notes, '. . . sudden and potent that proved, first as an emetic, ending in a purgative. The lax continued after a fortnight, and wasted both men to shadows.'[86]

Perry does everything possible for them, as for all the others, dispensing Peruvian bark, 'bleeding' the worst of them, giving them as much water as they will take – and getting the worst of the patients lifted on canvas and put outside their tents to get as much fresh air as possible, away from the vapours killing them . . . and for the lucky ones, a slow recovery beneath the shady trees.

And yet, whatever the skills of Mr Perry, crew member after crew member falls ill and quickly dies, with the pale, weakened survivors wondering at every funeral just who among them will be next.

Many suspect it will be . . . Tupia and Tayeto, who are getting worse every day battling a kind of dysentery completely unknown in the South Pacific, with the younger one, Tayeto, saying frequently in his half delirium, '*Tyau mate oee*' . . . 'My friends, I am dying.'[87]

And he really is. Beyond everything else, Tupia is desperately home-sick, 'regretting in the highest degree that he had left his own country'.[88]

To compare the green splendour, white beaches and fresh breezes of his native land with the tropical torpor of this horrid place, the dead dogs, the stinking carcasses of oxen in the street – the wonder of the place had soon faded – is to die by degrees.

Please, he begs Joseph Banks, put me back on the *Endeavour*, which will at least get me out of this land of sickness. Banks, very ill himself, declines – though at least promises Tupia that a special sick tent will be set up for him on the shore, where the breeze can soothe his fever. Tupia is even able to pick the spot himself, 'in a place he chose where both sea breeze and land breeze blew right over him, a situation in which he expressed great satisfaction'.[89]

Many of the sick seamen seek the same solution, and they 'now fell sick fast so that the tents ashore were always full of sick'.[90]

Alas, poor Tayeto succumbs to his illness, and on 9 November he breathes his last.

William Perry provides a tender narrative to Tayeto's death, '. . . the death, unexpected, of . . . a lively boy . . . of ingenuity and manners to deserve his master's regard. A short illness hurried him off, and he died like a Patriarch, taking leave of us pathetically, each by his name.'[91]

Goodbye, Toote. Goodbye, Mr Banks. Goodb . . . and Tayeto farewells no more, rasps no more and weeps no more for his homeland. Which is more than can be said of Joseph Banks, as he holds the child's hand even in death and shakes with sadness.

It is now the melancholy duty of Banks to journey down to the shore to break the news as gently as he can to Tupia. Alas, such news has a far from gentle reaction and Tupia immediately weeps and cries out 'Tayeto! Tayeto!'[92] over and over.

Tupia insists that the boy's body be removed to his own tent, 'that he might chant a certain funereal or death-song in his country's fashion'.[93]

It is a woeful incantation that unnerves Banks, and surprises him, for when Tayeto had been alive, Tupia had not been above listing the shortcomings of his faithful servant. But nothing will quell Tupia's grief, not even his beloved lorikeet, whose impossibly colourful plumage has never failed to bring a smile to the Tahitian priest's face, until now. He wails so hard and so long it even seems to weaken him further as the hours pass.

Thus begins Tupia's own rapid descent, his despondency lending strength to his illness, and just two days after the death of his boy, William Perry must recount with rather poetic sorrow . . .

'His last sigh, was breathed over Tayeto lying dead at his feet.'[94]

The two will remain buried, side by side for eternity, here in Batavia, a place far worse than the hell of their worst imaginings. For his part, Captain Cook's conscience is clouded, and he wishes to make clear to the Admiralty that, whatever else, it is not his fault.

'Tupia's death, indeed, cannot be said to be owing wholly to the unwholesome air of Batavia; the long want of a Vegetable Diet, which he had all his life before been used to, had brought upon him all the Disorders attending a Sea life. He was a shrewd, sensible, ingenious man, but proud and obstinate, which often made his situation on board both disagreeable to himself and those about him, and tended much to promote the diseases which put a Period to his Life.'[95]

As Tupia and Tayeto are only two of many of the *Endeavour* who keep succumbing to sickness, Joseph Banks decides – on the advice of the personal physician he has hired, Dr Jaggi – to retreat to the country, as he does back in England, escaping back to Revesby Abbey when he can. In the company of Dr Solander and Sydney Parkinson, he secures lodgings in a house nestled by a briskly running river, the jewel in a landscape that indeed reminds him fondly of the low country of his native Lincolnshire.

Although Dr Solander himself is desperately ill, it is decided that it is worth the risk to remove him to the new house in a gently handled carriage, while not long after they arrive they 'received from the ship Mr Sporing our writer, a Seaman, and the Captain's own servant who he had sent on hearing of our melancholy situation'.[96] Here, at least, they should all be able to get fresh air, far from the fetid canals and their lurking diseases.

All up, Banks and his companions are attended by 10 Malay servants – of whom five are the landlord's slaves.

It is as well, for, from the first night in the new premises, Dr Solander is so ill that the servants and slaves must attend him in shifts, applying 'fresh blisters . . . to the inside of his thighs'[97] while he lies there completely insensible to their ministrations. Yes, time and again, Dr Jaggi applies to Dr Solander's thighs a particular concoction of pasted powder made from blister beetles, otherwise known as Spanish Fly, which causes blisters to rise wherever it is applied. For you see, as all expert medical practitioners know, by allowing the body to be 'drained of ferous humours',[98] it should alleviate the sickness. And indeed, by the morning Dr Solander seems to be marginally better, and continues to recover a little each day thereafter, so it has clearly worked.[99]

'Myself,' Joseph Banks will note, 'either by the influence of the [Peruvian] Bark of which I had all along taken quantities or by the anxiety I suffered on Dr Solanders account, missed my fever, nor did it return for several days till he became better.'[100] But return it does to fell both Parkinson and Banks once more.

Banks hires yet more male slaves from the landlord, but is infuriated by their careful lack of comprehension and care. For not only are the 'Malay Slaves who alone we depended upon, naturally the worst attendants in nature',[101] but they cannot understand even the most basic of the scolds Mr Banks sends their way. Perhaps changing the genders of the slaves might help? Banks does exactly that, reasoning that at least the female slaves will have a maternal instinct, which will be a nice change from the studied indifference he has been paying for.

Captain Cook in the meantime has also fallen so desperately ill back aboard the *Endeavour* that Banks feels obliged to return to him his personal servant, William Howson.

All the men are now more desperate than ever to get underway, to return home – and the *Endeavour* is in fact now fully repaired and fit to leave, but the bitter irony is that the men themselves are not. In the words of Joseph Banks, 'the people were so sickly that not above 13 or 14 were able to stand to their work'.[102]

This is a dilemma. On the one hand, they have not really enough men to sail the ship, but on the other hand, if they stay much longer in this accursed place they may have none at all. As ill as he is, Captain Cook monitors the best he can the health of all, notes in his log the daily taking on of provisions, and tries to judge at just what point they will have enough men healthy to get underway – about 20, he judges.

Among his biggest worries, in fact, is Joseph Banks, who is now so gravely ill in his house by the river that no sooner has one fever broken than another takes its place.

Every day thus, Dr Jaggi must 'bleed him' – nicking a vein in his forearm and catching the resultant scarlet cascade in a bowl so as to purge him of bad humours and hopefully reinvigorate his constitution.

Could anything make the existence of Banks and his companions more miserable?

Yes, and it now comes thundering from the skies. An early monsoon season that sees deluge all day and all night, day after day, night after night.

Good *God*, why hast thou so forsaken us?

'The Frogs in the ditches,' Banks notes, 'whose voices were ten times louder than those of European ones, made a noise on those nights when rain was to be expected almost intolerable; and the Mosquitos, or Gnats, who had been sufficiently troublesome even in the dry time, now breeding in every splash of water became innumerable, especially in the Moonlight nights.'[103]

This rain is not mere splashes, it *bashes*; not a pitter-patter of no matter, but a sudden and stinging deluge of water that completely engulfs all beneath, a pounding precipitation that leaves everything not washed away completely sodden, before it suddenly . . . stops. And now, just as quickly, the roar of receding water is replaced once more by the buzzing of mosquitos and the *whap* and *slap* of damp English hands hitting slippery English skin, determined to slaughter the pests that plague them.

And then, another deluge.

Could they set off in weather like this?

Late December 1770, Batavia, come what may, on our way

Captain Cook feels he can no longer delay his decision.

As Christmas Day approaches, all the living, however sickly, are ordered aboard.

Joseph Banks and Dr Solander are carried on board, where they take to their bunks, both still gravely ill.

They are greeted and treated by, as ever, William Perry – *Merry Christmas, gentlemen!* – who in the time since taking over from the late Surgeon Monkhouse has barely stopped. And he has done well. Despite fears that they would lose dozens to the grim reaper, to this point they have only lost seven: Surgeon Monkhouse, three sailors, the servant of Mr Green, and Tupia and Tayeto.

'Comparative success hitherto,' he will recount, 'had so puffed me up that, could the same call be made at this hour, after a long and painful experience in East India complaints, I should hardly feel more self-confidence.'[104]

Now that he has Joseph Banks and Dr Solander on board, he has little doubt that – though they are still gripped by dreadful fevers – he will be able to save them, too.

And yet, and yet . . .

'Lo! The froth of youthful vanity how soon put down . . .'[105]

For he has underestimated how badly their fevers have gripped them. He tends to them both, while also offering what succour he can to the other ill ones who have arrived back on the ship, but before long it becomes clear that it is in the hands of the Lord as to whether or not men will pull through. They heat up till it seems they must burn. They shake so badly they must be held down. They shiver as if caught in a raging blizzard on a South American mountain. They perspire to the point that the only thing left is to expire . . . but they pull through.

And yet while Mr Banks and Dr Solander have made it for the moment, whether they can make it all the way to England, or even the next port, is another matter entirely. For just when it seems these cursed illnesses appear to let go, they tend to rebound and reclaim their victims.

It takes some time, the few healthy men all helping the many sick men aboard, but finally it is done and they are indeed all aboard.

But say, between them all, do they have the collective strength to move the capstan around and lift the anchor, when Captain Cook gives the order at dawn the following morning, Christmas Day, 1770? The answer is . . . yes, just, and only because of the collective desire to leave.

At last underway from this infernal place – the best Christmas gift the men could have asked for from their Captain – pushed along by a propitious breeze from the South-west, the *Endeavour* makes its way out of Batavia Harbour, as an English ship, the *Earl of Elgin*, farewells it with three cheers and the firing of 13 cannon. Even the Batavia garrison joins in, firing 14 cannon. The *Endeavour* returns both salutes with the three cannon that remain to it, and is soon in the open sea once more.

At last.

Captain Cook takes stock.

'The number of Sick on board at this time amounts to 40 or upwards, all suffering fever and lethargy in varying degrees. The rest of the Ship's Company are in a weakly condition, having been every one sick except the Sailmaker [John Ravenhill], an old Man about 70 or 80 years of age; and what is still more extraordinary in this man is his being generally more or less drunk every day.'[106]

True! Perpetually pickled, like a barrel of sauerkraut, old Ravenhill is completely impervious to the sickness that continues to tighten its grips on the ship's company. Within nine days of leaving Batavia it gets to the point that, after passing through the Strait of Sunda, Cook makes the decision to stop when they reach Princes Island, near the Westernmost tip of Java, known as Java Head, 'in order to recruit our wood and water, and to procure refreshments for the people, which are now in a much worse state of health than when we left . . .'.[107]

Again Joseph Banks must retire to his cabin, taken down by a fresh dose of fever, even as, with every day in port, even more men take ill. In the face of it, Captain Cook resolves in his journal that the *Endeavour* must push on for the Cape of Good Hope on the southern tip of Africa, come what may – while recognising there is every chance they will lose still more men on the way.

The *Endeavour*, Captain Cook concedes ruefully, has now become my 'hospital ship'.[108]

CHAPTER FOURTEEN

HOMEWARD BOUND

One foot on sea, and one on shore, to one thing constant never.
William Shakespeare, *Much Ado About Nothing*

4 January 1771, East of Krakatoa, dire straits

Such is life aboard the *Endeavour*, filled with the creak of the masts, the swish of the waves . . . the groans of the men, the stench of vomit, blood and festering sores. As the ship threads her way between the islands in the Strait of Sunda, sailing East of Krakatoa and on towards Princes Island, the situation is grim and getting grimmer. Despite the hopes of Captain Cook that the open air and the sea would restore his men away from the vicious vapours of Batavia, quite the opposite has occurred. By the time they drop anchor at Princes Island on 6 January, it is clear that the sick list is longer and deeper than when they left Batavia.

Fresh and untainted supplies from here will help, and it is with equal parts hope and desperation that Captain Cook writes, 'The Natives seemed inclined to supply us with Turtle, Fowls, etc; Articles that I intended laying in as great a stock as possible for the benefit of the Sick, and to suffer every one to purchase what they pleased for themselves, as I found these people as easy to [trade] with as Europeans.'[1]

(It is a far cry from the swindling Rajah and his Dutch accomplice back on Savu.)

A little over a week later, the ship is fully re-supplied – the wood coffer filled and the water barrels groaning – and they are ready to leave once more, only to find that the only wind comes from the rasping breath and dysenteric bowels of their sick sailors, and that is not enough to fill their sails.

The following day they weigh anchor and sail West, leaving the Strait of Sunda on a light breeze.[2] It is with great relief that they are on their way as, despite many of them still being sick, it is imperative that they leave while they still can – entirely unaware that the spirit with the grim countenance, holding a scythe, is now on board, stalking the darker decks and looking for his next victim.

Joseph Banks, drawing on his last reserves of Peruvian bark, rallies a little, at least enough to chronicle how bad things are, writing on 20 January 1771: 'Missed my fever today, the people however in general grew worse and many had now the dysentery or bloody flux.'[3]

Oh, the bloody flux. Things are bad, so bad that for the first time since the voyage began, Charles Green is not on deck searching the stars or shooting the sun, but is instead unable to rise from his hammock at all. Yet again the sea air seems to do little to improve the health of those on board, and, on the morning of 24 January 1771, John Truslove, Corporal of Marines, who Captain Cook notes as 'a man much esteemed by every body on board',[4] dies.

'Many of our people at this time lay dangerously ill of Fevers and Fluxes,' Cook chronicles. 'We are inclinable to attribute this to the water we took in at Princes Island, and have put lime into the Casks in order to purify it.'[5]

It just might be too little too late, as one of Mr Banks' entourage, Herman Sporing, also dies the next day. For his part, Mr Banks only *feels* as though he is dying: 'Myself endured the pains of the Damned almost; at night they became fixed in one point in my bowels on which the surgeon of the ship thought proper to order me the hot bath, into which I went 4 times at the intervals of two hours and felt great relief.'[6]

Yes, a small triumph for William Perry, who once more experiences a sudden shift in favour from James Cook.

'Our captain,' Perry will proudly recount, 'turned to [our] profession for relief . . . Whatever slighting opinion of Doctor or of medicines he had imbibed was now palpably changed, and his old looks of scowl and contempt [gone].'[7]

Perry harbours his own theories about what is causing the men to drop and rise no more. In an irony the Natives of New Holland might offer a heart-felt *tut-tut* to, a batch of bad turtles bought at Princes Island might be the cause.

'Every morning the ceremony of a knife drawn across the throat of the turtles which had died in the night, or we thought dying, consigned some to the ship's cook; and this food hastened through the bowels like quicksilver, leaving as little nourishment. All those who had other than ship's provisions escaped the flux.'[8]

Malaria, typhoid, dysentery, flux, turtle, whatever the cause, the result is the same. The tragic deaths continue, as none other than Sydney Parkinson, the brilliant young artist who has brought to life countless scenes over the last two years, also rasps out his last agonised breath, the quiet Quaker now for eternity.

Banks grieves as much as Banks can – he fears he may well soon follow – but can only muster the energy to record: 'In the Evening Mr Parkinson died and one of the ships crew.'[9]

And yet far more upsetting to those with still enough of a grip on the day to care is the death of drunken John Ravenhill, the only man who did not get sick at Batavia. From Ravenhill feeling nauseous to rasping his last had taken only a couple of days, and there is a strong feeling aboard that if the current sickness can take *him*, it can take anyone. Sure enough, just the next day, astronomer Charles Green, who has spent his life observing the heavens, now heads there, his soul departing this Earth even while his wasted corpse is consigned to the depths with the two other men who die this day. All three are cased in canvas and cast off with a rapidity that allows no sentimentality – mortality trumping mourning as ever more men teeter between life and death.

For Captain Cook, the ongoing deaths are not simply a matter of grieving for good men lost, nor even the difficulties of continuing to sail the ship. Rather, it is a matter of these deaths reflecting on his captaincy.

'He had long been in a bad state of health,' Captain Cook records of Charles Green, 'which he took no care to repair, but, on the contrary, lived in such a manner as greatly promoted the disorders he had had long upon him; this brought on the Flux, which put a period to his life.'[10]

For indeed, perhaps harking back to Captain Cook's Quaker influences, illness is a moral failing, or at least a result of it. Those who follow instruction and embrace moderation are well, or at least they should be.

A certain uncharacteristic gloom settles upon Captain Cook. More than that, a desperate desolation about the deepening sickness on board settles on every sailor, and, as Captain Cook notes, 'increased to that degree that a Man was no sooner taken with it than he looked upon himself as Dead'.[11]

In one case, one of the crew who has been particularly helpful with other sick crew members without suffering any ill-effects, suddenly comes down with a fever and other symptoms himself.

'I have got the Gripes,' he cries again and again while stamping his feet. 'I have got the Gripes; I shall die, I shall die!'[12]

So overwhelmed is he by dread of death he actually falls into a fit and is carried to his hammock only to . . . rather sheepishly . . . recover within a couple of days. He is one of the lucky ones.

For Surgeon Perry, working in the gloom and stench, amid the oozing blood, mucus and excrement, it's as baffling as it is frustrating. 'No medicine I could give had the least effect – despondency gained ground.'[13]

Each deceased sailor has 'DD' written after their name on the muster roll, Discharged Dead, a very definitive discharge in the way of these things.

As sailors and Marines keep dying, Captain Cook and Master Molineux struggle more than ever to keep the *Endeavour* – now 200 miles South-west of the Strait of Sunda – fully manned every watch. It is now getting to the point that when William Perry shows Captain Cook the daily sick list, even the weary Commander must acknowledge the tragic truth and say, 'The vessel will shortly be left without hands to navigate her.'[14]

In the meantime, those tars who can still climb the rigging and see the sails trimmed to the foul Westerly wind must do so for ever longer hours on watch. Most are glad to stay up there for as long as they can, away from the deadly sickness that stalks the lower decks, prowls the cabins and makes its way through the messes of the *Endeavour*. Helpless and hapless, the ship sails on, the remaining crew red-eyed, weary and cowed – now bound for home or the shrouded depths of the ocean, it is just not clear which.

True to form, the sick but still buoyant Banks displays an entirely characteristic gallows humour on the whole appalling situation, noting in his journal on 30 January: 'One person only died today.'[15]

As it happens, Banks is wrong about the improving death toll, as before the day is done, amidst the groans and anguished cries seeping unrelentingly from the mess deck, another two more men die. Just a day later and Cook is in despair as more die.

'In the course of this 24 Hours,' Cook records on the last day of January, 'we have had 4 men died of the Flux, viz., John Thompson, Ship's Cook; Benjamin Jordan, Carpenter's Mate; James Nickolson and Archibald Wolf, Seamen; a melancholy proof of the calamitous situation we are at present in, having hardly well men enough to tend the sails and look after the sick, many of whom are so ill that we have not the least hopes of their recovery.'[16] Worse still than a hospital ship, the *Endeavour* is now on the edge of being a ghost ship, overwhelmed by sickness, with the last men left standing engaged with sailing the ship, tending the dying and . . . consigning the dead to the depths.

An optimistic word in the face of this calamity, Joseph Banks?
Yes.

'The wind which came to E and SE yesterday blew today in the same direction so we had little reason to doubt its being the true trade, a circumstance which raised the spirits of even those who were most afflicted with the tormenting disease, which now raged with its greatest violence.'[17]

The long longed for trade wind now filling their sails is the one that should push them all the way to the Cape of Good Hope on the Southern tip of Africa – with barely a need for tacking – the only question remaining being how many of them will be alive to see it?

'Since we have had a fresh Trade Wind,' Cook records, 'this fatal disorder hath seemed to be at a stand; yet there are several people which are so far gone, and brought so very low by it, that we have not the least hopes of their recovery.'[18]

Cook struggles to maintain dignity and discipline amidst the squalor of the situation, on 4 February punishing Marine Thomas Rossiter with 12 lashes for a drunken assault of the Officer of the Watch.

And yet, even a sympathetic commander stoically weathering the attending trials can incline to become blasé. As the lives of his sailors are extinguished with what has become monotonous regularity, on 27 February, Cook records, 'In the A.M. died of the Flux Henry Jeffs, Emanuel Parreyra, and Peter Morgan, Seamen; the last came Sick on board at Batavia, of which he never recovered, and the other 2 had long been past all hopes of recovery, so that the death of these 3 men in one day did not in the least alarm us.'[19]

At this point, there is clearly nothing to be done, although Captain Cook continues to insist on discipline – do something, *anything*, anyway – always ordering that the decks be scrubbed as clean as the day that they left England, using vinegar; that clothes be washed and dried, that copious lime be added to all the barrels of water, that the ports are to be opened regularly to allow fresh air to circulate.

The sailors keep dying anyway.

Early March 1771, His Majesty's Hospital Ship *Endeavour*, Good Hope, grim truth

Sailing on the same latitude as Natal on the east coast of Africa – perhaps some two days' sail away – some of the crew claim to have seen the land dead ahead, or at least land. It is thought so improbable, however, Captain Cook, below in the Great Cabin, is not even told about it until well after the sun has gone down. He at once orders the crew to swing the lead and take soundings, but finding the ship has no less than 80 fathoms of the Indian Ocean beneath her, concludes that land is nowhere near, and they are in fact still 60 leagues from Africa.[20]

First light, however, brings a different story. For not only can they see land, but they can see, and even hear, the surf crashing upon it. They are just a few hundred yards off.

All hands on deck!

At least all hands who are able. Up from the lower decks, up from the stinking bowels of bloody hell, comes every sailor who can help. But can they?

'The ship . . .' William Perry will recount, 'was stemming in upon breakers and the shore so close that little chance appeared of clawing off.'[21]

After everything they have overcome, is this to be their fate?

'The wind blew right upon the shore and with it a heavy sea ran which broke mountains high on the rocks with which it was every where lined,' Joseph Banks chronicles, 'so that though some in the ship thought it possible the major part did not hope to be able to get off.'[22]

Whatever the case, it won't be without a fight from Captain Cook to save her, and, as he bellows hasty orders to haul to the Eastward, the jacks scramble to his tune: *Prepare the anchors and cables! Trim the sails!* It is a close-run thing but, yard by yard clawing to windward, the ship somehow miraculously manages to avoid the breakers and the rocky outcrops, being carried off by a favourable current moving along the coast. As Captain Cook records, 'after 4 hours spent in the vicissitudes of hope and fear we found that we got gradually off and before night were out of Danger'.[23]

Against all odds, not for the first time, the *Endeavour* survives.

•

By the time the *Endeavour* limps into the port of Simon's Bay by the Cape of Good Hope on 14 March 1771, no fewer than 26 men have died on the journey from Batavia, while Captain Cook records that another 29 men remain extremely ill. (In fact, one ill sailor will die before he can even be brought ashore.) It means that of the original ship's complement of 94, an extraordinary 34 men – more than a third – have now died since James Cook sent his proud letter back to England from Batavia, in which he stated that he had not lost a single man in two years to illness. The only good thing is that, quite unlike Batavia, the Cape of Good Hope is a place of health, hygiene and help, with first-class medical care; a place where the men can at last rest and recover.

A sure sign that at least one of the ship's company is on the mend once more is that Joseph Banks is now well enough, and frisky enough, to record his positive appraisal of the ladies of the Cape of Good Hope: 'In general they are handsome with clear skins and high complexions and when married (no reflections upon my country women) are the best housekeepers imaginable and great child-bearers; had I been inclined for a wife I think this is the place of all others I have seen where I could have best suited myself.'[24]

(Perhaps under the circumstances – for she must have been at least 20 lovers ago – Banks appears to have forgotten that once upon a time, just three years ago, not only *was* he inclined for a wife, but is currently engaged to take one, Harriet Blosset.)

15 March 1771, Cape of Good Hope, ill met by daylight

At anchor in Table Bay now, Cook happily spies another English ship moored nearby – the *Houghton* East Indiaman, sailing home from India, he presumes – and orders his men to row him over, so he may present his compliments to the Captain. On board, James Cook is morbidly fascinated to learn from the *Houghton*'s Captain that although his ship left England a little over 12 months ago, she has already lost nearly 40 men to sickness, while a good many more are now suffering scurvy. This, the other Captain insists, is not unusual. It is simply what happens on long voyages; it is to be expected. Unless, as Captain Cook knows, you take strong measures to prevent it, as he has done. He had managed to go for nigh on three years without losing a single man to sickness. And if they had not been obliged to stop off in wretched, stinking Batavia, they might have been able to sail around the entire world without losing a man to sickness at all!

But will he get credit for that? Highly unlikely.

The *Houghton* has lost 40 men after 12 months, he had lost none after 23 months, and yet . . .

'Yet their sufferings will hardly, if at all, be mentioned or known in England,' he notes with uncharacteristic bitterness, but entirely standard defensiveness in his situation, upon returning to his ship, 'when, on the other hand, those of the *Endeavour*, because the Voyage is uncommon, will very probable be mentioned in every newspaper, and, what is not unlikely, with many Additional hardships we never Experienced.'[25]

It is quite true. As Captain Cook knows, the newspapers in England at this time are little more than scandal rags, making a hue and cry over nothing. It is just way the press has gone in recent years.

'For such are the disposition of men in general in these Voyages,' he writes, 'that they are seldom content with the Hardships and Dangers which will naturally occur, but they must add others which hardly ever had existence but in their imaginations by magnifying the most Trifling accidents and circumstances to the greatest Hardships and insurmountable dangers . . .'[26]

Captain Cook struggles on day by day, pondering the course of events nearly as much as he ponders the course for the day, worried his 'failure' will be made much of, that he is about to be lambasted for his 'hospital ship', the dead men, no Great Southern Land and having the *Endeavour* come to grief on a reef.

As the weather has turned sunny and calm, those crew who can are put to work fixing the topmast, overhauling the rigging, scrubbing the decks, repairing the sails and painting the ship. After Batavia, this place is a delight, and over the next three weeks the ship's company so make headway in recovering their health that Lieutenant Gore feels so hale and hearty that he climbs all 3600 feet of Table Mountain just for the pleasure of the view.

Captain Cook is able to fill out the ship's complement somewhat by hiring some of the itinerant sailors who can always be found at such ports – the flotsam and jetsam of the sea routes ready to go wherever they can get a berth, and even desperate enough to go on a sick ship like this.

Speaking of which, ever eager for fresh greens before getting underway, Captain Cook sends some men to nearby Robben Island – home to both incarcerated criminals and vegetable patches. Joseph Banks accompanies them in order to do yet more botanising, and yet they are all back in a remarkably short time, quite shaken. For not only had they been told not to land by six Dutch soldiers, the fact they were holding muskets pointed right at them rather made the point. Cook decides he can do without the cabbages.

Banks, in any case, has plenty of other things of great interest to concern himself with. Lately his scientific inquiries have occasioned him taking notes as to whether the Native women of Cape Town have very large clitorises or some sort of mini-penis at the top of their vaginas – for so the latter a sailor has told him. Banks firmly plumps for large clitorises. He also records a rumour he has heard whereby for marriage ceremonies the priest urinates on the happy couple, but he cannot definitively get to the bottom of either report before it is time to go again.

Onwards!

Not that the whole of the crew is so recovered and chipper, as Captain Cook records that when the *Endeavour* prepares to take its leave on 16 April 1771, a month after arriving, there remain 11 men too sick to walk aboard. Again, of these, one man, the Master himself, Mr Robert Molineux, dies just an hour after they are underway. Once more, Captain Cook is inclined to blame his death on his habits not his habitat of recent times, nor simply disease: '. . . at 4 departed this Life Mr. Robert Molineux Master, a young man of good parts, but had unfortunately given himself up to Extravagancy and intemperance, which brought on disorders that put a Period to his Life'.[27]

•

The *Endeavour* stops at just one more port between the Cape of Good Hope and England – St Helena, a tiny English colony in the South Atlantic, off Africa's West coast. The men of the *Endeavour* arrive just as a dozen English ships, 'East Indiamen' trading ships, are preparing to set sail back to the motherland as part of a convoy under the protection of HMS *Portland*, as there is fear of war with Spain. (Indeed, when Captain Cook spies so many ships together, his first thought is that it must be an armada and the *Endeavour* is about to intrude upon a war.)

The Captains of these ships prove to be most agreeable fellows, why, they even know of the journey of the *Endeavour* already! (Just how much they know puzzles Captain Cook and Mr Banks.) And they are honoured to agree to delay their departure by a few days so the late-coming newcomer can be safely escorted home.

Still, before they set off, the ever curious Mr Banks must set off himself on a quick excursion to the highest spot on St Helena: 'Spent this day in Botanizing on the Ridge where the Cabbage trees grow, visiting Cuckold's point and Diana's peak, the Highest land in the Island as settled by the Observations of Mr Maskelyne, who was sent out to this Island by the Royal Society for the Purpose of Observing the transit of Venus in the Year [1761].'[28]

In terms of the expedition, this excursion offers a neat symmetry, it is the spot where, effectively, the whole extraordinary journey had begun. And yes, when the Transit of Venus had occurred on Tahiti, Banks had had no particular interest. But this is different. The novelty of closing the circle in this manner appeals to him. As to Cook, he is simply too busy preparing the ship to sail . . .

> *Fill those barrels with water!*
> *Stack those supplies below!*
> *Stow the boats.*
> *Check the muster list.*
> . . .
> . . . to go on such a jolly jaunt.

•

On 3 May, the night before heading for home at last, both Cook and Banks get a shock. For one of the commercial captains of the East India Company *already has a copy* of many of the latitudes and longitudes that Captain Cook has made in his new discoveries! *How is such a thing possible?* They can't prove it, but Banks has his suspicions of an earless suspect: '. . . we found that many Particulars of it has transpired and particularly that a copy of the Latitudes and Longitudes of most or all the principal places we had been at had been taken by the Captain's clerk from the Captain's own Journals and given or sold to one of the India Captains'.[29]

Innocent or guilty, Mr Orton is robust in his denials, which surprises no-one. Captain Cook becomes doubly determined to get home as soon as possible to give a firsthand account of their achievements before they are pirated out of their credit.

The voyage home, by the *Endeavour*'s rather dramatic standards – hitting a reef in the middle of the night, anyone? – is singularly undramatic. The sailing is easy, the wind is with them, and some nights Cook and Banks take a cutter to dine aboard one of the other vessels, enjoying the hospitality and new conversation of their convoy comrades. But on 24 May it becomes clear that their battered Whitby cat *Endeavour*, so versatile yet sluggish . . . simply can't keep up with these Indiamen in the open sea with a good wind blowing. The *Endeavour* loses sight of its company as the sun starts to sink in the West, 'and notwithstanding we kept close upon a wind all night, with as much Sail out as we could bear, there was not one Sail in sight in the Morning'.[30]

While most of Cook's men are on the mend and out sailing, still some of them remain confined and ailing, none more than Lieutenant Zachary Hicks. The trusty Lieutenant is so bad – critically ill with consumption – that at 1 o'clock on 25 May he dies, and that evening is 'committed to the Sea with the usual ceremonies'.[31]

Captain Cook feels the loss of this loyal Lieutenant, so close to home and the chance to recover, very keenly. The only positive note is that it enables him to record the promotion of a most deserving replacement, 'This day I gave Mr. Charles Clerke an order to act as Lieutenant in the room of Mr. Hicks, deceased, he being a Young Man extremely well qualified for that Station.'[32]

It is a death five weeks later that most affects Joseph Banks, however.

'My bitch, Lady, was found dead in my Cabin laying upon a stool on which she generally slept,' Mr Banks writes with a tear in his eye. 'She had been remarkably well for some days; in the night she shrieked out very loud so that we who slept in the great cabin heard her, but becoming quiet immediately no one regarded it. Whatever disease was the cause of her death it was the most sudden that ever came under my Observation.'[33]

(As a point of order and a point of wonder, given that Joseph Banks is on this night sleeping in the Great Cabin – he finds it roomier – Lady is actually sleeping in what should have been Cook's cabin, while the Commander of the entire vessel continues in his lesser quarters. Somehow, the man who has presided over the whole voyage is in little more than a doghouse, while his proper cabin is currently occupied by a dead dog and a now weeping Banks.)

•

Sail ho! Sail fine on the starboard bow!

From this passing ship, outbound from Liverpool, Captain Cook learns on 7 July, 'that no account had been received in England from us, and that Wagers were held that we were lost'.[34]

As improbable as it seems, the letters and documents he had sent upon the fast Dutch ships while still at Batavia have not arrived yet, and the *Endeavour*'s arrival will come as a surprise, and a relief, to all.

10 July 1771, aboard the *Endeavour*, this blessed plot, this Earth, this realm, this England . . .[35]

At noon, 'Young Nick', Nicholas Young, the very fellow who had been the first to spot New Zealand off the starboard bow, is at the masthead when he again spots a smudge, this time off the port bow.

Could it be . . . ?

Is it possible . . . ?

Decidedly yes!

Two years and 11 months after leaving England, with 30,000 miles travelled, 5000 miles of coastline charted and many lands visited, the *Endeavour* is now approaching the most blessed destination of all – *home*.

The cry goes up – 'Land ahoy!' And better still, 'Eng-land!' – and is taken up around the ship. As ever, men come from below, crowd to the bow, and strain their eyes as that distant dawn blob comes ever closer, greener, and more pleasant looking.

England!

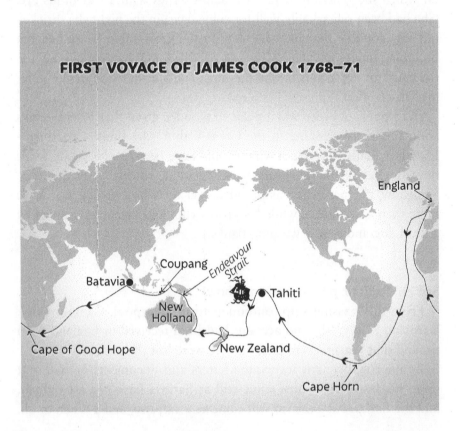

FIRST VOYAGE OF JAMES COOK 1768–71

12 July 1771, Land's End to the Downs, Home, James, and don't spare the horses!

They can practically *smell* home! It is a wonderful thing to make the English Channel proper and by dawn of this day they are off Beachy Head, which, as everyone aboard knows, means they are just hours from dropping anchor in the Downs, the English anchorage just off Kent.

At 3 o'clock that afternoon they do precisely that. And yes, the maritime tradition is that if a ship is sinking, the captain should be last off, making sure that everyone else is safe, but so too does the reverse apply.

That is, when completing a successful trip around the entire planet, when you have achieved all your goals and ensured the safety of your crew to the best of your manifest abilities, so too do you have the privilege of being the *first* off the ship if you want it, once home, and Captain Cook certainly does want it. He wants to move fast, and his heavy sea chest can be sent on to him at a more leisurely pace.

Only minutes after anchoring, thus, Captain Cook, accompanied by Joseph Banks and the still seriously ill Dr Solander, gingerly climbs into the long-boat and is rowed to the docks, even as his crew crowd the gunwale to cheer him off. Awaiting them at the docks is a carriage, in which they settle for the seven-hour journey to London, each feeling extremely fortunate to have made it, and for good reason. Of the original 94 men who had left England two years and 11 months ago only 56 have made it home.

Unfolding their limbs and hopping down from the cramped carriage, the three sun-tanned explorers look out of place on the Piccadilly street ... and they feel out of place, suffering an instant culture shock. After everything they have seen over these last three years, these lost lands on the other side of the world, it is an extraordinary thing to find themselves once more in London – *The streets! The houses! The lanterns in the middle of the night!* The coachman climbs to the roof to get down James Cook's small bag as the Captain prepares to head for the Admiralty, while the other two keep going on to Banks' mansion in New Burlington Street.

This is it. They have come a long way. They have accomplished much. But now is the time to say goodbye. There were times – on the reef, in Batavia and afterwards – where they were certain they would never make it back alive. But, well, here they are. Oddly, there is not a lot to say. They simply shake hands, wish each other well, and then Banks' coach is on its way back to the botanist's Mayfair mansion, leaving Cook with his bag on the street, gazing at its receding form.

What now?

No Mayfair for him. Just returned from circumnavigating the world, humble James Cook picks up his small bag – as anonymous as a lost dog – and walks the darkened streets of London all the way to the Admiralty, some two and a half miles away in Whitehall.

Certainly, Lieutenant James Cook has been away from his home, wife and children for no less than two years and 11 months and is anxious to be in the bosom of his family once more. But he is in no doubt as to where his priorities are. As a naval officer returned from such a long time away, his first duty is to report his return, and hand over the precious journals that are the record of all that he has seen.

He hands the night clerk his letter for Mr Philip Stephens, Secretary of the Admiralty, then takes a seat in one of the drawing rooms.

> *Endeavour Bark, Downs,*
> Sir,
> It is with pleasure I have to request that you will be pleased to acquaint my Lords Commissioners of the Admiralty with the arrival of His Majesty's Bark under my Command at this place, where I shall leave her to wait until further orders. And in obedience to their Lordship's orders immediately, and with this Letter, repair to their office, in order to lay before them a full account of the proceedings of the whole voyage . . .
> You will herewith receive my Journals containing an account of the proceedings of the whole voyage, together with all charts, plans and drawings I have made of the respective places we have touched at, which you will be pleased to lay before their Lordships. I flatter myself that the Latter will be found sufficient to convey a tolerable knowledge of the places they are intended to illustrate, & that the discoveries we have made, though not great, will apologise for the length of the Voyage. I have the honour to be, Sir
> Your most Obedient
> humble Servant
> James Cook[36]

So, following his orders to the letter, and to the last drop, the extraordinary James Cook waits patiently through the night to tell his tale and apologise for the length of his voyage. While Joseph Banks sleeps late in his

Mayfair mansion, James Cook, after handing everything to the delighted Admiralty Secretary Philip Stephens, at last heads home in the late morning, via Whitechapel Road . . .

Mid-July 1771, London, Banksia Man

Have you heard?

The great Joseph Banks has returned to us! He is, of course, the talk of London, the toast of no less than the British Empire – which has expanded, thanks to his genius and courage. Everyone is talking of the 'Immortal Banks',[37] this 'unequalled man',[38] who has discovered worlds unknown, together with plants, flowers, trees, species of animals, birds and fish beyond number and – just quietly? – women beyond wonder.

No less than Samuel Johnson boasts of spending time in the esteemed company of Banks, and composes poems to amuse him, while His Majesty King George III is delighted to receive Mr Banks at Buckingham Palace and receive his advice on plants, particularly for his pet project, Kew Gardens.

In the meantime, every London gentlemen's club – which is to say every club – longs to see him walk through their doors in the hope he will regale all those gathered round with tales fantastical and – just loudly – ribald. As the port flows and the air becomes thick with cigar smoke, he will lean in and move to the climax of the story.

And then we saw it: Completely severed!

A collective gasp. Can you imagine?

And then I showed him my musket!

And so it goes.

No serious society soiree is complete without Lords, Ladies, Dukes and Duchesses hovering nervously by the entrance waiting for the man of the moment, the main attraction, the handsome, brilliant, rich, famous and deliciously infamous Joseph Banks to arrive.

Infamous, you say? Well, yes, there is the rather more delicate matter of his broken engagement with Mademoiselle Harriet Blosset, who had heard *rien* from him since that night at the opera, when he had left her without explanation and sailed the next day. After she had written to the gay young blade on his return, requiring an 'interview or explanation',[39] Banks comes back with a three-page letter, centring on one primary message: 'I love you, I profess it, but I am of too volatile a temper to marry.'[40] The nerve of the bounder! She, however, will not take *Non* for an answer. She has spent three years of her glorious and perfumed youth waiting for him, and demands a meeting, so the scoundrel may say it to her face. Banks obliges, arriving unannounced just as she is sewing him a waistcoat.

'Miss Blosset swooned,' one of the botanist's great friends will recall ruefully, '& Mr Banks was so affected that Marriage was again concluded upon.'[41]

Alas, alas, a few days later the cad, the *bounder*, sends another letter calling the whole thing off again! *Quelle horreur!*

London society is scandalised. Deliciously. As one man in the Banks' circle gossips to another: he 'leaves poor Miss Bl. In the most distressing as well as ridiculous situation imaginable'.[42]

As a bare beginning, she refuses to sew another button to the waistcoat, though her feelings are slightly less mortified and just a *soupçon* more mollified when Banks makes a payment to her of £5000. With that payment, 'poor Miss Bl'[43] agrees to let the affair pass.

And when it comes to affairs, Banks has other titillating tales . . .

Let us, gents, just lean in to talk sotto voce of the anthropological nature of the sexual customs of Tahiti (*Three women! At the same time!*), and the interesting customs in this field of the Tahitian Royal Court (*The Queen and her maid and her male lover, you say, all at once?*), and how surprisingly open it all is (*A girl and her lover performing, in daylight, in front of the Queen? And the Queen yelling out encouragement? Extraordinary*). So please, do go on, Mr Banks. Whatever you can tell us will be repeated endlessly by us in coming weeks, in strictest confidence, of course. The whole thing is fantastic . . . but marvellously *true*!

At one royal dinner – of course held in honour of Mr Banks – a prominent visitor and guest from the American colonies, a Mr Benjamin Franklin, chronicles that Banks had unveiled important new learning upon the new world. For the Tahitians, Banks recounts to his enthralled audience, 'had no idea of Kissing with the Lips . . . though they liked it when they were taught it!'[44]

(And so do many of the beautiful women of London when Banks offers them instruction too!)

As a matter of fact, however, the women of Tahiti have taught Mr Banks sexual techniques that an English naval officer visiting Tahiti a short time later, one William Bligh, will chronicle as a 'sensual and beastly act of gratification, [whereby] even the mouths of women are not exempt from the pollution'.[45]

For his part, Banks had been much less horrified at the time.

But of course we have forgotten someone. For never let it be said that Mr Banks achieved his feats on his ownsome. There is someone else who deserves to be toasted – not as much as Banks of course – for he too brought England glory.

Gentlemen, I ask you to raise your glass to . . . Dr Solander!

Yes, *Mr Banks and Dr Solander, and not to forget Banks*; the celebrated duo are bound together in public acclaim, as they shall surely be for all time! Raise a glass, I say!

Why, one cannot open a newspaper without reading all about them! See here in *The Public Advertiser* of 6 August 1771:

> We are creditably informed that the *Endeavour* which carried Mr. Banks and Dr. Solander round the World, sailed many hundred Leagues with a large Piece of Rock sticking in her Bottom, which had it fallen out must have occasioned the inevitable Destruction to them all, and deprived the World of the agreeable Discoveries they have Reason to expect from this Voyage.[46]

Glory be to God! For He appears most certainly to have preserved Mr Banks and Dr Solander for more of their wonderful work to come. And did you hear about this whole 'fothering' business? Extraordinary, how Mr Banks managed to pull it off. It allowed them to once more stand on the solid ground of 'New Holland', speaking of which, the world's greatest botanist, Dr Carl Linnaeus himself, suggests that 'New Holland' be renamed 'Banksia' for the man who conquered its last mysteries and brought such wonders from it. Why not?

The *Westminster Journal* announces that, 'No less than seventeen thousand plants, of a kind never before seen in this kingdom, have been brought over by Mr Banks, which, we hear, are very likely to live in the royal gardens of Richmond.'[47]

Why Mr Banks might as well live in the royal gardens himself, so much time does he spend with the King and Queen of England, and so well is he nourished while there.

The Queen, so says the *Public Advertiser*, has been shown Mr Banks' wondrous drawings from the voyage, full of curiosities, and they were 'viewed by her with peculiar pleasure'.[48]

Ah, but when it comes to this voyage, there is another thing that is overlooked. For of course this voyage has not just produced enormous strides in the field of botany, but also whole leaps forward in the evolving science of navigation, and, as a direct result, whole new sections of the globe have been discovered and mapped.

The *Gazetteer* helps to put the record straight: 'We are told on the best Authority, that Mr Banks and Dr Solander's Voyage may be made extremely subservient to the Purposes of Navigation. They passed through two Straits, which were before unknown. Former Sailors had always doubled the Land which contains them, and thereby performed several hundred Leagues more sailing than, had they known these Straits, would have been necessary.'[49]

I tell you, there is nothing these two masters of the sea cannot do. King George himself is clearly of this view as he is seen to apply His Majesterial wiles to encouraging the discovering duo to embark on yet another voyage for the greater glory of Britain.

Banks is to sail once more? Oh yes, the hope is now truth as the *Gazetteer and New Daily Advertiser* tells its readers: 'Mr Banks is to have two ships from government to pursue his discoveries in the South Seas, and will sail upon his second voyage next March.'[50]

But, say, who is that rather strapping fellow who sits in a London coffee shop every morning reading these reports, a shiny shilling gripped in his palm, ready for payment after he finishes perusing the praises of Mr Banks?

Well, they say he is an obscure naval Lieutenant by the name of Cook, James Cook, and he apparently had *something* to do with the voyage himself. Still, there is little mention of him in any of the newspaper accounts, while Banks' fame grows daily.

And yet, to be fair, it is not as if Cook's feat of sailing around the world and charting a fresh 5000 miles of coastline across starkly different realms has gone entirely without notice. As a matter of fact, just two days after he arrived back in England, the *London Evening Post* of 15 July informed its readers of, 'the agreeable news of the arrival in the Downs of the *Endeavour*, with Captain Cooke, from the East-Indies. This ship sailed in August 1768 with Mr Banks, Dr Solander . . .'[51]

And that is just the way the Cook crumbles. Mr Banks and Dr Solander are celebrated famed adventurers, the toasts of London. Cook is the man who had the honour of taking them.

James Cook is, however, deeply treasured by his family, as he deeply treasures them and that is enough. As it happens, his family needs him more now than ever as he has returned home to the shocking news that his darling daughter, Elizabeth, named for her blessed mother and mourned by her, has died at the age of four, just three months before Cook returned to England.

And . . . the baby due only a few days after I sailed from Plymouth?

We called him Joseph, Elizabeth tells her husband softly, *but we lost him two weeks after he arrived.*

James Cook has stared death in the face for months, has buried at sea and on land dozens of his ship's company, but nothing has affected him as much as this devastating news.

At least his two lively young sons, Nathaniel and James – now so strong, so much taller – dance with delight in his presence.

It is, thus, something of a bittersweet homecoming, the sweetness coming when he had knocked on the door of his own small terraced house to have it opened by the blessed Elizabeth, who tumbles into his arms, followed shortly afterwards by his boisterous and amazingly *big* boys – and the bitterness, the quiet tears coming when he hears the news of his other sweet children lost.

This life of a navy man is hard and his family have done it hard without him.

•

When things are more settled, by which time Elizabeth Cook is newly pregnant with their fifth child, James Cook is sure to make a rare visit back to Whitby. Now, of course, he is a land-lubbing lad no more, but returns a seafarer for the ages, here to tell the tale.

He does go out of his way to proudly shake the hand of his old master, John Walker, who had been so good to him all those years ago. And yet James Cook's own pride is as nothing to the pride of Mary Prowd, the Walker's old housekeeper. Now, she has been told today to *remember*, Mary, that the boy you doted on all those years ago (and brought a candle to late at night when he pored over his mathematics) is now not only a grown man, but a sea-captain who has travelled the world. *And must be treated with respect, reverence and deference, Mary, do you hear?*

But on seeing him in the flesh, so grand, so big, so esteemed, she cannot hold back, and joyfully greets the great Captain Cook with the name she greeted him with when he was but a lad, 'Oh Honey James! How glad I is to see thee!'[52]

The years fall away, and for a moment Captain Cook is no longer an esteemed naval Commander. For it is Honey James himself who returns her warm greeting in kind, embracing this wonderful old woman with the respect and reverence *she* deserves. And yet Mary is not the only one eager to see him. For while London may be falling over for Joseph Banks, the people of Whitby regard James Cook as nothing less than their favourite son. This ship-building, sea-breathing folk know better than London what he has done, and certainly how he has done it – he has sailed a humble coal carrier, one of their own Whitby cats, *around the world*, and discovered whole worlds – him, a shop boy, our James Cook!

And yes, Mary, our Honey James!

•

And yet it is not as if James Cook is completely forgotten in London circles. On 10 August 1771, a month after arriving home, he receives a letter from the great Joseph Banks, *himself*, who is pleased to inform this fellow that he has put in a word with Lord Sandwich – who has recently been re-appointed as First Lord of the Admiralty, his third stint in the role – and has managed to secure him a promotion!

Yes, in short order he will officially be 'Captain Cook' – not just as the captain of a ship, but as an *actual* rank of Captain in His Majesty's Royal Navy.

Sure enough, when James Cook is ushered into the presence of Lord Sandwich the next day, his promotion is confirmed.

Thank you, Lord Sandwich. Most gratified, Lord Sandwich.

A few hours later *Captain* Cook writes a humble letter of thanks to his benefactor Joseph Banks:

> *Will's Coffee-house*
> *Charing Cross*
> *Sunday morning*
> Your very obliging letter was the first Messenger that conveyed to me Lord Sandwich's intentions. Promotion unsolicited to a man of my station in life must convey a satisfaction to the mind that is better conceived than described – I had this morning the honour to wait upon his Lordship who renewed his promises to me, and in so obliging and polite a manner as convinced me that he approved of the Voyage. The reputation I may have acquired on this account by which I shall receive promotion calls to my mind the very great assistance I received therein from you, which will ever be remembered with most grateful acknowledgements by,
> Dear Sir,

Your most obliged Humble Servant,
James Cook[53]

August 1771, Mayfair, clubbed by Sandwich

What Captain Cook does not realise – because to this point the botanist has only confided in his dear friend Lord Sandwich – is that Joseph Banks has no desire for him to be a Captain *at all*, let alone of Banks' next voyage, to the South Pole. (Yes, the South Pole! Banks is quite taken with the notion, as he writes to a friend, 'Oh how Glorious would it be to set my heel upon the Pole! And turn myself round 360 degrees in a second!'[54]).

For you see, by going to the South Pole, Banks will either have the glory of finding the elusive Great Southern Land, which Alexander Dalrymple still personally assures him is right there, just waiting for an explorer brave enough – not James Cook (*sniff*) – to find it, or at the very least expose it as a myth, which would be a lesser glory.

Yes, as expected, Alexander Dalrymple has not accepted Cook's expedition as proving that the Great Southern Land does not exist and so, just as Captain Cook had envisioned, a second expedition around the bottom of the world must be mounted, this time on a grander scale with two ships – as added insurance against one of them coming to grief.

So who should be the overall Commander of such an expedition? Why, Joseph Banks knows just the man . . . Joseph Banks.

No, of course *he* will not be the one doing petty things like setting specific courses and giving orders as to the sails and so forth, but nor will he be just the moneyed master, instead he will be the crowned *Commander* of the Royal Naval vessels in this planned second journey. Why, look at the portrait that he has just had painted of himself, by the finest British society painter of the lot, Sir Joshua Reynolds.

For Joseph Banks knows precisely the look he wants and stages the whole thing. Yes, he was a botanist on this voyage, but for this portrait there will not be a plant, or even a leaf to be seen and not even any of the amazing animals or birds they have discovered.

No, what Mr Banks wants for this portrait is to look like . . . well, like an *explorer* . . . like one who has just returned from charting huge tracts of the previously unknown world. So we'll have a globe at my left elbow, a window behind where I can gaze without flinching onto the stormy restless sea that awaits, and my logs before me, where I can document all the things I have discovered.

For yes, he *is* the man to command the next voyage, born for the part.

'Captain Cook shall be ordered to follow my directions as to the time of sailing, from the several places we shall touch in the course of the voyage,' Banks informs his friend, Lord Sandwich.

'In other words giving you the absolute command of the expedition?' Sandwich responds. It is ridiculous! It is 'a thing that was never done and I believe never attempted before'.[55]

Indeed? Well, Mr Banks is used to attempting things others have never done before, precedent be damned.

'It is to be a condition of my proceeding or not proceeding on the expedition,' Mr Banks replies.

'I suggest to you,' replies Sandwich 'that it would be fatal to the undertaking that the command should be in the hands of persons not under Military Law.'[56] Just as Alexander Dalrymple was not put in charge of the *Endeavour*, Lord Sandwich will be damned if he puts a civilian in charge of this next endeavour.

Not to mention fatal to all if command of a ship is given to a botanist who does not actually know very much about sailing. Banks could see that Sandwich would not budge, and undaunted had gone onto press his next demand 'in the strongest manner'.

'The officers in both ships shall receive promotion by my means,' he offers.

What? A civilian giving out promotion to naval men? While their Captain stands neutered? *No.*

On he goes . . .

'If they don't look up to me for preferment, I shall be considered a nobody!' argues Banks.

'This is another attempt on your part to get possession of the command!'[57] replies Sandwich.

No. You *are* a nobody, when it comes to the Navy, Mr Banks. Your money and fame will not change that. Influence is one thing, formal command is another.

I don't think Mr Banks could be more clear, Lord Sandwich, hold the relish?

Indeed not.

No, I am sorry, Joseph, this is the way it must be. If this second expedition is to proceed at all, it will do so under the same structure as last time, with Captain James Cook in full naval command, while you will be in charge of matters animal, vegetable and mineral.

Banks now has no choice.

He desperately wants to go on the second expedition, but the way it has been broken down, the only way he can do so is to accept James Cook as the Commander once more, the very man who has proved how capable he is in such climes. Is Banks desperate enough to accept a berth under Cook's command once more?

Reluctantly . . . yes.

At least, however, this time Banks insists on travelling in the style befitting one of his eminence, and now proceeds to lavish thousands of pounds re-modelling the two ships for his next voyage. On this voyage, we will have a French horn player – no, in fact, let us make it *two* French horn players – to accompany each other, and us, for the duration of the voyage.

For I, Joseph Banks Esq., hero of the *Endeavour* expedition, wish to hear music when I please this time. And I shall also have my personal physician, more painters, secretaries, draughtsmen and servants, some 15 in all.

Now to accommodate such a large party will not be easy. And it doesn't matter to Joseph Banks that on 28 November 1771, not six months since arriving home from the *Endeavour* voyage, James Cook is commissioned as Captain and has already selected a ship, the *Resolution*, another Whitby cat, which Cook is so happy with he will chronicle it as, 'the ship of my choice and as I thought the fittest for service she was going upon of any I had ever seen'.[58]

At 462 tons she is 100 tons heavier than the *Endeavour*.

The *Resolution* will be joined by HMS *Adventure*, under command of Captain Tobias Furneaux, former Second Lieutenant to Captain Wallis on the *Dolphin*.

And yet Joseph Banks is far from delighted with the *Resolution*, regarding it as too small. Far too cramped for his increased entourage, and he is underwhelmed as only he can be.

'Instead of having provided a ship in which an extraordinary number of people might be accommodated,' he will later recount, 'they had chosen one with a low and small cabin and remarkably low between decks.'[59]

Mr Banks, of course, objects, only to be told that there is no remedy for what he complains of.

Well, we'll see about that.

After Banks meets with his still dear friend Lord Sandwich, the First Lord of the Admiralty decides there is a remedy after all, and, as

Mr Banks will recount, 'ordered the cabin to be raised eight inches for our convenience and a spar deck to be laid the whole length of the ship for the accommodation of the people'.[60]

Now we are getting somewhere!

Joseph Banks also insists that an upper deck be built at the back of the ship, and he does not care even if it does cost £14,000.

An *extra upper deck*? A *new* deck invented, on a *sailing vessel*, to accommodate you, Mr Banks?

No, no, you misunderstand, Captain Cook.

The new deck will be to accommodate my party, my specimens and various animals I hope to bring back. *I* shall take the Great Cabin entirely.

But . . . But . . . But . . .

But Banks will hear no buts, the building must begin *at once*. If not the whole expedition will be doing without Banks' fortune and without the great Banks himself.

Very well then, Mr Banks.

A force of nature, by nature forceful, and backed by his extreme wealth and influence, even the Admiralty must reluctantly agree in these early months of 1772 to Joseph Banks' plans. The sailing date of the *Resolution* is delayed two full months to accommodate the changes to the accommodation.

Captain Cook is ordered to supervise the labours.

And so Mr Banks' wooden castle in the air is actually constructed, even as he regularly brings various Lords and Ladies on board for luncheon parties to give them a tour of inspection.

'Scarce a day passed,' Cook notes dryly, 'when [the *Resolution*] was not crowded with strangers, who came on board for no other purpose but to see the ship in which Mr Banks was to sail around the world.'[61]

And it is true that there are some with Captain Cook who wonder at the wisdom of all the changes.

And they also wonder where on Earth all of Mr Banks' considerable goods for this three-year voyage will go.

And yet, as Charlie Clerke will later recount, 'Captain Cook never expressed his scheme of Stowage to any of us.'[62]

Which is odd, because it simply seems impossible they'll be able to get it all in, and yet Captain Cook shows no interest at all.

There is one detail, however, that Captain Cook has a more than usual interest in. No ship may leave on assignment for the Royal Navy until an official pilot has taken it for a trial, with full crew, and declared it to be seaworthy.

Captain James Cook can't wait. And sure enough, on 13 May 1772, after just a few hours on the water, the pilot at the Nore, the naval anchorage of the Thames, orders the *Resolution* to be turned round as it is in danger of capsizing. The ship is unsafe.

Lieutenant Charlie Clerke – his promotion to Acting Lieutenant by Cook while at sea had been confirmed by the Admiralty as soon as they arrived to England – breaks the news to Banks in a witty, jovial letter:

> *Resolution* in Sea Reach
> Sir,
> We weighed anchor at Graves-End this morning about 10 O'clock, with a fine Breeze from the Eastward, the wind from that quarter, laid us under the necessity of working down the Reaches which work, I'm sorry to tell you, we found the *Resolution* very unequal to [the task]; ... for whilst several light Colliers were working down with their whole Topsails, Staysails &c. one small Brig in particular with her Top Gallant Sails; these Light Vessels so upright, that a Marble would hardly roll from Windward to Leeward, the *Resolution*, I give you my honour, under her reefed Topsails, Jibb & Main Top Mast Staysail, heeled within three Streaks of her Gun Ports.[63]

Indeed, Mr Banks! Even in just a light wind, the water was within three plank widths – no more than a foot – of the gun port! They were lucky to get out of it alive!

> She is so very bad, that the Pilot declares, he will not run the risk of his Character so far, as to take charge of her, farther than the Nore without a fair Wind, that he cannot with safety to himself attempt working her to the Downs.
> Hope you know me too well, to impute my giving this intelligence to any ridiculous apprehensions for myself, by God I'll go to Sea in a Grog Tub if desired, or in the *Resolution* as soon as you please; but must say, I do think her by far the most unsafe Ship, I ever saw or heard of: however, if you think proper to embark for the South Pole in a Ship, which a Pilot, (who I think is, by no means a timorous man) will not undertake to carry down the

River; all I can say is that you shall be most cheerfully attended, so long as we can keep her above water.
Sir,
Your much obliged and humble servant,
Chas. Clerke[64]

In short, she is, to use that most withering of maritime expressions, 'a crank ship'.

Mr Banks is not well pleased.

Yes, Charlie likes to joke, but there is no mistaking that he has a serious message. Banks must reluctantly tear himself away from his society for a short time, and down to the Nore to see what minor modifications might be made to his luxurious accommodations. Fear not, it should not take too long to give whatever orders are necessary. I will just nip down.

And yet, as quick as he is, Banks is too late.

For as Midshipman John Elliot records, while too many cooks might spoil the broth, it only takes one determined Cook to right the wrongs of the past in a few short hours and – after having received permission from the Navy Board to make seaworthy alterations – 'the next morning at daylight, I believe two hundred shipwrights were cutting and tearing the ship to pieces'.[65]

It means that when Banks' carriage arrives at the dock, the great man has no sooner alighted than he looks up to see . . . an ordinary ship.

The *Resolution* is back to being as it was, without a raised cabin ceiling and an extra poop deck – which will shortly see the poop hitting the fan.

What follows would have allowed Banks to go to a fancy-dress party dressed as Vesuvius. For in terms of sound and fury, the explosions of rage causing people to scatter in all directions, he is all that and more.

If only Cook could be there to see it, he would no doubt be impressed. In fact, with discretion being the better part of valour, he has discreetly removed himself for the day. (It had been, nevertheless, a day he had been expecting to come for some time, having noted as far back as 28 November 1771 in his private journal, 'we had reason to think that she would prove Crank'.[66])

No matter. Mr Joseph Banks, this man of the Enlightenment, has become the man of enraged Entitlement and his tantrum is a wonder for the ages as Midshipman Elliot breathlessly chronicles: 'He swore and stamped upon the Wharf, like a Mad Man, and instantly ordered his Servants and all of things out of the Ship. To find himself under the necessity of taking such a step must no doubt have been a very great mortification to him, for he had put himself to great expense, in all kinds of curious things, for use, amusement and pleasure . . .'[67]

Within minutes after the worst of the tantrum is over, there begins a kind of reverse Noah's Ark, as a parade of painters and popinjays leaves the ship, followed by doctors and draughtsmen, silks and servants, and sailors laden down with baubles, bangles, beads, jars, tubs, instruments, canvases, lace and finery, not to forget the underwater telescope. And finally off goes Mr Banks to have a *bloody word* with Lord Sandwich and the Admiralty.

With exquisite, if slightly suspicious, timing, Captain Cook reappears just as Joseph Banks recedes in the distance – still aflame atop his exceedingly high dudgeon – and pens a short letter of regret to Mr Joseph Banks, late of the *Resolution*:

> Sir,
> I received your letter by one of your people, acquainting me that you had ordered everything belonging to you removed out of the ship, and desiring my assistance therein.
> I hope, Sir, you will find this done to your satisfaction, and with the care the present hurry and confused state of the ship required . . . [68]

Oh, and not to forget:

> The Cook & two French Horn men are at liberty to go when ever they please . . .
> Your most obedient and very humble servant,
> James Cook[69]

The letter is well constructed, with exactly the right buttoned-down, disciplined tone of Captain James Cook. While it contains nothing but the strictest civility, each sentence hits Banks like a slap in the face. Cook, a man who he could buy and sell ten thousand times over, is mocking him!

Of course Joseph Banks tries to get his friend Lord Sandwich to intervene, but after bitter correspondence between the two, the good Lord comes down firmly on the side of Captain James Cook, his final letter to Mr Banks finishing:

> Upon the whole I hope that for the advantage of the curious part
> of Mankind, your zeal for distant voyages will not yet cease,

I heartily wish you success in all your undertakings, but I would
advise you in order to ensure that success to fit out a ship *yourself*; that and *only that* can give you the absolute command of the
whole Expedition ...
I am &c.[70]

In other words; don't let the cabin door hit you on the way out, Mr Banks,
and good luck forming your own venture, which you can entirely pay
for yourself.

In a blind fury, Joseph Banks proceeds to take Lord Sandwich's likely
sarcastic advice and decides in an instant to fund an entire voyage himself,
beginning with buying a private ship for a voyage to Iceland – the South
Pole being judged as too difficult in the short term – and determines
to hire away Cook's officers as well. Lieutenant John Gore is only too
happy to take Mr Banks' shilling. Lieutenant Charlie Clerke declines
Banks' poaching attempt. It is too late, he is on deck and in His Majesty's
service and it would not be seemly to cut and run at such short notice,
despite Mr Banks' tempting bags of money. But Charlie Clerke does
have some gossip about Captain Cook to pass on. It happened like this:

Busy with the seemingly never-ending task of stowing, Charlie had
taken it upon himself to ask Joseph Gilbert, the Master, how, given
things are so tight without Mr Banks and his party and things, 'What
the devil should we have done if we had all gone?'

'Oh, by God,' Gilbert had replied off-hand, 'that was impossible.'[71]

Charlie knew it! The whole thing was a farce from the start, and
Captain Cook never intended to take Joseph Banks at all. The humble
Yorkshireman simply gave in to all the rich Londoner's whims, knowing
the ship would be unseaworthy.

Simple, honest, plain Lieutenant James Cook has outwitted the great
Mr Banks.

This report infuriates Banks, doubly so as he realises that he, an
Etonian, has been outfoxed by ... a Yorkshire farm boy!

And so Banks readies himself for what he has no doubt will be a
famous trip to Iceland.

James Cook?

He sails off into nothing less than greatness.

EPILOGUE

I whose ambition leads me not only farther than any man has been before me, but as far as I think it is possible for a man to go . . .[1]

Captain James Cook, 30 January 1774

For my purpose holds,
To sail beyond the sunset, and the baths.
Of all the Western stars, until I die.[2]

'Ulysses', Lord Tennyson

In the early days after Federation in 1901, Captain Cook was a useful symbol to reassert British identity and imperial belonging. In his reimagined majesty he became the semi-divine presence invoked in statuary and art – an anaesthetising balm for a hapless nation of arriviste white-skinned ex-colonials earnest to deny the antiquity of prior inhabitation by a peoples they were engaged in supplanting, and troubled by their isolation in a region teeming with other peoples they feared would do the same to them.[3]

Bruce Buchan, 'Cooking the Books', *Inside Story*

July 1772, Madeira, neither Arthur nor Martha, but gone

Well, Mr Banks is gone from the Second Voyage, but it seems that some of his party linger. For when Captain Cook arrives at the Portuguese island of Madeira at the end of July 1772, he hears the extraordinary story of 'Mr Burnett', a 30-year-old of curious appearance who is singularly dismayed by Mr Banks' absence, as he has been waiting for the botanist for three months. Apparently, Mr Burnett has been hired as an assistant to Mr Banks, by Mr Banks . . . The really odd thing is, however, that Mr Burnett is . . .

'Every part of Mr Burnett's behaviour and every action,' Captain Cook chronicles, 'tended to prove that he was a Woman.'[4]

Mr Banks has had the *sheer nerve* to send his *mistress* on ahead, dressed as a man, so she could join him aboard! With the news that Joseph Banks is not on board the *Resolution*, so 'Mr Burnett' vanishes.

Captain Cook smiles wryly before busying himself with the inevitable – ordering more fresh greens to be brought on board.

18 November 1772, Cape of Good Hope, to whom it is of no concern

It has been eight months since Joseph Banks' spectacular dockside exit from the Second Voyage, meaning, surely, he must have cooled down by now. So James Cook, Captain and Commander of the *Resolution*, on stopover on the Southern tip of Africa, resolves to mend fences and, sitting in his cabin, writes Mr Banks a letter:

> Dear Sir,
> Some Cross circumstances which happened at the latter part of the equipment of the *Resolution* created, I have reason to think, a coolness betwixt you and I, but I can by no means think it sufficient to me to break off all correspondence with a Man I am under many obligations to . . .
> I wish you all the Success you can wish yourself and am with great esteem and respect,
> Dear Sir,
> Your most Obliged Humble Servant
> JAMES COOK[5]

Joseph Banks does not deign to respond.

•

Three years and 17 days after setting forth on his Second Voyage, on 30 July 1775, Captain Cook returns to London with much to report to the Admiralty . . .

> I had now made the circuit of the Southern Ocean in a high Latitude and traversed it in such a manner as to leave not the least room for the Possibility of there being a continent, unless near the Pole and out of the reach of Navigation; by twice visiting the Pacific Tropical Sea, I had not only settled the situation of some old discoveries but made there many new ones and left, I conceive, very little more to be done even in that part. Thus I flatter my self that the

intention of the Voyage has in every respect been fully Answered, the Southern Hemisphere sufficiently explored and a final end put to the searching after a Southern Continent, which has at times engrossed the attention of some of the Maritime Powers for near two Centuries past and the Geographers of all ages.[6]

The grand endeavour is resolved.

•

At the time of Cook's return to London town, Joseph Banks is sailing on his yacht on the Thames with one of his oldest and now reconciled friends, Lord Sandwich.

Breathless with the excitement of Captain Cook's arrival, the good Dr Daniel Solander rushes to the Admiralty to meet his old shipmate. The Doctor sends off a note to Banks, handed to him now as his yacht docks, bursting with staccato summation and excitement, the sheer thrill of Captain Cook's triumph.

> 260 new Plants collected and preserved under the auspices of the expedition's naturalist, Johann Reinhold Forster, and his son, Georg – 200 new animals – 71 degrees 10' farthest Sth – no continent – Many Islands, some 8- Leagues long . . . Glorious voyage – No man lost by sickness.[7]

Et tu, Brute?

You mean the trip that I declined to go on is characterised even by you, my most faithful ally, as a '*Glorious voyage*'. Captain Cook's glory. And you mean the ship that I warned Lord Sandwich – the man now right beside me, talking too attentively to my mistress – would kill many of the men who sailed on it, has returned, safe and sound to a hero's welcome?

And '*No man lost by sickness*' you say? In three years! It is unheard of!

A triumph, from top to bottom, first to last, North to South and back again, round and round, up and down, and all surveyed, recorded and charted by Captain James Cook?

Yes.

In terms of public acclaim, Captain Cook is lauded as the man of the hour, the day, the decade, the *era* . . . London has seen nothing like it since the days of Sir Francis Drake. Cook has turned into the greatest explorer since Christopher Columbus, nearly 300 years ago!

In lieu of Joseph Banks claiming all the glory for himself, all the acclaim for the voyage goes to the rightful recipient this time, the good – no, the great – Captain Cook. Green with jealousy, red with rage, and sick with shame, Joseph Banks is left to ponder these developments all alone in his mansion in New Burlington Street, surrounded by the relics of the *Endeavour* voyage, *his* voyage, dammit.

How quickly London forgets. And how quickly London realises that Cook was also truly responsible for the success of the *Endeavour* expedition, not Joseph Banks.

Compounding it all is Captain Cook's wretched, unforgivable *kindness* to Banks. For the next post brings another letter from Doctor Solander: 'Captain Cook desires his best compliments to you, he express himself in the most friendly manner towards you that could be. He said "Nothing could have added to the satisfaction he has had, in making this tour but having had your company."'[8]

Monstrous!

Solander goes on, noting that Captain Cook has a present for Banks, some birds he had caught on his voyage, and 'he would have wrote to you himself about them, if he had not been kept too long at the Admiralty and at the same time wishing to see his wife. He rather looks better than when he left England.'[9]

Shoot me, now!

No matter where Joseph Banks goes, all he hears is the name of his former cabin-mate, the newly esteemed James Cook. For the great man is, after all, single-handedly responsible for delivering into the laps of high society – 'Philosophers of all kinds, naval administrators, ocean-sailing mariners'[10] – the final answer to one of the longest-standing speculative sagas throughout human history: the question of whether there is or isn't a Great Southern Land.

Captain Cook, sir, you have the floor.

It does not exist, my Lords, says the Yorkshireman, humble as Yorkshire pudding and gravy.

It is all nonsense.

As his great biographer JC Beaglehole will summate: 'Simply as comment on the great classical hypotheses of geography – familiar through two millennia, on the maps that adorned the famous atlases – there is something magnificent in the amplitude and completeness of the voyage. There was something almost cruelly final about it, in relation to the myth that had gripped geographers with such tenacity.'[11]

But what about those whimpering protests, receding in the distance? That is just Alexander Dalrymple. But nobody is listening.

All the glory is for this great man, this toast of the British Empire, ladies and gentlemen, I give you . . . Captain Cook!

In the meantime, wounded, suffering, Mr Banks cannot bring himself to make reply to Cook's kind offer, not even when a fortnight later the Doctor writes hopefully one more time, urging Joseph to join the party for Captain Cook. When Joseph declines, Solander writes again, saying of the party, 'all our friends look as well as if they had been all the while in clover. All enquired after you.'[12]

Yes, where IS Banks?

James Cook guesses correctly: he is sulking.

With still no reply, the next note from the Doctor to Mr Banks advises that all of Captain Cook's presents to him have been sent to the Doctor's own apartment at the British Museum, if Mr Banks would care to collect them? It is a ridiculous situation, and Cook will not wait further for Mr Banks' presence or grace. He requires neither anymore.

Finally, Mr Banks plumps on collecting the gifts himself, swallowing his pride, climbing down from his high dudgeon to eat huge lashings of humble pie and greet an old comrade who has become a great man.

They meet under the auspices of one of Banks's clubs, the Royal Philosophers' Club, where, for the first time, they face each other as near social equals.

Mr Banks, despite himself, has many questions.

As obliging as ever, James Cook is only too happy to chat.

And you didn't lose a single soul, James?

Of the 118 men who embarked, Mr Banks, we actually lost four – two drownings, a fall, and a long descent with disease – but none to scurvy.

Amazing.

Yes, it has been an extraordinary trip filled with many great achievements. As the two talk intimately in the corner, other gentlemen are sure to point them, and particularly *him*, out.

Why look, there! In the corner, it is that strapping fellow, that imposing figure, *Captain Cook!* Dining with young Banks! Do you suppose Mr Banks could persuade Captain Cook to join our club, if the great man would do us the great honour?

On behalf of the club, Joseph Banks makes the approach and Captain Cook agrees. And so the two Englishmen are reconciled, friends once more.

Joseph Banks finally accepts the age-old adage, if you can't beat a man, join him ... or at least try to bask in his reflected glory. Not long after their meeting at the club, the great naturalist personally commissions no fewer than three portraits of James Cook that he hangs in his house.

James Cook? We sailed the world together! Fine man.

The most iconic of his portraits will be done by the famed Nathaniel Dance in 1776, 'for a few hours before dinner',[13] on 25 May 1776.

Here is Captain Cook resplendent in his full-dress uniform, holding his own chart of the Southern Ocean on the table while his right hand points to the East coast of New Holland. The painter omits to record the scar on his right hand. (One person is not happy with Nathaniel Dance's effort and that is Elizabeth Cook, who regrets 'that a portrait in all other respects so perfect, should convey this erroneous expression to the eye of a stranger. For she ... regards him still with the lively recollection of a husband uniformly kind and affectionate, and of a father dearly loving his children.'[14])

Such portraits, however, are among the least of the plaudits he receives from a grateful nation. In this Age of Enlightenment and Endeavour, Cook is judged to have done more than any man to expand the British frontiers of geography, while demonstrating dominance of the high seas and so opening up imperial expansion of new lands with potentially bountiful resources and riches. In the House of Lords, in 1775, Lord Sandwich refers to him as no less than 'the first navigator in Europe'.[15]

Seven years earlier Cook had appeared, to many of the Members of the Royal Society, as little more than the knock-kneed supplicant for their regal blessing, now *they* are supplicants to *him* to become a Member himself. He graciously accepts, and becomes a part of that august circle of gentlemen in November 1775. His recommendation reads:

> Captain James Cook of Mile-end, a gentleman skilful in astronomy, and the successful conductor of two important voyages for the discovery of unknown countries, by which geography and natural history have been greatly advantaged and improved ... we whose names are underwritten, do, from our personal knowledge testify, that we believe him deserving of such honour, and that he will become a worthy and useful member.[16]

'A gentleman' now, no less!

And say, whose names do you read right there, crowding to the front of the 25 distinguished members sponsoring the proposal? Why yes, no less than Joseph Banks himself, followed by Dr Daniel Solander.

James Cook's first act as a Member of the Royal Society is to pen a six-page letter titled, 'How health was kept aboard the *Resolution*', detailing how 'with plenty of fresh water and proper attention to cleanliness, a ship's company will seldom be much afflicted with the scurvy, even though they are not provided with any of the anti-scorbutics above mentioned'.[17]

The Royal Society publishes Captain Cook's letter in volume 66 of the *Philosophical Transactions* journal, and further awards him the prestigious Copley Gold Medal, for 'outstanding achievements in research', in recognition for having completed the entire Second Voyage without losing a man to scurvy. After all these years, James Cook is not only recognised but celebrated as an accomplished 'Man of Science', an extraordinary achievement for one with so little formal education.

The Admiralty also recognises his newly exalted status by promoting him to the rank of post-Captain, while also awarding him an honorary retirement from the Navy. Yes, he is posted as an officer at Greenwich Hospital, which, despite its name, is actually a home for retired sailors and soldiers. Here, the revered Captain could have an easy sinecure, a land posting close to his family (Elizabeth had given birth to a baby boy named George just after he left for the Second Voyage. Alas, the infant survived just a few weeks, leaving only the Cooks' two eldest boys, James Jnr and Nathaniel). For surely he has done enough, risked enough by now, to go to his rest?

And that is indeed the idea.

James Cook agrees, with the sole condition that should a tempting opportunity come up to go to sea again, he be able to quit his post and take it up and . . .

And here it is now.

Having solved the remaining riddles of the Pacific and the far-flung, frozen South, the next major navigational challenge is one that has lured men to their death for centuries. Is there, perchance, a Northwest Passage, a route across the frozen top of the Americas, but below the Arctic, a passage that could revolutionise trade in Britain's favour? For if this passage is found it will surely forge a much shorter route between the Pacific and Atlantic Oceans that would mean ships could avoid having to go around Cape Horn.

When asked to a dinner to give advice on who should lead the voyage, Captain James Cook leaps to his feet and volunteers his *own* services, with much the same enthusiasm as he had when, as a 17-year-old he had told Mr Sanderson – 'I want to go to sea, sir!'

The Admiralty has its man. They had hoped he would respond in precisely this manner, so things move quickly and Captain Cook sails off on his Third Voyage in July 1776, at the age of 47. He commands the lead ship, his ever trusty Whitby cat, *Resolution*, while his long-time colleague, Charlie Clerke – now *Captain* Charles Clerke, if you please – will command HMS *Discovery*. (As it happens, Clerke is actually in debtors' prison, taking the place of his brother who he had acted as guarantor for, when Cook sails, meaning the departure of *Discovery* is delayed. Unbeknownst to Clerke, he contracts tuberculosis while there.)

But is it all too soon? Has the good Captain not been given the time needed to recover from the last two gruelling voyages, to get his bearings, regain his equilibrium and energy? As the voyage gets underway, Captain Cook appears worn down, suffers bilious complaints, and is desperately missing his family – Elizabeth had been pregnant, again, when he left – a perpetually dissatisfied man; a grumpy and rash version of the mild and just James Cook of the *Endeavour*.

'Right against me stands Capt. Cook, like the knight of the woeful countenance,' one of his sailors, James Trevenen, writes to his family, 'and pointing to a map of the South Sea.'[18]

The good Captain's temper tantrums become volcanic in nature – suddenly erupting with violent force, hurting all those too close, and with a good deal of angry rumbling in between explosions. Such tantrums see him mercilessly punish Indigenous people and recalcitrant seamen alike.

In October 1777, on the small island of Moorea, just West of Tahiti, Captain Cook is so infuriated by the theft of his ship's goats – yes, its goats, not its boats – that he has the *Resolution*'s Marines burn many of the Natives' houses and canoes in wanton retaliation, an extraordinary overreaction to the temporary absence of two beasts. It shocks his men greatly.

Cook's reputation as a calm and just man is under threat of being torched as well.

For his full-blooded tantrums on the quarter-deck have such remarkably writhing rhythms they remind the veterans of a Tahitian *heiva* – and that's how the amused if scared jacks refer to them: the Captain's throwing a '*heiva*' again. (One possible explanation for Cook not being himself bears citing. Medical experts who studied Cook's medical ailments on the Third Voyage – including stomach cramps and nausea – have speculated that he picked up a parasite on his Second Voyage and was likely in chronic discomfort.)

But it is not just his temper.

It is also his judgement that appears to have gone awry.

For example, on 26 June 1778, in quest of the North-west Passage, the two ships are sailing through the Unalga Passage in the Catherine Islands. Cook is at the helm as they head through so heavy a fog that visibility is reduced to just 100 yards. Despite being in uncharted territory, on Cook's orders both the *Resolution* and the *Discovery* are sailing at a fierce clip. Master William Bligh is of the strong if silent view that this is *madness* as he looks for Cook to respond to these absurdly dangerous conditions, but the Captain, with full faith in his own star, stands calmly on deck displaying an air of perfect contentment, almost as if bemused by the nervousness of his officers.

He is Captain Cook, the most venerated sea-captain of his age, he knows what he is doing when others do not, he . . .

'Breakers!'[19] comes the alarmed cry of the lookout, high up in the rigging. Captain Cook instantly springs into action bellowing orders to heave to. It is a close-run thing. The real shock comes when the ships indeed manage to halt by furling all sails and dropping anchors, only for the fog to clear so they can all see that not only are they barely a cable's length from the breakers, and hence large and jagged rocks, but towering over them on both sides are high cliffs.

The last time a miracle this large had occurred, a star had appeared in the East. A touch either way would have seen their certain destruction.

'Very nice pilotage,' Charlie Clerke would dryly remark, 'considering our perfect ignorance of our situation and the total darkness which prevented our attaining any knowledge of it.'[20]

Captain Cook himself is shocked. His log reads almost like a confessional, as he really does thank the Lord that they have somehow chanced 'through between these rocks, where I would not have ventured on a clear day, and to such an anchoring place that I could not have chosen a better'.[21] Cook might still have the luck of the gods with him, but God knows his fine judgement and natural caution have deserted him.

Though his crew might secretly wonder at his decline, the world waits with bated breath to see what discoveries Cook will produce this time, even in the parts of the world that are in conflict with Great Britain.

And the trusty Captain has indeed already made a significant discovery. In January 1778, on their way North, Captain Cook and the men on his two ships are the first Europeans to make landfall on islands that feel a little like the Tahiti of the Northern hemisphere, a place called *Hawaii* – though Cook christens them the Sandwich Islands. It is a paradise . . .

10 March 1779, Paris, 'common friends to mankind'

Of course the United States of America's Ambassador to France, Benjamin Franklin, wants to win the current war with Great Britain. And so it follows he wants any British ship that is sighted by an American ship on the high seas to be sunk or captured. There is, however, one exception, one English ship that His Excellency Benjamin Franklin wants spared. In his inimitable manner, he writes a unique 'passport' to be sent to all American sea-captains forthwith:

Gentlemen,

A Ship having been fitted out from England before the Commencement of this War, to make Discoveries of new Countries, in Unknown Seas, under the Conduct of that most celebrated Navigator and Discoverer Captain Cook; an Undertaking truly laudable in itself, as the Increase of Geographical Knowledge, facilitates the Communication between distant Nations, in the Exchange of useful Products and Manufactures, and the Extension of Arts, whereby the common Enjoyments of human Life are multiplied and augmented, and Science of other kinds increased to the Benefit of Mankind in general. This is therefore most earnestly to recommend to every one of you; that in case the said Ship which is now expected to be soon in the European Seas on her Return, should happen to fall into your Hands, you would not consider her as an Enemy, nor suffer any Plunder to be made of the Effects contained in her, nor obstruct her immediate Return to England, by detaining her or sending her into any other Part of Europe or to America; but that you would treat the said Captain Cook and his People with all Civility and Kindness, affording them as common Friends to Mankind, all the Assistance in your Power which they may happen to stand in need of . . .

I have the honour to be Gentlemen, Your most obedient humble Servant,

B Franklin[22]

Yes, Captain Cook is nothing less than a servant of humanity to the eyes of Benjamin Franklin. Alas, what His Excellency doesn't know at the time is that his letter is already academic . . .

14 February 1779, Karakakooa Bay, Hawaii, into the undiscovered country

After being stopped by ice in the Bering Sea, Captain Cook has decided to return to Hawaii to rest and repair the ships before trying again next summer. And all had gone well until today, when they had woken to find that the *Discovery*'s large cutter has been stolen by the Natives during the night.

Enraged, Captain Cook despatches two boats to make sure no canoe leaves the bay, while he goes ashore intending to bring the local Grand Chief aboard until the boat is returned.

Alas, while the Captain is with the Chief, the word comes through that a neighbouring minor Chief has been shot and killed by Cook's men out in the bay. Immediately, the Hawaiians dress for war, donning armour made of plants woven into mats then soaked in water, 'arming themselves with long spears, clubs, and daggers'.[23] They start closing in on the Captain as he attempts to escort the head Chief, Terreeoboo, down the beach and into the waiting boat, and the situation becomes explosive when the crowd of Natives press around, begging their Chief not to go with the white men.

Straining for diplomacy, Captain Cook tries to keep everything calm, insisting to the Chief that no harm is intended, even as yet more Natives arrive. In short order Cook and his small armed band of officers and Marines are surrounded by no fewer than 400 Natives knocking together large stones in a menacing rhythm, the quickening beat of an attack that is surely building.

Clack, clack, clack-clack . . .

Cook can see no way forward. He quickly decides to let the whole affair, and the Chief, go.

'Lieutenant Phillips,' Cook says quietly. 'Withdraw the men, and get them into the boats.'[24]

The mob starts to close in on Cook and his men, swirling around them, beating their rocks, yelling, shaking their fists and weapons.

Captain Cook has had enough. He fires his musket loaded with small shot at a man, although the Native is unharmed thanks to his plant armour.

A Chief lunges at Lieutenant Phillips with a spear as stones begin to fly, knocking down a Marine. Phillips fires, sparking an attack from the Hawaiians.

As Captain Cook, close to the water's edge, turns to signal to the waiting boats, a Native wielding a club strikes him square in the back of the head.

Captain James Cook staggers forward, drops his musket and falls to one knee, his hands in the lapping water.

He attempts to stand, but a dagger cuts swiftly down into the middle of his back. The blade passes 'quite through'[25] James Cook, and his whole body seizes in shock and pain.

Only days before, these same Hawaiian Natives believed that Cook was the living incarnation of the great god *Lono*. But the blood that now pours forth from him in angry spurts shows him to be no more than a man, and now a mortally wounded one at that.

In a moment of blurred fury, other Native warriors rush forward and deal further blows to Captain Cook and the Marines who struggle to defend him.

Retreat!

It is the Captain's last order, his hand waving away the boats heading to rescue him.

Captain Cook falls, face first, into knee-deep, clear water.

A dark red stain spreads around him like an ink blot.

Home is the sailor, home from the sea . . .

Captain James Cook is dead.

The process of retrieving Captain Cook's body to give him as Christian a burial as possible is as grisly as it is draining, for his men quickly learn that his remains have been hacked to pieces, with individual chunks shared among the Chiefs of the different tribes. It takes a combination of negotiations and threats of reprisals for the moment to arrive in the forenoon of 20 February when one of the more high-ranking of the Hawaiian Chiefs, Eappo, is rowed out to HMS *Resolution* and comes on deck, 'bearing in his hands, with great solemnity, the bones of the illustrious Captain, wrapped up in a new cloth, and covered with a cloak of black and white feathers . . . The parcel contained the two hands entire, most of the head, with the bones of the arms, thighs and legs.'[26]

They know it is Captain Cook's remains by the cruel scar on the right hand. When some more bones arrive the next morning it is decided they are enough and, after all the remains are placed in a coffin and covered in a Union Jack, Captain James Cook's body is 'committed to the deep, with the funeral service, and military honours; amidst the tears and sobs of the officers and crew, whom he had so long and so honourably commanded'.[27]

The two European ships leave Karakakooa Bay to find safe harbour elsewhere, before making their second attempt, later in the spring, to find the North-west Passage.

As for the crew, despite their misgivings about the Captain's *heivas*, they are now devastated without exception. For they recognise that as well as being a good man, he was no less than a great man, as his achievements on this final voyage alone will attest.

'He explored the unknown part of the North American coast from lat. 43 N. to Lat. 70 N – that is to say 3500 miles,' one of his officers, Lieutenant James King, chronicles. 'He proved the proximity of the continents of Asia and America; passed the straits between them and surveyed the coast on each side to such a height of northern latitude as to demonstrate the impracticability of a passage in that hemisphere from the Atlantic into the Pacific Ocean either by an eastern or a western course. In short, if we accept the Sea of Amoor and the Japanese Archipelago, which still remain imperfectly known to Europeans, he has completed the hydrography of the habitable globe.'[28]

Yes, Captain Cook's men feel lost without their guiding star. Midshipman George Gilbert will note that Cook's death 'appeared to us somewhat like a dream that we could not reconcile ourselves to ... Grief was visible in every countenance, some expressing it by tears, and others by a kind of gloomy dejection.'[29]

Surgeon David Samwell notes of their fallen Commander: 'He was beloved by his people, who looked up to him as to a father, and obeyed his commands with alacrity. The confidence we placed in him was unremitting; our admiration of his great talents unbounded; our esteem for his good qualities affectionate and sincere.'[30]

•

With Captain Cook's death, **Captain Charles Clerke,** who has been ill for some time, is now in command of the voyage. The ships stop briefly in June 1779, on the Kamchatka Peninsula, in far Eastern Russia, where Captain Clerke writes a letter informing the Admiralty of the tragic news.

It takes seven months for the letter to be taken overland across Siberia, arriving at the Admiralty on 10 January 1780, and so goes to the Earl of Sandwich, who writes a shocked letter to his friend Joseph Banks:

> Dear Sir,
> What is uppermost in our mind always must come first, poor Captain Cook is no more, he was massacred with four of his people by the Natives of an Island where he had been treated if possible with more hospitality than at Tahiti . . . Captain Clerke now commands the *Resolution*; he means to make one more attempt for a northern passage but does not seem to have much hopes of success.[31]

•

A senior officer of the Admiralty knocks on the door of the unassuming terraced house, Number 7 Assembly Row, Mile End.

Elizabeth Cook sits in her armchair sewing a waistcoat of the finest Tahitian cloth for her fine husband. She places it aside and answers the door.

When she resumes her seat some minutes later, she closes her eyes and weeps.

•

On 11 January 1780, the *London Gazette* breaks the tragic news of Captain Cook's death to the public, and in the same edition prints an obituary, noting, 'This untimely and ever to be lamented fate of so intrepid, so able, and so intelligent a Sea-Officer, may justly be considered as an irreparable loss to the public, as well as to his family, for in him were united every successful and amiable quality that could adorn his profession; nor was his singular modesty less conspicuous than his other virtues. His successful experiments to preserve the health of his crews are well known, and his discoveries will be an everlasting honour to his country.'[32]

Of course, newspapers around Great Britain pick up the story to reprint it far and wide.

•

Up on the windswept North Sea coast, in the village of Redcar – just a day's walk from Whitby – James Cook's little sister Margaret stares sadly at an empty armchair. Heartbroken, she is yet grateful that her father, James Cook Senior, had died some eight months earlier, at the remarkable age of 85, and is so spared the agony of hearing the news. He had actually outlived his son by just two months. Oh, how her recent memories of him are cherished. There he goes, this venerable old man, hobbling to secure every newspaper he can mentioning his son, and bringing them home to slowly devour. For in the last years of his life, James Cook Senior had indeed learnt to read, purely to be able to keep track of his son's fantastic voyages, something that had filled those years with great joy. And now, both of them are gone.

Many around Great Britain mourn for the fallen Captain Cook, and King George III himself weeps upon receipt of the news.

•

Alas, in her grief, **Elizabeth Cook**'s greatest pleasures, her sons, will all bring her tremendous sorrows. Just 18 months after the death of her husband, their second eldest, Nathaniel, a 16-year-old Midshipman, dies serving aboard the HMS *Thunderer* when it founders with all hands in 1780 after being struck by a vicious hurricane in the West Indies.

Then in December 1793, her youngest boy, Hugh, who had been born a month after his father left on his Third Voyage, dies of scarlet fever while studying at Christ College, Cambridge, age 17.

Just the following month, January 1794, Elizabeth Cook's last surviving child of the six she had given birth to, her eldest, 30-year-old Captain James Cook Jnr of the Royal Navy, is ordered to join his vessel, the sloop *Spitfire*, anchored in Yarmouth Harbour, Isle of Wight, and attempts to do so in a small boat travelling from nearby Poole, despite a storm bearing down at the time. He did not arrive on the ship, and the following day his body washed up on shore with a grievous wound in his head, all of his money gone, as are the crew of his small boat – and neither they, nor the boat, are ever seen again. It is never clear whether a terrible crime has been committed, or it is simply a terrible accident. But it matters little either way to Elizabeth Cook, whose entire family are now gone to the grave before her.

She mourns them all, but none more than her dear, late, great husband, James Cook – though to her many visitors who continue to come to pay their respect over the decades, she is wont to refer to him as 'Mr Cook'. Theirs had been an extraordinarily close and loving bond, despite the fact that in their 17 years of marriage James and Elizabeth spent no more than four years under the one roof. She keeps a lock of her husband's hair in a ring to feel close to him, and every 14 February, the anniversary of his death, she stays completely alone in her room, reading Mr Cook's bible and fasting for the entire day, as she does on the anniversary of each of the deaths of her three sons, James, Nathaniel and Hugh.

In honour of the service rendered by her late, great, husband, the Admiralty awarded Elizabeth Cook an annual pension of £200 for life. It is a life alone.

Now, had James Cook been a member of the nobility and lived, even a minor aristocrat, there is little doubt he would certainly have been raised to the peerage. And yet, though born of the common herd, and now deceased, still the King grants his family a coat of arms.

'I think,' his second biographer Walter Besant will note, 'that this must have been the last occasion when a coat of arms was granted as a recognition of service . . . the old notion that the gentility can be conferred by the sovereign as the fountain of honour is clean forgotten. But it was not then forgotten . . . Cook's family, therefore, were rewarded with a shield: they were advanced to the first step of nobility. The shield is thus described. "Azure, between two polar stars or, a sphere on the plane of the meridian, showing the Pacific Ocean, his track thereon marked by red lines. And for crest, on a wreath of the colours, is an arm bowed, in the uniform of a Captain of the Royal Navy. In the hand is the Union Jack on a staff proper. The arm is encircled by a wreath of palm and laurel".'[33]

In the last months of Elizabeth Cook's life, when she is nudging 93, there comes a day when she slowly stoops by the fire of her fine home in Surrey. Despite her age – near unprecedented in these parts – she remains a handsome, venerable woman with an oval face and an aquiline nose, dressed, as ever, in long black satin. Clutched tightly in her veiny hand are letters, most of them love letters from a handsome young man written as long as 70 years ago, a man whose memory she still cherishes.

Mrs Cook carefully reads each dog-eared letter one last precious time before . . . casting them into the flames. Hundreds of letters from her James, a man that only she truly knows, a man whose intimate thoughts history will never fully be privy to, thanks to the very act she is now performing. Still she does not hesitate as the flames consume each letter in an instant – flaring up with extraordinary speed, just like he had described the bush in New Holland flaring up when the Natives had set fire to it. After all, history already has Captain Cook, the monument, the statue, the icon, and in many ways the demands of the historical tides had claimed him to make her a widow all these long decades.

But she has James Cook the man, and she will keep him for herself. And yes, for years people had asked after such papers and letters, but she had always denied their existence. They were no-one's affair bar her and dear James'. And now he is gone, their children are gone, just as she will soon be gone and, as the last of the greedy flames devours the last letter, crackling in satisfaction, those last insights into his soul, his life and his work are gone, too. She retires for the evening.

Elizabeth Cook outlived 'Mr Cook' by nearly six decades, dying on 13 May 1835.

She was buried in Cambridge's St Andrew the Great Church with her beloved sons James and Hugh. A measure of the goodness of the woman with whom James Cook had fallen in love with was that a large part of her final Will & Testament bequeathed over £1000 to keep the family monument in good repair from the interest, to give the minister an annual stipend to oversee the terms of the trust, and, most importantly, have the remainder of the interest divided equally and given to five poor aged women of the parish every St Thomas' Day.

•

In the meantime, what a life **Joseph Banks** led, what an influence he wielded! The dashing young naturalist who cut such a swathe through the Tahitian maidens on his first visit with Captain Cook in 1769 went on to be perhaps the most influential man of science of his time, becoming President of the Royal Society in 1778, a position he held for an extraordinary 42 years.

His own scientific pursuits were, of course, monumental. On his *Endeavour* voyage he and his fellow naturalists had gathered an extraordinary 30,000 exotic plant specimens – together with endless zoological specimens – and all of them had to be sorted and catalogued. In the hectic first years after the *Endeavour*'s return, Mr Banks had been far too occupied with social engagements, not to mention trying to lord it over Captain Cook before going on his collecting trip to Iceland, to really make headway.

Nevertheless, 'in late 1773 Banks finally committed himself to a sumptuous publication documenting the botanical results of the expedition. The collections represented at least 3000 different species, with perhaps 1400 new to science.'[34]

Banks also oversaw the legacy of the work of the late Sydney Parkinson, hiring a team of artists to take his original sketches and compose 900 gloriously colourful illustrations from them, all now held at the Natural History Museum in London.[35]

Banks was knighted in 1795 and was the key mover behind such initiatives as the expansion of the Royal Botanic Gardens at Kew and The Royal Horticultural Society. Oh, and a *Bounty* Mutiny and a Rum Rebellion resulted from Bank's enthusiastic patronage of one William Bligh.

Banks lived to the ripe old age of 77, finally dying at his house, Spring Grove, in Isleworth, London, on 19 June 1820.

One measure of just how extraordinary was the work of Banks and his entourage is that, *to this day*, there are still unopened specimens from the *Endeavour* voyage in the British Museum! Drawer after drawer after drawer of them . . .

Even history was exhausted by Banks.

•

Captain Cook's trusty Whitby cat, **HM Bark *Endeavour*,** conqueror of the globe? She became little more than a glorified ferry, renamed the *Lord Sandwich* to hide just how many sea miles she had done, going back and forth from England to the Falkland Islands, before being sold into private hands.

The ultimate ignominy came in 1778, when, during the American War of Independence, she was scuttled in a river mouth off Rhode Island by Captain Brisbane as part of an attempt to blockade American ships. She lay lost and rotting on the sea floor for over 200 years, until one day in September 2018, a group of marine archaeologists, came across – *hulloa!* – some sunken wrecks in the spot the blockade had taken place. The testing of which of the wrecks is the *Endeavour* is underway as we speak. In the meantime, the Rhode Island State Government has claimed ownership.

Still, it is extraordinary to reflect that 250 years after she rounded New Zealand and bashed into the Great Barrier Reef, the mighty *Endeavour* may be seen once more, her ancient deck displayed in a maritime museum, and surely – at midnight, when all is locked up, and the decks are clear – attracting the spirits of those men long gone. For if William Shakespeare was right, that 'All the world's a stage/And all the men and women merely players', what better stage to return to for the spiritual encore of those who once sailed upon her, than the reconstituted deck of the *Endeavour*, particularly those whose names no longer resonate like Cook and Banks . . .

Taking command of the Third Voyage after the death of Captain Cook, **Charlie Clerke** died of tuberculosis a short time later. The witty and beloved Captain Clerke managed a touching letter of farewell to Joseph Banks before he left this world, with the final paragraph reading:

> Now my dear & honored friend, I must bid you a final adieu, may you enjoy many happy years in this world, & in the end attain the fame your indefatigable industry so richly deserves. These are most sincerely the warmest & sincerest departing wishes of your most devoted, affectionate and departing servant,
> Chas. Clerke[36]

In 1772 **Lieutenant John Gore** joined Banks on his scientific expedition to Iceland and the two remained lifelong friends. In 1776, Gore put behind him the tensions of the First Voyage and joined Cook for his Third Voyage. Upon the death of Cook in Hawaii, it was Gore who not only assumed command of *Discovery*, but, when Charles Clerke died, took responsibility for the entire expedition, bringing the ships home on 4 October 1780. He was promoted to Captain, and continued with his Royal Navy career, until having circumnavigated the globe four times, he'd at last had enough. Upon retirement, he took up Captain Cook's old berth at Greenwich Hospital, with his wife, where he died 10 years later on 10 August 1790, aged 60.

It would be a hundred years before another sailor would go around the globe four times.

Likely the second longest lived of the *Endeavour*'s company and crew was **Isaac Smith**, who owned the first two English feet to set foot on Australian soil. He stayed with the Royal Navy, retiring with the rank of Rear-Admiral and for many years lived with his cousin, Elizabeth Cook, in her cottage in Clapham, caring for her in her final years, at least while he was able. In 1820 he inherited Merton Abbey from his brother and died in July 1831, aged 81.

Millions of lives were changed forever in the wake of James Cook's voyages.

Following a wave of arrivals of French Christian missionaries in Tahiti around the turn of the 19th century, the archipelago moved into the orbit of French imperialism and soon became part of 'French Polynesia'.

Though New Zealand was colonised by the English from the early 1800s, the Māori continued to fiercely fight for their land and were numerous enough to be able to negotiate a kind of peace. This culminated in the signing of the Treaty of Waitangi on 6 February 1840 between the Māori Chiefs and the British Crown, which gave the Crown the right to make law for all, while stipulating that the Māori could retain self-management of certain material and cultural resources, and had equal rights to the white settlers.

But perhaps nowhere was more affected, nor a native population more devastated, by Captain Cook's First Voyage than New Holland.

Before the American War of Independence in 1775, Britain was transporting a thousand convicts a year to the United States, which suddenly had to stop. With no further outlet for Britain's groaning prisons, in 1776 the Hulks Bill was passed, which saw Britain's excess convicts incarcerated in decommissioned ships at anchor, mostly on the Thames – only ever an extremely temporary measure.

What could be the permanent solution?

In 1779 the House of Commons set up the 'Bunbury Committee' – after Sir Charles Bunbury, a long-term member of the House of Commons with an interest in justice – to look for places in the British Empire where a penal colony could be set up. Joseph Banks is called to testify, and offers a suggestion. Botany Bay on the East coast of New Holland. To begin with, there are very few people there, while it boasts a good supply of fresh water, arable land with grassy plains, and 'the proportion of rich soil is sufficient to support a very large number of people'.[37]

But what of the Natives, Mr Banks?

'I apprehend there will be little probability of any opposition from Natives,' says Banks reassuringly. 'As during my stay there, in the year 1770, I saw very few and did not think there was above fifty in all the neighbourhood.'[38]

Indeed?

Oh yes.

So much for that little problem of the people who actually live in this land the British are about to take.

In fact, when the Bunbury Committee looks at Banks' notes from 1770, it seems that Botany Bay in fact has rather poor quality soil, 'the Soil wherever we saw it consisted of either swamps or light sandy soil on which grew very few species of trees',[39] wrote Banks on 1 May 1770.

Ahem . . .

Which is perhaps the reason the committee does not immediately embrace the notion of New South Wales as a place to send convicts. In fact, it proves to be another member of Cook's First Voyage, much more junior than Joseph Banks, who will prove decisive in establishing New South Wales as a settlement, a most unlikely fellow, a man who on a bad day can closely resemble a scoundrel.

Why, it is none other than the *Endeavour*'s Midshipman, **James Magra!** The years since the *Endeavour* have been good to the man strongly suspected of cutting off Richard Orton's ears, Mr Magra – now known as Mr James Matra. He had taken up a minor diplomatic post as British Consul in the Canary Islands before shrewdly beginning a long and warm correspondence with Sir Joseph Banks that would last decades. Mr Matra has an idea. Why not establish a new colony on the East coast of New Holland, around Botany Bay? It could be a place both for British Loyalists like himself who feel they no longer belong in the traitorous and newly declared 'United States of America', and, yes, also a place for Britain to send her convicts, to labour and establish a settlement. Banks is delighted to find an ally in this notion.

Encouraged, Matra writes to the Home Secretary, Lord Sydney, in 1783, with a detailed plan on how such a penal colony could be established.

> I am going to offer an object to the consideration of our Government which may in time atone for the loss of our American colonies. By the discoveries and enterprise of our officers, many new countries have been found which know no sovereign, and that hold out the most enticing allurements to European adventurers. None are more inviting than New South Wales . . . The Climate and soil are so happily adapted to produce every various and valuable production of Europe and of both the Indies, that with good management and a few settlers, in twenty or thirty years they might cause a revolution in the whole system of European commerce, and secure to England a monopoly of some part of it, and a very large share of the whole.[40]

The idea is so well received that in 1785 both Matra and Joseph Banks appear before a parliamentary committee at Westminster to make their case. The combination of passion and influence in these two *Endeavour* men wins the day and decides the fate of a continent. For in August 1786 it is the administration of William Pitt the Younger that formally decides to adopt 'Matra's Plan'. New South Wales *will* be a colony and in Mr Matra's opinion *he* is suited to be the colony's first Governor.

Mind you, in the opinion of no few others, the ear-lopping Matra is damn lucky not to be one of the first convicts who arrive upon the First Fleet under the command of Captain Arthur Phillip in mid-January 1788.

Captain Arthur Phillip, who assumes the role of Governor of the colony, is certain that he has been sent to the wrong place when he arrives, as, 'no place was found in the whole circuit of Botany Bay which seemed at all calculated for the reception of so large a settlement'.[41]

In short order Governor Phillip decides to look for a better place to settle and begins by exploring what Captain Cook had marked on the chart as Port Jackson. Entering the headlands to find a capacious harbour, he famously described today's Sydney Harbour as 'one of the finest harbours in the world, in which a thousand sail of the line might ride in perfect security'.[42]

The fleet is moved there days later, with the Union Jack being raised at 'Sydney Cove' on 26 January 1788.

As for the Wangal lad, Bennelong, by the time the *Berewalgal* come back again he has been initiated into manhood, scars raised on his 24-year-old chest and down his wiry arms, his front tooth knocked out, able to hunt kangaroos with the other men.

Like all of his clan and neighbouring clans, there is no little confusion and alarm when it becomes apparent that this time the *Berewalgal* are not just here to visit for a few days – white spirits on huge water birds, no sooner here than they are gone again. Instead, they come into *Birrabirragal* on a full flock of birds and *stay*. The white ghosts come on to the shore, and take a large pole – perhaps some kind of spear? – and, after driving the pole into *Warrane*, a munificent cove on the land of the Gadigal people, put up some kind of coloured cloth which flaps from it. On that same terrible day, for no apparent reason, the white intruders start to hack down the trees of the ancestors, causing animals and birds to flee. *Warrane* is desecrated.

And to the dismay of all the Natives, the intruders soon start to dig in, building curious kinds of very large lean-tos that don't actually seem to lean.

Five months after the arrival of the First Fleet, on 23 June 1788, one of the mates on HMS *Sirius*, Daniel Southwell, wrote from Sydney Cove to his uncle, the Reverend Weeden Butler, who lived in Chelsea, London: 'On June 23 . . . the King's birthday was celebrated with great state and solemnity, and large bonfires – we had plenty of wood – were burning all night. The ships saluted at sunrise, noon, and sunset, which must have frightened the warra warras, for so we call the blacks, from their constant cry of "warra warra" at everything they see that is new.'[43]

It is not just the desecration of the land the Natives need fear. For no more than two years after the arrival of the *Berewalgals*, Bennelong's people are ravaged by smallpox, dying in droves, his wife included.

Bennelong survives the epidemic, but the year after the arrival of the Europeans, his life and that of his friend Colebee, take a dramatic turn . . .

One day in late 1789, First Lieutenant William Bradley is ordered by Governor Phillip to capture a Native, and later recalling of the scene, 'they eagerly took the fish [we were offering], they were dancing together when the Signal was given by me, and the two poor devils were seiz'd & handed into the boat in an instant . . . They were bound with ropes and taken by boat to Sydney Cove . . . It was by far the most unpleasant service I was ever ordered to Execute . . . all that could be said or done was not sufficient to remove the pang they naturally felt at being torn away from their friends; or to reconcile them to their situation.'[44]

The men are brought before Governor Phillip and compelled to act as a kind of shackled liaison point with the 'warras'. From this moment, *Birrabirragal* will go on. But the life of Bennelong and all those of the Eora nation are changed forever.

•

Having come from that speck on the map which is Whitby, James Cook has accomplished nothing less than filling out the map for about a quarter of the *globe*.

His achievements were well captured by his second biographer, Sir Walter Besant:

> No other sailor has ever so greatly enlarged the borders of the earth.
> He discovered the Society Islands; he proved New Zealand to be

two islands and he surveyed its coasts; he followed the unknown
coast of New Holland for two thousand miles and proved that it
was separated from New Guinea; he traversed the Antarctic Ocean
on three successive voyages, sailing completely around the globe in
its high latitudes, and proving that the dream of the great southern
continent had no foundation, unless it was close around the pole
and so beyond the reach of ships; he discovered and explored a
great part of the coast of New Caledonia, the largest island in
the South Pacific next to New Zealand; he found the desolate
island of Georgia, and Sandwich-land, the southernmost land
yet known; he discovered the fair and fertile archipelago . . . the
Sandwich Islands; he explored three thousand five hundred miles
of the North American coast, and he traversed the icy seas of the
North Pacific, as he had done in the South, in search of the passage
which he failed to discover. All this, without counting the small
islands which he found scattered in the Pacific.[45]

Not surprisingly Cook iconography has thrived, his image wound into
modern national 'foundation' stories, meaning that all things related to
the man and his voyages are highly valued.

•

The **cannon** thrown off the *Endeavour* that terrible night after it hit the
Great Barrier Reef, destined to lie there forever and a day? Well, that
day actually came in 1969, when a project launched by the American
Academy of Natural Sciences managed to bring all six cannon to the
surface, together with the other ballast that had been dropped. Those
cannon are now in several museums around the world, including the
National Museum of Australia.

•

The **Aboriginal shield and spears** wielded by the Gweagal warriors on the
day of first contact? Joseph Banks bequeathed the spears to Trinity College,
Cambridge. Their return to Australia is requested, and is being considered.

Also still in the British Museum, to my amazement, is the shield. Is it
not bizarre and unjust that such an iconic and quintessentially Australian
artefact, should be in British possession, and not Australia's? One person
who has led the charge to bring it back is Rodney Kelly,[46] an Indigenous
man claiming to be a direct descendant of the elder warrior who was

shot in the legs by Captain Cook even before the Englishman set foot on shore. In 2016, Kelly travelled to Canberra to see the shield when it was on loan to the National Museum of Australia, and staged a peaceful protest, insisting the British had stolen it and that it should be returned to no less than its traditional owners. He then travelled to London to meet with museum officials, to be told no in person.

The British Museum now claims the shield they have may not have been brought back on the *Endeavour* – which goes directly against what it has claimed for the last 50 years while having it on display. In May 2017, the shield was taken from its usual cabinet, with a sign left behind saying it had been 'removed for study'. At last call the museum was holding a two-day workshop 'to test the argument – or widely-held belief – that the shield was collected at Botany Bay in 1770'.[47]

•

One measure of how highly Captain Cook remains regarded, even in the modern era by those on the cusp of explorative science, is that in 1984 NASA's third space shuttle was named *Discovery*, after one of the two ships used by Cook on the Third Voyage, while the last shuttle to fly, in 2011, was named nothing less than '*Endeavour*'.

•

Which leaves us with the original questions with which I began the book.

Who was James Cook? What sort of a man was he? Most importantly for the ongoing 'history wars', was he a hero? An anti-hero? A great man? An imperialist villain? The verdict keeps evolving with every generation, as more voices are heard and more views are realised. So it goes ... and keeps going.

What seems clear to me is that Cook, personally, was not an imperialist, at least in the sense of claiming such lands with any enthusiasm. He would later express strong regrets about the effect of imperialism on native peoples, after he had witnessed what the outcome of just a few years interaction with Europeans had been on their culture. The most obvious example is what he saw on his Second Voyage when it came to the previously relatively chaste women of New Zealand now being pushed forward for sexual services by their own husbands and fathers, in return for such things as a single spike nail.

'Such are the consequences,' Cook writes with real regret, 'of a commerce with Europeans and what is still more to our shame, civilised

Christians. We debauch their morals already too prone to vice and we introduce among them wants and perhaps diseases which they never before knew and which serves only to disturb that happy tranquility they and their forefathers have enjoyed. If anyone denies the truth of this assertion let him tell me what the Natives of the whole extent of America have gained by the commerce they have had with Europeans.'[48]

Does *that* sound like an enthusiastic imperialist?

Nor, for that matter, did he make any personal claim to having 'discovered' the Australian continent, in fact specifically rejecting the very idea when he wrote, 'Having satisfied myself of the great Probability of a passage, thro' which I intend going with the Ship, and therefore may land no more upon this Eastern coast of New Holland, and on the Western side I can make no new discovery, the honour of which belongs to the Dutch Navigators . . .'[49]

That honour may have belonged to the Dutch, but Australia soon belonged to the British, something that never would have happened if James Cook had not landed in New South Wales. Yet here are some ironic words from Cook's Second Voyage, concerning the fierce opposition of the Natives of New Hebrides, but a parallel will occur to many of the Indigenous peoples of Australia, New Zealand and Hawaii: '. . . one cannot blame them for when one considers the light in which they must look upon us in, its impossible for them to know our real design, we enter their Ports without their daring to make opposition, we attempt to land in a peaceable manner, if this succeeds its well, if not we land nevertheless and maintain the footing we thus got by the Superiority of our fire arms, in what other light can they then at first look upon us but as invaders of their Country; time and some acquaintance with us can only convince them of their mistake.'[50]

No less than 250 years later, in Australia, that very issue of invasion is being widely discussed, with the idea growing that the only way forward is by some measure of Treaty, as we are still the only nation settled by the British without one.

If we accomplish such a great thing, perhaps the motif at the top could be the broken spear proffered by the 'little old man', the great tribal elder, to Captain Cook.

We must live together in peace.

ENDNOTES

Epigraph

1 Beaglehole, 'On the Character of Captain James Cook', *The Geographical Journal*, Vol. 122, No. 4, December 1956, p. 417.
2 Besant, *Captain Cook*, Macmillan & Co., London, 1890, p. 33.

Introduction

1 Beaglehole, 'On the Character of Captain James Cook', p. 420.
2 Dugard, *Farther Than Any Man: The Rise and Fall of Captain James Cook*, Pocket Books, New York, 2001, p. 237.
3 Beaglehole, *The Life of Captain James Cook*, Adam & Charles Black, London, 1974, p. 289.
4 Beaglehole, *The Life of Captain James Cook*, p. 289.
5 Beaglehole, 'On the Character of Captain James Cook', p. 420.
6 Buchan, 'Cooking the Books', *Inside Story*, 14 June 2018, http://insidestory.org.au/cooking-the-books/.

Prologue

1 Hough, *Captain James Cook: A Biography*, Hodder & Stoughton, London, 1994, p. 5 [reported speech].
2 Defoe, *A Tour Through England and Wales*, Dent, London, 1928, p. 247.
3 Author's note: At this time, the North Sea was called the 'German Sea' but I have chosen to use the more familiar North Sea which became commonly used in the early 19th century.
4 Beaglehole, 'On the Character of Captain James Cook', p. 419.
5 Besant, *Captain Cook*, p. 10.
6 Besant, *Captain Cook*, p. 15. Author's note: Although Cook's second biographer, Sir Walter Besant, says that James Cook ran away from his apprenticeship with William Sanderson, I have decided to go with J.C. Beaglehole, who says that Mr Sanderson helped the lad to secure an apprenticeship at Whitby. I have also taken the liberty of consulting the world's most famous Yorkshireman, Sir Michael Parkinson, for the likely way of saying the words in the old Yorkshire dialect.
7 Hough, *Captain James Cook: A Biography*, p. 5.
8 Author's note: Local lore has it that this was a common refrain among Whitby locals or those who visited the town. For example: https://www.thenorthyorkshiregallery.co.uk/whitby-harbour/.
9 Besant, *Captain Cook*, p. 21.
10 Hough, *Captain James Cook: A Biography*, p. 8.
11 Besant, *Captain Cook*, p. 2.
12 Kippis, *A Narrative of the Voyages round the World performed by Captain James Cook, with an Account of His Life during the previous and intervening periods*, Porter and Coates, Philadelphia, 1850, p. 10.
13 Besant, *Captain Cook*, p. 22.

14 Hough, *Captain James Cook: A Biography*, p. 6.

15 Beaglehole, *The Life of Captain James Cook*, p. 284.

16 Besant, *Captain Cook*, p. 24.

17 Hough, *Captain James Cook: A Biography*, p. 9.

18 Smyth, *The Sailor's Word-Book: An Alphabetical Digest of Nautical Terms, including Some More Especially Military and Scientific, but Useful to Seamen; as well as Archaisms of Early Voyagers, etc.*, Blackie and Son, London, 1867.

19 Author Unknown, 'Notes', *The Journal of Geography*, Vol. 6, No. 6, 1908, pp. 194–208.

20 Apperson and Manser, *Dictionary of Proverbs*, Wordsworth, London, 2007, p. 630.

21 Hough, *Captain James Cook: A Biography*, p. 11.

Chapter 1

1 Scadding, Surveyor-General [unnamed publisher], Toronto, 1896, p. 4.

2 Hough, *Captain James Cook: A Biography*, p. 13.

3 Beaglehole, *The Life of Captain James Cook*, p. 17.

4 Hough, *Captain James Cook: A Biography*, p. 16.

5 Besant, *Captain Cook*, p. 37.

6 Lockett, *Captain James Cook in Atlantic Canada: The Adventurer and Map Maker's Formative Years*, Formac Publishing Company Ltd, Halifax, 2010, p. 52.

7 Chipman, 'The Life and Times of Major Samuel Holland, Surveyor-General 1764–1801', Reprinted from Ontario Historical Society's 'Papers and Records', Vol. XXI, p .9, http://www.islandlives.ca/fedora/repository/ilives%3A188913/PDF/ilives%3A188913/Full%20Text.pdf.

8 Lockett, *Captain James Cook in Atlantic Canada*, p. 48.

9 Author's note: In truth, a quarter-century before, the Navy had acquired some surveying equipment, but it had simply sat, unused, in the Portsmouth dockyards after that. But change is afoot, in no small part thanks to the current First Lord of the Admiralty, George Anson, who, after his circumnavigation of the globe from 1740 to 1744, which encountered successive navigation disasters – losing five out of six ships and the vast majority of his 1000 men – has strong and influential views, pinpointing the Admiralty's lack of interest in furthering the science of Marine navigation as a key cause for the losses. In his written report about the voyage, he had gone on a full four pages on the subject.

10 Beaglehole, *The Life of Captain James Cook*, p. 33.

11 Beaglehole, *The Life of Captain James Cook*, p. 33.

12 O'Brian, *Joseph Banks: A Life*, University of Chicago Press, Chicago, 1997, p. 23.

13 O'Brian, *Joseph Banks: A Life*, p. 17.

14 O'Brian, *Joseph Banks: A Life*, p. 17.

15 Smith, *The life of Sir Joseph Banks, president of the Royal society, with some notices of his friends and contemporaries*, John Lane, London, 1911, p. 6.

16 Burnet, *Where Australia Collides with Asia*, Rosenberg Publishing Sydney, 2017, p. 21 [reported speech].

17 Burnet, *Where Australia Collides with Asia*, p. 21 [reported speech].

18 O'Brian, *Joseph Banks: A Life*, p. 30.

19 Brougham, *Lives of men of letters & science, who flourished in the time of George III*, Vol II, Henry Colburn, London, 1846, p. 340 [reported speech].

20 Brougham, *Lives of men of letters & science, who flourished in the time of George III*, p. 340 [reported speech].

21 Gascoigne, *Joseph Banks and the English Enlightenment: Useful Knowledge and Polite Culture*, Cambridge University Press, UK, 1994, p. 22.

22 Gascoigne, *Joseph Banks and the English Enlightenment: Useful Knowledge and Polite Culture*, p. 22.

23 Lockett, *Captain James Cook in Atlantic Canada*, p. 39.

24 Suthren, *To Go Upon Discovery: James Cook and Canada, from 1758 to 1779*, Dundurn, Toronto, 2000, p. 59.

25 Chipman, 'The Life and Times of Major Samuel Holland, Surveyor-General 1764–1801', p. 11.

26 Suthren, *To Go Upon Discovery: James Cook and Canada, from 1758 to 1779*, p. 59 [reported speech].

27 Leadbetter, *A Compleat System of Astronomy*, J. Wilcox, London, 1728, p. [n/a].

28 Leadbetter, *A Compleat System of Astronomy*, p. iii.

29 Beaglehole, *The Life of Captain James Cook*, p. 50 [reported speech].

30 Lockett, *Captain James Cook in Atlantic Canada*, p. 63.

31 Hough, *Captain James Cook: A Biography*, p. 24.

32 Hough, *Captain James Cook: A Biography*, p. 24.

Chapter 2

1 Beaglehole, *The Life of Captain James Cook*, p. 59.

2 Smith, *The Life of Sir Joseph Banks*, p. 16.

3 Lockett, *Captain James Cook in Atlantic Canada*, p. 67.

4 Hough, *Captain James Cook: A Biography*, p. 26.

5 Stacey, *Quebec 1759: The Siege and the Battle*, Pan Books, London, 1959, p. 153.

6 Stacey, *Quebec 1759: The Siege and the Battle*, p. 153.

7 Beaglehole, *The Life of Captain James Cook*, p. 34.

8 Suthren, *To Go Upon Discovery: James Cook and Canada, from 1758–1779*, p. 108.

9 Hough, *Captain James Cook: A Biography*, p. 283.

10 Hough, *Captain James Cook: A Biography*, p. 283.

11 Beaglehole, *The Life of Captain James Cook*, p. 52.

12 Beaglehole, *The Life of Captain James Cook*, p. 59.

13 Beaglehole, *The Life of Captain James Cook*, p. 59.

14 Lockett, *Captain James Cook in Atlantic Canada*, p. 8.

15 Smith, *The Life of Sir Joseph Banks*, p. 7.

16 Boenigk, Wodniok and Glücksman, *Biodiversity and Earth History*, Springer, Heidelberg, 2015, p. 232.

17 Brougham, *Lives of men of letters & science, who flourished in the time of George III*, Vol II, p. 341.

18 Brougham, *Lives of men of letters & science, who flourished in the time of George III*, p. 341.

19 Brougham, *Lives of men of letters & science, who flourished in the time of George III*, pp. 341–42.

20 Brougham, *Lives of men of letters & science, who flourished in the time of George III*, p. 342.

21 Smith, *The Life of Sir Joseph Banks*, p. 16.

22 Murray, *The Celebrated Miss Fanny Murray*, S. Smith, Dublin, 1759.

23 Stockdale, *The Memoirs of the Life and Writings of Percival Stockdale*, Vol. 1, Longman, Hurst, Rees and Orme, London, 1809, p. 318.

24 Beaglehole, *The Life of Captain James Cook*, p. 80.

25 Cook and Bevis, 'An Observation of an Eclipse of the Sun at the Island of New-Found-Land, August 5, 1766, by Mr. James Cook, with the Longitude of the Place of Observation Deduced from It,' *Philosophical Transactions of the Royal Society*, 1767, p. 215.

26 Cook and Bevis, 'An Observation of an Eclipse of the Sun', p. 215.

27 Gascoigne, *Joseph Banks and the English Enlightenment: Useful Knowledge and Polite Culture*, p. 22.

28 Hough, *Captain James Cook: A Biography*, p. 61 [reported speech].

29 O'Brian, *Joseph Banks: A Life*, p. 36.

30 O'Brian, *Joseph Banks: A Life*, p. 36.

31 Kirk, *Paradise Past: The Transformation of the South Pacific, 1520–1920*, McFarland & Company, North Carolina, 2012, p. 37.

32 Kirk, *Paradise Past*, p. 37 [reported speech].

33 Kirk, *Paradise Past*, p. 37.

34 Kirk, *Paradise Past*, p. 37.

35 Kirk, *Paradise Past*, p. 36.

36 Hough, *Captain James Cook: A Biography*, p. 41.

37 Hough, *Captain James Cook: A Biography*, p. 39.

Chapter 3

1 Author's note: This motto is an expression of the determination of Fellows to withstand the domination of authority and to verify all statements by an appeal to facts determined by experiment.

2 Beaglehole, *The Life of Captain James Cook*, p. 107.

3 Firth, *Naval Songs and Ballads*, Navy Records Society, London, 1908, p. 244.

4 Halley, 'A New Method of Determining the Parallax of the Sun, or His Distance from the Earth', Sec. R. S., *Philosophical Transactions*, Vol. XXIX, No. 348, 1716, p. 454.

5 Halley, 'A New Method of Determining the Parallax of the Sun', p. 454.

6 Weld, *A History of the Royal Society: With Memoirs of the Presidents*, Vol. II, John W. Parker, London, 1848, p. 13.

7 Weld, *A History of the Royal Society*, p. 32.

8 Weld, *A History of the Royal Society*, pp. 33–34.

9 Weld, *A History of the Royal Society*, p. 19.

10 Kitson, *Captain James Cook*, E.P. Dutton and Company, New York, 1907, p. 88.

11 Author's note: In fact, the Admiralty officially renamed the ship the *Endeavour Bark* as there was already a Royal Navy ship named 'Endeavour' stationed at the Nore. But as Cook's voyage unfolded, the ship became simply referred to as the *Endeavour*.

12 Kitson, *Captain James Cook*, p. 88.

13 Weld, *A History of the Royal Society*, p. 34.

14 Beaglehole, *The Life of Captain James Cook*, , p. 103.

15 Kitson, *Captain James Cook*, p. 87.

16 Kitson, *Captain James Cook*, p. 87 [reported speech].

17 Beaglehole, *The Life of Captain James Cook*, p. 104.

18 Carter, 'The Royal Society and the Voyage of HMS "Endeavour" 1768–71', *Notes and Records of the Royal Society of London*, Vol. 49, No. 2, July 1995, p. 253.

19 Kitson, *Captain James Cook*, p. 90 [reported speech].

20 Hough, *Captain James Cook: A Biography*, p. 38 [reported speech.].

21 Hawkesworth, *An account of the voyages undertaken by the order of His present Majesty for making discoveries in the Southern Hemisphere*, Vol. I, W. Strahan and T. Cadell, London, 1773, p. 519.

22 Author's note: Although the British initially referred to Tahiti as 'Otaheite', I have generally made it Tahiti throughout, for the sake of consistency.

23 Hough, *Captain James Cook: A Biography*, p. 39.

24 Hough, *Captain James Cook: A Biography*, p. 55.

25 Hough, *Captain James Cook: A Biography*, p. 55.

26 Besant, *Captain Cook*, pp. 70–71.

27 Hough, *Captain James Cook: A Biography*, p. 42.

28 Hough, *Captain James Cook: A Biography*, p. 42.

29 Firth, *Naval Songs and Ballads*, p. 243.

30 Beaglehole, *The Life of Captain James Cook*, Stanford University Press, 1992, p. 140.

31 Cook to Stephens, Letter, 8 July 1768, in 'Letters from Captains, Surnames C. Includes letter from Captain James Cook', The National Archives, Kew, ADM 1/1609, p. 1.

32 Kodicek and Young, 'Captain Cook and Scurvy', *Notes and Records of the Royal Society of London*, Vol. 24, No. 1, 1969, p. 47, www.jstor.org/stable/530740.

33 Kodicek and Young, 'Captain Cook and Scurvy', *Notes and Records of the Royal Society of London*, p. 47.

34 Carter, 'The Royal Society and the Voyage of HMS "Endeavour" 1768–71', *Notes and Records of the Royal Society of London*, p. 255.

35 Author's note: 'Black servants' is a euphemistic term for indentured labourers or slaves used by the British in mid to late 18th century, a time when the abolition movement was beginning to gain traction and the notion of 'slaves' on British soil became too much for the polite British sensibility to publicly bear. And so they called them the far more palatable 'black servants'. It was common for wealthy merchants, Navy officers and high society folk like the Banks family to have domestic slaves or 'black servants' at least up until slavery on English soil was confirmed to be unsupported in English law in the Somersett case in 1772. Despite that, many indentured black people remained in

English households beyond this time under the moniker of 'servants'. (Slavery remained legal in most of the British Empire until the *Slavery Abolition Act* of 1833 came into force.) The personal details of people taken from Africa by the British and sold in the slave trade were not recorded.

36 Lysaght, 'Some Early Letters from Joseph Banks (1743–1820) to William Philp Perrin', *Notes and Records of the Royal Society of London*, Vol. 29, No. 1, October 1974, p. 95, https://discovery. nationalarchives.gov.uk/details/r/2c6214a4-5363-48a2-9637-e4765da8161c.

37 Salmond, *The Trial of the Cannibal Dog: Captain Cook in the South Seas*, Penguin, Auckland, 2004, p. 31.

38 Author's note: These are generic commands consistent with the terminology of the times.

39 Morton, James Douglas, Earl, 'Hints offered to the consideration of Captain Cooke, Mr. Bankes, Doctor Solander and other gentlemen who go upon the expedition on board the Endeavour. Chiswick', National Library of Australia, Papers of Sir Joseph Banks, 1745–1923, MS 9, Series 3/Item 113–113h, p. 1, http://nla.gov.au:80/tarkine/nla.obj-222969577.

40 Hough, *The Murder of Captain James Cook*, Macmillan, Hong Kong, 1979, p. 70.

41 Author's note: There is evidence to suggest one of the Marine privates came on board two days later than the rest. In any case, the *Endeavour* sailed with a total of 12 Marines on board.

42 Cook, Log of H.M.S. *Endeavour*, 1768–1770 [manuscript] NLA, Reference no.: MS 3, 16 August 1768.

43 Cook, Log, 16 August 1768.

44 Cook, Log, 16 August 1768.

45 Moore, *Endeavour: The Ship and Attitude that Changed the World*, Random House, Sydney, 2018, p. 142.

46 Freshfield, *The Life of Horace Benedict de Saussure*, Edward Arnold, London, 1920, pp. 105–106.

47 Freshfield, *The Life of Horace Benedict de Saussure*, pp. 105–106.

Chapter 4

1   Whall, *Ships, Sea Songs and Shanties*, J. Brown and Son, Glasgow, 1913, pp. 29–30.

2   Byrn, *Naval Courts Martial, 1793–1815*, Ashgate Publishing, England, 2009, p. 5.

3   Byrn, *Naval Courts Martial, 1793–1815*, p. 5.

4   Byrn, *Naval Courts Martial, 1793–1815*, p. 11.

5   Cook, Journal of H.M.S. *Endeavour*, 1768–1771, 16 August 1768 [reported speech], NLA, Ms 1, http://nla.gov.au/nla.obj-228983242/view.

6   Cook, Journal, 16 August 1768.

7   Cook, Journal, 26 August 1768.

8   Banks, The *Endeavour* Journal of Joseph Banks (25 August 1768 – 12 July 1771), 14 April 1769, SLNSW, Papers of Sir Joseph Banks, Section 2, Series 03.01, [no page numbers], http://www2.sl.nsw. gov.au/banks/series_03/03_231.cfm., 25 August 1768.

9   Banks, Journal, 26 August 1768.

10 Banks, Journal, 27 August 1768.

11 Banks, Journal, 29 August 1768.

12 Banks, Journal, 30 August 1768.

13 Cook, Log, 1 September 1768.

14 Banks, Journal, 6 September 1768.

15 Banks, Journal, 7 September 1768.

16 Hough, *Captain James Cook: A Biography*, p. 61.

17 Banks, Journal, 10 September 1768.

18 Perry, 'Voyage to Batavia', *The Gentleman's Magazine*, Vol. 78, Part 1, 1808, p. 22.

19 Cook, Log, 14 September 1768 [reported speech].

20 Cook, Log, 14 September 1768.

21 Banks, Journal, 13 September 1768.

22 Cook, Log, 15 September 1768.

23 Cook, Log, 16 September 1768.

24 Cook, (transcribed by Richard Orton), A Journal of the proceedings of His Majesty's Bark *Endeavour* on a voyage round the world, commencing the 25th of May 1768 – 23 Oct. 1770, 24 June 1770, SLNSW, Manuscript Safe 1/71, p. 59.

25 Cook, Log, 13 April 1769.

26 Banks, Journal, 25 September 1768.
27 Banks, Journal, 29 September 1768.
28 Banks, Journal, 29 September 1768.
29 Banks, Journal, 21 October 1768.
30 Banks, Journal, 10 October 1768.
31 Banks, Journal, 23 September 1768.
32 Banks, Journal, 7 October 1768.
33 Banks, Journal, 25 October 1768.
34 Banks, Journal, 25 October 1768.
35 Banks, Journal, 25 October 1768.
36 Banks, Journal, 25 October 1768.
37 Banks, Journal, 25 October 1768 [reported speech].
38 Banks, Journal, 25 October 1768.
39 Cook, Log, 25 October 1768.
40 Banks, Journal, 29 October 1768.
41 Banks, Journal, 29 October 1768 [reported speech].
42 Banks, Journal, 29 October 1768 [reported speech].
43 Banks, Journal, 29 October 1768.
44 Cook, Log, 6 November 1768.
45 Cook, Log, 9 November 1768.
46 Banks, Journal, 12 November 1768.
47 Cook, Log, 13 November 1768 [reported speech].
48 Chambers (ed.), The Letters of Sir Joseph Banks: A Selection, 1768–1820, World Scientific, 2000, p. 8.
49 Banks, Journal, 13 November 1768 [reported speech].
50 McNab (ed.), Historical Records of New Zealand Vol. II., John Mackay, Wellington, 1914, p. 64 [reported speech].
51 McNab (ed.), Historical Records of New Zealand, p. 64 [reported speech].
52 McNab (ed.), Historical Records of New Zealand, p. 64.
53 McNab (ed.), Historical Records of New Zealand, p. 64.
54 McNab (ed.), Historical Records of New Zealand, p. 64 [reported speech].
55 Hough, The Murder of Captain James Cook, p. 67.
56 Cook, Log, 14 November 1768.
57 Cook, Log, 14 November 1768.
58 Cook, Log, 17 November 1768.
59 Cook, Log, 17 November 1768.
60 Chambers (ed.), The Letters of Sir Joseph Banks, p. 4.
61 Cook, Log, 18 November 1768.
62 Cook, Log, 17 November 1768.
63 Cook, Log, 20 November 1768 [reported speech].
64 Cook, Log, 20 November 1768.
65 Banks, Journal, 23 November 1768.
66 Cook, Log, 23 November 1768.
67 Parkinson, Sydney; Kenrick, William, A Journal of a Voyage to the South Seas, in His Majesty's Ship, the Endeavour: Faithfully Transcribed from the Papers of the Late Sydney Parkinson, Draughtsman to Joseph Banks, Esq., on His Late Expedition with Dr. Solander, Round the World, Stanfield Parkinson, London, 1773, p. 4.
68 Banks, Journal, 26 November 1768.
69 Banks, Journal, 26 November 1768.
70 Beaglehole, (ed.), The Journals of Captain James Cook on His Voyages of Discovery, Vol. I, Cambridge University Press, London, 1955, p. 495.
71 Banks, Journal, 27 November 1768.
72 Banks, Journal, 27 November 1768.
73 Banks, Journal, 3 October 1769.
74 Banks, Journal, 2 December 1768.
75 Beaglehole, The Life of Captain James Cook, Stanford University Press, 1992, p. 159.

Chapter 5

1 Johnson, *The Rambler: A Periodical Paper Published in 1750, 1751, 1752*, Vol. 1, Jones and Company, London, 1826, p. 16.
2 Cook, Log, 5 December 1768.
3 Cook, Log, 5 December 1768.
4 Cook, Log, 5 December 1768.
5 Cook, Log, 26 December 1768.
6 Cook, Log, 11 January 1769.
7 Whall, *Ships, Sea Songs and Shanties*, pp. 37–39.
8 Banks, Journal, 20 January 1769.
9 Cook, Log, 16 January 1769.
10 Cook, Log, 16 January 1769.
11 Banks, Journal, 20 January 1769.
12 Cook, Log, 16 January 1769.
13 Banks, Journal, 16 January 1769.
14 Banks, Journal, 16 January 1769.
15 Banks, Journal, 16 January 1769.
16 Banks, Journal, 16 January 1769.
17 Banks, Journal, 16 January 1769.
18 Banks, Journal, 16 January 1769.
19 Banks, Journal, 16 January 1769.
20 Banks, Journal, 16 January 1769.
21 Banks, Journal, 16 January 1769.
22 Banks, Journal, 16 January 1769.
23 Banks, Journal, 16 January 1769 [reported speech].
24 Banks, Journal, 16 January 1769.
25 Banks, Journal, 16 January 1769 [reported speech].
26 Banks, Journal, 16 January 1769.
27 Banks, Journal, 16 January 1769 [reported speech].
28 Banks, Journal, 16 January 1769 [reported speech].
29 Banks, Journal, 16 January 1769 [reported speech].
30 Banks, Journal, 16 January 1769 [reported speech].
31 Banks, Journal, 16 January 1769 [reported speech].
32 Banks, Journal, 16 January 1769 [reported speech].
33 Banks, Journal, 16 January 1769 [reported speech].
34 Banks, Journal, 16 January 1769.
35 Banks, Journal, 16 January 1769.
36 Banks, Journal, 16 January 1769.
37 Banks, Journal, 16 January 1769.
38 Banks, Journal, 16 January 1769.
39 Banks, Journal, 16 January 1769.
40 Banks, Journal, 17 January 1769.
41 Banks, Journal, 17 January 1769 [reported speech].
42 Banks, Journal, 17 January 1769.
43 Banks, Journal, 17 January 1769.
44 Banks, Journal, 17 January 1769.
45 Hough, *Captain James Cook: A Biography*, pp. 78–79.
46 Cook, *Captain Cook's Journal During his First Voyage Around the World*, 1893, p. 36.
47 Cook, Log, 13 February 1769.
48 Cook, Log, 13 February 1769.
49 Cook, Log, 25 January 1769.
50 Cook, Log, 25 January 1769.
51 Cook, Log, 28 January 1769.
52 Banks, Journal, 5 February 1769.

53 Cook, Log, 13 February 1769.

54 Cook, Log, 26 February 1769 [reported speech].

55 Cook, Log, 28 February 1769.

56 Cook, Log, 1 March 1769.

57 Banks, Journal, 11 March 1769.

58 Banks, Journal, 25 March 1769 [reported speech].

59 Banks, Journal, 25 March 1769 [reported speech].

60 Banks, Journal, 25 March 1769 [reported speech].

61 Banks, Journal, 25 March 1769.

62 Banks, Journal, 25 March 1769 [reported speech].

63 Banks, Journal, 25 March 1769.

64 Cook, Log, 26 March 1769 [reported speech].

65 Banks, Journal, 25 March 1769.

66 Cook, Log, 26 March 1769.

67 Cook, Log, 26 March 1769.

68 Banks, Journal, 25 March 1769.

69 Cook, Log, 13 April 1769.

70 Letter from Surgeon William Perry to Lieutenant James Cook, July 1771, in McNab (ed.), *Historical Records of New Zealand*, p. 7.

71 Banks, Journal, 11 April 1769.

72 Hawkesworth, *An account of the voyages undertaken by the order of His present Majesty for making discoveries in the Southern Hemisphere*, p. 473.

73 Cook, Log, 13 April 1769 [reported speech].

74 Hawkesworth, *An account of the voyages undertaken by the order of His present Majesty for making discoveries in the Southern Hemisphere*, p. 473. Author's note: This is taken from Gore's account of his expedition inland at Tahiti on 25 July 1767.

75 Hawkesworth, *An account of the voyages undertaken by the order of His present Majesty for making discoveries in the Southern Hemisphere*, p. 473. Author's note: This is taken from Gore's account of his expedition inland at Tahiti on 25 July 1767.

76 Hawkesworth, *An account of the voyages undertaken by the order of His present Majesty for making discoveries in the Southern Hemisphere*, p. 473. Author's note: This is taken from Gore's account of his expedition inland at Tahiti on 25 July 1767.

77 Banks, Journal, 11 April 1769.

78 Banks, Journal, 11 April 1769.

79 Cook, Log, 13 April 1769.

80 Cook, Log, 13 April 1769.

Chapter 6

1 Hawkesworth, *An account of the voyages undertaken by the order of His present Majesty for making discoveries in the Southern Hemisphere*, p. 435.

2 Banks, 'Thoughts on the manners of [the women of] Otaheite', 1773, in Joseph Banks Papers, NLA, MS 9, Series 1, Item 4_4e, p. 3, http://nla.gov.au/nla.obj-222973317/view.

3 Parkinson, *A Journal of a Voyage to the South Seas*, p. 13.

4 Bligh, *A Voyage to the South Sea*, Hutchinson, Richmond, 1979, p. 59.

5 Cook, Log, 13 July 1769.

6 Banks, 'Thoughts on the manners of [the women of] Otaheite', p. 4, http://nla.gov.au/nla.obj-222973317/view.

7 Banks, Journal, 20 April 1769.

8 Banks, Journal, 20 April 1769.

9 Cook, Log, 20 April 1769.

10 Banks, Journal, 13 April 1769.

11 Cook, Log, 13 April 1769.

12 Banks, Journal, 13 April 1769 [reported speech].

13 Cook, Log, 13 April 1769.

14 Banks, Journal, 13 April 1769. Author's note: I presume Lieutenant Gore interpreted the actions of the Natives for James Cook, given he had already spent time in Tahiti and was aware of certain customs.
15 Banks, Journal, 13 April 1769.
16 Banks, Journal, 13 April 1769.
17 Banks, Journal, 14 April 1769.
18 Banks, Journal, 14 April 1769.
19 Banks, Journal, 14 April 1769.
20 Banks, Journal, 14 April 1769.
21 Banks, Journal, 14 April 1769.
22 Banks, Journal, 13 April 1769.
23 Cook, Log, 14 April 1769.
24 Cook, Log, 14 April 1769.
25 Banks, Journal, 14 April 1769.
26 Banks, Journal, 14 April 1769.
27 Banks, Journal, 14 April 1769.
28 Cook, Log, 14 April 1769.
29 Banks, Journal, 14 April 1769.
30 Banks, Journal, 14 April 1769.
31 Cook, Log, 14 April 1769.
32 Cook, Log, 15 April 1769.
33 Banks, Journal, 15 April 1769.
34 Cook, Log, 15 April 1769 [reported speech].
35 Banks, Journal, 15 April 1769.
36 Parkinson, A Journal of a Voyage to the South Seas, p.15.
37 Parkinson, A Journal of a Voyage to the South Seas, p.15.
38 Cook, Log, 15 April 1769.
39 Banks, Journal, 15 April 1769.
40 Parkinson, A Journal of a Voyage to the South Seas, 17 April 1769, p. 15.
41 Parkinson, A Journal of a Voyage to the South Seas, 17 April 1769.
42 Banks, Journal, 17 April 1769.
43 Banks, Journal, 17 April 1769.
44 Magra, A journal of a voyage round the world, in His Majesty's ship Endeavour, in the years 1768, 1769, 1770, and 1771, Becket and Hondt, London, 1771, pp. 41–42, https://nla.gov.au/nla.obj-631282051/view?partId=nla.obj-633672640#page/n55/mode/1up.
45 Banks, Journal, 'Manners and Customs of South Sea Islands', 1769.
46 Cook, Log, 18 April 1769.
47 Banks, Journal, 18 April 1769.
48 Cook, Log, 6 June 1769.
49 Salmond, Aphrodite's Island: The European Discovery of Tahiti, University of California Press, Berkeley, 2009, pp. 162–63.
50 Perry, 'Voyage to Batavia', The Gentleman's Magazine, p. 221.
51 Parkinson, A Journal of a Voyage to the South Seas, 4 May 1769.
52 Banks, Journal, 12 May 1769.
53 Salmond, Aphrodite's Island, p. 156.
54 Driessen, 'Dramatis Personae of Society Islanders, Cook's Endeavour Voyage 1769', The Journal of Pacific History, Vol. 17, No. 4, 1982.
55 Cook, Journal, 'Description of King George's Island', 13 July 1769.
56 Banks, 'Thoughts on the manners of [the women of] Otaheite', p. 3.
57 Banks, Journal, 19 April 1769.
58 Banks, Journal, 20 April 1769.
59 Parkinson, A Journal of a Voyage to the South Seas, 21–26 April 1769.
60 Banks, 'Thoughts on the manners of [the women of] Otaheite', pp. 2–3.
61 Author's note: Tiare means flower in Tahitian.
62 Cook, Log, 22 April 1769.

63 Cook, Log, 13 July 1769.
64 Banks, Journal, 10 May 1769.
65 Banks, Journal, 10 May 1769.
66 Banks, Journal, 10 May 1769.
67 Cook, Log, 28 April 1769 [reported speech].
68 Banks, Journal, 28 April 1769.
69 Cook, Log, 28 April 1769.
70 Cook, Log, 28 April 1769.
71 Cook, Log, 28 April 1769.
72 Cook, Log, 13 April 1769.
73 Molineux, Log, The National Archives, Kew, ADM 55/41, https://discovery.nationalarchives.gov.uk/details/r/C2976713, 29 April 1769.
74 Banks, Journal, 29 April 1769.
75 Cook, Log, 1 May 1769.
76 Banks, Journal, 2 May 1769.
77 Parkinson, *A Journal of a Voyage to the South Seas*, 2 May 1769.
78 Banks, Journal, 2 May 1769.
79 Banks, Journal, 2 May 1769.
80 Cook, Log, 2 May 1769 [reported speech].
81 Banks, Journal, 2 May 1769.
82 Parkinson, *A Journal of a Voyage to the South Seas*, 2 May 1769.
83 Banks, Journal, 2 May 1769.
84 Cook, Log, 2 May 1769.
85 Cook, Log, 2 May 1769.

Chapter 7

1 Cook, Log, 3 June 1769.
2 Banks, Journal, 28 May 1769.
3 Banks, Journal, 28 May 1769 [reported speech].
4 Banks, Journal, 28 May 1769.
5 Banks, Journal, 28 May 1769 [reported speech].
6 Cook, Journal, 13 July 1769.
7 Cook, Journal, 13 July 1769.
8 Cook, Journal, 'Manners and Customs of Tahiti', 13 July 1769.
9 Cook, Log, 28 May 1769 [reported speech].
10 Cook, Log, 29 May 1769.
11 Cook, Journal, 'Manners and Customs of Tahiti', 13 July 1769.
12 Cook, Log, 13 July 1769.
13 Banks, Journal, 29 May 1769.
14 Cook, Log, 30 May 1769.
15 Cook, Log, 2 June 1769 [reported speech].
16 Cook, Log, 3 June 1769.
17 Green and Cook, *Observations Made by Appointment of the Royal Society at King George's Island in the South Sea*, Royal Society Publishing, 1771, p. 176.
18 Cook, Journal, 3 June 1769.
19 Cook, Journal, 3 June 1769.
20 Cook, Journal, 3 June 1769.
21 Banks, Journal, 3 June 1769.
22 Banks, Journal, 4 June 1769.
23 Banks, Journal, 4 June 1769.
24 Cook, Log, 13 April 1769.
25 Stephens, 'Secret Instructions for Lieutenant James Cook Appointed to Command His Majesty's Bark the *Endeavour*', 30 July 1768, NLA, MS 2, https://www.foundingdocs.gov.au/scan-sid-252.html.
26 Cook, Log, 6 June 1769 [reported speech].

27 Perry, 'Voyage to Batavia', *The Gentleman's Magazine*, p. 102 [reported speech].
28 Perry, 'Voyage to Batavia', *The Gentleman's Magazine*, p. 102.
29 Cook, Log, 6 June 1769.
30 Cook, Log, 6 June 1769.
31 Cook, Log, 6 June 1769.
32 Banks, Journal, 8 June 1769.
33 Parkinson, *A Journal of a Voyage to the South Seas*, 19 June 1769 [reported speech].
34 Parkinson, *A Journal of a Voyage to the South Seas*, 19 June 1769.
35 Cook, Log, 1 July 1769.
36 Cook, Log, 29 June 1769.
37 Banks, Journal, 29 June 1769.
38 Cook, Log, 29 June 1769.
39 Banks, Journal, 29 June 1769.
40 Banks, Journal, 29 June 1769.
41 Banks, Journal, 29 June 1769.
42 Banks, Journal, 29 June 1769.
43 Banks, Journal, 29 June 1769.
44 Cook, Log, 13 July 1769.
45 Cook, Log, 13 July 1769.
46 Cook, Log, 13 July 1769.
47 Cook, Log, 13 July 1769.
48 Cook, Log, 13 July 1769.
49 Cook, Log, 13 July 1769.
50 Cook, Log, 13 July 1769.
51 Banks, Journal, 5 July 1769.
52 Banks, Journal, 5 July 1769.
53 Banks, Journal, 12 July 1769 [reported speech].
54 Banks, Journal, 12 July 1769.
55 Banks, Journal, 12 July 1769 [reported speech].
56 Banks, Journal, 12 July 1769 [reported speech].
57 Banks, Journal, 12 July 1769.
58 Banks, Journal, 12 July 1769.
59 Parkinson, *A Journal of a Voyage to the South Seas*, p. 95.
60 Cook, Log, 13 July 1769.
61 Salmond, *The Trial of the Cannibal Dog*, p. 107.
62 Cook, Journal, 17 July 1769.
63 Cook, Log, 17 July 1769.
64 Cook, Log, 19 July 1769.
65 Cook, Log, 21 July 1769.
66 Hawkesworth, *An account of the voyages undertaken by the order of His present Majesty for making discoveries in the Southern Hemisphere*, p. 227.
67 Hawkesworth, *An account of the voyages undertaken by the order of His present Majesty for making discoveries in the Southern Hemisphere*, p. 227.
68 Hawkesworth, *An account of the voyages undertaken by the order of His present Majesty for making discoveries in the Southern Hemisphere*, p. 227.
69 Cook, Journal, 1 July 1769.
70 Parkinson, *A Journal of a Voyage to the South Seas*, p. 67.
71 Salmond, *The Trial of the Cannibal Dog*, p. 96.
72 Salmond, *The Trial of the Cannibal Dog*, pp. 111–12.
73 Forster, *Observations Made During a Voyage Round the World, On Physical Geography, Natural History, and Ethic Philosophy*, G. Robinson, London, 1778, p. 511.
74 Forster, *Observations Made During a Voyage Round the World, On Physical Geography, Natural History, and Ethic Philosophy*, p. 511.
75 Cook, Log, 2 September 1769.
76 Cook, Log, 13 September 1769.

77 Banks, Journal, 5 April 1770.
78 Tasman, Journal, 19 December 1642.
79 Banks, Journal, 6 October 1769.
80 Banks, Journal, 6 October 1769.
81 Banks, Journal, 6 October 1769.
82 Cook, Log, 8 October 1769.

Chapter 8

1 Beaglehole, *The Journals of Captain James Cook on his Voyages of Discovery: Volume II: The Voyage of the Resolution and Adventure 1772–1775*, Routledge, Oxfordshire, 2017.
2 Banks, Journal, 20 January 1770.
3 Author's note: In fact, as a people, cultivation was widespread.
4 Banks, Journal, 'Account of New Zealand', 31 March 1770.
5 Banks, Journal, 8 October 1769.
6 Banks, Journal, 8 October 1769.
7 Cook, Log, 9 October 1769 [reported speech].
8 Cook, Log, 9 October 1769 [reported speech].
9 Mackay, *Life in Early Poverty Bay: Trials and Triumphs of its Brave Founders*, The Gisborne Publishing Company, Gisborne, 1927, p. 4.
10 Banks, Journal, 8 October 1769.
11 Banks, Journal, 8 October 1769.
12 Banks, Journal, 9 October 1769.
13 Hough, *Captain James Cook: A Biography*, p. 140.
14 Hough, *Captain James Cook: A Biography*, p. 140.
15 Hough, *Captain James Cook: A Biography*, p. 140.
16 Stephens, 'Secret Instructions for Lieutenant James Cook', 30 July 1768.
17 Banks, Journal, 9 October 1769 [reported speech].
18 Banks, Journal, 9 October 1769 [reported speech].
19 Cook, Log, 10 October 1769.
20 Banks, Journal, 9 October 1769 [reported speech].
21 Banks, Journal, 9 October 1769 [reported speech].
22 Banks, Journal, 9 October 1769.
23 Banks, Journal, 9 October 1769 [reported speech].
24 Banks, Journal, 9 October 1769.
25 Banks, Journal, 9 October 1769 [reported speech].
26 Banks, Journal, 9 October 1769.
27 Banks, Journal, 9 October 1769.
28 Banks, Journal, 'Account of New Zealand', March 1770. Author's note: I have taken the liberty of modernising the pidgin English vocabulary of Banks, to present I hope a more accurate translation of what was said, while retaining the recorded Māori words that were spoken.
29 Banks, Journal, 9 October 1769.
30 Parkinson, Journal, 9 October 1769.
31 Cook, Log, 10 October 1769 [reported speech].
32 Banks, Journal, 9 October 1769.
33 Cook, Log, 10 October 1769.
34 Cook, Log, 10 October 1769.
35 Banks, Journal, 9 October 1769.
36 Banks, *The Endeavour Journal*, 9 October 1769 [tense changed].
37 Cook, Log, 10 October 1769.
38 Banks, Journal, 9 October 1769.
39 Cook, Journal, 9 October 1769.
40 Banks, *The Endeavour Journal*, 1 December 1769
41 Banks, Journal, 9 October 1769.
42 Banks, Journal, 10 October 1769.

43 Cook, Log, 10 October 1769.
44 Cook, Log, 10 October 1769.
45 Cook, Log, 10 October 1769.
46 Cook, Log, 10 October 1769.
47 Banks, Journal, 10 October 1769.
48 Banks, Journal, 10 October 1769.
49 Banks, Journal, 10 October 1769 [reported speech].
50 Banks, Journal, 10 October 1769 [reported speech].
51 Banks, Journal, 10 October 1769.
52 Banks, Journal, 10 October 1769.
53 Cook, Log, 11 October 1769.
54 Banks, Journal, 11 October 1769.
55 Cook, Log, 11 October 1769.
56 Banks, Journal, 11 October 1769.
57 Banks, Journal, 11 October 1769.
58 Parkinson, A Journal of a Voyage to the South Seas, 13 October 1769.
59 Parkinson, A Journal of a Voyage to the South Seas, 11 October 1769.
60 Cook, Log, 12 October 1769.
61 Banks, Journal, 11 October 1769.
62 Banks, Journal, 12 October 1769.
63 Banks, Journal, 12 October 1769.
64 Parkinson, A Journal of a Voyage to the South Seas, 15 October 1769.
65 Banks, Journal, 14 October 1769.
66 Parkinson, A Journal of a Voyage to the South Seas, 15 October 1769.
67 Parkinson, A Journal of a Voyage to the South Seas, 14–15 October 1769.
68 Banks, Journal, 15 October 1769.
69 Cook, Log, 15 October 1769.
70 Cook, Log, 15 October 1769.
71 Banks, Journal, 15 October 1769.
72 Parkinson, A Journal of a Voyage to the South Seas, 15 October 1769.
73 Parkinson, A Journal of a Voyage to the South Seas, 15 October 1769.
74 Banks, Journal, 15 October 1769 [reported speech].
75 Cook, Log, 15 October 1769.
76 Banks, Journal, 21 October 1769.
77 Banks, Journal, 'Account of New Zealand', March 1770.
78 Banks, Journal, 21 October 1769.
79 Banks, Journal, 'Account of New Zealand', March 1770.
80 Banks, Journal, 'Account of New Zealand', March 1770.
81 Banks, Journal, 'Account of New Zealand', March 1770.
82 Banks, Journal, 'Account of New Zealand', March 1770.
83 Cook, Journal, 21 October 1769.
84 Polack, New Zealand: being a narrative of travels and adventures during a residence in that country between the years 1831 and 1837, Richard Bentley, London, 1838, p. 135, https://archive.org/details/newzealandbeingn00pola/page/134.
85 Banks, Journal, 24 October 1769.
86 Salmond, The Trial of the Cannibal Dog, p. 125.
87 Cook, Log, 11 November 1769.
88 Cook, Log, 29 October 1769.
89 Cook, Journal, 29 October 1769.
90 Cook, Log, 1 November 1769.

Chapter 9

1 Letter from Cook to Latouche-Tréville, 6 September 1775, in Hamy, 'James Cook et Latouche-Tréville', Bulletin de Geographie Historique et Descriptive, 1904, pp. 207–208.

2   Dalrymple, *An Historical collection of the several voyages and discoveries in the South Pacific Ocean*, T. Payne, London, 1770, p. xxiv.

3   'The Account of Cook's Visit By Te Horeta te Taniwha', 1770, p. xxiv, in White, *Ancient History of the Māori*, Vol. V, Cambridge University Press, UK, 2011, pp. 121–28.

4   'The Account of Cook's Visit By Te Horeta te Taniwha' in White, *Ancient History of the Māori*, pp. 121–28 [reported speech].

5   'The Account of Cook's Visit By Te Horeta te Taniwha' in White, *Ancient History of the Māori*, pp. 121–28. Author's note: The people who settled Aotearoa were isolated from other ethnic groups. They therefore lacked a collective term to describe themselves. The term *Tangata Māori* was originally a simple reference to a human being or used as a wider reference to normal things. In the wake of the arrival of Europeans, another measure of 'humanness' grew into common usage. *Tangata tupua* was used to describe a foreigner or supernatural being, an unknown entity – a goblin. The term was first recorded during an 1801 visit by the ship *Royal Admiral* to the Hauraki district.

6   Author's note: These are generic commands, consistent with the terminology of the time.

7   Cook, Log, 4 November 1769.

8   Banks, Journal, 3 November 1769.

9   Banks, Journal, 3 November 1769.

10 Banks, Journal, 3 November 1769.

11 Banks, Journal, 3 November 1769.

12 Banks, Journal, 3 November 1769 [reported speech].

13 Banks, Journal, 4 November 1769.

14 Banks, Journal, 4 November 1769.

15 Banks, Journal, 6 November 1769.

16 Salmond, 'Tupaia the Priest-Navigator' in Mallon (ed.), *Tangata o le Moana: The Story of Pacific People in New Zealand*, Te Papa Press, Wellington, 2012.

17 'The Account of Cook's Visit By Te Horeta te Taniwha' in White, *Ancient History of the Māori*, pp. 121–28.

18 'The Account of Cook's Visit By Te Horeta te Taniwha' in White, *Ancient History of the Māori*, pp. 121–28.

19 Stephens, Secret Instructions from the Admiralty to Captain Cook, 30 July 1768.

20 'The Account of Cook's Visit By Te Horeta te Taniwha' in White, *Ancient History of the Māori*, pp. 121–28.

21 'The Account of Cook's Visit By Te Horeta te Taniwha' in White, *Ancient History of the Māori*, pp. 121–28.

22 'The Account of Cook's Visit By Te Horeta te Taniwha' in White, *Ancient History of the Māori*, pp. 121–28.

23 'The Account of Cook's Visit By Te Horeta te Taniwha' in White, *Ancient History of the Māori*, pp. 121–28.

24 'The Account of Cook's Visit By Te Horeta te Taniwha' in White, *Ancient History of the Māori*, p. 121.

25 'The Account of Cook's Visit By Te Horeta te Taniwha' in White, *Ancient History of the Māori*, p. 123

26 'The Account of Cook's Visit By Te Horeta te Taniwha' in White, *Ancient History of the Māori*, p. 124

27 'The Account of Cook's Visit By Te Horeta te Taniwha' in White, *Ancient History of the Māori*, p. 127.

28 Banks, Journal, 9 November 1769.

29 'The Account of Cook's Visit By Te Horeta te Taniwha' in White, *Ancient History of the Māori*, p. 127.

30 'The Account of Cook's Visit By Te Horeta te Taniwha' in White, *Ancient History of the Māori*, p. 127.

31 Parkinson, *A Journal of a Voyage to the South Seas*, 9 November 1769.

32 Banks, Journal, 9 November 1769.

33 Banks, Journal, 9 November 1769.

34 Stephens, Secret Instructions from the Admiralty to Captain Cook, 30 July 1768.

35 Salmond, *The Trial of the Cannibal Dog*, p. 130.

36 Cook, Log, 9 November 1769.

37 Salmond, *The Trial of the Cannibal Dog*, p. 130.

38 'The Account of Cook's Visit By Te Horeta te Taniwha' in White, *Ancient History of the Māori*, p. 124.

39 'The Account of Cook's Visit By Te Horeta te Taniwha' in White, *Ancient History of the Māori*, p. 124.

40 'The Account of Cook's Visit By Te Horeta te Taniwha' in White, *Ancient History of the Māori*, p. 124.

41 'The Account of Cook's Visit By Te Horeta te Taniwha' in White, *Ancient History of the Māori*, p. 125.
42 'The Account of Cook's Visit By Te Horeta te Taniwha' in White, *Ancient History of the Māori*, p. 125.
43 'The Account of Cook's Visit By Te Horeta te Taniwha' in White, *Ancient History of the Māori*, p. 125.
44 'The Account of Cook's Visit By Te Horeta te Taniwha' in White, *Ancient History of the Māori*, p. 125.
45 Banks, Journal, 18 November 1769.
46 Banks, Journal, 18 November 1769.
47 Banks, Journal, 'Account of New Zealand', March 1770.
48 Parkinson, Journal, 23 October 1769.
49 Banks, Journal, 'Account of New Zealand', March 1770.
50 Cook, Log, 21 November 1769.
51 Banks, Journal, 20 November 1769.
52 Banks, Journal, 25 November 1769 [reported speech].
53 Banks, Journal, 26 November 1769.
54 Cook, Log, 25 November 1769. Author's note: 'Whangarei Bay' to the Natives.
55 Banks, Journal, 25 November 1769.
56 Banks, Journal, 26 November 1769.
57 Beaglehole (ed.), *The Journals of Captain James Cook*, pp. 211–12.
58 Beaglehole (ed.), *The Journals of Captain James Cook*, pp. 211–12.
59 Cook, Log, 27 November 1769.
60 Banks, Journal, 29 November 1769.
61 With thanks to Julian Wilcox of the *Ngāpuhi* people.
62 Banks, Journal, 29 November 1769.
63 Banks, Journal, 9 December 1769 [reported speech].
64 Banks, Journal, 9 December 1769 [reported speech].
65 Banks, Journal, 9 December 1769 [reported speech].
66 Banks, Journal, 9 December 1769 [reported speech].
67 Banks, Journal, 9 December 1769 [reported speech].
68 Cook, Log, 10 December 1769.
69 Cook, Log, 10 December 1769.
70 Cook, Log, 14 December 1769.
71 Cook, Log, 14 December 1769.
72 Banks, Journal, 24 December 1769.
73 Banks, Journal, 25 December 1769.
74 Banks, Journal, 25 December 1769.
75 Cook, Log, 26 December 1769.
76 Cook, Log, 15 January 1770.
77 Banks, Journal, 16 January 1770. Author's note: This is Banks' account of the fate of the woman seen floating offshore at Queen Charlotte's Sound. Cook's account gives a different version. He writes that those present were given to understand that the dead woman was among a group of enemies who had arrived in a boat, and had subsequently been attacked and killed by the local tribe at this spot. Broadly, I find Banks' accounts the more real – written without a view to the Admiralty looking over his shoulder. Banks also constantly notes things that Cook misses, and his journal is candid, spontaneous and unrevised, while Cook's is ever cautious.
78 Banks, Journal, 16 January 1770.
79 Banks, Journal, 16 January 1770.
80 Banks, Journal, 16 January 1770
81 Banks, Journal, 16 January 1770.
82 Banks, Journal, 16 January 1770.
83 Banks, Journal, 16 January 1770 [reported speech].
84 Banks, Journal, 16 January 1770.
85 Banks, Journal, 16 January 1770.
86 Beaglehole (ed.), *The Journals of Captain James Cook*, p. 282.
87 Banks, Journal, 17 January 1770 [reported speech].
88 Banks, Journal, 17 January 1770 [reported speech].
89 Parkinson, *A Journal of a Voyage to the South Seas*, 6 February 1770.

90 Banks, Journal, 'Account of New Zealand'.
91 Banks, Journal, 20 January 1770.
92 Banks, Journal, 20 January 1770.
93 Cook, Journal, 31 January 1770.
94 Cook, Journal, 31 January 1770.
95 Cook, Journal, 31 January 1770 [reported speech].
96 Cook, Journal, 31 January 1770.
97 Cook, Journal, 31 January 1770.
98 Cook, Journal, 31 January 1770.
99 Cook, Journal, 31 January 1770.
100 Author's note: Dr Monkhouse is not named by Banks, but due to their long-running sexual rivalry, with Banks a perpetually amused winner, one can discern the delight in this gentleman's misfortune that points towards Banks' familiar foil.
101 Banks, Journal, 3 February 1770 [reported speech].
102 Banks, Journal, 3 February 1770 [reported speech].
103 Banks, Journal, 3 February 1770.
104 Parkinson, Journal, 6 February 1770.
105 Cook, Log, 8 February 1770.
106 Cook, Log, 9 February 1770.
107 Banks, Journal, 16 February 1770.
108 Salmond, *The Trial of the Cannibal Dog*, p. 130.
109 Beaglehole, *The Life of Captain James Cook*, Stanford University Press, p. 217.
110 Banks, Journal, 24 February 1770.
111 Banks, Journal, 5 March 1770.
112 Banks, Journal, 10 March 1770
113 Cook, Log, 23 March 1770.
114 Banks, Journal, 'Account of New Zealand', March 1770.
115 Banks, Journal, 'Account of New Zealand', March 1770.
116 Cook, Log, Account of New Zealand, 31 March 1769.
117 Banks, Journal, 25 March 1770.
118 Cook, Log, 27 March 1770.
119 Cook, Log, 31 January 1770.
120 Cook, Log, 31 January 1770.
121 Hough, *Captain James Cook: A Biography*, pp. 134–35.
122 Cook, Log, 31 March 1770.
123 Cook, Log, 31 March 1770.
124 Cook, Log, 31 March 1770.
125 Banks, Journal, 'Account of New Zealand', March 1770.

Chapter 10

1 Cook, Journal, 30 April 1770.
2 Banks, Journal, 'Notes on New Holland', August 1770.
3 Banks, Journal, 3 April 1770.
4 Banks, Journal, 17 April 1770.
5 Banks, Journal, 17 April 1770.
6 Cook, Log, 19 April 1770.
7 Cook, Log, 19 April 1770.
8 Cook, Log, 22 April 1770.
9 Banks, Journal, 22 April 1770.
10 Cook, Log, 22 April 1770.
11 Banks, Journal, 27 April 1770.
12 Banks, Journal, 27 April 1770.
13 Cook, Log, 28 April 1770.
14 Banks, Journal, 27 April 1770.

15 Parkinson, Journal, 27 April 1770.

16 *Sydney Morning Herald*, 27 April 1863, p. 5. Author's note: This tale is told by a Catholic priest, Archdeacon John McEncroe. About 1833, he interviewed a man whom he described as being of the 'Botany Bay tribe', asking him if he had any recollections connected to the landing of Captain Cook in 1770. Being too young himself to have witnessed anything firsthand, the man told the clergyman that his father had passed on the story of the day the *Endeavour* arrived, and of subsequent interactions between the crew and the local tribe.

17 Author's note: Dr Shayne Williams notes of the use of the term Berewalgal. 'It is hard to say if this is a word created by local Aboriginal people or made up by the colonists, as they were doing language engineering of their own. In the early days of the colony Watkin Tench explains what Aboriginal people were referring to the colonist as: "It may be remarked that they translate the epithet white, when they speak of us, not by the name which they assign to this white earth, but by that which they distinguish the palms of their hands."' (*A Complete Account of the Settlement at Port Jackson*, Watkin Tench, 1793.)

18 Banks, Journal, 28 April 1770.

19 Parkinson, Journal, 28 April 1770.

20 Banks, Journal, 28 April 1770.

21 Banks, Journal, 28 April 1770.

22 Banks, Journal, 28 April 1770.

23 Banks, Journal, 28 April 1770.

24 Banks, Journal, 28 April 1770.

25 Banks, Journal, 28 April 1770.

26 Banks, Journal, 28 April 1770.

27 Parkinson, *A Journal of a Voyage to the South Seas*, 28 April 1770.

28 Parkinson, *A Journal of a Voyage to the South Seas*, 28 April 1770.

29 Parkinson, *A Journal of a Voyage to the South Seas*, 28 April 1770.

30 Parkinson, *A Journal of a Voyage to the South Seas*, 28 April 1770.

31 Parkinson, *A Journal of a Voyage to the South Seas*, 28 April 1770.

32 Banks, Journal, 28 April 1770.

33 Cook, Log, 29 April 1770.

34 Cook, Log, 29 April 1770.

35 Cook, Log, 29 April 1770.

36 Banks, Journal, 28 April 1770.

37 Cook, Journal, 29 April 1770: 'Saw, as we came in, on both points of the bay, several of the Natives and a few hutts; Men, Women, and Children on the South Shore abreast of the Ship, to which place I went in the Boats in hopes of speaking with them, accompanied by Mr. Banks, Dr. Solander, and Tupia. As we approached the Shore they all made off, except 2 Men, who seem'd resolved to oppose our landing. As soon as I saw this I order'd the boats to lay upon their Oars, in order to speak to them; but this was to little purpose, for neither us nor Tupia could understand one word they said. We then threw them some nails, beads, etc., a shore, which they took up, and seem'd not ill pleased with, in so much that I thought that they beckon'd to us to come ashore; but in this we were mistaken, for as soon as we put the boat in they again came to oppose us, upon which I fir'd a musquet between the 2, which had no other Effect than to make them retire back, where bundles of their darts lay, and one of them took up a stone and threw at us, which caused my firing a Second Musquet, load with small Shott; and altho' some of the shott struck the man, yet it had no other effect than making him lay hold on a Target. Immediately after this we landed, which we had no sooner done than they throw'd 2 darts at us; this obliged me to fire a third shott, soon after which they both made off, but not in such haste but what we might have taken one; but Mr. Banks being of Opinion that the darts were poisoned, made me cautious how I advanced into the Woods. We found here a few small hutts made of the Bark of Trees, in one of which were 4 or 5 Small Children, with whom we left some strings of beads, etc. A quantity of Darts lay about the Hutts; these we took away with us.'

Banks, Journal, 28 April 1770: 'After dinner the boats were mann'd and we set out from the ship intending to land at the place where we saw these people, hoping that as they regarded the ships coming in to the bay so little they would as little regard our landing. We were in this however mistaken, for as soon as we aproachd the rocks two of the men came down upon them, each armd with a lance of about 10 feet long and a short stick which he seemd to handle as if it was a machine to throw the lance. They calld to us very loud in a harsh sounding Language of which neither us or Tupia understood a word, shaking their lances and menacing, in all appearance resolvd to dispute our landing to the utmost tho they were but two and we 30 or 40 at least. In this manner we parleyd with them for about a quarter of an hour, they waving to us to be gone, we again signing that we wanted water and that we meant them no harm. They remaind resolute so a musquet was fird over them, the Effect of which was that the Youngest of the two dropd a bundle of lances on the rock at the instant in which he heard the report; he however snatchd them up again and both renewd their threats and opposition. A Musquet loaded with small shot was now fird at the Eldest of the two who was about 40 yards from the boat; it struck him on the legs but he minded it very little so another was immediately fird at him; on this he ran up to the house about 100 yards distant and soon returnd with a shield. In the mean time we had landed on the rock. He immediately threw a lance at us and the young man another which fell among the thickest of us but hurt nobody; 2 more musquets with small shot were then fird at them on which the Eldest threw one more lance and then ran away as did the other. We went up to the houses, in one of which we found the children hid behind the shield and a piece of bark in one of the houses. We were conscious from the distance the people had been from us when we fird that the shot could have done them no material harm; we therefore resolvd to leave the children on the spot without even opening their shelter. We therefore threw into the house to them some beads, ribbands, cloths etc. as presents and went away. We however thought it no improper measure to take away with us all the lances which we could find about the houses, amounting in number to forty or fifty.'

   Parkinson, A Journal of a Voyage to the South Seas, 28 April 1770: On the 28th, we got into a fine bay, and some of our people went on shore on one side of it, where we saw some houses. On our approaching the shore, two men, with different kinds of weapons, came out and made toward us. Their countenance bespoke displeasure; they threatened us, and discovered hostile intentions, often crying to us, Warra warra wai. We made signs to them to be peaceable, and threw them some trinkets; but they kept aloof, and dared us to come on shore. We attempted to frighten them by firing off a gun loaded with small shot; but attempted it in vain. One of them repaired to a house immediately, and brought out a shield, of an oval figure, painted white in the middle, with two holes in it to see through, and also a wooden sword, and then they advanced boldly, gathering up stones as they came along, which they threw at us. After we had landed, they threw two of their lances at us; one of which fell between my feet. Our people sired again, and wounded one of them; at which they took the alarm and were very frantic and furious, shouting for assistance, calling Hala, hala, mae; that is, (as we afterwards learned,) Come hither; while their wives and children set up a most horrid howl. We endeavoured to pacify them, but to no purpose, for they seemed implacable, and, at length, ran howling away, leaving their wives and children, who hid themselves in one of the huts behind a piece of bark. After looking about us a little while, we left some nails upon the spot and embarked, taking with us their weapons.'

38 Cook, Journal, 29 April 1770.
39 Cook, Journal, 29 April 1770.
40 Cook, Log, 28 April 1770.
41 Kitson, Captain James Cook, p. 133.
42 Parkinson, A Journal of a Voyage to the South Seas, 28 April 1770.
43 Banks, Journal, 28 April 1770.
44 Parkinson, A Journal of a Voyage to the South Seas, 28 April 1770.
45 Parkinson, A Journal of a Voyage to the South Seas, 28 April 1770.
46 Cook, Log, 29 April 1770.
47 Cook, Log, 29 April 1770.
48 Cook, Log, 29 April 1770.
49 Magra, A journal of a voyage round the World, p. 112.
50 Parkinson, A Journal of a Voyage to the South Seas, 28 April 1770.
51 Banks, Journal, 28 April 1770.
52 Banks, Journal, 28 April 1770.
53 Banks, Journal, 28 April 1770.

54 Banks, Journal, 28 April 1770.
55 Banks, Journal, 28 April 1770.
56 Cook, Log, 29 April 1770.
57 Cook, Log, 29 April 1770.
58 Banks, Journal, 28 April 1770.
59 Cook, Log, 29 April 1770.
60 Cook, Log, 29 April 1770.
61 Cook, Log, 29 April 1770.
62 Cook, Log, 29 April 1770.
63 Cook, Journal, 6 May 1770.
64 Parkinson, *A Journal of a Voyage to the South Seas*, 28 April 1770.
65 Banks, Journal, 30 April 1770.
66 Banks, Journal, 30 April 1770.
67 Cook, Journal, 6 May 1770.
68 Cook, Log, 1 May 1770.
69 Williams, 'An Indigenous Australian Perspective on Cook's Arrival', British Library, https://www.bl.uk/the-voyages-of-captain-james-cook/articles/an-indigenous-australian-perspective-on-cooks-arrival.
70 Henry Kendall, 'Sutherland's Grave', 1866, https://www.poetrylibrary.edu.au/poets/kendall-henry/sutherland-s-grave-0007076.
71 Cook, Journal, 1 May 1770.
72 Cook, Log, 1 May 1770.
73 Cook, Log, 1 May 1770.
74 Banks, Journal, 1 May 1770.
75 Banks, Journal, 1 May 1770.
76 Cook, Log, 1 May 1770.
77 Banks, Journal, 1 May 1770.
78 Banks, Journal, 1 May 1770.
79 Parkinson, *A Journal of a Voyage to the South Seas*, 28 April 1770.
80 Banks, Journal, 1 May 1770.
81 Banks, Journal, 2 May 1770.
82 Banks, Journal, 1 May 1770.
83 Banks, Journal, 1 May 1770.
84 Parkinson, *A Journal of a Voyage to the South Seas*, 5 May 1770.
85 Cook, Log, 3 May 1770.
86 Cook, Log, 3 May 1770.
87 Banks, Journal, 3 May 1770.
88 Banks, Journal, 3 May 1770.
89 Banks, Journal, 4 May 1770.
90 Banks, Journal, 4 May 1770.
91 Cook, Log, 6 May 1770.
92 Cook, Log, 6 May 1770.
93 Cook, Log, 6 May 1770.
94 Cook, Log, 6 May 1770.
95 Banks, Journal, 6 May 1770.

Chapter 11

1 Cook to Captain John Walker, Letter, 13 September 1771 in Beaglehole, *The Journals of Captain James Cook on His Voyages of Discovery*, pp. 508–509.
2 Banks, Journal, 11 June 1770.
3 Cook, Journal, 15 May 1770.
4 Banks, Journal, 15 May 1770.
5 Banks, Journal, 15 May 1770.
6 Banks, Journal, 23 May 1770.
7 Banks, Journal, 23 May 1770.

8   Cook, Log, 23 May 1770.
9   Perry, 'Voyage to Batavia', *The Gentleman's Magazine*, p. 221.
10 Cook, Journal, 23 May 1770.
11 Cook, Journal, 23 May 1770.
12 Cook, Journal, 23 May 1770.
13 Cook, Log, 23 May 1770.
14 Cook, Log, 23 May 1770.
15 Cook, Log, 23 May 1770.
16 Perry, 'Voyage to Batavia', *The Gentleman's Magazine*, p. 221.
17 Perry, 'Voyage to Batavia', *The Gentleman's Magazine*, p. 221.
18 Perry, 'Voyage to Batavia', *The Gentleman's Magazine*, p. 221.
19 Perry, 'Voyage to Batavia', *The Gentleman's Magazine*, p. 221.
20 Parkinson, *A Journal of a Voyage to the South Seas*, 21–23 May 1770.
21 Perry, 'Voyage to Batavia', *The Gentleman's Magazine*, p. 221.
22 Banks, Journal, 1 June 1770 [reported speech].
23 Banks, Journal, 1 June 1770.
24 Cook, Log, 4 June 1770.
25 Banks, Journal, 9 June 1770.
26 Cook, Log, 11 June 1770.
27 Cook, Log, 11 June 1770.
28 Banks, Journal, 10 June 1770.
29 Banks, Journal, 10 June 1770.
30 Banks, Journal, 11 June 1770.
31 Cook, Log, 11 June 1770.
32 Banks, Journal, 11 June 1770.
33 Banks, Journal, 10 June 1770.
34 Banks, Journal, 11 June 1770.
35 Banks, Journal, 11 June 1770.
36 Banks, Journal, 11 June 1770.
37 Banks, Journal, 11 June 1770.
38 Cook to Sir John Pringle, Letter, 8 April 1776, *Philosophical Transactions of the Royal Society of London*, Vol. 66, pp. 447–49.
39 Cook, Log, 11 June 1770.
40 Cook, Log, 11 June 1770.
41 Author's note: The correct terminology is actually 'bower anchors' but, for ease of understanding, I have used their position, rather than their formal name.
42 Cook, Log, 11 June 1770.
43 Banks, Journal, 11 June 1770.
44 Banks, Journal, 11 June 1770.
45 Banks, Journal, 11 June 1770.
46 Banks, Journal, 11 June 1770.
47 Banks, Journal, 11 June 1770.
48 Banks, Journal, 11 June 1770.
49 Banks, Journal, 12 June 1770.
50 Boswell, *The Life of Samuel Johnson*, L.L.D., Vol. 3, 1791.
51 Banks, Journal, 11 June 1770.
52 Banks, Journal, 12 June 1770.
53 Cook, Journal, 12 June 1770.
54 Banks, Journal, 12 June 1770.
55 Shakespeare, *Macbeth*, Act 4, Scene 1, Lyons and Carnahan, New York, 1913, p. 78.
56 Banks, Journal, 12 June 1770.
57 Banks, Journal, 12 June 1770 [reported speech].
58 Banks, Journal, 12 June 1770.
59 Banks, Journal, 12 June 1770.
60 Banks, Journal, 12 June 1770.

61 Banks, Journal, 13 June 1770.

62 Cook, Journal, 18 June 1770.

63 Cook, *A Voyage Towards the South Pole and Round the World*, Strahan and Cadell, London, 1777, p. 338.

64 Cook, Log, 22 June 1770.

65 Cook, Log, 22 June 1770.

66 Cook, Log, 4 August 1770.

67 Banks, Journal, 29 June 1770.

68 Banks, Journal, 'Account of New Holland', 31 August 1770.

69 Banks, Journal, 3 July 1770.

70 Banks, Journal, 22 June 1770.

71 Cook (transcribed by Richard Orton), 'A Journal of the proceedings of His Majesty's Bark *Endeavour* on a voyage round the world, commencing the 25th of May 1768 – 23 Oct. 1770, 24 June 1770, SLNSW, Manuscript Safe 1/71).

72 Cook, 'A Journal of the proceedings of His Majesty's Bark *Endeavour*', 24 June 1770.

Chapter 12

1 Cook, Journal, 30 June 1770.

2 Banks, Journal, 30 June 1770.

3 Cook, Log, 1 July 1770.

4 Cook, Journal, 6 July 1770.

5 Banks, Journal, 5 July 1770.

6 Banks, Journal, 7 July 1770.

7 Banks, Journal, 14 July 1770.

8 Banks, Journal, 7 July 1770.

9 Banks, Journal, 7 July 1770.

10 Banks, Journal, 7 July 1770.

11 Banks, Journal, 8 July 1770.

12 Banks, Journal, 9 July 1770.

13 Cook, Log, 10 July 1770.

14 Cook, Log, 10 July 1770 [reported speech].

15 Banks, Journal, 10 July 1770.

16 Banks, Journal, 10 July 1770.

17 Cook, Journal, 23 August 1770.

18 Cook, Log, 12 July 1770.

19 Banks, Journal, 10 July 1770.

20 Cook, Log, 10 July 1770.

21 Parkinson, *A Journal of a Voyage to the South Seas*, 'Account of New Holland', 4 July–3 August 1770.

22 Parkinson, *A Journal of a Voyage to the South Seas*, 'Account of New Holland', 4 July–3 August 1770.

23 Parkinson, *A Journal of a Voyage to the South Seas*, 'Account of New Holland', 4 July–3 August 1770.

24 Cook, Log, 10 July 1770.

25 Cook, Log, 10 July 1770.

26 Cook, Journal, 10 July 1770.

27 Banks, Journal, 11 July 1770.

28 Banks, Journal, 11 July 1770.

29 Morton, James Douglas, Earl,' Hints offered to the consideration of Captain Cooke, Mr. Bankes, Doctor Solander and other gentlemen who go upon the expedition on board the Endeavour. Chiswick', National Library of Australia, Papers of Sir Joseph Banks, 1745–1923, MS 9, Series 3/Item 113–113h, p. 1, http://nla.gov.au:80/tarkine/nla.obj-222969577.

30 Banks, Journal, 'New Holland Observations', 1770.

31 Hill, *New Words from Endeavour*, Penguin Books, Australia, 2018.

32 Parkinson, *A Journal of a Voyage to the South Seas*, 'Vocabulary of the language of New-Holland', 4 July–3 August 1770.

33 Banks, Journal, 12 July 1770.

34 Parkinson, *A Journal of a Voyage to the South Seas*, August 1770 [reported speech].

35 Parkinson, *A Journal of a Voyage to the South Seas*, August 1770.

36 Banks, Journal, 'New Holland Observations', 1770.

37 Banks, Journal, 'New Holland Observations', 1770.

38 Banks Journal, 'New Holland Observations', 1770.

39 Banks Journal, 'New Holland Observations', 1770.

40 Banks, Journal, 'New Holland Observations', 1770.

41 Cook, Log, 14 July 1770.

42 Parkinson, *A Journal of a Voyage to the South Seas*, 3 August 1770.

43 Banks, Journal, 15 July 1770.

44 Banks, Journal, 15 July 1770.

45 Banks, Journal, 15 July 1770.

46 Banks, Journal, 17 July 1770.

47 Banks, Journal, 18 July 1770.

48 Banks, Journal, 18 July 1770.

49 Banks, Journal, 12 July 1770.

50 Cook, Log, 18 July 1770.

51 Banks, Journal, 19 July 1770.

52 Banks, Journal, 19 July 1770.

53 Banks, Journal, 19 July 1770.

54 Banks, Journal, 19 July 1770.

55 Banks, Journal, 19 July 1770.

56 Cook, Log, 19 July 1770.

57 Cook, Log, 19 July 1770.

58 Banks, Journal, 19 July 1770.

59 Cook, Log, 19 July 1770.

60 Cook, Log, 19 July 1770.

61 Banks, Journal, 19 July 1770.

62 Cook, Journal, 'Account of New Zealand'.

63 Banks, Journal, 19 July 1770.

64 Banks, Journal, 19 July 1770.

65 Banks, Journal, 19 July 1770.

66 Banks, Journal, 19 July 1770.

67 Banks, Journal, 19 July 1770.

68 Banks, Journal, 19 July 1770.

69 With thanks to Guugu Yimithirr man Harold Ludwick, this oral history comes from Eric Deeral, Gamay Warra clan elder of the Guugu Yimithirr nation, 2001.

70 Banks, Journal, 19 July 1770.

71 Interview between David Phoenix and Guugu Yimithirr man Harold Ludwick, 22 July 2019.

72 Cook, Log, 19 July 1770.

73 Banks, Journal, 19 July 1770 [reported speech].

74 Banks, Journal, 19 July 1770 [reported speech].

75 Banks, Journal, 19 July 1770.

76 Cook, Journal, 19 July 1770.

77 Cook, Journal, 19 July 1770.

78 Cook, Journal, 19 July 1770.

79 Banks, Journal, 20 July 1770.

80 Cook, Log, 20 July 1770.

81 Cook, Log, 20 July 1770.

82 Banks, Journal, 20 July 1770.

83 Cook, Journal, 23 July 1770.

84 Banks, Journal, 22 July 1770.

85 Banks, Journal, 22 July 1770.

86 Cook, Log, 4 August 1770.

87 Cook, Log, 4 August 1770.

88 Banks, Journal, 7 August 1770.
89 Cook, Log, 7 August 1770.
90 Cook, Log, 7 August 1770.
91 Banks, Journal, 11 August 1770.
92 Perry, 'Voyage to Batavia', *The Gentleman's Magazine*, p. 299.
93 Perry, 'Voyage to Batavia', *The Gentleman's Magazine*, p. 299.
94 Perry, 'Voyage to Batavia', *The Gentleman's Magazine*, p. 299.
95 Perry, 'Voyage to Batavia', *The Gentleman's Magazine*, p. 299.
96 With thanks to Guugu Yimithirr man Harold Ludwick, this oral history comes from Eric Deeral, Gamay Warra clan elder of the Guugu Yimithirr nation, 2001.

Chapter 13

1 Banks, Journal, 14 August 1770.
2 Parkinson, *A Journal of a Voyage to the South Seas*, 'Description of Batavia', October 1770.
3 Cook, Journal, 26 December 1770.
4 Cook, Journal, 16 August 1770.
5 Cook, Log, 16 August 1770.
6 Cook, Log, 16 August 1770.
7 Cook, Log, 16 August 1770.
8 Banks, Journal, 16 August 1770.
9 Cook, Log, 16 August 1770.
10 Cook, Log, 16 August 1770.
11 Cook, Log, 16 August 1770.
12 Banks, Journal, 16 August 1770.
13 Banks, Journal, 16 August 1770.
14 Banks, Journal, 16 August 1770.
15 Banks, Journal, 16 August 1770.
16 Kitson, *Captain James Cook*, p. 190.
17 Banks, Journal, 16 August 1770 [reported speech].
18 Cook, Log, 16 August 1770.
19 Cook, Log, 17 August 1770.
20 Cook, Log, 17 August 1770.
21 Cook, Log, 17 August 1770.
22 Cook, Log, 17 August 1770.
23 Cook, Log, 17 August 1770.
24 Cook, Log, 17 August 1770.
25 Banks, Journal, 21 August 1770.
26 'Possession Island', http://www.australiaforeveryone.com.au/cairns/possession-isld.html.
27 Stephens, 'Secret Instructions to Captain Cook from the Admiralty', 30 July 1768.
28 Letters Patent to Sir Humfrey Gylberte, 11 June 1578, https://avalon.law.yale.edu/16th_century/humfrey.asp.
29 Cook, Journal, 22 August 1770.
30 Author's note: As with some other significant Cook naming, 'New South Wales' has inspired much academic debate as to exactly when it was coined or settled upon. The pre-eminent Cook scholar Beaglehole notes that the 'earliest' draft of the Log (the safety version Cook sent on from Batavia) has no mention of New South Wales, so therefore it must be a later addition on paper. But Cook first called the East coast 'New Wales' in his retained version of the log and the matter is complicated by the fact that this 'New Wales' was erased, or rather cut out, presumably by Cook or his clerk, Orton, and then the final title 'New South Wales' was written in their place, in a space too small for all three words. None of this precludes the name 'New South Wales' as being in Cook's head, he was clearly musing on what would be a significant nomenclature, but as with 'Botany Bay' it is a peculiar quirk that Cook would change his mind on the very naming that would become his legacy.
31 Banks, Journal, 'New Holland Observations', 1770.
32 Banks, Journal, 'New Holland Observations', 1770.

33 Banks, Journal, 'New Holland Observations', 1770.
34 Banks, Journal, 'New Holland Observations', 1770.
35 Banks, Journal, 'New Holland Observations', 1770.
36 Banks, Journal, 'New Holland Observations', 1770.
37 Cook to Captain John Walker, Letter, 13 September 1771 in Beaglehole, *The Journals of Captain James Cook on His Voyages of Discovery*, p. 509.
38 Cook, Journal, 17 September 1770.
39 Banks, Journal, 18 September 1770 [reported speech].
40 Banks, Journal, 19 September 1770 [reported speech].
41 Banks, Journal, 19 September 1770 [reported speech].
42 Banks, Journal, 19 September 1770.
43 Banks, Journal, 'Account of the Island of Savu' 1770.
44 Banks, Journal, 'Account of the Island of Savu' 1770.
45 Banks, Journal, 'Account of the Island of Savu' 1770.
46 Banks, Journal, 9 October 1770.
47 Cook, Log, 15 October 1770.
48 Cook, Journal, 10 October 1770.
49 Cook, Journal, 10 October 1770.
50 Cook, Journal, 12 October 1770.
51 Cook, Journal, 12 October 1770.
52 Cook, Log, 16 October 1770.
53 Perry, 'Voyage to Batavia', *The Gentleman's Magazine*, p. 27.
54 Perry, 'Voyage to Batavia', *The Gentleman's Magazine*, p. 26.
55 Perry, 'Voyage to Batavia', *The Gentleman's Magazine*, p. 26.
56 Parkinson, *A Journal of a Voyage to the South Seas*, 'Description of Batavia', October 1770.
57 Banks, Journal, 10–20 October 1770.
58 Parkinson, *A Journal of a Voyage to the South Seas*, 'Description of Batavia', October 1770.
59 Banks, Journal, 'Account of Batavia'.
60 Banks, Journal, 10–20 October 1770.
61 Cook, Journal, 15 October 1770.
62 Banks, Journal, 'Account of Batavia'.
63 Parkinson, *A Journal of a Voyage to the South Seas*, 'Description of Batavia', October 1770.
64 Banks, Journal, 10–20 October 1770.
65 Perry, 'Voyage to Batavia', *The Gentleman's Magazine*, p. 598.
66 Banks, Journal, 'Account of Batavia', 31 December 1770.
67 Banks, Journal, 'Account of Batavia', 31 December 1770.
68 Cook, Journal, 'Description of Batavia', 26 December 1770.
69 Beaglehole, *The Life of Captain James Cook*, Stanford University Press, 1992, p. 261.
70 Beaglehole, *The Life of Captain James Cook*, Stanford University Press, 1992, p. 262.
71 Banks, Journal, 10–20 October 1770.
72 Banks, Journal, 10–20 October 1770.
73 Banks, Journal, 10–20 October 1770.
74 Cook, Journal, Letter to Philip Stephens (Secretary of the Admiralty), 23 October 1770.
75 Cook, Journal, Letter to Philip Stephens (Secretary of the Admiralty), 23 October 1770.
76 Banks, Journal, 10–20 October 1770.
77 Perry, 'Voyage to Batavia', *The Gentleman's Magazine*, pp. 221–22.
78 Perry, 'Voyage to Batavia', *The Gentleman's Magazine*, pp. 221–22.
79 Banks, Journal, 30 October 1770.
80 Perry, 'Voyage to Batavia', *The Gentleman's Magazine*, p. 27.
81 Cook, Log, 7 November 1770.
82 Perry, 'Voyage to Batavia', *The Gentleman's Magazine*, p. 101.
83 Perry, 'Voyage to Batavia', *The Gentleman's Magazine*, p. 102.
84 Perry, 'Voyage to Batavia', *The Gentleman's Magazine*, p. 102.
85 Perry, 'Voyage to Batavia', *The Gentleman's Magazine*, p. 597.
86 Perry, 'Voyage to Batavia', *The Gentleman's Magazine*, p. 299.

87 Parkinson, *A Journal of a Voyage to the South Seas*, 'Description of Batavia', October 1770.
88 Parkinson, *A Journal of a Voyage to the South Seas*, 'Description of Batavia', October 1770.
89 Banks, Journal, 28 October 1770.
90 Banks, Journal, 28 October 1770.
91 Perry, 'Voyage to Batavia', *The Gentleman's Magazine*, p. 299.
92 Parkinson, *A Journal of a Voyage to the South Seas*, 'Description of Batavia', October 1770.
93 Perry, 'Voyage to Batavia', *The Gentleman's Magazine*, p. 299 [reported speech].
94 Perry, 'Voyage to Batavia', *The Gentleman's Magazine*, p. 299.
95 Cook, Journal, 26 November 1770.
96 Banks, Journal, 13 November 1770.
97 Banks, Journal, 13 November 1770.
98 Walton, 'Medical Blistering in the Georgian Era', Unique Histories from the 18th and 19th Centuries, 2015, https://www.geriwalton.com/medical-blistering-in-georgian-era/.
99 Banks, Journal, 13 November 1770.
100 Banks, Journal, 13 November 1770.
101 Banks, Journal, 7 November 1770.
102 Banks, Journal, 14 November 1770.
103 Banks, Journal, 24 November 1770.
104 Perry, 'Voyage to Batavia', *The Gentleman's Magazine*, p. 766.
105 Perry, 'Voyage to Batavia', *The Gentleman's Magazine*, p. 766.
106 Cook, Log, 26 December 1770.
107 Cook, Journal, 6 January 1771.
108 Cook, Journal, 'Description of Batavia', 26 December 1770.

Chapter 14

1 Cook, Journal, 6 January 1771.
2 Cook, Log, 16 January 1771.
3 Banks, Journal, 20 January 1771.
4 Cook, Log, 24 January 1771.
5 Cook, Log, 24 January 1771.
6 Banks, Journal, 25 January 1771.
7 Perry, 'Voyage to Batavia', *The Gentleman's Magazine*, p. 597.
8 Perry, 'Voyage to Batavia', *The Gentleman's Magazine*, p .766.
9 Banks, Journal, 26 January 1771.
10 Cook, Journal, 29 January 1771.
11 Cook, Journal, 15 March 1771.
12 Cook, Journal, 15 March 1771.
13 Perry, 'Voyage to Batavia', *The Gentleman's Magazine*, p. 766.
14 Perry, 'Voyage to Batavia', *The Gentleman's Magazine*, p. 766.
15 Banks, Journal, 30 January 1771.
16 Cook, Journal, 31 January 1771.
17 Banks, Journal, 31 January 1771.
18 Cook, Journal, 2 February 1771.
19 Cook, Journal, 27 February 1771.
20 Cook, Journal, 5 March 1771.
21 Perry, 'Voyage to Batavia', *The Gentleman's Magazine*, p. 767.
22 Banks, Journal, 4 March 1771.
23 Cook, Log, 4 March 1771.
24 Banks, Journal, 'Account of the Cape of Good Hope'.
25 Cook, Log, 20 March 1771.
26 Cook, Log, 20 March 1771.
27 Cook, Log, 16 April 1771.
28 Banks, Journal, 3 May 1771.
29 Banks, Journal, 4 May 1771.

30 Cook, Journal, 24 May 1771.
31 Cook, Journal, 26 May 1771.
32 Cook, Journal, 27 May 1771.
33 Banks, Journal, 1 July 1771.
34 Cook, Journal, 7 July 1771.
35 Shakespeare, *Richard II*, Act 2, Scene 1.
36 Beaglehole, (ed.), *The Journals of Captain James Cook on His Voyages of Discovery*, pp. 504–505.
37 Salmond, *The Trial of the Cannibal Dog*, p. 168.
38 Salmond, *The Trial of the Cannibal Dog*, p. 167.
39 Moore, *Endeavour: The Ship and Attitude that Changed the World*, Vintage, Sydney, 2018, p. 253.
40 Salmond, *The Trial of the Cannibal Dog*, p. 168 [reported speech].
41 Moore, *Endeavour: The Ship and Attitude that Changed the World*, p. 253.
42 Moore, *Endeavour: The Ship and Attitude that Changed the World*, p. 253.
43 Banks, *Joseph Banks in Newfoundland and Labrador, 1776: His Diary, Manuscripts, and Collections*, University of California Press, Berkeley and Los Angeles, 1971, p. 49.
44 Salmond, *The Trial of the Cannibal Dog*, p. 169.
45 Bligh, Extract from the logbook HMS *Bounty* (16 August 1787–20 August 1789), 15 January 1789, The National Archives, Kew, ADM 55/151, p. 257.
46 Beaglehole (ed.), *The Journals of Captain James Cook on His Voyages of Discovery*, p. 651.
47 Beaglehole (ed.), *The Journals of Captain James Cook on His Voyages of Discovery*, p. 651.
48 Beaglehole (ed.), *The Journals of Captain James Cook on His Voyages of Discovery*, p. 652.
49 Beaglehole, (ed.), *The Journals of Captain James Cook on His Voyages of Discovery*, p. 652.
50 Beaglehole, (ed.), *The Journals of Captain James Cook on His Voyages of Discovery*, p. 652.
51 Beaglehole, (ed.), *The Journals of Captain James Cook on His Voyages of Discovery*, p. 643.
52 Beaglehole, *The Life of Captain James Cook*, p. 284.
53 Beaglehole, (ed.), *The Journals of Captain James Cook on His Voyages of Discovery*, p. 637.
54 Beaglehole, *The Life of Captain James Cook*, p. 284.
55 O'Brian, *Joseph Banks*, p. 161.
56 Beaglehole (ed.), *The Journals of Captain James Cook on His Voyages of Discovery*, Vol. 2, Cambridge University Press, London, 1961, p. 713.
57 Beaglehole, (ed.), *The Journals of Captain James Cook on His Voyages of Discovery*, Vol. 2, pp. 713–14 [reported speech].
58 Hough, *Captain James Cook: A Biography*, p. 225.
59 Smith, *The Life of Sir Joseph Banks, president of the Royal Society, with some notices of his friends and contemporaries*, p. 26.
60 Smith, *The Life of Sir Joseph Banks, president of the Royal Society, with some notices of his friends and contemporaries*, p. 26. Hough, *Captain James Cook: A Biography*, p. 187.
61 McLynn, *Captain Cook: Master of the Seas*, Yale University Press, USA, 2011, p. 174.
62 Beaglehole, (ed.), *The Journals of Captain James Cook on His Voyages of Discovery*, Vol. 2, pp. 930–31.
63 Beaglehole, (ed.), *The Journals of Captain James Cook on His Voyages of Discovery*, Vol. 2, pp.930–31.
64 Salmond, *The Trial of the Cannibal Dog*, p. 171.
65 Salmond, *The Trial of the Cannibal Dog*, pp. 169–70.
66 Cook, *Journal*, 28 November 1771.
67 Salmond, *The Trial of the Cannibal Dog*, pp. 171–72.
68 Beaglehole (ed.), *The Journals of Captain James Cook on His Voyages of Discovery*, Vol. 2, p. 938.
69 Beaglehole (ed.), *The Journals of Captain James Cook on His Voyages of Discovery*, Vol. 2, p. 938.
70 Beaglehole (ed.), *The Journals of Captain James Cook on His Voyages of Discovery*, Vol. 2, pp. 936–37.
71 Beaglehole (ed.), *The Journals of Captain James Cook on His Voyages of Discovery*, Vol. 2, p. 297.

Epilogue

1 Beaglehole, *The Life of Captain James Cook*, Stanford University Press, 1992, p. 365.
2 Van Dyke (ed.), *Poems of Tennyson*, Ginn and Company Publishers, Boston, 1903, p. 117.
3 Buchan, 'Cooking the Books', *Inside Story*, June 2018.
4 Beaglehole, *The Journals of Captain James Cook on his Voyages of Discovery: Volume II*, p. 685.

5 Cook to Joseph Banks, Letter, 18 November 1772, SLNSW, Sir Joseph Banks Papers, Section 03, Series 07.02, p. 2.

6 Cook, *Three Voyages of Captain James Cook Round the World*, Vol. 1, Longman, 1821, London, p. 219.

7 Salmond, *The Trial of the Cannibal Dog*, p. 299.

8 O'Brian, *Joseph Banks*, p. 187.

9 O'Brian, *Joseph Banks*, p. 187.

10 Beaglehole, *The Life of Captain James Cook*, p. 443.

11 Beaglehole, *The Life of Captain James Cook*, p. 443.

12 O'Brian, *Joseph Banks*, p. 189.

13 The Collection, Royal Museums Greenwich, 'Portrait of Captain James Cook' by Nathaniel Dance. https://collections.rmg.co.uk/collections/objects/14102.html

14 Beaglehole, *The Life of Captain James Cook*, p. 695.

15 Lord Sandwich addressing the House of Lords, *The Gentleman's Magazine*, Vol. 45, 1775, p. 511.

16 James Taylor, *Picturing the Pacific*, Adlard Coles, London, 2018, p. 71.

17 Cook to Sir John Pringle, Letter, Undated, in Robert McNab (ed.), *Historical Records of New Zealand*, Vol. II, John Mackay, Wellington, 1914, p. 129.

18 Penrose, *Lives of Vice-Admiral Sir Charles Vinicombe Penrose, K. C. B,. and Captain James Trevenen, Knight of the Russian Orders of St. George and St. Vladimir*, John Murray, London, 1850, p. 196.

19 Hough, *Captain James Cook: A Biography*, p. 325.

20 Hough, *Captain James Cook: A Biography*, p. 289.

21 Hough, *Captain James Cook: A Biography*, p. 289.

22 Franklin, *The Works of Benjamin Franklin*, Vol. 5, Tappan & Whittemore, Boston, 1837, pp. 123–124.

23 Samwell, *A Narrative on the Death of Captain Cook*, G. G. J. & J. Robinson, London, 1786, p. 11.

24 Account of John Ledyard, in Jarves, *History of the Hawaiian or Sandwich Islands*, Tappan and Dennett, Boston, 1843, p. 126 [reported speech].

25 Jarves, *History of the Hawaiian or Sandwich Islands*, p. 126.

26 Young, *The Life and Voyages of Captain James Cook, Drawn Up from His Journals, and Other Authentic Documents*, Whittaker Treacher & Co., London, 1836, p. 441.

27 Young, *The Life and Voyages of Captain James Cook*, p. 441.

28 Besant, *Captain Cook*, p. 171.

29 Gilbert, 'The Death of Captain James Cook', *Hawaiian Historical Society Reprints*, No. 5, p. 13.

30 Samwell, 'Some Particulars Concerning the Life and and Character of Captain James Cook', *The European Magazine and London Review*, Vol. 9, May 1786, p. 323.

31 Beaglehole (ed.), *The Journals of Captain James Cook on His Voyages of Discovery*, Vol. 3, 1967, p. 1552.

32 *London Gazette*, 11 January 1780.

33 Besant, *Captain Cook*, pp. 186–187.

34 Brownsy, 'The Banks and Solander Collections – a Benchmark for Understanding the New Zealand Flora', *Journal of the Royal Society of New Zealand*, Vol. 42, No. 2, 2012, p. 131.

35 Brownsy, 'The Banks and Solander Collections', *Journal of the Royal Society of New Zealand*, p. 131.

36 Clerke to Joseph Banks, 10 August 1779 SLNSW, Sir Joseph Banks Papers, Section 04, Series 11.04, p. 2.

37 Tink, 'The Role of Parliamentary Witnesses in the Foundation of Australia', *Australasian Parliamentary Review*, Spring, 2005 Vol. 20, No. 2, pp. 33–38 [tense changed] [reported speech].

38 Tink, 'The Role of Parliamentary Witnesses in the Foundation of Australia', Australasian Parliamentary Review, pp. 33–38 [tense changed] [reported speech].

39 Banks, Journal, 1 May 1770.

40 Magra, 'A Proposal for Establishing a Settlement in New South Wales', 1783, in Arthur Phillip, *Historical Records of New South Wales*, Vol. I, Part 2, 1783–1792, Charles Potter, Government Printer, Sydney, 1892, p. 1.

41 Stockdale, *The Voyage of Governor Phillip to Botany Bay*, London, 1789, p. 46.

42 Stockdale, *The Voyage of Governor Phillip to Botany Bay*, p. 55.

43 Southwell to his uncle, Letter, 23 June 1788, Daniel Southwell, Journal, Historical Records of New South Wales, Vol. 2, 692.17.

44 Bradley, 'A Voyage to New South Wales: December 1786 – May 1792', Journal, 25 November 1789, SLNSW, Safe 1/14, p. 182.

45 Besant, *Captain Cook*, pp. 184–5.
46 Morelli, 'A Step Closer to Winning Bank Gweagal Shield', NITV News, 24 August 2016.
47 Keenan, 'How the British Museum Changed its Story About the Gweagal Shield', Australian Critical Race and Whiteness Studies Association, 2018.
48 Cook, Journal, 3 June 1773.
49 Cook, Log, 22 August 1770.
50 Beaglehole, *The Journals of Captain James Cook on his Voyages of Discovery: Volume II*, Routledge, p. 685.

BIBLIOGRAPHY

Books

Anson, George, *A voyage round the world, in the years MDCCXL, I, II, III, IV,* [no publisher], London, 1748

Apperson, George Latimer and Martin H. Manser, *Dictionary of Proverbs,* Wordsworth, London, 2007

Banks, Joseph, *Joseph Banks in Newfoundland and Labrador, 1766: His Diary, Manuscripts, and Collections,* University of California Press, Berkeley and Los Angeles, 1971

Beaglehole, J. C. (ed.), The Endeavour Journal of Joseph Banks, 1768–1771, Trustees of the Public Library of NSW/Angus & Robertson, Sydney, 1963

Beaglehole, J. C. (ed.), *The Journals of Captain James Cook on His Voyages of Discovery, Vol. I,* Cambridge University Press, London, 1955

Beaglehole, J. C. (ed.), *The Journals of Captain James Cook on His Voyages of Discovery, Vol. 2,* Cambridge University Press, London, 1961

Beaglehole, J.C., (ed.), *The Journals of Captain James Cook on His Voyages of Discovery, Vol. 3,* Cambridge University Press, London, 1967

Beaglehole J. C., *The Journals of Captain James Cook on his Voyages of Discovery: Volume II: The Voyage of the Resolution and Adventure 1772–1775,* Routledge, Oxfordshire, 2017

Beaglehole, J. C., *The Life of Captain James Cook,* Adam & Charles Black, London, 1974

Beaglehole, J. C., *The Life of Captain James Cook,* Stanford University Press, 1992

Besant, Walter, *Captain Cook,* Macmillan & Co., London, 1890

Bligh, William, *A Voyage to the South Sea,* Hutchinson, Richmond, 1979

Boenigk, Jens, Sabina Wodniok and Edvard Glücksman, *Biodiversity and Earth History,* Springer, Heidelberg, 2015

Boswell, James, *The Life of Samuel Johnson LL.D.,* Vol. 3, 1791

Brougham, Henry, *Lives of men of letters & science, who flourished in the time of George III,* Vol II, Henry Colburn, London, 1846

Burnet, Ian, *Where Australia Collides with Asia,* Rosenberg Publishing, Sydney, 2017

Burney, James, *The Private Journal of James Burney,* National Library of Australia, Canberra, 1975

Byrn, John D., *Naval Courts Martial, 1793–1815,* Ashgate Publishing, England, 2009

Chambers, Neil (ed.), *The Letters of Sir Joseph Banks: A Selection, 1768–1820,* World Scientific, 2000

Chipman, Willis, *The Life and Times of Major Samuel Holland, Surveyor-General 1764–1801,* Reprinted from Ontario Historical Society's 'Papers and Records' Vol. 21

Cook, James, *A Voyage Towards the South Pole and Round the World,* Strahan and Cadell, London, 1777

Cook, James, *Three Voyages of Captain James Cook Round the World, Vol. 1,* Longman, London, 1821

Cook, James and Wharton, W. J. L. (ed.), *Captain Cook's Journal During his First Voyage Around the World,* Elliot Stock, London, 1893

Dalrymple, Alexander, *An Historical collection of the several voyages and discoveries in the South Pacific Ocean,* T. Payne, London, 1770

Defoe, Daniel, *A Tour Through England and Wales*, Dent, London, 1928

Dugard, Martin, *Farther Than Any Man*, Washington Square Press, New York, 2002

Firth, Charles Harding, *Naval Songs and Ballads*, Navy Records Society, London, 1908

Forster, Johann Reinhold, *Observations Made During a Voyage Round the World, On Physical Geography, Natural History, and Ethic Philosophy*, G. Robinson, London, 1778

Franklin, Benjamin, *The Works of Benjamin Franklin*, Vol. 5, Tappan & Whittemore, Boston, 1837

Freshfield, D. W., *Life of H.B. de Saussure*, Edward Arnold, London, 1920

Gascoigne, John, *Joseph Banks and the English Enlightenment: Useful Knowledge and Polite Culture*, Cambridge University Press, UK, 1994

Gilbert, George and Hawaiian Historical Society, *The Death of Captain James Cook*, Paradise of the Pacific Press, Honolulu, 1926

Green, Charles, and Lieutenant James Cook, *Observations Made by Appointment of the Royal Society at King George's Island in the South Sea*, Royal Society Publishing, London, 21 November 1771

Hawkesworth, John, *An account of the voyages undertaken by the order of His present Majesty for making discoveries in the Southern Hemisphere, and successively performed by Commodore Byron, Captain Wallis, Captain Carteret, and Captain Cook, in the Dolphin, the Swallow, and the Endeavour: drawn up from the journals which were kept by the several commanders, and from the papers of Joseph Banks, Esq., Vol. I*, W. Strahan and T. Cadell, London, 1773

Hill, Anthony, *New Words from Endeavour*, Penguin Books, Australia, 2018

Hough, Richard, *The Murder of Captain James Cook*, Macmillan, Hong Kong, 1979

Hough, Richard, *Captain James Cook: A Biography*, Hodder & Stoughton, London, 1994

Jarves, James, *History of the Hawaiian or Sandwich Islands*, Tappan and Dennett, Boston, 1843

Johnson, Samuel, *The Rambler: A Periodical Paper Published in 1750, 1751, 1752, Vol. 1*, Jones and Company, London, 1826

Kennedy, Gavin, *The Death of Captain Cook*, Duckworth, London, 1978

Kippis, Andrew, *A Narrative of the Voyages round the World performed by Captain James Cook, with an Account of His Life during the previous and intervening periods*, Porter and Coates, Philadelphia, 1850

Kirk, Robert W., *Paradise Past: The Transformation of the South Pacific, 1520–1920*, McFarland & Company, North Carolina, 2012

Kitson, Arthur, *Captain James Cook*, E.P. Dutton and Company, New York, 1907

Leadbetter, Charles, *A Compleat System of Astronomy*, J. Wilcox, London, 1728

Lockett, Jerry, *Captain James Cook in Atlantic Canada: The Adventurer and Map Maker's Formative Years*, Formac Publishing Company Ltd, Halifax, 2010

Mackay, Joseph Angus, *Life in Early Poverty Bay: Trials and Triumphs of its Brave Founders*, The Gisborne Publishing Company, Ltd, Gisborne, 1927

McLynn, Frank, *Captain Cook: Master of the Seas*, Yale University Press, USA, 2011

McNab, Robert (ed.), *Historical Records of New Zealand, Vol. II*, John Mackay, Wellington, 1914

Magra, James, *A journal of a voyage round the world, in His Majesty's ship* Endeavour, *in the years 1768, 1769, 1770, and 1771*, T. Becket and P.A.D. Hondt, London, 1771

Matra, James, 'A Proposal for Establishing a Settlement in New South Wales, 1783', in *Arthur Phillip, Historical Records of New South Wales, Vol. I, Part 2, 1783–1792*, Charles Potter, Government Printer, Sydney, 1892

Megaw, J. V. S, *Employ'd as a Discoverer*, A. H. & A. W. Reed, Sydney, 1971

Moore, Peter, *Endeavour: The Ship and Attitude that Changed the World*, Random House, Sydney, 2018

Murray, Fanny, *The Celebrated Miss Fanny Murray*, S. Smith, Dublin, 1759

Nugent, Maria, *Captain Cook Was Here*, Cambridge University Press, Melbourne, 2009

O'Brian, Patrick, *Joseph Banks*, Harvill, London, 1994

O'Brian, Patrick, *Joseph Banks: A Life*, University of Chicago Press, Chicago, 1997

Parkinson, Sydney, Kenrick, William, *A Journal of a Voyage to the South Seas, in His Majesty's Ship, the Endeavour: Faithfully Transcribed from the Papers of the Late Sydney Parkinson, Draughtsman to Joseph Banks, Esq., on His Late Expedition with Dr. Solander, Round the World*, Stanfield Parkinson, London, 1773

Penrose, The Rev. John, *Lives of Vice-Admiral Sir Charles Vinicombe Penrose, K. C. B,. and Captain James Trevenen, Knight of the Russian Orders of St. George and St. Vladimir*, John Murray, London, 1850

Polack, Joel Samuel, *New Zealand: being a narrative of travels and adventures during a residence in that country between the years 1831 and 1837*, Richard Bentley Publisher, London, 1838

Price, A. Grenfell, *The Explorations of Captain James Cook in the Pacific*, Dover, New York, 1971.

Reed, A. W. (ed.), *Captain Cook in Australia*, A. H. & A. W. Reed, Melbourne, 1969

Salmond, Anne, *Aphrodite's Island: The European Discovery of Tahiti*, University of California Press, Berkeley, 2009

Salmond, Anne, *The Trial of the Cannibal Dog: Captain Cook in the South Seas*, Penguin, Auckland, 2004

Salmond, Anne, 'Tupaia the Priest-Navigator' in Mallon (ed.), *Tangata o le Moana: The Story of Pacific People in New Zealand*, Te Papa Press, Wellington, 2012

Samwell, David, *A Narrative on the Death of Captain Cook*, G.G.J. & J. Robinson, London, 1786

Scadding, Henry, *Surveyor-General Holland*, Toronto, 1896

Shakespeare, William, *Julius Caesar*, Cambridge University Press, 1907

Shakespeare, William, *Macbeth*, Lyons and Carnahan, New York, 1913

Shakespeare William, *Richard II*, Oxford University Press, 2011

Smith, Edward, *The Life of Sir Joseph Banks, President of the Royal society, With Some Notices of his Friends and Contemporaries*, John Lane, London, 1911

Smyth, William Henry, *The Sailor's Word-Book: An Alphabetical Digest of Nautical Terms, including Some More Especially Military and Scientific, but Useful to Seamen; as well as Archaisms of Early Voyagers, etc.*, Blackie and Son, London, 1867

Stacey, C. P., *Quebec 1759: The Siege and the Battle*, Pan Books, London, 1959

Stockdale, John, *The Voyage of Governor Phillip to Botany Bay, with an Account of the Establishment of the Colonies of Port Jackson and Norfolk Island*, London, 1789

Stockdale, Percival, *The Memoirs of the Life and Writings of Percival Stockdale, Vol. 1*, Longman, Hurst, Rees and Orme, London, 1809

Suthren, Victor, *To Go Upon Discovery: James Cook and Canada, from 1758 to 1779*, Dundurn, Toronto, 2000

Tasman, Abel Janszoon, *Abel Janszoon Tasman's Journal of His Discovery of Van Diemens Land & New Zealand in 1642*, N. A. Kovach, Los Angeles, 1965

Taylor, James, *Picturing the Pacific*, Adlard Coles, London, 2018

Thomas, Nicholas, *Discoveries: The Voyages of Captain Cook*, Allen Lane, London, 2003

Van Dyke, Henry (ed.), *Poems of Tennyson*, Ginn and Company Publishers, Boston, 1903

Weld, Charles Richard, *A History of the Royal Society: With Memoirs of the Presidents, Vol. II*, John W. Parker, London, 1848

Whall, W. B., *Ships, Sea Songs and Shanties*, J. Brown and Son, Glasgow, 1913

White, John, *Ancient History of the Māori, His Mythology and Traditions, Vol. V*, Cambridge University Press, UK, 2011

Young, George, *The Life and Voyages of Captain James Cook, Drawn Up from His Journals, and Other Authentic Documents*, Whittaker Treacher & Co., London, 1836

Manuscripts/Letters

Banks, Joseph, The Endeavour Journal of Joseph Banks (25 August 1768 – 12 July 1771), SLNSW, Papers of Sir Joseph Banks, Section 2, Series 03.01, [no page numbers], http://www2.sl.nsw.gov.au/banks/series_03/03_231.cfm

Banks, Joseph, 'Thoughts on the manners of [the women of] Otaheite', 1773, in Joseph Banks Papers, NLA, MS 9, Series 1, Item 4_4e, pp. 2–3, http://nla.gov.au/nla.obj-222973317/view

Bligh, William, Extract from the logbook HMS *Bounty* (16 August 1787-20 August 1789), The National Archives, Kew, ADM 55/151, http://discovery.nationalarchives.gov.uk/details/r/C2976823

Bradley, William, 'A Voyage to New South Wales: December 1786 – May 1792', Journal, 25 November 1789, SLNSW, Safe 1/14

Clerke Charles, to Joseph Banks, Letter, 10 August 1779, SLNSW, Sir Joseph Banks Papers, Section 04, Series 11.04, p. 2, https://www.sl.nsw.gov.au/banks/section-04/series-11/11-04-letter-received-by-banks-from-charles

Cook, James, (transcribed by Richard Orton), A Journal of the proceedings of His Majesty's Bark *Endeavour* on a voyage round the world, commencing the 25th of May 1768 – 23 Oct. 1770, 24 June 1770, SLNSW, Manuscript Safe 1/71

Cook, James, Journal of H.M.S. *Endeavour*, 1768–1771, 3 June 1769, NLA, Ms 1, http://nla.gov.au/nla.obj-228983242/view

Cook, James, to Philip Stephens, Letter, 8 July 1768, in Letters from Captains, Surnames C. Includes letter from Captain James Cook, The National Archives, Kew, ADM 1/1609

Cook, James, to Sir John Pringle, Letter, 8 April 1776, Philosophical Transactions of the Royal Society of London, Vol. 66, 1776

Cook, James, to Latouche-Treville, Letter, 6 September 1775, in E. T. Hamy, 'James Cook et Latouche-Tréville', *Bulletin de Geographie Historique et Descriptive*, 1904

Cook, James to Joseph Banks, Letter, 18 November 1772, SLNSW, Sir Joseph Banks Papers, Section 03, Series 07.02, p. 2, https://www.sl.nsw.gov.au/banks/section-03/series-07/07-02-letter-received-by-banks-from-james-cook

Cook, James, Log of H.M.S. *Endeavour*, 1768–1770 [manuscript] NLA, Reference no.: MS 3

Cook, James, to Sir John Pringle, Letter, Undated, in Robert McNab (ed.), Historical Records of New Zealand, Vol. II, John Mackay, Wellington, 1914

Molineux, Log, The National Archives, Kew, ADM 55/41, https://discovery.nationalarchives.gove.uk/details/r/C2976713, 29 April 1769.

Morton, James Douglas, Earl, 'Hints offered to the consideration of Captain Cooke, Mr. Bankes, Doctor Solander and other gentlemen who go upon the expedition on board the *Endeavour*. Chiswick', National Library of Australia, Papers of Sir Joseph Banks, 1745–1923, MS 9, Series 3/Item 113–113h, p. 1, http://nla.gov.au:80/tarkine/nla.obj-222969577

Southwell, Daniel, to his uncle, the Reverend Weeden Butler, Letter, 23 June 1788, Journal, Historical Records of New South Wales, Vol. 2, 692.17

Stephens, Philip, 'Secret Instructions for Lieutenant James Cook Appointed to Command His Majesty's Bark the Endeavour', 30 July 1768, NLA, MS 2, https://www.foundingdocs.gov.au/scan-sid-252.html

Periodicals/Journals

Author Unknown, 'Notes', *The Journal of Geography*, Vol. 6, No. 6, 1908

Beaglehole, John Cawte, 'On the Character of Captain James Cook', *The Geographical Journal*, Vol. 122, No. 4, 1956

Brownsy, P. J., 'The Banks and Solander Collections – a Benchmark for Understanding the New Zealand Flora', *Journal of the Royal Society of New Zealand*, Vol. 42, No. 2, 2012

Carter, Harold B., 'The Royal Society and the Voyage of HMS "Endeavour" 1768–71', *Notes and Records of the Royal Society of London*, Vol. 49, No. 2, July 1995

Cook, James and Bevis, John, 'An Observation of an Eclipse of the Sun at the Island of New-Found-Land, August 5, 1766, by Mr. James Cook, with the Longitude of the Place of Observation Deduced from It', Philosophical Transactions of the Royal Society, Vol. 57, 1767

Driessen, H. A. H., 'Dramatis Personae of Society Islanders, Cook's "Endeavour" Voyage 1769', *The Journal of Pacific History*, Vol. 17, No. 4, 1982

The Gentleman's Magazine, Lord Sandwich addressing the House of Lords, Vol. 45, 1775

Halley, Edmund, 'A New Method of Determining the Parallax of the Sun, or His Distance from the Earth, Sec. R. S.', Philosophical Transactions Vol. 29, No. 348, 1716

Kodicek, Egon H., and Frank G. Young, 'Captain Cook and Scurvy', *Notes and Records of the Royal Society of London*, Vol. 24, No. 1, 1969

London Gazette, 11 January 1780

Lysaght, Averil, 'Some Early Letters from Joseph Banks (1743–1820) to William Philp Perrin', *Notes and Records of the Royal Society of London*, Vol. 29, No. 1, October 1974

Perry, William, 'Voyage to Batavia', *The Gentleman's Magazine*, Vol. 78, Part 1, 1808

Samwell, David, 'Some Particulars Concerning the Life and Character of Captain James Cook', *The European Magazine and London Review*, Vol. 9, May 1786

Sydney Morning Herald, 27 April 1863, https://trove.nla.gov.au/newspaper/article/13077664

Tink, Andrew, 'The Role of Parliamentary Witnesses in the Foundation of Australia', *Australasian Parliamentary Review*, Spring, Vol. 20, No. 2, 2005

Other

Buchan, Bruce, 'Cooking the Books', *Inside Story*, 14 June 2018, http://insidestory.org.au/
cooking-the-books/

Daley, 'The Gweagal Shield and the Fight to Change the British Museum's Attitude to Seized Artefacts',
The Guardian, 25 September 2016, https://www.theguardian.com/australia-news/2016/sep/25/
the-gweagal-shield-and-the-fight-to-change-the-british-museums-attitude-to-seized-artefacts

Keenan, Sarah, 'How the British Museum Changed its Story About the Gweagal Shield', Australian
Critical Race and Whiteness Studies Association, 2018, https://acrawsa.org.au/2018/05/18/
how-the-british-museum-changed-its-story-about-the-gweagal-shield/

Kendall, Henry, 'Sutherland's Grave', 1866, https://www.poetrylibrary.edu.au/poets/kendall-henry/
sutherland-s-grave-0007076

Letters Patent to Sir Humfrey Gylberte June 11, 1578, https://avalon.law.yale.edu/16th_century/humfrey.asp

Morelli, 'A Step Closer to Winning Back Gweagal Shield', NITV News, 24 August 2016, https://www.sbs.
com.au/nitv/article/2016/08/24/step-closer-winning-back-gweagal-shield

Walton, Geri, 'Medical Blistering in the Georgian Era', Unique Histories from the 18th and 19th Centuries,
2015, https://www.geriwalton.com/medical-blistering-in-georgian-era/

Williams, Shayne, T., 'An Indigenous Australian Perspective on Cook's Arrival', British Library,
https://www.bl.uk/the-voyages-of-captain-james-cook/articles/an-indigenous-australian-
perspective-on-cooks-arrival

Oral History

Ludwick, Harold, Guugu Yimithirr man, interview with David Phoenix 22 July 2019. Oral history comes
from Eric Deeral, Gamay Warra clan elder of the Guugu Yimithirr nation, 2001.

INDEX